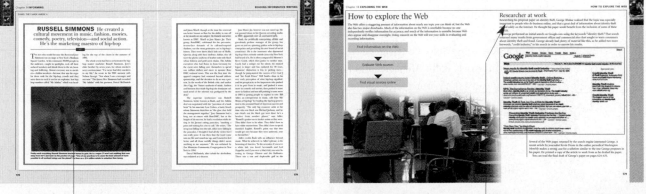

Dynamic readings that model writing for different purposes

Examples of a student "Researcher at work"

A TEXT & TECHNOLOGY SYSTEM FOR WRITING & RESEARCH SUCCESS

Lester Faigley's writing guide offers a unique, integrated text and technology learning system that combines the power of the textbook's instruction with the interactive tools of MyCompLab, Longman's market-leading online composition resource.

A book-specific version of MyCompLab includes an **E-book of *Writing*** by Lester Faigley that links you to relevant **MyCompLab activities, quizzes, tutorials and instruction.** The MyCompLab multimedia tutorials enable you to learn about grammar, writing and research topics in a new way, while the self-grading quizzes and in-depth exercises allow you to practice and improve skills. All scores and work are captured in MyCompLab's **Grade Tracker** so you can assess your progress and track your success.

Set yourself on the path to writing and research success today. Register for the Faigley *Writing* version of MyCompLab!

www.mycomplab.com

PLEASE NOTE: Access to MyCompLab comes packaged with your text at no additional cost only if your instructor has ordered it that way. If your text did not come with an access card, you can ask your bookstore to order one for you, or you can purchase access at <u>www.mycomplab.com</u> using a credit card.

RESOURCES TO HELP YOU SUCCEED!

Not all resources are listed here. For the full list of resources, go to www.mycomplab.com

- **My Book Resources.** Additional activities and materials (downloadable worksheets, additional readings) that supplement Faigley's *Writing*.

GRAMMAR

- **Diagnostics.** Two Comprehensive and four Targeted Diagnostics test student skills in basic grammar, sentence grammar, style/usage and punctuation/mechanics. For both types of Diagnostics, results pages provide a study plan for the student with overall proficiency scores, question-by-question feedback, and links to appropriate areas in ExerciseZone to improve skills.

- **ExerciseZone.** Over 4,600 self-grading questions allow students to improve skills in basic grammar, sentence grammar, punctuation and mechanics, and usage and style.

- **Grammar Video Tutorials.** For each of the 20 most common grammar errors, an animated clip with voiceover shows students on-screen editing, including tips for identifying and correcting errors.

WRITING

- **"Office Hours" Writing Video Tutorials.** This unique and engaging video series shows real students tackling the stages of the writing process (prewriting, drafting, editing, revising, peer review) and learning useful strategies from their instructor.

- **Writing Process Exercises.** Offering in-depth instruction and practice opportunities for each stage of the writing process, this section also provides a series of "guided" exercises that walk students from one step to the next, allowing them to bring a writing project to completion.

RESEARCH

- **Citation Diagnostics and Exercises.** Offering 2 MLA diagnostic tests and 2 APA diagnostic tests, this new section features follow-up, self-grading exercises in both styles.

- **Evaluating Sources Tutorial.** This section features instruction, exercises and an interactive tutorial that helps students master the challenging skills of using and evaluating sources.

- **Avoiding Plagiarism.** These self-guided tutorials—in both MLA and APA formats—offer strategies, self-tests and quizzes to help students recognize plagiarism and avoid it.

- **"Office Hours" Research Video Tutorials.** These videos show real students tackling stages of the research process (Avoiding Plagiarism, Evaluating Sources, Citing Sources, Finding and Narrowing a Topic) and learning useful strategies from their instructor.

WRITING

A Guide for College and Beyond

BRIEF EDITION

LESTER FAIGLEY
University of Texas at Austin

PEARSON
Longman

New York Boston San Francisco
London Toronto Sydney Tokyo Singapore Madrid Mexico City Munich
Paris Cape Town Hong Kong Montreal

Dorling Kindersley Education
Text design and page layout by Stuart Jackman
DTP: David McDonald
Cover design by Stuart Jackman

Longman Publishers
Executive Editor: Lynn M. Huddon
Development Editor: Katharine Glynn
Senior Supplements Editor: Donna Campion
Media Supplements Editor: Jenna Egan
Senior Marketing Manager: Sandra McGuire
Production Manager: Bob Ginsberg
Project Coordination: Pre-Press Company, Inc.
Cover Design Manager: Wendy Ann Fredericks
Cover Photographs: Lester Faigley
Visual Researcher: Rona Tuccillo
Senior Manufacturing Buyer: Dennis J. Para
Printer and Binder: Quebecor World/Taunton
Cover Printer: Phoenix Color Corporation

Library of Congress Cataloging-in-Publication Data
Faigley, Lester, (date)
Writing : a guide for college and beyond / Lester Faigley.
p. cm.
Includes index.
ISBN 0-321-39626-X (full-length ed.) – ISBN 0-321-40896-9 (brief ed.)
1. English language–Rhetoric. 2. English language–Grammar. 3. Academic writing. 4. Critical thinking. I. Title.
PE1408.F255 2006
808'.042--dc22
2006025510

Visit us at www.ablongman.com

ISBN 0-321-40896-9

345678910—QWT—090807

PART 1
The Writer as Explorer

PART 2
The Writer as Guide

CONTENTS

11. Analyzing Causes

12. Evaluating

CONTENTS

PART 3
The Writer as Researcher

CONTENTS

PART 4
The Writer as Designer

Preface

When I was asked to serve as the founding director of the Division of Rhetoric and Writing at the University of Texas at Austin, I began regularly teaching the practicum course for new graduate instructors and, along with my colleagues, redesigning our curriculum. These tasks made me aware of how much I didn't know about what students were getting out of our courses. I began conducting exit interviews and organizing focus groups with students along with looking at many examples of their writing. I learned many things from these interviews and focus groups, but I always was struck by students' comments about their textbooks. Students found them frustrating to use and dull in content. The more I thought about the textbook problem, the more I became convinced that textbooks could be better if they were rethought from the students' perspective. I saw a need for a guide to writing that offers instruction to students both visually and verbally, and thus is better suited for students with different learning styles.

I started from these beliefs:

A guide to writing should be student oriented.	It should start from the student's point of view, not the teacher's.
A guide to writing should be easy to use.	No matter where you open the book, the content on a particular page and the place of that content in the overall organization should be evident.
A guide to writing should show what readers and writers actually do.	Students learn best by seeing what readers and writers do, not by reading discussions of what they do.
A guide to writing should be engaging.	Textbooks don't have to be dull. Furthermore, students learn faster and remember longer when a book is well designed.

I did not know if I could actually create the guide I imagined until the opportunity came to work with designers at Dorling Kindersley. You may not know the name, Dorling Kindersley (I didn't for a long time), but you probably recognize their books if you browse the travel and reference sections in your bookstore. DK books are easy to use and handsome in presentation. Their visual format allows readers to find quickly what they are looking for. They provide just the right amount of information in a stimulating format. In other words, the DK books typically achieve what we, as writing teachers, hope our students might achieve—to produce high-quality and engaging writing.

DK books are accessible and inviting because they pay a great deal of attention to how words and images work together on the page. The designers at DK think hard about how design can improve learning. They are experts in taking something complicated and breaking it down into uncomplicated steps and elements. I wanted to bring this expertise to guide students in the complex processes of reading, writing, and researching in college.

Most writing teachers agree that the broad goals for a first-year college writing course are those identified in the Outcomes Statement from the Council of Writing Program Administrators.

The WPA goals include:

1. Rhetorical knowledge.	Students should respond to different situations and the needs of different audiences, understand how genres shape reading and writing, and write in several genres.
2. Critical thinking, reading, and writing.	Students should find, evaluate, analyze, and synthesize sources and integrate their ideas with those of others.
3. Processes.	Students should develop flexible strategies for generating, revising, editing, and proofreading, and should understand how to collaborate effectively with others.
4. Knowledge of conventions.	Students should learn the common formats for different kinds of texts, practice appropriate documentation, and control surface features of grammar, mechanics, and spelling.

Writing: A Guide for College and Beyond helps students to achieve these goals by using a combination of concise, accessible instruction, visual explanations, plentiful examples, and appealing assignments and readings. Important concepts and processes are presented in concise spreads, letting students see at a glance the key points they should master.

You'll find these key features in *Writing: A Guide for College and Beyond*

Process guides

Like most writing teachers, I have found over my many years of teaching that students struggle most with writing when they lack effective strategies. When students internalize an overview of the process of writing, they are far better able to monitor what they need to do to produce successful writing. The writing guides in each of the eight chapters on writing aims in Part 2 are designed as "Process Maps" to give a visual organization. Students first see an overview of how to write in each of the eight major "aims," and then the process is presented in detail with specific strategies for invention, drafting and revising, all with reference to the process as a whole.

Writers at work

Even though strategies can guide the process of writing, the process is nevertheless messy and for any significant piece of writing nearly always involves going back and forth among activities. The "Writer at work" sections in Part 2 show examples of student writers working through the whole messy, creative process of writing. These examples demonstrate how strategies of invention can produce the necessary raw material that leads to a manageable topic, and how strategies for revision can focus and develop a writer's ideas. "Staying on Track" boxes focus on common writing problems and give students concrete advice for how to avoid such problems.

Dynamic readings

The experience of stimulating reading inspires good writing. The 57 readings offer diverse models of writing for different purposes, including selections by such well-known writers as Bharati Mukherjee, David Sedaris, Amy Tan, Annie Dillard, Dagoberto Gilb, Alice Walker, Edward Tufte, Frederick Douglass, and Steven Johnson. Most reading selections are designed to look like original publications (an editorial looks like a page from a newspaper, a Web article looks like a Web page, and so on), reminding students of the original context and the importance of design and visual elements.

Engaging writing projects

More and more, college students are expected to be able to write in different genres as well as for different purposes. Furthermore, I have discovered in my teaching that students better grasp the conventions of the academic essay if they have opportunities to write in more than one genre. The "Projects" that conclude the eight aims chapters in Part 2 offer a variety of assignments, ranging from essays to a field observation paper, a profile, a film review, and a position argument. Eleven student papers, all with sources and citations and many with images, give students realistic, accurate models to learn from.

Guides for researching

I concluded from my interviews with students and discussions with colleagues that the processes of research and documenting sources are the most confusing aspects of college writing. Students in my classes best learn these processes by seeing concrete examples. In Part 3, students see a "Researcher at work" complete an assignment by using the strategies given in the chapters, including avoiding plagiarism, evaluating sources, and using the Internet as a research tool. Documentation guidelines for MLA and APA styles are provided in Chapters 21 and 22, as well as model research papers in both formats. These chapters feature several visual "source samples," which show students how to find the essential information needed to put together a citation.

Practical instruction on design and using visuals

Concise chapters on design and using visuals are included in Part 4, which encourage students to think of design and images to be rhetorically motivated and which offer practical advice for making design and visuals part of the composing process.

Resources for teachers and students

Writing: A Guide for College and Beyond is accompanied by many helpful supplements for both teachers and students. Please contact your local Longman representative for a complete listing of all available supplements.

Instructor's Resource Manual

The *Instructor's Resource Manual*, prepared by Susan Schorn of the University of Texas at Austin, offers detailed chapter-by-chapter suggestions to help both new and experienced instructors. For every chapter in the student text, this manual includes chapter goals and chapter challenges, suggestions for different ways to use the assignments and boxed tips in the chapter, additional activities and resources, and more. It also features an overall discussion of teaching a writing class, including discussion of the Writing Program Administrators Outcomes for first-year composition. Finally, the manual offers suggested syllabi and ideas for teaching students with different learning styles.

MyCompLab

MyCompLab, Longman's premier site for college writing teachers and students, provides the best multimedia resources for writing, research, and grammar in one easy-to-use site. In this site, students will find guided assistance through each step of the writing process; interactive tutorials and videos that illustrate key concepts; over 30 model documents from across the curriculum; "Exchange", Longman's online peer-review program; the "Avoiding Plagiarism" tutorial; diagnostic grammar tests and thousands of practice questions; and Research Navigator™, a database with thousands of magazines and academic journals, the subject-search archive of the *New York Times*, "Link Library," library guides, and more. Tour the site at www.mycomplab.com.

E-book

An E-book of *Writing: A Guide for College and Beyond*, available within MyCompLab, offers a complete, engaging multimedia learning experience for students. In almost every chapter of the E-book, students will find links to relevant MyCompLab tutorials, quizzes, and instruction. In addition, students can access unique, book-specific materials that supplement the key writing chapters in this text (look for the "My Book Resources" icon in the E-book), including downloadable worksheets, writing activities, additional readings and more. Visit the site at www.mycomplab.com and select Lester Faigley's *Writing*.

Acknowledgments

It takes a village to create a book, and for this book the village was global, relying on daily collaboration with my co-creators in London, New York, New Jersey, Massachusetts, Maine, and here at home in Austin. The list of people to thank is long. I'll begin with Lynn Huddon, executive editor for Longman Publishers, with whom I have written seven previous books and editions and whom I have come to know as one of the best in her profession. Lynn is an extraordinarily talented editor, and this book results from those talents: her vision of taking a radical new approach to a guide for writing, her managerial ability in assembling and organizing a diverse group of people, and her editorial skills and attention to detail. I told her at the outset that I would not attempt to write this book with anyone else because it seemed way too ambitious for the time we allowed ourselves, but I knew that if she began the project, she would do everything necessary to make it happen. My development editor, Katharine Glynn, has been a delight to write with because she is not only highly competent but also makes the process fun. She has kept stress to a minimum in what could have been a highly stressful project. And she too is one of the best at what she does.

Others at Longman who contributed their wisdom and experience include Roth Wilkofsky, president; Tim Stookesberry, vice president of marketing; Joseph Opiela, editorial director; Megan Galvin-Fak, executive marketing manager; Sandra McGuire, senior marketing manager; Laura Coaty, market research director; Donna Campion, senior supplements editor; Jenna Egan, media supplements editor; Mary Ellen Curley, director of development for English; Wendy Ann Fredericks, cover design manager; Rona Tuccillo, photo researcher; Bob Ginsberg, production manager; Michael Greer, development editor; and Nicole Solano, editorial

assistant. At Pre-Press, two other excellent people whom I have enjoyed working with in the past guided the book into print: Melissa Mattson, production manager, and copy editor Elsa van Bergen. Margery Niblock compiled the index.

The process of writing this book has been unlike anything I have ever done before because the book was designed in London at Dorling Kindersley at the same time it was written in Austin, with megabytes of pixels crossing the Atlantic day and night. The experience of working with Stuart Jackman, design director of DK Education, was nothing short of magical. While writing this book, my first act of the morning, even before coffee, was to see what creative gifts Stuart had sent me overnight. Even more than his artistry, Stuart taught me a great deal about using effective design for learning. Sophie Mitchell, publisher for DK Education, also made editorial contributions and helped to initiate and keep the DK collaboration running smoothly.

I also benefited from collaborators in Austin, especially Susan "George" Schorn, who contributed ideas and her prose in many places in the first three parts of the book and has written the Instructor's Resource Manual. Grace Bernhardt and Kelly Kessler also helped in the early stages. Russell Cobb created resources to accompany the E-book version of this text. I cannot say enough about how much I have learned over the years from colleagues and students at the University of Texas, a few of whom are represented by their writing here. Colleagues across the country have also given me advice and encouragement by reviewing chapters, testing chapters in their classes, and participating in focus group. And special thanks go to the students who participated in the class tests and contributed their thinking to the book.

I am most grateful to these colleagues:
Melissa P. Aaron, *California State Polytechnic University, Pomona*; Susan Achziger, *Community College of Aurora*; Diana Marie Agy, *Jackson Community College*; Jeffrey Andelora, *Mesa Community College*; Melissa Batai, *Triton College*; David Beach, *George Mason University*; Adrienne Bliss, *Ball State University*; Louise Bown, *Salt Lake Community College*; Virginia Brackett, *Park University*; Stuart Brown, *New Mexico State University*; Sandra Camillo, *Finger Lakes Community College*; Ron Christiansen, *Salt Lake Community College*; Kevin Eric De Pew, *Old Dominion University*; Stephanie Dowdle, *Salt Lake Community College*; Anthony Edgington, *University of Toledo*; Gary Enns, *Cerro Coso Community College*; Kristin Garaas-Johnson, *North Dakota State University*; Beth Erika Gulley, *Johnson County Community College*; Ella Hairston, *Guilford Technical Community College*; Rick Hansen, *California State University, Fresno*; Kimberly Harrison, *Florida International University*; Anne Helms, *Alamance Community College*; Jeffrey Hillard, *College of Mount St. Joseph*; Maurice Hunt, *Baylor University*; Richard A. Iadonisi, *Grand Valley State University*; Deborah Kehoe, *Northeast Mississippi Community College*; Bonnie Kyburz, *Utah Valley State College*; Bill Lamb, *Johnson County Community College*; John Larkin, *Castleton State College*; Nancy(Ramirez) Lenihan, *Pima College Downtown*; Shawna Lichtenwalner, *Eastern Tennessee State University*; Peggy Lindsey, *Wright State University*; Brett McInelly, *Brigham Young University*; Bryan Moore, *Arkansas State University*; Martha Petry, *Jackson Community College*; Larry Riley, *Ball State University*; Deidre Farrington Schoolcraft, *Pikes Peak Community College*; Liz Skrabacz, *Laramie County Community College*; Regina St. John, *Ball State University*; Lynn Sykes, *College of DuPage*; Teresa Trevathan, *South Plains College*; Pat Tyrer, *West Texas A&M University*; Janice Vierk, *Metropolitan Community College*; Patricia Webb, *Arizona State University*; Dan Wiley, *Hastings College*; Kristen Yonko, *Delaware Technical and Community College*; Pavel Zemliansky, *James Madison University*; and William Ziegler, *J. Sargeant Reynolds Community College*.

Finally, without my wife Linda's deep reserves of patience in putting up with a husband who becomes distracted and grumpy when he is writing, the book would never have been written.

Part 1

The Writer as Explorer

1
Making Discoveries

Go outside. Don't plan where to go. Wander toward nothing in particular. Walk slowly. Pause often. Look up. Look down. Widen your field of vision. Shield your eyes with your hands and look as far as you can see in the distance. No matter how familiar you are with the place, you'll see something that you have never seen before.

Look with new eyes

Walk long enough so you forget about what is most pressing at the moment. Look for secrets that no one else sees. The dance of light in the canopy of a tree. A second-story cornice on a building. The clarity of reflections in dark puddles. The faint outline of a chalk drawing on the sidewalk. The date stamped on a fire hydrant. The dark blue of a distant slope dotted with blue-green trees.

Take in the sounds. What can you hear besides human-made noises? Even in the middle of a city you may hear birds claiming territories. Listen to the sounds wind makes. Take in the smells. Close your eyes and focus. You can distinguish different smells. Feel the leaves on different plants. Touch the trunks of trees. The world is full of distinct textures.

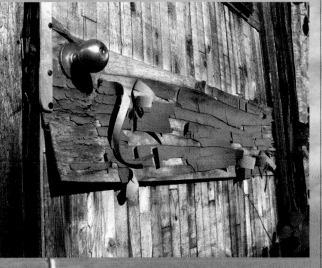

A city's pride can be expressed on its water meter covers. A water meter cover is also a historical document of American industry. Over the decades the manufacturers of water meters moved from New England to the Midwest, and more recently to India and Taiwan.

An aging door reveals the secrets of its construction and the rates of deterioration of its materials.

3

Explore the world

Ralph Waldo Emerson observed that "the writer is an explorer. Every step is an advance into a new land." Walking in a strange city or hiking in a forest for the first time is exciting because each step reveals something new. But you can experience the same excitement in places you know well if you see them with new eyes.

Cities display ongoing conversations— in the short term with words

. . . and in the long term with competing architectural styles.

4

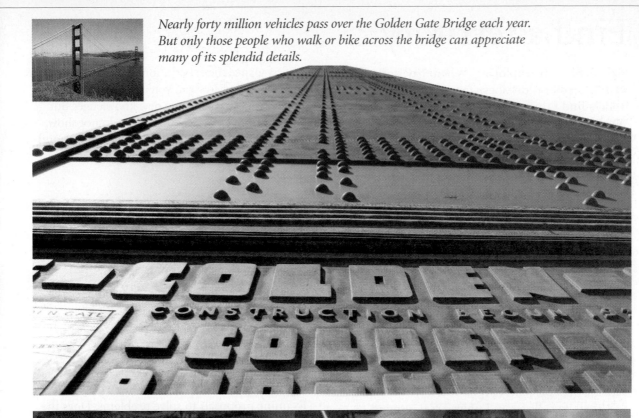

Nearly forty million vehicles pass over the Golden Gate Bridge each year. But only those people who walk or bike across the bridge can appreciate many of its splendid details.

Discovering history

Go to the oldest part of your city or town. Take a notebook with you. Your assignment is to learn as much as you can about the history of particular buildings from observing. For some buildings with visible signs of their past, it will be easy to find their history. But for others you will have to dig deeper. Small details give clues. For example, between 1900 and 1950, experts believed that green paint had a calming effect. The interiors of hospitals, asylums, schools, government buildings, and even kitchens in houses were painted the same shade of light green. Look closely at the colors under peeling paint. (Remember that old paint is often lead-based and hazardous to small children.)

If your town has a railroad track, walk along it. Before the automobile became dominant, towns were organized around railroads. Look for evidence such as the concrete foundation of a loading dock torn down long ago. If you live in a newer suburban environment, take a close look at strip malls, which typically have a high turnover of businesses. Often you can find traces of earlier occupants.

Describe three details about three buildings (or about one building if you can identify separate details) or other man-made structures as precisely as you can. Give their exact location. Then write what you can infer about the history of each building or object from the details.

Find a territory

Writers begin by exploring. When they start writing, exploration doesn't stop. Once they start, writers find things they could not have imagined. Where writers end up is often far away from where they thought they were going.

Most writing in college concerns exploration because academic disciplines seek to create new knowledge and to rethink what is known. Colleges and universities bring together people who ask interesting questions: How does recent archaeological evidence change our understanding of Homer's *Iliad* and *Odyssey*? Why does eyesight deteriorate with age? How do volcanoes affect the world climate? How do chameleons regenerate lost body parts? How do Rousseau's ideas about nature continue to shape notions about wilderness? How do electric eels generate voltage and not get shocked in the process? How can a poll of a thousand people represent 295 million Americans with only a 3 percent margin of error?

Writers in colleges and universities respond to these questions and many others. They challenge old answers and contribute new answers. Readers of college writing expect to learn something when they read—new knowledge, a fresh interpretation, another point of view that they had not considered.

At first glance the expectations of college writing seem impossible. How can you as an undergraduate student expect to contribute new knowledge? But just as there is a great deal that maps do not show, you can find many uncertainties, controversies, and unresolved problems in any field of study. You just have to ask the right questions.

Ask interesting questions

Good questions can take you to places that will interest you and your readers alike.

- Focus on an area you don't know and want to know more about.

- Find out where experts disagree. What exactly is the source of the disagreement? Why do they come to different conclusions using the same evidence?

- Analyze explanations of current trends and events. What possible causes might be left out?

- Examine proposals to solve problems. Does the solution fix the problem? Will people support the solution if it costs them effort or money?

- Compare what people claim and the reality. Often people (especially politicians) represent things and their role in making them as much better than they actually are.

Determine what do you want to accomplish

Writers, like explorers, start with what they think they want to accomplish. Often the assignment will contain key words such as *analyze*, *argue*, *describe*, *evaluate*, *propose*, *reflect* and *report* that will assist you in determining what direction to take.

Analyze	Find connections among a set of facts, events, or readings and make them meaningful (see Chapters 10 and 11).
Argue	Convince others to accept or reject a particular position (see Chapter 13).
Describe	Observe details carefully and select details that create a dominant impression (see Chapter 8).
Evaluate	Argue that something is good, bad, best, or worst in its class according to criteria that you set out (see Chapter 12).

Propose	Identify a particular problem and explain why your solution is the best one (see Chapter 14).
Reflect	Narrate personal experience and personal insights (see Chapter 7).
Report	Organize and communicate information (see Chapter 9).

A specific audience might be mentioned in the assignment. If you are writing for a specific audience, what will those readers know about your topic? What will they likely have read about your topic? What attitudes are they likely to have about your topic?

Use strategies for finding a topic

Sometimes your instructor will assign a topic, but more often you will have to come up with your own topic. Look first at material from your course. You might find a topic to explore from the readings or from class discussion.

Start with what interests you. It's hard to write about topics that you care little about. If your assignment gives you a range of options, make more than one list.

Personal	1. History of Anime in Japan 2. Cave exploration and conservation 3. Learning to windsurf
CAMPUS	1. Pros and cons of computer fees 2. Excessive litter on campus 3. Fellowships for study-abroad programs
COMMUNITY	1. Safe bicycle commuting 2. Bilingual education programs 3. Better public transportation
NATION/WORLD	1. Advertising aimed at preschool children 2. Censorship of the Internet 3. Genetically altered crops

WRITE NOW

Mapping your campus

Your campus likely has an information desk for students and visitors. Information centers typically will have several brochures with maps. Visit the information desk and collect everything that includes a map. Then compare the maps. Make a checklist for what the maps show and don't show (building names, streets, shuttle bus routes, bicycle routes, parking, landmarks, hotels, and more).

Create a map for new students on your campus that contains insider knowledge that would not appear on the maps your school produces. For example, where can you find the best burger on or close to campus? The best cup of coffee or cookies? A quiet place to study? A great place to meet friends? Make a list of places that need to be included on your map. Then draw the map.

Take inventory when you have a topic

A good way to begin writing about a subject is to take inventory of what you know about it. The classic reporters' questions can assist you in thinking about it.

1. *Who* is doing it?
2. *What* is happening or at issue?
3. *When* is it happening?
4. *Where* is it happening?
5. *How* is it happening?
6. *Why* is it happening?

If you don't know the answers to all the questions, you'll know where to start looking.

DECLINE OF FROGS AND TOADS

<u>WHO?</u> Frogs and toads populations worldwide

<u>WHAT?</u> Declined by 50% according to scientists

<u>WHERE?</u> Worldwide but especially in the Americas

<u>WHEN?</u> Since 1950

<u>HOW?</u> Deadly skin infection for tropical frogs and toads; pesticides and pollution worldwide

<u>WHY?</u> (1) Frogs and toads breathe partially through their skin, making them more vulnerable to disease, pollution, and toxic chemicals.

(2) A tropical fungus that causes disease in frogs has spread because of climate change due to global warming.

Brainstorm

Another way to determine what you are looking for is to brainstorm a list. For example, opposite is a list of observations and questions on lyme disease.

- A friend had lyme disease for a year and went to many doctors before it was diagnosed.

- Why is lyme disease hard to diagnose?

- Overpopulation of deer spreads lyme disease.

- Are deer the only animals that spread the ticks that transmit lyme disease?

- What methods can control the deer population in suburbs?

- How can you control ticks in yards?

WRITE NOW

Write nonstop

Another way to find out how much you know about a topic is to write nonstop.

1. Put a tentative topic at the top of the page. Then write as fast as you can for five to ten minutes.

2. Don't stop to correct mistakes. Let your ideas flow wherever they take you, even if they take you well outside the boundaries of your topic. The idea is that the constant flow of words will generate ideas—some useful, and some not.

3. If you get stuck, write the same sentence over again, or write about how hungry you are or how hard it is to write. Thoughts will eventually start reappearing.

4. After you've finished, read what you have written and underline any key ideas.

5. Select one of the ideas and put it at the top of the page. Then write nonstop again for five to ten minutes.

Use guides

Writers can take advantage of guides developed by libraries. Your library's online subject catalog often divides big subjects into smaller and more manageable ones. For example, if you type "nanotechnology" into the subject search window in your online catalog, you likely will get results similar to those below.

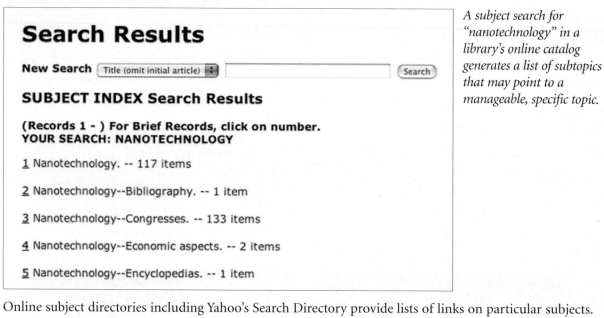

A subject search for "nanotechnology" in a library's online catalog generates a list of subtopics that may point to a manageable, specific topic.

Online subject directories including Yahoo's Search Directory provide lists of links on particular subjects.

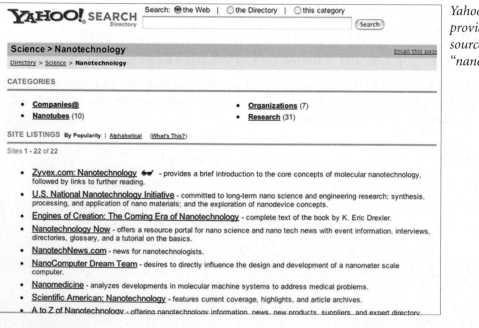

Yahoo's subject directory provides links to online sources for "nanotechnology."

Make an idea map

Start with the general subject you plan to write about. State it in a few words. Draw a box around it.

Next think about what can be said about this topic. At this point you don't want specifics but general categories.

The third stage is to generate topics about each category.

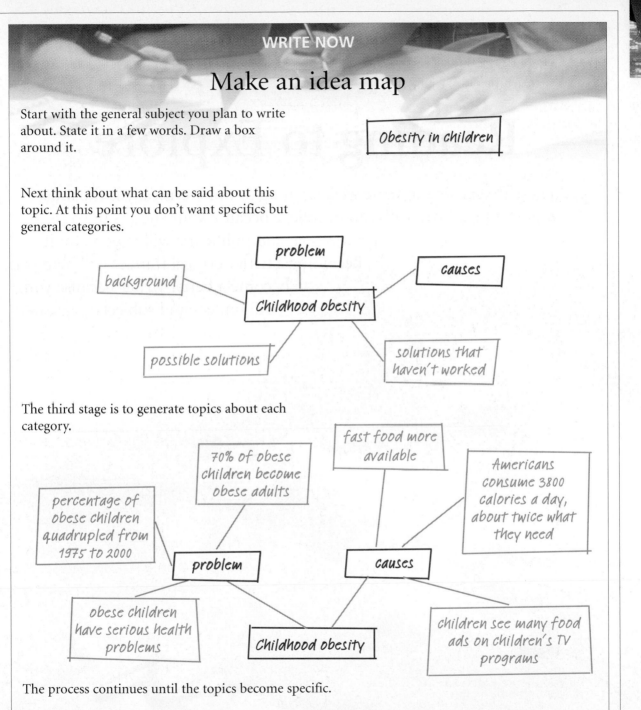

The process continues until the topics become specific.

When you finish the map, look at how it might be translated into writing. Probably you don't want to include everything that is in the map. Get a colored marker and put a line around those parts you intend to write about.

2
Reading to Explore

Along with learning to write well, learning to think critically is the most important skill you will gain in college because your success in your professional and public life will depend on it. Becoming a better critical thinker will help you to become a better writer because you will understand subjects in greater complexity and you will be better able to evaluate and revise what you write.

Become a critical reader

Critical thinking begins with critical reading. For most of what you read, one time through is enough. When you start asking questions about what you are reading, you are engaging in critical reading. Critical reading is a four-part process. First, begin by asking where a piece of writing came from and why it was written. Second, read the text carefully to find the author's central claim or thesis and the major points. Third, decide if you can trust the author. Fourth, read the text again to understand how it works.

1. Where did it come from?
- Who wrote this material?
- Where did it first appear? In a book, newspaper, magazine, or online?
- What else has been written about the topic or issue?
- What do you expect after reading the title?

2. What does it say?
- What is the topic or issue?
- What is the writer's thesis or overall point?
- What reasons or evidence does the writer offer?
- Who are the intended readers? What does the writer assume the readers know and believe?

3. Can you trust the writer?
- Does the writer have the necessary knowledge and experience to write on this subject?
- Do you detect a bias in the writer's position?
- Are the facts relevant to the writer's claims?
- Can you trust the writer's facts? Where did the facts come from?
- Does the writer acknowledge opposing views and unfavorable evidence? Does the writer deal fairly with opposing views?

4. How does it work?
- How is the piece of writing organized? How are the major points arranged?
- How does the writer conclude? Does the conclusion follow from the evidence the writer offers? What impression does the writer take away?
- How would you characterize the style? Describe the language that the writer uses.
- How does the writer represent herself or himself?

WRITE NOW

Analyze information for students on your campus

No doubt your school mailed you a great deal of information when you were admitted. Schools continue to distribute information to students when they get to campus. You can find informative brochures and flyers at your school's student services building and in the health center.

Pick one of the brochures or flyers to analyze. Remember that you are the intended audience.

Write a one-page evaluation about why the brochure or flyer is effective or ineffective for an audience of college students. If it is ineffective, what changes need to be made to make it effective? If it works, what does it do well?

13

Look with a critical eye

Critical viewing, like critical reading, requires thinking about where the image or visual came from. Begin by asking the following.

- What kind of an image or visual is it?

- Who created this image (movie, advertisement, television program, and so on)?

The Pharaoh Menkaure (Mycerinus) and his queen, Giza, Old Kingdom, 2548–2530 BCE. One of the finest statues from ancient Egypt depicts a royal couple. Compare the statue to formal portraits of couples today. Why does the queen have one arm around his waist and the other touching the king's arm? Do you think it depicts how they looked in real life? Or how they might have wanted to look in the afterlife? How do you think people in ancient Egypt might have viewed this statue?

The following questions are primarily for still images. For animations, movies, and television, you also have to ask questions about how the story is being told.

- What attracts your eye first? If there is an attention-grabbing element, how does it connect with the rest of the image?

- What impression of the subject does the image create?

- How does the image appeal to the values of the audience? (For example, politicians love to be photographed with children.)

- How does the image relate to what surrounds it?

- Was it intended to serve purposes besides art and entertainment?

- What is it about? What is portrayed in the image?

- Where did it first appear? Where do you usually find images like this one?

- When did it appear?

14

Arthur Rothstein made this photograph of black clouds of dust rising over the Texas Panhandle in March 1936. Look closely at the photo. What attracts your eye first? Snapshots usually put the horizon line in the center. Why did Rothstein put the horizon at the bottom? What impression does this photo convey to you?

WORKING TOGETHER

Analyze political cartoons

Political cartoons make comments on politics in drawings combined with words. Bring a political cartoon to class. You can find many political cartoons on the Web in addition to ones in newspapers and magazines.

Answer these questions.

1. What is the point of the cartoon?

2. What do you need to know to understand the cartoon? Political cartoons usually make reference to current events, television shows, and popular culture.

3. Political cartoons often exaggerate physical attributes. Is anything exaggerated?

4. Political cartoons are often ironic—pointing to the difference between the way things really are and what they are expected to be. Is the cartoon ironic?

5. Why is the cartoon funny or not funny?

Organize in groups of three or four students. Exchange your cartoons and answer the same questions for your classmates' cartoons.

When all finish, compare your answers for each cartoon. Where there is disagreement, stop to discuss why you came up with different answers.

Read actively

If you own what you are reading (or are able to make yourself a photocopy of borrowed materials), read with a pencil in hand. Pens and highlighters don't erase, and often you don't remember why you highlighted a particular sentence.

Annotate what you read

Using annotating strategies will make your effort more rewarding.

Mark major points and key concepts	Sometimes major points are indicated by headings, but often you will need to locate them.
Connect passages	Notice how ideas connect to each other. Draw lines and arrows. If an idea connects to something a few pages before, write a note in the margin with the page number.
Ask questions	Note anything that puzzles you, including words to look up.

Annotate difficult readings

Much of what you read in college will deal with unfamiliar concepts, which are often defined by other concepts. Annotating a difficult reading will help you understand the relationship of concepts, and the annotations will be valuable in remembering key points when you come back to the reading later. In this passage from John Heskett's *Toothpicks and Logos, Design in Everyday Life*, the author defines function in terms of two other concepts.

A more inclusive definition of function is needed, which can be opened up by breaking the concept of function into a twofold division: the key concepts of utility and significance.

definition of function – utility and significance

definition of utility

Utility can be defined as the quality of appropriateness in use. This means it is concerned with how things work, of the degree to which designs serve practical purposes and provide affordances or capabilities. A simple example is a professional kitchen knife used to prepare food: its primary utility value is as a cutting tool. In order for it to work effectively, the blade needs to possess material qualities enabling a sharp edge to be maintained and for it to remain stable in use.

affordances? odd word – author is British

example – kitchen knife

definition of significance

Significance as a concept in design, explains how forms assume meaning in the ways they are used, or the roles and meaning assigned them, often becoming powerful symbols or icons in patterns of habit and ritual. In contrast to the emphasis on efficiency, significance has more to do with expression and meaning.

other examples:
computer keyboard,
pencil,
traffic light

examples of
designs for
significance

It is possible to find designs of many kinds defined solely in terms of utility or significance. Many examples of the former are products related to the performance of professional services, tools with highly specific purposes, such as a hand saw or a lathe, or medical equipment, such as an ultrasound machine. Where information has to perform a highly specific task, as in a railway timetable, the layout and type forms should be clean, simple, and directed wholly to imparting essential facts. A primary condition of utilitarian design is that it must effectively execute or support certain tasks. In contrast, a piece of jewelry, a porcelain figurine, or a frame for a family pho-tograph has no such specific purpose—instead their pur-pose can be described in terms of contemplative pleas-ure or adornment.

examples of
designs for
utility

Map what you read

Drawing a map of a text can help you to identify key points and understand the relationships of concepts.

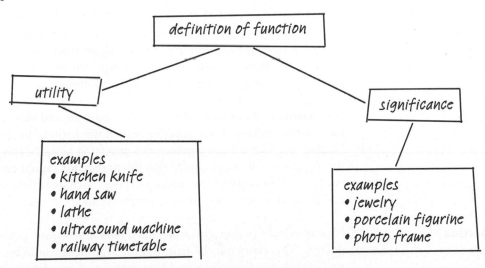

Make notes

Write down your thoughts as you read. Often you will find that something you read reminds you of something else. Jot that down. It might give you ideas for writing. Think about what impresses as you read. And think about what else you might read if you want to write about this subject.

Recognize fallacies

Reasoning depends less on proving a claim than it does on finding evidence for that claim that readers will accept as valid. The kinds of faulty reasoning called logical fallacies reflect a failure to provide sufficient evidence for a claim that is being made.

Fallacies of logic

Begging the question	*Politicians are inherently dishonest because no honest person would run for public office.* The fallacy of begging the question occurs when the claim is restated and passed off as evidence.
Either-or	*Either we eliminate the regulation of businesses or else profits will suffer.* The either-or fallacy suggests that there are only two choices in a complex situation. Rarely, if ever, is this the case. (In this example, the writer ignores the fact that Enron was unregulated and went bankrupt.)
False analogies	*Japan quit fighting in 1945 when we dropped nuclear bombs on them. We should use nuclear weapons against other countries.* Analogies always depend on the degree of resemblance of one situation to another. In this case, the analogy fails to recognize that circumstances today are very different from those in 1945; many countries now possess nuclear weapons, and we know their use could harm the entire world.
Hasty generalization	*We have been in a drought for three years; that's a sure sign of climate change.* A hasty generalization is a broad claim made on the basis of a few occurrences. Climate cycles occur regularly over spans of a few years; climate trends must be observed over centuries.
Non sequitur	*A university that can raise a billion dollars from alumni should not have to raise tuition.* A *non sequitur* (which is a Latin term meaning "it does not follow") ties together two unrelated ideas. In this case, the argument fails to recognize that the money for capital campaigns is often donated for special purposes such as athletic facilities and is not part of a university's general revenue.
Oversimplification	*No one would run stop signs if we had a mandatory death penalty for doing it.* This claim may be true, but the argument would be unacceptable to most citizens. More complex, if less definitive, solutions are called for.
Post hoc fallacy	*The stock market goes down when the AFC wins the Super Bowl in even years.* The *post hoc* fallacy (from the Latin *post hoc ergo hoc,*

	which means "after this, therefore this") assumes that things that follow in time have a causal relationship.
Rationalization	*I could have finished my paper on time if my printer was working.* People frequently come up with excuses and weak explanations for their own and others' behavior that often avoid actual causes.
Slippery slope	*We shouldn't grant citizenship to illegal immigrants now living in the United States because no one will want to obey our laws.* The slippery slope fallacy maintains that one thing inevitably will cause something else to happen.

Fallacies of emotion and language

Bandwagon appeals	*It doesn't matter if I copy a paper off the Web because everyone else does.* This argument suggests that everyone is doing it, so why shouldn't you? But on close examination, it may be that everyone really isn't doing it—and in any case, it may not be the right thing to do.
Name calling	Name calling is frequent in politics and among competing groups (*radical, tax-and-spend liberal, racist, fascist, right-wing ideologue*). Unless these terms are carefully defined, they are meaningless.
Polarization	*Feminists are all man-haters.* Polarization, like name-calling, exaggerates positions and groups by representing them as extreme and divisive.
Straw man	*Environmentalists won't be satisfied until not a single human being is allowed to enter a national park.* A straw man argument is a diversionary tactic that sets up another's position in a way that can be easily rejected. In fact, only a small percentage of environmentalists would make an argument even close to this one.

WRITE NOW

Analyze opinion writing

Examine writing that expresses opinions: blogs, discussion boards, editorials, advocacy Web sites, the letters to the editor on the editorial pages of your campus or local newspaper. Read with a pencil in hand, and mark where you think there may be fallacies.

Select the example that has the clearest fallacy. Explain in a paragraph the cause of the fallacy.

Respond as a reader

Engage in a dialog with what you read. Talk back to the author. If you are having trouble understanding a difficult section, read it aloud and listen to the author's voice. Hearing something read will sometimes help you to imagine being in a conversation with the author.

Make notes

As you read, write down your thoughts. Something you read may remind you of something else. Jot that down.

- Imagine that the author is with you. What points does the writer make that you would respond to in person?

- What questions would you have of the author? These indicate what you might need to look up.

- What ideas do you find that you might develop or interpret differently?

Write summaries

When you summarize, you state the major ideas of an entire source or part of a source in your own words. Most summaries are much shorter than the original because they include just the main points, not most of the examples and supporting material.

The keys to writing a good summary are identifying the main points and then putting those points into your own words. If you use words from the source, you have to put those words in quotation marks.

John Heskett argues that the concept of function in design should be understood in terms of "utility" and "significance." He defines utility as the degree a design accomplishes its purpose, such as how well a knife cuts. Significance is defined as the degree to which an object is designed to give pleasure or create meaning. A piece of art is an example of something designed exclusively for significance.

Build on what you read

Keeping a reading journal is a good practice for a writer. You'll have a record of your thinking as you read that you can return to later. Often you can connect different ideas from different readings. A reading journal is a great place to test ideas that you can later develop for a writing assignment.

Heskett says, "It is possible to find designs of many kinds defined solely in terms of utility and significance." I'll grant the distinction, but his examples suggest that most things have elements of both.

He uses tools as objects designed strictly for utility, but look at a tool catalog and you'll see lots of bright colors and handsome cases. He uses a photograph frame as an example of significance. True enough that frames are often decorative, but a frame also has to fit the picture. The frame should use non-glare glass to reduce reflected light. A frame has to do more than just look good.

But a bigger point is that anything can have significance for a particular person. I have my grandfather's hammer. It is nearly worthless because the handle is so old and worn that it would snap if you swung it hard against a nail. I took the hammer to work one day to hang a picture, and it shortly disappeared. I searched and couldn't find it. I forgot about it, but then I noticed it in a storeroom months later and recovered it.

WRITE NOW

Respond to what you read

Select a reading in one of the chapters in Part 2 that interests you. Write a one-paragraph summary of either the entire reading or of a part that contains a stimulating idea.

Write a second paragraph that develops one or more of the ideas in the reading. Think of some way of expanding or extending one of the author's ideas, either by relating it to your own experience or to something else you have read.

3

Planning a Journey

How often do you find yourself lost in buildings on your campus? In some buildings, you feel comfortable and at ease right away. But in others you always feel disoriented, even after you memorize the route to your classroom. The rooms may be fine once you are in them. The problem is the layout or plan of the building.

A disorienting building lacks central spaces and signs. Directions are missing at intersections. All the hallways look alike.

Strong central spaces, like the Piazza Navona in Rome, organize neighborhoods and attract people.

Determine your direction

Poorly organized writing is like a poorly designed building. It takes too much effort to get to where you want to go. Effective writing keeps readers oriented. Writing that succeeds is organized around a central idea, much as successful buildings and even thriving neighborhoods are.

Identify your center

Often the challenge in writing is finding the center that connects your sentences and paragraphs. Probably you have had the experience of driving around looking for a store or a house without having the address. Unless you were lucky, it was probably frustrating. Knowing your center is like having an address. It makes the journey far easier.

Having a big topic like privacy is like knowing only the general area of where something is located.

BROAD TOPIC:
privacy and surveillance

SPECIFIC TOPIC:
Which public spaces should be under constant surveillance with micro-devices invisible to the human eye?

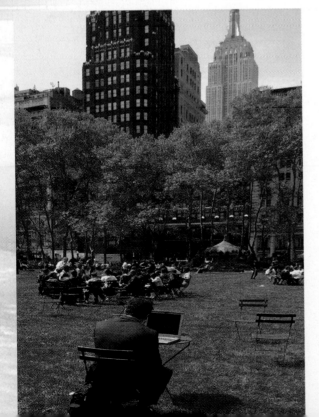

Think about where you are headed

Writing is a dynamic activity that goes back and forth between your mind and the page. Nevertheless, it helps to have an overall strategy that enables your thinking to evolve into writing that communicates with your readers.

Read your assignment again. Often the assignment will tell you which direction to go.

Reflect
You will need to think about an idea or concept in terms of your own history and life experience (see Chapter 7).

Describe
Often you will need to visit a site, observe details, and make notes, which you will later use to write a description (see Chapter 8).

Inform
You will need to report information or explain a concept or idea (see Chapter 9).

Analyze
You will need to interpret a text or a set of data to find connections and reach conclusions (see Chapter 10).

Analyze causes
You will need to identify probable causes of a trend or phenomenon and give evidence for your analysis (see Chapter 11).

Evaluate
You will need to determine whether something is good or bad based on criteria that you identify (see Chapter 12).

Argue
You will need to take a position on an issue or propose a course of action (see Chapters 13 and 14).

Write a thesis

Central ideas in writing are often expressed in a thesis statement. Just as many urban neighborhoods grow up around strong central spaces, most writing you will do in college and later in your career will have an explicit thesis, usually stated near the beginning. The thesis announces your topic and indicates what points you want to make about that topic.

Write a working thesis

Your thesis should follow the direction your assignment calls for. These examples show how the broad subject of databases and privacy can be approached from different directions, depending on your purpose.

Describe

THESIS: My Amazon.com account has a list of every book I have purchased from them dating back ten years, plus Amazon records every item I browse but don't buy. No wonder Amazon's recommendations of what I might like are so uncannily accurate!

Analyze

THESIS: Understanding how the concept of privacy is legally defined is critical for strengthening privacy laws.

Inform

THESIS: Imagine a government that compels its citizens to reveal vast amounts of personal data, including your physical description, your phone number, your political party, your parents' and spouse's names, where you work, where you live, what property you own, what it is worth, and every legal transaction in your life, and then making that data available to anyone on the Web—which is exactly what federal, state, and local governments are doing today in the United States.

Argue

THESIS: Unlike the government, companies have almost no restrictions on what information they collect or what they do with that information. Laws should be passed that make companies responsible for the misuse of personal information and allow people to have greater participation in how that information is used.

Evaluate

THESIS: Using personal consumer data to refuse service or offer inferior service to customers who likely will not spend much money is an example of the misuse of personal information.

Reflect

THESIS: I had never thought about the consequences of data profiling until I read about Netflix's policy of "throttling" frequent users, which explained why deliveries of movies I had requested from Netflix grew slower and slower.

Analyze causes

THESIS: Many laws to protect privacy are on the books, but these laws are ineffective for the digital era because they were written to protect people from government spying and intrusion rather than from the collection and selling of personal information by companies.

Evaluate your working thesis

Ask yourself these questions about your working thesis.

1. Is it specific?
2. Is it manageable in terms of the assigned length and the amount of time you have?
3. Is it interesting to your intended readers?

Example 1

THESIS: Steroids are a problem in Major League Baseball.

- **Specific?** The thesis is too broad. What exactly is the problem? Is the problem the same now as it was a few years ago?
- **Manageable?** Because the thesis is not limited, it cannot be discussed adequately.
- **Interesting?** The topic is potentially interesting, but many people are aware that baseball players used steroids. How can you lead readers to think about the topic in a new way?

Example 1 revised

THESIS: Home run records from 1993 through 2004 should be placed in a special category because of the high use of steroids in Major League Baseball before testing began in 2004.

Example 2

THESIS: "Nanotechnology'" refers to any technology that deals with particles measured in units of a nanometer, which is one billionth (10^{-9}) of a meter.

- **Specific?** The thesis is specific, but it is too narrow. It offers only a definition of nanotechnology.
- **Manageable?** The thesis states a fact.
- **Interesting?** Nanotechnology could be interesting if some of its potential effects are included.

Example 2 revised

THESIS: Nanotechnology may soon change concepts of social identity by making it possible for individuals to alter their physical appearances either through cosmetic surgery performed by nanorobots or changes in genetic sequences on chromosomes.

WRITE NOW

Write a bold thesis

Too much of what we read says what we've all heard before. Instead of serving up what readers likely know, try challenging readers. For example, in *Everything Bad Is Good for You*, Steven Johnson argues that video games are not a total waste of time but teach children valuable problem-solving skills.

Think of something that many people accept as common sense or general wisdom—that junk food is bad for you, reality television is garbage, or graffiti is vandalism—and argue the opposite. Or that something thought of as boring might be really interesting: bird watching, classical Indian music, or ancient Greek drama. Write a thesis that stands that common wisdom on its head.

Then write a paragraph about how you might argue for your controversial thesis. What evidence might you supply?

Plan your route

Experienced travelers have multiple strategies for getting to their destinations. Sometimes they have the route planned in advance and follow it exactly. In other cases, they know they have to be flexible, just as when you find traffic stopped and you take an alternate route. Experienced writers work in much the same way, using different strategies for different writing tasks.

Determine a plan

Get out your notes and all the information you have collected. You may find it helpful to write major points on sticky notes so you can move them around. If your topic is the effects of nanotechnology on the body, you might produce an organization plan similar to this one.

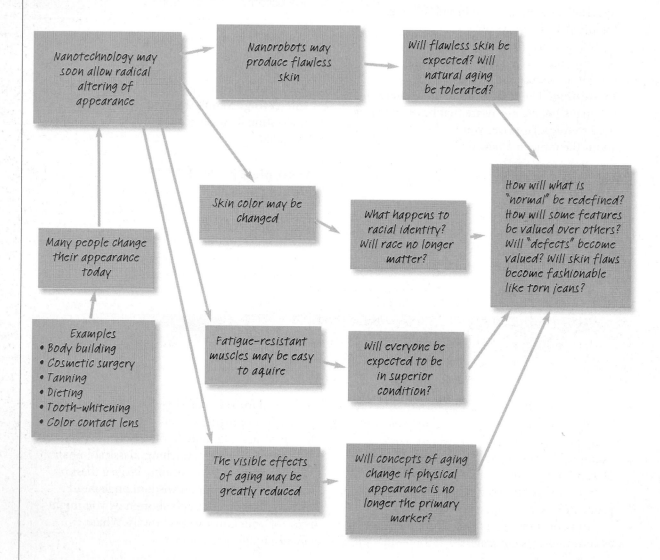

Make a writing plan

Writing plans often take the form of outlines, either formal outlines or working outlines.

A formal outline typically begins with the thesis statement, which anchors the entire outline.

A working outline is a sketch of how you will arrange the major sections.

THESIS: Nanotechnology may soon allow radical altering of the human body, which will have major social consequences.

I. Altering the appearance of the body has become common.
    A. Cosmetic surgery is now routine.
    B. Body building is popular.
    C. Most people are aware of diet and many attempt to control their weight.
    D. Tanning, changing eye color, and tooth-whitening are frequent.

II. Nanotechnology may soon radically accelerate these trends.
    A. Nanorobots may produce flawless skin.
    B. Skin color may be changed.
    C. Wrinkles and other signs of aging may be eliminated or reduced.
    D. Muscle tissue may be enhanced.

Effects of nanotechnology on the body

SECTION 1: Begin with how people change the appearance of their bodies today.

SECTION 2: Discuss how nanotechnology will accelerate these trends, giving people the potential for perfect skin, changing their skin color, and reducing aging.

SECTION 3: Move to the questions these technologies raise, such as how aging will be perceived and how race will be understood.

SECTION 4: Raise the issue of how "normal" will be defined if people can choose how they look.

SECTION 5: Expand the idea of "normal" to who will control what is desirable and how social hierarchies might be changed or reinforced.

SECTION 6: End by connecting body issues to larger issues such as who gets to live for how long.

WRITE NOW

Make a plan

First, write a working thesis. Ask the questions on page 25.
- Is the thesis specific?
- Is it manageable?
- Is it interesting?

Revise your thesis if necessary.

Then use two of the three methods—a visual organization plan, a formal outline, or a working outline—to develop a plan for writing a paper based on the thesis. When you finish, compare the plans. Which will be easier to use for writing your paper?

4

Returning and Revising

When you return to a place after you have been away for some time, often you gain enough distance to "re-see" it in a totally different way. The same is true for writing. Skilled writers know that they often have to revise several times to get the results they want. In order to revise effectively, they must "re-see," which, after all, is what revision means.

See again

Pretend you are someone who is either uninformed about your subject or else someone who is informed but is likely to disagree with you. If possible, think of an actual person and pretend to be that person. Read your draft aloud all the way through. When you read aloud, you often hear clunky phrases and catch errors, but do no more in this stage than put checks in the margins that you can return to later. You don't want to get bogged down with the little stuff. You want an overall sense of how well you accomplished what you set out to do.

Evaluate your draft

Use these questions to evaluate your draft. Note any places where you might make improvements.

Does your paper or project meet the assignment?

- Look again at your assignment and especially at the key words such as *analyze, define, evaluate,* and *propose.* Does your paper or project do what the assignment asks for? If not, how can you change it?
- Look again at the assignment for specific guidelines including length, format, and amount of research. Does your work meet these guidelines? If not, how can you change it?

Do you have a clear focus?

- Underline your thesis. Think how you might make your thesis more precise.
- Underline the main idea of each paragraph. Check how each paragraph connects to your thesis. Think about how you can strengthen the connections.

Are your main points adequately developed?

- Put brackets around the reasons and evidence that support your main points.
- Can you find places to add more examples and details that would help to explain your main points?

Is your organization effective?

- Make a quick outline of your draft if you have not done so already.
- Mark the places where you find abrupt shifts or gaps.
- Think about how you might rearrange sections or paragraphs to make your draft more effective.

Do you consider your potential readers' knowledge and points of view?

- Where do you give background if your readers are unfamiliar with your subject?
- Where do you acknowledge any opposing views your readers might have?

Do you represent yourself effectively?

- To the extent you can, forget for a moment that you wrote what you are reading. What impression do you have of you, the writer?
- Does the writer have an appropriate tone?
- Is the writer visually effective? Has the writer selected an attractive and readable font? Does the writer use headings and illustrations where they are helpful?

When you finish, make a list of your goals in the revision. You may have to scrap the draft and start over, but you will have a better sense of your subject and your goals.

Learn strategies for rewriting

Now it's time to go through your draft in detail. You should work on the goals you identify in your review. Also, look for other opportunities using this checklist.

1. Keep your audience in mind.	Reread each of your paragraphs' opening sentences and ask yourself whether they are engaging enough to keep your readers interested.
2. Sharpen your focus wherever possible.	You may have started out with a large topic but most of what you wrote concerns only one aspect. You may need to revise your thesis and supporting paragraphs.
3. Check if key terms are adequately defined.	What are your key terms? Are they defined precisely enough to be meaningful?
4. Develop where necessary.	Key points and claims may need more explanation and supporting evidence. Look for opportunities to add support without becoming redundant.
5. Check links between paragraphs.	Look for any places where you make abrupt shifts and make the transitions better. Check if you signal the relationship from one paragraph to the next.
6. Consider your title.	Many writers don't think much about titles, but they are very important. A good title makes the reader want to see what you have to say. Be as specific as you can in your title, and if possible, suggest your stance.
7. Consider your introduction.	In the introduction you want to get off to a fast start and convince your reader to keep reading. Cut to the chase.
8. Consider your conclusion.	Restating your thesis usually isn't the best way to finish; conclusions that offer only summary bore readers. The worst endings say something like "in my paper I've said this." Effective conclusions are interesting and provocative, leaving readers with something to think about.
9. Improve the visual aspects of your text.	Does the font you selected look attractive using your printer? Would headings and subheadings help to identify key sections? If you include statistical data, would charts be effective? Would illustrations help to establish key points?

Respond to others

Your instructor may ask you to respond to the drafts of your classmates. Responding to other people's writing requires the same careful attention you give to your own draft. To write a helpful response, you should go through the draft more than once.

First reading:
Read at your normal rate the first time through without stopping. When you finish you should have a clear sense of what the writer is trying to accomplish.

- Main idea: Write a sentence that summarizes what you think is the writer's main idea in the draft.
- Purpose: Write a sentence that summarizes what you think the writer was trying to accomplish in the draft.

Second reading:
In your second reading, you should be most concerned with the content, organization, and completeness of the draft. Make notes as you read.

- Introduction: Does the writer's first paragraph effectively introduce the topic and engage your interest?
- Thesis: Where exactly is the writer's thesis? Note in the margin where you think the thesis is located.
- Focus: Does the writer maintain focus on the thesis? Note any places where the writer seems to wander off to another topic.
- Organization: Are the sections and paragraphs ordered effectively? Do any paragraphs seem to be out of place? Do you note any abrupt shifts? Can you suggest a better order for the paragraphs?
- Completeness: Are there sections and paragraphs that lack key information or adequate development? Where do you want to know more?
- Sources: If the draft uses outside sources, are they cited accurately? If there are quotations, are they used correctly and worked into the fabric of the draft?

Third reading:
In your third reading, turn your attention to matters of audience, style, and tone.

- Audience: Who is the writer's intended audience? What does the writer assume the audience knows and believes?
- Style: Is the writer's style engaging? How would you describe the writer's voice?
- Tone: Is the tone appropriate for the writer's purpose and audience? Is the tone consistent throughout the draft? Are there places where another word or phrase might work better?

When you have finished the third reading, write a short paragraph on each bulleted item above, referring to specific paragraphs in the draft by number. Then end by answering these two questions:

1. **What does the writer do especially well in the draft?**
2. **What one or two things would most improve the draft in a revision?**

Pay attention to details last

When you finish revising, you are ready for one final careful reading keeping the goals of improving your style and eliminating errors in mind.

Edit for particular goals

1. Check the connections between sentences.	Notice how your sentences are connected. If you need to signal the relationship from one sentence to the next, use a transition word or phrase.
2. Check your sentences.	If you notice that a sentence doesn't sound right, think about how you might rephrase it. Often you will pick up problems by reading aloud. If a sentence seems too long, then you might break it into two or more sentences. If you notice a string of short sentences that sound choppy, then you might combine them.
3. Eliminate wordiness.	Writers tend to introduce wordiness in drafts. Look for long expressions that can easily be shortened ("at this point in time" –> "now") and for unnecessary repetition. Remove unnecessary words like *very*, *really*, and *totally*. See how many words you can take out without losing the meaning.
4. Use active verbs.	Anytime you can use a verb besides a form of be (*is*, *are*, *was*, *were*) or a verb ending in –ing, take advantage of the opportunity to make your style more lively. Sentences that begin with "There is (are)" and "It is" often have better alternatives.

Proofread carefully

In your final pass through your text, eliminate as many errors as you can. To become an effective proofreader, you have to learn to slow down. Some writers find that moving from word to word with a pencil slows them down enough to find errors. Others read backwards to force concentration on each word.

1. Know what your spelling checker can and can't do.	Spelling checkers are the greatest invention since peanut butter. They turn up many typos and misspellings that are hard to catch. But spelling checkers do not catch wrong words (e.g. "to much" should be "too much), where you leave off endings ("three dog"), and other similar errors.
2. Check for grammar and punctuation.	Nothing hurts your credibility more than leaving many errors in what you write. Many job application letters get tossed in the reject pile because an applicant made a single, glaring error. Readers probably shouldn't make such harsh judgments when they find errors, but in real life they do.

WRITE NOW

Write a helpful response

Read the following first draft and use the guidelines on page 31 to write a response that will help the writer to revise the paper. Resist the urge to edit sentences and correct mechanical errors. The assignment asked the student to analyze an ad. The revised version of this paper is on pages 49–51.

Analysis of an Ad

In our modern world of today, Americans see thousands of advertisements every year, we buy many products because of ads. One of the products advertised a lot is milk. I chose an Andy Roddick ad for this assignment because he is my very favorite tennis player. There was another totally awesome milk ad with Stone Cold Steve Austin, but I couldn't find it.

I found the picture of Andy in Seventeen magazine. I don't read Seventeen any more, but my younger sister does, and I needed to find an ad. Andy looks totally cool in this photo. He was on the court with his tennis racquet. His milk mustache is visible to the eye.

I suppose the milk people wanted him because he is popular and good looking. The milk ads all have celebrities and sports stars. I read that the milk people were worried that younger people aren't drinking milk and they wanted young stars to pitch milk and praise it's benefits. I guess its working because the ad campaign has been around as long as I can remember. I've even heard copycats use slogans like "Got cookies?" "Got fish?" "Got fish?" "Got sports?" and even "Got Jesus?"

The Roddick ad probably works because Roddick is good looking. As I said before, the milk people like good looking stars. He has kind of a sexy pose too. He looks like a movie star.

In conclusion, the Andy Roddick ad is a good ad because young people like Andy Roddick. If they see Andy Roddick drinking milk, they want to drink milk to.

Part 2

The Writer as Guide

5
Writing in College

Writers today do many different kinds of writing for multiple purposes.

Understand the demands of writing in college

Writing in college changes from course to course depending on the requirements of the course's discipline. What is expected in a philosophy course differs from what is expected in a biology course.

Nevertheless, there are some common expectations about writing in college that extend across disciplines.

Writing in college . . .	Writers are expected to . . .
States explicit claims	Make a claim that isn't obvious. The claim is often called a thesis statement.
Develops an argument	Support their claims with facts, evidence, reasons, and testimony from experts.
Analyzes with insight	Analyze in depth what they read and view.
Investigates complexity	Explore the complexity of a subject, challenging their readers by asking "Have you thought about this?" or "What if you discard the usual way of thinking about a subject and take the opposite point of view?"
Organizes with a hierarchical structure	Make the major parts evident to readers and to indicate which parts are subordinate to others.
Signals with transitions	Indicate logical relationships clearly so readers can follow a pathway without getting lost.
Document sources carefully	Provide the sources of information so readers can consult the same sources the writer used.

Think about your aim

What you want to accomplish guides your choices as a writer. You may want to reflect on your experience or the experiences of others. You may want to inform your readers about a subject. Or you may want to change your readers' attitudes about a subject or persuade them to take action. You will find out more about these aims for writing in the remaining chapters in Part 2.

AIM	FOCUS	EXAMPLES OF GENRES
Reflecting Chapter 7 page 52	Narrating personal experience and personal insights for a public audience	Journals, personal letters, blogs, memoirs, reflective essays
Observing Chapter 8 page 108	Describing accurately and vividly to create a dominant impression	Ethnographies, travel accounts, case studies, photo essays, on-the-scene articles
Informing Chapter 9 page 166	Communicating information clearly in a form suited for the reader	Newspaper and magazine articles, academic articles, brochures, government reports, profiles, informational Web sites
Analyzing texts Chapter 10 page 232	Analyzing what makes a text effective or ineffective and why the author made particular choices	Rhetorical analysis, short story analysis, visual analysis, academic essays
Analyzing causes Chapter 11 page 304	Exploring why an event, phenomenon, or trend happened	Causal analysis, accident analysis, financial analysis, history
Evaluating Chapter 12 page 366	Assessing whether something is good or bad according to particular criteria	Reviews, evaluative essays, performance evaluations, product evaluations
Arguing for a position Chapter 13 page 424	Convincing others through reasoned argument to accept or reject a position	Speeches, letters to the editor, op-ed columns, editorials, essays
Arguing for change Chapter 14 page 484	Convincing others through reasoned argument to take action	Speeches, business proposals, grant proposals, letters of application, advocacy Web sites, advertisements

Use your aim as a guide

In many cases, if you know your aim in advance, you have a good start toward how to structure your paper or project.

For example, you might want to evaluate a Shetland Sheepdog (sheltie) as a breed. For an evaluation, you know that your thesis will take the form of _____ is a good/bad, better/best/worst _____ according to these criteria: _____, _____, _____. With this guide, you come up with the following: *The sheltie is one of the best breeds because shelties are highly intelligent, extremely loyal, responsive, and easy to train.*

Chapters 7 through 14 show you how to use your aim to guide the development of your paper or project.

WORKING TOGETHER

Use aims to create thesis statements

In a group of three or four students

Come up with a list of subjects that your group has some interest in and knows something about. They could be big subjects like global warming or more limited subjects like your school's shuttle bus system.

As a group, brainstorm thesis statements for at least three aims. For example, on the subject of eating disorders, you might come up with something like the following.

Reflecting
My younger sister overcame her bulimia disorder during her last two years of high school when successes in school and in music improved her self-esteem.

Informing
Anorexia nervosa is diagnosed when patients weigh 15% under the normal body weight for their height and is characterized by starvation, excessive exercise, and sometimes forced vomiting.

Analyzing Causes
The causes of eating disorders are not a failure of will but are medical illnesses that take on a life of their own.

Arguing for Change
Less money and effort should be spent to find drugs to treat eating disorders, and more effort should go toward teaching adolescents to deal with negative thoughts about their bodies and to develop a positive body image.

Think about your genre

Be aware of genre

Genre is a term for a kind of writing or form of communication. When you walk into your video store, you find movies classified by genre: action, animation, comedy, documentary, drama, family, horror, sci-fi, and so on. The music industry classifies music by genre: alternative, blues, classical, country, electronic, folk, gospel, jazz, rap, reggae, rock, world, and so on.

Most of the time we recognize genre in writing immediately—junk mail, a letter of application, a novel, a lease for an apartment, an informative brochure. We know a great deal more than just the form. We know, for example, that junk mail is trying to sell something, and we know to be suspicious of any offers of free products. Likewise, we know that the person writing a letter of application wants to get a job or enter a selective program.

Be aware of how genre influences style

The genre you select has a strong influence on the style you use. Compare the first paragraphs of a research report, a news article, and a blog on beach erosion.

Research report

Coastal management as a distinct practice emerged just a few decades ago, when ideas and information were exchanged through mostly conventional means. Scientists and coastal planners gave talks and presented posters at conferences and workshops, as they still do. Field trips and tours organized as part of these events highlighted problems and success stories. Agency experts prepared and distributed reports and guidelines. Academics researched problems and systematically evaluated methods to address them, reporting their results in new periodicals like the *Coastal Zone Management Journal*. Face-to-face meetings, telephone conversations, the U.S. Postal Service, and later the fax machine played key roles in the development of ideas and movement of information to address coastal problems. Working with these communication tools, professionals and concerned citizens alike drew from their personal experience, new state and federal legislative mandates, and a palpable sense of urgency to create a new practice called coastal zone management. At the time, the demand was great for scientific data and information about coastal resources and use, for tools to interpret this information, and for strategies and processes to apply it for problem solving. And the information flowed freely, albeit by slower and less sophisticated means than today.

The H. John Heinz III Center for Science, Economics and the Environment, *Innovation by Design: Improving Learning Networks in Coastal Management,* 2004.

News article

> When scientists consider the possible effects of global warming, there is a lot they don't know. But they can say one thing for sure: sea levels will rise.
>
> Cornelia Dean, "Next Victim of Global Warming: The Beaches," *New York Times online*, June 20, 2006.

Blog

B Blogger   Push-Button Publishing

> First it was the State Legislature in Albany. Then it was the County Legislature in Mineola.
>
> Now, the dysfunction has spread to the Long Beach City Council, which voted last week—unanimously, no less—not to proceed with plans to protect the seashore of the barrier island on which this city by the sea is located.
>
> The Community Alliance Blog, "Legislative Dysfunction Under The Boardwalk." May 8, 2006 (http://the communityalliance.blogspot.com/2006/05/ by-sea-by-sea-by-beautiful-sea.html).

Even though each writer is writing about the same subject, notice what is different.

Sentence length	• The report has much longer sentences than the newspaper article or the blog.
Paragraph length	• The report has long paragraphs compared to the short paragraph of the newspaper article and the blog.
Word choice	• The report uses much more formal language than the blog. The newspaper language is neutral.
Relationship with the reader	• The report and newspaper writers are distant and objective. The blog writer is passionately involved with the issue.

WRITE NOW

Compare styles across genres

Find a newspaper article on a current social, economic, political, or scientific issue. Then find a scholarly article on the same subject using scholar.google.com/ or one of the databases on your library's Web site. Next, search blogs for the same subject using blogsearch.google.com.

Compare the styles of the scientific article, the newspaper article, and the blog using the following criteria: overall length, paragraph length, sentence length, word choice, relationship with the reader, and use of graphics and images. Write a summary of your analysis.

6
Writing Effectively

When people write for others to read, they become guides for others.
They show readers new places and help readers see places where they've
been with new eyes.

Understand the rhetorical situation

At the most basic level, communication involves the interaction of three things: the writer or speaker, the audience, and the subject. These three elements are often represented by a triangle.

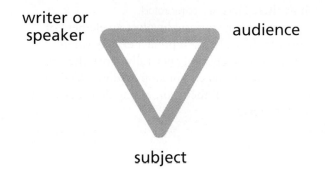

writer or speaker

audience

subject

All three elements—speaker, subject, and audience—are necessary for an act of communication to occur. Think about all the times you talk and listen in a day. Who are the people you talk with regularly? What do you talk about? Even if you are talking to or writing to yourself, you still have an audience. And all three elements are in a dynamic relationship. Every one of us makes adjustments depending on our audience (think of how you talk to small children). Just as speakers adjust to audiences, audiences continually adjust to speakers (think of how your attitude toward a speaker changes for the better when that person can make you laugh).

Persuade others

The ancient Greeks recognized that the dynamic nature of the rhetorical triangle is the key to understanding how an audience is persuaded. Aristotle (384–323 BCE) defined rhetoric as the art of finding the best available means of persuasion in any situation. He set out three primary tactics of persuasion: appeals based on the trustworthiness of the speaker (ethos); appeals to the emotions and deepest-held values of the audience (pathos); and appeals to logic, reasoning, and evidence (logos).

These appeals likewise can be represented using the rhetorical triangle.

Aristotle's insight about how people can be persuaded remains relevant today. To give an example, imagine that you drive every day on Lakeside Boulevard, a divided highway with a grass median. You've read about numerous accidents on Lakeside Boulevard and witnessed two horrible accidents, when cars and trucks skidded across the median and collided head-on with traffic in the opposite lanes. You want your city council to vote to erect a concrete barrier that will prevent these frequent head-on collisions. One approach would be to use logic and evidence, documenting that Lakeside Boulevard has far more fatal accidents per mile than other streets in your city (logos). Another would be to invite an expert on traffic safety to speak to the city council (ethos). A third way would be to appeal to the council about the unnecessary loss of life caused by the unsafe street (pathos). Often you will use all of these appeals to gain support of an audience.

Ethos
appeals to the character and expertise of the writer or speaker

Pathos
appeals to the beliefs and values of the audience

Logos
appeals based on logic, reasoning, and evidence concerning the subject

Think about your audience

When you talk with someone face-to-face, you receive constant feedback from that person, even when you're doing all the talking. Your listener may nod in agreement, frown, act bored, and give you a variety of other signals.

Unless your listener is deliberately acting, you have a sense of how they are responding to what you are saying. If your listener looks puzzled, for example, you can try explaining again.

Imagine your readers

When you write, you rarely receive immediate response from readers. Most of the time you don't know exactly how readers will react to what you write. You have to think consciously about your readers and anticipate how they might respond.

Write for college readers

Readers of college writing expect more than what they can find out from a Google search or an online encyclopedia. Facts are easy to obtain from databases and print sources. Readers want to know how these facts are connected.

Good college writing involves an element of surprise. If readers can predict exactly where a writer is going, even if they fully agree, they will either skim to the end or stop reading. Readers expect you to tell them something that they don't know already.

WORKING TOGETHER

Analyze advertisements

Magazines sell advertising by targeting specific readers. Bring to class a magazine that you read regularly or one that you find interesting. Organize in groups of three or four students and exchange magazines with each other. Look at the articles and the advertising in the magazine.

Analyze your classmate's magazine for these criteria.

1. What is the target age group?
2. What percentages of men and women are likely to read the magazine?
3. What income level is targeted?
4. Is a particular ethnicity being targeted?
5. What else is being assumed about the audience? For magazines that cover a specific subject or activity (for example, backpacking, beauty, snowboarding, parenting, fitness, cats, and so on), what other products and services do you find being advertised?

Share your analysis with other members of your group. Ask the person who brought the magazine you analyzed if he or she agrees with your description of the target audience.

STAYING ON TRACK

Know what college readers expect

Readers expect to be challenged.
Simple answers that can be easily looked up are not adequate.

OFF TRACK
The United States entered World War II when the Japanese attacked Pearl Harbor on December 7, 1941. *(This fact is well known and not informative for college readers.)*

ON TRACK
The war with Japan actually began on July 25, 1941, when President Franklin Roosevelt froze Japanese assets and declared an oil embargo, leaving the Japanese with the choices of abandoning the war with China or neutralizing the United States Navy in order to secure oil resources in Indonesia.

Readers expect claims to be backed up with reasons and evidence.
Simple explanations without support are not adequate.

OFF TRACK
New York City is an exciting place to live, but I wouldn't want to move there because of the crime. *(Is crime really that much higher in New York City?)*

ON TRACK
Many people don't know that New York City is the safest large city in the United States according to FBI crime statistics. It even ranks in the top 20 safest cities among the 210 cities with populations over 100,000.

Readers expect complex answers for complex problems.
Simple solutions for complex problems are not adequate.

OFF TRACK
We need posters urging students not to litter so much on campus. *(Are posters alone likely to solve the problem?)*

ON TRACK
Most of the litter on our campus is paper, bottles, and cans—all recy-clable—yet there are almost no recycle containers on campus. Putting recycle containers in high-litter locations along with a "don't litter" campaign could go a long way toward making our campus cleaner.

Readers expect writers to be engaged.
Readers expect writers to be curious and genuinely concerned about their subjects.

OFF TRACK
Older people have to deal with too much bureaucracy to obtain health care. *(The statement rings true but doesn't motivate readers.)*

ON TRACK
After spending seven hours with my 78-year-old aunt on hold on a help line that never answered while sorting through stacks of booklets and forms, I became convinced that the Medicare prescription drug program is an aging American's worst nightmare.

Think about your credibility

Some writers begin with credibility because of who they are. If you wonder what foods compose a balanced meal for your dog, you probably would listen carefully to the advice of a veterinarian. Most writers, however, have to convince their readers to keep reading by demonstrating knowledge of their subject and concern with their readers' needs.

Think about how you want your readers to see you

To get your readers to take you seriously, you must convince them that they can trust you. You need to get them to see you as

Concerned

Readers want you to be committed to what you are writing about. They also expect you to be concerned with them as readers. After all, if you don't care about them, why should they read what you write?

Well informed

Many people ramble on about any subject without knowing anything about it. If they are family members, you have to suffer their opinions, but it is not enjoyable. College writing requires that you do your homework on a subject.

Fair

Many writers look at only one side of an issue. Readers respect objectivity and an unbiased approach.

Ethical

Many writers use only the facts that support their positions and often distort facts and sources. Critical readers often notice what is being left out. Don't try to conceal what doesn't support your position.

STAYING ON TRACK

Build your credibility

Know what's at stake
What you are writing about should matter to your readers. If its importance is not evident, it's your job to explain why your readers should consider it important.

OFF TRACK

We should be concerned about two-thirds of Central and South America's 110 brightly colored harlequin frog species becoming extinct in the last twenty years. *(The loss of any species is unfortunate, but the writer gives us no other reason for concern.)*

ON TRACK

The rapid decline of amphibians worldwide due to global warming may be the advance warning of the loss of cold-weather species such as polar bears, penguins, and reindeer.

STAYING ON TRACK

Have your readers in mind

If you are writing about a specialized subject that your readers don't know much about, take the time to explain key concepts.

OFF TRACK

Reduction in the value of a debt security, especially a bond, results from a rise in interest rates. Conversely, a decline in interest rates results in an increase in the value of a debt security, especially bonds. *(The basic idea is here, but it is not expressed clearly, especially if the reader is not familiar with investing.)*

ON TRACK

Bond prices move inversely to interest rates. When interest rates go up, bond prices go down, and when interest rates go down, bond prices go up.

Think about alternative solutions and points of view.

Readers appreciate a writer's ability to see a subject from multiple perspectives.

OFF TRACK

We will reduce greenhouse gas and global warming only if we greatly increase wind-generated electricity. *(Wind power is an alternative energy source, but it is expensive and many people don't want windmills in scenic areas. The writer also doesn't mention using energy more efficiently.)*

ON TRACK

If the world is serious about limiting carbon emissions to reduce global warming, then along with increasing efficient energy use, all non-carbon-emitting energy sources must be considered, including nuclear power. Nuclear power now produces about 20 percent of U.S. electricity with no emissions—the equivalent of taking 58 million passenger cars off the road.

Write well

Nothing impresses readers more than graceful, fluent writing that is clear, direct, and forceful. Even if readers don't agree with you in the end, they still will appreciate your writing ability.

OFF TRACK

Nobody can live today without taking some risks, even very rich people. After all, we don't know what we're breathing in the air. A lot of food has chemicals and hormones in it. There's a big hole in the ozone, so more people will get skin cancer. And a lot of people have sexually transmitted diseases these days. *(The impact of the point is lost with unfocused writing.)*

ON TRACK

We live in a world of risks beyond our control to the extent that it is difficult to think of anything that is risk free down to the most basic human acts—sex in an era of AIDS, eating in an era of genetically altered food, walking outside in an ozone-depleted atmosphere, drinking water and breathing air laden with chemicals whose effects we do not understand.

Become an effective writer

Learning how to write well may be the most important part of your college education. Many surveys that ask college graduates what they most value about their education report that they rank writing and communication skills far above anything else they learned. If you write well, you will become more confident and more successful in whatever you do.

What makes college writing effective

You can become a successful college writer if you do two things: write regularly and learn what makes writing effective. Effective writing is judged by the following criteria.

On task
The paper or project does what the assignment asks for.

Focused
The paper or project has a clear thesis or main point, and all paragraphs are relevant to that main point.

Organized
The order of the major points and paragraphs is clear to the reader.

Developed
Major points are supported with reasons, evidence, and examples.

Linked
Paragraphs and sentences have transitions that mark relationships.

Stylistically fluent
The sentences are varied and energetic, with active verbs.

Concise
The language is efficient without unnecessary words.

Correct
The final version is free from major errors.

Well designed
The format should be correct, the font readable, the headings consistent, and all photographs and charts clearly labeled.

Effective writing

The qualities of effective writing are evident in Angela Yamashita's essay "Got Roddick?" Her assignment was to select an advertisement and analyze how it makes appeals to ethos, pathos, and logos.

Yamashita 1

Angela Yamashita

Dr. Sanchez

English 15

12 December 2005

Got Roddick?

Andy Roddick is one of the hottest professional athletes today. In 2003 he became the youngest American to finish ranked number one in the ATP rankings, and he's known not only for his excellent playing skills but also for his good looks and easygoing attitude. Ex-boyfriend to popular singer Mandy Moore, Roddick has been thrown into the spotlight and is now a teenage crush. It was his picture that stopped me while leafing through Seventeen and made me take a longer look. Roddick stands staring at the viewer, racquet over his shoulder, leaning against the net on the court. More prominent than his white pants, white tennis shirt, and white towel draped around his neck is the white milk mustache above his upper lip. The ad reads: "Now serving. I'm into power. So I drink milk. It packs 9 essential nutrients into every glass. Which comes in handy whether you're an athlete or an energetic fan." At the bottom of the page is the ad slogan (also in white) "Got Milk?"

The "Got Milk?" campaign has published numerous ads that try to convince adults to drink more milk. Everyone from rock groups to actors to athletes have participated in this campaign. In today's caffeine-obsessed society of coffee and soda drinkers, America's Dairy Farmers and Milk Processors (the association that sponsors the "Got Milk?" campaign) felt the need to reverse the decline in milk consumption by advertising milk in a new way. The catchy "Got Milk?" proved to be highly successful, and the campaign has been

The heading is in the correct MLA format. The paper is free of major errors.

The title plays off the theme of the ad and suggests the content.

The writer gets off to a fast start, introducing her subject in the first sentence.

The writer engages her subject.

Angela describes the ad with specifics.

Angela provides background information

49

Yamashita 2

"Got Milk?" ad featuring Andy Roddick

Angela includes the ad along with the caption.

mimicked by many others including "Got cookies?" "Got fish?"
"Got sports?" and even "Got Jesus?" (Philpot). The Andy Roddick ad
is typical of the "Got Milk?" series, urging people young and old to
drink milk to remain healthy and strong. The Roddick ad primarily
uses the appeals of ethos and pathos to persuade its audience. (The
one gesture toward logos in the ad is the mention that milk has nine
nutrients.)

Angela cites the source of her information.

Thesis of paper

    To establish the ethos of their ads, America's Dairy Farmers and
Milk Processors use celebrity endorsements. The "Got Milk?"
campaign has enlisted a range of celebrities popular with young
audiences from Kelly Clarkson to Sheryl Crow, Bebe Neuwirth to
Ben Roethlisberger, T-Mac (Tracy McGrady) to Bernie Mac.
Choosing Andy Roddick, the dominant young male player in
American tennis, fits squarely in this lineup. Admired by a strong
following of young adults (girls for his looks, boys for his athletic
ability), Roddick is an ideal spokesman for establishing that milk is a
healthy drink. Implicit in the ad is that milk will help you become a
better athlete and better looking too.

Repeating "ethos" makes a smooth transition.

Angela explains why Andy Roddick was chosen as a spokesperson.

Yamashita 3

Pathos in the ad is conveyed not simply through Roddick's good looks. His pose is casual, almost slouching, yet his face is serious, one that suggests that he not only means business about playing tennis but also about his drink of choice. The words "I'm into power" don't mess around. They imply that you too can be more powerful by drinking milk. "Now serving" is also in your face, making a play on the word "serving" both as a tennis and a drink term.

The effectiveness of the "Got Milk?" campaign is demonstrated in gallons of milk sold. The campaign began in California in 1993 at a time when milk sales were rapidly eroding. A San Francisco ad agency developed the milk mustache idea, which is credited for stopping the downward trend in milk consumption in California. In 1995 the campaign went national. By 2000 national sales of milk remained consistent in contrast to annual declines in the early 1990s (Stamler). "Got Milk?" gave milk a brand identity that it had previously lacked, allowing it to compete with the well-established identities of Pepsi and Coca-Cola. Milk now has new challengers with more and more people going out to Starbuck's and other breakfast bars. Nonetheless, the original formula of using celebrities like Andy Roddick who appeal to younger audiences continues to work. Milk isn't likely to go away soon as a popular beverage.

Angela analyzes the appeals to pathos.

Angela looks closely at the language the ad uses.

The history of the "Got Milk?" campaign is given briefly and the source is documented.

Angela's style is efficient and appropriate for college readers.

The ending provides new ideas for readers to think about rather than simply summarizing what has been said.

Yamashita 4

Works Cited

"Andy Rodick." Got Milk? 2003. Milk Processor Education Program. 18 Nov. 2005 <http://www.whymilk.com/celebrity_archive.htm>.

Philpot, Robert. "Copycats Mimic 'Got Milk' Ads." Milwaukee Journal Sentinel 12 May 2002, final ed.: D3.

Stamler, Bernard. "Got Sticking Power?" New York Times 30 July 2001, late ed.: C11.

Angela includes a list of works cited in the correct MLA format. If readers want to look at her sources, they should be able to find them easily.

7

Reflecting

A successful reflection engages readers and allows them to see an event, person, or thing through your eyes, but more important, by thinking about your reflections, readers often find out something about themselves.

Chapter contents

Writing reflections

When we reflect, we consider an idea or experience in order to come to a greater understanding of its significance. Unless we are writing in a private diary or journal, we use reflective writing to share our experience and its significance with others. Reflecting is also a way of understanding ourselves. By connecting memories of the past to our knowledge in the present, we learn about who we were and who we have become.

Reflective essays can address deeply emotional issues like family relationships, personal failings, and dramatic crises. But reflection does not always involve personal topics. In some cases, being too personal or confessional can limit a writer's ability to connect to his or her audience.

The goal of reflection should not be simply to vent pent-up emotions or to expose secrets (although when done well, these techniques can be effective). Instead, it should allow the audience to share with the writer a discovery of significance. A reflection on an important event in the history of a family should do more than focus on the writer's feelings; it should explore how each family member changed as a result.

Components of reflections

What people, places, and events stand out in my memory?

Find a reflective topic

Listing is one way to identify possible topics for reflective writing. You might list people, events, or places that have been significant in your life, then look back over your list and check the items that seem especially vivid to you.

Will my readers be interested?

Consider your readers

How interesting will this topic be to your readers? Will they want to share in your experience?

What is my purpose?

Identify a purpose

A clear purpose makes the reflection coherent. Your purpose is not to teach a lesson about life but rather to convey the significance of the experience—why it is important or memorable and why it is worth writing and reading about.

What key details communicate the significance of my reflection?

Provide concrete details

Concrete details stimulate readers' imagination and make your reflection come alive. Use factual details such as dates to provide background information. Augment visual details with your other senses: smells, sounds, tastes, and feelings.

Use dialog when possible

Convey interaction between people with their words.

How do I organize my reflection?

Think about your organization

Telling what happened in a chronological order is the simplest organization for writers to use, but it is not the only one possible. Conceptual order explores different points and links them together. For example, you might reflect on a photograph, examining details one by one and discussing how they related to your family's past.

What is the most engaging way to begin?

Start fast

The beginning of a reflection must show the writer's involvement and gain the reader's interest.

Finish strong

Effective conclusions invite readers to reflect further. Ending with a question or an issue to think about is usually better than trying to sum up with a moral lesson.

Keys to reflections

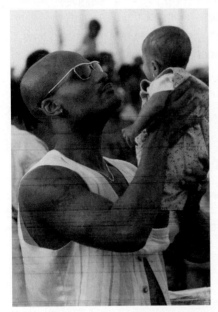

Snapshots freeze important moments in people's lives.

Tell a good story

Readers have to be interested in your story to understand the significance. Often reflections gain and keep readers' interest by presenting a conflict or a difficult decision that must be resolved.

Let the details convey the significance

Select details carefully to communicate meaning. Identify people by more than how they look. Think about mannerisms, gestures, and habits to suggest their character.

Be honest

Telling the truth about your thoughts and actions can build a strong rapport with your audience, but beware of becoming sentimental. Too much emotion may turn readers off.

Focus on the little things in life

A reflection need not reveal earth-shattering secrets or teach crucial life lessons. It may be as simple as describing something that makes you happy. Remember that small moments of significance can be just as rewarding for readers as great events.

For a reflection on an image or object, let the reflection grow out of the details

Your close reading of details and your explanation of the significance of the experience is critical.

WORKING TOGETHER

Reflecting on photographs

In a group of three or four students

- Look at a selection of photographs from newspapers, magazines, or a photo Web log such as **www.chromasia.com.**
- Have each person work with two or three photos, making a list of the people each image reminds you of, the things the image makes you think about, and the places you associate with the image. Write a brief narrative for each image.
- Share your memories and narratives with the group. Which ones strike you as the most engaging and interesting? How would you develop or change the narratives of other students?

An effective reflection

Effective reflective writing can only come after honest examination of memories, perceptions, and meanings.

Some Lines for a Younger Brother . . .
Sue Kunitomi Embrey

Sue Kunitomi Embrey was born in Los Angeles and lived there until she and her family were forced to move to the Manzanar War Relocation Camp on May 9, 1942, where she stayed until the end of World War II. She has become a spokeswoman for the thousands of Japanese-Americans who were incarcerated during the anti-Japanese hysteria of that time. In this essay, she recalls the life and death of her youngest brother Tets, who spent three years of his childhood in Manzanar.

Some Lines for a Younger Brother . . .

I still remember the day he was born. It was early April and Papa came into the kitchen with a smile on his face. He said we had a baby brother. In the months to follow, we were busy carrying and cuddling the brother who was many years younger than the rest of us. When he cried from hunger and Mama was busy, one of us would run into the bedroom and rock the bed or pick him up and quiet him.

We were a family of five sons and three daughters. Money was scarce. My father ran a moving and transfer business in L'il Tokyo, the Japanese community in the shadow of City Hall in Los Angeles, but people had little money to pay him. He came home with boxes of books bartered for his services, and we spent many hours curled up in a corner reading some popular fiction story.

Tets, as we called him, was eight years old when Papa was killed in an automobile accident a week before Christmas. Tets cried because he could not give his dad the present he had made at school. The bullies would beat him up now that he had no father, he said.

Pearl Harbor was attacked by the Japanese when Tets was in elementary school. Rumors of sabotage couldn't be separated from the facts. Soon there was a

Embrey begins with her earliest memory of her brother, making it clear that he will be the focus of her reflection.

Outside events are fitted into the family's personal chronology. Embrey shows vividly the impact of the decision to intern Japanese-Americans.

clamor on the West Coast for wholesale evacuation of all Japanese into inland camps. The democratic process was lost in hysteria. The grocery store which we had purchased only a year before was sold at a loss. All the furniture we couldn't sell, the plants my mother had tenderly cared for, our small personal treasures went to a neighborhood junk dealer. Tears came when we saw the truck being loaded.

On the first Sunday in May, 1942, Manzanar Relocation Center became our war-time home. Before breakfast, we walked around the dry, dusty land, to get acquainted with the landscape. The sun sparkled against the Sierra Nevada mountains to the west. The brown Inyo hills were high-rising barriers, more formidable than the barbed wire which was soon to enclose us. As we wondered how the pioneers had crossed over the Sierras, someone asked, "How long do we have to stay here?" and someone quoted from the military instructions, "For the duration of the war, and six months thereafter." Six months are forever, and forever is a long, long time.

Some order became evident within a few months after the fear, confusion and shock of transplantation from the big city to the arid land of Manzanar. Catholic nuns, who had joined the evacuees, found empty barracks and started a school. The War Relocation Authority recruited teachers from the "outside." Many of them were Quakers with a real desire to serve their fellow man.

When I asked Tets what he was studying, he shrugged his shoulders. There were no chairs, no desks, no supplies, he said. "What's the use of studying American history when we're behind barbed wires?" he asked. I tried to tell him that it would matter some day, but I was not sure any more. "Someday," I said, "the government would realize it had made a mistake and would try to correct it." His eyes were narrow against the noon sun, his whole body positioned badly to the right as he looked at me and said, "You 'da kind'? I lose fight." The colloquial speech was everywhere among the second generation. "Da kind" categorically placed me among those who argued for and defended American democracy. The second expression was used

Details about the relocation camp reinforce the sense of isolation and hopelessness it evokes.

Embrey uses dialog to recount a significant conversation she had with her brother, one that she has remembered for many years.

constantly, but it meant different things to different people.

"Try walking out that gate," he added. "See if they don't shoot you in the back." With that, he walked away.

The rest of us managed to get out of confinement— to Chicago, to Madison, Wisconsin. Three brothers entered the United States Army. Tets was left with his aging mother and he was to spend almost three years behind barbed wires.

By 1948 when the family was partially reunited and settled in Los Angeles, Tets was in high school, or we thought he was. One day a school counselor came to the door. He reported that Tets had not been in school for several weeks and that he had been missing school sporadically for several months. He saw the shock on our faces. We had been too busy working to be suspicious.

"I'm looking for a job," Tets said, when confronted.

"But you can't find a job without a high school diploma," I protested. ←

"So I found out," he answered. "Learning to say 'isn't' instead of 'ain't' doesn't get you a job. They want us to have experience to land a job, but how can we get experience if we can't get a job?"

I asked him what he was going to do.

"I'm going to join the Army," was his reply.

Day in and day out, this was his argument. "I'm going to join the Army when I'm eighteen. You won't have me around to bother you and I'll be doing some traveling. I'm tired of holding up the buildings in L'il Tokyo. There's nothing to do and no place to go where I can be with my friends."

He was sure that wars were over for a while and there would be no danger. He signed up one day and was gone the next. He came home on furlough, husky and tanned, a lot taller and more confident than when he had left. He had been in training camp in Louisiana and had seen much of the country. Before he left, he broke the news to us that he had signed up for another three years so he wouldn't have to serve in the reserves. He was transferred to the West Coast and we saw him often when he hitch-hiked home on

Again, Embrey uses dialog to show viewers a turning point in her brother's life. As in the internment camp, this argument centers on whether he should go to school, but it is clear there are deeper issues at play for Embrey and for Tets.

weekends. One day he phoned collect from San Jose. He was being shipped out to Japan and it would probably be a year before he would be back.

His hitch was almost over when the Korean War broke out. Soon after his 22nd birthday, he wrote that he hoped to be home for Christmas. He explained that he had not been sleeping well lately since some veterans had been brought into his barracks. They had nightmares and they screamed in the night. The stories of war they told could not be shut out of his mind. There was a rumor going around that his company might be going over to replace the first groups. He hoped his timetable for discharge would not change. He was worried and that was why he had not written.

Tets came home before Christmas. He came home in a flag-draped coffin, with one of his buddies as a military escort. The funeral at the Koyasan Buddhist Church was impressive. There was a change of guards every few minutes. Their soft-spoken order mixed with the solemn chants. The curling incense smoke made hazy halos of the young faces who came mourning a dead friend.

Embrey uses vivid detail to re-create her dead brother's funeral.

On December 27, 1969, I joined several hundred young people who made a day-long pilgrimage to the Manzanar cemetery. While I helped clean out the sagebrush and manzanilla, pulled tumbleweeds out of my boots, I was interrupted many times to recall facts and figures for the NBC and CBS television crews who were there to record the event.

Mt. Williamson's peak crested somewhere in the grey clouds that drew menacingly closer as the hours passed. Soon there was no sun. No seven-mile shadow lay across Owens Valley.

Dedication services ended that freezing, windswept and emotional day. I looked beyond the crowd and the monument. Out of the painful memories my mind dusted out of the past, I saw again the blurred impressions of the barbed-wire fence, the sentry towers and the tar-papered barracks. For a moment I saw again the 12-year-old boy with his head cocked, his shoulders sagging, his eyes fighting to keep open in the sun, while the long and lonely desert stretched out behind him.

Embrey ends with an almost wistful recollection of her brother.

How to read reflections

Make notes as you read, either in the margins or on paper or a computer file. Circle any words or references that you don't know and look them up.

What is it?	• What kind of a text is it? A memoir? a letter? a diary? an essay? a short story? a photographic essay? What are your expectations for this kind of text? • What media are used? (Web sites, for example, often combine images, words, and sounds.)
Where did it come from?	• Who wrote the reflection? • What do you know about the writer's background that might have influenced the reflection?
Who is the intended audience?	• What clues do you find about whom the writer had in mind as the readers? • What does the writer assume that the readers already know about the subject? • What new knowledge is the writer providing?
What is the significance of the reflection?	• Does the writer give precise, objective, concrete details? • Does the writer comment on the reflections? • What did you learn or come to understand differently by reading the reflection?
How is the reflection organized?	• Chronologically? In order of perceived importance? Or some other way?
How is it composed?	• How does the writer represent herself or himself? • How would you characterize the style? • How effective is the design? Is it easy to read? • If there are any photographs or other graphics, what information do they contribute?

Two Ways to Belong to America
(EDITORIAL)
Bharati Mukherjee

The New York Times

Novelist Bharati Mukherjee moved to the United States when she was 21 to study at the University of Iowa, and she later became a professor at the University of California at Berkeley. She wrote the following opinion piece in response to changes in federal immigration law in the 1990s. The article originally appeared in the *New York Times* in 1996.

Analyzing and Connecting
Return to these questions after you have finished reading.

1. What does Mukherjee reveal or explain in this essay that is new to you? How does this essay change or add to your feelings about immigration?

2. How is the focus of her reflection revealed in the essay's title?

3. Mukherjee is an obvious choice to author an editorial on immigration, since she herself is an immigrant to America. But why did Mukherjee choose to write this piece about herself and her sister? How does the wealth of detail about their lives contribute to the impact of the essay?

4. Why do you think Bharati Mukherjee's sister Mira clung to her Indian identity while Bharati was not interested in preserving her Indian roots?

TWO WAYS TO BELONG TO AMERICA

Bharati Mukherjee

IOWA CITY -- This is a tale of two sisters from Calcutta, Mira and Bharati, who have lived in the United States for some 35 years, but who find themselves on different sides in the current debate over the status of immigrants.

I am an American citizen and she is not. I am moved that thousands of long-term residents are finally taking the oath of citizenship. She is not.

Mira arrived in Detroit in 1960 to study child psychology and pre-school education. I followed her a year later to study creative writing at the University of Iowa. When we left India, we were almost identical in appearance and attitude. We dressed alike, in saris; we expressed identical views on politics, social issues, love and marriage in the same Calcutta convent-school accent. We would endure our two years in America, secure our degrees, then return to India to marry the grooms of our father's choosing.

Instead, Mira married an Indian student in 1962 who was getting his business administration degree at Wayne State University. They soon acquired the labor certifications necessary for the green card of hassle-free residence and employment.

Mira still lives in Detroit, works in the Southfield, Mich., school system, and has become nationally recognized for her contributions in the fields of pre-school education and parent-teacher relationships. After 36 years as a legal immigrant in this country, she clings passionately to her Indian citizenship and hopes to go home to India when she retires.

In Iowa City in 1963, I married a fellow student, an American of Canadian parentage. Because of the accident of his North Dakota birth, I bypassed labor-certification requirements and the race-related "quota" system that favored the applicant's country of origin over his or her merit.

I was prepared for (and even welcomed) the emotional strain that came with marrying outside my ethnic community. In 33 years of marriage, we have lived in every part of North America. By choosing a husband who was not my father's selection, I was opting for fluidity, self-invention, blue jeans and T-shirts, and renouncing 3,000 years (at least) of caste-observant, "pure culture" marriage in the Mukherjee family. My books have often been read as unapologetic (and in some quarters overenthusiastic) texts for cultural and psychological "mongrelization." It's a word I celebrate.

Mira and I have stayed sisterly close by phone. In our regular Sunday morning conversations, we are unguardedly affectionate. I am her only blood relative on this continent. We expect to see each other through the looming crises of aging and ill health without being asked. Long before Vice President Gore's "Citizenship U.S.A." drive, we'd had our polite arguments over the ethics of retaining an overseas citizenship while expecting the permanent protection and economic benefits that come with living and working in America.

Like well-raised sisters, we never said what was really on our minds, but we probably pitied one another. She, for the lack of structure in my life, the erasure of Indianness, the absence of an unvarying daily core. I, for the narrowness of her perspective, her uninvolvement with the mythic depths or the superficial pop culture of this society. But, now, with the scapegoating of "aliens" (documented or illegal) on the increase, and the targeting of long-term legal immigrants like Mira for new scrutiny and new self-consciousness, she and I find ourselves unable to maintain the same polite discretion. We were always unacknowledged adversaries, and we are now, more than ever, sisters.

"I feel used," Mira raged on the phone the other night. "I feel manipulated and discarded. This is such an unfair way to treat a person who was invited to stay and work here because of her talent. My employer went to the I.N.S. and petitioned for the labor certification. For over 30 years, I've invested my creativity and professional skills into the improvement of this country's pre-school system. I've obeyed all the rules, I've paid my taxes, I love my work, I love my students, I love the friends I've made. How dare America now change its rules in midstream? If America wants to make new rules curtailing benefits of legal immigrants, they should apply only to immigrants who arrive after those rules are already in place." To my ears, it sounded like the description of a long-enduring, comfortable yet loveless marriage, without risk or recklessness. Have we the right to demand, and to expect, that we be loved? (That, to me, is the subtext of the arguments by immigration advocates.) My sister is an expatriate, professionally generous and creative, socially courteous and gracious, and that's as far as her Americanization can go. She is here to maintain an identity, not to transform it.

I asked her if she would follow the example of others who have decided to become citizens because of the anti-immigration bills in Congress. And here, she surprised me. "If America wants to play the manipulative game, I'll play it too," she snapped. "I'll become a U.S. citizen for now, then change back to Indian when I'm ready to go home. I feel some kind of irrational attachment to India that I don't to America. Until all this hysteria against legal immigrants, I was totally happy. Having my green card meant I could visit any place in the world I wanted to and then come back to a job that's satisfying and that I do very well."

In one family, from two sisters alike as peas in a pod, there could not be a wider divergence of immigrant experience. America spoke to me—I married it—I embraced the demotion from expatriate aristocrat to immigrant nobody, surrendering those thousands of years of "pure culture," the saris, the delightfully accented English. She retained them all. Which of us is the freak?

Mira's voice, I realize, is the voice not just of the immigrant South Asian community but of an immigrant community of the millions who have stayed rooted in one job, one city, one house, one ancestral culture, one cuisine, for the entirety of their productive years. She speaks for greater numbers than I possibly can. Only the fluency of her English and the anger, rather than fear, born of confidence from her education, differentiate her from the seamstresses, the domestics, the technicians, the shop owners, the millions of hardworking but effectively silenced documented immigrants as well as their less fortunate "illegal" brothers and sisters.

Nearly 20 years ago, when I was living in my husband's ancestral homeland of Canada, I was always well-employed but never allowed to feel part of the local Quebec or larger Canadian society. Then, through a Green Paper that invited a national referendum on the unwanted side effects of "nontraditional" immigration, the Government officially turned against its immigrant communities, particularly those from South Asia.

I felt then the same sense of betrayal that Mira feels now.

I will never forget the pain of that sudden turning, and the casual racist outbursts the Green Paper elicited. That sense of betrayal had its desired effect and drove me, and thousands like me, from the country.

Mira and I differ, however, in the ways in which we hope to interact with the country that we have chosen to live in. She is happier to live in America as expatriate Indian than as an immigrant American. I need to feel like a part of the community I have adopted (as I tried to feel in Canada as well). I need to put roots down, to vote and make the difference that I can. The price that the immigrant willingly pays, and that the exile avoids, is the trauma of self-transformation.

A Blizzard Under Blue Sky
(SHORT STORY)
Pam Houston

Pam Houston is a teacher and writer who has also worked as a hunting and raft guide in the American West and Alaska. She often writes about the relationships women have with animals, in particular horses and dogs. In this story from her first collection, *Cowboys Are My Weakness* (1992), she addresses the personal topic of depression with humor.

Analyzing and Connecting

Return to these questions after you have finished reading.

1. Houston uses "dialog" between herself and her dogs to enliven her reflection. Apart from humor, what do these "conversations" contribute to readers' understanding of the events she describes?

2. Note all the different sensory details Houston provides. See if you can find descriptions of sights, sounds, smells, tastes, and feelings. Which does Houston use most? Which ones stand out the most to you?

3. "I wish I could tell you I dropped right off to sleep," the narrator says. Why does Houston call attention to the contrast between real and ideal here? Why does she wish the truth were shaped differently? Why does she feel she "can't" tell readers she fell asleep?

4. Houston alerts readers to the revelation in her reflection at the very end. "I was five miles down the trail before I realized what had happened," she says. What exactly did happen? What changed for Houston during her camping trip? Does she adequately communicate this change to the reader? What might the reader learn from Houston's experience?

A Blizzard Under Blue Sky

The doctor said I was clinically depressed. It was February, the month in which depression runs rampant in the inversion-cloaked Salt Lake Valley and the city dwellers escape to Park City, where the snow is fresh and the sun is shining and everybody is happy, except me. In truth, my life was on the verge of more spectacular and satisfying discoveries than I had ever imagined, but of course I couldn't see that far ahead. What I saw was work that wasn't getting done, bills that weren't getting paid, and a man I'd given my heart to weekending in the desert with his ex.

The doctor said, "I can give you drugs."

I said, "No way."

She said, "The machine that drives you is broken. You need something to help you get it fixed."

I said, "Winter camping."

She said, "Whatever floats your boat."

One of the things I love the most about the natural world is the way it gives you what's good for you even if you don't know it at the time. I had never been winter camping before, at least not in the high country, and the weekend I chose to try and fix my machine was the same weekend the air mass they called the Alaska Clipper showed up. It was thirty-two degrees below zero in town on the night I spent in my snow cave. I don't know how cold it was out on Beaver Creek. I had listened to the weather forecast, and to the advice of my housemate, Alex, who was an experienced winter camper.

"I don't know what you think you're going to prove by freezing to death," Alex said, "but if you've got to go, take my bivvy sack; it's warmer than anything you have."

"Thanks," I said.

"If you mix Kool-Aid with your water it won't freeze up," he said, "and don't forget lighting paste for your stove."

"Okay," I said.

"I hope it turns out to be worth it," he said, "because you are going to freeze your butt."

When everything in your life is uncertain, there's nothing quite like the clarity and precision of fresh snow and blue sky. That was the first thought I had on Saturday morning as I stepped away from the warmth of my truck and let my skis slap the snow in front of me. There was no wind and no clouds that morning, just still air and cold sunshine. The hair in my nostrils froze almost immediately. When I took a deep breath, my lungs only filled up halfway.

I opened the tailgate to excited whines and whimpers. I never go skiing without Jackson and Hailey: my two best friends, my yin and yang of dogs. Some of you might know Jackson. He's the oversized sheepdog-and-something-else with the great big nose and the bark that will shatter glass. He gets out and about more than I do. People I've never seen before come by my house daily and call him by name. He's all grace, and he's tireless; he won't go skiing with me unless I let him lead. Hailey is not so graceful, and her body seems in constant indecision when she runs. When we ski she stays behind me, and on the downhills she tries to sneak rides on my skis.

The dogs ran circles in the chest-high snow while I inventoried my backpack one more time to make sure I had everything I needed. My sleeping bag, my Thermarest, my stove, Alex's bivvy sack, matches, lighting paste, flashlight, knife. I brought three pairs of long underwear—tops and bottoms—so I could change once before I went to bed, and once again in the morning, so I wouldn't get chilled by my own sweat. I brought paper and pen, and Kool-Aid to mix with my water. I brought Mountain House chicken stew and some freeze-dried green peas, some peanut butter and honey, lots of dried apricots, coffee and Carnation instant breakfast for morning.

Jackson stood very still while I adjusted his backpack. He carries the dog food and enough water for all of us. He takes himself very seriously when he's got his pack on. He won't step off the trail for any reason, not even to chase rabbits, and he gets nervous and angry if I do. That morning he was impatient with me. "Miles to go, Mom," he said over his shoulder. I snapped my boots into my skis and we were off.

There are not too many good things you can say about temperatures that dip past twenty below zero, except this: They turn the landscape into a crystal palace and they turn your vision into Superman's. In the cold thin morning air the trees and mountains, even the twigs and shadows, seemed to leap out of the background like a 3-D movie, only it was better than 3-D because I could feel the sharpness of the air.

I have a friend in Moab who swears that Utah is the center of the fourth dimension, and although I know he has in mind something much different and more complicated than subzero weather, it was there, on that ice-edged morning, that I felt on the verge of seeing something more than depth perception in the brutal clarity of the morning sun.

As I kicked along the first couple of miles, I noticed the sun crawling higher in the sky and yet the day wasn't really warming, and I wondered if I should have brought another vest, another layer to put between me and the cold night ahead.

It was utterly quiet out there, and what minimal noise we made intruded on the morning like a brass band: the squeaking of my bindings, the slosh of the water in Jackson's pack, the whoosh of nylon, the jangle of dog tags. It was the bass line and percussion to some primal song, and I kept wanting to sing to it, but I didn't know the words.

Jackson and I crested the top of a hill and stopped to wait for Hailey. The trail stretched out as far as we could see into the meadow below us and beyond, a double track and pole plants carving though softer trails of rabbit and deer.

"Nice place," I said to Jackson, and his tail thumped the snow underneath him without sound.

We stopped for lunch near something that looked like it could be a lake in its other life, or maybe just a womb-shaped meadow. I made peanut butter and honey sandwiches for all of us, and we opened the apricots.

"It's fabulous here," I told the dogs. "But so far it's not working."

There had never been anything wrong with my life that a few good days in the wilderness wouldn't cure, but there I sat in the middle of all those crystal-coated trees, all that diamond-studded sunshine, and I didn't feel any better. Apparently clinical depression was not like having a bad day, it wasn't even like having a lot of bad days, it was more like a house of mirrors, it was like being in a room full of one-way glass.

"Come on, Mom," Jackson said. "Ski harder, go faster, climb higher."

Hailey turned her belly to the sun and groaned.

"He's right," I told her. "It's all we can do."

After lunch the sun had moved behind our backs, throwing a whole different light on the path ahead of us. The snow we moved through stopped being simply white and became translucent, hinting at other colors, reflections of blues and purples and grays. I thought of *Moby Dick*, you know, the whiteness of the whale, where white is really the absence of all color, and whiteness equals truth, and Ahab's search is finally futile, as he finds nothing but his own reflection.

"Put your mind where your skis are," Jackson said, and we made considerably better time after that.

The sun was getting quite low in the sky when I asked Jackson if he thought we should stop to build the snow cave, and he said he'd look for the next good bank. About one hundred yards down the trail we found it, a gentle slope with eastern exposure that didn't look like it would cave in under any circumstances. Jackson started to dig first.

Let me make one thing clear. I knew only slightly more about building snow caves than Jackson, having never built one, and all my knowledge coming from disaster tales of winter camping fatalities. I knew several things *not* to do when building a snow cave, but I was having a hard time knowing what exactly to do. But Jackson helped, and Hailey supervised, and before too long we had a little cave built, just big enough for three. We ate dinner quite pleased with our accomplishments and set the bivvy sack up inside the cave just as the sun slipped away and dusk came over Beaver Creek.

The temperature, which hadn't exactly soared during the day, dropped twenty degrees in as many minutes, and suddenly it didn't seem like such a great idea to change my long underwear. The original plan was to sleep with the dogs inside the bivvy sack but outside the sleeping bag, which was okay with Jackson the super-metabolizer, but not so with Hailey, the couch potato. She whined and wriggled and managed to stuff her entire fat body down inside my mummy bag, and Jackson stretched out full-length on top.

One of the unfortunate things about winter camping is that it has to happen when the days are so short. Fourteen hours is a long time to lie in a snow cave under the most perfect of circumstances. And when it's thirty-two below, or forty, fourteen hours seems like weeks.

I wish I could tell you I dropped right off to sleep. In truth, fear crept into my spine with the cold and I never closed my eyes. Cuddled there, amid my dogs and water bottles, I spent half of the night chastising myself for thinking I was Wonder Woman, not only risking my own life but the lives of my dogs, and the other half trying to keep the numbness in my feet from crawling up to my knees. When I did doze off, which was actually more like blacking out than dozing off, I'd come back to my senses wondering if I had frozen to death, but the alternating pain and numbness that started in my extremities and worked its way into my bones convinced me I must still be alive.

It was a clear night, and every now and again I would poke my head out of its nest of down and nylon to watch the progress of the moon across the sky. There is no doubt that it was the longest and most uncomfortable night of my life.

But then the sky began to get gray, and then it began to get pink, and before too long the sun was on my bivvy sack, not warm, exactly, but holding the promise of warmth later in the day. And I ate apricots and drank Kool-Aid-flavored coffee and celebrated the rebirth of my fingers and toes, and the survival of many more important parts of my body. I sang "Rocky Mountain High" and "If I Had a Hammer," and yodeled and whistled, and even danced the two-step with Jackson and let him lick my face. And when Hailey finally emerged from the sleeping bag a full hour after I did, we shared a peanut butter and honey sandwich and she said nothing ever tasted so good.

We broke camp and packed up and kicked in the snow cave with something resembling glee.

I was five miles down the trail before I realized what had happened. Not once in that fourteen-hour night did I think about deadlines, or bills, or the man in the desert. For the first time in many months I was happy to see a day beginning. The morning sunshine was like a present from the gods. What really happened, of course, is that I remembered about joy.

I know that one night out at thirty-two below doesn't sound like much to those of you who have climbed Everest or run the Iditarod or kayaked to Antarctica, and I won't try to convince you that my life was like the movies where depression goes away in one weekend, and all of life's problems vanish with a moment's clear sight. The simple truth of the matter is this: On Sunday I had a glimpse outside of the house of mirrors, on Saturday I couldn't have seen my way out of a paper bag. And while I was skiing back toward the truck that morning, a wind came up behind us and swirled the snow around our bodies like a blizzard under blue sky. And I was struck by the simple perfection of the snowflakes, and startled by the hopefulness of sun on frozen trees.

Arrival: 1960

(MEMOIR)

Pablo Medina

Novelist, essayist, and poet Pablo Medina was born in Cuba in 1948 and immigrated to New York in 1960. He teaches in the creative writing program at the New School for Social Research in New York City. In 1990 he published a book, *Exiled Memories: A Cuban Childhood,* which reflects on his memories of Cuba decades earlier. "Arrival: 1960" is the first three pages of the book.

Analyzing and Connecting

Return to these questions after you have finished reading.

1. These particular memories stand out for Medina nearly thirty years later. Think back to your earliest memories. What makes these events, people, and places stick in your mind?

2. Well-written memoirs use details to describe the significance of the remembered experience. Which details are especially important in Medina's narrative?

3. What lessons does 12-year-old Pablo learn on his first day of school?

4. All of us experienced first days at new schools. What in your memory stands out about first-day-of-school experiences? Think about which details would convey the significance of your memories.

SNOW. Everywhere the snow and air so cold it cracks and my words hang stiffly in the air like cartoons. After that first stunning welcome of the New York winter, I rush down the steps of the plane and sink my bare hands into the snow, press it into a ball, and throw it at my sister. I miss by a few yards. The snowball puffs on the ground. I make another and miss again. Then I can make no more, for my hands are numb. I look down at them: red and wet, they seem disembodied, no longer mine. A few flakes land on them, but these flakes are not the ones I know from *Little LuLu* or *Archie*; they are big lumpy things that melt soon after landing. On closer look, I can make out the intricate crystals, small and furry and short lived. As if from a great distance, I hear my mother calling. Her voice seems changed by the cold and the words come quicker, in shorter bursts, as if there might be a limited supply of them. I follow the family into the airport building. It is early February. It is El Norte.

The drive into Manhattan is a blur. We piled into a cab and took a wide and busy highway in, most probably the Grand Central Parkway. Once over the East River, my first impression was of riding down into a canyon, much of it shadowy and forbidding, where the sky, steel gray at the time, was a straight path like the street we were on, except bumpier and softer: old cotton swabbed in mercury. It seemed odd that out of that ominous ceiling came the pure white snow I had just touched.

But the snow on the ground did not stay white very long. Nothing does in New York. It started graying at the edges four days after our arrival when my father took my sister and me to school, Robert F. Wagner Junior High, on East 72nd Street. It was a long brick building that ran the length of the block. Inauspicious, blank, with shades half-raised on the windows, it could have been a factory or a prison. Piled to the side of the entrance steps was a huge mound of snow packed with children like fruit on supermarket ice. J.H.S. 167 was a typical New York school, a microcosm of the city where all races mingled and fought and, on occasion, learned. The halls were crowded, the classes were crowded, even the bathroom during recess was packed to capacity.

On that first day I was witness to a scene that was to totally alter my image of what school was. On my way from one class to the next, I saw a teacher—who, I later learned, was the prefect of discipline—dragging a girl away by the arm. The girl, trying to tug herself free, was screaming curses. He slapped her across the face several times. Most students, already practicing the indifference that is the keynote of survival in New York, barely turned their heads. I, however, stared, frozen by violence in a place previous experience had deluded me into thinking ought to be quiet and genteel and orderly. It was the loud ring of the bell directly overhead that woke me. I was late for English class.

When I entered the room, the teacher, a slightly pudgy lady with silver white hair, asked if I had a pass. I did not know what a pass was but I answered no anyway. It was my first day and I had gotten lost in the halls.

"Well, in that case, young man, you may come in."

She spoke with rounded vowels and smooth, slightly slurred r's rolling out of her mouth from deep in the throat. Years later I was to learn to identify this manner of speech as an affectation of the educated.

"Next time, however, you must have a pass."

Not that it mattered if one was late to English class. Much of the time was spent doing reading or writing assignments while Mrs. Gall, whose appearance belied that she was close to retirement, did crossword puzzles. A few days later, in fact, something happened that endeared me to her for the rest of the term. Speaking to herself, not expecting any of the students to help her, she said, "A nine letter word for camel." Almost instantaneously, as if by magic, I responded, "Dromedary."

She looked up at me. "That's very good. You have a nice complexion. Where are you from?"

"Complexion?" I asked.

"Yes, skin."

Skin? What does skin have to do with any of this? I had never thought of my skin, let alone considered it a mark of foreignness.

"Cuba."

"Ah, I was there once."

Then she went off on a monologue of beaches and nightlife and weather.

Let It Snow
(ESSAY)
David Sedaris

David Sedaris is a writer, playwright, and radio commentator whose work often has an autobiographical focus. He became famous for *The Santaland Diaries,* a play about his job as a Christmas elf in Macy's department store. In this essay, from his collection *Dress Your Family in Corduroy and Denim,* he recalls a single day from his childhood in North Carolina.

Analyzing and Connecting

Return to these questions after you have finished reading.

1. On the surface, this story centers around a snowstorm, and children playing in it. Underlying these events are the much darker issues of the narrator's mother, her drinking, and her treatment of her children. How exactly does the snowstorm focus Sedaris's investigation of his family's past?

2. The narrator, as a fifth-grader, thinks that having his sister get hit by a car would be "the perfect solution" to their problem. What do you believe the adult narrator thinks of this "solution"? Are there any other clues that the narrator feels differently now?

3. The humor turns a potentially sad story into a ridiculous one. Think about how this essay might have been written without the humor. Could it be as effective?

4. Although this story deals with intensely personal issues, the tone is quite ironic and detached. Given the tone, what do you make of the story's ending, with the children surrounding their mother "tightly on all sides," finally going back to their house?

Let It Snow

In Binghamton, New York, winter meant snow, and though I was young when we left, I was able to recall great heaps of it, and use that memory as evidence that North Carolina was, at best, a third-rate institution. What little snow there was would usually melt an hour or two after hitting the ground, and there you'd be in your windbreaker and unconvincing mittens, forming a lumpy figure made mostly of mud. Snow Negroes, we called them.

The winter I was in the fifth grade we got lucky. Snow fell, and for the first time in years, it accumulated. School was canceled and two days later we got lucky again. There were eight inches on the ground, and rather than melting, it froze. On the fifth day of our vacation my mother had a little breakdown. Our presence had disrupted the secret life she led while we were at school, and when she could no longer take it she threw us out. It wasn't a gentle request, but something closer to an eviction. "Get the hell out of my house," she said.

We reminded her that it was our house, too, and she opened the front door and shoved us into the carport. "And stay out!" she shouted.

My sisters and I went down the hill and sledded with other children from the neighborhood. A few hours later we returned home, surprised to find that the door was still locked. "Oh, come on," we said. I rang the bell and when no one answered we went to the window and saw our mother in the kitchen, watching television. Normally she waited until five o'clock to have a drink, but for the past few days she'd been making an exception. Drinking didn't count if you followed a glass of wine with a cup of coffee, and so she had both a goblet and a mug positioned before her on the countertop.

"Hey!" we yelled. "Open the door. It's us." We knocked on the pane, and without looking in our direction, she refilled her goblet and left the room.

"That bitch," my sister Lisa said. We pounded again and again, and when our mother failed to answer we went around back and threw snowballs at her bedroom window. "You are going to be in so much trouble when Dad gets home!" we shouted, and in response my mother pulled the drapes. Dusk approached, and as it grew colder it occurred to us that we could possibly die. It happened, surely. Selfish mothers wanted the house to themselves, and their children were discovered years later, frozen like mastodons in blocks of ice.

My sister Gretchen suggested that we call our father, but none of us knew his number, and he probably wouldn't have done anything anyway. He'd gone to work specifically to escape our mother, and between the weather and her mood, it could be hours or even days before he returned home.

"One of us should get hit by a car," I said. "That would teach the both of them." I pictured Gretchen, her life hanging by a thread as my parents paced the halls of Rex Hospital, wishing they had been more attentive. It was really the perfect solution. With her out of the way, the rest of us would be more valuable and have a bit more room to spread out. "Gretchen, go lie in the street."

"Make Amy do it," she said.

Amy, in turn, pushed it off onto Tiffany, who was the youngest and had no concept of death. "It's like sleeping," we told her. "Only you get a canopy bed."

Poor Tiffany. She'd do just about anything in return for a little affection. All you had to do was call her Tiff and whatever you wanted was yours: her allowance money, her dinner, the contents of her Easter basket. Her eagerness to please was absolute and naked. When we asked her to lie in the middle of the street, her only question was "Where?"

We chose a quiet dip between two hills, a spot where drivers were almost required to skid out of control. She took her place, this six-year-old in a butter-colored coat, and we gathered on the curb to watch. The first car to happen by belonged to a neighbor, a fellow Yankee who had outfitted his tires with chains and stopped a few feet from our sister's body. "Is that a person?" he asked.

"Well, sort of," Lisa said. She explained that we'd been locked out of our house and though the man appeared to accept it as a reasonable explanation, I'm pretty sure it was him who told on us. Another car passed and then we saw our mother, this puffy figure awkwardly negotiating the crest of the hill. She did not own a pair of pants, and her legs were buried to the calves in snow. We wanted to send her home, to kick her out of nature just as she had kicked us out of the house, but it was hard to stay angry at someone that pitiful-looking.

"Are you wearing your *loafers*?" Lisa asked, and in response our mother raised her bare foot. "I was wearing loafers," she said. "I mean, really, it was there a second ago."

This was how things went. One moment she was locking us out of our own house and the next we were rooting around in the snow, looking for her left shoe. "Oh, forget about it," she said. "It'll turn up in a few days." Gretchen fitted her cap over my mother's foot. Lisa secured it with her scarf, and surrounding her tightly on all sides, we made our way back home.

Just Another Soldier

(BLOG)

Jason Christopher Hartley

Jason Christopher Hartley grew up in Salt Lake City and joined the Army National Guard when he was 17. Thirteen years later in 2003 he was called to active duty. From March 2004 to January 2005 he served as an infantry soldier in Iraq, where he kept a blog (**blog.justanothersoldier.com**) that was later assembled as a book, *Just Another Soldier.* The entry for April 23, 2004, was written after he had been in Iraq for five weeks.

Analyzing and Connecting

Return to these questions after you have finished reading.

1. Everyone did what seemed rational at the time: the soldiers fired at what they thought were fleeing terrorists, the Iraqi driver attempted to get his family out of danger, and the Iraqi women attempted to shield the 3-year-old girl with their bodies, only to smother her. What is the significance of everyone doing what they believed was the right action only to have things turn out so terribly?

2. Hartley asks himself, "Now what am I doing here again?" How does he answer his question?

3. Hartley regrets that he didn't get to witness the tragedy. Why would he want to "bear witness" to a family riddled with bullets?

4. In the last paragraph, Hartley considers "how the *drive* to be violent seems to precede the *purpose* to be violent." What does he mean?

5. In the last sentence, Hartly uses an unfamiliar word, *kludge,* which is an engineering term for a pieced-together solution. Is kludge a good word to describe his efforts to explain to himself what happened to the Iraqi family?

HARTLEY: JUST ANOTHER SOLDIER

April 23, 2004

The man in the passenger seat lay slumped against the dashboard, a massive wound to his head. Kirk pulled the body upright and cut the man's pockets open looking for ID. When he was done and let the body fall back against the dashboard, he said that what was left of the man's brain fell out of the opening in the back of his head and onto the ground. He could handle the guy with the brain and both the dead women, but it was the three-year-old girl, he said, that got to him.

Roughly an hour earlier, a convoy of fuel tankers and Humvees came to a halt a little north of our forward operating base when what looked like an improvised explosive device (IED) was spotted on the side of the road. Since the suspected IED was spotted mid-convoy, the vehicles were split, part to the north and part to the south, leaving the area around the IED open to prevent any of the trucks from being destroyed. Our explosive ordinance disposal team was being called in, and our quick-reaction force (QRF) was going to escort them. I was in the QRF staging area that day, but I wasn't on the mission. We were listening to the radio in a Humvee as one of the officers in the convoy was communicating with our headquarters about the IED when the convoy started to take small arms fire. Then the mortar rounds started to fall. The people who attack convoys seem to have no end to their supply of mortar rounds. Thankfully they don't know how to aim them any better than they do their rifles.

When our QRF made it to the scene, shots were still being fired, so they laid down suppressive fire as best they could. Even though this attack took place in daylight, there was much difficulty pinpointing the location of the enemy assailants.

But to the north, another QRF also responded to this ambush, an active-duty unit newly in country. This was their first mission. Since this other QRF was on a separate communications net, the response attacks were not coordinated.

They also spotted a vehicle, a white pickup, a small Toyota, one like most Iraqis stack their families in the back of, just as this family was. Everyone has these trucks in Iraq; it's like the national vehicle. I can imagine that the man driving it, most likely the father of those on board, just wanted to get his family out of the area of the fighting as quickly as possible. I can also imagine that the other QRF got word that a fast-moving vehicle was our attackers' likely means of attack and escape, a completely plausible and reasonable possibility.

The Humvee gunships engaged the pickup with a load of machine gun fire. The truck contained six people: two men, two women, and two young girls. As is the custom in Iraq, the men were in the cab as the females huddled together in the bed of the truck. Among the dead were one of the men, both women, and a three-year-old girl, apparently smothered to death by the two women's bullet-riddled bodies as the women tried to shield the girl from the fusillade of gunfire—the tragic irony being that this ultimate protective act was the very thing that killed the girl. The man driving was still alive when the casualty evacuation team got there, but he was probably on his way out. Matt said the man had numerous wounds to his legs and a gunshot wound to the scrotum, an entry wound for a bullet that had no visible exit and was most likely lodged in his pelvis or abdomen. As Matt held a pressure dressing to the man's bleeding thigh, he felt the shattered pieces of femur grind against each other. The only one who seemed certain to survive was an eight-year-old girl who had gunshot wounds in both of her upper arms.

As I try to fathom what it must feel like to be a poverty-stricken eight-year-old girl and to experience the epic pain of having your family suddenly and violently killed in front of you, I have to pause and ask myself, Now what am I doing here again? I know this kind of thing happens in combat, and I kind of expected to see it, but, Jesus, the record is pretty bad so far. Since I've been in Iraq, in situations that my platoon has responded to, there have been three dead bad guys, two wounded civilians (one critically), and seven dead civilians, including four women, one three-year-old girl, and one mentally unstable man on a moped.

Like I said, I wasn't with the QRF that day and didn't see any of this first-hand, and all the information I got was gleaned from the guys in my squad who were. Even though Matt said it was better that I hadn't seen any of it, I wish I had been there—to bear witness, I suppose. So tell me, why would I wish for this?

I've been stewing over this dead family thing for a couple of weeks now. I've been painstakingly mulling over in my mind the things these insurgents do and the things we, the U.S. Army, do and the unintuitive peculiarity of how the *drive* to be violent seems to precede the *purpose* to be violent, and how rampant it is to meaninglessly develop one's identity through injury, but frankly I don't think I've figured it all out well enough yet to even kludge together a coherent line of thought.

Why I Hunt: A Predator's Meditation

(ESSAY)

Rick Bass

Texas-born Rick Bass now lives on an isolated ranch in Montana, where he writes about the wilderness, animals, and environmental issues. He received a degree in geology from Utah State University and worked as a petroleum geologist, prospecting for oil. In his most recent book, *Caribou Rising: Defending the Porcupine Herd, Gwich-'in Culture, and the Arctic National Wildlife Refuge* (2004), Bass describes how drilling for oil in the Arctic National Wildlife Refuge in Alaska will adversely affect the Gwich-'in tribe, who depend on caribou hunting for their survival.

Analyzing and Connecting

Return to these questions after you have finished reading.

1. Bass gives several reasons for why he hunts. Go through the essay and note them. How well do they fit together? Do you find any contradictions?

2. In the first five paragraphs Bass describes hunting as an activity critical to his life. His essay starts as a straightforward defense of hunting. But later he says he feels "guilty" and "ashamed." Why does Bass use the strategy of going back and forth about his feelings about hunting?

3. A central claim is that humans are predators. But isn't it more accurate to claim that humans are farmers? After all, human civilizations emerged when people learned to domesticate plants and animals. Very few people get most of their nourishment from hunting. Does Bass make an effective case that humans are hunters by nature?

4. In the last two paragraphs Bass compares ravens to humans. Does this strategy make an effective conclusion?

Why I Hunt: A Predator's Meditation

IN THE FALL, it's what I want to do. It would be unnatural and dishonest to sit on my hands; I'm a hunter, a predator (in the fall), with eyes in front of my head, like a bear's, or a wolf's, or even an owl's. Prey have their eyes on the sides of their heads, in order to see in all directions, in order to be ready to run. But predators—and that's us, or at least some of us—have our eyes before us, out in front, with which to focus, to a single point. For two months of the year—or until I have killed one deer and one elk—that's what I do. I want to be out in the woods, walking quietly, walking slowly—or not walking at all but just sitting in some leaves, completely hidden and motionless—waiting, and waiting. To not pursue the thing one wants would be a waste of one's life.

In the fall, I can do things I couldn't do in my normal, civilized life. I can disappear into the woods, and over the next mountain, the next ridge. My roaming has meaning—it's no longer just roaming, but *hunting*. The year's meat supply is in question. My meat, my family's meat—not some rancher's heifer from Minnesota. Meat from my valley, where I hope to live and die—where I cut firewood, where I pick huckleberries, where I walk, where I watch the stars—my valley.

For those two months, I am *after* something: something tangible, something that's moving away from me, and something that I must have, for the coming year. It's as simple as that.

Over the next ridge. The new life of stores and towns falls away, and the old life returns. There's a loveliness to looking ahead—looking *straight* ahead—that only hunting brings out.

The other ten months are okay, too—I can be the artist, can loll around eating grapes and reading poetry, but the fall comes like a splash of water to my face on a hot, dusty day; and the dust, and my new ways, new feelings—the ones bound by rules—are washed away, leaving the old ways revealed.

I keep eating those lovely candlelit dinners—grouse and potatoes, and the red, almost *purple* heartthrob steaks from elk; fried trout for break-fast, and homemade huckleberry jam. . . . I feel alive. . . . I draw immense strength from those meals, strength to live my life, and it feels *good*. I eat about a pound and a half of meat a day. The cancer studies for this kind of diet alarm me, but I have to trust that they apply to fatty steroid beef, and cattle that must have been raised in pesticide fields. I was seven miles into the mountains when I shot last year's elk, and I carried him out in three trips over a twenty-four-hour period.

Into those same dark woods I go each year, looking straight ahead, and stopping, and listening, and turning my head. . . .

Of course, it's possible that there's a greater life force that judges us; and of course, sometimes I feel guilty about being a hunter, a killer—a killer of deer and elk, though not moose, because they're too easy, and not bears, because . . . well, bears them-selves are meant to hunt. During part of the year they're predators, not prey. It seems unnatural to hunt predators.

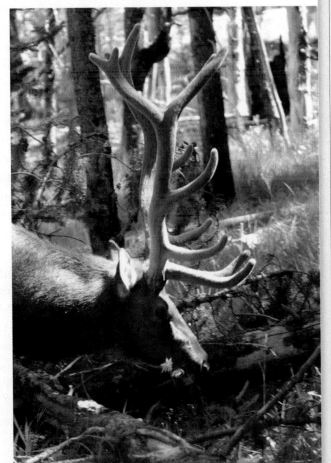

I'm scared, sometimes, that all the animals I've killed—few as they are—add up, and that I'm liable for them.

I wouldn't mind paying for them with my life someday—we must all give up our lives—but sometimes I get scared I may have to pay afterward, in the afterlife, for my gluttony, my insatiable hunger for clean meat, and so much of it.

Nonetheless, I've studied it, and have come up with this: I

am who I am, and I've come from the place we all come from—the past—but I still remember, and love, that place. Some of us are glad to be away from that place, but I'm not one of those people—not in the fall.

The worst day I ever had hunting was when I shot an elk in the neck, where I was aiming, but it made me feel strangely ashamed, after it was over. I broke the elk's neck, the way I always try to do—that instant drop—but he groaned when I walked up to him. He couldn't have been feeling anything, and I hope it was just air leaving his lungs—but it was still a groan.

For a fact—or rather, for me—hunting's better than killing. It takes a while, after it's over—sometimes a long while—before you can think of it as meat. You can't go straight from a living animal to 250 pounds of elk steaks. There's too much knife and ax work involved—and you're the one who has to do it—skinning the animal, and pulling the hide back to reveal your crime, the meat—and already, sometimes, the call of ravens drifting in, black-winged shapes flying through the treetops, past the sun. . . .

Instead of trying to make that instantaneous conversion—which I cannot do—life to meat—what I do is pray, sort of. I give heartfelt, shaky thanks to the animal as I clean it—ravens calling to ravens—and I do this with deer and grouse too, and even, if I can remember—which I don't always—with fish. A man or a woman who apologizes for hunting is a fool. It's a man's, or a woman's, choice, and he or she must live with it.

I don't do it for profit or gain; and rarely do I tell anyone about it after I've done it.

I watch ravens in the off-season. I think ravens have more of a soul than humans—and I think ravens understand the hunt better than I ever will. Sometimes ravens, in Alaska, lead hunters—wolves, or humans— to prey, and then they eat the pickings from the kill.

Ravens, black as coal, shiny and greasy, flying in the sun, like winged, black devils. . . I feel as if I'm on their side, and it scares me, but it would be a lie, in the fall, to switch sides: to pretend that I'm not. I'm a killer, sometimes. I wish I weren't, but I am. I've wrestled with it but can't escape it, any more than—until death—one can escape one's skin.

Mother Tongue
(ESSAY)
Amy Tan

Amy Tan is a world-renowned writer for her novels that concern the bonds between Chinese-American mothers and daughters. She has introduced a rich world of Chinese myth and history to a global audience, but her themes of love and forgiveness are universal. Tan began writing fiction along with playing the piano to curb her workaholic tendencies, but with the publication of *The Joy Luck Club* in 1989, her talent as a writer became widely celebrated. She reflects on her career in this essay.

Analyzing and Connecting

Return to these questions after you have finished reading.

1. How did Tan's attitude toward her mother's language change over the years? Use evidence from the text to support your statements.

2. Tan writes about value judgments based on language. How does Tan account for these judgments?

3. Why was Tan's awareness of different Englishes important to her development as a writer?

4. Near the end, Tan says an insight she had as a beginning writer was to imagine a reader. Why was imagining a reader so important?

I am not a scholar of English or literature. I cannot give you much more than personal opinions on the English language and its variations in this country or others. I am a writer. And by that definition, I am someone who has always loved language. I am fascinated by language in daily life. I spend a great deal of my time thinking about the power of language—the way it can evoke an emotion, a visual image, a complex idea, or a simple truth. Language is the tool of my trade. And I use them all—all the Englishes I grew up with.

Recently, I was made keenly aware of the different Englishes I do use. I was giving a talk to a large group of people, the same talk I had already given to half a dozen other groups. The nature of the talk was about my writing, my life, and my book, *The Joy Luck Club*. The talk was going along well enough, until I remembered one major difference that made the whole talk sound wrong. My mother was in the room. And it was perhaps the first time she had heard me give a lengthy speech, using the kind of English I have never used with her. I was saying things like, "The intersection of memory upon imagination" and "There is an aspect of my fiction that relates to thus-and-thus"—a speech filled with carefully wrought grammatical phrases, burdened, it suddenly seemed to me, with nominalized forms, past perfect tenses, conditional phrases, all the forms of standard English that I had learned in school and through books, the forms of English I did not use at home with my mother.

Just last week, I was walking down the street with my mother, and I again found myself conscious of the English I was using, the English I do use with her. We were talking about the price of new and used furniture and I heard myself saying this: "Not waste money that way." My husband was with us as well, and he didn't notice any switch in my English. And then I realized why. It's because over the twenty years we've been together I've often used that same kind of English with him, and sometimes he even uses it with me. It has become our language of intimacy, a different sort of English that relates to family talk, the language I grew up with.

So you'll have some idea of what this family talk I heard sounds like, I'll quote what my mother said during a recent conversation which I videotaped and then transcribed. During this conversation, my mother was talking about a political gangster in Shanghai who had the same last name as her family's, Du, and how the gangster in his early years wanted to be adopted by her family, which was rich by comparison. Later, the gangster became more powerful, far richer than my mother's family, and one day showed up at my mother's wedding to pay his respects. Here's what she said in part:

Du-Yusong having business like fruit stand. Like off the street kind. He is Du like Du Zong—but not Tsung-ming Island people. The local people call putong, the river east side, he belong to that side local people. That man want to ask DuZong father take him in like become own family. Du Zong father wasn't look down on him, but didn't take seriously, until that man big like become a mafia. Now important person, very hard to inviting him. Chinese way, came only to show respect, don't stay for dinner. Respect for making big celebration, he shows up. Mean gives lots of respect. Chinese custom. Chinese social life that way. If too important won't have to stay too long. He come to my wedding. I didn't see, I heard it. I gone to boy's side, they have YMCA dinner. Chinese age I was nineteen.

You should know that my mother's expressive command of English belies how much she actually understands. She reads the *Forbes* report, listens to *Wall Street Week*, converses daily with her stockbroker, reads all of Shirley MacLaine's books with ease—all kinds of things I can't begin to understand. Yet some of my friends tell me they understand 50 percent of what my mother says. Some say they understand 80 to 90 percent. Some say they understand none of it, as if she were speaking pure Chinese. But to me, my mother's English is perfectly clear, perfectly natural. It's my mother tongue. Her language, as I hear it, is vivid, direct, full of observation and imagery. That was the language that helped shape the way I saw things, expressed things, made sense of the world.

Lately, I've been giving more thought to the kind of English my mother speaks. Like others, I have described it to people as "broken" or "fractured" English. But I wince when I say that. It has always bothered me that I can think of no way to describe it other than "broken," as if it were damaged and needed to be fixed, as if it lacked a certain wholeness and soundness. I've heard other terms used, "limited English," for example. But they seem just as bad, as if everything is limited, including people's perceptions of the limited English speaker.

I know this for a fact, because when I was growing up, my mother's "limited" English limited my perception of her. I was ashamed of her English. I believed that her English reflected the quality of what she had to say. That is, because she expressed them imperfectly her thoughts were imperfect. And I had plenty of empirical evidence to support me: the fact that people in department stores, at banks, and at restaurants did not take her seriously, did not give her good service, pretended not to understand her, or even acted as if they did not hear her.

My mother had long realized the limitations of her English as well. When I was fifteen, she used to have me call people on the phone to pretend I was she. In this guise, I was forced to ask for information or even to complain and yell at people who had been rude to her. One time it was a call to her stockbroker in New York. She had cashed out her small portfolio and it just so happened we were going to go to New York the next week, our very first trip outside California. I had to get on the phone and say in an adolescent voice that was not very convincing, "This is Mrs. Tan."

And my mother was standing in the back whispering loudly, "Why he don't send me check, already two weeks late. So mad he lie to me, losing me money."

And then I said in perfect English, "Yes, I'm getting rather concerned. You had agreed to send the check two weeks ago, but it hasn't arrived."

Then she began to talk more loudly. "What he want, I come to New York tell him front of his boss, you cheating me?" And I was trying to calm her down, make her be quiet, while telling the stockbroker, "I can't tolerate any more excuses. If I don't receive the check immediately, I am going to have to speak to your manager when I'm in New York next week." And sure enough, the following week there we were in front of this astonished stockbroker, and I was sitting there red-faced and quiet, and my mother, the real Mrs. Tan, was shouting at his boss in her impeccable broken English.

We used a similar routine just five days ago, for a situation that was far less humorous. My mother had gone to the hospital for an appointment, to find out about a benign brain tumor a CAT scan had revealed a month ago. She said she had spoken very good English, her best English, no mistakes. Still, she said, the hospital did not apologize when they said they had lost the CAT scan and she had come for nothing. She said they did not seem to have any sympathy when she told them she was anxious to know the exact diagnosis, since her husband and son had both died of brain tumors. She said they would not give her any more information until the next time and she would have to make another appointment for that. So she said she would not leave until the doctor called her daughter. She wouldn't budge. And when the doctor finally called her daughter, me, who spoke in perfect English—lo and behold—we had assurances the CAT scan would be found, promises that a conference call on Monday would be held, and apologies for any suffering my mother had gone through for a most regrettable mistake.

I think my mother's English almost had an effect on limiting my possibilities in life as well. Sociologists and linguists probably will tell you that a person's developing language skills are more influenced by peers. But I do think that the language spoken in the family, especially in immigrant families which are more insular, plays a large role in shaping the language of the child. And I believe that it affected my results on achievement tests, IQ tests, and the SAT. While my English skills were never judged as poor, compared to math, English could not be considered my strong suit. In grade school I did moderately well, getting perhaps B's, sometimes

B-pluses, in English and scoring perhaps in the sixtieth or seventieth percentile on achievement tests. But those scores were not good enough to override the opinion that my true abilities lay in math and science, because in those areas I achieved A's and scored in the ninetieth percentile or higher.

This was understandable. Math is precise; there is only one correct answer. Whereas, for me at least, the answers on English tests were always a judgment call, a matter of opinion and personal experience. Those tests were constructed around items like fill-in-the-blank sentence completion, such as, "Even though Tom was _____, Mary thought he was _____." And the correct answer always seemed to be the most bland combinations of thoughts, for example, "Even though Tom was shy, Mary thought he was charming," with the grammatical structure "even though" limiting the correct answer to some sort of semantic opposites, so you wouldn't get answers like, "Even though Tom was foolish, Mary thought he was ridiculous." Well, according to my mother, there were very few limitations as to what Tom could have been and what Mary might have thought of him. So I never did well on tests like that.

The same was true with word analogies, pairs of words in which you were supposed to find some sort of logical, semantic relationship—for example, "*Sunset* is to *nightfall* as _____ is to _____." And here you would be presented with a list of four possible pairs, one of which showed the same kind of relationship: *red* is to *stoplight, bus* is to *arrival, chills* is to *fever, yawn* is to *boring.* Well, I could never think that way. I knew what the tests were asking, but I could not block out of my mind the images already created by the first pair, "*sunset* is to *nightfall*"—

and I would see a burst of colors against a darkening sky, the moon rising, the lowering of a curtain of stars. And all the other pairs of words—red, bus, stoplight, boring—just threw up a mass of confusing images, making it impossible for me to sort out something as logical as saying: "A sunset precedes nightfall" is the same as "a chill precedes a fever." The only way I would have gotten that answer right would have been to imagine an associative situation, for example, my being disobedient and staying out past sunset, catching a chill at night, which turns into feverish pneumonia as punishment, which indeed did happen to me.

I have been thinking about all this lately, about my mother's English, about achievement tests. Because lately I've been asked, as a writer, why there are not more Asian Americans represented in American literature. Why are there few Asian Americans enrolled in creative writing programs? Why do so many Chinese students go into engineering? Well, these are broad sociological questions I can't begin to answer. But I have noticed in surveys—in fact, just last week—that Asian students, as a whole, always do significantly better on math achievement tests than in English. And this makes me think that there are other Asian-American students whose English spoken in the home might also be described as "broken" or "limited." And perhaps they also have teachers who are steering them away from writing and into math and science, which is what happened to me.

Fortunately, I happen to be rebellious in nature and enjoy the challenge of disproving assumptions made about me. I became an English major my first year in college, after being enrolled as pre-med. I started writing nonfiction as a freelancer the week after I was told by my former boss that writing was my worst skill and I should hone my talents toward account management.

But it wasn't until 1985 that I finally began to write fiction. And at first I wrote using what I thought to be wittily crafted sentences, sentences that would finally prove I had mastery over the English language. Here's an example from the first draft of a story that later made its way into *The Joy Luck Club*, but without this line: "That was my mental quandary in its nascent state." A terrible line, which I can barely pronounce.

Fortunately, for reasons I won't get into today, I later decided I should envision a reader for the stories I would write. And the reader I decided upon was my mother, because these were stories about mothers. So with this reader in mind— and in fact she did read my early drafts—I began to write stories using all the Englishes I grew up with: the English I spoke to my mother, which for lack of a better term might be described as "simple"; the English she used with me, which for lack of a better term might be described as "broken"; my translation of her Chinese, which could certainly be described as "watered down"; and what I imagined to be her translation of her Chinese if she could speak in perfect English, her internal language, and for that I sought to preserve the essence, but neither an English nor a Chinese structure. I wanted to capture what language ability tests can never reveal: her intent, her passion, her imagery, the rhythms of her speech and the nature of her thoughts.

Apart from what any critic had to say about my writing, I knew I had succeeded where it counted when my mother finished reading my book and gave me her verdict: "So easy to read."

How to write a reflection

These steps for the process of writing a reflection may not progress as neatly as this chart might suggest. Writing is not an assembly-line process. Writing about a remembered event, place, or person is, in itself, a powerful way to reflect. Be open to uncovering insights and understanding more broadly the significance.

1 CHOOSE A SUBJECT

- Analyze the assignment.
- Explore possible topics.
- Remember places and objects.
- Consider the significance.

2 DEVELOP A RESPONSE

- Generate details.
- Make people come alive.
- Think about the context.
- Relate your experience to the experiences of others.

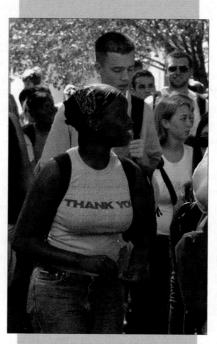

PLEIADES ISLANDS FROM 7/21 CAMP

US BETWEEN BIG ROCKS WITH WAVES CRASHING OVER THEM WITH KELP BEDS IN BETWEEN. IAN HAD A WET RIDE WHEN WAVES CAME OVER OUR DECK. HE SAID "OUR BOAT IS TOO SMALL FOR WATER THIS ROUGH." WHEN WE MADE IT TO THE BAINBRIDGE PASSAGE, WE FOUND TWO PLEASURE BOATS WAITING OUT THE STORM. THE BIG BOATS STAYED IN; THE LITTLE BOATS BRAVED IT. WE PADDLED BACK UP BAINBRIDGE PASSAGE UNTIL WE FOUND A CAMPSITE ON A COVE LOOKING OUT TOWARD THE PLEIADES. IT WAS OUR FIRST BEACH WITH BAD BUGS. IAN CRAWLED IN THE TENT WHILE I COOKED NOODLES WITH TOMATO PESTO. WE HAD A RORSARCH TEST FOR THE PLEIADES:
- A FLEET
- MOTHER TURTLE WITH BABIES
- COVERED WAGONS

Analyze your potential readers

- *What do your readers likely know about the subject?*
- *How can you engage readers?*
- *What will they gain from reading your reflection?*

3 WRITE A DRAFT

- Select vivid details and dialog.
- Decide on an organization.
- Craft a strong beginning.
- Conclude by inviting further reflection.
- Consider your voice and tone.
- Choose a title that will interest readers.

4 REVISE, REVISE, REVISE

- Check that your paper or project fulfills the assignment.
- Make sure that the subject is focused.
- Add details, description, or dialog.
- Make sure your voice and tone will engage readers.
- Examine your organization and think of possible better ways to organize.
- Review the visual presentation.
- Proofread carefully.

5 SUBMITTED VERSION

- Make sure your finished writing meets all formatting requirements.

1: Find a reflective topic and a focus for writing about it

Analyze the assignment

- Read your assignment slowly and carefully. Look for key words like *reflect, reminisce,* or *contemplate.* These key words tell you that you are writing a reflective essay.

- Identify any information about the length specified, date due, formatting, and other requirements. You can attend to this information later. At this point you want to give your attention to your topic and the focus of your reflection.

Explore possible topics

- Think about your family. What memories stand out about your parents? your brothers and sisters? your own child or children? your grandparents and other close relatives? your pets? your shared family experiences including vacations and holidays? Make a list of events and situations associated with your family.

- Think about work experience. What was your first job? Did you ever have a great boss or a horrible boss? Do any other workers stand out? What important learning experiences did you have on the job? Make a list of events and situations associated with work.

- Think about your school experience. What school memories stand out? Did a teacher have a strong influence on you? Did a coach make a difference in your life? What were the social groups in your school? Make a list of events and situations associated with school.

- Think about friends and social relationships. What memories stand out about your friends? about people you've met? about people you've dated? Make a list of events and situations associated with friends and social relationships.

- Review all of your lists and put a check beside any items that look like interesting possibilities for writing.

Remember places and objects	• Is a particular place important? Why is it critical? For example, how did you gain an understanding of your mother's attitudes when you visited the place where she grew up?
	• Is a particular object important? For example, can you describe the locket that belonged to your great-grandmother and was passed down to you?
Consider the significance	• Ask yourself: Why is this person, event, place, or object significant to me?
	• Think about why the person, place, event, or object seems more important now than in your initial experience. How did your view change?
	• How did you change as a result of being around this person, event, place, or object?
Analyze your potential readers	• What do your readers likely know about the subject?
	• What might you need to tell readers about your background?
	• How can you engage readers?
	• What will they gain from reading your reflection?

WRITE NOW

Explore memories

• Select one of the items that you have checked on your lists.
• Write nonstop for five minutes to explore the event, situation, place, or object.
  What was your initial reaction? Who else was there? Did you share your reaction at the time?
• Write nonstop for five minutes to explore your current perspective. How did an experience change you? Why do you remember this person, event, place, or object so well? Looking back, what do you see now that you didn't recognize at the time?
• Stop and read what you have written. Do you see possibilities for writing at length about this person, event, or situation? If you do, then begin generating more content. If the idea seems limited, try writing nonstop about another person, event, place, or object.

Writer at work

Janine Carter received the following assignment in her Introduction to Archeology class.
She made notes on her assignment sheet as the class discussed the assignment.

Archeology 201
Reflection on an Artifact

We have read about and discussed (artifacts) at great length in this unit—how and where they are
found, what they indicate about human cultures, and what they mean to archeologists. But not
all artifacts are found in museums. Almost any human-made object can be considered an artifact,
because it contains information about its makers. Archeologists study artifacts because they
teach us about people we do not know, and because they teach us things about ourselves.

For your first paper, I would like you to find an artifact in your daily life. This might be a   *Use*
family heirloom with a great deal of personal meaning, or it might be something you have no   *lots of*
emotional attachment to at all, like a soda can or a discarded newspaper. Write a 4-6 page   *detail*
essay reflecting upon your artifact. Describe it in as much detail as you can. Consider what its
construction tells you about its maker. Why was it made? When? By whom? What clues does
the artifact contain about its own history?   *"Think like a detective"*

Spend some time considering what the artifact means to you. What is your relationship to the
person who created the artifact? What can you construct about the culture and conditions in
which it was created? What sorts of things can you not figure out about it?

Writing Process
Bring in a good draft of your essay on October 3rd. We will discuss them in class so you can
revise carefully before you turn your essay in on October 10.   *Two weeks for first draft*
                                                                                                                     One week for revision

Grading
I will look for the following qualities in your essay: detailed description, logical deduction,
and an interesting account of the artifact's significance or meaning.

Then Janine made a list of possible objects to write about.

<u>HEIRLOOMS/EMOTIONAL CONNECTION</u>
• Aunt Marie's tulip quilt--shows my connection to
  a long line of quilters
• ~~Sea shells from Girl Scout camp~~--NOT MAN-MADE
• Bracelet from graduation
• Terry's photo
• Stuffed elephant--shows how much I have grown up.
  Where was it made?
✓ • Garage sale quilt--don't know much about this;
  could guess a lot though.
• Diploma

<u>LESS IMPORTANT OBJECTS</u>
• Cereal box--ingredients show lack of
  nutrition. Pictures show how kids are
  bombarded with cartoons and colorful images.
  Expiration date and other clues to where it was
  made.
• Desk in dorm room--Must have been used by
  dozens of people like me (?)
• Old calendar
• Old cookbook
• A floppy disk--Could talk about how fast
  technology is changing. Do I have one?

2: Develop a response

Generate details

- Write down all the sights, sounds, smells, tastes, and tactile sensations you associate with your topic.
- If you are using a photograph or other object, write a detailed description of it.
- If you are remembering a past event, write down everything that happened: what people said and did, how you felt as things happened, and anything else you remember or feel is significant.

Make people come alive

- Use dialog to let readers hear people talk, which reveals much about character.
- Record the little mannerisms, gestures, clothing, and personal habits that distinguish people.
- Don't forget to make yourself come alive. If you are reflecting on an incident from your childhood, how old were you? What do you remember about yourself at that age?

Think about the context

- How does your memory compare with similar experiences you have read or heard about from others?
- Does your memory connect to any larger trends or events going on at the time?

Relate your experience to the experiences of others

- The very fact that you find the topic memorable means there is something there you can share with others. Think about how to make it obvious to them.
- How is your subject particular to you? What do you notice, as you reflect, that other people might not notice? This is the "added value" that will make your reflection more than a mere description or memory.

Writer at work

Janine Carter sat down with her garage-sale quilt and a pen and paper. She observed it carefully and made a list of detailed observations about its physical appearance. Then, she added her conclusions and guesses about the quilt, its history, and its maker, based on these clues.

   Janine thought about her relationship to the quilt. She jotted down, in no particular order, what she remembered about buying the quilt, conversations she had had with her grandmother about quilting, and ideas that occurred to her.

- Unbleached muslin, pink calico, coral calico
- Most stitching is white thread and quilting is pink thread
  - All these materials are very cheap

- Nine-patch plus a 5-patch alternating throughout; binding is plain muslin
  - I do not know the name of this pattern. Looks a little like Churn Dash.

- Batting is coming through in many areas
- Lots of stains, even some paint
  - Has been used a lot and has been used for unintended purposes—discarded?

- Large muslin patches are cut on bias
  - Means the person knew what she was doing and planned ahead

- Quilting is in nested L-blocks. Is there a name for that?

- 1372 patches (approx.) Small squares are 1-1/2 inches

- Quilting is about 5 stitches/inch on average, 1" apart. Over 100 yards total.

- The two colors clash and are not mixed together; one runs out and the other starts. Why?

  - New quilter? Poor planning? To make it bigger? Unforeseen accident?
  - Grandma would have had a fit if I ever made a quilt this ugly. So why did I buy it?

3: Write a draft

Select vivid details and dialog	• Don't rely solely on visual memory. Include sounds, smells, tastes, and tactile feelings. • Describe people's mannerisms, gestures, and voices. • Use dialog to reveal character.
Decide on an organization	• Use chronological order to help readers re-live events with you. • Use conceptual order to show connections and links between ideas.
Craft a strong beginning	• Start with an incident or a place that is the focus.
Conclude by inviting further reflection	• Have you discovered anything new in the process of writing the reflection to share in your conclusion? • A conclusion can sometimes change the entire tone of a reflection. Do you want to surprise your readers? • Above all, your conclusion should help readers make sense of your reflection.
Consider your voice and tone	• Who are you writing for? How do you want your audience to feel upon reading your reflection? • How interested will your readers be in your reflection? Can you add details or something else to draw them in?
Choose a title that will interest readers in your essay	• Your title should suggest the direction or the significance of your reflection.

Writer at work

Janine Carter tried several organizational patterns for her essay. Because she knew so little about the quilt's history, she did not feel chronological organization would be a good strategy. However, as she worked through her draft she realized that readers would appreciate a first-hand account of her purchase of the quilt. She decided to include this story near the beginning of her essay, after describing the quilt. She organized the rest of her essay around the questions that occurred to her as she considered the quilt's appearance. As she worked, she referred back to her assignment frequently to make sure she was fulfilling all its terms. She decided to cut one section, about the names of various quilt patterns, because it was too general and distracted from the main focus of her essay. Here is the original outline Janine began working from, along with revisions she made.

I.   Intro—describe quilt with detail

< *tell story of "Miracle" salesman*

II. Cheap material and clashing colors–poor person, or some other reason?

III. Bias-cut material indicates experienced quilter

IV. ~~Names and meanings of quilt patterns.~~

V.   Number of patches, stitching: this information means more to quilters than to average people. Explain.

VI. Quilting's meaning for women (cultural use). Tell Grandma's story about the work on the farm.

VII. My relationship with the quilt

< *contrast w/how much I know about quilts in our family*
< *add more detail here, and talk about quilt's probable history*

4: Revise, revise, revise

Skilled writers know that the secret to writing well is rewriting. Even the best writers often have to revise several times to get the result they want. You also must have effective strategies for revising if you're going to be successful. The biggest trap you can fall into is starting off with correcting errors. Leave the small stuff for last.

Does your paper or project meet the assignment?	• Look again at the assignment for specific guidelines, including length, format, and amount of research. Does your work meet these guidelines?
Is the subject focused?	• Will readers find your subject early on? • Is the significance evident?
Can you add dialog, description, and other details?	• Can you make events and memories from the past more concrete?
Is your tone engaging?	• Will readers sympathize and identify with you, or will they find your tone too negative, angry, or intensely personal? • Does your tone fit your topic? Some intensely personal topics may not be suited to humorous treatment.
Is your organization effective?	• Are links between concepts and ideas clear? • Are there any places where you find abrupt shifts or gaps? • Are there sections or paragraphs that could be rearranged to make your draft more effective?
Is the writing project visually effective?	• Is the font attractive and readable? • Are the headings and visuals effective? • If you have included an image associated with your reflection, where should it be placed for maximum impact?
Save the editing for last	• When you have finished revising, edit and proofread carefully.

A peer review guide is on page 31.

Writer at work

Janine Carter was not satisfied with her opening paragraph, or her title. After talking to a consultant at her campus writing center, she worked on ending her opening paragraph with a surprising twist that would engage readers. She also realized that she could draw out the concept of "miracles" from within her essay to tie together the beginning and end. Here are the first drafts of Janine's opening and concluding paragraphs, with her notes.

My Mystery Quilt   *This is so boring!*

[introduction]   *Too obvious. That's sort of the point of the assignment, looking for clues.*

The quilt folded at the foot of my bed is a mystery. It is made of cotton: plain muslin and two patterns of calico, with a cotton batt inside, sewn by hand with careful stitches. Some of its thread is white and some is pink. It is frayed around the edges, so someone has obviously used it. But unlike quilts in my own family, this quilt was not handed down as a cherished heirloom. I rescued it from a garage sale and have tried to "piece together" its history.

consultant says puns are usually a bad idea—especially in opening

[conclusion]

When I am cold at night I pull the quilt up over my knees and think about the stranger who made it, wondering who she was, who her loved ones were, whether she was happy. Her quilt gives me warmth, and I give her thanks. There is a bond between us because of this quilt.

This is boring/obvious. Can I make it more special?

5: Submitted version

Carter 1

Janine Carter
Dr. Shapiro
Archaeology 201
10 October 2006

The Miracle Quilt

The quilt folded at the foot of my bed has a long history. It is made of cotton: plain muslin and two patterns of calico, with a cotton batt inside, sewn by hand with careful stitches. Some of its thread is white and some is pink. It is frayed around the edges and has obviously lived a long, useful life. It is steeped in memories. Unfortunately, I don't know what any of them are.

I found the quilt at a city-wide garage sale. At the end of the auditorium, taking up half of the bleachers, was a vendor's booth called "Miracles by the Pound." The gentleman who ran the booth went around buying up vintage fabrics in bad condition. He would dump huge piles of them on the bleachers for people to pick through. When you had found what you wanted, he would weigh it on a scale and tell you how much it cost. Everything was five dollars per pound. As he weighed your purchase, he would call out the price so everyone at the garage sale could hear what a good deal you were getting. My quilt weighed three pounds. "Fifteen dollar miracle!" the vendor sang out as I opened my purse.

My quilt had already been dug out of the pile and discarded by another woman at the garage sale, who had two or three other vintage quilts in her

Fig. 1. Detail of the miracle quilt.

arms. She told me she bought old, damaged quilts and cut them up to make sofa pillows. My quilt didn't interest her because it wasn't in very good shape, and the blocks were the wrong size for the pillow forms she used. I come from a family of quilters, so when I saw the quilt I felt it needed a good home. I didn't like the idea of someone using it to wrap around furniture in a moving van, or even cutting it up for pillows. I took it home and washed it, and put it on my bed, and took a good look at it.

The quilt was probably made by someone poor, or at least very frugal, I decided. The muslin, which provides the background, is the cheapest unbleached kind. Even the binding around the edges, which in most quilts is a bright, contrasting color, is plain muslin. Whoever pieced the quilt—and it was almost certainly a woman, because quilting has always been women's work—started out using a coral-toned calico. But before she finished, she ran out and had to switch to a rose-colored calico. The effect is jarring, as the colors do not complement each other. The coral marches two-thirds of the way across the quilt, and then stumbles into rose. I do not know why the quiltmaker did not work the two colors evenly throughout the quilt; this is what my own grandmother taught me to do when I didn't have enough of one color. Perhaps she was inexperienced; perhaps this was her first quilt, or perhaps she hadn't intended to make the quilt as large as it is. The coral would have been sufficient to cover a single bed; maybe, I think to myself, someone proposed to her while she was making it, and she ended up enlarging it to fit a double bed after she got married.

But there are other clues that suggest experience and planning. The octagon-shaped patches of muslin that center the five-patch blocks are cut so that the lines of quilting cross them on the bias—that is, diagonally across the up-and-down and side-to-side warp and woof threads of the fabric. Fabric is more flexible on the bias (this, my grandmother once explained to me, is why clothing cut on the bias fits and looks better, and is more expensive). A needle slips in and out between the threads more easily, so a quilter is wise to arrange pieces so as to maximize bias quilting. The quilting itself (that is the stitching through all the layers of the quilt) is respectable enough, about five stitches per inch. No fancy 12-stitch-per-inch quilting like you would see in a showpiece quilt, but quite firm and straight, in neat pink rows spaced an inch apart. The quilting pattern is in L-shaped blocks, which I have never seen before. There must be over one hundred yards of quilting all together; the length of a football field, taken one stitch at a time.

The quilt's pattern looks like a variation of wagon tracks, but it uses an octagonal block like a "churn-dash" pattern that sets it apart from a more straightforward Irish chain. Nine-patch and five-patch blocks alternate across it. By my count it contains 1,372 separate pieces, all cut, sewn, and quilted by hand. The nine-patch blocks use 1-1/2-inch patches. These may seem like insignificant details to most people, but to quilters they are important. They tell you how much work went into the quilt. The first nine-patch quilt I made with my grandmother contained a grand total of 675 patches, and I thought it would take forever to sew it (even using a sewing machine!). I remember asking my grandmother how she ever made her more complicated quilts: the flower garden with its thousands of tiny hexagons; the Dutchman's puzzle that was so mesmerizing you could hardly stop your eyes from running over it, trying to pick out the "real" pattern. "Doesn't quilting drive you crazy sometimes?" I asked her. She thought that was pretty funny. "Quilting was how we used to keep from going crazy," she told me.

When she first married my grandfather and moved to a farm in the Brazos River bottom over sixty years ago, there was no television and no neighbors for miles. In the spring, rain would turn the roads to thick clay mud and no one could get off their property for days at a time. Quilting was the way women dealt with the isolation. "That is what the pioneer women did too," she told me. Stuck out alone on the prairies and in the mountains, they kept their sanity by cutting and arranging hundreds of pieces of cloth in different patterns, methodically assembling quilts to bring some order into their own bleak lives.

"It looks like hard work to you now," my grandmother explained, "but for us it was like a vacation. So much of women's work was never done, but you could sit down after dinner in the evening and finish a quilt block and feel like you had done something that would last. You might have spent the whole day dirtying and washing the same set of dishes three times, feeding the same chickens and milking the same cows twice, and you knew you'd have to get up in the morning and do the same things all over again, from top to bottom. But quilt blocks added up to something. Nobody was going to take your finished quilt block and sit down at the breakfast table and pick it apart, and expect you to sew it back together again before lunch. It was done, and it stayed done. There wasn't much else you could say that about, on a farm."

In my family, quilts are heirlooms and are handed down with stories about who made them, who owned them, what they were used for, and what events they had been part of. Some were wedding presents, others were made for relatives when they were first born. I don't know the stories that go with my miracle quilt. It has had a hard life; that is easy to see. Most of the binding has frayed off and there are some spots where the quilt has holes worn straight through it—top, batting, and backing. There are stains that suggest coffee or tea or perhaps medicines from a sickbed spilled on it. There are some spots of dried paint. Evidently at some point it was used as a drop-cloth. But at least, I tell myself, it has found a home with someone who appreciates the work that went into it, and can guess at some of its history.

When I am cold at night I pull the quilt up over my knees and think about the stranger who made it, wondering who she was, who her loved ones were, whether she was happy. Her quilt gives me warmth, and I give her thanks. Though we will never meet, or even know each other's identity, there is a bond between us because of this quilt. And so it seems that the man who sold me this quilt was right: it is a sort of miracle.

Projects

Reflections focus on people, places, events, and things—past and present—that have significance in the writer's life. Successful reflections engage readers in their subjects and convey the importance of the person, event, or place.

These projects are frequently written kinds of reflections.

REFLECTION ON THE PAST
For an example of a reflective essay, see pages 85–89.

List people, events, or places that have been significant in your life or in some way changed you. Many reflections focus on a conflict of some kind and how it was resolved. Look back over your list and check the items that seem especially vivid to you.

Take a few minutes to write first about the person, event, or place as you remember it, and then write about how you regard it today. What was your initial reaction? Did your initial reaction change over time? Why do you feel differently now?

Think about the significance of the person, event, or place in your life. What details best convey that significance? If conversations were involved, remember what was said and create dialog.

Organize your essay around the focus. Start fast to engage your readers. If there is a conflict in your reflection, get it up front.

Show the significance through describing, vivid details, and dialog. Make the characters and the places come to life.

For additional reading, writing, and research resources, go to **www.mycomplab.com** and choose **Lester Faigley's** *Writing.*

FAMILY PHOTOGRAPH

For an example of a reflection on a family, see pages 74–76.

Family photographs and cherished objects can be subjects for reflection. Try carefully observing (or picturing in your mind) an object or photograph that has special meaning for you. Write down all the details you can. What memories does each observation evoke? Do you find that different aspects of the photograph make you feel different ways?

Choose as a topic something that is significant to you, and which you can recall with a reasonable amount of detail. But also consider how interesting this topic will be to others. Will an audience want to share in your experience?

Write a reflective essay about that photograph. What does the photograph convey that other similar snapshots do not? What does it hide or not show? What does it say about your family?

REFLECTION ON THE PRESENT

For an example of a reflection on the present, see pages 81–84.

Not all reflective writing is about the past. You can visit a place or go to an event and focus on your interaction with it instead of the place or event itself. How do you feel when you walk through a local cemetery? What do you think about? What do you notice about the grounds, headstones, and grave decorations? Do you come away from the experience with any interesting realizations about yourself and your life?

Connect the place or event with your life. You are "reading" it in terms of experiences in your life. These connections should be at the center.

Identify a focus. Then write the most vivid introduction you can that will indicate this focus. Select your strongest observations and reactions, and elaborate on that material.

Describe the experience in an essay. Use description and details to express your feelings.

107

8

Observing

Effective observations capture readers' attention through details that may be unfamiliar or surprising but always fresh and vivid.

Chapter contents

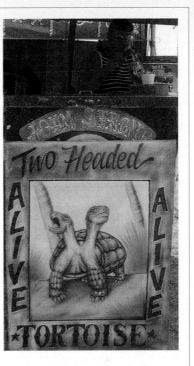

Writing observations

Observing is often the first step to understanding. In fields such as anthropology, sociology, and psychology, scientists observe people and processes, and use their observations to answer questions: How is death regarded in Navajo societies? What groups of people are most likely to visit an urban parkland? How do primates interact?

In everyday life, we use our observational skills to learn more about people and places we encounter. We learn about coffee-break protocol by watching how our co-workers tidy up the break room before they leave, and by listening to them complain about those who leave dirty cups and napkins behind. We learn how our neighbors feel about certain political issues by observing the signs they put up on their lawn. Businesses and governments also use observation to learn more about the people they serve. City officials might observe children playing on a public playground to see what kinds of equipment are used. They might also talk to the children's parents to learn why they bring their children to the playground at particular times of the day.

Observations begin with thorough research. Your firsthand impressions must be carefully recorded in as much detail as possible. These observations, often called field notes, provide your raw material. When you write as an observer, you place yourself in the background, and give readers the clearest, most detailed view you can of your subject. What you see, what you hear, what you smell, taste, and feel as an observer can provide valuable information to your readers.

Components of observations

Where exactly is the place and who are the people?	**Identify your subject** Be specific about who or what you are observing. If it is a certain group of people, what sets them apart as a group? Do they share a common interest? Do they all use a particular space? Explain to readers how and why you limited your observations.
What background do I need to provide? Do I need to explain why I chose this place or these people?	**Provide background on the subject** Readers need some idea of why your observations are significant. Is there a question that could be answered by your observations? Give readers the context they need to appreciate the picture you are about to present and to understand your motivation for observing.
How do I organize my observations?	**Assemble your observations** You may approach your observations chronologically, leading readers through your day-to-day or hour-by-hour experience as an observer. Or you may find other ways to organize that work better for your purposes: perhaps starting with the most surprising discovery you made while observing would interest readers, for example, and draw them into your writing.
What do my observations add up to?	**Place your observations in a larger context** Firsthand observation is a powerful tool for understanding, but it has its limits. What questions are left unanswered by your observations? How might your observations be atypical? Should they change the way people think or act? Give your readers a framework within which to understand your observations.

How many of my reactions and comments should I include?

Know when you are expected to be objective

Field observations in the sciences and social sciences keep the writer in the background, focusing instead on the subject. But essays often allow for personal reflection. Find out from your instructor what is expected.

Keys to observations

Photographs are valuable for providing concrete examples. For instance, Frank Lloyd Wright's attention to detail is evident in his 1905 design for the lobby of the Rookery Building in Chicago.

Build a strong sense of place

Help readers locate themselves along with you as you describe your observations. Tell them the date, time, and exact location of your observations, if possible. Give the names of the objects present.

Provide vivid, well-chosen details

Concrete imagery and descriptions of what you see, hear, smell, taste, and feel during your observation will ground your writing, helping readers "see" as if through your eyes.

Create an overall impression

Select your details to create an overall impression that grows out of the details. Think about which details will best build a coherent image for your readers.

Build trust with your audience by being precise and objective

Begin your observations with an open mind. The goal of observing is not to judge the people or your subjects but to learn as much about them as possible. Being precise about what you observe—not jumping to conclusions or relying on stereotypes—will heighten your objectivity. Precision will also enhance your credibility.

Provide visuals if needed

Photographs and other images can work in combination with words to enhance observations. Close attention to details is critical for both descriptive writing and descriptive visuals.

WORKING TOGETHER

Visit a place or event

In a group of three or four students

First make a visit individually to the same place or event, such as a museum, a parade or festival, or a political rally. Each group member should make notes about what he or she observes and write a 1–2 page synopsis of the visit. Then, as a group, read each other's synopses. How different was each person's experience? What, if anything, did they have in common?

Working together, draft a short introduction that summarizes the different perspectives your observations provide. What can an audience learn by reading multiple accounts of the same experience?

An effective observation

Effective observations do not present a mass of unorganized details but instead select details carefully to convey to readers a vivid sense of the subject.

Living Like Weasels
Annie Dillard

Annie Dillard was born in Pittsburgh and earned a degree in creative writing at Hollins College in Virginia. She lived in a cabin on Tinker Creek in the Roanoke Valley after she graduated, where she spent months observing the beauty and violence of the natural world. Her observations were collected and published in 1974 in the prize-winning *Pilgrim at Tinker Creek*.

"Living Like Weasels" appeared in *Teaching a Stone to Talk: Expeditions and Encounters*, a collection of her essays published in 1982.

A weasel is wild. Who knows what he thinks? He sleeps in his underground den, his tail draped over his nose. Sometimes he lives in his den for over two days without leaving. Outside, he stalks rabbits, muskrats, and birds, killing more bodies than he can eat warm, and often dragging the carcasses home. Obedient to instinct, he bites his prey at the neck, either splitting the jugular vein at the throat or crunching the brain at the base of the skull, and he does not let go. One naturalist refused to kill a weasel who was socketed into his hand deeply as a rattlesnake. The man could in no way pry the tiny weasel off, and had to walk half a mile to water, the weasel dangling from his palm, and soak him off like a stubborn label.

And once, says Ernest Thompson Seton, a man shot an eagle out of the sky. He examined the eagle and found the dry skull of a weasel fixed by the jaws to his throat. The supposition is that the eagle had pounced on the weasel and the weasel swiveled and bit as instinct taught him, tooth to neck, and nearly won. I would like to have seen that eagle from the air a few weeks or months before he was shot: was the whole weasel still attached to his feathered

Dillard introduces her subject and provides a context for viewing it; the weasel is ferocious.

Another incident attests to the ferocity and tenacity of weasels.

throat, a fur pendant? Or did the eagle eat what he could reach, gutting the living weasel with his talons before his breast, bending his beak, cleaning the beautiful airborne bones?

Dillard places herself at the center with the weasel. If she were writing field notes for a biology paper, the focus would be exclusively on the weasel.

I have been reading about weasels because I saw one last week. I startled a weasel who startled me, and we exchanged a long glance.

Twenty minutes from my house, through the woods by the quarry and across the highway, is Hollins Pond, a remarkable piece of shallowness, where I like to go at sunset and sit on a tree trunk. Hollins Pond is also called Murray's Pond; it covers two acres of bottomland near Tinker Creek with six inches of water and six thousand lily pads. In winter, brown and white steers stand in the middle of it, merely dampening their hooves; from the distant shore they look like miracle itself, complete with miracle's nonchalance. Now in summer, the steers are gone. The water lilies have blossomed and spread to a green horizontal plane that is terra firma to plodding blackbirds, and tremulous ceiling to black leeches, crayfish, and carp.

Dillard uses a chronological organization until the final section.

She provides many specific details including the names of the plants, animals, and fish that live in and around Hollins Pond.

This is, mind you, suburbia. It is a five-minute walk in three directions to rows of houses, though none is visible here. There's a 55 mph highway at one end of the pond, and a nesting pair of wood ducks at the other. Under every bush is a muskrat hole or a beer can. The far end is an alternating series of fields and woods, threaded everywhere with motorcycle tracks—in whose bare clay wild turtles lay eggs.

She points out the contradictions of the natural world in close proximity to the human world.

So. I had crossed the highway, stepped over two low barbed-wire fences, and traced the motorcycle path in all gratitude through the wild rose and poison ivy of the pond's shoreline up into high grassy fields. Then I cut down through the woods to the mossy

Carefully chosen adjectives allow us to picture where she is sitting.

fallen tree where I sit. This tree is excellent. It makes a dry, upholstered bench at the upper, marshy end of the pond, a plush jetty raised from the thorny shore between a shallow blue body of water and a deeper blue body of sky.

The sun had just set. I was relaxed on the tree trunk, ensconced in the lap of lichen, watching the lily pads at my feet tremble and part dreamily over the thrusting path of a carp. A yellow bird appeared to my right and flew behind me. It caught my eye; I swiveled around—and the next instant, inexplicably, I was looking down at a weasel, who was looking up at me.

Weasel! I'd never seen one wild before. He was ten inches long, thin as a curve, a muscled ribbon, brown as fruitwood, soft-furred, alert. His face was fierce, small and pointed as a lizard's; he would have made a good arrowhead. There was just a dot of a chin, maybe two brown hairs' worth, and then the pure white fur began that spread down his underside. He had two black eyes I didn't see, any more than you see a window.

> Dillard conveys the surprise of encountering the weasel with vivid details. She compares the weasel's head to an arrowhead.

The weasel was stunned into stillness as he was emerging from beneath an enormous shaggy wild rose bush four feet away. I was stunned into stillness twisted backward on the tree trunk. Our eyes locked, and someone threw away the key.

Our look was as if two lovers, or deadly enemies, met unexpectedly on an overgrown path when each had been think-ing of something else: a clearing blow to the gut. It was also a bright blow to the brain, or a sudden beating of brains, with all the charge and intimate grate of rubbed balloons. It emptied our lungs. It felled the forest, moved the fields, and drained the pond; the world dismantled and tumbled into that black hole of eyes. If you and I looked at each other that way, our skulls would split and drop to our shoulders. But we don't. We keep our skulls. So.

> The passion that Dillard feels is expressed by comparisons with unexpected meetings of lovers or enemies, literally taking the breath away.

He disappeared. This was only last week, and already I don't know what shattered the enchantment. I think I blinked, I think I retrieved my brain from the weasel's brain, and tried to memorize what I was seeing, and the weasel felt the yank of separation, the careening splashdown into real life and the urgent current of instinct. He vanished under the wild rose. I waited motionless, my mind suddenly full of data and my spirit with pleadings, but he didn't return.

Please do not tell me about "approach-avoidance conflicts." I tell you I've been in that weasel's brain for sixty seconds, and he was in mine. Brains are private places, muttering through unique and secret tapes—but the weasel and I both plugged into another tape simultaneously, for a sweet and shocking time. Can I help it if I was blank?

Dillard speaks directly to the reader about the significance of meeting the weasel.

What goes on in his brain the rest of the time? What does a weasel think about? He won't say. His journal is tracks in clay, a spray of feathers, mouse blood and bone: uncollected, unconnected, loose-leaf, and blown.

I would like to learn, or remember, how to live. I come to Hollins Pond not so much to learn how to live as, frankly, to forget about it. That is, I don't think I can learn from a wild animal how to live in particular—shall I suck warm blood, hold my tail high, walk with my footprints precisely over the prints of my hands?—but I might learn something of mindlessness, something of the purity of living in the physical senses and the dignity of living without bias or motive. The weasel lives in necessity and we live in choice, hating necessity and dying at the last ignobly in its talons. I would like to live as I should, as the weasel lives as he should. And I suspect that for me the way is like the weasel's: open to time and death painlessly, noticing everything, remembering nothing, choosing the given with a fierce and pointed will.

She ponders what she could learn from this encounter; at this point observation becomes reflection. Purely scientific observation would not engage in reflection.

115

I missed my chance. I should have gone for the throat. I should have lunged for that streak of white under the weasel's chin and held on, held on through mud and into the wild rose, held on for a dearer life. We could live under the wild rose wild as weasels, mute and uncomprehending. I could very calmly go wild. I could live two days in the den, curled, leaning on mouse fur, sniffing bird bones, blinking, licking, breathing musk, my hair tangled in the roots of grasses. Down is a good place to go, where the mind is single. Down is out, out of your ever-loving mind and back to your careless senses. I remember muteness as a prolonged and giddy fast, where every moment is a feast of utterance received. Time and events are merely poured, unremarked, and ingested directly, like blood pulsed into my gut through a jugular vein. Could two live that way? Could two live under the wild rose, and explore by the pond, so that the smooth mind of each is as everywhere present to the other, and as received and as unchallenged, as falling snow?

We could, you know. We can live any way we want. People take vows of poverty, chastity, and obedience—even of silence—by choice. The thing is to stalk your calling in a certain skilled and supple way, to locate the most tender and live spot and plug into that pulse. This is yielding, not fighting. A weasel doesn't "attack" anything; a weasel lives as he's meant to, yielding at every moment to the perfect freedom of single necessity.

I think it would be well, and proper, and obedient, and pure, to grasp your one necessity and not let it go, to dangle from it limp wherever it takes you. Then even death, where you're going no matter how you live, cannot you part. Seize it and let it seize you up aloft even, till your eyes burn out and drop; let your musky flesh fall off in shreds, and let your very bones unhinge and scatter, loosened over fields, over fields and woods, lightly, thoughtless, from any height at all, from as high as eagles.

The concluding section takes an imaginative flight: could she live like a weasel? As absurd as the idea sounds, Dillard points out that people choose how they live.

How to read observations

Make notes as you read, either in the margins or on paper or a computer file. Circle any words or references that you don't know and look them up.

What is it?	• What kind of a text is it? An article? an essay? a Web site? field notes? a photographic essay? What are your expectations for this kind of text? • What media are used? (Web sites, for example, often combine images, words, and sounds.)
Where did it come from?	• Who wrote the observation? • How and when were the observations made?
Who is the intended audience?	• What clues do you find about whom the writer had in mind as the readers? • What does the writer assume that the readers already know about the subject? • What new knowledge is the writer providing?
What is the overall impression?	• Does the writer give precise, objective, concrete details? • Does the writer comment on the observations?
How are the observations organized?	• Chronologically? In order of perceived importance? Or some other way?
What is the larger context surrounding the writer's observations?	• For what purposes were the observations made?
How is it composed?	• How does the writer represent herself or himself? • How would you characterize the style? • How effective is the design? Is it easy to read? • If there are any photographs or other graphics, what information do they contribute?

The First Descent of the Grand Canyon
(TRAVEL ACCOUNT)
John Wesley Powell

Tau-gu, Chief of the Paiutes, and John Wesley Powell

John Wesley Powell (1834–1902) had a deep interest in the natural sciences throughout his life. After losing an arm in the Civil War, he led a series of expeditions into the Rocky Mountains and around the Green and Colorado rivers. In 1869 he set out to explore the Colorado River and the Grand Canyon, which were then unknown. He gathered nine men in four sturdy rowboats (Powell named his boat *Emma Dean* after his wife) and set out from Green River, Wyoming, on May 24. One man quit after the first month and another three left only days before the group reached the mouth of the Virgin River in Arizona on August 30, where they met settlers.

Powell was lucky to survive. His boats were unsuited for running rapids and the men lacked experience. None could swim, and they didn't have life jackets. But they made up in bravery and determination for what they lacked in knowledge and equipment. They learned through trial and error how to get down rapids, often by floating the boats with ropes attached or hauling them when the rapids were beyond their ability. By the time they reached the Grand Canyon on August 13, where the excerpt below begins, they had lost one of the boats, their food had nearly run out, and the rapids were becoming more violent.

Analyzing and Connecting

Return to these questions after you have finished reading.

1. Powell described a place none of his readers had ever seen and an activity—running rapids—that none had ever done. How does he attempt to describe both?

2. Adventurers today are still making first descents down rivers in remote places. Powell's account was first published in *Scribner's Magazine* in 1874. An account of descending an unknown river today likely would be a documentary film or at least contain photographs. How else might a travel adventure account today be different from Powell's?

3. Powell didn't have a photographer on his first trip down the Colorado River. How might have photographs changed what Powell wrote?

4. Look in your textbooks for other courses for examples of authors explaining unfamiliar concepts or objects. What strategies do they use to describe what is unfamiliar?

AUGUST 13.

We are now ready to start on our way down the Great Unknown. Our boats, tied to a common stake, are chafing each other, as they are tossed by the fretful river. They ride high and buoyant, for their loads are lighter than we could desire. We have but a month's rations remaining. The flour has been resifted through the mosquito net sieve; the spoiled bacon has been dried, and the worst of it boiled; the few pounds of dried apples have been spread in the sun, and reshrunken to their normal bulk; the sugar has all melted, and gone on its way down the river; but we have a large sack of coffee. The lightening of the boats has this advantage; they will ride the waves better, and we shall have but little to carry when we make a portage.

We are three quarters of a mile in the depths of the earth, and the great river shrinks into insignificance as it dashes its angry waves against the walls and cliffs that rise to the world above; they are but puny ripples, and we but pigmies, running up and down the sands, or lost among the boulders.

We have an unknown distance yet to run, an unknown river yet to explore. What falls there are, we know not; what rocks beset the channel, we know not; what walls rise over the river, we know not. Ah, well! we may conjecture many things. The men talk as cheerfully as ever; jests are bandied about freely this morning; but to me the cheer is somber and the jests are ghastly.

With some eagerness, and some anxiety, and some misgiving, we enter the canyon below, and are carried along by the swift water through walls which rise from its very edge. They have the same structure as we noticed yesterday—tiers of irregular shelves below, and, above these, steep slopes to the foot of marble cliffs. We run six miles in a little more than half an hour, and emerge into a more open portion of the canyon, where high hills and ledges of rock intervene between the river and the distant walls. Just at the head of this open place the river runs across a dike; that is, a fissure in the rocks, open to depths below, has been filled with eruptive matter, and this, on cooling, was harder than the rocks through which the crevice was made, and, when these were washed away, the harder volcanic matter remained as a wall, and the river has cut a gateway through it several hundred feet high, and as many wide. As it crosses the wall, there is a fall below, and a bad rapid, filled with boulders of trap; so we stop to make a portage. Then on we go, gliding by hills and ledges, with distant walls in view; sweeping past sharp angles of rock; stopping at a few points to examine rapids, which we find can be run, until we have made another five miles, when we land for dinner.

Then we let down with lines, over a long rapid, and start again. Once more the walls close in, and we find ourselves in a narrow gorge, the water again filling the channel, and very swift. With great care, and constant watchfulness, we proceed, making about four miles this afternoon, and camp in a cave.

AUGUST 14.

At daybreak we walk down the bank of the river, on a little sandy beach, to take a view of a new feature in the canyon. Heretofore, hard rocks have given us bad river; soft rocks, smooth water; and a series of rocks harder than any we have experienced sets in. The river enters the granite!

We can see but a little way into the granite gorge, but it looks threatening.

After breakfast we enter on the waves. At the very introduction, it inspires awe. The canyon is narrower than we have ever before seen it; the water is swifter; there are but few broken rocks in the channel; but the walls are set, on either side, with pinnacles and crags; and sharp, angular buttresses, bristling with wind and wave-polished spires, extend far out into the river.

Ledges of rocks jut into the stream, their tops sometimes just below the surface, sometimes rising few or many feet above; and island ledges, and island pinnacles, and island towers break the swift course of the stream into chutes, and eddies, and whirlpools. We soon reach a place where a creek comes in from the left, and just below, the channel is choked with boulders, which have washed down this lateral canyon and formed a dam, over which there is a fall of thirty or forty feet; but on the boulders we can get foothold, and we make a portage.

Three more such dams are found. Over one we make a portage; at the other two we find chutes, through which we can run.

As we proceed, the granite rises higher, until nearly a thousand feet of the lower part of the walls are composed of this rock.

About eleven o'clock we hear a great roar ahead, and approach it very cautiously. The sound grows louder and louder as we run, and at last we find ourselves above a long, broken fall, with ledges and pinnacles of rock obstructing the river. There is a descent of, perhaps, seventy-five or eighty feet in a third of a mile, and the rushing waters break into great waves on the rocks, and lash themselves into a mad, white foam. We can land just above, but there is no foothold on either side by which we can make a portage. It is nearly a thousand feet to the top of the granite, so it will be impossible to carry our boats around, though we can climb to the summit up a side gulch, and, passing along a mile or two, can descend to the river. This we find on examination; but such a portage would be impracticable for us, and we must run the rapid, or abandon the river. There is no hesitation. We step into our boats, push off and away we go, first on smooth but swift water, then we strike a glassy wave, and ride to its top, down again into the trough, up again on a higher wave, and down and up on waves higher and still higher, until we strike one just as it curls back, and a breaker rolls over our little boat. Still, on we speed, shooting past projecting rocks, till the little boat is caught in a whirlpool and spun around several times. At last we pull out again into the stream, and now the other boats have passed us. The open compartment of the "Emma Dean" is filled with water, and every breaker rolls over us. Hurled back from a rock, now on this side, now on that, we are carried into an eddy, in which we struggle for a few minutes, and are then out again, the breakers still rolling over us. Our boat is unmanageable, but she cannot sink, and we drift down another hundred yards, through breakers; how, we scarcely know. We find the other boats have turned into an eddy at the foot of the fall, and are waiting to catch us as we come, for the men have seen that our boat is swamped. They push out as we come near, and pull us in against the wall. We bail our boat, and on we go again.

The walls, now, are more than a mile in height—a vertical distance difficult to appreciate. Stand on the south steps of the Treasury building, in Washington, and look down Pennsylvania Avenue to the Capitol Park, and measure this distance overhead, and imagine cliffs to extend to that altitude, and you will understand what I mean; or, stand at Canal Street, in New York, and look up Broadway to Grace Church, and you have about the distance; or, stand at Lake Street bridge in Chicago, and look down to the Central Depot, and you have it again.

A thousand feet of this is up through granite crags, then steep slopes and perpendicular cliffs rise, one above another, to the summit. The gorge is black and narrow below, red and gray and flaring above, with crags and angular projections on the walls, which, cut in many places by side canyons, seem to be a vast wilderness of rocks. Down in these grand, gloomy depths we glide, ever listening, for the mad waters keep up their roar; ever watching, ever peering ahead, for the narrow canyon is winding, and the river is closed in so that we can see but a few hundred yards, and what there may be below we know not; but we listen for falls, and watch for rocks, or stop now and then, in the bay of a recess, to admire the gigantic scenery. And ever, as we go, there is some new pinnacle or tower, some crag or peak, some distant view of the upper plateau, some strange-shaped rock, or some deep, narrow side canyon. Then we come to another broken fall, which appears more difficult than the one we ran this morning.

A small creek comes in on the right, and the first fall of the water is over boulders, which have been carried down by this lateral stream. We land at its mouth, and stop for an hour or two to examine the fall. It seems possible to let down with lines, at least a part of the way, from point to point, along the right-hand wall. So we make a portage over the first rocks, and find footing on some boulders below. Then we let down one of the boats to the end of her line, when she reaches a corner of the projecting rock, to which one of the men clings, and steadies her, while I examine an eddy below. I think we can pass the other boats down by us, and catch them in the eddy. This is soon done and the men in the boats in the eddy pull us to their side. On the shore of this little eddy there is about two feet of gravel beach above the water. Standing on this beach, some of the men take the line of the little boat and let it drift down against another projecting angle. Here is a little shelf, on which a man from my boat climbs, and a shorter line is passed to him, and he fastens the boat to the side of the cliff. Then the second one is let down, bringing the line of the third. When the second boat is tied up, the two men standing on the beach above spring into the last boat, which is pulled up alongside of ours. Then we let down the boats, for twenty-five or thirty yards, by walking along the shelf, landing them again in the mouth of a side canyon. Just below this there is another pile of boulders, over which we make another portage. From the foot of these rocks we can climb to another shelf, forty or fifty feet above the water.

On this bench we camp for the night. We find a few sticks, which have lodged in the rocks. It is raining hard, and we have no shelter, but kindle a fire and have our supper. We sit on the rocks all night, wrapped in our ponchos, getting what sleep we can.

Photographs of Japanese-Americans at Manzanar
(PHOTO ESSAY)
Ansel Adams

Ansel Adams (1902–1984), one of the most famous American photographers, is best known for his black-and-white landscape photography. During World War II, he made murals for the Department of Interior. He was distressed about the relocation and internment of American citizens of Japanese descent, many of whom lost everything they owned. In 1943, Adams obtained permission to photograph one of the internment camps, the Manzanar War Relocation Center, located in the Owens Valley in eastern California. Adams published a book in 1944 with the photographs, *Born Free and Equal,* and he later donated the images to the Library of Congress. He wrote, "The purpose of my work was to show how these people, suffering under a great injustice, and loss of property, businesses and professions, had overcome the sense of defeat and despair by building for themselves a vital community in an arid (but magnificent) environment."

Manzanar is now a National Historic Site administered by the National Park Service.

Analyzing and Connecting
Return to these questions after you have finished reading.

1. You can read an account of life in Manzanar, Sue Kunitomi Embrey's "Some Lines for a Younger Brother . . . ," on pages 56–59. Embrey uses words to describe Manzanar while Adams uses pictures. What do you learn from Embrey about Manzanar that you could not learn from Adams's photographs? Likewise, what does Adams show you that you don't find in the Embrey account?

2. Adams's specialty was photographing landscapes, especially mountains. Look at the landscape in these images. How does Adams represent the relationship of the people interned at Manzanar to their environment?

3. Great photographers pay close attention to details. Adams used a bulky, large-format camera and spent a great deal of time setting up his shots. What details caught his eye?

4. All Adams's pictures of people were posed. He had to coach the people in each of his pictures. What do you think he might have told them? What was Adams trying to convey with his portraits of individuals?

ADAMS: PHOTOGRAPHS OF JAPANESE-AMERICANS AT MANZANAR

Manzanar from guard tower, view west

Dressmaking class: Mrs. Ryie Yoshizawa, instructor

Catholic church

Yonehisa Yamagami, electrician

ADAMS: PHOTOGRAPHS OF JAPANESE-AMERICANS AT MANZANAR

Joyce Yuki Nakamura, eldest daughter

Farm workers, Mt. Williamson in background

Richard Kobayashi, farmer with cabbages

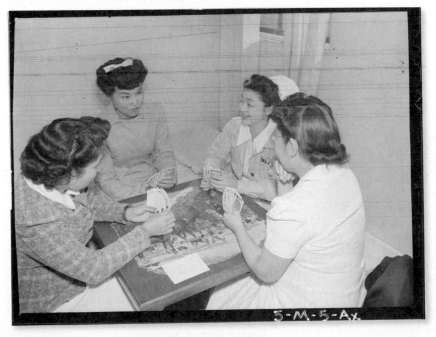

Bridge game

A Small Place
(ESSAY)
Jamaica Kincaid

Jamaica Kincaid was born in Antigua in 1949, and she moved to New York City at age 18 to work as an au pair, taking care of rich people's children. She had planned to become a nurse, but while supporting herself with odd jobs, she began publishing her writing. She shortly gained wide acclaim for two works of fiction about life in Antigua, *At the Bottom of the River* (1983) and *Annie John* (1985). In 1988 she published *A Small Place,* a short, polemical nonfiction book about Antigua, from which the excerpt below is taken.

Analyzing and Connecting

Return to these questions after you have finished reading.

1. Kincaid describes Antigua, the place where she was born and grew up, from the perspective of a tourist just arriving on her island. Why does she describe Antigua from the point of view of the second-person "you"?

2. Examine places where Kincaid contrasts what a tourist sees and what the local sees. What causes the differences?

3. Kincaid writes, "A tourist is an ugly human being." Many readers have taken offense at her bitter tone; perhaps you will too. Why is she so deliberately provocative?

4. What is the alternative for an island like Antigua that offers little economic opportunity besides tourism? Is tourism necessarily bad? Should tourists be concerned about issues such as the sewage system of beach resorts?

If you go to Antigua as a tourist, this is what you will see. If you come by aeroplane, you will land at the V. C. Bird International Airport. Vere Cornwall (V. C.) Bird is the Prime Minister of Antigua. You may be the sort of tourist who would wonder why a Prime Minister would want an airport named after him—why not a school, why not a hospital, why not some great public monument? You are a tourist and you have not yet seen a school in Antigua, you have not yet seen the hospital in Antigua, you have not yet seen a public monument in Antigua. As your plane descends to land, you might say, What a beautiful island Antigua is—more beautiful than any of the other islands you have seen, and they were very beautiful, in their way, but they were much too green, much too lush with vegetation, which indicated to you, the tourist, that they got quite a bit of rainfall, and rain is the very thing that you, just now, do not want, for you are thinking of the hard and cold and dark and long days you spent working in North America (or, worse, Europe), earning some money so that you could stay in this place (Antigua) where the sun always shines and where the climate is deliciously hot and dry for the four to ten days you are going to be staying there; and since you are on your holiday, since you are a tourist, the thought of what it might be like for someone who had to live day in, day out in a place that suffers constantly from drought, and so has to watch carefully every drop of fresh water used (while at the same time surrounded by a sea and an ocean—the Caribbean Sea on one side, the Atlantic Ocean on the other), must never cross your mind.

You disembark from your plane. You go through customs. Since you are a tourist, a North American or European—to be frank, white—and not an Antiguan black returning to Antigua from Europe or North America with cardboard boxes of much needed cheap clothes and food for relatives, you move through customs swiftly, you move through customs with ease. Your bags are not searched. You emerge from customs into the hot, clean air: immediately you feel cleansed, immediately you feel blessed (which is to say special); you feel free. You see a man, a taxi driver; you ask him to take you to your destination; he quotes you a price. You immediately think that the price is in the local currency, for you are a tourist and you are familiar with these things (rates of exchange) and you feel even more free, for things seem so cheap, but then your driver ends by saying, "In U.S. currency." You may say, "Hmmmm, do you have a formal sheet that lists official prices and destinations?" Your driver obeys the law and shows you the sheet, and he apologises for the incredible mistake he has made in quoting you a price off the top of his head which is so vastly different (favoring him) from the one listed. You are driven to your hotel by this taxi driver in his taxi, a brand-new Japanese-made vehicle. The road on which you are traveling is a very bad road, very much in need of repair. You are feeling wonderful, so you say, "Oh, what a marvelous change these bad roads are from the splendid highways I am used to in North America." (Or, worse, Europe.) Your driver is reckless; he is a dangerous man who drives in the middle of the road when he thinks no other cars are coming in the opposite direction, passes other cars on blind curves that run uphill, drives at sixty miles an hour on narrow, curving roads when the road sign, a rusting, beat-up thing left over from colonial days, says 40 MPH. This might frighten you (you are on your holiday; you are a tourist); this might excite you (you are on your holiday; you are a tourist), though if you are from New York and take taxis you are used to this style of driving: most of the taxi drivers in New York are from places in the world like this.

Oh, but by now you are tired of all this looking, and you want to reach your destination—your hotel, your room. You long to refresh yourself; you long to eat some nice lobster, some nice local food. You take a bath, you brush your teeth. You get dressed again; as you get dressed, you look out the window. That water—have you ever seen anything like it? Far out, to the horizon, the color of the water is navy-blue; nearer, the water is the color of the North American sky. From there to the shore, the water is pale, silvery, clear, so clear that you can see its pinkish-white sand bottom. Oh, what beauty! Oh, what beauty! You have never seen anything like this. You are so excited. You breathe shallow. You breathe deep. You see a beautiful boy skimming the water, godlike, on a Windsurfer. You see an incredibly unattractive, fat, pastry-

like-fleshed woman enjoying a walk on the beautiful sand, with a man, an incredibly unattractive, fat, pastrylike-fleshed man; you see the pleasure they're taking in their surroundings. Still standing, looking out the window, you see yourself lying on the beach, enjoying the amazing sun (a sun so powerful and yet so beautiful, the way it is always overhead as if on permanent guard, ready to stamp out any cloud that dares to darken and so empty rain on you and ruin your holiday; a sun that is your personal friend). You see yourself taking a walk on that beach, you see yourself meeting new people (only they are new in a very limited way, for they are people just like you). You see yourself eating some delicious, locally grown food. You see yourself, you see yourself . . . You must not wonder what exactly happened to the contents of your lavatory when you flushed it. You must not wonder where your bathwater went when you pulled out the stopper. You must not wonder what happened when you brushed your teeth. Oh, it might all end up in the water you are thinking of taking a swim in; the contents of your lavatory might, just might, graze gently against your ankle as you wade carefree in the water, for you see, in Antigua, there is no proper sewage-disposal system. But the Caribbean Sea is very big and the Atlantic Ocean is even bigger; it would amaze even you to know the number of black slaves this ocean has swallowed up. When you sit down to eat your delicious meal, it's better that you don't know that most of what you are eating came off a plane from Miami. And before it got on a plane in Miami, who knows where it came from? A good guess is that it came from a place like Antigua first, where it was grown dirt-cheap, went to Miami, and came back. There is a world of something in this, but I can't go into it right now.

The thing you have always suspected about yourself the minute you become a tourist is true: A tourist is an ugly human being. You are not an ugly person all the time; you are not an ugly person ordinarily; you are not an ugly person day to day. From day to day, you are a nice person. From day to day, all the people who are supposed to love you on the whole do. From day to day, as you walk down a busy street in the large and modern and prosperous city in which you work and live, dismayed, puzzled (a cliché, but only a cliché can explain you) at how alone you feel in this crowd, how awful it is to go unnoticed, how awful it is to go unloved, even as you are surrounded by more people than you could possibly get to know in a lifetime that lasted for millennia, and then out of the corner of your eye you see someone looking at you and absolute pleasure is written all over that person's face, and then you realize that you are not as revolting a presence as you think you are (for that look just told you so). And so, ordinarily, you are a nice person, an attractive person, a person capable of drawing to yourself the affection of other people (people just like you), a person at home in your own skin (sort of; I mean, in a way; I mean, your dismay and puzzlement are natural to you, because people like you just

seem to be like that, and so many of the things people like you find admirable about yourselves—the things you think about, the things you think really define you—seem rooted in these feelings): a person at home in your own house (and all its nice house things), with its nice back yard (and its nice back-yard things), at home on your street, your church, in community activities, your job, at home with your family, your relatives, your friends—you are a whole person. But one day, when you are sitting somewhere, alone in that crowd, and that awful feeling of displacedness comes over you, and really, as an ordinary person you are not well equipped to look too far inward and set yourself aright, because being ordinary is already so taxing, and being ordinary takes all you have out of you, and though the words "I must get away" do not actually pass across your lips, you make a leap from being that nice blob just sitting like a boob in your amniotic sac of the modern experience to being a person visiting heaps of death and ruin and feeling alive and inspired at the sight of it; to being a person lying on some faraway beach, your stilled body stinking and glistening in the sand, looking like something first forgotten, then remembered, then not important enough to go back for; to being a person marveling at the harmony (ordinarily, what you would say is the backwardness) and the union these other people (and they are other people) have with nature. And you look at the things they can do with a piece of ordinary cloth, the things they fashion out of cheap, vulgarly colored (to you) twine, the way they squat down over a hole they have made in the ground, the hole itself is something to marvel at, and since you are being an ugly person this ugly but joyful thought will swell inside you: their ancestors were not clever in the way yours were and not ruthless in the way yours were, for then would it not be you who would be in harmony with nature and backwards in that charming way? An ugly thing, that is what you are when you become a tourist, an ugly, empty thing, a stupid thing, a piece of rubbish pausing here and there to gaze at this and taste that, and it will never occur to you that the people who inhabit the place in which you have just paused cannot stand you, that behind their closed doors they laugh at your strangeness (you do not look the way they look); the physical sight of you does not please them; you have bad manners (it is their custom to eat their food with their hands; you try eating their way, you look silly; you try eating the way you always eat, you look silly); they do not like the way you speak (you have an accent); they collapse helpless from laughter, mimicking the way they imagine you must look as you carry out some everyday bodily function. They do not like you. *They do not like me!* That thought never actually occurs to you. Still, you feel a little uneasy. Still, you feel a little foolish. Still, you feel a little out of place. But the banality of your own life is very real to you; it drove you to this extreme, spending your days and your nights in the company of people who despise you, people you do not like really, people you would not want to have as your actual neighbor. And so you must devote yourself to puzzling out how much of what you are told is really, really true (Is ground-up bottle glass in peanut sauce really a delicacy around here, or will it do just what you think ground-up bottle glass will do? Is this rare, multicolored, snout-mouthed fish really an aphrodisiac, or will it cause you to fall asleep permanently?). Oh, the hard work all of this is, and is it any wonder, then, that on your return home you feel the need of a long rest, so that you can recover from your life as a tourist?

That the native does not like the tourist is not hard to explain. For every native of every place is a potential tourist, and every tourist is a native of somewhere. Every native everywhere lives a life of overwhelming and crushing banality and boredom and desperation and depression, and every deed, good and bad, is an attempt to forget this. Every native would like to find a way out, every native would like a rest, every native would like a tour. But some natives—most natives in the world—cannot go anywhere. They are too poor to escape the reality of their lives; and they are too poor to live properly in the place where they live, which is the very place you, the tourist, want to go—so when the natives see you, the tourist, they envy you, they envy your ability to leave your own banality and boredom, they envy your ability to turn their own banality and boredom into a source of pleasure for yourself.

Low Wages, Strong Backs

(ARTICLE)

Tom Meagher and Suzanne Travers

Journalist Tom Meagher spent one month living and working as a low-wage day laborer in Passaic County, New Jersey. His story idea is not new. George Orwell wrote about his experiences of living among the desperately poor in the 1930s in *Down and Out in London and Paris,* and Barbara Ehrenreich has written recently about surviving on low-paying jobs in *Nickle and Dimed.* Nevertheless, Meagher describes vividly how difficult it is to start over with nothing in the bank. Meagher and cowriter Suzanne Travers reported his experience in a series of articles in 2005 for the *New Jersey Herald.*

Analyzing and Connecting

Return to these questions after you have finished reading.

1. Meagher takes an approach to reporting that is similar to the method that anthropologists call "ethnography." It requires living among the subjects you write about and learning firsthand about their world. What does Meagher learn about low-wage workers that he could not have found out by interviewing them?

2. The key to a live-the-experience article is to be believable. What strategies does Meagher use to convince his readers that he is telling the truth?

3. Another challenge in writing these articles is describing mind-numbing work. Look for specific description of jobs. What writing strategies do Meagher and Travers use?

4. How does Meagher's experience of living at the edge of homelessness differ from how politicians and the media represent poor people?

LOW WAGES, STRONG BACKS

Today I face the clock. Standing on an assembly line in a warehouse in Mount Olive, I wear safety goggles and stack boxes full of Euphoria perfume on a wooden pallet as they come off the conveyor belt. Women in white lab coats scurry around downstairs, pulling bottles randomly off the line to test them in the quality assurance room.

Folding or stacking or filling these boxes I am a cog in the production wheel, repeating motions that get my bit of the work done. Yesterday, it was open box, pull out bag, pull box from bag, pivot. Today it's fold, stack, slide. Everybody is interchangeable, especially temps like me.

My feet are tired from standing, but even worse is today's spot on the line: I'm directly in front of the clock. I don't think I can watch eight hours drag by, second by second. I keep my head down and force myself to fold 50 boxes before I look up again. When I do, it's only five minutes later. OK then, I'll do 100 boxes.

This job pays $8 an hour. That's nearly $3 more than I made last week stacking boxes of foam padding at a factory in Moonachie. This is temp work in the "light industrial" sector: warehouses and boxes and hours that stretch forever for dollars that don't.

Tom Meagher gets his evening call from his fiancée at a pay phone on Main Avenue in Passaic. KYE-RYUNG LEE/NEW JERSEY HERALD

I'm a newspaper reporter, though nobody in this warehouse knows it. I'm three weeks into a month-long project aimed at showing what life is like for people starting over in Passaic County: the thousands of new immigrants who arrive each year, or people who've lost jobs. What kind of work and housing exist for those who need both, fast? This is my assignment: Find a job and a place to live and write about the experience.

Last year, 85,069 Passaic County residents—17 percent of the county's population—lived below the federal poverty line, as compared with 722,300 —8.5 percent—statewide. Legal Services of New Jersey's Poverty Research Institute estimates that a single person living in

Passaic County needs to make $9.64 an hour to meet all his or her needs. Can I do that?

My experience won't be a perfect example of the temp life. I'm white, American-born, English-speaking and college-educated. I have health insurance through North Jersey Media Group, which owns the *Herald News*. I know if things get bad, I can go home. That's hardly the profile of most people in this situation. Still, I hope this project will illuminate the lives and challenges of those who come here, seeking a future, and those, born here, who struggle to live near the poverty line.

As a reporter, I make about $33,000. Like everyone I know, I work really hard just to scrape by. In the days before this assignment starts, I'm nervous and excited. I'm burnt out from months of cranking out stories, and I think that a few weeks at a no-stress job will be just what I need.

I begin on August 1, a Monday. I leave behind my checkbook, my ATM card, my credit card, my cell phone, my car keys, my fiancée and our apartment in Brooklyn. I've got $424 to get started, an amount based on a week's wages at the Poverty Research Institute's self-sufficiency level. I board a jitney shuttle bus in New York City and head for Paterson with a backpack full of clothes. Now I'm depressed to be alone and scared of what's ahead.

I get off on Main Street in South Paterson and go to the library to check the classifieds. There are rooms for rent in Haledon, Clifton and Passaic. I make calls at a payphone across the street. An agency in Fair Lawn will find me a room for a $100 fee, but that's almost a quarter of the money I have right now—not worth it.

Today is a scorcher, the beginning of a month of a dozen 90-plus-degree days. My backpack weighs about 40 pounds. I lug it down Main Avenue in Clifton. I don't want to waste money on sunblock, but I can feel my skin turning red. As the day goes by, my legs chafe against each other into a stinging rash. I make more calls. People want more money than I've got for a room: One place asks $165 a week, plus a $330 security deposit and $100 for the key.

I don't have a car to check out apartments, and every phone call or jitney ride chips away at my wad of cash. I check out a rooming house in the city of Passaic, then walk to another on Paulison Avenue. The house contains 11 of the 569 licensed rooming house units left in Passaic.

"You welfare? You work?" asks the landlady, Señora Maria Ortega. Work, I tell her. I don't have a job yet, but I'm going to get one.

She shows me a second-floor room. The house is a rambling Victorian. I can see a hint of its past in the bathroom's stained-glass windows. The room she shows me is spacious, spare and worn. A patchwork of brown carpet pieces, woven and shag, covers the floor. There's a faint stench of mold and urine in the hallway, but it's tough to argue with $125 a week.

Señora Maria tells me I seem nice, but I can't have the room until tomorrow.

I take the jitney to see another place. No luck. It's 5 p.m., and I don't know where I'm going to sleep yet.

I start to panic.

I find a payphone and call my fiancée, Ginger, almost in tears. I'm scared and dejected. The heat has sucked the life out of me. I'm sore and sunburned and my legs are so chafed I can hardly walk. I spend $1.79 for dinner at White Castle and start calling hotels. The cheapest costs $70 a night, plus tax. I don't want to risk spending that much for one night when I still have to pay a security deposit.

In the end, I find a place to stay like most people do: through a friend. Ginger's friend's cousin's boyfriend lives in Jersey City and agrees to let me crash on his floor. The cousin picks me up, and I'm so relieved. I feel safe, and happy that I can relax, and so grateful I could cry.

The next day I am too spent to look for work. At 4 p.m., I move into Señora Maria's house. I have to give her two weeks' rent plus a $20 key deposit. In just two days, my $424 has dwindled to $110. It all adds up: jitney rides to look for apartments, phone cards to answer job ads. I eat a dinner of $2 cheeseburgers, unpack and go over every inch of the room. There's a flimsy wooden dresser and a plywood entertainment center where I stack my clothes. On the closet wall I later find a trace of who's been here before:

"Rainbow Lesbians Yelly n Jessie," someone has carved.

"2gether til eternity Was here 6/30/03 left 8/9/04"

I sleep with a hammer next to my pillow in case the door lock is as flimsy as it looks. I try to ignore the people outside, yelling and honking their car horns.

ON THE JOB

I spend the next two days looking for work. Up and down Main Avenue, through Clifton and Passaic, I fill out applications and stop at places with help-wanted signs. I use my real name, but I'm vague about my background. I try about 20 businesses, with little success. A taxi company needs drivers, but it takes four weeks to get a license. I've washed dishes for restaurants, but Venezia's needs only waiters. I stop by Brickforce Staffing, one of a few temporary employment agencies in the city of Passaic. A woman tells me to come in at 6 a.m. and ask for Nelson. I'm sick of walking everywhere. My employment opportunities would double if I had a bike. I see a few and am tempted to take one—why don't kids lock up their bikes? I call it a day and head home.

The next morning I'm up a few minutes after 5 a.m. It's still dark as I walk the mile downtown. At the Brickforce office, I sign a couple of forms and show my Social Security card. That's all it takes: I'm hired. The morning rush there is busy. People trickle in and, by 6 a.m., workers crowd around Nelson, the dispatcher, angling to be sent out on a job. Nelson takes calls from clients on a cell phone while juggling others on a speakerphone, all the while talking to jitney drivers over a Nextel walkie-talkie.

Later, I learn that Brickforce is well known, thanks to a word-of-mouth network. Brickforce acts as the middle-man between warehouses and factories across North Jersey and a pool of laborers. The warehouses, or clients, use temps when regular workers are absent or when there's a big shipment coming in and not enough people to get the job done.

In economic terms, Brickforce supplies a product—workers—to its clients for a fee. The boxes we fold and move and stack are the clients' product, but I am Brickforce's product: a worker ready to work. Temporary agencies give the labor market flexibility to respond to demand: Their people can fill one factory's need one week, another factory's the next. At its best, it means flexibility for employees who may be between jobs or unable to take a full-time job. The light-industrial sector pays the lowest wages in the temp industry: between $5.15 and $9 an hour at Brickforce.

I pile into a jitney with about 20 other temps. There are no seat belts, and the bus rattles like a dishwasher—we shake back and forth like we're on Mr. Toad's Wild Ride. Brickforce sub-contracts with a jitney service as an essential part of business. Because the agency transports us to the ware-houses, it can promise on-time delivery of the necessary number of workers each day. Some temp agencies expect workers to get to the work site them-selves, a problem for clients and agen-cies if workers show up late or not at all.

FINE PRINT

While Brickforce sells clients this competitive advantage, it charges employees for the ride. The rationale is that if Brickforce didn't shuttle us to warehouses, we'd have to pay to get there ourselves. I don't have a car and public transportation could take hours. Brickforce subtracts between $4 and $7 a day from my wages to pay for the rides to and from work. No one tells me this directly, but the arrangement is explained in a section of the application I signed on my first day.

Still, the deduction doesn't register until I get my first paycheck. The company jitney costs less than if I had to ride New Jersey Transit to Secaucus, where my first assignment is. But the jitney also means getting up at 5 a.m., in the dark, so I can walk to Brickforce. There I wait up to 30 minutes for the ride, then spend an hour or so onboard—sometimes standing in the aisle—as the driver drops off a few workers at one factory, a few more at another. Some afternoons I wait 90 minutes after my shift ends—all off the clock—to get picked up.

My co-worker Priyank says he doesn't mind the jitney, except when the driver forgets to pick him up. He's had to walk more than three miles home from a factory in Wood-Ridge to the city of Passaic.

Almost all the other temp workers speak Spanish and little English. I'm assigned to work with one man, and we develop a kind of sign language. I'm raring to go and working quickly, but it's only 8 a.m. My partner gestures with his hands, and the message is clear: Ease up a little. It turns out to be an unspoken rule of temping. Don't work too hard or too fast. The day is long and the work exhausting. No one pays you enough to wear yourself out. As it is, I can't pay my second week's rent. I make a deal with Señora Maria to pay her installments until I get a full paycheck.

I spend my first full week at a warehouse near Teterboro airport. It's ridiculously hot. We're assigned busy work while we wait more than a week for a truck carrying 1,000 boxes to arrive from California. When the driver gets in, Steve, my supervisor, tells him the delay has cost him $2,000 a day. Now there's work to do. Steve and I stand deep inside the trailer loading boxes onto pallets. We work through the afternoon break. My arms are sore and I'm soaked with sweat, but the action, the constant scooping, tossing, turning, feels exhilarating. When we're done I'm almost a little sad to see it end. We finish in two hours, for which I earn $14, before taxes.

LIFE OUT OF REACH

Another temp named Julio and I sort the 1,000 boxes, then assemble them in smaller stacks and label them. The radio blares commercials that advertise a life out of reach: Take your family to Dorney Park; buy a computer; invest in real estate. I put on gloves and grab a 2-foot-long roll of shrinkwrap. I tuck one end under the corner of a box and run around the stack in circles, wrapping it for transport. By the time I'm done, I'm dizzy.

Everything that comes through the warehouse—mostly women's clothes, shoes, handbags—is made in other countries. Basically, we take large shipments and repackage them into smaller ones that go out to discount clothing stores.

We break when the lunch truck arrives. I buy a slice of pizza. Julio eats his box lunch quickly and then sleeps. He sleeps on breaks, on the jitney, every moment he can. I pull out a Spanish phrase book and tell Julio I am trying to learn Spanish; he says he needs to learn English and we begin to talk. He's from Peru, where he used to be an accountant. He had a business and rented out apartments, but Peru's sour economy left him unable to find work to put his son through medical school. He came here last year on a tourist visa and started working at Brickforce.

SHEER EXHAUSTION

Julio, who does not use his real name for fear of deportation, lives with his aunt and her husband in Passaic. At 49, he's left behind his wife and children in Peru, but exhaustion keeps him from feeling lonely. He sleeps only four hours a night. "I work and work," he tells me.

He works at Brickforce from 6 a.m. to 4 p.m., then at McDonald's from 5 to 11 p.m., except on weekends, when he works the overnight shift. He takes home $375 a week for 78 hours of work. He pays no rent, so most of his paycheck goes back to his family in Peru, nearly $1,300 a month.

Julio's plan is to work in the U.S. for five years. He wants to work here legally, but he has no time to find out how to get the proper documents. He took a year preparing his family for his departure. They didn't want him to go. "That's a father's sacrifice," he says. You want your children to have a better life.

He calls home every Sunday. He misses his wife so much. Every time they talk, they cry. He carries photos of his wife, parents, sisters and children in a knapsack, wherever he goes. In some, they're smiling because it's Christmas, or they're relaxing with friends. Two pictures show Julio with his family at the airport the day he left Lima. Their faces have a stony, blank look of worry and disbelief.

AT HOME

Tenants in my rooming house have no kitchen access, and we aren't allowed appliances in our rooms. (The rules say no microwaves, no air conditioning.) My first paycheck, for the first day I worked, comes to $35.16 after taxes and the jitney fee. My second paycheck, for a full week's work, comes to $196.46. After paying $125 a week in rent, I'll have $5 a day to live on. I skip breakfast and decide to ration my money between lunch and dinner.

Fast-food dollar menus and value meals are a salvation, and I'm grateful for cheap slices of pizza. At the grocery store, two days of food money buys enough bread, peanut butter and jelly for 10 sandwiches—a couple days' worth. One payday, I treat myself to a two-piece fried chicken combo from KFC for $5.29. I think about food all the time.

In the evenings it's hot in my room, and I'm lonely. I've got a standing phone date with my girlfriend, Ginger. In the beginning I buy $5 phone cards so I can call her. They're supposed to charge 10 cents a minute, but there's a 90-cent surcharge every time I use the card at a payphone, so I can only make three or four calls per card. I miss her an almost unhealthy amount, even though she comes to visit every week or so. The fact that I can't call her when I want to is making our separation painful. I think of Julio. I can't imagine what it would be like to leave her behind and go to another country.

AN ODDITY

I've been at Brickforce a couple of weeks when Nelson tells me I'm a good worker. I get the sense that "good" means mostly that I'm on time. Nelson says he doesn't want me to be bounced between $8-an-hour jobs and $5-an-hour ones. He'll try to get me $8 an hour from now on.

Turns out the best-paying job is at the perfume factory in Mount Olive. After a few days, the regimentation there reminds me of high school. We're transported in buses, profanity's not allowed, we keep our bags in lockers, and the women constantly leave the assembly line in pairs to go to the bathroom. At day's end, everyone stops, waits for the end-of-shift buzzer and runs for the front door.

When he announced the job, Nelson said he needed five men and 10 women. Nobody questions this division of labor, and there are more women than men.

Later, I learn this segregation may be discrimination, banned by state and federal law. Last week, when I asked the company to comment on this story, it said, "Brickforce Staffing complies with all federal and state laws pertaining to hiring practices, wage and hour guidelines and any other applicable regulation and/or statute."

There also seems to be a hierarchy based on language. To work here, you're supposed to know English. I don't think Julio was even considered for this job for that reason. Most line workers are Spanish speakers with only basic English: hello, yes, no, thank you. The line supervisors are bilingual Latinos; the managers speak English only.

This makes me an oddity on the line. I'm the only white guy, and the only native English speaker, on the Brickforce jitney in the morning. Nobody talks to me. I imagine people assume I've just gotten out of jail. In the warehouses, though, I get a few questions.

"Why are you working for the agency?" asks one of the regulars at one warehouse. "It doesn't pay anything."

"Are you Polish? From Polonia?" someone else asks.

I've got dirty blond hair and a pink complexion, but a Latino co-worker asks me: "Are you white?"

The questions puzzle me until I realize what's behind them. It's rare to see white people in the Brickforce temp world. In downtown Passaic, someone with blond hair is probably from Poland. White Americans don't work these jobs; Caucasians who do are usually immigrants from Eastern Europe. My co-workers are trying to fit me into the categories that define their lives and this work. I think about the guy who asked if I'm white and marvel. The segregation of class along racial lines is so strong it's made him question what he can see before his eyes.

WINDING DOWN

By the two-week mark, I can't wait for this project to end. I begin to count down: two days until the weekend, one week until an overnight trip to Baltimore for my grandfather's memorial service; a few days more and I'll be done. I wake up every day, go to work, come home to shower, go to the library, then wait for Ginger's call.

Finally, it's August 31. I tell Nelson it's my last day and tell the rooming-house super I'm moving out on Sept. 1. The super says if I'm ever back in town I can stay there. I pack my things, take the jitney to Paterson and walk up Grand Street. I trudge onto New Street, over Interstate 80, to the *Herald News* office.

I kept a job and a roof over my head and my belly mostly full—a life of minimalist survival. I couldn't have supported a child or taken a vacation, a day off or a sick day. To do better, I'd need to do what so many, like Julio, do: work a second job. An illness or work slowdown could have plunged me into homelessness.

At the office, I put my bags down and hug my colleagues. In the weeks ahead, I'll find I'm still scraping by at the paper, but it's different than temping in Passaic. I can eat when I want to, see my girlfriend and friends, talk to my co-workers instead of laboring in silence. I feel connected to the world, and that makes a huge difference.

I'm relieved it's over. In a second, I step out of one life and back into my own.

The Travelogue of an Astronomer

(TRAVEL ACCOUNT)

Salman Hameed

Salman Hameed is an astronomer who teaches at Hampshire College in Amherst, Massachusetts. His main research interest is star formation, and in addition to astronomy, he has taught courses on public policy, supernatural phenomena, and science in the Islamic world. Hameed is a regular contributor to the online journal *Chowk*, where "The Travelogue of an Astronomer" was published in May 2004.

Analyzing and Connecting

Return to these questions after you have finished reading.

1. In this account Hameed writes little about what he observes through the telescope and a great deal about the Canary Islands. Why does he include so much history about the islands?

2. Do you find any clues in the description about why Hameed might have wanted to become an astronomer?

3. List all references to time in the essay. Why is time important to the overall effect of Hameed's account?

4. How do you interpret his conclusion, "telescopes are the new altars for humanity"?

CH☀WK
at chowk all are welcome to read, write and think !

RELIEF INTERNATIONAL
Saving Lives, Sustaining Livelihoods

please sign-in !
Sign-in
forgot password?
new to chowk?

home | civic center | leafyglade inn | chaathouse | gulberg | university ave | market street | gymkhana
archives | sitemap | contribute | community | unplugged | about chowk

articles   all articles▶university ave articles▶God in Vedas and Upanishads

The Travelogue of an Astronomer
Salman Hameed

Roughly 3 million years back, a series of volcanic eruptions raised a huge mass of land to a height of over 3000 meters. The primary volcano lost its fight to gravity and eventually collapsed 500,000 years ago to form a huge caldera. Today this is the most dominant feature on the island of La Palma in the Spanish Canary Islands, located in the Atlantic Ocean off the coast of Morocco. The rim of the caldera is now populated with instruments designed to answer some of humanity's most profound questions about our place in the universe. Three million years of landscaping has provided astronomers an ideal place to gaze at the heavens.

I was awarded 4 nights to use the 2.5-meter Isaac Newton Telescope, one of the ten telescopes located at La Palma. The size denotes the diameter of the main mirror of the telescope; the bigger the mirror the more powerful is the telescope. The 10-meter Keck telescope is the largest in the world and is located in Hawaii.

My journey started from Amherst, Massachusetts. I packed my observing notebook in the backpack along with other travel essentials, and just like my passport and my toothbrush, I was not going to let it separate from me at any cost. In order to get to La Palma, I had to fly first from Boston to Madrid, then from Madrid to the island of Tenerife, and finally on a small propeller plane to La Palma. Observatories are usually located in such remote and exotic locations because astronomers seek places that have little or no light pollution, are high up on the mountain and are close to the ocean. The tall peaks of the mountains provide the necessary dry conditions and the ocean smoothes the air that, as a result, improves the quality of the pictures taken through the telescope. Thus, volcanic islands, like La Palma and Hawaii, are some of the world's best locations for astronomy and provide astronomers an excuse to visit these visually stunning places.

Before getting to La Palma, I spent a night in Tenerife. I was expecting Tenerife to be a small sleepy island geared solely for entertaining tourists from western Europe. While tourism is indeed one of its main industries, Tenerife turned out to be a busy port with a population of over half a million. I stayed in a small university town, La Laguna, located roughly 6 km from the capital city of Santa Cruz. It was in Santa Cruz I learnt that, despite its remote location, Tenerife has played its role in history. The legendary British naval officer, Lord Nelson (1758–1805) or better known as Horatio Nelson, lost his arm in the battle for Tenerife in

HAMEED: THE TRAVELOGUE OF AN ASTRONOMER

Astronomers study the barred spiral structure of NGC 210 and other unusually shaped galaxies to better understand how galaxies evolve.

1797. The guilty cannon has been preserved and is now one of the tourist attractions on the island. Horatio Nelson survived the cannon shot, but died at the hands of a French sniper in the battle of Trafalgar in 1805. I don't know what happened to the rifle of the sniper, but the Trafalgar Square in London can be seen as a memorial to the war achievements of Lord Nelson.

Tenerife also has a footnote in relatively recent Spanish history. General Franco, who was in exile on the island, flew from Tenerife to take control of Spanish troops in Morocco, an event that started the bloody Spanish civil war in 1936, leading ultimately to the Fascist victory in 1939.

After staying overnight in Tenerife, I flew to La Palma on a small plane that braved the winds of the Atlantic ocean. Even though the flight lasted only 20 minutes, the turbulence made it seem much longer. Perhaps this is the only occasion when I not only paid attention to the instructions given by the air-hostess regarding life-jackets, but also read additional material on plane safety and escape routes. At La Palma airport I was relieved to see a smiling taxi driver holding a sign of the telescope with my name on it.

La Palma is a small island with a population of roughly 80,000. This volcanic island is the youngest amongst the Canary islands and is still geologically active. I don't think I felt completely reassured to know that the last major volcanic eruption on the island occured in 1971. The landscape of the island is dominated by the Caldera of Taburiente, formed by the collapse of the primary volcano. The rim of the caldera, roughly 10,000 feet above sea level, was my destination. The road up the mountain had endless twists and turns and the landscape changed dramatically in the hour long drive from the airport to the observatory. The sight and sound of waves crashing on the beach gave way to our passage through a forest of dense pine trees leading up to an almost barren top. Reflection of sunlight from one of the telescope domes provided the first greeting from the observatory while secrets of the night sky seemed safely hidden in the stunningly beautiful dark-blue sky.

The taxi dropped me at the residential area for astronomers, which is like a small hostel with a cafeteria. My telescope was located a few kilometers away but I could see its dome from the window of my room. I was given keys to a car and my first afternoon was spent checking instruments at the telescope. Everything was ready now. All I had to do was wait for the Sun to go down.

Meal times at observatories are dictated by the Sun. Dinner is usually served two hours before the sunset. Fish was on the menu for the first night. I got my plate and looked for a table with English conversation; this is usually the table of astronomers. It is exciting to meet astronomers from all over the world and to learn about their research. The astronomer sitting next to me had flown from England and was working on galaxies that formed when our universe was "only" a billion years old. A Dutch astronomer was searching for exploding stars in nearby galaxies, while giant eruptions from stars was the interest of another. The conversation at dinner ranged from the latest science results to politics and local culture. Now we were all ready to go to our respective telescopes.

After dinner I waited outside for the sky to get dark. My mind wandered off thinking about the indigenous people that lived here several centuries ago and how they would have looked up and interpreted the sky. La Palma and the other Canary Islands were first settled by native Canarians, called Gaunches, whose origin is still controversial. Gaunches are now extinct, but are thought to be an offshoot of the race of Berbers from northern Africa. The Spanish conquest of the Canary Islands began in 1402 and went on until 1496. Despite having enormous technological advantage, the Spanish Conquistadors faced stiff resistance from the natives, in particular from legendary Tanausu, who ruled the Kingdom of Acero on the island of La Palma. Tanausu fought from the base of the caldera and was finally defeated with treachery in 1493. The sight of a majestic sunset brought me back to the present. Earth's rotation was taking the rays of the Sun away from the Earth. A layer of clouds could be seen covering the ocean below us. Like the eyes of giant but curious beasts, I could see the slits of the neighboring telescope domes open up.

I pointed my telescope first at a galaxy named NGC 210, the two hundred and tenth object in the New General Catalogue of galaxies. Apart from a few nearby galaxies, most galaxies have numerical numbers assigned to them. Still, that does not take away the majesty of an individual galaxy containing roughly a hundred billion stars. I am searching for new-born stars in some of these galaxies. My journey to the Canary Islands took only two days from Massachusetts, but the light photons hitting the mirror of the telescope, in the case of NGC 210, started their journey 17 million years ago. The light has taken so long to get to us that some of the stars are probably already dead but we are just getting the news of their birth. After taking several images of NGC 210, I turned my attention to NGC 660 followed by other galaxies.

The first night goes smoothly, and my work is interrupted only by the increasing brightness of the sky due to dawn. I close off the telescope dome and walk outside to look at the caldera. Inside the caldera stands the monolith Idafe, an altar for the original indigenous people to worship their god Abora. I could not help but wonder if, in our quest to understand our origins, the telescopes are the new altars for humanity.

How to write an observation

These steps for the process of writing an observation may not progress as neatly as this chart might suggest. Writing is not an assembly-line process. As you write, you are constantly reading what you have written and rethinking.

Writing may help you to remember details about what you have observed.

1 CHOOSE A SUBJECT

- Analyze the assignment.
- Identify your goals.
- Choose a person or people.
- Choose a place.
- Plan your observations.

2 MAKE OBSERVATIONS AND ANALYZE THEM

- Make observations.
- Analyze the observations.
- Analyze patterns and draw implications.
- Be a "participant observer."

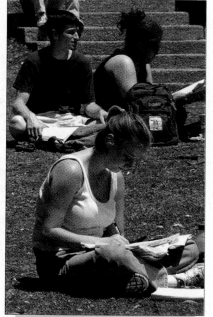

Analyze your potential readers

- *What do your readers likely know about the place?*
- *What are your readers' expectations of the genre?*

3 WRITE A DRAFT

- Determine your thesis or the overall impression you want to convey.
- Determine your point of view.
- Determine an organizational strategy.
- Select details.
- Grab readers at the beginning, and leave them with something to think about.

4 REVISE, REVISE, REVISE

- Check that your paper or project fulfills the assignment.
- Make sure that you have a focused thesis or a clear overall impression.
- Revise your introduction, if needed, to draw readers in.
- Examine the organization.
- Add details to make the description more concrete.
- Check that the conclusion gives a sense of significance of the observations.
- Review the visual presentation.
- Proofread carefully.

5 SUBMITTED VERSION

- Make sure your finished writing meets all formatting requirements.

1: Choose a subject or place to observe

Analyze the assignment

- Read your assignment slowly and carefully. Look for the key words *observe, field research,* or *field observation.* These key words tell you that you are writing about your firsthand observations.
- Note any specifics about what you should observe.

Identify your goals

- Different kinds of observing have different goals. What makes an observation effective for this assignment?
- Think about what categories of subjects or places would fit the assignment.

Choose a person or people

- If your assignment asks you to observe a person or people, think about whom you might observe—a supervisor, a front-desk person, an athlete on and off the court or field, players of video games or other games, viewers of television or performances, people exercising, and so on.
- Consider how each person interacts with others or how a group maintains its identity.

Choose a place

- If your assignment asks you to observe a place, think about where you might observe—a park, a downtown street, a market, a mall, a restaurant, a factory, a bowling alley, a game room, and so on.
- Consider what recurring activities that you can observe happen at the place.

Plan your observations

- Allow a considerable amount of time for making your observations.
- Determine at what times you will need to visit and what will be going on.
- Determine the logistics: How will you get there? What will you need to take with you.

Analyze your potential readers and genre expectations

- What do your readers likely know about the place?
- What are your readers' expectations of the genre? If you are doing observations in the sciences or social sciences, your readers will expect you to be objective and not to concentrate on your reactions.

WRITE NOW

Find a place

Think about possible places that might work for your assignment. Divide a sheet of paper into four columns and label them place, people, activities and times. List your places in the first column. Then list the people who go there, their behavior, and the times they are present.

PLACE	PEOPLE	ACTIVITIES	TIMES
Television room in student union.	Some of the same people everyday.	They view particular programs but also talk.	Most busy around lunch time.

When you have at least five possible places, select the one you feel will work best.

Writer at work

Megan Garza was asked to write a micro-ethnography for her Curriculum and Instruction class. She made notes on and highlighted important parts of her assignment sheet.

Megan began by circling key words in the assignment.

Focus is on student-instructor interaction

EDC 332
Paper #2: Classroom Cultures

Now that we have covered the basics of field observation, you can use it to further your understanding of classroom dynamics. For this assignment, you will make field observations in a classroom, and write about what you observe. You will then go on to hypothesize about how the particular classroom culture you observe developed. *Don't leave out any: what's normal? How common is deviation?*

She also made notes to herself about important aspects of the assignment.

Points to pay attention to in making your observations:

- What is the standard procedure in the class you observe? How similar is it to other classes? How is it different?
- How many students follow established procedures? How many do not? Does the professor diverge from established procedures?
- How does the professor interact with the class as a whole?
- How does the professor interact with individual students?
- How do these relationships affect the overall culture of the classroom?

Schedule

The final version of your field research is due on April 7th. I suggest you plan out the time between now and then, making sure you have adequate time to observe, to synthesize your observations, to draft your paper, to discuss it with me or a writing consultant, and to revise it.

Grading Criteria

I will grade your field research on the following criteria:

1) Nuance and detail in your observations.
2) Connection of observed behaviors to overall classroom culture.
3) Plausibility of your hypothesis about the factors contributing to the classroom culture you observe.

After she felt she understood the assignment, Megan made a list of classes she was taking, and chose the one she thought would yield the best results.

English   <u>Advantage</u> Lots of interaction—conversation

                 <u>Disadvantage</u> I talk a lot—would be hard to take good notes and still pay attention.

EDS   <u>Advantage</u> Would be interesting to look at Dr. Anzalone's interaction with us.

                 <u>Disadvantage</u> Everyone in the class will want to do this.

*Chemistry <u>Advantage</u> Lots to observe—chaotic atmosphere would be interesting to hypothesize about.

                 <u>Disadvantage</u> Will be hard to observe and keep up with notes for class.

Math   <u>Advantage</u> Smaller class size would allow more observation of professor's interaction with individual students.

                 <u>Disadvantage</u> I really need to focus exclusively on math when I'm in there.

<u>*Best choice. Ask Chris to help review notes if necessary.</u>

2: Make observations and analyze them

Make observations

- Take notes that record what you observe in detail.
- Write on the right side of your notebook only, saving the left side for observation and commentary after your observations are complete.
- Pay attention to all your senses—smell, taste, touch, and hearing as well as sight. Take photos if possible, or make recordings of sounds.

Be a "participant observer"

- Talk to the people you observe. Ask them questions about their activities, opinions, and feelings. If you are polite and unobtrusive, you will learn a great deal more than if you keep silent.
- Keep your own language distinct, in your notes, from the language of your subjects.

Analyze the observations

- How many different activities were going on during your observations?
- Which activities were particular to this place?
- Were there significant differences among the subjects you observed? Were these differences behavioral or of some other type?
- Did anything unusual happen?
- Why were the subjects there?

Analyze patterns and draw implications

- What patterns can you identify?
- What implications can you draw from these patterns?

Writer at work

Megan spent several weeks making observations of her class. Once a week, she would go back over her observations and makes comments on them, or note links between various days' observations. Here is a page from her notebook:

Monday 2/13

Prof. Kennedy late by 5 min. Students talking when she gets here. Many have already turned in homework, gotten new homework sheets, and left.

Third time so far she has been several minutes late.

PowerPoint slides are very complicated. Some people can't take notes fast enough. Everyone else whispers while they wait.

Threats to stop lecturing are now occurring in every class—up from about once a week early in the semester.

3:52—Prof. turns off projector and waits for everyone to get quiet. Says, "We won't continue this if you aren't willing to participate." Points to last few rows and says, "I can hear you perfectly well from up here, and you are disturbing the rest of the class."

Professor is also more likely to single out students—increasing frequency

Wednesday 2/15

Prof. Kennedy 3 min. late.

The class seems to get louder every day.

3:35—Prof. answers question about home work assignment from student in front row. No one else can hear the answer. Someone in back yells "Speak up!"

4:05—Prof. turns off projector during PowerPoint lecture and demands quiet. People keep talking. Finally, someone in front yells "Shut up!" Everyone laughs (except prof.).

13 minutes between threats.

4:30—people start packing up their books. Prof. says loudly, "This class runs until 4:45, and anything I cover from now until then may be on your next exam."

3: Write a draft

I. Introduction
Answer the main question: How is this class like or unlike other classes on campus?
It is noisier and has a higher level of direct conflict between instructor and students.
II. Professor-Class Relationship
  A. Large class size
    1. Large auditorium
    2. Only half full
  B. Timing
    1. Professor often late
    2. Students ready to go home for the day
  C. Format
    1. PowerPoint is hard to read and copy
    2. Instructor goes too fast sometimes
  D. Noise
    1. Gets worse when professor goes slower
    2. Professor has trouble stopping it (give examples)
  E. Homework
    1. Students turn in early
    2. Distribution is chaotic
    3. Some students try to turn in late
III. Understanding the Professor-Class Relationship (hypothesize here)
  A. Lack of respect
    1. Professor lacks confidence
    2. Students resent lecture style
    3. Professor does not treat students as equals when they ask questions
  B. Student motivation
    1. Students from other majors who have to take the course resent it
    2. Students who want to take the course don't find it rewarding
  C. Setting
    1. Large class makes students more anonymous
    2. Misbehavior escalates
IV. The Professor-Individual Student Relationship
  A. In one-on-one settings, students treat professor with respect
  B. Likewise, professor treats students as adults
  C. As these interactions increase, some behavior has changed in the classroom
V. Changing the Classroom Relationship
  A. Instructor could ask for help from colleagues
  B. Lecture material could be made more readily available
  C. Professor could arrange more one-on-one or small group interaction to foster respectful relationships

Determine your thesis or the overall impression you want to convey	• If your assignment asks you to observe for particular purpose, likely you will need to provide a clear, significant thesis early on. • If you are writing a travel account or describing a place, you may not have an explicit thesis, but you will want to convey an overall impression through the details you select.
Determine your point of view	• If you are observing for a science or social science class, focus on when and what you observed. • If you are writing a travel account or describing a place, you may want to foreground yourself as a participant—why you went there and how you responded to the place and people.
Determine an organization	• You might organize by chronology or by special location. • You may need to classify your observations into subtopics and organize accordingly.
Select details	• Give accurate, specific information about the place and, if present, the people. • Include short quotations if you record conversations, and attribute them accurately.
Grab readers at the beginning, and leave them with something to think about	• Choose an appropriate title that will immediately get readers' attention. • Conclude by leaving your readers with a sense of why your observations matter. Press beyond the superficial.

Work for precise description

Show, not tell

OFF TRACK

It is very difficult to hike cross country in the Arctic National Wildlife Refuge.

ON TRACK

Every inch of ground challenges human walking: meadows of waist-high muskeg brush, quicksand beside the streams and slick rocks in them, loose shale on the hillsides, and uneven tundra hillocks on flat sections that offer no good way to negotiate—plant your foot on them and they collapse sideways, step between them and you sink to your calf.

Provide exact details

OFF TRACK

Grizzly bears and black bears look different.

ON TRACK

Rely on body shape rather than size and color to distinguish grizzly bears from black bears. Grizzlies have a hump above their front shoulders; black bears lack this hump. In profile, grizzlies have a depression between their eyes and nose, while black bears have a "Roman" profile with a straight line between the forehead and nose.

Give names where possible

OFF TRACK

The courthouse stands in the center of the town square, bordered by streets named for Civil War generals.

ON TRACK

The courthouse stands in the center of the town square, bordered by streets named for Confederate heroes: Lee, Jackson, Stuart, and Davis.

Writer at work

Megan realized that the format of her assignment would require her to re-organize her chronological observations. She decided to divide her observations into two main categories, following each one with a section of interpretation. Megan made a brief outline of the section headings she planned to use, and then filled in information from her observations pertaining to each section.

Professor–class relationship

- Large lecture—impersonal
- Professor lectures with PowerPoint, which students copy
- Students talk during class, annoying professor
- Strategies for getting students to be quiet are not effective
- Homework procedure disruptive to class

Professor–individual student relationship

- Students more respectful in one-on-one interaction
- Professor more patient in one-on-one interactions
- Some carryover of mutual respect to lectures for certain students

Interpretation

- Lack of mutual respect—neither students nor professor want to be there
- Required course for nonmajors
- Large lecture format makes the class impersonal

Interpretation

- Situation would be better if class were small
- Changing homework procedure and posting PowerPoints to Web site would help

I. Introduction
Answer the main question: How is this class like or unlike other classes on campus? It is noisier and has a higher level of direct conflict between instructor and students.

II. Professor-Class Relationship
    A. Large class size
        1. The class is held in a large auditorium.
        2. The auditorium is only half full.
    B. Timing
        1. Professor is often late.
        2. Students are ready to go home for the day.
    C. Format
        1. PowerPoint is hard to read and copy.
        2. Instructor goes too fast sometimes.
    D. Noise
        1. Noise gets worse when professor goes slower.
        2. Professor has trouble stopping it (give examples).
    E. Homework
        1. Students turn in early.
        2. Distribution is chaotic.
        3. Some students try to turn in late.

III. Understanding the Professor-Class Relationship (hypothesize here)
    A. Lack of respect
        1. Professor lacks confidence.
        2. Students resent lecture style.
        3. Professor does not treat students as equals when they ask questions.
    B. Student motivation
        1. Students from other majors who have to take the course resent it.
        2. Students who want to take the course don't find it rewarding.
    C. Setting
        1. Large class makes students more anonymous.
        2. Misbehavior escalates.

IV. The Professor-Individual Student Relationship
    A. In one-on-one settings, students treat professor with respect.
    B. Likewise, professor treats students as adults.
    C. As these interactions increase, some behavior has changed in the classroom.

V. Changing the Classroom Relationship
    A. Instructor could ask for help from colleagues.
    B. Lecture material could be made more readily available.
    C. Professor could arrange more one-on-one or small group interaction to foster respectful relationships.

4: Revise, revise, revise

1 → **2** → **3** → **4**

4

Don't use first person—be more of an observer than a participant

Be more specific?

One day when our class was loud, Dr. Kennedy succeeded in restoring order by calling out two of my friends who happened to be among the approximately 150 students attending. She singled them out merely because they had stood up to switch seats and were clearly talking. When they sat down, Dr. Kennedy screamed at them, "If you want to have a private conversation, go outside! You're not required to be here!" The entire class fell silent, and we all stared at the professor for several seconds while she stared back at us. My friends did not leave, but the remainder of the class was horrible. After that, whenever she yelled at someone, people started whispering nasty comments. Everyone blames the professor for the noise problem and the breakdown in the classroom atmosphere.

This was kind of distracting. Also, she had aircraft turned off the projector and no one paid any attention.

Be more specific?

→ **5**

Skilled writers know that the secret to writing well is rewriting. Even the best writers often have to revise several times to get the result they want. You also must have effective strategies for revising if you're going to be successful. The biggest trap you can fall into is starting off with the little stuff first. Leave the small stuff for last.

Does your paper or project meet the assignment?	• Look again at the assignment for specific guidelines, including length, format, and amount of research. Does your work meet these guidelines?
Do you have a focused thesis or a clear overall impression?	• Is it clear to readers what is most important about your observations?
Is your introduction effective?	• Will your title grab people's attention? • Does your introduction draw readers in?
Is your organization effective?	• Is the order the best for your purpose? Possibly you may need to shift the order of some of your paragraphs.
Do you provide vivid, well-chosen details?	• Can you add details to increase interest and paint a clearer picture?
Is your conclusion effective?	• Do you place your observations in a larger overall context? • Do you leave readers with the feeling that they have learned something valuable?
Is the writing project visually effective?	• Is the font attractive and readable? • Are the headings and visuals effective?
Save the editing for last	• When you have finished revising, edit and proofread carefully.

A peer review guide is on page 31.

Writer at work

Megan took a draft of her paper to her instructor's office hours and talked with him about it. She made notes during their conversation and used his comments to guide her revisions. Here, she noted a passage with an overly personal and emotional tone:

Don't use first person—be more of an observer than a participant.

Be more specific?

One day when our class was loud, Dr. Kennedy succeeded in returning order by calling out two of my friends who happened to be among the approximately 150 students attending. She singled them out merely because they had stood up to switch seats and were clearly talking. When they sat down, Dr. Kennedy screamed at them, "If you want to have a private conversation, go outside! You're not required to be here!" The entire class fell silent, and we all stared at the professor for several seconds while she stared back at us. My friends did not leave, but the remainder of the class was horrible. After that, whenever she yelled at someone, people started whispering nasty comments. Everyone blames the professor for the noise problem and the breakdown in the classroom atmosphere.

This was kind of distracting. Also, she had already turned off the projector and no one paid any attention.

Be more specific?

Here is how Megan revised the passage:

On one occasion when the class was loud and ignored her initial attempt to quiet them by turning off the projector, Dr. Kennedy succeeded in returning order by calling out two young men among the approximately 150 students attending. These men were singled out because they had stood up to switch seats and were clearly talking. When they sat down, Dr. Kennedy screamed at them, "If you want to have a private conversation, go outside! You're not required to be here!" The entire class fell silent, and the students and professor stared at each other for several seconds. The young men did not leave, and the remainder of the class was tense. Similar incidents are frequent, and the students react with hostility and complaints. They blame the professor for the noise problem and the breakdown in the classroom atmosphere.

5: Submitted version

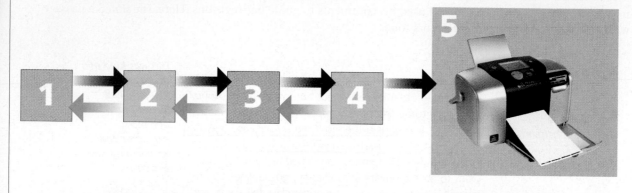

Garza 1

Megan Garza
Professor Anzalone
EDC 332
April 3, 2006

Chemistry 105:
An Analysis of Classroom Dynamics in a Large Lecture Course

Classroom student behavior on our campus is similar from one class to the next. Most classes establish routines early, and students follow them obediently. Dr. Kennedy's Chemistry for Non-majors, CH 105, is like many other classes with standard procedures, but unlike most other classes, students often don't follow the procedures. The differences between CH 105 and other classes stem directly from the ways the students and the professor interact. Analyzing the professor-class relationship and the professor-individual student relationship suggests why students behave differently in CH 105.

The Professor-Class Relationship

The professor-class relationship sets the tone for the classroom environment and the professor's lecture style. The classroom is a large auditorium, and during most classes it is only half full. Students have plenty of room to spread out, and they relax and talk before class begins. Dr. Kennedy usually arrives a few minutes late, contributing to the students' restlessness, already at a high level because the class begins at 3:30 p.m. when students are ready for the school day to be over.

When the lecture begins, students often do not stop talking. The format of the lectures also contributes to the noise. Dr. Kennedy stands behind a podium with PowerPoint slides projected on a screen behind her. The majority of students find it necessary to copy the points on the slides verbatim. Dr. Kennedy often appears nervous and speaks rapidly, moving to the next slide before students are finished copying the previous one. When she moves too quickly, students howl in protest. Often she becomes impatient and continues anyway, causing resentment. But if she waits for everyone to finish writing, she encounters another problem: noise.

Student talking is the source of most of the conflicts during class. When Dr. Kennedy waits for slower writers to finish copying, the noise begins to build. In turn, the professor becomes annoyed and her patience wears thin. Her most frequent methods are to

1. turn off the projector,
2. stare impatiently,
3. threaten not to lecture,
4. make angry demands for order,
5. single out a loud group and denounce them.

Often she will combine methods if her first attempt is not successful.

On one occasion when the class was loud and ignored her initial attempt to quiet them by turning off the projector, Dr. Kennedy succeeded in returning order by calling out two young men among the approximately 150 students attending. These men were singled out because they had stood up to switch seats and were clearly talking. When they sat down, Dr. Kennedy screamed at them, "If you want to have a private conversation, go outside! You're not required to be here!" The entire class fell silent, and the students and professor stared at each other for several seconds. The young men did not leave, and the remainder of the class was tense. Similar incidents are frequent, and the students react with hostility and complaints. They blame the professor for the noise problem and the breakdown in the classroom atmosphere.

Another source of conflict is the homework procedure. The teaching assistants (TAs) for the class distribute homework assignments each Monday, which are due on the following Monday. The TAs sit on stage before class with stacks of homework assignments. Students often do not wait for the assignments to be passed out but instead rush the stage, collect the new assignment, and submit the completed assignment. Many then leave. The harried TAs rush up and down the aisles passing out assignments, continually interrupted with questions and latecomers. The chaotic procedure prompts Dr. Kennedy to ask repeatedly to get the assignments distributed and collected.

After the TAs have finished walking up and down the aisles, homework is no longer collected. Late students rush up to the stage in an attempt to get Dr. Kennedy to accept their work. At the beginning of the semester, she allowed work to be turned in after the class has started, but she shortly began to refuse because of the delays the late work was causing. Students who come late and are unable to submit their work grow angry and walk away from the stage with looks of disgust. Nevertheless, Monday's classes are always late getting started with the professor agitated.

Understanding the Professor-Class Relationship

The keys to understanding the professor-class relationship lie in the degree of mutual respect, the reason students are enrolled, and the impersonal nature of a large lecture hall.

Mutual respect is critical for a successful class. Students do not take courses seriously if they believe that the material has no value and the professor is not competent. Many students use the excuse of an inexperienced or ineffective teacher to let their work suffer. Likewise, a professor does not give her best effort if she dislikes the class and finds the students lacking in intelligence. In this case, both the professor and the students have contributed to the generally hostile atmosphere. Dr. Kennedy's lecture method causes many problems because students insist in copying her slides and because many students resent the procedure. She evidently finds the lecture method necessary because of all the chemical equations and examples she must provide.

The professor's attitudes toward the students and the material are reflected in her lectures. The course is a simplified introduction to chemistry for non-science majors with no background in chemistry. In particular, when students ask questions, her response is often taken as condescending. Her tone of voice changes, and she often oversimplifies answers. If she considers the answer obvious, she will talk very slowly, as if she were responding to a small child.

An additional difficulty is the reason students are taking the course. Required courses outside of a student's major are rarely popular. Nevertheless, students do have options in fulfilling the science requirement, and many students in the class want to learn more about chemistry. The class is unrewarding for these students because it seems to be aimed at the lowest level possible, rendering it dull for professor and student alike.

Finally, the large lecture hall makes students anonymous. In a large group students are more likely to behave disrespectfully toward the professor and to flaunt Dr. Kennedy's weak authority. Students often mock her and call her rude names, behavior that would be unlikely to occur in a small class.

The Professor-Individual Student Relationship

The professor relates to individual students more successfully than to the class as a whole. When students meet with the professor one-on-one or in groups of three or four, the atmosphere is one of mutual respect. Students call the professor Dr. Kennedy instead of the rude names they use in class, and Dr. Kennedy in turn speaks to them in a normal tone of voice and gives detailed answers to questions. She recognizes that the students are intelligent, even if they are novices at chemistry, and the students understand that she is genuinely concerned about their learning.

Some of this change in attitude has carried over to the classroom. Dr. Kennedy has begun to recognize individually some of the students in the class. Their questions are answered first and with a friendly tone. Dr. Kennedy is more likely to slow down when these students make a request. In turn, the students refrain from talking and behave politely.

Changing the Classroom Relationship

The causes of the breakdown of the student-professor classroom relationship in CH 105 are no doubt complex. Why an inexperienced professor was assigned to a potentially difficult class lies beyond the scope of this paper, but it is a contributing factor. The professor could use the advice of experienced colleagues on the basics of classroom management such as an improved procedure for distributing and collecting homework assignments. The content of PowerPoint slides should be made available to students on the class Web site. Certainly these changes would lead to immediate improvement.

The immediate cause of the poor classroom atmosphere is the lack of mutual respect. Both students and the professor are capable of respecting each other and communicating effectively in small group interactions. But in the large lecture hall, the mutual respect breaks down. More small group interactions could help students and the professor to get to know each other and consequently gain the respect of the other.

Projects

Observations span a wide range of writing, from objective scientific reports to highly personal descriptions of places. Accurate, detailed description is valued in all kinds of observations.

These projects are frequently written kinds of observations.

DESCRIPTION OF A PLACE

For an example of a description of a place, see pages 128–132.

Write an essay describing a place. Select one of these options:

Visit an urban neighborhood that is not familiar to you. Pay close attention to what distinguishes this neighborhood from other neighborhoods in the city.

or

Visit a small town near you, preferably one that is not on a major highway. Likely you will find that many of the businesses that once thrived on Main Street or on the courthouse square are gone. Pay close attention to signs and other things that give indications to what goes on in the town.

Visit some stores, a local coffee shop, and other places where you can talk to people. Ask them about their neighborhood or their town. Then reconstruct conversations in your notebook. Include some dialog in your paper. If you go with someone else from your class, walk around independently. You should not come up with the same observations and conversations.

For additional reading, writing, and research resources, go to **www.mycomplab.com** and choose **Lester Faigley's** *Writing*.

NATURAL OBSERVATION

For an example of a natural observation, see pages 112–116.

Find a setting in which you can observe animals or natural phenomena such as tides, weather patterns, or erosion. In a large city, you might watch pigeons interacting with people in a park, observe feeding time at a zoo, or watch how insects behave during a rainstorm.

↓

Use your observations to generate a list of questions that would help you fill in any gaps in what you observed. Can you explain the behavior of any animals you observed? If not, how could you determine the causes of their behavior? Can your localized observation of a spring-fed pool uncover the causes of the heavy algae growth there, or do you need to look further to find an explanation?

↓

Write a brief description about what you observed, including the questions your observation raised, and any answers you found.

FIELD OBSERVATION

For an example of a field observation, see pages 133–141.

Observe people in a public setting you frequent, such as your student union, a library, a coffee shop, a dormitory lounge, a gym, a basketball court, or bus route. Think of one or more questions that field observation might answer. For example, students who use your campus library go there for multiple reasons: to study, to find books, to find journal articles, to use a computer, to watch movies on DVD, to meet their friends, and others.

↓

Collect field notes by observing. Take a notebook and write only on the righthand pages. Use the lefthand pages later to analyze your data. Plan to spend at least three hours a week at your site for two weeks. You should gather at least ten pages of notes per week. Listen carefully to conversations and record direct quotations. After you leave the site, make comments on your notes on the lefthand page.

↓

Analyze your notes after two weeks of observations. What constitutes abnormal behavior? How do people learn the normal behavior for that setting? What happens when the norm is violated by someone?

↓

Write a detailed field observation that includes concrete details and quotations from people at your site. Make your paper interesting to readers by showing them something about the setting they didn't already know, or had never noticed.

9
Informing

Good informative writing begins with what the reader needs to know and how that information can be most effectively presented.

Chapter contents

Reporting information

Whether reading the news, following a recipe, hooking up a new computer, deciding which course to take, or engaging in a multitude of other events in our daily lives, we depend on reliable and clear information. Reporting information takes many forms, ranging from newspaper articles and reports of experimental research to tables, charts, and simple lists of information.

In one sense, most kinds of writing, including writing to reflect and writing to persuade, also report information. The main difference is that the focus of a report and other informative kinds of writing is on the subject, not on the writer's reflections or on changing readers' minds or on getting them to take action.

Components of informative writing

Where do I find information?

Find information

Reports require research. Scientists make observations in the field and conduct experiments to create new knowledge. Journalists interview people for the information to include in articles. Accountants assemble financial information in order to write reports on the financial status of companies and organizations. Knowing where to find information and knowing how much you need is critical for writing reports.

What does it mean?

Interpret information

Writers not only report what they read and observe. They construct meaning through selecting what and what not to include and in organizing that information.

How can I explain it?

Explain information

Often what you know well is difficult to explain to others. In order to do so effectively, you will need to break down a process into steps that you can describe. Explaining a process sometimes requires you to think about something familiar in a new way.

What are the implications?

Explore questions and problems

Not all informative writing is about topics with which you are familiar or ones that you can bring to closure. Often college writing involves issues or problems that perplex us and for which we cannot come to a definitive conclusion. The goal in such writing is not the ending but the journey. Difficult issues often leave you conflicted; readers appreciate writers who deal honestly with those conflicts.

Keys to informative writing

Narrow the topic

A central difficulty in writing to inform is knowing where to stop. For any large subject, a lifetime may be insufficient. The key to success is limiting your topic to one you can cover adequately in the space you have.

Start fast

The title and introduction should entice readers to want to read the rest. Dull generic titles and vague, general introductory paragraphs discourage further reading. Offer a new viewpoint that challenges the usual, commonplace viewpoint.

Keep readers interested

Readers become bored quickly if they have heard it all before. Once you have made your readers curious to know more about your subject, don't disappoint them.

Define key terms

Writers should define clearly any key terms and concepts that might be unfamiliar.

Provide relevant examples, illustrations, and details

The examples, illustrations, and details make or break informative writing, whether it is a news article, a profile, or even a set of instructions or a cookbook. Select them carefully.

Remain objective

Writers whose purpose is to inform usually stay in the background, taking the stance of an impartial, objective observer. An objective tone and the absence of bias help readers to believe the information is accurate and the writer is trustworthy.

Provide accurate information

Informative writing frequently draws on outside sources of information, including library research, Web research, interviews, surveys, and observations. Even if writers are familiar with a subject, they often find out what experts have to say about it.

Document the sources of information

If you use sources in a college assignment, you will be expected to document those sources. Lakshmi Kotra's essay at the end of this chapter (see pages 222–229) follows an academic format for citing sources.

Conclude with strength

Besides just stopping, a plain summary is the weakest possible conclusion. Leave your readers with something to think about— a memorable example, an anecdote that illustrates a key point, implications of the information you have provided, a quotation that expresses a main point vividly, or a projection into the future.

Satellite photography helped the world to understand the damage caused by the tsunami that struck Indonesia on December 28, 2004.

Explain with charts and graphs

Charts and graphs show facts and relationships that are often difficult to communicate using words alone. A good chart makes the significance of the data clear at a glance.

Explain with images

Pictures don't always tell a thousand words; indeed, we need words to understand what is represented in pictures. Nevertheless, photographs, drawings, maps, and other graphics can provide concrete evidence to support what is being explained in words.

WORKING TOGETHER

Explain a concept or activity

In a group of three or four students

First select a concept or activity that you know a great deal about (through your courses, your work experience, or your personal interests) but your classmates likely do not. Subjects might range from the second law of thermodynamics and postmodern architecture to competitive ballroom dancing and growing your own herbs. In your group give each person five minutes to explain the concept or activity.

Listen carefully to each classmate, and when each finishes, stop for a minute to note

- what you knew already
- what you found engaging
- what you wanted to know more about
- what you didn't understand

After the last person finishes, share your notes with the group. You'll have an immediate audience response to your explanation.

Effective informative writing

Informative writing succeeds when readers can connect new facts and concepts to what they know already.

The Emperor's Giraffe
Samuel M. Wilson

Samuel Wilson, a professor of anthropology, wrote "The Emperor's Giraffe" for the magazine *Natural History* in 1992. It was later collected with other essays and published in a book with the same title. Wilson had the challenge of writing about a subject unfamiliar to most of his readers, and moreover, he wanted to make a larger point. Notice how he leads his readers to his unexpected conclusion.

A HUGE FLEET LEFT PORT in 1414 and sailed westward on a voyage of trade and exploration. The undertaking far surpassed anything Columbus, Isabella, and Ferdinand could have envisioned. The fleet included at least sixty-two massive trading galleons, any of which could have held Columbus's three small ships on its decks. The largest galleons were more than 400 feet long and 150 feet wide (the *Santa Maria*, Columbus's largest vessel, was about 90 by 30 feet), and each could carry about 1,500 tons (Columbus's ships combined could carry about 400 tons). More than one hundred smaller vessels accompanied the galleons. All told, 30,000 people went on the voyage, compared with Columbus's crew of 90-some.

> The 500th anniversary of Columbus's first trip to America was celebrated in 1992. Wilson uses the occasion to introduce his readers to a major Chinese voyage of discovery in 1414 that was massively larger in ships and personnel.

The commander's name was Zheng He (Cheng Ho), the Grand Eunuch of the Three Treasures and the most acclaimed admiral of the Ming dynasty. He was sailing from the South China Sea across the Indian Ocean, heading for the Persian Gulf and Africa. As the historian Philip Snow notes in his wonderful book *The Star Raft*, "Zheng He was the Chinese Columbus. He has become for China, as Columbus has for the West, the personification of maritime endeavour" (21). The flotilla was called the star raft after the luminous presence of the emperor's ambassadors on board.

Zheng He did not really set out to explore unknown lands— neither did Columbus, for that matter—for the Chinese were aware of most of the countries surrounding the Indian Ocean.

> Wilson begins challenging commonly held views by pointing out that neither Zheng He nor Columbus was exploring unknown territory.

For centuries, China had been a principal producer and consumer of goods moving east and west from Mediterranean, African, and Middle Eastern trading centers. With this trade came cultural and ideological exchange.

Zheng He, like many Chinese of his time, was a Muslim, and his father and his father before him had made the pilgrimage to Mecca. But in Zheng He's day, the trade routes were controlled by Arabian, Persian, and Indian merchants. Private Chinese traders had been barred from traveling to the West for several centuries. China had been conquered by Ghengis Khan and his descendants in the 1200s, and the Mongol emperors of the subsequent Yuan dynasty were the first to impose these constraints. In 1368 the Chinese expelled the Mongol rulers and established the Ming dynasty, which was destined to rule for the next 300 years. (Thus, in 1492 Columbus was searching for a "Grand Khan" who had been put out of business 124 years earlier.)

After the period of Mongol rule, China became strongly isolationist, placing even more severe restrictions on Chinese traders. In 1402 an outward-looking emperor named Yong'le (Yung-lo) came to power. Seeking to reassert a Chinese presence on the Western seas and to enhance the prestige of his rule and dynasty, he began funding spectacular voyages by Zheng He. As sociologist Janet Abu-Lughod notes in *Before European Hegemony*, "The impressive show of force that paraded around the Indian Ocean during the first three decades of the fifteenth century was intended to signal the 'barbarian nations' that China had reassumed her rightful place in the firmament of nations—had once again become the 'Middle Kingdom' of the world" (343).

As Zheng He pressed westward in 1414, he sent part of his fleet north to Bengal, and there the Chinese travelers saw a wondrous creature. None like it had ever been seen in China, although it was not completely unheard of. In 1225 Zhao Rugua, a customs inspector at the city of Quanzhou, had recorded a secondhand description of such a beast in his

A parenthetical aside—that Columbus was looking for the "Grand Khan" who had long ceased to exist—speaks to the lack of knowledge of China among Europeans.

strange and wonderful *Gazetteer of Foreigners*. He said it had a leopard's hide, a cow's hoofs, a ten-foot-tall body, and a nine-foot neck towering above that. He called it a *zula*, possibly a corruption of *zurafa*, the Arabic word for giraffe.

> The account of how a giraffe was described for those who had never seen one adds interest.

The giraffe the travelers saw in Bengal was already more than 5,000 miles from home. It had been brought there as a gift from the ruler of the prosperous African city-state of Malindi, one of the several trading centers lining the east coast of Africa (Malindi is midway along modern Kenya's coast, three degrees south of the equator). Zheng He's diplomats persuaded the Malindi ambassadors to offer the animal as a gift to the Chinese emperor. They also persuaded the Malindi ambassadors to send home for another giraffe. When Zheng He returned to Beijing, he was able to present the emperor with two of the exotic beasts.

A pair of giraffes in Beijing in 1415 was well worth the cost of the expedition. In China they thought the giraffe (despite its having one horn too many) was a unicorn (*ch'i-lin*), whose arrival, according to Confucian tradition, meant that a sage of the utmost wisdom and benevolence was in their presence. It was a great gift, therefore, to bring to the ambitious ruler of a young dynasty. The giraffes were presented to the emperor Yong'le by exotic envoys from the kingdom of Malindi, whom the Chinese treated royally. They and the marvelous gift so excited China's curiosity about Africa that Zheng He sent word to the kingdom of Mogadishu (then one of the most powerful trading states in East Africa and now the capital of modern Somalia) and to other African states, inviting them to send ambassadors to the Ming emperor.

> Wilson explains why the giraffes took on great significance beyond their novelty.

The response of the African rulers was overwhelmingly generous, for China and Africa had been distant trading partners from the time of the Han dynasty (206 BC to AD 220). In the *Universal Christian Topography*, written about AD 525 by Kosmos, a Byzantine monk known as the Indian Traveler, Sri Lanka is described as a trading center frequented by both Chinese and Africans. Envoys from a place called

> Wilson refutes another common view that sub-Saharan Africa was not engaged in international trade before Europeans arrived.

Zengdan—the name translates as "Land of Blacks"—visited China several times in the eleventh century. And a Chinese map compiled in the early fourteenth century shows Madagascar and the southern tip of Africa in remarkable detail, nearly two centuries before the Portuguese "discovered" the Cape of Good Hope. Archeologists find china (why the English word came to be synonymous with glazed pottery and porcelain, instead of silk or spices, is unclear) from the Han and later dynasties all along the east coast of Africa.

The African emissaries to the Ming throne came with fabulous gifts, including objects for which entrepreneurs had long before managed to create a market in the Far East: tortoise shell, elephant ivory, and rhinoceros-horn medicine. On their many visits they also brought zebras, ostriches, and other exotica. In return, the Ming court sent gold, spices, silk, and other presents. Zheng He was sent with his fleet of great ships on yet another voyage across the Indian Ocean to accompany some of the foreign emissaries home. This escort was the first of several imperially supported trips to Africa. According to official records, they went to Mogadishu, Brava, and perhaps Malindi; Snow (in *The Star Raft*) suggests that these Chinese expeditions may have gone farther—to Zanzibar, Madagascar, and southern Africa.

Meanwhile, as the Chinese were pushing down the east coast of Africa, Portuguese mariners were tentatively exploring the west coast. They had started the process in the early fifteenth century and were steadily working their way south. Bartolomeu Dias reached the Cape of Good Hope in 1488 and was the first of these mariners to see the Indian Ocean. Surely the Europeans and Chinese were poised to meet somewhere in southern Africa, where perhaps they would have set up trading depots for their mutual benefit.

This did not happen, however. Emperor Yong'le died in 1424, and by 1433 the Ming dynasty discontinued its efforts to secure tributary states and trading partners around the Indian Ocean. In Beijing, those favoring an isolationist foreign policy

That Chinese sailors might have met the Portuguese in Africa and established trade is a "what if?" that leads to Wilson's conclusion.

won out, and the massive funding needed to support Zheng He's fleet—difficult to sustain during what was a period of economic decline in China—was canceled. As Edwin Reischauer and John Fairbank note in *East Asia: The Great Tradition:*

> The voyages must be regarded as a spectacular demonstration of the capacity of early Ming China for maritime expansion, made all the more dramatic by the fact that Chinese ideas of government and official policies were fundamentally indifferent, if not actually opposed, to such an expansion. This contrast between capacity and performance, as viewed in retrospect from the vantage point of our modern world of trade and overseas expansion, is truly striking. (478)

Wilson uses the conclusion of other scholars to set up the point he makes in the following paragraph.

The contrast also refutes the argument that as soon as a country possesses the technology of overseas trade and conquest it will use it. Zheng He's fleet was 250 times the size of Columbus's, and the Ming navy was many times larger and more powerful than the combined maritime strength of all of Europe. Yet China perceived her greatest challenges and opportunities to be internal ones, and Yong'le's overseas agenda was forgotten. Restrictions on private trade were reimposed, and commercial and military ventures in the Indian Ocean and South China Sea in subsequent centuries were dominated by the Portuguese, Arabs, Indians, Spaniards, Japanese, Dutch, British, and Americans. Zheng He's magnificent ships finally rotted at their moorings.

Wilson concludes his essay by making a significant point. He refutes the idea that those who have the best technology necessarily will use it to conquer others. Had he started with this point, readers might have been skeptical, but he gives the impression that his conclusion logically follows from the data.

Works Cited

Abu-Lughod, Janet L. *Before European Hegemony: The World System AD 1250-1350*. New York: Oxford UP, 1989.

Reischauer, Edwin O., and John K. Fairbank. *East Asia: The Great Tradition*. Boston: Houghton, 1958.

Snow, Philip. *The Star Raft: China's Encounter with Africa*. London: Weidenfeld, 1988.

How to read informative writing

Make notes as you read, either in the margins, if it is your copy, or on paper or a computer file. Circle any words or references that you don't know and look them up.

What is it?	• What kind of a text is it? An article? an essay? a profile? a set of instructions? a chart? a brochure? a Web site? an executive summary? What are your expectations for this kind of text?
	• What media are used? (Web sites, for example, often combine images, words, and sounds.)
Where did it come from?	• Who wrote this material?
	• Where did it first appear? In a book, newspaper, magazine, online, in a company, or in an organization?
What is the writer's thesis or main idea?	• Where is the thesis or main idea located?
	• If you cannot find a specific claim, what is the main focus?
	• What are the key ideas or concepts that the writer considers?
	• What are the key terms? Are they defined?
Who is the intended audience?	• What clues do you find about whom the writer had in mind as the readers?
	• What does the writer assume that the readers already know about the subject?
	• What new knowledge is the writer providing?
How is the piece of writing organized?	• Look for the main idea in each paragraph. It helps to write them down. Then examine how each paragraph connects to the others.
	• Where are the details and examples located? Do they support the main points?
What kinds of sources are cited?	• Are they from books, newspapers, periodicals, or the Web?
	• Are they completely documented?
How is it composed?	• How does the writer represent herself or himself?
	• How would you characterize the style?
	• How effective is the design? Is it easy to read?
	• If there are any photographs, charts, or other graphics, what information do they contribute?

Russell Simmons

(PROFILE)

Harold Evans

Harold Evans's profile of Russell Simmons was first published in a collection of profiles of famous inventors titled *They Made America: Two Centuries of Innovators from the Steam Engine to the Search Engine*. Others profiled in the book include John Fitch, inventor of the steamboat; Charles Goodyear, the inventor of vulcanized rubber; Wilbur and Orville Wright, Henry Ford, Walt Disney, and Estée Lauder. Russell Simmons didn't invent hip-hop, but he became its most successful marketer.

Analyzing and Connecting

Return to these questions after you have finished reading.

1. Evans opens the essay with a vivid description of a social, visual spectacle. What does this opening lead readers to expect from the rest of the piece? What kind of connection does Evans seem to be establishing with his audience?

2. Note the lengthy introductory caption to this essay: "He created a cultural movement in music, fashion, movies, comedy, poetry, television—and social action. He's the marketing maestro of hip-hop." These two sentences neatly summarize Evans's main claim about Simmons's career. Why do you think the author chose to express his main point in the title of the piece? Remember that this essay appears in a larger anthology containing many similar biographical sketches.

3. The person mentioned in the first sentence of the essay is not its subject, Russell Simmons, but his brother Joey. The remainder of the essay jumps back and forth between events, people, and anecdotes. Compare the organization of this essay with that of the executive summary on pages 194–196. What effect does Evans's more indirect method have on readers? Why might he have chosen this structure over something more straightforward?

4. Harold Evans accommodates his audience by defining words they may not be familiar with. How many such definitions or explanations can you find? What do these examples reveal about the audience the author was reaching out to? What did he expect them to know or not know? Who did he consider to be his core audience, and who else might he have wanted to appeal to?

5. Consider two types of readers: one who knows a great deal about the careers of Run-DMC, Public Enemy, and the Beastie Boys, and one who is only vaguely familiar with rap and hip-hop music and culture. What could each person learn from this profile?

RUSSELL SIMMONS He created a cultural movement in music, fashion, movies, comedy, poetry, television—and social action. He's the marketing maestro of hip-hop

1957 –

THE MAN who would become the Reverend Joey Simmons was on stage at New York's Madison Square Garden. At his command, 20,000 people in the audience, caught in spotlights, took off their unlaced sneakers and shook them in the air, hooting and hollering. Almost everyone was in sneakers—Adidas sneakers—because that was the regular dress code for the hip-hop crowds and they were there to rock it out for an explosive, hot hip-hop number called "My Adidas," which was heading for the top of the charts in the summer of 1986.

The whole event had been orchestrated by hip-hop master marketer Russell Simmons, Joey's elder brother by seven years, for whom sneakers were a serious issue: "I've never had dirty sneakers in my life," he wrote in his 2001 memoir with Nelson George. "Not when I was a teenager and not now." The future Rev. Simmons had recorded "My Adidas" with his partners, Darryl McDaniels

Pretty much everything Russell Simmons touched turned to gold. He is a vegan ("I won't eat anything that runs away from me") and keen on the practice of yoga: "One of our practices is to cause the least amount of harm possible to all sentient beings and the planet." He lives on a $14 million estate in suburban New Jersey.

and Jason Mizell, though at the time the reverend was better known as Run for his ability to run off at the mouth on any subject; McDaniels was better known as DMC, Mizell as Jam Master Jay. Their group, Run-DMC, celebrated for the percussive, in-your-face dynamic of its call-and-respond rhythms, was the most generative act in hip-hop's history. They were three black kids out of Hollis, Queens; along with their shell-toe Adidas, they all wore the ghetto uniform of leather suits with black velour fedoras and gold neck chains. The Adidas executives who had flown in from Germany for the event were falling over themselves to spend one million dollars and more to sponsor Run-DMC national tours. This was the first time the apparel company had ventured beyond athletic sponsorship, and the decision to do so was a portent. In the words of the British critic and author Alex Ogg, the "future synthesis of music, fashion and business that made hip-hop the dominant cultural trend of the nineties was prefigured by the deal."

The supreme synthesizer was Russell Simmons, better known as Rush, and the Adidas deal was negotiated with the "precision of a bank heist" by his associate Lyor Cohen, a lanky Israeli whom Simmons describes as "the glue that held the management together." Joey Simmons had a long run as emcee with Run-DMC, but at the height of his success, he had a revelation while sitting in his Jacuzzi eating pancakes, "smoking a joint and waiting for a ho to call." He writes, "The syrup was falling into the tub, ashes were falling in the pancakes. I thought I had all the riches but I was really poor. It was then that the Lord came into my life and raised me up, and I started to feel better and all those worldly things didn't mean anything to me anymore." He was ordained by Zoe Ministries Community Congregation in New York in 1994.

Darryl McDaniels, after rehab for alcoholism, was ordained as a deacon.

Jam Master Jay, however, was not raised up. He was gunned down in his Queens recording studio in 2002, apparently over an unresolved debt.

Rush, the prolifically enterprising, affable and garrulously profane manager of the group, has gone on and on, spinning golden webs in hip-hop enterprises and preaching his own brand of social conscience. He is the innovator who discovered hip-hop when nobody outside inner-city New York had heard of it. He is often compared to Motown's Berry Gordy, which does justice to neither man. Gordy had a unique ear for talent; his musical legacy is larger and has endured for 40 years. Simmons' distinction is less in picking stars—though he jump-started the careers of LL Cool J and "the Fresh Prince" Will Smith—than in his very early perception of what hip-hop signified, and his perspicacity as the impresario who pushed it in its pure form in music, and pushed it some more in comedy and movies, then pushed it some more in fashion and was still pushing it some more in 2004 in getting people to register to vote. Bill Adler, an entrepreneur in music, calls him "the Moses of hip-hop" for leading the hip-hop generation to the promised land of American success and prosperity. "The only big crossover artist at the time who was black was Michael Jackson, and he was clearly not the black guy next door; he's a brother from another planet," says Adler. "Russell's genius was to broker artists as they were. They didn't have to be white. They didn't have to have white mannerisms. They didn't have to speak standard English. Russell's point was that they would get over because they were authentic, true to themselves."

Adler credits Rush with an influence beyond music. What he achieved, in Adler's phrase, is the browning of America. "In the seventies, if you were a white kid, you loved Aerosmith and Led Zeppelin, and if you were a black kid, you were listening to George Clinton and the Delfonics. There was a vast and deplorable gulf in the

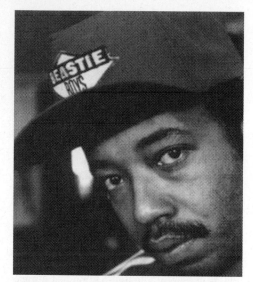

A lot of people were mad at him, he says, for managing the white hip-hop group the Beastie Boys, but to him they were honest. They were doing their version of black music. "They weren't rip-off artists . . . they were ultimately accepted by black people because they were good."

culture, and what hip-hop has done is to reunite the races on a shared affection for this music and this culture. I think this is a much more integrated society at ground level because of Russell Simmons."

Russell Simmons had a great start in life—and almost threw it away. His father was a history professor at Pace University, his mother a Howard University graduate in sociology and the family lived in a pleasant part of Queens. The white population was on the move out, but Rush attended an integrated school that he says had a very important effect. "It taught me to see people for what they were. I never let race affect my judgment of a person's character. The family said prayers every day and went to church on Sunday. But hidden in the bushes of the front garden there were little bags of marijuana Russell would sell for $5 apiece

to indulge his passion for fly clothing—three-stripe Pro-Ked sneakers, $32 silk-and-wool pants. "At the time I thought having the right sneakers and pants meant I was a future Rolls-Royce nigga." Inevitably, the drug pushing led to running with a gang, in his case the Seven Immortals, a Queens branch of the more violent Bronx founding chapter. "For my father," Rush writes in his memoir, "everything I was into . . . meant I was heading straight to prison." He knows he was lucky to come through. When he was robbed once, one of his gang put a .45 in his hand, and he took a wild shot at the fleeing robber. "In my heart I knew missing Red was the best thing I ever did," he said in an interview. "I only shot a gun one time. I shot over his head. I told everybody I tried to kill him. He was murdered a week later, he and his brother. The sad thing is how many of my Hollis crew peers were killed by the drug lifestyle. Some got hit in the head by thieves one time too many. Some got shot. Some died of AIDS in jail."

Around the time he headed off to City College (located in Harlem) in 1975, the ghettos of South Bronx and Harlem were undergoing a sea change. Coming from the parks and community centers of these written-off, depressed, burned-out neighborhoods was a song unlike any heard before. Led by Afrika Bambaataa's Zulu Nation, the hip-hop culture slowly began to replace the gang warfare of knives and guns with battles of sound systems, words and dance moves. At first the music sounded like the disco and funk hits being played in the downtown nightclubs, but the drumbeats and the chants were like nothing else.

Rush describes the epiphany he had one night hanging out in Charles' Gallery on 125th Street when Eddie Cheeba started rhyming and the crowd of black and Hispanic college kids chanted along, moving harder to the beat because the emcee said so. "It wasn't a sophisticated rhyme by current standards, but seeing Eddie spitting them flames on the mike made me feel I'd just witnessed the invention of the wheel. Just like that I saw how I could turn my life into another, better way. All the street entrepreneurship I'd learned I decided to put into promoting music."

He stopped selling drugs. Instead, he promoted club parties, sticking "Rush Productions" flyers on lamp posts, talking up a storm about artists who could only be heard in person: The recording industry had no interest in the rappers who inspired Rush. "I just looked up to people like the great DJ Hollywood, Melle Mel, Lovebug Starski, Kurtis Blow and Grandmaster Flash ('introducing the disco dream on the mean machine, a Darth Vader on the slide fader. No one cuts it straighter, than New York's number one creator')." One afternoon in Queens, Billboard magazine's black music writer Robert "Rocky" Ford spotted Rush's brother Joey hanging posters along Jamaica Avenue. He hooked up with Simmons, who says he learned marketing from Ford. "He taught me to have integrity, build the artists, build the truth. A lot of the disco records out there were fake. They put together a group and that was the end of it."

The first artist Rush managed was Kurtis Blow, the name he gave to Curtis Walker, a student at City College. He sold him in Queens as "a smooth Harlem native with a booming low tenor voice and real charisma," but he could not get him on radio or vinyl. The shock that propelled Rush into even more determined efforts came in October 1979. At the Armory in Queens, a DJ played a new record, "Rapper's Delight," from a New Jersey group, the Sugarhill Gang; it went on to sell 14 million copies. "We were just stunned," writes Rush. "Someone had taken our rhymes, our attitude, our culture and made a record. And not one of us in the community had anything to do with it. I remember after the record played, DJ Starski got on the mike and said, 'Y'all know we started this shit. Don't worry. We're gonna go to the moon.'"

Four credits short of his sociology degree, Rush upset his father by pulling out of school to concen-trate on hip-hop. He and Ford cut a record with Kurtis Blow spoofing "The Night Before Christmas" ("he was roly, he was poly, and I said, 'Holy molie, you've got a lot of whiskas on your chinny, chin chin' "). The clubs loved "Christmas Rappin'" but the buyers in the record industry had all concluded that the big sales for "Rapper's Delight" were a fluke. Rush and Ford jimmied open the door by going into retailers and placing fake orders for "Christmas Rappin'," saying it was a Polygram recording. Dealers ordered from Polygram, which persuaded the company buyers to have second thoughts about hip-hop. Kurtis Blow became the first rapper on a major label. The song was a hit. The door was open.

In 1983, Rush got together with his brother and McDaniels to form Run-DMC. They wanted to call themselves the Sure Shot Two; he insisted on the odd name to establish that a new genre was taking wing. Mizell came onboard as the duo's DJ. "Of all the stylistic innovations to shape modern rap," writes Ogg, "the most indelible contribution came from Run-DMC." The group members were bright, well-adjusted suburban kids, he notes, "but their brooding and confrontational records spoke

One of the future Beastie Boys found a demo tape made by 16-year-old LL (or Ladies Love) Cool J, left, in the dorm room of Rick Rubin, and Rubin sold his talent to Simmons.

of an alternative reality that fellow suburbanites were happy to take as the gospel of the street." Rush says, "The band and I weren't concerned with reaching blacks or whites but with making new sounds for people who wanted to listen to them." By 1984, Simmons thought Rush Management, Inc., ruled the scene; he managed many acts, including Blow, Whodini, Stetasonic and Jekyll and Hyde. Then he heard a record that rocked him back with its raw quality, "It's Yours" by T La Rock and Jazzy J. He was even more astounded when he met the producer—Rick Rubin, a white, long-haired punk rocker from a well-to-do Jewish family in Lido Beach, Long Island. Rubin had organized the hit out of his scruffy dorm room at New York University, the headquarters of a label he had called Def Jam, def being the vernacular for definitive (and also hip-hop slang for "cool"), and jam from the free-wheeling breakouts in classic jazz.

Simmons' strength has always been his readiness to recognize and then associate with people whose talents complemented his own. It was Rubin who would see the promise in 16-year-old James Todd Smith (LL Cool J) when Rush didn't. The two of them, for an investment of $4,000 each, started Def Jam Records in the fall of 1984. Over four years of their association, they developed stars like Public Enemy, a group with a conscience and antidrug message; Slick Rick; and the first successful white hip-hop act, the Beastie Boys. Run-DMC, then on the Profile label, could earn $150,000 a night on tour. Rush talked hip-hop onto MTV. He pointed out that the channel had no black artists to speak of beyond Michael Jackson, and a suburban audience that had been isolated from the urban movement. He and Rubin made a video featuring Run-DMC and the already well-known rock band Aerosmith. It bowled over MTV's Ted Demme. "It was fantastic. They took hip-hop into the video millennium."

In 1985, Rush and Rubin signed a major distribution deal with CBS for $600,000. Several coownership deals followed—Rubin departed in 1988—then in 1999, the label was sold to Universal for $120 million. In 2002, Def Jam—under Lyor Cohen—was the second largest label in the industry, with sales of more than $700 million. Nelson George commented: "Def Jam has become an institution and Simmons a role model for a generation of hip-hop entrepreneurs."

After a few false starts in Hollywood, Simmons again found smashing success with Russell Simmons Def Comedy Jam, the HBO comedy series developed, he likes to point out, by two black men (Simmons and veteran television producer Stan Lathan) and two white men (agents Brad Grey and Bernie Brillstein). Originally slated as a miniseries, it aired for seven years, providing HBO with its highest rated weekly show until The Sopranos.

So much for entertainment. Rush Communications has recognized no boundaries, venturing into every area of popular culture. In 1992, having enjoyed chasing fashion models, Rush married one of the most beautiful, Kimora Lee, and started a clothing line with hip-hop inflections based on a flagship boutique he opened in Soho. He called it Phat Farm. It was a worrying struggle. Year after year he lost money he could not afford to lose. He refused to sell into big-city department stores that intended to place Phat Fashions in "ethnic (aka 'nigger clothing') sections." In the sixth year, with $10 million invested, he turned a profit, and by then Phat Farm had bred eight divisions, including Baby Phat, a line for women and babies run by Kimora Lee, and Phat Farm Footwear, run by Run, i.e., the Reverend Joey Simmons. Phat Farm clothing was finally integrated in stores with the likes of Polo, Hilfiger, Klein and Nautica. He sold Phat Fashions for $140 million in January 2004 to Kellwood, one of the largest and staidest of manufacturers. He remained CEO.

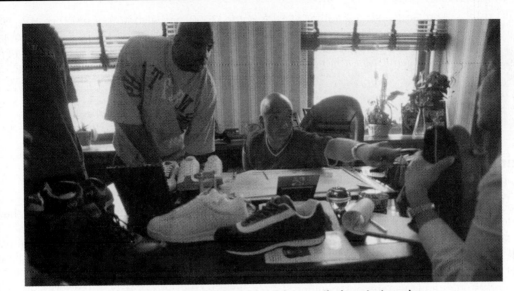

Rush Communications Headquarters: A focus on the important sneaker.

According to BusinessWeek, in 2003 one-quarter of all discretionary spending in the United States was influenced by hip-hop. "Coke, Pepsi, Heineken, Courvoisier, McDonald's, Motorola, Gap, CoverGirl—even milk: They all use hip-hop to sell themselves." Simmons has become the go-to guy for corporations like these trying to reach the young urban and suburban market.

The reason it is hard to get ahold of him, though he seems to have a cell phone permanently stitched to both ears, is that while he is doing all this, he is also thinking about the Def Poetry Jam enterprise he started in 2001, doing for "slam" poets what he did for comedians; or his DefCon 3 carbonated beverage in 7-Eleven stores; or his Rush Philanthropic Arts Foundation, which distributes $350,000 a year to stimulate arts education for disadvantaged youth. Def Poetry Jam on HBO won a Peabody Award in 2002. He is proud of that. "If you had asked kids in a class five years ago how many of y'all write poetry, nobody would have raised a hand. Now sixty percent of kids in inner-city schools write poetry."

Bill Stephney, president of StepSun Records and cofounder of Public Enemy, describes what happens when he drops in on classrooms of young black kids. "If you asked them what they want to do, and I do it rather frequently, they say, 'Well, I want to run my own business.' The notion of controlling your destiny, as much as you possibly can, basically did not exist within the community until Russell came along."

How Do I Love Thee?
(ESSAY)
Lori Gottlieb

Lori Gottlieb is the author of *Stick Figure* (2000) and a co-author of *I Love You, Nice to Meet You* (2006). She is a regular commentator on NPR's *All Things Considered* and has written for many newspapers and magazines. A longer version of this essay appeared in *The Atlantic Monthly* in March 2006.

Analyzing and Connecting

Return to these questions after you have finished reading.

1. Why does Gottlieb begin with the story of her visit to Dr. Neil Clark Warren's office rather than her central question: can cold, hard science be a facilitator of romance?

2. How does Gottlieb answer her central question?

3. Buckwalter's studies and Warren's observations conclude that happy couples have many similarities. Think about happy and unhappy couples you know. Is their degree of happiness a result of what they have in common?

4. Online dating and relationship Web sites have become some of the fastest-growing businesses on the Internet. Compare eHarmony.com with Perfectmatch.com, Chemistry.com, Match.com, and others. What does each promise on the first page? What does each claim to distinguish it from other similar online dating sites?

HOW DO I LOVE THEE?

LORI GOTTLIEB

I'd been sitting in Dr. Neil Clark Warren's office for less than fifteen minutes when he told me he had a guy for me. It wasn't surprising that the avuncular seventy-one-year-old founder of eHarmony.com, one of the nation's most popular online dating services, had match-making on his mind. The odd thing was that he was eager to hook me up without having seen my eHarmony personality profile.

I'd come to the eHarmony headquarters in Pasadena, California, in early October to learn more about the site's "scientifically proven" and patented Compatibility Matching System. Apparently, the science wasn't working for me. The day before, after I'd taken the company's exhaustive (and exhausting) 436-question personality survey, the computer informed me that of the approximately 9 million eHarmony members, more than 40 percent of whom are men, I had zero matches. Not just in my city, state, region, or country, but in the entire world. So Warren, who looks like Orville Redenbacher and speaks with the folksy cadence of Garrison Keillor, suggested setting me up with one of his company's advisory board members, whom he described as brilliant, Jewish, and thirty-eight years old. According to Warren, this board member, like me, might have trouble finding a match on eHarmony.

"Let me tell you why you're such a difficult match," Warren said, facing me on one of his bright floral sofas. He started running down the backbone of eHarmony's predictive model of broad-based compatibility, the so-called twenty-nine dimensions (things like curiosity, humor, passion, intellect), and explaining why I and my prospective match were such outliers.

"I could take the nine million people on our site and show you dimension by dimension how we'd lose people for you," he began. "Just on IQ alone—people with an IQ lower than 120, say. Okay, we've eliminated people who are not intellectually adequate. We could do the same for people who aren't creative enough, or don't have your brilliant sense of humor. See, when you get on the tails of these dimensions, it's really hard to match you. You're too bright. You're too thoughtful. The biggest thing you've got to do when you're gifted like you are is to be patient."

After the over-the-top flattery wore off— and I'll admit, it took an embarrassingly long time—I told Warren that most people I know don't join online dating sites to be patient. Impatience with real-world dating, in fact, is precisely what drives many singles to the fast-paced digital meat market. From the moment Match.com, the first such site, appeared in 1995, single people suddenly had twenty-four-hour access to thousands of other singles who met their criteria in terms of race, religion, height, weight, even eye color and drinking habits.

Nearly overnight, it seemed, dozens of similar sites emerged, and online dating became almost de rigueur for busy singles looking for love. According to a recent Pew survey, 31 percent of all American adults (63 million people) know someone who has used a dating Web site, while 26 percent (53 million people) know someone who has gone out with a person he or she met through a dating Web site. But was checking off boxes in columns of desired traits, like an à la carte Chinese take-out menu, the best way to find a soul mate?

Enter eHarmony and the new generation of dating sites, among them PerfectMatch.com and Chemistry.com. All have staked their success on the idea that long-term romantic compatibility can be predicted according to scientific principles—and that they can discover those principles and use them to help their members find lasting love. To that end they've hired high-powered academics, devised special algorithms for relationship-matching, developed sophisticated personality questionnaires, and put into place mechanisms for the long-term tracking of data. Collectively, their efforts mark the early days of a social experiment of unprecedented proportions, involving millions of couples and possibly extending over the course of generations. The question at the heart of this grand trial is simple: In the subjective realm of love, can cold, hard science help?

Although eHarmony was the first dating site to offer science-based matching, Neil Clark Warren seems like an unlikely pioneer in the field. Even though he earned a Ph.D. in clinical psychology from the University of Chicago, in 1967, he never had much of a passion for academic research—or an interest in couples. "I was scared to death of adults," he told me. "So I did child therapy for a while." With a master's degree in divinity from Princeton Theological Seminary, he went on to Fuller Theological Seminary's Graduate School of Psychology, in southern California, where he taught and practiced humanistic psychology (what he calls "client-centered stuff") in the vein of his University of Chicago mentor, Carl Rogers. "I hated doing research," he admitted, before adding with a smile, "In fact, I was called 'Dr. Warm.' "

Fittingly, it was Warren's family, not academia, that piqued his interest in romantic compatibility. "When my daughters came along, that was a big pivot in my life in thinking about how do two people get together," he told me. "I started reading in the literature and realizing what a big chance they had of not having a satisfying marriage. I started trying to look into it."

Soon he began a private practice of couples therapy—with a twist. "People have always thought, wrongly, that psychotherapy is a place to go deal with problems," he said. "So when a couple would come in, I'd say, 'Tell me how you fell in love. Tell me the funniest thing that's happened in your marriage.' If you want to make a relationship work, don't talk about what you find missing in it! Talk about what you really like about it."

Warren is a big proponent of what he likes to call "folksy wisdom." One look at the shelves in his office confirms this. "I've been reading this little book about the Muppets—you know, Jim Henson," he said. "And I've been reading another book about Mister Rogers. I mean, Mister Rogers was brilliant beyond belief! He got a hold of concepts so thoroughly that he could transmit them to six-year-old kids! Do you know how much you have to get a hold of a concept to transmit it simply? His idea of simple-but-profound has had a profound influence on me."

The basis of eHarmony's matching system also sounds simple but profound. In successful relationships, Warren says, "similarities are like money in the bank. Differences are like debts you owe. It's all right to have a few differences, as long as you have plenty of equity in your account."

He leaned in and lowered his voice to a whisper. "Mister Rogers and Jim Henson," Warren continued, "they got a hold of the deep things of life and were able to put them out there. So that's what we want to do with our products. We want to put them out there in a way that you'd say, 'This is common sense. This seems right, this seems like it would work.' Our idea of broad-based compatibility, I put it out there in front of you. Does that seem right?"

Whether or not it seems right on an intuitive level is almost beside the point. After all, eHarmony's selling point, its very brand identity, is its scientific compatibility system. That's where Galen Buckwalter comes in.

A vice president of research and development for the company, Buckwalter is in charge of recruiting what he hopes will be twenty to twenty-five top relationship researchers away from academia—just as he was lured away by Warren nine years ago. A former psychology graduate student at Fuller Theological Seminary (his dissertation was titled "Neuropsychological Factors Affecting Survival in Malignant Glioma Patients Treated with Autologous Stimulated Lymphocytes"), Buckwalter had become an assistant professor at the University of Southern California, where he was studying the effects of hormones on cognition, when he got the call from Warren.

"Neil knew I lived and breathed research, and he had this idea to try to develop some empirically based model to match people," Buckwalter said when I visited him at his office at eHarmony. He wore a black T-shirt and wire-rimmed glasses, and had a hairstyle reminiscent of Einstein's. "He wasn't necessarily thinking, over the Internet—maybe a storefront oper-ation like Great Expectations." Relationships weren't Buckwalter's area, but he welcomed the challenge. "A problem is a problem, and relationships are a good problem," he said. "In the research context, it's certainly an endlessly fascinating question."

With the help of a graduate student, Buckwalter reviewed the psychological literature to identify the areas that might be relevant in predicting success in long-term relationships. "Once we identified all those areas, then we put together a questionnaire—just a massively long questionnaire," he said.

"It was probably close to a thousand questions. Because if you don't ask it, you're never gonna know. So we had tons of questions on ability, even more on interest. Just every type of personality aspect that was ever measured, we were measuring it all."

Because it wasn't practical to execute a thirty-year longitudinal study, he and Warren decided to measure existing relationships, surveying people who were already married. The idea was to look for patterns that produce satisfaction in marriages, then try to reproduce them in the matching of singles.

Buckwalter's studies soon yielded data that confirmed one of Warren's longtime observations: namely, that the members of a happy couple are far more similar to each other than are the members of an unhappy couple. Compatibility, in other words, rests on shared traits. "I can't tell you how delighted I was," Warren said, "when the factor-analytic studies started bringing back the same stuff I'd seen for years."

But could this be true across the board? I told Warren that my most successful relationships have been with men who are far less obsessive than I am. Warren assured me that's not a similarity their system matches for. "You don't want two obsessives," he explained. "They'll drive each other crazy. You don't find two control freaks in a great marriage. So we try to tweak the model for that. Fifty percent of the ball game is finding two people who are stable."

For Warren, a big question remained: What should be done with these findings? Originally, he had partnered with his son-in-law, Greg Forgatch, a former real-estate developer, to launch the business. Their first thought was to produce educational videotapes on relationship compatibility. After all, Warren had recently written his book, *Finding the Love of Your Life*.

"We tried so hard to make videotapes and audiotapes," Warren said. "I went into the studio and made lists. We came up with a hundred things singles need. But singles don't want education; they want flesh! They want a person. So that's when, in 1997, we said, 'We've gotta help people find somebody who would be good for them. Some body?' "

To connect singles and create a data pool for more research, the Internet seemed the best option. Based on a study of 5,000 married couples, Warren put together the compatibility model that became the basis for eHarmony. "We got encouraged by everybody, 'Get out there, get out there! The first person to market is going to be the most successful,' " Warren recalled. But he insisted on getting the matching system right before launching the site—and that didn't happen until August of 2000, during the dot-com bust. By 2001 he was contemplating declaring bankruptcy.

"And then," Warren recalled, "we found an error in our matching formula, so a whole segment of our people were not getting matched. It was an error with all the Christian people on the site."

This is a sensitive topic for Warren, who bristles at the widely held opinion that eHarmony is a Christian dating site. The company's chief operating officer, he offered by way of rebuttal, is Jewish, and

Buckwalter, who became a quadriplegic at age sixteen after jumping into a river and breaking his neck, is agnostic. And while Warren describes himself as "a passionate Christian" and proudly declares, "I love Jesus," he worried about narrowing the site with too many questions about spiritual beliefs. Which is where the error came in.

"We had seven questions on religion," he explained, "and we eliminated four of them. But we forgot to enter that into the matching formula! These were seven-point questions. You needed twenty-eight points to get matched with a Christian person, but there was no way you could get them! We only had three questions! So every Christian person who had come to us had zero matches."

Fortunately, a wave of positive publicity, featuring married couples who'd met through eHarmony and the naturally charismatic Warren, turned things around. Still, Warren said of the innocent mistake, "you kind of wonder how many relationships fall apart for reasons like this—how many businesses?"

Today, eHarmony's business isn't just about using science to match singles online. Calling itself a "relationship-enhancement service," the company has recently created a venture-capital-funded think tank for relationship and marital research, headed up by Dr. Gian Gonzaga, a scientist from the well-known marriage-and-family lab at the University of California at Los Angeles. The effort, as Gonzaga put it to me recently, is "sort of like a Bell Labs or Microsoft for love."

An energetic, attractive thirty-five-year-old, Gonzaga thought twice about leaving the prestige of academia. "It seemed cheesy at first," he said. "I mean, this was a dating service." But after interviewing with Warren, he realized that conducting his research under the auspices of eHarmony would offer certain advantages. He'd be unfettered by teaching and grant-writing, and there would be no sitting on committees or worrying about tenure. More important, since his research would now be funded by business, he'd have the luxury of doing studies with large groups of ready subjects over many years—but without the constraints of having to produce a specific product.

"We're using science in an area most people think of as inherently unscientific," Gonzaga said. So far, the data are promising: a recent Harris Interactive poll found that between September of 2004 and September of 2005, eHarmony facilitated the marriages of more than 33,000 members—an average of forty-six marriages a day. And a 2004 in-house study of nearly 300 married couples showed that people who met through eHarmony report more marital satisfaction than those who met by other means. The company is now replicating that study in a larger sample.

"We have massive amounts of data!" Warren said. "Twelve thousand new people a day taking a 436-item questionnaire! Ultimately, our dream is to have the biggest group of relationship psychologists in the country. It's so easy to get people excited about coming here. We've got more data than they could collect in a thousand years."

But how useful is this sort of data for single people like me? Despite Warren's disclaimer about what a tough eHarmony match I am, I did finally get some profiles in my inbox. They included a bald man with a handlebar moustache, who was fourteen inches taller than me; a five-foot-four-inch attorney with no photos; and a film editor whose photo shows him wearing a kilt—and not in an ironic way. Was this the best science could do?

When I asked Galen Buckwalter about this, he laughed, indicating that he'd heard the question before. "The thing you have to remember about our system is we're matching on these algorithms for long-term compatibility," he said. "Long-term satisfaction is not the same as short-term attraction. A lot of people, when they see their initial matches, it's like, 'This is crap!' "

In ads and on his Web site, Warren talks about matching people "from the inside out." Was eHarmony suggesting that I overlook something as basic as romantic chemistry? "When we started out," Buckwalter said, "we were almost that naive." But now, he added, eHarmony is conducting research on the nature of physical attraction.

"We're trying to find out if we can predict physical chemistry with the same degree of statistical certainty that we've used to predict long-term satisfaction through our compatibility matching. In general, people seem to be attracted to people who share their physical attributes," Buckwalter explained, noting that he has found some exceptions, like height preference. "There's a lot of variability on that dimension," he

said. "A person's height, it turns out, is not a consistent predictor of short-term attraction." Meanwhile, Buckwalter's team is in the process of testing new hypotheses.

"We're still convinced that our compatibility-matching process is essential for long-term satisfaction, so we're not going to mess with that," he insisted. "But if we can fit a short-term attraction model on top of that, and it's also empirically driven, that's the Holy Grail."

Over at Chemistry.com, a new site launched by Match.com, short-term attraction is already built into the system. This competitor of eHarmony's was developed with help from Match.com's chief scientific adviser, Dr. Helen Fisher, an anthropologist at Rutgers University, whose research focuses on the brain physiology of romantic love and sexuality. Chemistry.com is currently assembling a multidisciplinary group of psychologists, relationship counselors, sociologists, neuroscientists, and sexologists to serve as consultants.

The company sought out Fisher precisely because its market research revealed that although a large segment of singles wanted a scientific approach, they didn't want it to come at the expense of romantic chemistry. "On most of the other sites, there's this notion of 'fitness matching,' " Fisher said from her office in New York City. "You may have the same goals, intelligence, good looks, political beliefs. But you can walk into a room, and every one of those boys might come from the same background, have the same level of intelligence, and so on, and maybe you'll talk to three but won't fall in love with any of them. And with the fourth one, you do. What creates that chemistry?"

It's a constellation of factors, Fisher told me. Sex drive, for instance, is associated with the hormone testosterone in both men and women. Romantic love is associated with elevated activity of the neurotransmitter dopamine and probably also another one, norepinephrine. And attachment is associated with the hormones oxytocin and vasopressin. "It turns out," she said, "that seminal fluid has all of these chemicals in it. So I tell my students, 'Don't have sex if you don't want to fall in love.'"

Romantic love, Fisher maintains, is a basic mating drive—more powerful than the sex drive. "If you ask someone to go to bed with you, and they reject you," she says, "you don't kill yourself. But if you're rejected in love, you might kill yourself."

For Chemistry.com's matching system, Fisher translated her work with neurotransmitters and hormones into discrete personality types. "I've always been extremely impressed with Myers-Briggs," she said, referring to the personality assessment tool that classifies people according to four pairs of traits: Introversion versus Extroversion, Sensing versus Intuition, Thinking versus Feeling, and Judging versus Perceiving. "They had me pinned to the wall when I took the test, and my sister, too. So when Chemistry.com approached me, I said to myself, I'm an anthropologist who studies brain chemistry, what do I know about personality?'"

The 146-item compatibility questionnaire on Chemistry.com correlates users' responses with evidence of their levels of these various chemicals. One question, for instance, offers drawings of a hand, then asks:

Which one of the following images most closely resembles your left hand?

The relevance of this question might baffle the average online dater accustomed to responding to platitudes like, "How would you describe your perfect first date?" But Fisher explains that elevated fetal testosterone determines the ratio of the second and fourth finger in a particular way as it simultaneously builds the male and female brain. So you can actually look at someone's hand and get a fair idea of the extent to which they are likely to be a Director type (ring finger longer than the index finger) or a Negotiator type (index finger longer or the same size).

Another question goes like this:

How often do you vividly imagine extreme life situations, such as being stranded on a desert island or winning the lottery?

Almost never
Sometimes
Most of the time
All the time

"Someone who answers 'All the time' is a definite Negotiator," Fisher said. "High estrogen activity is associated with extreme imagination."

While other sites gather data based on often unreliable self-reports ("How romantic do you consider yourself to be?"), many of the Chemistry.com questions are designed to translate visual interpretation into personality assessment, thus eliminating some of the unreliability. In one, the user is presented with a book's jacket art. We see a woman in a sexy spaghetti-strapped dress gazing at a man several feet away in the background, where he leans on a stone railing. The sky is blue, and they're overlooking an open vista. "What is the best title for this book?" the questionnaire asks, and the choices are as follows:

A Spy in Rimini
Anatomy of Friendship:
    A Smart Guide for Smart People
A Scoundrel's Story
Things Left Unsaid

According to Fisher, each response is correlated with one of the four personality types: Choice A corresponds to Explorer, B to Builder, C to Director, and D to Negotiator.

Even sense of humor can be broken down by type, with questions like "Do you sometimes make faces at yourself in the mirror?" (people with a sense of humor do) and "At the zoo, which do you generally prefer to watch?" (the reply "monkeys and apes" indicates more of a funny bone than "lions and tigers"). According to Fisher, a Director likes people to laugh at his or her jokes; a Negotiator likes to be around someone funny so he or she can laugh at that person's jokes; an Explorer is spontaneous and laughs at just about anything; and a Builder, she suspects, generally isn't as funny as the others.

But how to match people up according to Fisher's four personality types, and under what circumstances, isn't so straightforward. Another question, for instance, presents four smiling faces and asks:

Take a look at the faces below. Are their smiles sincere?

Fisher says that people with high levels of estrogen—usually women—have better social skills, and are better at reading other people. So users who choose the correct "real" smiles (pictures two and three) will be the Negotiators. This, Fisher says, is an area where "complementarity" might be important. The problem with sites like eHarmony, she believes, is that they place too much emphasis on similarity, whereas, in her view, falling in love depends on two elements: similarity and complementarity. "We also want someone who masks our flaws," she explained. "For example, people with poor social skills sometimes gravitate toward people with good social skills. I'm an Explorer, so I don't really need a partner who is socially skilled. That's not essential to me. But it may be essential to a Director, who's generally less socially skilled."

Chemistry.com's compatibility questionnaire also examines secondary personality traits. To illustrate, Fisher cited her own relationship. "I'm currently going out with a man," she said, "and of course I made him take the test instantly. We're both Explorers and older. I'm not sure two Explorers want to raise a baby together, because nobody will be home. But in addition, I'm a Negotiator and he's a Director type. Our dominant personality is similar, but underneath, we're complementary."

Determining which works best—similarity or complementarity—may change with the circumstances. A young woman who's an Explorer, Fisher said, might be attracted to a Builder, someone who's more of a homebody, loyal, dependable, and protective. But the pair will be more compatible if their secondary personalities match—maybe they're both Negotiators underneath.

"Nobody is directly locked into any one of these temperament types," Fisher said. "That's why we provide each person with both a major and a minor personality profile. Do Explorers go well together? Do likes attract likes? Sometimes they do and sometimes they don't."

If this sounds a bit, well, unscientific, Fisher is the first to admit it. "I have theories about what personality type a person would be most ideally suited with," she told me, "but I also trust people to tell me what they are looking for. All throughout the questionnaire are checks and balances to what are just Helen Fisher's theories."

This is why she decided to include an item on the Chemistry.com questionnaire that asks about the traits of a person's partner in his or her most successful former relationship: Was that person an Explorer, a Builder, a Director, a Negotiator? "Anybody can match somebody for values. But I'm hoping to create a system so that five years later they still fascinate each other."

At the same time, Fisher wants couples to be fascinated by each other early on. In other words, why waste time e-mailing back and forth to get to know a potential match over the course of several weeks, as eHarmony encourages its users to do, if there won't be any chemistry when they finally meet? Chemistry.com's guided 1-2-3-Meet system provides a step-by-step

structure to get couples face to face as soon as possible for that all-important "vibe check." Then there's a post-meeting "chemistry check," where each person offers feedback about the date.

The goal is to incorporate this information into the algorithm to provide better matches, but it can also serve as an accuracy check of the data. Say, for instance, that Jack describes himself as a fashionable dresser, but Jill reports that he showed up for their date in flip-flops, cut-offs, and a do-rag. If the feedback from a number of Jack's first meetings indicates the same problem, Chemistry.com will send him an e-mail saying, "Jack, wear a pair of trousers."

Still, even a thoroughly researched biochemical model won't prevent glitches in the matching system. In Fisher's view, for example, no scientifically based site would pair her with the men she's dated, because, as she put it, "they're all better-looking than me."

"It would be preposterous for anyone to say they can create a formula that works perfectly," she said emphatically. "But I do believe that science can help us get close, and that there's a lot more to be learned."

Meanwhile, until these sites start sending me better dating prospects, I figured I'd take Neil Clark Warren up on his offer to introduce me to the thirty-eight-year-old single board member he thought would be such a good match for me. But when I asked a company spokesman about him, I was told that he had recently begun seeing someone. Did they meet through eHarmony? My potential soul mate declined to answer.

Writing: A Ticket to Work . . . Or a Ticket Out

(EXECUTIVE SUMMARY)

National Commission on Writing for America's Families, Schools, and Colleges

Writing: A Ticket to Work . . . Or a Ticket Out was issued in September 2004 by a commission of the nonprofit association The College Board. The College Board is perhaps best known for administering the SAT. Starting with this information, what can you infer about the report's intended audience? Who would find this information useful or interesting? Who has a stake in this issue?

Analyzing and Connecting

Return to these questions after you have finished reading.

1. An executive summary is written for busy upper-level managers. It typically makes its main point quickly and clearly, condensing the bulk of the report that follows. Where is the main point of the study expressed in this summary, and what is it?

2. This report provides a great deal of evidence to support its main point. The summary also takes pains to provide some background on the sources cited. What kinds of information about sources are included in the summary?

3. Note the specificity with which the authors report their findings. Are any of the statistics they cite particularly striking to you? Which ones, and why? Do you get the sense that their data are reliable? Do you think their conclusions are justified? Why or why not?

4. Notice that the summary also includes a number of direct quotations from survey respondents. What do these quotes add to the summary? How do they fit together with the statistical data?

5. Reflect on the survey findings reported in this summary. Do they surprise you at all, or change your perspective on writing?

6. An executive summary is, of course, only a summary. It leaves out much of the detailed information found in the rest of the report. Think about what this summary does and does not tell readers. What questions does it leave unanswered? What gaps does it leave in your knowledge of the issue? What kinds of follow-up would you like to see in the remainder of the report? What more would you like to find out about the issue?

The entire report can be downloaded at **www.writingcommission.org/pr/writing_for_employ.html.** You can explore the rest of the report and see how well it answers your questions.

SUMMARY

A survey of 120 major American corporations employing nearly 8 million people concludes that in today's workplace writing is a "threshold skill" for hiring and promotion among salaried (i.e., professional) employees. Survey results indicate that writing is a ticket to professional opportunity, while poorly written job applications are a figurative kiss of death. Estimates based on the survey returns reveal that employees spend billions annually correcting writing deficiencies. The survey, mailed to 120 human resource directors in corporations associated with Business Roundtable, produced responses from 64 companies, a 53.3 percent response rate.

Among the survey findings:

- Writing is a "threshold skill" for both employment and promotion, particularly for salaried employees. Half the responding companies report that they take writing into consideration when hiring professional employees. "In most cases, writing ability could be your ticket in . . . or it could be your ticket out," said one respondent.

- People who cannot write and communicate clearly will not be hired and are unlikely to last long enough to be considered for promotion. "Poorly written application materials would be extremely prejudicial," said one respondent. "Such applicants would not be considered for any position."

- Two-thirds of salaried employees in large American companies have some writing responsibility. "All employees must have writing ability . . . Manufacturing documentation, operating procedures, reporting problems, lab safety, waste-disposal operations—all have to be crystal clear," said one human resource director.

- Eighty percent or more of the companies in the service and finance, insurance, and real estate (FIRE) sectors, the corporations with the greatest employment-growth potential, assess writing during hiring. "Applicants who provide poorly written letters wouldn't likely get an interview," commented one insurance executive.

- A similar dynamic is at work during promotions. Half of all companies take writing into account when making promotion decisions. One succinct comment: "You can't move up without writing skills."

- More than half of all responding companies report that they "frequently" or "almost always" produce technical reports (59 percent), formal reports (62 percent), and memos and correspondence (70 percent). Communication through email and PowerPoint presentations is almost universal. "Because of email, more employees have to write more often. Also, a lot more has to be documented," said one respondent.

- More than 40 percent of responding firms offer or require training for salaried employees with writing deficiencies. Based on the survey responses, it appears that remedying deficiencies in writing may cost American firms as much as $3.1 billion annually. "We're likely to send out 200-300 people annually for skills-upgrade courses like 'business writing' or 'technical writing'," said one respondent.

Business Roundtable (**www.businessroundtable.org**) is an association of the chief executive officers of some of the leading U.S. corporations. The chief executives are committed to advocating public policies that foster vigorous economic growth and a dynamic global economy. The Roundtable's members represent corporate leaders in manufacturing, finance, services, and high technology. The Roundtable encouraged its members to participate in the survey, which was developed and administered by the National Commission on Writing for America's Families, Schools, and Colleges.

Building a Shelter

(INSTRUCTION)

Hugh McManners

"Building a Shelter" was published in Hugh McManners's *The Complete Wilderness Training Book*, a practical guide to outdoor skills. McManners was born in Oxford, England, and spent 16 years in the British army, serving in many countries with the Commando Forces, including running the army's jungle warfare school in Belize. After his years in the army, he has become a prolific writer of books and articles on the outdoors.

Analyzing and Connecting

Return to these questions after you have finished reading.

1. How well does McManners explain how to build a shelter? What else might he have included? What could he have left out?

2. McManners could have given the instructions without photographs. What difference do the photographs make?

3. How much does McManners assume his readers know about wilderness survival? A great deal? some? very little? How do you determine the level of knowledge?

4. Building a lean-to shelter out of available materials is one of the oldest forms of human architecture, and the knowledge to build a shelter was passed down from generation to generation. Think of a practical skill your grandparents, aunts, uncles, or parents taught you. How did they teach you the steps? What special knowledge or tips did they share with you?

5. Instructions for technology-related products often frustrate users. Have you had a bad experience with instructions? What was incomplete or confusing? How did you compensate for the bad instructions? Call the help line? trial and error? ask a friend?

McMANNERS: BUILDING A SHELTER

LIVING IN THE WILD

BUILDING A SHELTER

GETTING OUT OF the wind, rain, and sun, and being able to rest and sleep are vital for survival. The better you build your shelter, the more comfortable you will be – and the more rest you will be able to get. Being rested is essential for your physical health, as well as for your psychological well-being, which determines how sensibly and logically you think and how strongly you are resolved to survive. A lean-to shelter is probably the

easiest and quickest type of shelter to build and is suitable for most terrain. It should be erected on a sheltered, safe, level site, and built so that the roof faces into the wind. The construction of your shelter will depend entirely on the materials at your disposal. If you have a tarpaulin or plastic sheeting, you should use that to make the roof of your shelter, but otherwise you will have to improvise with whatever items you find.

Ridge pole should be taller than you can reach

1 To make a lean-to shelter, first cut a long branch as a ridge pole. Measure the correct length by reaching up as high as possible and cutting it another 2 ft (60 cm) or so above that. Try to get as straight a branch as possible for the ridge pole, and trim off all projecting twigs. Do not use a dead branch, which may snap and break in a high wind.

2 Cut two Y-shaped supports to about chest height, each with an extra 1 ft (30 cm) that will be hammered into the ground. Sharpen the bottom ends.

Sharpen post ends so that they can be hammered into the ground

3 Hammer both the supports into the ground with a heavy rock until they are secure and will not fall over. The distance between them should be about 2 ft (60 cm) less than the length of the ridge pole.

4 Lay the ridge pole between the two forks of the support posts, allowing equal overlap at the ends. The ridge pole must be fairly light, but sturdy enough to take the weight of the finished roof and withstand heavy rain and strong winds without collapsing.

5 Cut several fairly strong branches long enough to lean against the ridge pole at an angle of about 45 degrees to the ground. This will allow maximum rainwater runoff from the roof. Space them 8 in (20 cm) apart. They should overhang the ridge pole by about 4 in (10 cm).

BUILDING A SHELTER

6 Cut plenty of straight, fairly sturdy saplings. Weave the saplings over and under alternate sloping roof branches, until all the branches are joined fairly firmly together in a lattice. Weave a row of saplings over and under the ridge pole, as well, to hold it in place.

Weave the top saplings over and under the ridge pole to hold it in place, thus giving the structure tensile strength

7 Weave whole branches, complete with foliage to keep out the wind and rain, into the roof lattice. Using whole branches will make the roof strong and keep the foliage alive longer, especially if it is deciduous.

8 Continue weaving the foliage into the lattice until you are content with the density of your roof. Some types of foliage die faster than others, and may have to be replaced after a few days. It is best to weave new branches over the old ones to build up the layers of the roof. Branches from small-leaved trees are preferable, since large leaves tear, die quickly, and are hard to weave into a flat mat.

9 The finished shelter may require further improvement – for example you may want to place large rocks along the back to hold down the bottom of the roof in high winds, or to add side walls. Light your camp fire in front of the shelter, but keep the flames away from the thatch. Rethatch as the roof foliage withers.

USING MANMADE MATERIALS

Manmade materials should be used if available, and augmented by natural ones where necessary. Plastic bags and sheets of polyethylene are common forms of rural litter. Wooden boxes, plywood, cardboard, and galvanized metal sheets can also be used.

Other materials
Shelters can be made from all kinds of discarded manmade materials.

View Lava Safely

(INFORMATIONAL WEB SITE)

Hawai'i Volcanoes National Park Visitor Information

View Lava Safely is a page on the Hawai'i Volcanoes National Park Web site sponsored by the National Park Service. This national park is unusual because it has active volcanoes that spew red molten lava flows. These spectacular flows pose many dangers to the visitors who come to view them; thus the Web site takes on the additional mission of providing specific safety information along with general information about the park.

Analyzing and Connecting

Return to these questions after you have finished reading.

1. This Web page is designed to help park visitors view volcanic activity safely. Notice that the site contains current, regularly updated information on lava flows as well as generic safety information. Why did the site's designers choose to combine both types of information here?

2. This page contains a number of striking photographs. Apart from showing the natural beauty of the park, what purpose do the images serve in the context of this site?

3. Consider the tone of this Web page. While the designers are concerned with warning visitors of potential dangers, they also do not want to discourage people from visiting the park and enjoying their experience. Are they successful in striking a balance between these two goals?

4. Explain why you think the designers chose to include the map of Flows from Pu'u O'o on this page. What information from the map is likely to influence visitors' behavior in terms of safety? Consider in particular the route of Chain of Craters Road.

5. This site demonstrates how important informational writing can be. Most people who are injured while viewing lava are simply unaware of the hazards. How many potential volcanic hazards explained in this site were you previously aware of? Would this information make you more or less likely to visit Hawai'i Volcanoes National Park?

Visitor Information

View Lava Safely

- Visit
- Lava
- Drive
- Maps
- Camp
- Hike
- Bike
- Lodging
- Programs
- Climate
- Travel
- Accessibility
- Park Facts
- Statistics
- Links
- Site Index
- Search
- Contact Us
- Bookstore

Where is the lava?

Gear

Dangers

Volcanic Fumes

View Lava Safely

Eruption Update

Live Com – Pu'O'o' Vent

Eruption History

Image Archive

Lava Flow Map

Earthquakes

Lava is currently entering the ocean 3 miles from the ranger station at the end to the Chain of Craters Road.
Click on the photo for larger version. NPS photo by Elizabeth Bell 03/04/2005

Where can we see red lava?

Currently lava flowing in a remote area of the park, 3 miles beyond the ranger station at the end of Chain of Craters Road: The eruption update for Friday, July 22, 2005 from Don Swanson, Research Scientist at the Hawaiian Volcano Observatory, reports that:

"Two moderately large areas of breakouts occur this morning on the coastal flat about 900 m inland of the East Lae'apuki. They are in the east branch of the PKK flow, which otherwise exhibits only weak surface activity farther upstream."

"The other two branches of the flow aren't doing so well. Each hosts several small breakouts high on Pulama pali, and that's about it."

Areas to the right and seaward of the dotted lines are closed due to the potential for major land collapses. Click on the map for a larger version.

"Both entry areas are aglow this morning, particularly East Lae'apuki, where a large plume of laze reflects back the glow from several places along the delta front where lava streams into the water. East Kamoamoa is much smaller, but nonetheless its glow shines through some fairly nasty laze."

View from the end of Chain of Craters road:
After nightfall (7:30 p.m.), visitors may see spots of red incandescence on the distant hillside from the "steam plume" viewing area, a $\frac{1}{2}$ mile walk on the roadway from the ranger station at the end of Chain of Craters Road and an additional 5 minute walk on a trail. Lava is currently entering the ocean in multiple places and from the viewing area at the end of this moderate walk, one may see glow or lava from a distance. Binoculars would be useful at this viewpoint.

To view lava up close, visitors must hike out from the end of the road (see hike information below). Lava viewing conditions are constantly changing. Check with rangers at the Kilauea Visitor Center or at the ranger station at the end of Chain of Craters road for the most current report.

The new land where lava enters the ocean is poised to collapse without warning. The area has been closed to the public. USGS photo 06/28/2005. Click on the picture for a larger version.

- Visit
- Lava
- Drive
- Maps
- Camp
- Hike
- Bike
- Lodging
- Programs
- Climate
- Travel
- Accessibility
- Park Facts
- Statistics
- Links
- Site Index
- Search
- Contact Us
- Bookstore

Be safe- Be prepared – Plan carefully! Read:
Viewing Lava Safely – Common Sense is Not Enough!

What do we take on the hike? What do we wear?

Flashlight 1 for EACH person with extra batteries – if you will be viewing lava after 6:00 p.m. Headlamps are helpful.	**Clothing** Long lightweight hiking pants and gloves (gives added protection in case you fall), raingear, and hat.
Binoculars to see lava from a safe distance.	**Boots** or other sturdy closed-toed shoes.
First Aid Kit The slightest fall can cause deep cuts. Falling on lava is like falling on broken glass.	**Water** 2 to 3 quarts/liters, per person.
Sun Screen SPF 15 or greater.	**Food** You will be gone from your car for several hours. Food gives you energy.

For Your Safety, Know the Dangers!
Be Prepared, Be Aware, Stay Alive!

DANGERS INCLUDE:	REQUIRED READING:
- VOLCANIC FUMES - STEAM AND EXPLOSIONS - METHANE GAS EXPLOSIONS - COASTLINE COLLAPSE	- View Lava Safely - Printable Pdf version

VOLCANIC FUMES

Learn more about volcano gas and "vog"

Volcanic fume/gasses (VOG) are not only found where lava enters the ocean but may be evident in other areas of the park. For current air quality conditions, click on this link:

VOG Monitoring So2 Data

Volcanic fumes (VOG) are hazardous to your health. Persons with breathing and heart difficulties, pregnant women, infants, and young children are especially at risk. All persons should avoid breathing these fumes. They contain hydrochloric acid, sulfuric acid, and glass particles.

DO NOT STAND OR WALK IN OR UNDER THE FUMES

Real-time VOG Data

Link to current air quality conditions

STEAM AND EXPLOSIONS WHERE LAVA ENTERS THE OCEAN

Lava enters the ocean at 210°F (1,140°C). Sea water explodes into steam and boiling water. Molten lava and rocks explode sky-wards. Blocks the size of microwave ovens are tossed hundreds of yards/meters inland. Ocean waves wash onto hot lava and flash to steam. In June 1998, large violent steam explosions began without warning, throwing molten lava in all directions. Falling debris built a 30 foot (10 m) spatter cone at the lava entry within

Additional information:

- For the Eruption Update recorded message, phone (805) 985-6000 and press 1 for eruption update. This message is recorded at about 8:00 p.m. Hawai'i time when the rangers return from their shift at the lava flow.
- Visit the Hawaiian Volcano Observatory's Eruption Update for daily information on lava flow activity:

Map of Flows from Pu'u'O'o: May 15, 2005

Map prepared by the U.S. Geological Survey Hawaiian Volcano Observatory and shows areas that have been covered by lava flows from the current eruption of Kilauea -- January 1983 through May 15, 2005.

Map of Pu'u'O'o and Vicinity: August 24, 2004

Map shows vents, flows, and other features referred to in the scientist's daily eruption updates. These features change frequently and the map will be updated as needed. Click on the map to view a larger version.

How to write to inform

These steps for the process of informative writing may not progress as neatly as this chart might suggest. Writing is not an assembly-line process. As you write, you are constantly reading what you have written and rethinking.

Keep your readers in mind while you are writing, and if you don't know who your readers might be, imagine someone. What questions might that person have? Where would they appreciate a more detailed explanation?

1 ASSESS THE WRITING TASK & BEGIN RESEARCH

- Read the assignment, carefully noting key words.

- Determine what kind of writing is required. Who are the potential readers?

- Find the limits of your topic. What do you not need to cover? How far do you need to go in breaking down your explanations?

- Review class notes and textbooks; talk to instructor and peers.

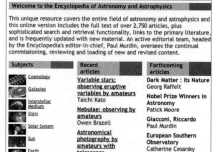

Do background research

Search library subject indexes and catalogs, periodicals, indexes, and online indexes.

2 CHOOSE A TOPIC & WRITE A THESIS

- Within the scope of the assignment, explore what interests you.

- Ask yourself, "Who else will be interested in this topic?"

- Make a list of issues, questions, or problems associated with the topic area.

- Make idea maps about possible topics.

- Discuss possible choices with your peers, co-workers, or instructor.

- Ask questions:

  What happened? What do people need to know?

  Who is my audience?

  How can I connect with them on this topic?

- Narrow your topic. When you learn more about your topic, you should be able to identify one aspect or concept that you can cover thoroughly.

- Write a working thesis that describes what you plan to report or explain.

- If you are unsure if you can follow through with your thesis, do additional research and revise your thesis.

3 WRITE A DRAFT

- Write your revised thesis and main points.
- Think about how you will organize your main points.
- Draft an introduction that will make readers interested in your subject.
- Build the organization by identifying the topic of each paragraph.
- Draft a conclusion that does more than summarize.
- Write an engaging title.

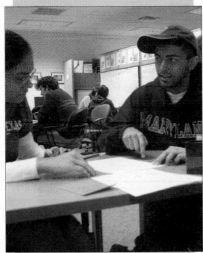

4 REVISE, REVISE, REVISE

- Reorganize your ideas for clarity.
- Add detail or further explanation where needed.
- Cut material that distracts from your thesis.
- Check that all key terms are defined.
- Frame your report with an introduction that interests readers and a conclusion that makes a point or raises an interesting question.
- Check that any sources are appropriately quoted or summarized and that they are documented correctly.
- Revise the title to be more accurate and to make readers more interested.
- Review the visual presentation of your report for readability and maximum impact.
- Proofread carefully.

5 SUBMITTED VERSION

- Make sure your finished writing meets all formatting requirements.

1: Assess the writing task and begin research

Analyze the assignment

Read your assignment slowly and carefully. Mark off any information about the length specified, date due, formatting, and other requirements. You can attend to this information later. At this point you want to zero in on the subject you will write about and how you will approach that subject.

What kind of writing is required?

Look for key words such as *analyze, compare and contrast, define, discuss,* or *explain*. Often these key words will help you in determining what direction to take. Highlight key words in all questions and commands.

Analyze
Find connections among a set of facts, events, or things, and make them meaningful.

Compare and contrast
Examine how two or more things are alike and how they differ.

Define
Make a claim about how something should be defined, according to features that you set out.

Discuss
Summarize what is known about a particular subject or issue, including research findings.

Explain
Go into detail about how something works or make an unfamiliar subject comprehensible.

Is the audience specified?	If the audience is mentioned in the assignment, how much will they know about your subject? How much background will you need to provide? What attitudes are they likely to have about your subject?
Find a topic	Sometimes you know immediately what you want to write about, but most often, it takes some time to find the right topic. Think first about what is most interesting to you. Give yourself some time to identify the right topic for you.
What do you know about the general topic?	A good first step is to make an inventory of what you know. Make a list of possible ideas. After you write down as many ideas as you can, go back through the list and place a star beside the ideas that seem most promising.
What ideas can you find in your course notes, class discussions, and your textbooks?	Often you need to look no further than your course materials for possible topics. Think about subjects raised in lectures, in class discussions, or in your textbooks for potential ideas.
What might you find in a print or online library?	Subject directories in your library's online catalog are a valuable source of potential topics. See Chapters 16 and 17.
What might you find on the Web?	Google searches and other search engines often turn up promising ideas to pursue. Yahoo has a subject directory that breaks down large topics into subtopics. See Chapter 18.
What might you find doing field research?	Sometimes the information you need cannot be found in libraries or on the Web, and you have to collect the information firsthand through interviews, surveys, or observations. See Chapter 19.

WRITE NOW

Explore possible topics

1. Make a list of concepts in your courses. Textbooks usually highlight key concepts, so use them and your course notes to develop your list.
2. Put a check beside the concepts that look most interesting to write about or the ones that mean the most to you.
3. Put a question mark beside the concepts that you don't know much about. If you choose one of these concepts, you will probably have to do in-depth research—by talking to people, by using the Internet, or by going to the library.
4. Select a possible concept. Write nonstop for five minutes about why this concept is interesting to you and how it affects you and other people.

Writer at work

Astronomy 101
Writing Assignment #2

Use examples (Show, don't just tell) Galaxy 999 shows this process at work, b/c

Explain an astronomical process, and the current theory that accounts for it, to a general audience. Use examples of specific phenomena to illustrate the process. Be sure to discuss observations or data that aren't well understood or don't fit the theory. Your paper should seek to make an astronomical process accessible and interesting to an average adult.

Do not "dumb down" your topic. Though you may choose to leave out more dry and complex aspects of a process, such as precise temperature ranges or time spans, your essay must be as accurate as possible given existing theories.

Keep it simple but be accurate. Interest

You should use reputable sources. As we discussed in class, newsmagazines and newspaper articles are fine as supporting sources, but you should make an attempt to get your information "from the horse's mouth." Given the ready availability of astronomical information from NASA and other publicly funded programs, this should not be difficult.

Check NASA

You may use any kind of visual features that you think helps you explain your topic to a general audience. If you reproduce a graph or chart from another source, be sure to cite the source. The same goes for photographs.

Due dates
Have two weeks for research and writing rough draft
Rough drafts will be due on April 22. We will have peer review in class on that day.
Final drafts are due at the beginning of class on May 6.

Two more weeks to revise

Grading criteria
You will be graded on the accuracy of your descriptions and explanations, the clarity of your writing, your success in appealing to a general audience, and the extent to which grammatical and mechanical considerations help, rather than hinder, your essay.

Assess the assignment
Lakshmi Kotra wrote a report in response to this assignment in her Introduction to Astronomy course. She made the following notes and observations to help determine what her essay needed to accomplish, and to explore how she might find a good topic.

Highlight key words
Lakshmi began by highlighting the words in the assignment that gave her specific information about the writing tasks she was to perform.

Identify goals
Then, she made notes on the assignment sheet to specify what she needed to do.

Note time frame
She also made notes about the time frame she has to work in.

Plan strategy
Lakshmi made notes about possible sources for her paper. Then she sketched out a brief time line to follow.

SOURCES
- Go back over lecture notes—Unit 3 was easiest for me to understand so may be best for a general audience?
- Review theories—what makes an idea a theory; who decides what is the accepted theory?
- See book also, esp. Table of contents, for topic ideas.
- Library subject index
- Online subject index
- Check NASA archives online for good pictures. Maybe categories there would help too.
- Ask Dr. Jenson if we can do something we haven't covered in class yet.

***Get to the library by <u>Friday</u> so topic is ready over the weekend. See if Karen wants to go too. Check reference librarian hours first, just in case.

- Outline over the weekend so I have next week to ask Dr. Jenson for help with the rough draft, if I need it.
- Visuals will help make the essay interesting and appealing to a general audience, and also can help explain. So maybe pick two or three topics and then look at NASA images and other visuals to see what is available. This should help narrow down my choices.

2: Choose a topic and write a thesis

Connect your ideas

After you have done preliminary research and collected ideas, it's time to list possible topics and begin making connections. Circle the most interesting possibilities.

Choose a topic you will enjoy writing about

Writing is fun when you discover new things along the way. Choose a topic you want to explore. If your topic isn't interesting for you, it likely won't be for your readers either.

Choose a topic that your readers will enjoy reading about

Readers may ask, "Why are you telling me this?" Your subject should be interesting to your readers. If the subject isn't one that is immediately interesting, think about ways you can make it so.

Choose a topic that either you know something about or for which you can find the information you need

A central difficulty with writing to inform is determining where to stop. The key to success is to limit the topic. Choose a topic for which you can find the information you need and which you can cover thoroughly in the space you have. If you choose an unfamiliar topic, you must be strongly committed to learning much about it in a short time.

Narrow your topic and write a thesis

Look for ways of dividing large topics into smaller categories, and select one that is promising.

1. What is your topic exactly? (Try to state your answer in specific terms.)

2. What points do you want to make about your topic?

3. What exactly is your purpose in this project? To inform? explain? compare?

4. Develop a working thesis that draws on your answers to questions 1 and 2 and that reflects the purpose you described in your answer to question 3.

STAYING ON TRACK

Evaluate your thesis

Your thesis should fulfill the assignment

If your assignment is informative, your purpose is not to argue something is good or bad (see Chapter 12), not to argue for a position (see Chapter 13), and not to argue for change (see Chapter 14).

OFF TRACK

"The electoral college is an antiquated system that results in unfair election results."
(evaluates rather than informs)

ON TRACK

"Considering the huge impact the electoral college system has on American presidential elections, it is surprising that few people understand how it actually works."

Your thesis should be interesting

If your readers already know everything that you have to say, you will bore them. Likewise, your thesis should be significant. Readers will care little about what you have to say if they find your subject trivial.

OFF TRACK

"There are many steps involved before a bill becomes a law."
(vague, bland)

ON TRACK

"Only a tiny fraction of the bills proposed in Congress will ever become laws, and of those, most will accrue so many bizarre amendments and riders that they will barely resemble the original document."

Your thesis should be focused

You cannot tell the story of the Cold War in five pages. Narrow your thesis to a topic you can treat in-depth.

OFF TRACK

"Many new products were developed in the 1950s to support the boom in housing construction."
(possibly interesting if particular products are described)

ON TRACK

"The rush to create new housing for returning WWII veterans in the 1950s resulted in many houses that are now extremely hazardous to live in."

Writer at work

groups of things
- binary stars
- star clusters
- colliding galaxies
- galaxy clusters

violent phenomena
- supernovae
- novae
- quasars
- pulsars
- black holes
- neutron stars

these might be too complicated for
a general audience in 7 pages

visible phenomena
- colors of stars
- shooting stars
- eclipses
- meteors
- comets
- sunspots

most of these are pretty
simple processes. Could I
get 5–7 pages?

How things form or evolve
- plants
- stars
- galaxies
- the universe (string theory, Big
Bang) too hard to do in 7 pages
- solar system

Is formation of planets a normal part of stellar formation or a fluke?
Can binary star systems have planets?
How common are supernovae? Or black holes?
What will happen to the Sun when it runs out of hydrogen?
How do sunspots fit in with atomic processes in stars?
Why do stars start forming in the first place?

Map possible topics

Lakshmi Kotra began by reviewing her class notes and her textbooks. She also looked in the library's online catalog subject index and an online subject index. She listed all the possible topics she came across in these sources. Then she made an idea map of the topics that appealed to her, clustering types of theories, and adding new ones as they occurred to her. She made a few notes on some of her topic areas, describing how well they would meet the needs of her assignment. And she jotted down questions she had about some topics as well.

Narrow the search

Lakshmi narrowed her search by considering how complicated a topic she wanted to take on. Since she had to explain the theory to a general audience, she ruled out topics like black holes and string theory. She noticed that stellar processes showed up several times in her lists of interesting topics.

Identify the topic

Lakshmi settled on stellar formation as a theory that interested her and which she felt confident she could explain in layman's terms. Her preliminary research also indicated there was a wealth of observational data and photos that she could use in her report.

Find images and get source information

Lakshmi wanted to include photographs of star formation, and she located images that she could use legally on NASA's Web site. She carefully recorded all the information she would need to find the images again and to document the images in her paper.

GRIN
GREAT IMAGES IN NASA

Browse by Subject
Browse by Center
Search by Keywords
Frequent Questions
How to Use GRIN
Copyright Information

National Aeronautics and Space Administration

NASA Center: Hubble Space Telescope Center
Image # : PR95-44A
Date : 04/01/1995

Title

The Eagle Nebula

Full Description

These eerie, dark pillar-like structures are columns of cool interstellar hydrogen gas and dust that are also incubators for new stars. The pillars protrude from the interior wall of a dark molecular cloud like stalagmites from the floor of a cavern. They are part of the "Eagle Nebula" (also called M16 -- the 16th object in Charles Messier's 18th century catalog of "fuzzy" objects that aren't comets), a nearby star-forming region 7,000 light-years away in the constellation Serpens. Ultraviolet light is responsible for illuminating the convoluted surfaces of the columns and the ghostly streamers of gas boiling away from their surfaces, producing the dramatic visual effects that highlight the three dimensional nature of the clouds. The tallest pillar (left) is about a light-year long from base to tip. As the pillars themselves are slowly eroded away by the ultraviolet light, small globules of even denser gas buried within the pillars are uncovered. These globules have been dubbed "EGGs." EGGs is an acronym for "Evaporating Gaseous Globules," but it is also a word that describes what these objects are. Forming inside at least some of the EGGs are embryonic stars, stars that abruptly stop growing when the EGGs are uncovered and they are separated from the larger reservoir of gas from which they were drawing mass. Eventually, the stars themselves emerge from the EGGs as the EGGs themselves succumb to photoevaporation. The picture was taken on April 1, 1995 with the Hubble Space Telescope Wide Field and Planetary Camera 2. The color image is constructed from three separate images taken in the light of emission from different types of atoms. Red shows emission from singly-ionized sulfur atoms. Green shows emission from hydrogen. Blue shows light emitted by doubly- ionized oxygen atoms.

AUTHOR: U.S. National Aeronautics and Space Administration

DATE: April 1, 1995

PAGE TITLE: The Eagle nebula.

SITE TITLE: Great Images in NASA

DATE OF RETRIEVAL: April 5, 2005

URL: http://grin.hq.nasa.gov/ABSTRACTS/GPN-000987.html

213

3: Write a draft

Organize your information

Gather your notes and other materials. Think about how you want to convey the information to your readers.

- If your subject matter occurs over time, you might want to use a chronological order.
- If you need to discuss several aspects, you likely will need to identify key concepts and think about how they relate to each other. An idea map can help you to determine these relationships.
- If you are comparing two or more things, you will want to think about how these things are similar and how they are different.

Make a working outline

A working outline is a tool that you can use as you write your first draft. The more detailed it is, the better. (If you would prefer to write a complete, formal outline before drafting your essay, by all means do so.) To make your outline, follow these steps:

1. List the sections of your essay, in the order that you expect them to appear.

2. Write two or three complete sentences describing the content and purpose of each section.

3. Now, review your outline. Does the project as you have described it here achieve the purpose you intend it to?

Think about a title

An effective title motivates your readers to want to read what you have written. Be as specific as you can.

Consider the use of visuals

Would a table or chart be helpful? photographs? a map? Do you need headings and subheadings?

STAYING ON TRACK

Write an effective introduction and conclusion

Write an effective introduction

Get off to a fast start. Cut to the chase: no empty sentences or big generalizations at the beginning.

OFF TRACK

"Because we all live such busy, hectic lives in these modern times, everyone wants to know why we must wait for hours and hours at the airport before boarding a flight."
(boring, predictable beginning—a signal that the paper will be dull)

ON TRACK

"It's a traveler's worst nightmare: the long line of people at the security gate, snaking back and forth across the waiting area. What exactly goes on in an airport screening area, and how does it help to keep us safe?"

Write an effective conclusion

Remember that a summary of what you have just written is the weakest way to conclude. Think of something interesting for your reader to take away such as an unexpected implication or a provocative example.

OFF TRACK

"In conclusion, we have seen how peer-to-peer file sharing works."
(ineffective; says only that the paper is finished)

ON TRACK

"The peer-to-peer file sharing process is relatively simple. Unfortunately, in many cases it is also illegal. It is ironic that a technology intended to help people has resulted in turning many of them into *de facto* criminals."
(ends with a significant point, which helps readers remember the paper)

Writer at work

Lakshmi Kotra began with the following rough outline of the process she planned to write about.

Introduction—connect with audience and make them interested
(explain what the clouds are first—composed of what elements?)

I. molecular clouds—collapse begins

will need to explain HOW that happens. No one seems sure so this is a good place to "discuss things that don't fit the theory." Maybe start with one possibility and then describe an alternate explanation in the next paragraph, then go back to process.

II. protostar stage

describe cocoon nebulae—good image

III. fusion begins

will need to explain fusion process

IV. equilibrium

Before getting to equilibrium stage, describe how nebula is blown away and planetary disk forms (for some stars). Mention Earth's origin to interest readers again.

V. death
- ## white dwarfs
- ## supernova

End with supernova to connect back up with interstellar matter/cycle of star formation.

Conclusion can highlight "cycle," and that can be built in at beginning too.

Think about organization

Lakshmi recognized that the process she was describing naturally lent itself to chronological, or time-order, organization, because one thing has to happen after another for a star to form. However, she found that she had to "break out" from the simple time line of stellar formation at some points, to explain in more detail or to trace multiple possibilities.

Make notes on how to develop the subject

She made notes on her outline indicating where she would step away from the chronological pattern to do this explaining. As she considered how she wanted to end her essay, she realized the idea of a "life cycle" for stars could point back toward the essay's beginning. This strategy helped her focus her thesis.

Connect with readers

Lakshmi realized that stellar formation would probably seem like a distant and forbidding topic to a general audience, so she thought carefully about making a connection with her readers. She began by trying out some different ways to introduce her essay. Here are some of her initial attempts and the comments she made on them. Lakshmi decided to work with the last of these openings and see how well she could integrate it with the rest of her essay.

Stars have a complex and fascinating life cycle. Saying it's fascinating doesn't make it fascinating to readers.

Have you ever looked up at the stars at night and wondered why they are there? Vague. Kind of sounds like I'm going to talk about religious or spiritual issues.

Astronomers have spent many years studying the life cycle of stars. So? Anyway, I just want to talk about what they've found, not how long it took them.

If "sunshine on your shoulders" makes you happy, you will be even happier to know that the sun will keep shining for at least another 8 billion years. Too corny. Does anyone even remember that song? Anyway, "happy" isn't the way I want readers to feel. But using a familiar phrase might be good.

"Twinkle, twinkle little star. How I wonder what you are." Good—more personal than "Have you ever looked up at the stars and wondered . . ." Astronomers wonder too. That could be the connection between them and scientists' work. More familiar song, also.

4: Revise, revise, revise

Skilled writers know that the secret to writing well is rewriting. Even the best writers often have to revise several times to get the result they want. You also must have effective strategies for revising if you're going to be successful. The biggest trap you can fall into is starting off with the little stuff first. Leave the small stuff for last.

Does your paper or project meet the assignment?	• Look again at your assignment. Does your paper or project do what the assignment asks? • Look again at the assignment for specific guidelines, including length, format, and amount of research. Does your work meet these guidelines?
Is your title specific?	• Vague titles suggest dull treatment of the topic. Can you make your title more accurate?
Does your writing have a clear focus?	• Does your project have an explicitly stated thesis? If not, is your thesis clearly implied? • Is each paragraph related to your thesis? • Do you get off the track at any point by introducing other topics? • Are your main points adequately developed? • Do you support your main points with reasons and evidence? • Can you add more examples and details that would help to explain your main points?
Is your organization effective?	• Is the order of your main points clear to your reader? • Are there any places where you find abrupt shifts or gaps? • Are there sections or paragraphs that could be rearranged to make your draft more effective?
Is your introduction effective?	• Do you have any general statements that you might cut to get off to a faster start?

- Can you think of a vivid example that might draw in readers?
- Can you use a striking fact to get readers interested?
- Does your introduction make clear where you are headed?

Is your conclusion effective?

- Conclusions that only summarize tend to bore readers. Does your conclusion add anything new to what you've said already?
- Can you use the conclusion to discuss further implications?
- Have you left your audience with a final provocative idea that might invite further discussion?

Do you represent yourself effectively?

- To the extent you can, forget for a moment that you wrote what you are reading. What impression do you have of you, the writer?
- Does "the writer" create an appropriate tone?
- Has "the writer" done his or her homework?

Is the writing project visually effective?

- Is the font attractive and readable?
- Are the headings and visuals effective?

Save the editing for last

When you have finished revising, edit and proofread carefully.

STAYING ON TRACK

Reviewing your draft

Give yourself plenty of time for reviewing your draft. For detailed information on how to participate in a peer review, how to review it yourself, and how to respond to comments from your classmates, your instructor, or a campus writing consultant, see pages 28–32.

Some good questions to ask yourself when reviewing informative writing

- Are the explanations in the essay easy to follow?
- Are there gaps or places where you feel you need more information?
- Are any unusual or discipline-specific words defined for readers?
- Can the reader construct a clear picture of what the essay describes?
- Is the essay interesting enough to catch readers' attention and keep them reading?

Writer at work

Density increases much faster at the cloud's center

Once a section of a dust cloud starts to collapse, gravity relentlessly pulls the material together into a much smaller area. Gradually, <u>the cloud becomes denser</u> and less cloudlike. At this stage, astronomers refer to the object as a "protostar." For a star the size of our sun, the journey from cloud to protostar may take about 100,000 years (Chaisson and McMillan 429). <u>Bigger clouds of gas will develop faster—but they will also have shorter lives. The larger the star, the faster it uses up its "fuel." But first the fuel must start burning.</u> As the atoms of gas crowd into a smaller and smaller space, they bounce off one another faster and faster, and the protostar heats up. However, it is not a true star yet. That comes later, when nuclear <u>fusion begins. If a cloud segment is less than .08 solar masses, it won't get hot enough, and it will never become a star.</u>

When the protostar is dense enough, its nuclear heart finally starts to beat. This happens when hydrogen atoms are pushed close enough together to fuse into helium. This requires a total of six hydrogen atoms, which must combine in a specific sequence: hydrogen—deuterium—helium 3—helium + hydrogen. Every time fusion takes place, a small amount of energy is released.

You bring up a number of concepts here that don"t quite fit with the main idea of the paragraph. It might make sense to move the information about mass and lifespan to later in the paper

The "sequence" isn't clear. Can you break this down into simpler steps?

Read carefully your instructor's comments

Lakshmi Kotra gave a copy of her first draft to her instructor for feedback. She used his comments to guide her revision of the essay.

Determine a plan for revision in light of your instructor's comments

Based on her instructor's comments, Lakshmi decided to shift some information on the rates at which stars burn nuclear fuel from an earlier section of the paper to her later discussion of the fates of stars with different masses. This strategy also allowed her to flesh out the description of "brown dwarfs"—starlike objects that do not develop into stars.

Act on specific comments

She also took her instructor's advice about simplifying her explanation of hydrogen fusion.

Read your paper aloud to catch mistakes and awkward phrasing

Lakshmi also read her essay aloud to help identify spelling errors and missing or poorly chosen words.

Visit your writing center

Finally, Lakshmi visited her school's writing center. She asked for specific help in making the paper accessible for an audience without a scientific background. Working with a consultant, she recognized the need to define scientific terms, like *nebulae, protostar,* and *equilibrium,* that might not be familiar to a general audience.

5: Submitted version

Lakshmi Kotra

Professor Jenson

Astronomy 101

6 May 2005

The Life Cycle of Stars

"Twinkle, twinkle, little star; how I wonder what you are." This old nursery rhyme may not seem profound, but it echoes some of the biggest questions astronomers puzzle over: What are stars made of? How do they form? How are they born and how do they die? Current theories of star formation answer some of these questions, but not all of them. We do know that, even though stars are separated from one another by vast amounts of space, their life cycles are intertwined.

Twinkling stars are born in dark, cold clouds of dust and gas called nebulae. These clouds consist mainly of hydrogen, and may be as cold as 10 degrees Kelvin (Chaisson and McMillan 427). Nebulae are very dense compared to the near-vacuum of interstellar space. But something must concentrate this dust and gas even more if a star is to form. This first part of the star-forming process is not fully understood. Some force has to cause a portion of the nebula to begin collapsing. Magnetism and rotation are two forces already at work in most clouds, but astronomers have long thought that these forces are more likely to counteract the collapsing force of gravity (Chaisson and McMillan 427). However, new research may have found a solution to this problem. In some clouds, magnetic fields may cancel out some or all of the rotational force. This reorganization would allow gravity to begin collapsing the star (Farivar).

Another theory is that a shock wave from some outside event or object might trigger the collapse of a cloud. The Eagle Nebula provides a good illustration of this theory. Ultraviolet radiation from super-hot stars in the nebula has been observed bombarding the surrounding dust and gas. The radiation has stripped away a lot of dust but left dense columns of cloud where stars are believed to be forming. The impact of this "stellar wind" may have also triggered the star formation. Smaller clumps of denser gas are contracting within the columns, taking their first step on the journey to stardom (see fig. 1).

Once a section of a dust cloud starts to collapse, gravity relentlessly pulls the material together into a much smaller area. Gradually, the center of the cloud becomes denser and less cloudlike. At this stage, astronomers refer to the object as a "protostar." For a star the size of our sun, the journey from cloud to protostar may take about 100,000 years (Chaisson and McMillan 429). As the atoms of gas crowd into a smaller and smaller space, they bounce off one

Fig. 1. Eagle Nebula
The columns of interstellar gas in the Eagle Nebula are incubators for new stars (US, NASA, "Eagle").

another faster and faster, and the protostar heats up. However, it is not a true star yet. That comes later, when nuclear fusion begins. For now, the developing protostar is still surrounded by a shroud of dust that hides it from view. This dust mantle is called a cocoon nebula. Some protostars can be detected by the infrared glow of their cocoon nebulae (Chaisson and McMillan 435-36).

Over millions of years, the protostar continues to grow and change, like a butterfly in its cocoon. Gravity keeps compacting it, making it smaller in size and denser. When the protostar is dense enough, its nuclear heart finally starts to beat. This happens when hydrogen atoms are pushed close enough together to fuse into helium. The fusion process involves several steps. First, two hydrogen atoms will fuse to form an atom of deuterium, or heavy hydrogen. When a third hydrogen atom joins the deuterium atom, an isotope called helium 3 results. Finally, when two helium 3 atoms fuse together, an atom of regular helium plus two of hydrogen are created. But the crucial part of this process is that, every time fusion takes place, a small amount of energy is released. The radiation emitted from the fusion of hydrogen into helium is what makes the majority of stars shine. Fusion radiation from the Sun lights our planet in the daytime, makes the moon shine at night—and gives you sunburn.

Hydrogen atoms must be moving at extremely high speeds in order to fuse. Another way to say this is that the temperature in the core of a protostar must be very high for fusion to take place: at least 10 million degrees Kelvin (Chaisson and McMillan 431). Now nuclear forces, not just gravity's grip, are controlling the star's development. In fact, these two forces will compete throughout the star's life. Gravity tries to collapse the star, while the pressure of its fast-moving, superheated atoms pushes it outward. As long as the two forces balance each other, the star will remain stable. Astronomers call this state "equilibrium."

During the intense heating at the end of the protostar stage, and when hydrogen fusion is beginning, intense radiation streams off the young star. The dust and gas that have surrounded the protostar are swept away by this energy bombardment, and the star emerges from its cocoon. This phenomenon can be observed visually in NGC 4214. Young stars in this nebula are pouring out radiation that has created "bubbles" in the surrounding gas. Brighter and older stars have pushed away more of the dust and gas. The bubbles around these stars are bigger than those around younger or cooler stars in the nebula (see fig. 2).

Sometimes, not all of a protostar's dust cocoon blows away. According to one theory, you can look around our own solar system and see the remnants of the dust that once surrounded our Sun. In fact, you are standing on some of it. The Earth and the rest of the planets in our solar system are believed to have formed from a disk of dust and gas left over after the sun formed. The reasons this happens are not entirely clear, but astronomers now think that many stellar systems have planetary disks around them. The Orion Nebula provides some confirmation of this theory. There, astronomers have observed many

Fig. 2. Star Formation
Clusters of new stars form from interstellar gas and dust in galaxy NGC 4214 (US, NASA, "Star").

glowing disks of dust, called "proplyds." They think these disks are actually young stars surrounded by material that will eventually form a system of orbiting planets (see fig. 3).

The size of the original dust cloud a star is born from will also determine how it dies. Some protostars don't quite have what it takes to become a star. Clumps of dust and gas that are smaller than .08 solar masses never get hot enough to begin fusing hydrogen (Chaisson and McMillan 433). These "brown dwarfs" produce infrared radiation, but they never shine visibly.

True stars burn through their nuclear fuel at different rates. The larger the star, the faster its fuel is fused. Smaller stars, like our Sun,

Fig. 3. Orion Nebula
This composite photo of the Orion nebula assembled from images taken by the Hubble Space Telescope shows the beginnings of new solar systems surrounding young stars (US, NASA, "Orion").

are called "dwarf stars." If they began life with less than eight times the mass of our Sun, they will quietly burn hydrogen for perhaps ten billion years. Toward the end of their lives, as they begin to run out of fuel, they will swell briefly into red giant stars, fusing their helium into carbon, and cooling substantially. Finally, they will subside into "white dwarf" stars, about the size of the planet earth. Provided they do not have nearby neighboring stars that might interact with them, white dwarfs gradually dim and cool, until they go dark altogether (Chaisson and McMillan 459). This cooling process is what astronomers predict will some day happen to our Sun.

A star of more than about eight solar masses has a shorter but much more spectacular life. It will fuse all its available fuel in well under one billion years—perhaps in as little as one million years. When a giant star has run through all its available nuclear fuel, it develops a core of iron atoms, which cannot be fused into anything else. When this core has grown to about 1.4 solar masses, the star will explode in a supernova. All that will be left of the original star is a dark neutron star or black hole (Chaisson and McMillan 475). But the shock wave from the supernova may go on to trigger new star formation in dust clouds nearby. In this way, dying stars contribute to the birth of new ones, and the life cycle of stars continues.

Kotra 8

Works Cited

Chaisson, Eric, and Steve McMillan. <u>Astronomy Today</u>. 3rd ed.
    Upper Saddle River: Prentice, 1997.

Farivar, Cyrus. "Galactic Map Aids Stellar Formation Theory." <u>The</u>
    <u>Daily Californian</u> 23 Jan. 2002. 8 Apr. 2005 <http://www.daily-
    cal.org/article.php?id=7441>.

United States. National Aeronautics and Space Administration.
    "The Eagle Nebula." <u>Great Images in NASA</u>. 1 Apr. 1995. 5
    Apr. 2005 <http://grin.hq.nasa.gov/ABSTRACTS/GPN-2000-
    000987.html>.

- - -. - - -. "Fireworks of Star Formation Light Up a Galaxy."
    <u>Great Images in NASA</u>. 6 Jan. 2000. 5 Apr. 2005
    <http://grin.hq.nasa.gov/ABSTRACTS/GPN-2000-000877.html>.

- - -. - - -. "The Orion Nebula." <u>Great Images in NASA</u>. 20 Nov. 1995.
    5 Apr. 2005 <http://grin.hq.nasa.gov/ABSTRACTS/GPN-2000-
    000983.html>.

Projects

No matter how diverse its forms, successful informative writing begins with the basics.

- What do readers already know about a subject?
- What do readers need to know about a subject?
- What kind of writing is best suited for particular readers? a Web site? a brochure? an article? or something else?

You'll do many kinds of informative writing in your life after college. The following projects are common informative writing tasks.

INSTRUCTIONS
For an example,
see pages 197–199

Be aware that instructions are much harder to write than most people expect. They usually require a lot of detail, yet if they are too complex, people will be confused or intimidated. After all, how many times have you glanced at an instruction booklet for a new appliance, set it aside, and just started pushing buttons?

Think of a fairly simple device you have learned to use, like an iPod or a software application.

Imagine a friend who wants to learn to use the same device. How could you simply and accurately instruct him or her?

Write a one- or two-page set of instructions explaining how to perform a simple task, such as creating a play list on your iPod, using your school's Web-based email service, or changing the toner cartridge in your printer. When you are finished, have a friend volunteer to try out your instructions. How easy is it to follow them? Do they work?

For additional reading, writing, and research resources, go to **www.mycomplab.com** and choose **Lester Faigley's** *Writing.*

PROFILE

For an example, see pages 177–183

REPORT

For an example, see pages 171–175

Find several written profiles of people at your school—these might be your school president, a coach, and an award-winning student. Profiles often appear in school newspapers, on school Web sites, and in news reports about events on campus.

Read the profiles and note what information is included about each person, and what is left out.

- Are the profiles all written for the same audience?
- How does the information in each profile vary depending on the intended audience?

Choose someone else to write a profile about—a classmate, a staff member you have worked with, or even yourself— and interview that person. Choose someone you find interesting. A custodial worker or fellow student can be just as interesting as a college president, depending on the details you select to write about. Model your profile on the examples you have read.

Think carefully about the audience you wish to appeal to. How can you interest them in your subject?

Think of a subject you know a great deal about but one that most other people are either uninformed or misinformed, especially those who are your intended readers.

Your subject might come from your life experience

- What's it like to grow up on a family farm?
- What's it like to be an immigrant to the United States?

Your hobbies

- What's the best way to train for a marathon?
- How can you avoid injuries in sports by stretching?

Your personal interests

- Why everyone over age 20 should pay attention to cholesterol

A place that you have found fascinating, or a subject you have studied in college

- The misunderstood nature of conceptual art
- Breakthroughs in nanotechnology in the near future.

Consider what will likely be most interesting about your subject to your readers.

Engage your readers with a provocative title and a thesis that will challenge them to think about your subject in new ways.

Aim for a report of 700–1000 words or about 3–5 double-spaced pages.

10
Analyzing Texts

Every piece of writing, every painting, every building, every movie, every new product, every advertisement, is a response to what came before it.

Chapter contents

Writing to analyze

Critical reading and viewing are essential skills for all kinds of writing. Analysis is a more specific aim where those critical reading and viewing skills are applied to particular subjects. Analysis involves dividing a whole into parts that can be studied both as individual entities and as parts of the whole.

Rhetorical analysis is a kind of analysis that divides a whole into parts to understand how an act of speaking or writing conveys meaning. Thus the goal of a rhetorical analysis is to understand how a particular act of writing or speaking influenced particular people at a particular time.

Visual analysis is closely related to rhetorical analysis. The tools of rhetorical analysis have been applied to understanding how other human creations make meaning, including art, buildings, photographs, dance, memorials, advertisements—any kind of symbolic communication.

Literary analysis takes into account elements of literature such as plot, character, and setting, paying particular attention to language and metaphor. The goal of literary analysis is to interpret a literary text and support that interpretation with evidence or, more simply, to make a discovery about a text that you share with your readers.

Text and context

A rhetorical, visual, or literary analysis may be concerned with either text or context, but often it examines both. Textual analysis focuses on the features of a text—the words and evidence in a speech, the images and patterns in a picture, and so on. For a textual analysis, ask

- What is the subject?

- What is the author's claim or what are the main ideas?

- What is the medium of the text? a newspaper? a Web site? scholarly journal? a photograph? a short story?

- What appeals are used? What are the author's credentials, and how does he represent himself? What facts or evidence does he present? What values does he share with you and the rest of his audience? What emotions does he try to evoke?

- How is the text organized?

- What kind of style does the author use? Formal or informal, satirical or humorous? Are any metaphors used?

Contextual analysis reconstructs the cultural environment, or context, that existed when a particular rhetorical event took place, and then depends on that recreation to produce clues about persuasive tactics and appeals. For a contextual analysis, ask

- Who is the author? What else has she written or said on this subject? Who does she borrow from or quote? What motivated her to address this issue?

- Who is the audience? What are the occasion and forum for writing? Would the argument have been constructed differently if it had been presented in a different medium? What motivated the newspaper, magazine, or other venue to publish it?

- What is the larger conversation? When did the text appear? Why did it appear at that particular moment? Who or what might this text be responding to?

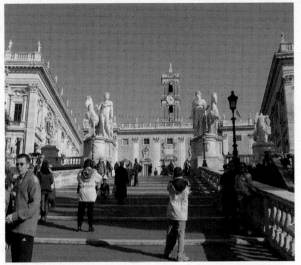

The statue of Castor stands at the entrance of the Piazza del Campidoglio in Rome. A textual analysis focuses on the statue itself. The size and realism of the statue makes it a masterpiece of classical Roman sculpture.

A contextual analysis focuses on the surroundings and the history of the statue. Legend has Castor and his twin brother Pollux, the mythical sons of Leda, assisting Romans in an early battle. Romans built a large temple in the Forum to honor them. The statues of Castor and Pollux were uncovered in sixteenth-century excavations and brought in 1583 to stand at the top of the Cordonata, a staircase designed by Michelangelo as part of a renovation of the Piazza del Campidoglio commissioned by Pope Paul III Farnese in 1536.

WORKING TOGETHER

Analyze text and context

In a group of three or four students

Find several examples of verbal and visual texts. These might be ads you have seen on television or heard on the radio, photos or editorials in the student newspaper, or Web sites.

- What is the context in which this text was produced?
- How was the creator of the text attempting to influence or persuade the audience? What appeals are made?
- In the visual texts, what connections or associations is the reader invited to create?
- In the verbal texts, what claims and reasons are explicitly stated?

235

Writing a rhetorical analysis

People often use the term *rhetoric* to describe empty language. "The Governor's speech was just a bunch of rhetoric," you might say, meaning that the Governor offered noble-sounding words but no real ideas. But rhetoric originated with a much more positive meaning. According to Aristotle, rhetoric is "the art of finding in any given case the available means of persuasion." Rhetoric is concerned with producing effective pieces of communication.

Rhetoric can also be used to interpret or analyze. Students of rhetoric know not only how to produce effective communication, but also how to understand communication. The two skills complement each other: Becoming a better writer makes you a better analyst, and becoming a better analyst makes you a better writer. For an example of rhetorical analysis, see pages 242–246.

Components of a rhetorical analysis

What is the author's purpose?	**Identify the purpose** Some texts have an obvious purpose; for example, an ad wants you to buy something. But texts can have more than one purpose. A politician who accuses an opponent of being corrupt may also be making a case for her own honesty.
Who is the audience?	**Examine the audience** The most effective texts are ones that are tailored specifically for an audience. What can you determine about the actual audience's values, attitudes, and beliefs? How does the author create an audience in the text by making assumptions about what the audience believes?
Who is the author of my text?	**Examine the author** How did the author come to this subject? Is the author an expert or an outsider?
What is the background of my text?	**Examine the context** What else has been said or written on this topic? What was going on at the time that influenced this text?
Which rhetorical appeals are used in my text?	**Analyze rhetorical appeals** Aristotle set out three primary tactics of argument: appeals to the emotions and deepest held values of the audience (pathos), appeals based on the trustworthiness of the speaker (ethos), and appeals to good reasons (logos).
How does the language and style contribute to the purpose?	**Examine the language and style** Is the style formal? informal? academic? Does the writer or speaker use humor or satire? What metaphors are used?

Keys to rhetorical analysis

Choose a text that you care about

Your paper will require close multiple readings of the text. Your interest (or lack of interest) in your text will come through in your paper.

Write a descriptive title
The title of your essay should indicate the focus of your analysis.

Check your thesis
Make sure your thesis is sensible and realistic as well as being supported by evidence and examples in the text.

Interrogate evidence
Look closely at the evidence supporting the writer's claims. Is it convincing? Are there gaps? Can it be interpreted in a different way? Is counterevidence acknowledged?

Examine underlying values, attitudes, and beliefs
When a writer or speaker neglects the audience's values, attitudes, and beliefs, the text is rarely persuasive.

Identify fallacies
Be aware when only one side of the story is being presented, when claims and accusations are grossly exaggerated, and when complex issues are oversimplified. See pages 18–19.

Identify relationships
An effective rhetorical analysis makes connections, showing how strategies in the text are responses to other texts and the larger context.

Recognize complexity
Many texts cannot be reduced to a sound bite. Successful rhetorical analyses often read between the lines to explain why a statement may be ironic or what is not being said. Readers appreciate being shown something they may not otherwise have noticed.

Writing a visual analysis

We are bombarded by images on a daily basis. They compete for our attention, urge us to buy things, and guide us on our way home from work. These visual texts frequently attempt to persuade us; to make us think, feel, or act a certain way. Yet we rarely stop to consider how they do their work.

Visual texts leave room for the audience to interpret to a greater degree than many verbal texts, which make them particularly rich subjects for analysis. For an example of visual analysis, see pages 49–51.

Components of a visual analysis

What kind of visual is it?	**Describe what you see** Is it a single image, part of a series, a sign, a building, or something else? What are the conventions for this kind of visual?
What is the image about?	**Consider the subject** What does the image depict? What is the setting? What is the purpose? Are words connected with the image?
How is the image arranged?	**Analyze the composition** What elements are most prominent? Which are repeated? Which are balanced or in contrast to each other? Which details are important?
What is the context?	**Examine the context** Who created the image? When and where did it first appear? Can you determine why it was created?
What visuals are like it?	**Look for connections** What is the genre? What kind of visual is it? What elements have you seen before? Which remind you of other visuals?

Keys to visual analysis

Choose a visual text that you care about
If an image or other visual text means something to you, you will find it easier to analyze.

Pay close attention to details
Identify the key details that keep the viewer's attention and convey meaning. Also, examine the point of view—the viewer's perspective of the subject.

Provide a frame for understanding
You will need to provide a context for understanding a visual text, giving a sense of how it is a response to events and trends going on at the time and how it was initially understood.

Go beyond the obvious
A successful visual analysis gets readers to make connections and see aspects that they otherwise would not have noticed.

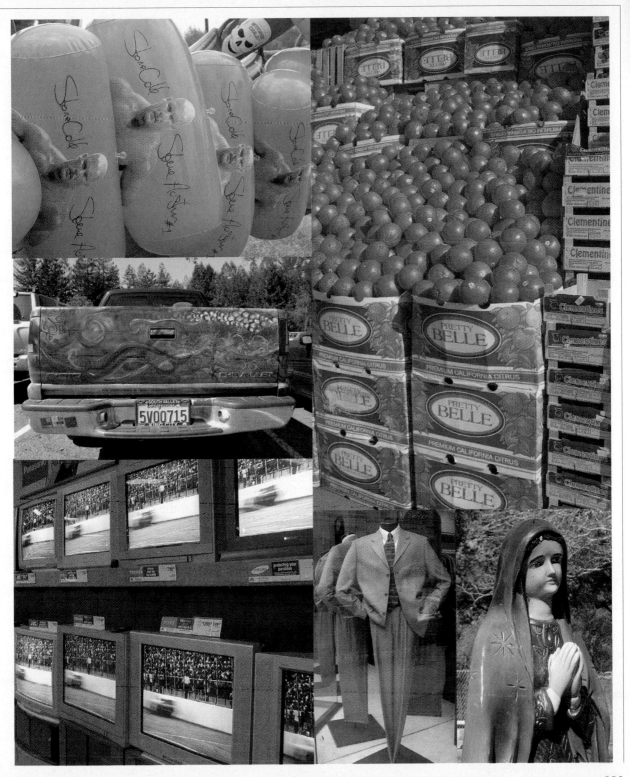

Writing a literary analysis

A literary analysis takes different forms. One form is to analyze patterns, such as how the repetition of particular images and even words contributes to the meaning. Another form is to pose a problem, such as why a particular character behaves in an odd way or why the narrator leaves out key information. Another approach is to use comparison and contrast to provide an analysis of two characters, two works of literature, or any pairs that help readers gain insight into a work. Finally, you can use one or more critical strategies as your approach. By using biographical criticism, for example, you might show how the life and times of the author shaped the literary work you are studying.

For an example of literary analysis, see pages 269–280.

Components of a literary analysis

What is my purpose?	**State an arguable thesis** Your purpose is to give your readers an arguable thesis and support-able interpretation that demonstrates you have closely read the text.
How do I support my thesis and interpretation?	**Provide as much relevant evidence as possible** You must show that your thesis and interpretation are supported by evidence from the text. Cite precise passages from the work and refer to specific details. Your instructor may ask you to use secondary sources in addition to the text.
What components should I look for?	**Use literary concepts to support your ideas** Take into account literary concepts such as character, setting, theme, motif, symbol, point of view, and imagery to express your ideas. Your analysis will likely answer such questions as who are the characters, what is the setting and what role does it play, what are themes or motifs in the text, from what point of view is the work told, what language choices are made, and what is the significance of the title?
Should I give a plot summary?	**Avoid plot summaries** Assume your readers are familiar with the literary work. Do not give plot summaries unless the summary relates directly to your thesis. Remember a plot summary is not an interpretation nor is it an arguable thesis.

Keys to literary analysis

Choose a topic that you care about
Your paper will require close multiple readings of the text. Make sure you are interested in your topic and feel that you have something to say about it.

Become familiar with your text
Convince your readers that you have closely read the work and that you have carefully annotated the work with pencil in hand as you read.

Write a descriptive title
The title of your analysis should provide clues as to your overall topic and thesis.

Evaluate and revise your thesis
Make sure your thesis is specific and significant. If you identify a pattern but say nothing about why it is important, your reader will ask "So what?" What does the pattern contribute to an overall interpretation?

Select your evidence and examples with an eye on your thesis
Make sure your evidence and examples are relevant to your thesis. Explain the significance of the evidence for your thesis.

Use the present tense
In writing about literature, refer to events in the present tense.

Document carefully
You will be quoting from the literary text and perhaps using secondary sources as well. Be sure to carefully document your sources using MLA format.

An effective analysis

A successful analysis can be generally textual or contextual in nature. But the two approaches are not mutually exclusive—in fact, most analysts consider the details of the text, but also attend to the particulars of context as well.

theguardian **Straight from the Heart**
Tim Collins

On July 11, 2005, a woman named Marie Fatayi-Williams made an immensely moving speech in London at the site where her son Anthony had been killed in a terrorist bombing four days earlier. Her speech was reported in numerous media outlets. *The Guardian,* a British newspaper, printed Fatayi-Williams's speech on July 13, with an analysis and commentary by Tim Collins. Collins considers the factors that make Fatayi-Williams's speech so powerful, and places it in a larger context of responses to terrorism.

Caught in the spotlight of history, set on the stage of a very public event, Marie Fatayi-Williams, the mother of Anthony Fatayi-Williams, 26 and missing since Thursday, appeals for news of her son. Her words are a mixture of stirring rhetoric, heartfelt appeal and a stateswoman-like vision, and so speak on many levels to the nation and the world. Her appeal is a simple one—where is my son? If he has been killed, then why? Who has gained?

Marie has found herself, as I did on the eve of the invasion of Iraq, an unwitting voice, speaking amid momentous events. Her appeal, delivered on Monday not far from Tavistock Square, where she fears her son died in the bomb attack on the number 30 bus, gives a verbal form to the whirlpool of emotions that have engulfed society as the result of last week's bombings. I suspect Marie, like myself, had no idea that her words would find such wide recognition, have fed such an acute hunger for explanation, have slaked such a thirst for expression of the sheer horror of Thursday's events.

This kind of speech is normally the preserve of the great orators, statesmen and playwrights, of Shakespeare, Churchill or Lincoln. It is often a single speech, a soliloquy or address from the steps of the gallows, that explains, inspires, exhorts and challenges. But always such addresses are crafted for effect and consciously intended to sway and influence, and often, as in the case of Shakespeare's Henry V, they are set in the mouth

Collins points out the appeal to pathos—the beliefs and values of the audience—that lies at the heart of Fatayi-Williams's speech.

Collins identifies the genre of the speech, which is usually crafted for a specific occasion. Marie's speech is remarkable because it is spontaneous.

of a long dead hero or delivered by wordsmiths who are masters of their craft. It is rare in history that such oratory is the genuine article, springing from the heart and bursting forth to an unwitting audience. In Marie's case, her speech gains its power as a vehicle of grief and loss, and of the angst of a mother who yearns for her beloved son. In my case it was the opposite emotion from which I drew inspiration—an appeal to understand, to empathize, to give courage and purpose. I was motivated by a need to warn and teach as well as to encourage. Marie's motivation is a reflection on loss and that most powerful of all emotions, a mother's love.

The form the address takes is as poignant as the language used. There is an initial explanation of the extraordinary circumstances of the loss, a cri de coeur for the innocent blood lost, a rejection of the act by its comparison to the great liberators, and the assertion that her loss is all our loss in the family of humanity. It ends with her personal grief for her flesh and blood, her hopes and pride. The language echoes verses of the Bible as well as from the Koran. It has raw passion as well as heart-rending pathos.

> Several rhetorical techniques used in the speech connect it to a larger historical tradition.

With only a photograph of her son and a sheet of paper as a prompt, Marie's words burst out with as much emotion as anger. Her speech stands in stark contrast to the pronouncements of politicians, prepared by aides and delivered from copious notes. It is indeed the raw originality and authentic angst that give the delivery such impact, the plea such effect. No knighted veteran of the Royal Shakespeare Company could deliver such an address without hours or even days of rehearsal. I know from my own experience that only momentous events can provoke such a moment, only raw emotion can inspire such a spontaneous plea. I am often asked how long it took me to write my speech, delivered to my regiment, the Royal Irish, on the eve of the invasion of Iraq on March 19, 2003, at Fort Blair Mayne camp in the Kuwaiti desert. My answer is simple—not one moment. There was no plan; I spoke without notes. For me there was only the looming specter of actual warfare and the certainty of loss and killing, and I was speaking to myself as well as to my men. I suspect for Marie there was only the yawning black void of loss, the cavern left behind in her life caused by the loss of a son who can never be replaced.

> Collins's own experience informs his understanding of what Fatayi-Williams might have been feeling. This helps assure his audience that he is qualified to comment on the meaning of her speech.

What, then, can we take from this? Marie's appeal is as important as it is momentous. Her words are as free from hatred as they are free from self-interest; it is clear that no man can give her her heart's desire—her son. I was also struck by the quiet dignity of her words, the clarity of her view and the weight of her convictions. She does not condemn, she appeals; her words act as an indictment of all war and violence, not just acts of terror but also the unnecessary aggression of nation states. Her message is simple: here is a human who only wanted to give, to succeed and to make his mother proud. Where is the victory in his death? Where is the progress in his destruction? In her own words: "What inspiration can senseless slaughter provide?"

Collins examines how Marie creates her ethos, which convinces her audience of her sincerity and lack of malice.

I am certain that Marie's appeal will go down as one of the great speeches of our new century. It will give comfort to the families and friends of the dead and injured, both of this act and no doubt, regrettably, of events still to come. It should act as a caution to statesmen and leaders, a focus for public grief and, ultimately, as a challenge to, as well as a condemnation of, the perpetrators.

Collins sees Fatayi-Williams's directness as perhaps the most important aspect of her speech. She responds to historic events in a way that personalizes them and shows their human cost.

Marie is already an icon of the loss of Thursday July 7. Having travelled from Africa to find a better life, Anthony Fatayi-Williams carried the hopes and pride of his family. Now, as his mother has traveled to London, arguably one of the most cosmopolitan and integrated cities in the world, and standing nearby a wrecked icon of that city, a red double-decker bus, she has made an appeal which is as haunting as it is relevant, as poignant as it is appealing. It is a fact that such oratory as both Marie and I produced is born of momentous events, and inspired by hope and fears in equal measure.

But Marie's appeal is also important on another level. I have long urged soldiers in conflict zones to keep communicating with the population in order to be seen as people—it is easier to kill uniforms than it is to kill people. On July 7 the suicide bombers attacked icons of a society that they hated more than they loved life, the red London bus and the tube. Marie's speech has stressed the real victims' identities. They are all of us.

Marie's speech

This is Anthony, Anthony Fatayi-Williams, 26 years old, he's missing and we fear that he was in the bus explosion ... on Thursday. We don't know. We do know from the witnesses that he left the Northern line in Euston. We know he made a call to his office at Amec at 9.41 from the NW1 area to say he could not make [it] by the tube but he would find alternative means to work.

Marie Fatayi-Williams

Since then he has not made any contact with any single person. Not New York, not Madrid, not London. There has been widespread slaughter of innocent people. There have been streams of tears, innocent tears. There have been rivers of blood, innocent blood. Death in the morning, people going to find their livelihood, death in the noontime on the highways and streets.

They are not warriors. Which cause has been served? Certainly not the cause of God, not the cause of Allah because God Almighty only gives life and is full of mercy. Anyone who has been misled, or is being misled to believe that by killing innocent people he or she is serving God should think again because it's not true. Terrorism is not the way, terrorism is not the way. It doesn't beget peace. We can't deliver peace by terrorism, never can we deliver peace by killing people. Throughout history, those people who have changed the world have done so without violence, they have won people to their cause through peaceful protest. Nelson Mandela, Martin Luther King, Mahatma Gandhi, their discipline, their self-sacrifice, their conviction made people turn towards them, to follow them. What inspiration can senseless slaughter provide? Death and destruction of young people in their prime as well as old and helpless can never be the foundations for building society.

My son Anthony is my first son, my only son, the head of my family. In African society, we hold on to sons. He has dreams and hopes and I, his mother, must fight to protect them. This is now the fifth day, five days on, and we are waiting to know what happened to him and I, his mother, I need to know what happened to Anthony. His young sisters need to know what happened, his uncles and aunties need to know what happened to Anthony, his father needs to know what happened to Anthony. Millions of my friends back home in Nigeria need to know what happened to Anthony. His friends surrounding me here, who have put this together, need to know what has happened to Anthony. I need to know, I want to protect him. I'm his mother, I will fight till I die to protect him. To protect his values and to protect his memory.

Innocent blood will always cry to God Almighty for reparation. How much blood must be spilled? How many tears shall we cry? How many mothers' hearts must be maimed? My heart is maimed. I pray I will see my son, Anthony. Why? I need to know, Anthony needs to know, Anthony needs to know, so do many other unaccounted for innocent victims, they need to know.

It's time to stop and think. We cannot live in fear because we are surrounded by hatred. Look around us today. Anthony is a Nigerian, born in London, worked in London, he is a world citizen. Here today we have Christians, Muslims, Jews, Sikhs, Hindus, all of us united in love for Anthony. Hatred begets only hatred. It is time to stop this vicious cycle of killing. We must all stand together, for our common humanity. I need to know what happened to my Anthony. He's the love of my life. My first son, my first son, 26. He tells me one day, "Mummy, I don't want to die, I don't want to die. I want to live, I want to take care of you, I will do great things for you, I will look after you, you will see what I will achieve for you. I will make you happy." And he was making me happy. I am proud of him, I am still very proud of him but I need to now where he is, I need to know what happened to him. I grieve, I am sad, I am distraught, I am destroyed.

He didn't do anything to anybody, he loved everybody so much. If what I hear is true, even when he came out of the underground he was directing people to take buses, to be sure that they were OK. Then he called his office at the same time to tell them he was running late. He was a multi-purpose person, trying to save people, trying to call his office, trying to meet his appointments. What did he then do to deserve this? Where is he, someone tell me, where is he?

How to read analyses

Make notes as you read, either in the margins, if it is your own copy, or on paper or a computer file. Circle any words or references that you don't know and look them up.

What kind of analysis is it?	• Is it a rhetorical analysis? a literary analysis? an analysis of a visual? an analysis of an object?
Where did it come from?	• Who wrote the analysis? • What do you know about the writer's background that might have influenced the analysis?
Who is the intended audience?	• What clues do you find about whom the writer had in mind as the readers? • What does the writer assume that the readers already know about the subject? • What new knowledge is the writer providing?
What is the focus of the analysis?	• What does the writer have to say about the context or background? • What does the writer have to say about how the text or object is composed?
What is the significance of the analysis?	• Does the writer make specific claims? • What did you learn or come to understand differently by reading the analysis?
How is it composed?	• How does the writer represent herself or himself? • How would you characterize the style? • If there are any photographs or other graphics, what information do they contribute?

The Collapse of Big Media: The Young and the Restless
(ESSAY)

David T. Z. Mindich

David T. Z. Mindich, a former assignment editor at CNN, is a professor of journalism and mass communication at St. Michael's College in Colchester, Vermont, and the author of *Tuned Out: Why Americans under 40 Don't Follow the News* (2005). "The Collapse of Big Media: The Young and the Restless" was published in the *Wilson Quarterly* in spring 2005.

Analyzing and Connecting

Return to these questions after you have finished reading.

1. Mindich's essay is an audience analysis in which he concludes that "Most of the young people I interviewed had almost no measurable interest in political news." First, from your experience do you agree with Mindich's claim? If you do agree, does having no measurable interest in political news mean that young people are not interested in news in general?

2. Make a log for one entire day on all the news you read, watch, or listen to: newspapers, radio, television news broadcasts, comedy reporting of news like *The Daily Show*, comic monologues commenting on events, news flashes at the bottom of other television programs, news on the Web, blogs, and personal news sources such as email. Make notes about what the news contained, and keep track of the time you spent reading, viewing, or listening. On the next day total the time for each category. Bring your analysis to class to compare with other students' totals. Do the results for the entire class surprise you in any way?

3. Watch the NBC, CBS, or ABC evening news and make a list of the ads. Then watch *The Daily Show* or another comedy news program and make a list of the ads. Compare the lists. What can you infer about the audiences for each program from the ads? What age group is being targeted? Are men or women being targeted? What income level?

4. Mindich speaks of the decline in newspaper readership and television news viewing as a cultural crisis. Do you believe this trend is something to worry about? Why or why not?

5. In the next-to-last paragraph, Mindich makes proposals that news should be a part of the school curriculum, high school seniors should take a civics test, and broadcasters should be required to produce a certain amount of children's news programming. Do you support these proposals? What suggestions do you have to raise the civic awareness of young people?

The Collapse of Big Media: The Young and the Restless

When news executives look at the decline over the past few decades in the number of people who read or watch the news, they're scared silly. But then they reassure themselves that the kids will come around. Conventional wisdom runs that as young men and women gain the trappings of adulthood—a job, a spouse, children, and a house— they tend to pick up the news habit, too. As CBS News president Andrew Heyward declared in 2002, "Time is on our side in that as you get older, you tend to get more interested in the world around you." Unfortunately for Heyward and other news executives, the evidence suggests that young people are not picking up the news habit— not in their teens, not in their twenties, not even in their thirties.

When they aren't reassuring themselves, editors and publishers are lying awake at night thinking about the dismaying trends of recent decades. In 1972, nearly half of 18-to-22-year-olds read a newspaper every day, according to research conducted by Wolfram Peiser, a scholar who studies newspaper readership. Today, less than a quarter do. That younger people are less likely to read than their elders is of grave concern, but perhaps not surprising. In fact, the baby boomers who came of age in the 1970s are less avid news consumers than their parents were. More ominous for the future of the news media, however, is Peiser's research showing that a particular age cohort's reading habits do not change much with time; in other words, as people age, they continue the news habits of their younger days. Thus, the real danger, Peiser says, is that cohort replacement builds in a general decline in newspaper reading. The deleterious effects of this phenomenon are clearly evident: In 1972, nearly three-quarters of the 34-to-37 age group read a paper daily. Those thirtysomethings have been replaced by successive crops of thirtysomethings, each reading less than its predecessor. Today, only about a third of this group reads a newspaper every day. This means that fewer parents are bringing home a newspaper or discussing current events over dinner. And fewer kids are growing up in households in which newspapers matter.

A similar decline is evident in television news viewership. In the past decade, the median age of network television news viewers has crept up from about 50 to about 60. Tune in to any network news show or CNN, and note the products hawked in the commercials: The pitches for Viagra, Metamucil, Depends, and Fixodent are not aimed at teenyboppers. Compounding the problem of a graying news audience is the proliferation of televisions within the typical household, which diminishes adult influence over what's watched. In 1970, six percent of all sixth graders had TVs in their bedrooms; today that number is an astonishing 77 percent. If you are in sixth grade and sitting alone in your room, you're probably not watching Peter Jennings.

One of the clearest signs of the sea change in news viewing habits was the uproar following the appearance last fall by Jon Stewart, host of *The Daily Show*, a parody of a news program, on CNN's *Crossfire*, a real one. With a median age of 34, *The Daily Show*'s audience is the envy of CNN, so when Stewart told *Crossfire*'s hosts that their show's predictable left/right approach to debates of current issues was "hurting America," one could have guessed that CNN bigwigs would pay attention. But who could have foreseen that CNN president Jonathan Klein would cancel *Crossfire*? "I agree wholeheartedly with Jon Stewart's overall premise," he told the *New York Times*. News executives are so desperate to get to consumers before the AARP does that they're willing to heed the advice of a comedian.

If the young (and not so young) are not reading newspapers or watching network television news, many assume that they are getting news online. Not so. Only 18 percent of Americans listed the Internet as a "primary news source" in a survey released earlier this year by the Pew Internet and American Life Project and the Pew Research Center for the People and the Press. And the theory that younger people are more reliant on the Internet for news than their elders doesn't hold up. Certainly an engaged minority of young people use the Net to get a lot of news, but studies show that most use it primarily for e-mailing, instant messaging, games, and other diversions. You only need to wander into a computer lab at your local college or high school and see what the students have on their screens for the dismal confirmation of these choices.

If the youth audience is tuned out of newspaper, television, and Internet news, what, exactly, is it tuning in to? To answer this question, I traveled the country in 2002 speaking with groups of young people about their news habits. My research confirmed what many people already suspect: that most young people tune in to situation comedies and "reality" TV to the exclusion of news. I was surprised, though, by the scope of the trend: Most of the young people I interviewed had almost no measurable interest in political news. At Brandeis University in Massachusetts, one student explained that watching the situation comedy *Friends* creates a "sense of emotional investment" and "instant gratification." This engagement contrasts with the "detachment" young people feel from public issues such as campaign finance reform and news sources such as CNN and Peter Jennings. And when the news and its purveyors are seen simply as alternative forms of entertainment, they can't compete with the likes of *CSI*, *Las Vegas*, *American Idol*, and *Fear Factor*.

The entertainment options competing with the news for the attention of the youth audience have multiplied exponentially. In the 1960s, there were only a handful of television stations in any given market. When Walter Cronkite shook the nation by declaring in a February 1968 report on the Vietnam War that the United States was "mired in stalemate," he spoke to a captive audience. New York City, for example, had only seven broadcast stations. At 10:30 p.m. on the night of Cronkite's remarks, channels 4 and 11 ran movies, channels 5 and 9 had discussion shows, and channel 7 was showing *N. Y. P. D.*, a cop show. In this media universe of limited competition, nearly 80 percent of all television viewers watched the nightly news, and from the late 1960s on, Cronkite won the lion's share of the total news audience. Today, young people can choose from hundreds of stations, less than a tenth of which are devoted to news. And that's not to mention the many competing diversions that weren't available in 1968, from video games to iPods. Amid this entertainment cornucopia, the combined network news viewership has shrunk significantly—from some 50 million nightly in the 1960s to about 25 million today. (In comparison, CNN's audience is minuscule, typically no more than a million or so viewers, while public television's *NewsHour with Jim Lehrer* generally reaches fewer than three million viewers.)

The effects of this diet are evident in how little Americans know about current events. True, Americans have been extremely uninformed for a long time. Most follow public affairs only in a vague way, and many don't bother to engage at all. In the 1950s and 1960s, at the height of the Cold War, a poll revealed that only 55 percent of Americans knew that East Germany was a communist country, and less than half knew that the Soviet Union was not part of NATO, report political scientists Michael X. Delli Carpini and Scott Keeter in *What Americans Know about Politics and Why It Matters* (1996). In short, there was never a golden age of informed citizenry. But in recent decades, Americans' ignorance has reached truly stupefying levels, particularly among young adults. A series of reports published over the past two decades by the Pew Research Center for the People and the Press (and its predecessor, the Times Mirror Center) suggest that young adults were once nearly as informed as their elders on a range of political issues. From 1944 to 1968, the interest of younger people in the news as reported in opinion surveys was less than five percent below that of the population at large. Political debates and elections in the 1940s, the Army-McCarthy hearings of the 1950s, and the Vietnam War in the 1960s generated as much interest among the young as among older people. But Watergate in the 1970s was the last in this series of defining events to draw general public attention. (Decades later, in 2001, the bombing of the World Trade Center towers revived general public engagement, at least for a few weeks.) Soon after Watergate, surveys began to show flagging interest in current affairs among younger people.

There is no single explanation for this sudden break. Many of the young people I spoke with in doing my research were disaffected with the political process and believed that it was completely insulated from public pressure. Why, in that case, keep up with public affairs? The blurring line between entertainment and journalism, along with corporate consolidation of big media companies, has also bred in some minds a deep skepticism about the news media's offerings. At bottom, however, the sense of community has declined as Americans are able to live increasingly isolated lives, spending long hours commuting to work and holing up in suburban homes cocooned from the rest of the world.

The extent of this withdrawal from civic involvement is evident in a poll conducted during the height of the 2004 Democratic presidential primaries. In response to the question, "Do you happen to know which of the presidential candidates served as an army general?" about 42 percent of the over-50 crowd could name Wesley Clark. Only 13 percent of those under 30 could. While these results reveal a general lack of political knowledge across ages, they also underscore the growing gap between ages.

The shrinking audience for news is undermining the health of many major news media outlets. The most recent symptom was the revelation last year that a number of major newspapers, notably the *Chicago Sun-Times* and New York's *Newsday*, had cooked their books, inflating circulation figures in order to mask declines and keep advertising revenues from falling. More insidious—and less widely decried—is the industry-wide practice of bolstering profits by reducing news content. In newspapers, this is done by cutting back on the number of reporters covering state government, Washington, and foreign affairs, and by shrinking the space in the paper devoted to news. The news media are, in a very real sense, making our world smaller. On the broadcast networks, this shrinkage is easily measurable: In 1981, a 30-minute nightly newscast on CBS, minus commercials, was 23 minutes and 20 seconds, according to Leonard Downie, Jr., and Robert G. Kaiser's *The News about the News: American Journalism in Peril* (2002). In 2000, the same newscast was down to 18 minutes and 20 seconds. That's a lot of missing news.

The failing health of the nation's news media is not only a symptom of Americans' low levels of engagement in political life. It is a threat to political life itself. "The role of the press," writes news media critic James W. Carey, "is simply to make sure that in the short run we don't get screwed." Independent, fair, and accurate reporting is what gives "We the People" our check on power. Reporters dig up corruption and confront power; they focus the public's attention on government policies and actions that are unwise, unjust, or simply ineffective. It was the news media that exposed the Watergate burglary and cover-up engineered by Richard Nixon, sparked the investigation of the Iran-Contra affair during the watch of Ronald Reagan and George H. W. Bush, ferreted out Bill

Clinton's Whitewater dealings, and turned a searchlight on George W. Bush's extrajudicial arrests of American citizens suspected of terrorism.

A shrinking audience impairs the news media's ability to carry out their watchdog role. It also permits the powers that be to undermine journalism's legitimate functions. Where was the public outrage when it was revealed that the current Bush administration had secretly paid journalists to carry its water, or when the White House denied a press pass to a real journalist, Maureen Dowd of the *New York Times*, and gave one to a political hack who wrote for purely partisan outlets using a fake identity? The whole notion of the news media as the public's watchdog, once an unquestioned article of the American civic faith, is now in jeopardy. A recent study commissioned by the John S. and James L. Knight Foundation showed that more than a third of high school students feel that newspaper articles should be vetted by the federal government before publication.

If we are entering a post-journalism age—in which the majority of Americans, young and old, have little interaction with mainstream news media—the most valuable thing we are losing is the marketplace of ideas that newspapers and news broadcasts uniquely provide, that place where views clash and the full range of democratic choices is debated. You usually don't get that on a blog. You don't get that in the left-leaning *Nation* or on right-wing talk shows. But any newspaper worth its salt, and there are plenty, presents a variety of views, including ones antithetical to its editorial page positions. These papers are hardly immune from criticism—they sometimes err, get sloppy, or succumb to partisan or ideological bias—but they do strive to be accurate and independent sources of fact and opinion, and more often than not they fulfill that indispensable public function.

America's newspapers and television news divisions aren't going to save themselves by competing with reality shows and soap operas. The appetite for news, and for engagement with civic life itself, must be nurtured and promoted, and it's very much in the public interest to undertake the task. It's not the impossible assignment it may seem. During the course of my research, I met a group of boys in New Orleans who were very unlikely consumers of news: They were saturated with television programs and video games, they were poor, and they were in eighth grade. Yet they were all reading the *New York Times* online. Why? Because one of their teachers had assigned the newspaper to them to read when they were in sixth grade, and the habit stuck. There's no reason why print and broadcast news shouldn't be a bigger part of the school curriculum, or why there shouldn't be a short civics/current affairs section on the SAT for college-bound students, or why all high school seniors shouldn't have to take a nonbinding version of the civics test given to immigrants who want to become U.S. citizens. And why shouldn't broadcasters be required to produce a certain amount of children's news programming in return for their access to the public airwaves? These are only the most obvious possibilities.

Reporters, editors, producers, and media business executives will all need to make their own adjustments to meet the demands of new times and new audiences, but only by reaching a collective judgment about the value and necessity of vigorous news media in American democracy can we hope to keep our public watchdogs on guard and in good health.

Race, Gender, and Civilization at the Columbian Exposition

(ESSAY)

Gail Bederman

Gail Bederman's book *Manliness and Civilization* examines the connections between gender, violence, and power in America. The first chapter, titled "Remaking Manhood through Race and Civilization," performs a detailed reading of the text and context of the World's Columbian Exposition in Chicago, Illinois, in 1893. In this excerpt, Bederman explains the fair's layout as a physical demonstration of the divisions between black and white, civilized and savage, that dominated public discourse at the time.

Analyzing and Connecting

Return to these questions after you have finished reading.

1. Note each piece of evidence Bederman uses to show the connection between whiteness and the fair's concept of civilization. What types of evidence does she provide? Why does she provide more than one kind of evidence? Does she provide enough evidence to convince you that the connection is more than a coincidence?

2. Bederman's book traces the lengthy history of American discussions about race, gender, and civilization. Given that there are many more overt examples of racism in America's history, why do you suppose Bederman chose to write about this event, the 1893 World's Columbian Exposition?

3. Note the physical descriptions of the fair in the fifth paragraph of the excerpt. How do these help the reader understand Bederman's argument?

4. Consider the passage from the *New York Times* Bederman quotes in the seventh paragraph. It provides her an opportunity for detailed textual analysis. What do you think of the quote? Without Bederman's analysis, would the quote strike you as significant in any way? How so?

5. Overall, how believable do you find Bederman's claim in this passage? What do you think about the evidence she presents to support it?

The millennial perfection embodied in the exposition was composed of equal parts white supremacy and powerful manhood. As Robert Rydell has shown, organizers divided the World's Fair into two racially specific areas. The White City depicted the millennial advancement of white civilization, while the Midway Plaisance, in contrast, presented the undeveloped barbarism of uncivilized, dark races. The civilized White City was intended to suggest a millennial future—what a city might look like as advanced white races worked toward a perfect civilization. Organizers employed the most eminent architects and city planners; and visitors commented upon the White City's breathtaking perfection.

In the White City, white racial perfection was repeatedly connected to powerful manhood. The White City's focal point was the majestic Court of Honor, a formal basin almost a half-mile long, surrounded by massive white beaux arts buildings. "Honorable," according to the 1890 *Century Dictionary*, was a synonym for "manly," and contemporaries would not have missed the Court's association with manhood. The seven huge buildings framing the Court of Honor represented seven aspects of civilization's highest scientific, artistic, and technological achievements—Manufactures, Mines, Agriculture, Art, Administrations, Machinery, and Electricity. All were presented as the domain of civilized white *men*. These buildings housed thousands of enormous engines, warships, trains, machines, and armaments—all self-consciously presented as artifacts built and employed by men, only. The White City also glorified the masculine world of commerce, exhibiting the most advanced products and manufacturing processes—"dynamos and rock drills, looms and wallpaper"—and housing these exhibits in magnificent white temples

Opening of the World's Columbian Exposition, Chicago, 1893.

BEDERMAN: RACE, GENDER, AND CIVILIZATION AT THE COLUMBIAN EXPOSITION

Egyptian dancing girl, World's Columbian Exposition, Chicago, 1893.

("World's Columbian" 169). Thus, by celebrating civilization, the organizers celebrated the power of white manhood. Men alone, as they saw it, were the agents who lifted their race toward the millennial perfection God and evolution intended for them. As one poet put it, the White City was "A Vision of Strong Manhood and Perfection of Society" (qtd. in Rydell 37).

The men who organized the Columbian Exposition made certain that the White City's advanced civilization appeared overwhelmingly male. They firmly excluded women's products from most of the exhibits, even though a large group of upper-class white women had worked tirelessly—if fruitlessly—to gain women equal representation. In 1889, over one hundred prominent women including Susan B. Anthony and the wives of three Supreme Court justices had petitioned Congress to name some women to the exposition's governing commission (Weimann 31). Congress refused. Instead, it established a "Board of Lady Managers." (Even the title was patronizing and ridiculous, many women complained [Weimann 36].) Congress gave them almost no authority, yet through persistent efforts the Lady Managers were able to make themselves an important part of the exposition. Led by Bertha Palmer, they organized and built one of the most well-attended exhibits in the White City, the Woman's Building.

The Columbian Exposition depicted white women as marginal to the White City; but at least white women got a building and an official Board of Lady Managers. Men and women of color, on the other hand, were not marginal but absent from the White City. Although African American men and women objected vehemently to this policy, the white organizers—including the Board of Lady Managers—ignored them. In the Columbian Exposition's schema of hegemonic civilization, only whites were civilized. All other races were uncivilized and belonged not in the White City but on the Midway Plaisance.

As Robert Rydell has demonstrated, the Midway specialized in spectacles of barbarous races—"authentic" villages of Samoans, Egyptians, Dahomans, Turks, and other exotic peoples, populated by actual imported "natives." Guidebooks advised visitors to visit the Midway only after visiting the White City, in order to fully appreciate the contrast between the civilized White City and the uncivilized native villages (Rydell 61–62). Where the White City spread out in all directions from the Court of Honor, emphasizing the complexity of manly civilization, the Midway's attractions were organized linearly down a broad avenue, providing a lesson in racial hierarchy. Visitors entering the Midway from the White City would first pass the civilized German and Irish villages, proceed past the barbarous Turkish, Arabic, and Chinese villages, and finish by viewing the savage American Indians and Dahomans. "What an opportunity was here afforded to the scientific mind to descend the spiral of evolution," enthused the *Chicago Tribune*, "tracing humanity in its highest places down almost to its animalistic origins" (qtd. in Rydell 65).

Where the White City celebrated the white man's civilization as outstandingly manly, the Midway depicted savagery and barbarism as lacking manliness entirely. In the Persian, Algerian, Turkish, and Egyptian villages, for example, unmanly dark-skinned men cajoled customers to shed manly restraint and savor their countrywomen's sensuous dancing ("Sights" 653). Male audiences ogling scantily clad belly dancers could have it both ways, simultaneously relishing the dancers' suggestiveness and basking in their own sense of civilized superiority to the swarthy men hawking tickets outside, unashamedly selling their countrywomen's charms ("World's Columbian" 169). Men who had just visited the White City would be especially conscious of their own racially superior manliness. Civilized womanliness, too, was absent on the Midway. Although few American women deigned to see the exotic belly dancers, they understood the message: White woman's place in civilization might be marginal, but at least it was moral and safe. Under barbarism, however, women experienced not respect and equality but sexual danger and indecent exploitation.

Least manly of all the Midway's denizens, according to many commentators, were the savage Dahomans, who seemed to lack gender difference entirely. *The New York Times* described "The Dahomey gentleman, (or perhaps it is a Dahomey lady, for the distinction is not obvious,) who may be seen at almost any hour . . . clad mainly in a brief grass skirt and capering nimbly to the lascivious pleasings of an unseen tom-tom pounded within . . . There are several dozen of them of assorted sexes, as one gradually makes out" ("Wonderful"). Asserting that he could only "gradually" make out the difference between the sexes, the columnist suggests that savages' sexual difference was so indistinct that the Dahomans might have a larger "assortment" of sexes than the usual two. Uncivilized, and thus unable to evince the self-restraint of true manliness, the Dahoman (who was clearly no "gentleman," despite the ironic appellation) publicly cavorts to the drums "lascivious pleasings." He even wears "skirts."

In short, the Columbian Exposition demonstrated, in a variety of ways, that "nonwhite" and "uncivilized" denoted "unmanly" and, conversely, that whiteness and civilization denoted powerful manhood. Whether they looked like women or pandered their women's sexuality, the "savage" and "barbarous" men of the Midway served as reminders that, in comparison, white American men were far more manly. At the same time, by relishing the exotic native dancing girls, white American men could savor their own primitive masculinity. Either way, the Midway's deployment of civilization allowed white men to see their own manhood as especially powerful.

Works Cited

"Manly." <u>Century Dictionary: An Encyclopedic Lexicon of the English Language</u>. 1890.

Rydell, Robert W. <u>All the World's a Fair: Visions of Empire at American International Expositions, 1876–1916</u>. Chicago: U of Chicago P, 1984.

"Sights at the Fair." <u>Century Magazine</u> 46 (5 Sept. 1893): 651–54.

Weimann, Jeanne Madeline. <u>The Fair Women</u>. Chicago: Academy Chicago, 1981.

"Wonderful Place for Fun," <u>New York Times</u> 19 June 1893: 9.

"The World's Columbian Exposition—A View from the Ferris Wheel." <u>Scientific American</u> 69 (9 Sept. 1893): 165–74.

The Ray and Maria Stata Center, Massachusetts Institute of Technology

(BUILDING)

Frank Gehry

Frank Gehry, born in Toronto in 1929, has become one of most famous architects in the world for his sculptural approach to building design. His buildings feature shiny, curved surfaces, bizarre color combinations, and warped forms. One of his most famous and most controversial buildings is The Ray and Maria Stata Center on the Massachusetts Institute of Technology campus, which opened in March 2004. Housed in the Stata Center are the Computer Science and Artificial Intelligence Laboratory, the Laboratory for Information and Decision Systems, and the Department of Linguistics and Philosophy.

The Stata Center has been controversial from the start. *The Kaplan College Guide* describes MIT has having the "hottest" architecture of any campus. *Boston Globe* architecture columnist Robert Campbell wrote that "the Stata is always going to look unfinished. It also looks as if it's about to collapse. Columns tilt at scary angles. Walls teeter, swerve, and collide in random curves and angles. Materials change wherever you look: brick, mirror-surface steel, brushed aluminum, brightly colored paint, corrugated metal. Everything looks improvised, as if thrown up at the last moment. That's the point. The Stata's appearance is a metaphor for the freedom, daring, and creativity of the research that's supposed to occur inside it." But others have criticized the Stata Center as poorly designed for day-to-day use, extremely overpriced (the official cost is $283.5 million), and garishly ugly.

Analyzing and Connecting

Return to these questions after you have looked at the images of the Stata Center.

1. A campus joke goes "No worry at Stata about earthquakes—it already had one." Why do you think MIT wanted a building so different and whimsical on its campus?

2. Some of the world's best-loved structures including the Statue of Liberty and the Eiffel Tower were hated by many when they were erected. Why do people have such strong feelings about buildings and statues when they first appear, only to accept them soon afterwards?

3. The Stata Center was built on the site of Building 20, which was hastily constructed during World War II for research on radar. Building 20 was plain and ugly, yet it has been claimed that it was the most productive building for research in the history of the United States. Does the architecture of a building influence what happens inside? Think of examples that you have experienced.

4. Does your campus or city have a "signature" building? What does that building say about your school or your city?

GEHRY: THE RAY AND MARIA STATA CENTER

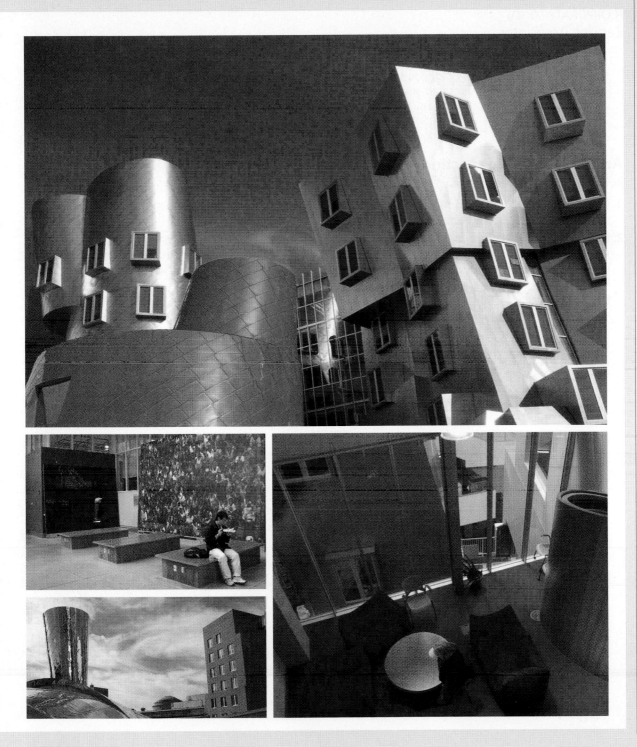

Federal Express Logo

(CORPORATE LOGO)

Landor Associates

Federal Express, founded in 1973, created a new market for rapid delivery of packages and documents. By 1993 the company had greatly expanded and operated around the world. Federal Express hired the design firm, Landor Associates, to create a new logo. By this time Federal Express had become universally known as FedEx, which Landor chose to use for the new logo. The FedEx logo quickly became one of the most recognizable in the world.

Analyzing and Connecting

Return to these questions after you have finished looking at the logos.

1. Make a list of all the logos you can think of. What makes these logos memorable?

2. Logos were originally designed to distinguish products and companies. Notice how many now look similar. Why do you think so many logos look alike?

3. Which logos suggest what a company actually does?

4. Your school probably has a logo. How frequently do you see the logo? What message does the logo convey about your school?

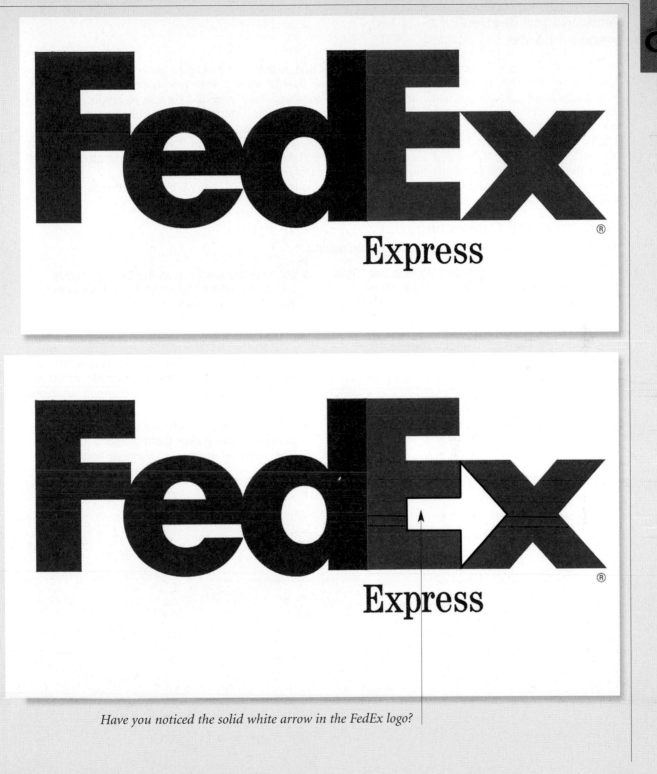

Have you noticed the solid white arrow in the FedEx logo?

Volkswagen Beetle

(PRODUCT DESIGN)

The Volkswagen Type 1, better known as the Beetle or Bug, is the most produced car in history. From 1938 until the last original Beetle came off an assembly line in Puebla, Mexico, over twenty-one million were built. The Beetle began in Nazi Germany, when Adolf Hitler commissioned Ferdinand Porsche to produce a car for common people. Only a handful were produced before World War II started in 1939. Volkswagen was soon back in production after the war, and by 1954, the number of Beetles passed a million. Volkswagen began shipping cars to the United States at a time when American cars were big and boxy. The VW Beetle was just the opposite—small and rounded, inexpensive, and three times as fuel efficient. Beetles dominated the small-car market until Japanese imports showed up in large numbers in the mid-1970s.

More than the story of a car, however, the Beetle demonstrates how what we buy reflects cultural attitudes and values.

Analyzing and Connecting

Return to these questions after you have finished reading.

1. Volkswagen ads in the United States in the 1960s appealed to simplicity—simple shape, simple technology—which grew out of long-standing American values of honesty, economy, and lack of pretense. Look at automobile ads today, both in print and on television. What values do they appeal to?

2. Your campus may have a building that is better known by a nickname than its official name. Is the building liked or disliked by students? How does the nickname change the image of the building? For example, is it more friendly or less friendly?

3. Look up the word *bug* in the *Oxford English Dictionary*, which traces the histories of words. Your library has the print OED and may allow access through the library's Web site. How has the meaning of *bug* changed over time? Think about how *bug* is used today. For example, a common saying among computer programmers is "It's not a bug, it's a feature." Identify examples of other words such as *pimp* that have changed meanings in recent years.

4. Think of other products that we find cute and loveable. What makes them cute and loveable? Does advertising promote these associations?

When Adolf Hitler became Chancellor of Germany in 1933, he declared that a centerpiece of Nazism would be the motorization of the country. He asked Ferdinand Porsche to design a car that would be affordable for everyone.

Clever advertising helped make the Beetle a hit in the 1960s. The American advertising firm Doyle Dane Bernbach (DDB) began a campaign in 1959 that emphasized the differences between the Beetle and bulky American cars that changed designs yearly.

VOLKSWAGEN BEETLE

In 1968, Walt Disney's *The Love Bug* created a new generation of Beetle fans and led to a series of *Herbie* sequels.

Beetles became part of the counterculture of the 1960s. Many were hand-painted and customized in various ways, even adding fins that mocked American cars.

Misery has enough company.
Dare to be happy.

In 1998 Volkswagen launched the New Beetle, which benefited from the lovable image of the original Beetle.

Everyday Use

(SHORT STORY)

Alice Walker

Alice Walker was born in Eatonville, Georgia, in 1944, and won a scholarship in 1961 to Spelman College in Atlanta. Her third novel, *The Color Purple*, published in 1982, became a best seller, won a Pulitzer Prize, and established her reputation as one of the finest living writers in America. "Everyday Use" is one of her best-loved short stories.

Analyzing and Connecting

Return to these questions after you have finished reading.

1. Who is the narrator in the story? How does the point of view of the narrator affect the information we are given in the story?

2. Describe each of the main characters in the story. Use specific evidence from the text to support your descriptions. Which character do you find the most sympathetic? Explain.

3. The idea of heritage plays a big role in the story. Compare and contrast the meaning of heritage from each of the main characters' point of view.

4. Another important theme in the story is the idea of intergenerational conflict. Read the story paying particular attention to examples of this conflict and describe the conflict in a few sentences.

5. Explain the symbolic meaning the quilts serve in the story.

6. Why do you think the story is titled "Everyday Use"?

Note: See page 278 for a student's analysis of the use of symbolism in "Everyday Use."

Everyday Use

For your grandmama

I will wait for her in the yard that Maggie and I made so clean and wavy yesterday afternoon. A yard like this is more comfortable than most people know. It is not just a yard. It is like an extended living room. When the hard clay is swept clean as a floor and the fine sand around the edges lined with tiny, irregular grooves anyone can come and sit and look up into the elm tree and wait for the breezes that never come inside the house.

Maggie will be nervous until after her sister goes: she will stand hopelessly in corners, homely and ashamed of the burn scars down her arms and legs, eyeing her sister with a mixture of envy and awe. She thinks her sister has held life always in the palm of one hand, that "no" is a word the world never learned to say to her.

You've no doubt seen those TV shows where the child who has "made it" is confronted, as a surprise, by her own mother and father, tottering in weakly from backstage. (A pleasant surprise, of course: What would they do if parent and child came on the show only to curse out and insult each other?) On TV mother and child embrace and smile into each other's faces. Sometimes the mother and father weep, the child wraps them in her arms and leans across the table to tell how she would not have made it without their help. I have seen these programs.

Sometimes I dream a dream in which Dee and I are suddenly brought together on a TV program of this sort. Out of a dark and soft-seated limousine I am ushered into a bright room filled with many people. There I meet a smiling, gray, sporty man like Johnny Carson who shakes my hand and tells me what a fine girl I have. Then we are on the stage and Dee is embracing me with tears in her eyes. She pins on my dress a large orchid, even though she has told me once that she thinks orchids are tacky flowers.

In real life I am a large, big-boned woman with rough, man-working hands. In the winter I wear flannel nightgowns to bed and overalls during the day. I can kill and clean a hog as mercilessly as a man. My fat keeps me hot in zero weather. I can work outside all day, breaking ice to get water for washing. I can eat pork liver cooked over the open fire minutes after it comes steaming from the hog. One winter I knocked a bull calf straight in the brain between the eyes with a sledge hammer and had the meat hung up to chill before nightfall. But of course all this does not show on television. I am the way my daughter would want me to be: a hundred pounds lighter, my skin like an uncooked barley pancake. My hair glistens in the hot bright lights. Johnny Carson has much to do to keep up with my quick and witty tongue.

But that is a mistake. I know even before I wake up. Who ever knew a Johnson with a quick tongue? Who can even imagine me looking a strange white man in the eye? It seems to me I have talked to them always with one foot raised in flight, with my head turned in whichever way is farthest from them. Dee, though. She would always look anyone in the eye. Hesitation was no part of her nature.

"How do I look, Mama?" Maggie says, showing just enough of her thin body enveloped in pink skirt and red blouse for me to know she's there, almost hidden by the door.

"Come out into the yard," I say.

Have you ever seen a lame animal, perhaps a dog run over by some careless person rich enough to own a car, sidle up to someone who is ignorant enough to be kind to him? That is the way my Maggie walks. She has been like this, chin on chest, eyes on ground, feet in shuffle, ever since the fire that burned the other house to the ground.

Dee is lighter than Maggie, with nicer hair and a fuller figure. She's a woman now, though sometimes I forget. How long ago was it that the other house burned? Ten, twelve years? Sometimes I can still hear the flames and feel Maggie's arms sticking to me, her hair smoking and her dress falling off her in little black papery flakes. Her eyes seemed stretched open, blazed open by the flames reflected in them. And Dee. I see her standing off under the sweet gum tree she used to dig gum out of; a look of concentration on her face as she watched the last dingy gray board of the house fall in toward the red-hot brick chimney. Why don't you do a dance around the ashes? I'd wanted to ask her. She had hated the house that much.

I used to think she hated Maggie, too. But that was before we raised the money, the church and me, to send her to Augusta to school. She used to read to us without pity; forcing words, lies, other folks' habits, whole lives upon us two, sitting trapped and ignorant underneath her voice. She washed us in a river of make-believe, burned us with a lot of knowledge we didn't necessarily need to know. Pressed us to her with the serious way she read, to shove us away at just the moment, like dimwits, we seemed about to understand.

Dee wanted nice things. A yellow organdy dress to wear to her graduation from high school; black pumps to match a green suit she'd made from an old suit somebody gave me. She was determined to stare down any disaster in her efforts. Her eyelids would not flicker for minutes at a time. Often I fought off the temptation to shake her. At sixteen she had a style of her own: and knew what style was.

I never had an education myself. After second grade the school was closed down. Don't ask me why: in 1927 colored asked fewer questions than they do now. Sometimes Maggie reads to me. She stumbles along good-naturedly but can't see well. She knows she is not bright. Like good looks and money, quickness passed her by. She will marry John Thomas (who has mossy teeth in an earnest face) and then I'll be free to sit here and I guess just sing church songs to myself. Although I never was a good singer. Never could carry a tune. I was a ways better at a man's job. I used to love to milk till I was hoofed in the side in '49. Cows are soothing and slow and don't bother you, unless you try to milk them the wrong way.

I have deliberately turned my back on the house. It is three rooms, just like the one that burned, except the roof is tin; they don't make shingle roofs any more. There are no real windows, just some holes cut in the sides, like the portholes in a ship, but not round and not square, with rawhide holding the shutters up on the outside. This house is in a pasture, too, like the other one. No doubt when Dee sees it she will want to tear it down. She wrote me once that no matter where we "choose" to live, she will manage to come see us. But she will never bring her friends. Maggie and I thought about this and Maggie asked me, "Mama, when did Dee ever *have* any friends?"

She had a few. Furtive boys in pink shirts hanging about on washday after school. Nervous girls who never laughed. Impressed with her they worshiped the well-turned phrase, the cute shape, the scalding humor that erupted like bubbles in lye. She read to them.

When she was courting Jimmy T she didn't have much time to pay to us, but turned all her faultfinding power on him. He *flew* to marry a cheap city girl from a family of ignorant flashy people. She hardly had time to recompose herself.

When she comes I will meet—but there they are!

Maggie attempts to make a dash for the house, in her shuffling way, but I stay her with my hand. "Come back here," I say. And she stops and tries to dig a well in the sand with her toe.

It is hard to see them clearly through the strong sun. But even the first glimpse of leg out of the car tells me it is Dee. Her feet were always neat-looking, as if God himself had shaped them with a certain style. From the other side of the car comes a short, stocky man. Hair is all over his head a foot long and hanging from his chin like a kinky mule tail. I hear Maggie suck in her breath. "Uhnnnh," is what it sounds like. Like when you see the wriggling end of a snake just in front of your foot on the road. "Uhnnnh."

Dee next. A dress down to the ground, in this hot weather. A dress so loud hurts my eyes. There are yellows and oranges enough to throw back the light of the sun. I feel my whole face warming from the heat waves it throws out. Earrings, too, gold and hanging down to her shoulders. Bracelets dangling and making noises when she moves her arm up to shake the folds of the dress out of her armpits. The dress is loose and flows, and as she walks closer, I like it. I hear Maggie go "Uhnnnh" again. It is her sister's hair. It stands straight up like the wool on a sheep. It is black as night and around the edges are two long pigtails that rope about like small lizards disappearing behind her ears.

"Wa-su-zo-Tean-o!" she says, coming on in that gliding way the dress makes her move. The short stocky fellow with the hair to his navel is all grinning and he follows up with "Asalamalakim, my mother and sister!" He moves to hug Maggie but she falls back, right up against the back of my chair. I feel her trembling there and when I look up I see the perspiration falling off her chin.

"Don't get up," says Dee. Since I am stout it takes something of a push. You can see me trying to move a second or two before I make it. She turns, showing white heels through her sandals, and goes back to the car. Out she peeks next with a Polaroid. She stoops down quickly and lines up picture after picture of me sitting there in front of the house with Maggie cowering behind me. She never takes a shot without making sure the house is included. When a cow comes nibbling around the edge of the yard she snaps it and me and Maggie *and* the house. Then she puts the Polaroid in the back seat of the car, and comes up and kisses me on the forehead.

Meanwhile Asalamalakim is going through the motions with Maggie's hand. Maggie's hand is as limp as a fish, and probably as cold, despite the sweat, and she keeps trying to pull it back. It looks like Asalamalakim wants to shake hands but wants to do it fancy. Or maybe he don't know how people shake hands. Anyhow, he soon gives up on Maggie.

"Well," I say. "Dee."

"No, Mama," she says. "Not 'Dee,' Wangero Leewanika Kemanjo!"

"What happened to 'Dee'?" I wanted to know.

"She's dead," Wangero said. "I couldn't bear it any longer, being named after the people who oppress me."

"You know as well as me you was named after your aunt Dicie," I said. Dicie is my sister. She named Dee. We called her "Big Dee" after Dee was born.

"But who was *she* named after?" asked Wangero.

"I guess after Grandma Dee," I said.

"And who was she named after?" asked Wangero.

"Her mother," I said, and saw Wangero was getting tired. "That's about as far back as I can trace it," I said. Though, in fact, I probably could have carried it back beyond the Civil War through the branches.

"Well," said Asalamalakim, "there you are."

"Uhnnnh," I heard Maggie say.

"There I was not," I said, "before 'Dicie' cropped up in our family, so why should I try to trace it that far back?"

He just stood there grinning, looking down on me like somebody inspecting a Model A car. Every once in a while he and Wangero sent eye signals over my head.

"How do you pronounce this name?" I asked.

"You don't have to call me by it if you don't want to," said Wangero.

"Why shouldn't I?" I asked. "If that's what you want us to call you, we'll call you."

"I know it might sound awkward at first," said Wangero.

"I'll get used to it," I said. "Ream it out again."

Well, soon we got the name out of the way. Asalamalakim had a name twice as long and three times as hard. After I tripped over it two or three times he told me to just call him Hakim-a-barber. I wanted to ask him was he a barber, but I didn't really think he was, so I didn't ask.

"You must belong to those beef-cattle peoples down the road," I said. They said "Asalamalakim" when they met you, too, but they didn't shake hands. Always too busy: feeding the cattle, fixing the fences, putting up salt-lick shelters, throwing down hay. When the white folks poisoned some of the herd the men stayed up all night with rifles in their hands. I walked a mile and a half just to see the sight.

Hakim-a-barber said, "I accept some of their doctrines, but farming and raising cattle is not my style." (They didn't tell me, and I didn't ask, whether Wangero (Dee) had really gone and married him.)

We sat down to eat and right away he said he didn't eat collards and pork was unclean. Wangero, though, went on through the chitlins and corn bread, the greens and everything else. She talked a blue streak over the sweet potatoes. Everything delighted her. Even the fact that we still used the benches her daddy made for the table when we couldn't afford to buy chairs.

"Oh, Mama!" she cried. Then turned to Hakim-a-barber. "I never knew how lovely these benches are. You can feel the rump prints," she said, running her hands underneath her and along the bench. Then she gave a sigh and her hand closed over Grandma Dee's butter dish. "That's it!" she said. "I knew there was something I wanted to ask you if I could have." She jumped up from the table and went over in the corner where the churn stood, the milk in it clabber by now. She looked at the churn and looked at it.

"This churn top is what I need," she said. "Didn't Uncle Buddy whittle it out of a tree you all used to have?"

"Yes," I said.

"Uh huh," she said happily. "And I want the dasher, too."

"Uncle Buddy whittle that, too?" asked the barber.

Dee (Wangero) looked up at me.

"Aunt Dee's first husband whittled the dash," said Maggie so low you almost couldn't hear her. "His name was Henry, but they called him Stash."

"Maggie's brain is like an elephant's," Wangero said, laughing. "I can use the churn top as a centerpiece for the alcove table," she said, sliding a plate over the churn, "and I'll think of something artistic to do with the dasher."

When she finished wrapping the dasher the handle stuck out. I took it for a moment in my hands. You didn't even have to look close to see where hands pushing the dasher up and down to make butter had left a kind of sink on the wood. In fact, there were a lot of small sinks; you could see where thumbs and fingers had sunk into the wood. It was beautiful light yellow wood, from a tree that grew in the yard where Big Dee and Stash had lived.

After dinner Dee (Wangero) went to the trunk at the foot of my bed and started rifling through it. Maggie hung back in the kitchen over the dishpan. Out came Wangero with two quilts. They had been pieced by Grandma Dee and then Big Dee and me had hung them on the quilt frames on the front porch and quilted them. One was in the Lone Star pattern. The other was Walk Around the Mountain. In both of them were scraps of dresses Grandma Dee had worn fifty and more years ago. Bits and pieces of Grandpa Jarrell's paisley shirts. And one teeny faded blue piece, about the size of a penny matchbox, that was from Great Grandpa Ezra's uniform that he wore in the Civil War.

"Mama," Wangero said sweet as a bird. "Can I have these old quilts?"

I heard something fall in the kitchen, and a minute later the kitchen door slammed.

"Why don't you take one or two of the others?" I asked. "These old things was just done by me and Big Dee from some tops your grandma pieced before she died."

"No," said Wangero. "I don't want those. They are stitched around the borders by machine."

"That'll make them last better," I said.

"That's not the point," said Wangero. "These are all pieces of dresses Grandma used to wear. She did all this stitching by hand. Imagine!" She held the quilts securely in her arms, stroking them.

"Some of the pieces, like those lavender ones, come from old clothes her mother handed down to her," I said, moving up to touch the quilts. Dee (Wangero) moved back just enough so that I couldn't reach the quilts. They already belonged to her.

"Imagine!" she breathed again, clutching them closely to her bosom.

"The truth is," I said, "I promised to give them quilts to Maggie, for when she marries John Thomas."

She gasped like a bee had stung her.

"Maggie can't appreciate these quilts!" she said. "She'd probably be backward enough to put them to everyday use."

"I reckon she would," I said. "God knows I been saving 'em for long enough with nobody using 'em. I hope she will!" I didn't want to bring up how I had offered Dee (Wangero) a quilt when she went away to college. Then she had told me they were old-fashioned, out of style.

"But they're *priceless*!" she was saying now, furiously; for she has a temper. "Maggie would put them on the bed and in five years they'd be in rags. Less than that!"

"She can always make some more," I said. "Maggie knows how to quilt."

Dee (Wangero) looked at me with hatred. "You just will not understand. The point is these quilts, *these* quilts!"

"Well," I said, stumped. "What would *you* do with them!"

"Hang them," she said. As if that was the only thing you *could* do with quilts.

Maggie by now was standing in the door. I could almost hear the sound her feet made as they scraped over each other.

"She can have them, Mama," she said, like somebody used to never winning anything, or having anything reserved for her. "I can 'member Grandma Dee without the quilts."

I looked at her hard. She had filled her bottom lip with checkerberry snuff and it gave her face a kind of dopey, hangdog look. It was Grandma Dee and Big Dee who taught her how to quilt herself. She stood there with her scarred hands hidden in the folds of her skirt. She looked at her sister with something like fear but she wasn't mad at her. This was Maggie's portion. This was the way she knew God to work.

When I looked at her like that something hit me in the top of my head and ran down to the soles of my feet. Just like when I'm in church and the spirit of God touches me and I get happy and shout. I did something I never had done before: hugged Maggie to me, then dragged her on into the room, snatched the quilts out of Miss Wangero's hands and dumped them into Maggie's lap. Maggie just sat there on my bed with her mouth open.

"Take one or two of the others," I said to Dee.

But she turned without a word and went out to Hakim-a-barber.

"You just don't understand," she said, as Maggie and I came out to the car.

"What don't I understand?" I wanted to know.

"Your heritage," she said. And then she turned to Maggie, kissed her, and said, "You ought to try to make something of yourself, too, Maggie. It's really a new day for us. But from the way you and Mama still live you'd never know it."

She put on some sunglasses that hid everything above the tip of her nose and her chin.

Maggie smiled; maybe at the sunglasses. But a real smile, not scared. After we watched the car dust settle I asked Maggie to bring me a dip of snuff. And then the two of us sat there just enjoying, until it was time to go in the house and go to bed.

Huff 1

Shaunte Huff
Dr. Logan
Introduction to Literature
5 May 2006

"Make Something of Yourself": Symbolism in Alice Walker's "Everyday Use"

In her short story "Everyday Use," Alice Walker uses symbolism to give readers a fuller understanding of the narrator's relationship with her two daughters. Household objects, clothing, and fire all work together in the story to depict the narrator's complicated feelings toward her older daughter Dee and her younger daughter Maggie. In some ways the two daughters represent the past and the future, and the narrator's complex attitude toward the two of them reflects her own position between her past heritage and the "new day" Dee talks about.

Although the narrator of the story clearly loves both her daughters, she is honest enough to admit that she has always been a little awed by Dee, the older sister. Dee has gone to school and moved away from home. Maggie, who has stayed at home with her mother, is an object of pity. She acts like "a lame animal" (271). Her mother sometimes forgets that she is not a child anymore. The dress that burned off of Maggie "in little black papery flakes" during the house fire (271) has left her scarred and vulnerable. Dee, on the other hand, comes back to visit wrapped in a bright, voluminous new dress that "throws out heat waves" of its own. Maggie and Dee's dresses are important symbols because they remind us of the dresses and other clothes used in the quilts Dee wants to take with her. The fabric of the quilts is a link to history—the dresses worn by Dee's grandmother, for whom she is named, older fabrics passed down from older relatives, and even a piece of a Union Army uniform from the Civil War. Dee's new dress is probably an African dashiki; she has appropriated it from a heritage so distant none of her family can remember it. And yet, the narrator admits, "as she walks closer, I like it" (273).

The narrator associates Dee with fire and burning. The old house that Dee hated burned down, and while Maggie was burned in the fire, Dee was unharmed. In fact, the way the narrator describes Dee staring at the burning house—"a look of concentration on her face as she watched the last dingy gray board of the house fall in toward the red-hot brick chimney"—leaves us wondering if perhaps Dee somehow caused the house to burn down, through sheer hatred. In high school, Dee read to her mother and Maggie and, according to the narrator, "burned us with a lot of knowledge we didn't necessarily need to know" (271). Dee's wit is a "scalding humor that erupted like bubbles in lye" (272).

Now that Dee has returned home for a visit, she seems to have changed. Instead of wanting to tear down the new house, as her mother fears, Dee takes picture after picture of it. Instead of scorning the old quilts that her mother had offered to her when she went off to college, now Dee wants to take them with her. But we soon see that Dee's new interest in the past consumes her family's history in much the same way a fire would. She takes away the cover and dasher from her mother's churn, even though the churn is full of milk ready to be made into butter. The narrator lets Dee have them, even though she won't be able to make butter without them. They are treasured family heirlooms and it is clear she will miss them from the way she considers the dasher carefully before handing it over to Dee:

> I took it for a moment in my hands. You didn't even have to look close to see where hands pushing the dasher up and down to make butter had left a kind of sink in the wood. In fact, there were a lot of small sinks; you could see where thumbs and fingers had sunk into the wood. It was a beautiful light yellow wood, from a tree that grew in the yard where Big Dee and Stash had lived. (275)

The family's history is physically imprinted on their possessions, through long years of everyday use. Dee wants to take these possessions away and enshrine them, but not touch or use them. Dee disassembles a very useful churn into knick-knacks for her house, saying she will "think of something artistic to do with the dasher" (275). Maggie and her mother live in the midst of their heritage, and use it, and leave their own imprint on it, while Dee relegates it to alcoves and corners.

Dee's disconnect with her history is evident in her own lack of memory. She "never knew" about the grooves in the benches until she sits in them after returning home (275). She doesn't remember that she wants the churn cover and dash until she sees and touches the butter dish. She doesn't remember who carved the dasher. She doesn't know why she is named Dee. She has to take photographs of everything, including her family. She does this even before she kisses her mother hello. She needs tangible things to stand in for her past as she moves forward. She sheds her family name and takes another, African one. She is moving back toward a more distant past that she has no real connection with.

Huff 3

Maggie, on the other hand, says. "I can 'member Grandma Dee without the quilts" (276). Maggie is truly attached to the quilts; she is upset that Dee wants them (she drops something in the kitchen and the door slams when Dee asks for them), but she does not need them in order to establish a connection to the past. Maggie knows how to quilt because she learned from her grandmother. "Maggie's brain is like an elephant's" says Dee (275), and she does not seem to mean it as a compliment.

Maggie can make quilts, but Dee is a quilt. She is a pastiche of names, dresses, tastes, loyalties, and desires. Ever since high school she has been re-making herself from the outside—demanding and getting a yellow organdy dress, making over a green suit handed down from someone else. Dee never learned to make quilts because she was too busy re-making herself. She has given up part of her past and wants to put it into a museum, whereas Maggie has kept the past alive. Maggie is all of one piece.

In the end, Walker seems to be saying that neither sister is "right" or "wrong" in living the way they do. Dee's selfish attempts to connect with her past on her own terms are part of her ongoing struggle to better herself, and live her life fearlessly—a trait her mother clearly admires in her. "Who can even imagine me looking a strange white man in the eye? . . . Dee, though. She would always look anyone in the eye" (271). But Maggie's stay-at-home, shy ways, which obviously irritate her mother sometimes, are unimportant when compared to Maggie's memory of her family, her ability to quilt, and her humility. The narrator's moment of inspiration in the story comes when she looks hard at Maggie, whose face has "a kind of dopey, hangdog look," "with her scarred hands hidden in the folds of her skirt" (277). Maggie, she realizes, has always assumed that Dee was better than her, more deserving of her. She is half afraid of her sister but she still loves her. It is at this moment that the narrator is able to see Maggie's worth clearly, in relation to Dee.

At the beginning of the story, the narrator says that Maggie "thinks her sister had held life always in the palm of one hand, that 'no' is a word the world never learned to say to her" (270). It is when Dee tries to take the quilts promised to Maggie that the world, in the form of the narrator, finally says "no" to Dee—or rather, "yes" to Maggie—by dumping the quilts in her lap.

Love in L.A.
(SHORT STORY)
Dagoberto Gilb

Dagoberto Gilb's mother was an illegal immigrant from Mexico who settled in Los Angeles, where she met his father, an ex-Marine sergeant of German ancestry, a relationship that ended quickly. Born in 1950, Gilb grew up in Los Angeles, attended college, and worked for many years as a carpenter, which gave him time to write. He now teaches at Texas State University and has published novels and collections of short stories and essays.

Analyzing and Connecting

1. From whose point of view is the story told? Do you think the narrator is a neutral observer?

2. Does Jake act responsibly after the accident? What other choices did he consider? What does his response tell you about his character?

3. What do we learn about Mariana from her response, her car, and her mention of her parents? Do you find her behavior credible and realistic? Support your response with evidence from the text.

4. How does the setting on a freeway shape how we understand the two characters? Imagine the story told in a rural setting. Do you think the main characters would behave differently?

5. Put forth an argument about whether the title is appropriate for the story. Use details from the story to support your position.

6. Gilb often writes about lives of working-class Latinos. Do you think Gilb is sympathetic to Jake's behavior? Explain.

LOVE IN L.A.

Jake slouched in a clot of near motionless traffic, in the peculiar gray of concrete, smog, and early morning beneath the overpass of the Hollywood Freeway on Alvarado Street. He didn't really mind because he knew how much worse it could be trying to make a left onto the onramp. He certainly didn't do that everyday of his life, and he'd assure anyone who'd ask that he never would either. A steady occupation had its advantages and he couldn't deny thinking about that too. He needed an FM radio in something better than this '58 Buick he drove. It would have crushed velvet interior with electric controls for the LA summer, a nice warm heater and defroster for the winter drives at the beach, a cruise control for those longer trips, mellow speakers front and rear of course, windows that hum closed, snuffing out that nasty exterior noise of freeways. The fact was that he'd probably have to change his whole style. Exotic colognes, plush, dark nightclubs, maitais and daquiris, necklaced ladies in satin gowns, misty and sexy like in a tequila ad. Jake could imagine lots of possibilities when he let himself, but none that ended up with him pressed onto a stalled freeway.

Jake was thinking about this freedom of his so much that when he glimpsed its green light he just went ahead and stared bye bye to the steadily employed. When he turned his head the same direction his windshield faced, it was maybe one second too late. He pounced the brake pedal and steered the front wheels away from the tiny brakelights but the smack was unavoidable. Just one second sooner and it would only have been close. One second more and he'd be crawling up the Toyota's trunk. As it was, it seemed like only a harmless smack, much less solid than the one against his back bumper.

Jake considered driving past the Toyota but was afraid the traffic ahead would make it too difficult. As he pulled up against the curb a few carlengths ahead, it occurred to him that the traffic might have helped him get away too. He slammed the car door twice to make sure it was closed fully and to give himself another second more, then toured front and rear of his Buick for damage on or near the bumpers. Not an impressionable scratch even in the chrome. He perked up. Though the car's beauty was secondary to its ability to start and move, the body and paint were clean except for a few minor dings. This stood out as one of his few clearcut accomplishments over the years.

Before he spoke to the driver of the Toyota, whose looks he could see might present him with an added complication, he signaled to the driver of the car that hit him, still in his car and stopped behind the Toyota, and waved his hands and shook his head to let the man know there was no problem as far as he was concerned. The driver waved back and started his engine.

"It didn't even scratch my paint," Jake told her in that way of his. "So how you doin? Any damage to the car? I'm kinda hoping so, just so it takes a little more time and we can talk some. Or else you can give me your phone number now and I won't have to lay my regular b.s. on you to get it later."

He took her smile as a good sign and relaxed. He inhaled her scent like it was clean air and straightened out his less than new but not unhip clothes.

"You've got Florida plates. You look like you must be Cuban."

"My parents are from Venezuela."

"My name's Jake." He held out his hand.

"Mariana."

They shook hands like she'd never done it before in her life.

"I really am sorry about hitting you like that." He sounded genuine. He fondled the wide dimple near the cracked taillight. "It's amazing how easy it is to put a dent in these new cars. They're so soft they might replace waterbeds soon." Jake was confused about how to proceed with this. So much seemed so unlikely, but there was always a possibility. "So maybe we should go out to breakfast somewhere and talk it over."

"I don't eat breakfast."

"Some coffee then."

"Thanks, but I really can't."

"You're not married, are you? Not that that would matter that much to me, I'm an openminded kinda guy."

She was smiling. "I have to get to work."

"That sounds boring."

"I better get your driver's license," she said.

Jake nodded, disappointed. "One little problem," he said. "I didn't bring it. I just forgot it this morning. I'm a musician," he exaggerated greatly, "and, well, I dunno, I left my wallet in the pants I was wearing last night. If you have some paper and a pen I'll give you my address and all that."

He followed her to the glove compartment side of her car.

"What if we don't report it to the insurance companies? I'll just get it fixed for you."

"I don't think my dad would let me do that."

"Your dad? It's not your car?"

"He bought it for me. And I live at home."

"Right." She was slipping away from him. He went back around to the back of her new Toyota and looked over the damage again. There was the trunk lid, the bumper, a rear panel, a taillight.

"You do have insurance?" she asked, suspicious, as she came around the back of the car.

"Oh yeah," he lied.

"I guess you better write the name of that down too."

He made up a last name and address and wrote down the name of an insurance company an old girlfriend once belonged to. He considered giving a real phone number but went against that idea and made one up.

"I act too," he lied to enhance the effect more. "Been in a couple of movies."

She smiled like a fan.

"So how about your phone number?" He was rebounding maturely.

She gave it to him.

"Mariana, you are beautiful," he said in his most sincere voice.

"Call me," she said timidly.

Jake beamed. "We'll see you, Mariana," he said holding out his hand. Her hand felt so warm and soft he felt like he'd been kissed.

Back in his car he took a moment or two to feel both proud and sad about his performance. Then he watched the rear view mirror as Mariana pulled up behind him. She was writing down the license plate numbers on his Buick, ones that he'd taken off a junk because the ones that belonged to his had expired so long ago. He turned the ignition key and revved the big engine and clicked into drive. His sense of freedom swelled as he drove into the now moving street traffic, though he couldn't stop the thought about that FM stereo radio and crushed velvet interior and the new car smell that would even make it better.

How to write a rhetorical analysis

These steps for the process of writing a rhetorical analysis may not progress as neatly as this chart might suggest. Writing is not an assembly-line process.

As you write, be open to new insights about the subject you are analyzing. Writing often generates new ideas that you can use to strengthen your analysis.

1 SELECT A TEXT TO ANALYZE

- Examine the assignment.
- Find a text.
- Make an analytical claim.
- Research the context.
- Research the author and audience.

2 ANALYZE CONTEXT AND TEXT

- Consider the medium and genre.
- Identify the main claim or claims.
- Consider the evidence.
- Analyze the appeals.
- Situate the text in its context.
- Consider the style and tone.

3 WRITE A DRAFT

- Select vivid details and dialog.
- Decide on an organization.
- Craft a strong beginning.
- Conclude by inviting further reflection.
- Consider your voice and tone.
- Choose a title that will interest readers.

4 REVISE, REVISE, REVISE

- Check that your paper or project fulfills the assignment.
- Make sure that the subject is focused.
- Add details, description, or dialog.
- Make sure your voice and tone will engage readers.
- Examine your organization and think of possible better ways to organize.
- Review the visual presentation.
- Proofread carefully.

5 SUBMITTED VERSION

- Make sure your finished writing meets all formatting requirements.

1: Select a text to analyze

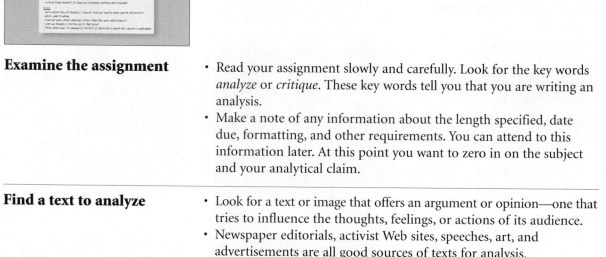

Examine the assignment

- Read your assignment slowly and carefully. Look for the key words *analyze* or *critique*. These key words tell you that you are writing an analysis.
- Make a note of any information about the length specified, date due, formatting, and other requirements. You can attend to this information later. At this point you want to zero in on the subject and your analytical claim.

Find a text to analyze

- Look for a text or image that offers an argument or opinion—one that tries to influence the thoughts, feelings, or actions of its audience.
- Newspaper editorials, activist Web sites, speeches, art, and advertisements are all good sources of texts for analysis.

Make an analytical claim

- Ask: What will my analysis reveal for readers that they might not otherwise have realized about the text?
- Think about the evidence you will need to support your claim. It may come from the text itself, or from your research into the piece's context.

Research the context

- What else was being written and said about this subject at the time the text was written?
- What events were taking place that might have influenced the author?

Research the author and audience

- Who is the author? What else has he or she said on this subject? What motivated him or her to produce this text?
- Who is the audience? Where did the text first appear (or, why was this image made or created)? Why did it appear at that particular moment?

WRITE NOW

Find a verbal text to analyze

Find at least three examples of verbal texts that intend to persuade you in some way. They may ask you to do something specific such as buy a product or vote for a candidate or else they may aim at changing your attitude. Note what makes each text interesting and make a tentative claim.

Text	Deadspin.com blog
What makes it interesting	Takes a humorous look at sports, exposing the pretensions and lack of honesty among sports figures.
Claim	Deadspin.com represents the spirit of many blogs in going for the truth underneath layers of hype and having fun along the way.

WRITE NOW

Find a visual text to analyze

Identify at least three visual texts for possible analysis. Look for a visual text that in some way attempts to influence the viewer—an advertisement, a public building, a statue, a controversial work of art, a dramatic photograph, a television commercial, a corporate logo, and so on. Note what makes it interesting and make a tentative claim

Text	Logos of competing political candidates
What makes it interesting	Candidate X's logo appears much better than candidate Y's logo among people I have asked, but they cannot explain why.
Claim	Candidate X has a better logo than candidate Y because the typeface and colors of X's logo express strength, energy, and movement while those on Y's logo suggest indecision and weakness.

Writer at work

Grace Bernhardt was asked to write a rhetorical analysis for her Rhetoric of the Nineteenth Century course. Upon receiving the assignment, she made the following notes and observations.

Grace began by highlighting key words in the assignment and noting specifics about the length, due date, and formatting of the essay.

RHE 309: Rhetoric of the Nineteenth Century
Rhetorical Analysis

Choose a speech, article, or essay dating from the nineteenth century, and analyze the techniques it uses to persuade its audience. Take a stand as to whether and how the techniques work (you will need to research audience to do this). I suggest you choose something fairly short, as you will need to analyze it in ten pages or fewer. Note how the text uses appeals to logos, ethos, and pathos, and point out any specific rhetorical techniques employed as well.

Discuss impact of rhetorical techniques on audience.

Important Dates
3/2—Rough drafts due   *Have two weeks for first draft.*
3/9—Final drafts due

Grading
We will use the standard rubric for papers distributed at the beginning of the semester. In addition to the usual distribution for reasoning, logic, organization, and mechanics, you will be graded upon the amount and applicability of the evidence you use to support your claim, the persuasiveness of your claim, and the thoroughness of your analysis.

Remember most evidence should come from the text itself.

She made some comments noting the types of texts she might write about.

After some preliminary research, Grace chose a speech to analyze and made a list of research she would need to do.

POSSIBILITIES:

- Abolitionist pamphlets and speeches--Douglass speeches have lots of personal anecdotes; his ethos is strong b/c he is an ex-slave. This bolsters the pathos of the anecdotes. Everyone used anecdotes in abolitionist speeches but his are more powerful. Maybe that could be a thesis? Also he knew professional speakers like W. L. Garrison and would prob ably have used some classical rhetorical techniques I could talk about. I think his best would be "What to the Slave Is the 4th of July?"***

- Political speeches. Lincoln-Douglass debates, pro- or anti-secession articles--some very important politically. Gettysburg Address is probably too short. Lincoln's inaugural speeches are really long though.

- Speeches on women's suffrage--haven't read any yet that I think are really great. Ask Prof. Morrison to recommend others?

- Section from Walden? Or Emerson (probably nothing short enough).

TO DO:

- Get a good copy of Douglass's speech. Find out exactly what year he delivered it, where, and to whom.

- Find out more about audience (other than they were abolitionists).

- Look up Douglass's history up to that point.

- Think about ways to summarize rhetoric of abolition in which this speech is embedded.

2: Analyze context and text

Consider the medium and genre

- What is the medium?
- What is the genre of the piece? Is it an editorial? a speech? an advertisement?

Consider the main claim or claims

- Summarize the claim, or describe the subject.

Consider the evidence

- Note all the reasons and evidence given to support the claim.

Analyze the appeals

- How is the author presented? As a credible, trustworthy person?
- How logical are the arguments? Are there any logical fallacies?
- What emotions, if any, does the author appeal to?
- How effective is each one of these appeals and techniques? How effective are they all together? Why are they effective or not effective?

Situate the text in its context

- Where do you find evidence that this text was responding to other texts and events?
- What does this text contribute to the ongoing conversation of which it is part?

Consider the style and tone

- How would you characterize the style? Is the style formal? informal? academic?
- How would you characterize the tone? Does the writer or speaker use humor or satire?
- How is language used to influence the audience? repetition? contrast? particular word choices? What metaphors are used?

Writer at work

Grace Bernhardt read her chosen text carefully several times, making notes in the margins about the rhetorical techniques she saw being used. She then summarized her findings and used her summary to help construct an overall approach to the analysis.

Religious language—very important in 19th C. See where else he does this—ethos.

What, to the American slave, is your 4th of July? I answer: a day that reveals to him, more than all other days in the year, the gross injustice and cruelty to which he is the constant victim. To him, your celebration is a sham; your boasted liberty, an unholy license; your national greatness, swelling vanity; your sounds of rejoicing are empty and heartless; your denunciations of tyrants, brass fronted impudence; your shouts of liberty and equality, hollow mockery; your prayers and hymns, your sermons and thanksgivings, with all your religious parade, and solemnity, are, to him, mere bombast, fraud, deception, impiety, and hypocrisy — a thin veil to cover up crimes which would disgrace a nation of savages. There is not a nation on the earth guilty of practices, more shocking and bloody, than are the people of these United States, at this very hour. (Prgph 46)

Pairs of words and phrases show sharp contrast: slave vs. free. Loaded words are an emotional appeal.

Also attacks Fugitive Slave Law and Church to show hypocrisy of government and churches. Hypocrisy is his big focus. See paragraph 37 where he shifts abruptly in tone to highlight difference between him and his white audience. Slavery is hypocritical in a democracy and Christian country and so the 4th of July is a hypocritical holiday while slavery exists. Uses a primary document of American independence, the Constitution, to argue against slavery. Speech is really emotional but also very very well constructed. Uses a lot of logic almost like building a legal case, but also pathos in the personal anecdotes. Shows he put a lot of thought into it, not just speaking impromptu. All the techniques feed into his task of showing the hypocrisy of the system.

3: Write a draft

Briefly describe the text you are analyzing	• Describe the medium and genre (newspaper editorial, blog on the Web, radio interview, and so on). • Who produced it? Where and when did it first appear?
Make a claim	• Analysis adds a new dimension to a text; what will your analysis reveal for readers? Be sure your claim is not an over-generalization and can be supported by textual and contextual evidence.
Analyze the context	• Through research find out what else was being said about the subject your text discusses. • Track down any references to other texts or events.
Analyze the text	• Select the most important parts of the text to focus on. Choose elements that will show a pattern or illustrate specific techniques you want to talk about. However, be honest: do not leave out evidence that might undercut your claims. • Build a critical mass of evidence. Supply the evidence and examples to support your claim. • Make larger patterns or contrasts visible for your readers. For example, does an author seem to be appealing to two different audiences in a single essay? What parts of the work appeal to one audience? What parts appeal to the other?
Build a strong conclusion	• Don't merely summarize what you have already said. Ask yourself "Have I learned anything new in this analysis?" A conclusion can be a good place to succinctly describe a larger pattern you have been tracing in a work. Or, it may be a good place to make conjectures about other works by the same artist, about the motivations of a school or movement, or to tie your analysis of this text to other texts.

Writer at work

Grace Bernhardt used note cards to determine an organization for her paper.

INTRO: CONTEXT OF SPEECH
- July 5, 1852.
- Speech to Rochester Ladies' Anti-Slavery Society.
- Douglass had been free 14 years; experienced orator by this time.
- Fugitive Slave Act passed < 2 years before.
- Uncle Tom's Cabin just published.

CLAIM:
- Douglass focuses on hypocrisy of slavery in speech.
- Uses shifts in tone, personal anecdote, contrasts to appeal to emotions.
- Uses his own background as ethical appeal.
- Uses historical examples, arguments from church and U.S. Constitution to make logical, legal-sounding case.

- Douglass's opening—sets tone.
- Downplays expectations.
- Comparison of America to England.
- Comparison of struggle for independence to struggle against slavery.

- First big change in tone: Paragraph 37.
- Quote parallel construction. Asks "Do you mock me?"

- Long parallel construction: Paragraph 37.
- Quote parallel construction.
- Note positive/negative word pairs.

- Comparison of slaves to animals, Par. 53.
- Quote "I hear the doleful wail . . ."
- Emotional language—"my soul sickens . . ."

Fugitive Slave law—hypocrisy of government (par. 57)

Failure of U.S. church to denounce Fugitive Slave Law—hypocrisy of Church.

Constitution
- Uses logic to show it doesn't support slavery.
- Doesn't even mention slavery.
- "GLORIOUS LIBERTY DOCUMENT" (par. 71).
- Uses primary U.S. document everyone would be thinking about on July 4.

Comparison to Church of England. England more advanced than U.S.—challenges moral superiority felt on 4th of July.

CONCLUSION
- Douglass concludes by returning to the beginning.
- Note long life and impact of speech.
- Speech was effective and became famous because it was highly emotional yet relentlessly logical at the same time.

4: Revise, revise, revise

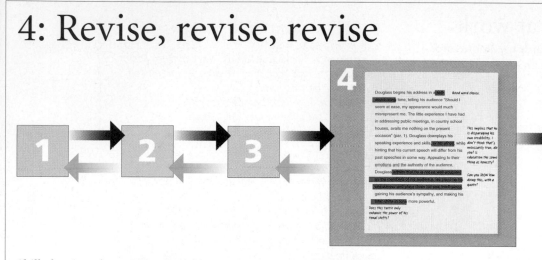

Skilled writers know that the secret to writing well is rewriting. Leave correcting errors for last.

Does your paper or project meet the assignment?	• Look again at your assignment. Does your paper or project do what the assignment asks? • Check the assignment for specific guidelines, including length, format, and amount of research. Does your work meet these guidelines?
Does your analysis have a clear purpose?	• Does it tell readers something they would not have otherwise noticed? • Do you make some kind of claim about the work you are analyzing? Is it a debatable claim?
Do you support your analysis with evidence?	• Do you provide a background about the author, intended audience, and the larger conversation surrounding the text you are analyzing? • Can you provide additional analysis to support your claims?
Is your organization effective?	• Is the order of your main points clear to your reader? • Are there any places where you find abrupt shifts or gaps? • Are there sections or paragraphs that could be rearranged to make your draft more effective?
Is the writing project visually effective?	• Is the font attractive and readable? • Are the headings and visuals effective?
Save the editing for last	• When you have finished revising, edit and proofread carefully.

A peer review guide is on page 31.

Writer at work

Grace Bernhardt received comments from her instructor on her rough drafts. She used his comments in conjunction with a visit to her campus writing center to revise her draft.

Grace received specific feedback on an important part of her essay: the paragraph where she describes Douglass's introduction and setting of tone.

To see how she responded to these comments, see her submitted draft of the analysis on page 296.

Grace found several other areas of her paper where she felt more quotations would help illustrate the claims she was making about Douglass's speech. She also re-ordered several paragraphs, removed one paragraph entirely, and carefully checked her grammar, spelling, and syntax.

Douglass begins his address in a self-deprecating tone, telling his audience "Should I seem at ease, my appearance would much misrepresent me. The little experience I have had in addressing public meetings, in country school houses, avails me nothing on the present occasion" (par. 1). Douglass downplays his speaking experience and skills, or his ethos, while hinting that his current speech will differ from his past speeches in some way. Appealing to their emotions and the authority of the audience, Douglass admits that he is not as well-educated as the members of his audience. He plays up his uneasiness and plays down his own intelligence, gaining his audience's sympathy, and making his later shifts in tone more powerful.

Good word choice.

This implies that he is disparaging his own credibility. I don't think that's necessarily true, do you? Is education the same thing as honesty?

Can you SHOW him doing this, with a quote?

Does this tactic only enhance the power of his tonal shifts?

5: Submitted version

Grace Bernhardt

Professor Morrison

Rhetoric of the Nineteenth Century

9 March 2006

Investigating "Independence": An Analysis of Frederick Douglass's Speech,

"What to the Slave Is the Fourth of July?"

On July 5, 1852, Frederick Douglass stood before a meeting of the Rochester Ladies' Anti-Slavery Society to give a speech that few expected but many deserved to hear. Douglass addressed his audience with an initial unease yet little timidity, revealing both his aversion to slavery and his passionate dedication to seeing it end. Douglass himself had escaped from slavery fourteen years earlier and had since become an influential voice for the abolitionist movement, giving powerful oratories both in America and abroad. Douglass spoke at an especially volatile time, with the Fugitive Slave Act passed less than two years prior, and Harriet Beecher Stowe's novel, <u>Uncle Tom's Cabin</u>, published a mere months prior (Blight).

While Douglass spoke that day to an audience of abolitionists who likely shared similar views, he speaks directly to all proud Americans. Its central purpose is to expose the hypocrisy of celebrating democracy in a country that allows the enslavement of part of its populace. Appealing to his audience's emotions with shifts in tone and direct comparisons between slave and free, Douglass gave a powerful speech that laid bare the hypocrisy of slavery. He brought his own unique credibility to the speech, speaking as a former slave and providing intimate anecdotes of his personal experiences with slavery. Finally, Douglass appealed to the audience's sense of logic as he detailed the ills of slavery and the pretense of its supporters, giving examples from America's history, the principles of the Christian Church, and the U.S. Constitution.

Douglass begins his address in a self-deprecating tone, telling his audience "Should I seem at ease, my appearance would much misrepresent me. The little experience I have had in addressing public meetings, in country school houses, avails me nothing on the present occasion" (par. 1). Douglass downplays his speaking experience and skills while hinting that his current speech will differ from his past speeches in some way. Subtly, he builds his own credibility by appealing to the "greater" authority of the audience. Douglass admits that he is not as well-educated as the members of his audience—"With little experience and with less learning, I have been able to throw my thoughts hastily and imperfectly together; and trusting to your patient and generous indulgence, I will proceed to lay them before you" (par. 3). Douglass admits his uneasiness and reduces expectations about his performance, gaining his audience's sympathy, and making his later rhetorical flourishes more powerful.

As Douglass continues, he describes America's colonial past, urging the audience to connect the oppression of America's forefathers by England to the current entrapment of slaves. Douglass points out that "there was a time when to pronounce against England, and in favor of the cause of the colonies, tried men's souls" but "Feeling themselves harshly and unjustly treated by the home government, your fathers, like men of honesty, and men of spirit, earnestly sought redress" (par. 6). By concentrating on the fight that gave Americans their freedom, Douglass intimates that the abolitionist cause is experiencing a similar struggle for freedom for slaves. However, Douglass feels that Americans are losing sight of their past and the principles laid forth in the Declaration of Independence, quickly forgetting their fight against oppression by Britain. By appealing to the audience's sense of pride and pointing out American's history of revolt against oppression and wrongdoing, Douglass foreshadows his later criticism of the nation's treatment of slaves.

It is at this point in his speech that Douglass does a quick turnaround, switching from praise of American's historical rebellion against wrong to condemnation of the current support of slavery. Douglass questions his invitation to speak on the 5th of July when his people lack the very independence and freedom being celebrated by those sitting before him. Douglass uses parallel construction to emphasize the discrepancy between the life of the free man and the life of the slave and to impress his point on the audience:

> Your high independence only reveals the immeasurable distance between us. The blessings in which you, this day, rejoice, are not enjoyed in common. The rich inheritance of justice, liberty, prosperity and independence, bequeathed by your fathers, is shared by you, not by me. The sunlight that brought life and healing to you, has brought stripes and death to me. This Fourth [of] July is yours, not mine. You may rejoice, I must mourn . . . Do you mean, citizens, to mock me, by asking me to speak today? (par. 37)

Douglass reminds his audience that his people do not share the same independence as white Americans, and cannot celebrate the Fourth of July. By analyzing the American holiday from the slave perspective, Douglass quickly reverses the feelings of pride which he had built up in his audience.

Douglass elaborates on the slave perspective, using point and counterpoint to highlight the slave's interpretation of the 4th of July and emphasize the hypocrisy of America's celebration of freedom:

> What, to the American slave, is your 4th of July? I answer: a day that reveals to him, more than all other days in the year, the gross injustice and cruelty to which he is the constant victim. To him, your celebration is a sham; your boasted liberty, an unholy license; your national greatness, swelling vanity; your sounds of rejoicing are empty and heartless; your denunciations of tyrants, brass fronted impudence; your shouts of liberty and equality, hollow mockery; your prayers and hymns, your sermons and thanksgivings, with all your religious parade, and solemnity, are, to him, mere bombast, fraud, deception, impiety, and hypocrisy—a thin veil to cover up crimes which would disgrace a nation of savages. (par. 46)

Douglass uses repeated criticism and parallel structure within his argument to hammer in his point and give his audience insight into the slave's point of view. He pairs positive words such as "celebration," "liberty," "greatness," and "rejoicing" with negative words and phrases like "sham," "unholy license," "vanity," and "heartless." He implies that the slave's perception of these words, the negative perception, is the more accurate one. Douglass continues on, detailing the horrors of the internal slave trade, using pathos again to gain the audience's sympathy. Reflecting on the slave trade, Douglass likens the practice to that of an animal trade show: "I hear the doleful wail of fettered humanity, on the way to the slave-markets, where the victims are to be sold like horses, sheep, and swine, knocked off to the highest bidder . . . My soul sickens at the sight" (par. 53).

As if the mere existence of such a practice is not enough, Douglass denounces the enactment of the Fugitive Slave Law which legalized the capture and return of slaves to their owner. Douglass states: "In glaring violation of justice, in shameless disregard of the forms of administering law, in cunning arrangement to entrap the defenseless, and in diabolical intent, this Fugitive Slave Law stands alone in the annals of tyrannical legislation" (par. 57). By criticizing the government, Douglass challenges his audience to question whether the principles that he praised in America's early heroes still exist, and whether the nation continues to value the same things they once did—freedom for all citizens, fairness and democracy.

However, Douglass's criticism does not end with the government—Douglass views the Fugitive Slave Law as not only a denial of civil rights, but also "one of the grossest infringements of Christian Liberty" (par. 58). Douglass points to the hypocrisy of the Church, claiming that "At the very moment that they are thanking God for the enjoyment of civil and religious liberty, and for the right to worship God according to the dictates of their own consciences, they are utterly silent in respect to a law which robs religion of its chief significance, and makes it utterly worthless to a world lying in wickedness" (par. 59). Douglass blames the Church for failing to speak out against slavery and for supporting the Fugitive Slave Law by failing to denounce its anti-Christian nature, raising issues of value for his audience to consider.

Douglass feels that the Church holds great power to abolish slavery, and points to the anti-slavery movement in England as an example. Douglass remarks:

> One is struck with the difference between the attitude of the American church
> towards the anti-slavery movement, and that occupied by the churches in England
> towards a similar movement in that country. There, the church, true to its mission
> of ameliorating, elevating, and improving the condition of mankind, came forward
> promptly, bound up the wounds of the West Indian slave, and restored him to his
> liberty. There, the question of emancipation was a high[ly] religious question . . .
> The anti-slavery movement there was not an anti-church movement, for the

reason that the church took its full share in prosecuting that movement: and the anti-slavery movement in this country will cease to be an anti-church movement, when the church of this country shall assume a favorable, instead of a hostile position towards that movement. (par. 66)

Douglass reveals the logical inconsistency in the American Church and hopes that his audience will see the logic in his argument—that unless the Church adopts a stance on slavery that is consistent with the core principles of Christianity, America will continue to deteriorate and destroy itself. In one last attempt to iron in his point, Douglass alludes to a lesson learned in the Bible, crying forth "Oh! be warned! be warned! a horrible reptile is coiled up in your nation's bosom; the venomous creature is nursing at the tender breast of your youthful republic; for the love of God, tear away, and fling from you the hideous monster, and let the weight of twenty millions crush and destroy it forever!" (par. 67). Douglass calls on his audience to examine the logical inconsistency between the Church's lessons and their stance on slavery, ultimately hoping to incite further action.

Finally, Douglass examines the Constitution using logical reasoning, questioning how the document can be considered pro-slavery when it makes no mention of the word "slave." Douglass emphasizes the original intent of the document—to provide a framework for the newly free country of America and implores his audience to remember that "the Constitution is a GLORIOUS LIBERTY DOCUMENT" (par. 71). He challenges his audience to search the document, and questions "if it be not somewhat singular that, if the Constitution were intended to be, by its framers and adopters, a slave-holding instrument, why neither slavery, slaveholding, nor slave can anywhere be found in it" (par. 71). Douglass uses logic to discount the argument that the Constitution supports the practice of slavery, and urges Northerners to reject arguments that claim to find support therein.

Despite the biting and critical tone of the majority of his speech, Douglass leaves his audience in a manner similar to that in which he greeted them. Douglass ends with hope and humility, and shows faith in the slow progress of the abolitionist movement, concluding his courageous speech with a poem from William Lloyd Garrison, an abolitionist. Douglass undoubtedly left an impression on his audience; moreover, he was successful in reaching an audience far beyond the members of the Rochester Ladies' Anti-Slavery Society. His speech was reprinted and distributed far and wide, reaching many more people. Clearly, the highly emotional and relentless logic of his speech caused many to reconsider the current state and direction of the United States.

Works Cited

Blight, David W. "What to the Slave Is the Fourth of July?" Historian David W. Blight on
Frederick Douglass's Greatest Speech. <u>Time</u> 26 June 2005. 22 Feb. 2006
<http://www.time.com/time/nation/article/0,8599,1077058,00.html>.

Douglass, Frederick. "What to the Slave Is the 4th of July?" <u>Archives of American Public
Address</u> 14 June 2002. 22 Feb. 2006 <http://douglassarchives.org/doug_a10.htm>.

Projects

Analyzing is valuable for clarifying and developing your own thinking as well as for giving your readers a broader understanding.

These projects are frequently written kinds of analyses.

RHETORICAL ANALYSIS

For an example of a rhetorical analysis, see pages 242–246.

Select a text to analyze—a speech, a sermon, an editorial, a persuasive letter, an essay, a Web site, a pamphlet, a brochure, or another kind of text.

Explain briefly what kind of text it is, when and where it was first published or spoken, and its main argument.

Make a claim about the text, which you support with close analysis.

Analyze the context. Is the text part of a larger debate? What other texts or events does it respond to? Who is the author? What motivated the author to write this text? What can you infer about the intended audience?

Analyze the appeals. What appeals to values and emotions are used? What appeals to logic are used? Do you find any logical fallacies (see pages 18–19)? Do you trust the writer?

Analyze the organization and style. What are the major parts and how are they arranged? Is the style formal, informal, satirical, or something else? Are any metaphors used?

For additional reading, writing, and research resources, go to **www.mycomplab.com** and choose **Lester Faigley's** *Writing.*

VISUAL ANALYSIS

For an example of a visual analysis, see pages 49–51.

Find a visual text to analyze. You might analyze a popular consumer product, a public building, advertising, art, or a map.

Make a claim about the visual text. Support your claim with close analysis. Describe key features.

Analyze the context. Where and when was the visual created? What was the purpose? Who created it? What can you infer about the intended audience?

Analyze the visual text. What kind of visual is it? What is the medium? How is it arranged? How would you characterize the style? Are any words connected?

CRITICAL LITERARY ANALYSIS

For an example of a critical literary analysis, see pages 269–280.

Read carefully a short story or other literary text. Map out the plot. What is the conflict and how is it resolved?

Examine the characterization, including the major and minor characters. Characters are not real people, but instead they are constructed for a purpose. What role does each character perform? The setting too is a character. What role does the setting play in the story?

Consider the point of view. Does a character tell the story? Or is the narrator an all-knowing observer? Describe the language, style, and tone of the story. Identify any important images, symbols, and metaphors.

Identify the story's central theme. How does the title of the story relate to the theme?

Write an arguable thesis that connects one or more elements—characters, setting, language, metaphors, and so on—to the overall theme. A paper that begins with an engaging thesis arouses the reader's interest. Support your thesis with evidence from the text. A successful paper shares a discovery with the reader.

11
Analyzing Causes

An effective causal analysis moves beyond the obvious to examine complex underlying causes.

Chapter contents

Writing to analyze causes

Have you ever wondered why your car is hard to start on a cold morning? Why all the shoppers in the supermarket seem to converge on the checkout stands at the same time? Why a company's stock price rises when it announces hundreds of layoffs?

Questions of causation confront us all the time. We spend much of our daily lives puzzling over them—trying to start the car, pick the best time to visit the supermarket, or buy the most valuable stock. Causal investigation also drives scientists, as they search for cures to diseases, try to explain certain behaviors in people and animals, and attempt to predict the weather. In your professional life, you will have to make many detailed causal analyses. You may need to find out why consumers have stopped buying your product suddenly, or why a particular sector of a factory is much more productive than others.

Answering these kinds of questions requires a causal analysis, which typically takes the form "SOMETHING causes (or does not cause) SOMETHING ELSE." The causal claim is at the center of a causal analysis. Therefore, to get started on a causal analysis, you need to propose one or more causes.

Methods of analyzing causes

Causal analyses can be challenging to write because any topic worth writing about is likely to be complex. Causes can be hard to identify, and there may be more than one cause behind any given phenomenon. The philosopher John Stuart Mill (1806–1873) developed four different methods for finding causes.

1 The Common Factor Method

If you look at all the cases of a phenomenon, and find a single factor that is common to all of them, that common factor is probably the cause. For example, if a number of people in your dormitory all develop symptoms of food poisoning, and it turns out they all ate the potato salad from the cafeteria salad bar the night before, the potato salad is probably the cause of their illness.

2 The Single Difference Method

This method is useful when you have two similar situations, with only one leading to an effect. Look for something that was present in one case and not the other. It is commonly used in scientific experiments under controlled conditions. You might grow a group of identical soybean plants, for example, giving them all equal amounts of light and water, but only feeding fertilizer to half of them. If the fertilized plants grow faster, the fertilizer is probably the cause.

3 Concomitant Variation

This method is also frequently used by scientists, especially when they cannot completely control the conditions they are observing. Investigators look for a similar pattern of variation between a possible cause and a possible effect. If you give different amounts of fertilizer to each soybean plant in the example, and the plants getting the most fertilizer grow the tallest, while the ones getting the least stay the smallest, a causal relationship between fertilizer and accelerated growth is likely.

4 The Process of Elimination

The more complex the set of causes behind a phenomenon, the more likely you are to use the process of elimination. Let's return to the soybean plants from the earlier example. You are fairly certain that adding fertilizer to the plants causes them to grow faster. Yet you notice that some plants have developed spots on their leaves. Some of the spotted plants get a lot of fertilizer, and some only get a little, but they all have a similar number of leaf spots, so the fertilizer is probably not the cause. Upon further investigation, you find that an absentminded professor has been emptying the remains of his diet soda into the spotted plants' pots every evening. Even though conditions among the spotted plants are not identical, it is reasonable to infer that the soda is causing the spotting. It is the only factor "left over" after you have accounted for all the others' impact on the plants.

Which method should I use?

You can use more than one of Mill's methods to evaluate possible causes. For example, the common factor and single difference methods are often combined: If everyone in your dorm who got sick had eaten the potato salad and the fruit cocktail, you would have to find someone who ate the fruit cocktail, but not the potato salad, to determine which food was the cause of illness. If anyone who ate fruit cocktail stayed healthy, you can eliminate it as a possible cause and focus on the potato salad.

Keys to causal analysis

Pay attention to effects

It's not enough to simply identify causes. In order for a causal analysis to matter, you must make clear why the effects are important. Otherwise, readers are apt to ask, "So what?" We often look for causes so that we can prevent something bad from happening, or facilitate something good. You may make the case that the film versions of *101 Dalmatians* led to an increase in the popularity of Dalmation dogs, but your analysis gains more stature if you further explore that effect: many of the puppies bred and sold to people who saw the movie ended up in animal shelters because their new owners were not prepared for such high-energy pets.

Identify what is at stake

Because a strong causal claim may inspire people to change policies or behaviors or take other action, you will find that some members of your audience hold different stakes in the outcome of your analysis. Their stakes can influence the ways, and the degree to which, they oppose your claim. For example, although the causal link between cigarette smoke and cancer was widely accepted in scientific circles for many years, tobacco companies argued vociferously that no such link existed. Their stake was financial: if their product was shown to cause a serious disease, they stood to lose customers and money.

Move beyond the obvious to identify underlying causes

When people are involved, you can expect causes to be complex. Perhaps the cause you are seeking to link to an effect is only one of several causes. You'll need to address all the contributing causes, not just the one you are focusing on. You should also consider whether one cause arises from another. For example, lower life expectancies among poor people are usually attributable to a number of factors, such as poor nutrition, restricted access to health care, and dangerous jobs. But some factors that affect life expectancy are indirectly linked to poverty: education level, for example, determines the type of job you can get—and poverty usually makes it much harder to get a good education. A well-thought-out causal analysis will trace multiple causes and consider their cumulative effect.

Avoid mistaking correlation for causation

A common pitfall of causal analysis is confusing causation with correlation. Events can be correlated, or mutually related in some way, without one being the cause of the other. Deaths by drowning and baseball games are correlated. But does one cause the other? Or is it because both occur most frequently in the summer?

Consider a visual explanation of causation

Investigators of accidents often use causal charts to identify the factors that lead to accidents. Accidents almost never happen from a single cause. Most often a combination of factors leads to accidents.

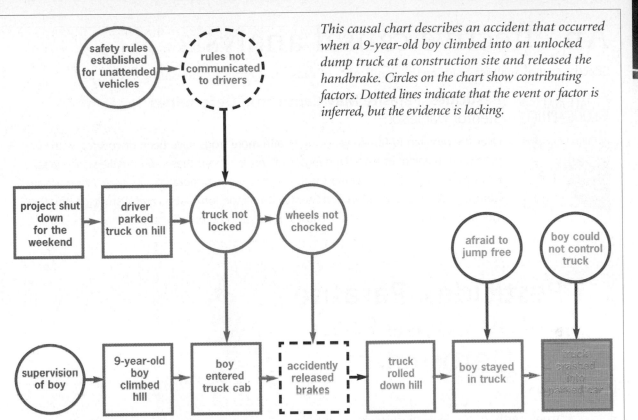

This causal chart describes an accident that occurred when a 9-year-old boy climbed into an unlocked dump truck at a construction site and released the handbrake. Circles on the chart show contributing factors. Dotted lines indicate that the event or factor is inferred, but the evidence is lacking.

WORKING TOGETHER

Find causes

In a group of three or four students

Brainstorm to create a list of "Why?" questions about causes. You list might include questions such as "Why is the sky blue?" or "Why do music CDs cost $15 when DVDs of entire films, with director's cuts, outtakes, and other extras only cost $19?" Try to come up with at least ten or fifteen questions.

Working together, come up with as many possible causes for each phenomenon as you can. Use your imagination, but stay within the realm of possibility. You might want to arrange your responses from the most plausible to the least plausible.

An effective causal analysis

Effective causal analyses examine the significance of cause-and-effect relationships.

Pesticides, Parasite May Cause Frog Deformities
Stentor Danielson

Over the past ten to fifteen years, more and more frogs have been discovered with deformed, missing, or extra hind legs. Concerned about these abnormalities, scientists worldwide have been searching for the cause. In this *National Geographic News* article from July 2002, science journalist Stentor Danielson looks at a careful study of the interplay between two potential causes: a waterborne parasite and common pesticides.

Pesticides, Parasite May Cause Frog Deformities

Frogs with extra legs or missing legs have been showing up with greater frequency over the past decade, and scientists have been baffled by the cause.

Some researchers have concluded that pesticide runoff from farms is to blame; others say a common parasite is the culprit. Now, a new study suggests that both these factors in combination have disturbed normal development in many frogs, leading to the abnormalities.

The study, published today in the *Proceedings of the National Academy of Sciences*, was based on tests in both the laboratory and the field that were designed to examine the interaction of parasites and pesticides. The research team, led by Joseph Kiesecker, found that only frogs infected by the larvae of a parasite, the trematode worm, developed deformities, but infected frogs exposed to pesticide runoff experienced much higher levels of deformities.

Danielson begins by briefly laying out the problem and by explaining how his article will add to previous discussions: new research indicates that two potential causes need to be considered together in order to get a clear picture of what is happening.

"It is not uncommon now for 20 to 30 percent of the frogs at many locations to have limb deformities," said Kiesecker, an assistant professor of biology at Penn State University.

Abnormalities have been documented in 52 species of amphibians, mainly frogs, in 46 U.S. states and four Canadian provinces, according to the U.S. Geological Survey. Reports of deformed frogs have been particularly common in New England and the Upper Midwest and on the Pacific coast.

Although there is some disagreement about what levels of deformities occur naturally in frog populations, most researchers agree that current levels are above normal.

Kiesecker and other researchers have warned that the physiological problems seen in frogs may foreshadow similar effects on humans.

Infected by Trematodes

During its life cycle, the parasitic trematode depends on several hosts, including pond snails. Tadpoles in ponds with snails pick up trematode larvae, called cercariae. In some cases the cercariae develop into hard cysts, which interfere with the tadpole's metamorphosis into a frog. When the cysts occur in tissue that later develops into legs, the cysts disrupt the animal's normal development and cause duplicate or missing legs.

The trematode also affects people—although not so dramatically as in developing frogs. It's the same parasite that causes "swimmer's itch," a common ailment in people who swim in ponds and lakes. Eventually, the human immune system defeats the cercariae, leaving the victim with just a rash.

Pesticides, Parasite May Cause Frog Deformities

In tropical climates trematodes cause schistosomiasis, a disease that kills millions of people. The World Health Organization estimates that 120 million people worldwide suffer from schistosomiasis.

Kiesecker's team took tadpoles from Centre County, Pennsylvania, and placed them in six local ponds—three affected by pesticide runoff and three pesticide-free. In each

Statistics provide a sense of the scope of the phenomenon. Notice the use of a government source for this information—sources which are usually credible and respected by readers.

At the end of this introductory section, Danielson places an important point about the issue: it could directly affect humans.

Details about one of the causes are explained step-by-step.

311

pond, the tadpoles were separated into two groups. One group was placed inside a fine mesh that kept out cercariae.

Only the tadpoles that were exposed to cercariae developed deformities. "We learned from the first field experiment that tadpoles have to be exposed to trematode infection for limb deformities to develop," Kiesecker said.

Pesticide Problems

Kiesecker's team then compared the rate of infection between trematode-exposed tadpoles in the different ponds. The team discovered that rates of infection were much higher in the ponds that received pesticide runoff.

This result parallels the finding of a study in 2000 in which frogs from the same pond—that is, those experiencing the same environmental conditions—were found to have similar deformities.

To examine the effects of pesticides on cercariae development, the team conducted lab experiments on four groups of tadpoles—three groups exposed to three common pesticides and a control group. The pesticides were Atrazine, the most commonly used pesticide in North America; Malathion, a common household pesticide that also is used to control insect pests in agricultural fields; and Esfenvalerate, a synthetic pyrethroid pesticide. The tadpoles were all exposed to cercariae.

When they counted the number of cysts that formed in the tadpoles, the researchers found much higher levels in the tadpoles exposed to pesticides. The team also took blood samples before and after the experiments to determine whether the tadpoles' white blood cell count—a measure of immune system health—was affected.

"The tadpoles that we exposed to pesticides had fewer of this particular kind of white blood cell compared to the tadpoles that we did not expose to pesticides, suggesting that pesticides make these animals more susceptible to parasitic infections," Kiesecker said.

Danielson explains how an experiment was designed to isolate possible causes of the limb mutations. The careful control of conditions led to a "single difference" method: the only difference between affected and unaffected frogs was their exposure to cercariae.

The additional variable of exposure to pesticides shows concomitant variation. The rate of malformation among affected frogs fluctuated in direct relation to the amount of exposure to pesticides.

Scientists repeated the pond test under controlled laboratory conditions and got similar results, with more detailed findings. In scientific causal analysis, repeatability of results strengthens the case for causality.

Pesticides have been found to have additional harmful effects on frogs. A study published in April in the *Proceedings of the National Academy of Sciences* found that Atrazine interfered with the sexual development of male frogs in the Midwest, reducing their levels of testosterone to below the levels found in female frogs.

"Atrazine-exposed frogs don't have normal reproductive systems," said Tyrone Hayes, the leader of a team from the University of California at Berkeley. "The males have ovaries in their testes and much smaller vocal organs."

Human Impacts?

Kiesecker said society can learn a lot from the experiments because "amphibians are particularly sensitive to environmental changes that appear to be associated with the recent emergence of new diseases and resurgence of old diseases that infect humans."

Especially disturbing, he added, is that the concentrations of two of the pesticides that caused the deformities in frogs, Esfenvalerate and Atrazine, were low enough for the water to be considered safe for human consumption under Environmental Protection Agency standards.

"Frogs may be a sentinel species that is warning us about the interplay between human-caused environmental change and disease susceptibility," he said, adding: "Hopefully, people will listen."

In other recent research on this problem, a study published in the July 1 issue of *Environmental Science & Technology* indicates that frog deformities may also occur as a result of exposure to ultraviolet (UV) radiation. At levels close to 60 percent of normal sunlight, frogs experienced deformities.

A survey of ponds in the Duluth, Minnesota, area showed that frogs in only three of 26 ponds were at risk of UV-induced deformities, because wetlands absorb a significant portion of the radiation. However, Steve Diamond of the Environmental Protection Agency's Duluth office and leader of the UV study said there may be cause for concern if human activities cause UV levels to rise.

Additional tests give scientists more information about the possible causal chain between pesticides and malformation.

Danielson closes by reminding readers of the possibility that the cause-and-effect relationship at work in frogs might have parallels for humans.

How to read causal analyses

Make notes as you read, either in the margins, if it is your copy, or on paper or a computer file. Circle any words or references that you don't know and look them up.

What is it?	• What kind of a text is it? An article? an essay? a chart? a scientific report? a Web site? an executive summary? What are your expectations for this kind of text? • What media are used? (Web sites, for example, often combine images, words, and sounds.)
Where did it come from?	• Who wrote the analysis? • Where did it first appear? In a book, newspaper, magazine, online, in a company, or in an organization?
What is the writer's thesis or main idea?	• What is the writer's topic? What effect is he or she trying to determine the cause of? • Why is this topic important? • What are the key ideas or concepts that the writer considers? • What are the key terms? How does the writer define those terms?
Who is the intended audience?	• What clues do you find about whom the writer had in mind as the readers? • What does the writer assume that the readers already know about the subject? • What new knowledge is the writer providing?
How are causes analyzed?	• What methods does the writer use to determine causation? • Does the writer consider multiple causes? • How complex is the analysis? Does the writer examine relationships between causes, or look at how one cause may arise from another? • Can you think of other causes that the writer doesn't consider?
What kinds of evidence are given?	• Is the evidence from books, newspapers, periodicals, the Web, or field research? • Is the evidence convincing that the causes given are the actual causes?
How is it composed?	• How does the writer represent herself or himself? • How would you characterize the style? • How effective is the design? Is it easy to read? • If there are any photographs, charts, or other graphics, what information do they contribute?

New Orleans' Blessing; New Orleans' Curse

(ESSAY)

Ari Kelman

Ari Kelman, a professor of history at the University of California, Davis, is the author of an environmental history of New Orleans *(A River and Its City: The Nature of Landscape in New Orleans)*. In 2005, just days after Hurricane Katrina devastated New Orleans and much of the Louisiana and Mississippi coasts, he wrote the following essay for the online magazine *Slate*. In his essay, Kelman explains the powerful economic forces that led to a major city being built in such a vulnerable location.

Analyzing and Connecting

Return to these questions after you have finished reading.

1. Why does Kelman begin by saying that moving New Orleans residents to the Superdome "was so stupid and yet so American"?

2. Kelman looks at two chains of cause and effect in this essay: how geography dictated the placement of New Orleans, and how developing technology allowed the city to grow so large. What links these two causal chains? How are they related?

3. In the immediate aftermath of Hurricane Katrina, there was speculation that New Orleans would not, or should not, be rebuilt. What does Kelman's analysis contribute to the question of whether to rebuild the city?

4. Could the same chain of causation Kelman describes in New Orleans be at work in other locations? Consider, for example, the city of San Francisco, built on a major geological fault zone and already devastated once by a major earthquake and fire. What ramifications does Kelman's essay have for people in cities like San Francisco?

Slate

Home
News & Politics
Arts & Life
Business & Tech
Health & Science
Style & Shopping
Travel & Food
Sports
Slate **on NPR**
Output Options
About Us

New Orleans' blessing; New Orleans' curse

By Ari Kelman
Wednesday, Aug. 31, 2005

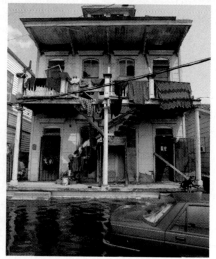

In retrospect, the idea was so stupid and yet so American: Move the homeless, the elderly, the impoverished, the unlucky, all those poor souls who couldn't get out of New Orleans in time to avoid Hurricane Katrina; move them into the city's cavernous domed football stadium. Anyone who has seen a disaster movie could have predicted what would happen next: Katrina slammed into the Superdome, ripped off the roof, and knocked out the power, cutting off the drinking water and the air conditioning. Those trapped inside had to be moved again—to Houston's Astrodome, of course.

If it's not too callous to say so while the tragedy on the Gulf Coast is still unfolding, the stadium mishap is an apt metaphor for New Orleans' environmental history. The sodden city has long placed itself in harm's way, relying on uncertain artifice to protect it from unpredictable environs.

New Orleans is utterly dependent for its survival on engineered landscapes and the willful suspension of disbelief that technology has allowed its citizens to sustain. As most people know by now, much of New Orleans lies well below sea level and also beneath the Mississippi River, which flows high above the city it helped create. If you visit New Orleans you can't actually see the river unless you're willing to climb its steep banks, mini-mountains that jut above the Mississippi's endlessly flat delta. From the relatively high ground of the French Quarter, you might catch a glimpse of a

Print | E-mail | Discuss | Newsletters | Podcast | RSS

Slate

- Home
- News & Politics
- Arts & Life
- Business & Tech
- Health & Science
- Style & Shopping
- Travel & Food
- Sports
- *Slate* on NPR
- Output Options
- About Us

huge container ship, seemingly levitating above the roofline of most houses. New Orleans is, in other words, a shallow bowl surrounded by a ridge of levees, which are supposed to keep out water from the Mississippi and from Lake Pontchartrain at the city's rear—and this week didn't. When the levees fail, as they have many times before, a flood occupies the recessed terrain in the city's center. Like the people trapped in the football stadium, water has no natural way to leave New Orleans. It must constantly be pumped over the lip of the bowl formed by the levees.

New Orleans' dysfunctional relationship with its environment may make it the nation's most improbable metropolis. It is flood prone. It is cursed with a fertile disease environment. It is located along a well-worn pathway that tropical storms travel from the Atlantic to the nation's interior. From this perspective, New Orleans has earned all the scorn being heaped upon it—the city is a misguided urban project, a fool's errand, a disaster waiting to happen.

But such insults miss why most American cities are built in the first place: to do business. In 1718, when the French first settled New Orleans, the city's earliest European inhabitants saw riches inscribed by the hand of God into the landscape of the vast

KELMAN: NEW ORLEANS' BLESSING; NEW ORLEANS' CURSE

Print | E-mail | Discuss | Newsletters | Podcast | RSS

Slate

Home
News & Politics
Arts & Life
Business & Tech
Health & Science
Style & Shopping
Travel & Food
Sports
Slate on NPR
Output Options
About Us

Mississippi valley. The Mississippi river system takes the shape of a huge funnel, covering nearly two-thirds of the United States from the Alleghenies to the Rockies. The funnel's spout lies at the river's outlet at the Gulf of Mexico, less than 100 miles downstream from New Orleans. In an era before railways, good highways, and long before air travel, much of the interior of the nation's commerce flowed along the Mississippi, fronting New Orleans. The river system's inexorable downstream current swept cotton, grain, sugar, and an array of other commodities to New Orleans' door. Because of the region's geography and topography, many 19th-century observers believed that God—working through nature, His favorite medium—would see to it that anyone shrewd enough to build and live in New Orleans would be made rich.

So, people built. Some lived. A lucky few even got rich. Many others, usually poor residents, died. They were carried away in floods. They were battered by catastrophic storms. They were snuffed out by yellow fever epidemics, like the great scourge of 1853 that killed nearly 10,000 people in the city. Over time, New Orleans developed a divided relationship with the environment: Nature, as embodied by the Mississippi, promised a bright future. But it also brought water, wind, and pathogens, elements of a fickle environment that in the past as now turned cruelly chaotic.

Geographers refer to this as the difference between a city's "situation"—the advantages its location offers relative to other cities—and its "site"—the actual real estate it occupies. New Orleans has a near-perfect situation and an almost unimaginably bad site. It's because of the former that people have worked endlessly to overcome the hazards of the latter.

From the first, New Orleans turned to technology to impose order on its environs. Since engineers began to figure out how to drain the city adequately in the mid-19th century, they have struggled mightily to do so. Over time they built a network of enormous pumps (several of which have failed in the face of Katrina) and hundreds of miles of canals—a quantity to make a Venetian feel at home. Their feats, however incomplete, have allowed the city to expand off the relatively high ground near the Mississippi and to spread out into what used to be a huge cypress swamp along the shore of Lake Pontchartrain.

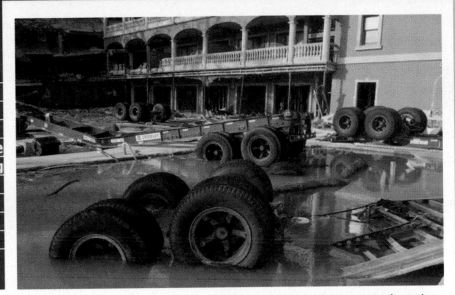

Print | E-mail | Discuss | Newsletters | Podcast | RSS

Slate

Home
News & Politics
Arts & Life
Business & Tech
Health & Science
Style & Shopping
Travel & Food
Sports
Slate on NPR
Output Options
About Us

New Orleans' early settlers also built artificial levees. At first they were little more than crude efforts to augment the natural riverbanks. But for more than two centuries, engineers steadily ramped up their project, and today the levees have grown so high that they loom over the city below. New Orleans has literally walled itself off from the Mississippi. This is all part of the effort to realize the promise of the city's situation while keeping at bay the forces that buffet its site. Of course, in its present condition, the city faces two truths: First, even today the levees are not impregnable. And second, the higher the defenses are built, the more difficult it becomes to remove water from New Orleans once it finds a way inside.

Most of the time, New Orleans can forget the perils of its environment. With the levees standing between the city and the Mississippi, it is possible to ignore the river peering down into town. And unless you happen upon one of the huge pumping stations that dot the city and manage to figure out what's inside the anonymous structure, there's no reason to consider the city's peculiar hydrology. But now, with water flowing 20 feet deep in some places, New Orleans is forced to remember that it is trapped in a cage of its own construction. Most of the city's residents will be saved, but its site cannot be airlifted to Texas.

If You Build It, They Will Come—on Foot

(ESSAY)

Jay Walljasper

Jay Walljasper was the editor of *Utne Magazine* for ten years and has written frequently about positive social and political initiatives for newspapers and magazines. He is now the Executive Editor of *Ode Magazine*, where this essay first appeared in 2005.

Analyzing and Connecting

Return to these questions after you have finished reading.

1. Notice how Walljaspar piles up examples beginning with Copenhagen. Why does he use this strategy? At what point do you know his thesis?

2. The trend of creating new public spaces runs counter to the trends of people spending more time in front of computers and watching television. How does Walljaspar explain the causes of this trend?

3. Architect Jan Gehl makes the claim that people anywhere will gather in public if you give them a good place to do it. Is a "good place" the only factor in getting people to gather? Why then have so many attempts at pedestrian malls and other public spaces been unsuccessful?

4. Visit a public space in your city or town. How new is it? Are people using it frequently? What kinds of activities do they do in this space?

If You Build It, They Will Come—on Foot

It's a dark and wintry night in Copenhagen, and the streets are bustling. The temperature stands above freezing, but winds blow hard enough to knock down a good share of the bicycles parked all around. Scandinavians are notorious for their stolid reserve, but it's all smiles and animated conversation here as people of many ages and affiliations stroll through the city center on a Thursday evening.

A knot of teenage boys, each outfitted with a slice of pizza, swagger down the main pedestrian street. Older women discreetly inspect shop windows for the coming spring fashions. An accomplished balalaika player draws a small crowd in a square as he jams with a very amateur guitarist. Earnest young people collect money for UNICEF relief efforts. A surprising number of babies in strollers are out for a breath of fresh January air. Two African men pass by, pushing a piano. Several stylishly dressed women sit at the edge of a waterless fountain, talking on mobile phones. Candlelit restaurants and cafes beckon everyone inside.

"Cultures and climates differ all over the world," notes architect Jan Gehl, "but people are the same. They will gather in public if you give them a good place to do it." Gehl, an urban design professor at the Danish Royal Academy of Fine Arts and international consultant, has charted the progress of Copenhagen's central pedestri- an district since it opened in 1962. At that time cars were overrunning the city, and the pedestrian zone was conceived as a way to bring vitality back to the declining urban center. "Shopkeepers protested vehemently that it would kill their businesses," he recalls, "but everyone was happy with it once it started. Some now even claim it was their idea."

The pedestrian zone has been expanded a bit each year ever since, with parking spaces gradually removed and biking and transit facilities improved. Cafes, once thought to be an exclusively Mediterranean institution, have become the center of Copenhagen's social life. Gehl documents that people's use of the area has more than tripled over the past 40 years. The pedestrian district is now the thriving heart of a reinvigorated city.

Copenhagen's comeback gives hope to growing numbers of citizens around the world who want to make sure that lively public places don't disappear in this era of rampant traffic, proliferating malls, heightened security measures, overpowering commercialization and the general indifference of many who think the internet and their own families can provide all the social interaction they need.

While only a century ago streets almost everywhere were crowded with people, many are now nearly empty— especially in the fast-growing suburbs sprouting all over the globe, but in some

WALLJASPER: IF YOU BUILD IT, THEY WILL COME—ON FOOT

Bryant Park in midtown Manhattan was neglected for much of the twentieth century and became the turf of drug dealers through the early 1980s. Today it is one of the most popular public spaces in New York City.

older towns and cities, too. Walking through the center of certain North American communities can be a profoundly alienating experience, as if the whole place had been evacuated for an emergency that no one told you about.

Even in the crowded urban quarters of Asia and Africa, public spaces are suffering under the onslaught of increasing traffic and misguided development plans imported from the West. The decline of public places represents a loss far deeper than simple nostalgia

for the quiet, comfortable ways of the past. "The street, the square, the park, the market, the playground are the river of life," explains Kathleen Madden, one of the directors of the New York-based Project for Public Spaces, which works with citizens around the world to improve their communities.

Public spaces are favorite places to meet, talk, sit, look, relax, play, stroll, flirt, eat, drink, smoke, peoplewatch, read, soak in sunshine and feel part of a broader whole. They are the starting point for all community, commerce and democracy. Indeed, on an evolutionary level, the future of the human race depends on public spaces. It's where young women meet and court with young men—an essential act for the propagation of the species.

Numerous studies in fields ranging from social psychology to magazine cover design have proved that nothing grabs people's attention more than other people, especially other people's faces. We are hard-wired with a desire for congenial places to gather. That's why it's particularly surprising how much we overlook the importance of public places today.

"If you asked people 20 years ago why they went to central Copenhagen, they would have said it was to shop," observes Jan Gehl, sitting in the former navy barracks that houses his "urban quality" consulting firm Gehl + Associates. "But if you asked them today, they would say it was because they wanted to go to town." That small change of phrase represents the best hope for the future of public spaces. Historically, Gehl explains, public spaces were central to everyone's lives. It's how people traveled about town, where they shopped and socialized.

Living in cramped homes, often with no yards, and certainly no cars or refrigerators, they had little choice but to use public spaces. Walking was most people's way to get around. Urban families depended on markets and shopping districts for the day's food. Parks were the only place for kids to play or see nature. Squares and churches and taverns were the few spots to meet friends.

But all that changed during the 20th century. Cars took over the streets in industrialized nations (and in wide swaths of the developing world too), putting many more places within easy reach but making walking and biking dangerous. Towns and cities spread out, with many merchants moving to outlying shopping malls. Telephones, refrigerators, television, computers, and suburban homes with big yards transformed our daily lives. People withdrew from the public realm.

No longer essential, public spaces were neglected. Many newly constructed communities simply forgot about sidewalks, parks, downtowns, transit, playgrounds, and people's pleasure in taking a walk after dinner and bumping into their neighbors. Today, many folks wonder if public spaces serve any real purpose anymore. "Some places have gone down the drain and become completely deserted," Gehl notes, brandishing a photo to prove his point. "See this, it's a health club in Atlanta, in America. It's built on top of seven stories of parking. People there don't go out on the streets. They even drive their cars to the health club to walk and get exercise.

"But other places have decided to do something about it—they fight back," he adds, pointing to another photo, a street scene in Norway, where dozens of people are enjoying themselves at an outdoor cafe alongside a sidewalk filled with people. Gehl ticks off a list of places that have revitalized themselves by creating great public places: Copenhagen; Barcelona, Spain; Lyon, France; Bogota, Colombia;

Vancouver, Canada; the American city of Portland, Ore.; and the small Danish city of Vejle. His definitive book *New City Spaces* (2000, Danish Architectural Press), written with partner Lars Gemzoe, includes more success stories from Cordoba, Argentina; Melbourne, Australia; Curitiba, Brazil; Freiburg, Germany; and Strasbourg, France.

Melbourne made great efforts to keep its streets pedestrian-friendly by widening sidewalks and adding attractive features that ignited a spectacular increase in people going out in public. Cordoba turned its riverfront into a series of popular parks. Curitiba pioneered an innovative bus rapid transit system that prevented traffic from overwhelming the fast-growing city.

Portland put curbs on suburban sprawl and transformed a ho-hum downtown into a bustling urban magnet, starting by demolishing a parking garage to build a town square. Barcelona and Lyon best illustrate the power of public spaces. Once thought of as dull industrial centers, both are now widely celebrated as sophisticated, glamorous places that attract international attention and instill local residents with a sense of pride.

Barcelona is now mentioned in the same breath as Paris and Rome as the epitome of a great European city. The heart of Barcelona—and of Barcelona's revival—is Las Ramblas, a pedestrian promenade so popular it has spawned a new Spanish word: Ramblistas, meaning the folks who hang out in the area. In the spirit of liberation following the end of the Franco dictatorship, during which time public assembly was severely discouraged, local citizens and officials created new squares and public spaces all across the city and suburbs to celebrate the return of democracy and heal the scars of political and civic repression. Some of them fit so well with the urban fabric of the old city that visitors often assume they are centuries old.

Creating popular public places yields substantial economic return in the form of business investment, strengthened local economies and tourism, while enhancing the quality of existing public spaces can bring rewards to an already prosperous area. Take New York's Bryant Park, which was off-limits to most citizens in the early 1980s due to non-stop drug dealing. A renovation of the park, which tore out the shrubbery that gave drug dealers a sense of privacy and added ample seating to invite everyone else back, has transformed the place into one of New York's most beloved gathering spots.

The key to restoring life to our public places—and our communities as a whole—is understanding that most people today have more options than in the past. A trip downtown or to the farmer's market or the local library is now recreational as much as it is practical—the chance to have fun, hang out with other folks, and enjoy the surroundings. "People are not out in public spaces because they have to but because they love to," Gehl explains.

If the idea of a new movement rising up to change the face of communities all around the planet strikes you as far-fetched, consider the Crossroads mall in Bellevue, Washington. A standard-issue, auto-dominated suburb east of Seattle, Bellevue seems way off-the-radar of any upsurge to promote lively public spaces. Especially Crossroads, a '70s-era enclosed mall surrounded by acres of parking a mile south of Microsoft's sprawling campus.

But look again. Whimsical public art dots the parking lot, and cafe tables and sidewalk merchandise displays flank the entrances—just like in a classic downtown. An impressively well-stocked newsstand greets you in the hall of the main entrance, right next to a used bookstore. Wandering through the mall you find the local public library, a police station and a branch of city hall, where I am told "you can do nearly everything they do at the main office." There are even comfy chairs stationed right outside the bathrooms and a giant-sized chess board where kids can push around pawns and bishops almost as big as they are.

Some of the usual franchise suspects are here: Bed, Bath and Beyond; a JoAnn fabrics superstore; a Pier One home furnishings store, but you'll find locally owned businesses too, like a wine shop and a ceramics studio. The food court—where you can choose among Indian, Russian, Thai, Mexican, Korean, Greek, barbecue, Vietnamese, Italian, a juice bar or a burger joint—features local restaurateurs. Breakfast, lunch or dinner arrive on a ceramic plate with metal (not plastic!) cutlery.

Many of the tables face a stage, where on this particular Thursday Black History Month is being observed with an impressive program of music, theatre and dance—all of it first rate. The audience is multiethnic, reflecting the changing demographics of American suburbia. The loudest applause comes from a delegation of preschoolers visiting from a nearby daycare center.

Ron Sher, who transformed Crossroads from a failing mall into a spirited gathering place, sits down with me for lunch and, in between greeting customers and conducting mini-meetings with shop owners, outlines the next phase of his vision. "I want a mix of upscale and affordable housing built on a part of the parking lot, so this could become a true town square that some people walk to." I pinch myself to make sure this is all real, that I am actually talking to a shopping center developer who is telling me, "I want to get people together with the city to discuss how to step this up to be even more of a community center."

Now, of course, I would prefer to hang out in Copenhagen, or Barcelona, or the famous Pike Place market in downtown Seattle. So would many of the people in Bellevue. But the fact is they live in Bellevue, and it's a great thing they have a mall where they can take care of their errands, meet their neighbors and have some fun. If a lively public place can take root here, it can happen anywhere.

Why Should I Be Nice To You? Coffee Shops and the Politics of Good Service

(ESSAY)

Emily Raine

Emily Raine recently received a Masters degree in Communication Studies at McGill University in Montreal. She also writes about graffiti and street art. This essay appeared in the online journal *Bad Subjects* in 2005.

Analyzing and Connecting

Return to these questions after you have finished reading.

1. What exactly is Raine's causal argument about why work in coffee chains is worse than in other kinds of service jobs?

2. Raine mixes technical terms with informal language. For example, she says "café labor is heavily grounded in the rationalism of Fordist manufacturing principles," which is the technical term for the method of assembly-line production developed by Henry Ford. But she says she "felt like an aproned Coke machine." Look for other examples of technical and informal language. Why does she mix them?

3. Why is it important that coffee shop employees not act like individuals from the employer's perspective?

4. Have you ever worked in a restaurant, coffee shop, retail store, or another service industry? If so, how was your experience similar to or different from Raine's? If not, think about your experiences as a customer in coffee shops and similar businesses. How did the employees behave?

5. Look at the last paragraph. Raine makes a new claim that rudeness allows workers to retain their individuality. Why does she put this claim in the conclusion? Does it lead to a strong conclusion?

home about articles authors books contact us **editorials** links news reviews

Why Should I Be Nice To You?
Coffee Shops and the Politics of Good Service

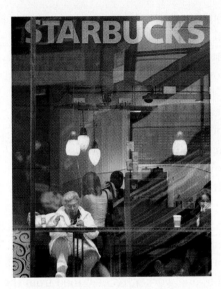

"There is no more precious commodity than the relationship of trust and confidence a company has with its employees."

–Starbucks Coffee Company
Chairman Howard Schultz

I actually like to serve. I'm not sure if this comes from some innate inclination to mother and fuss over strangers, or if it's because the movement and sociability of service work provides a much-needed antidote to the solitude of academic research, but I've always found something about service industry work satisfying. I've done the gamut of service jobs, from fine dining to cocktail waitressing to hip euro-bistro counter work, and the only job where I've ever felt truly whipped was working as a barista at one of the now-ubiquitous specialty coffee chains, those bastions of jazz and public solitude that have spread through urban landscapes over the last ten years or so. The pay was poor, the shifts long and oddly dispersed, the work boring and monotonous, the managers demanding, and the customers regularly displayed that unique spleen that emerges in even the most pleasant people before they've had the morning's first coffee. I often felt like an aproned Coke machine, such was the effect my sparkling personality had on the clientele. And yet, some combination of service professionalism, fear of termination and an imperative to be "nice" allowed me to suck it up, smile and continue to

Bad Subjects

home   about   articles   authors   books   contact us   **editorials**   links   news   reviews

provide that intangible trait that the industry holds above all else, good service.

Good service in coffee shops doesn't amount to much. Unlike table service, where interaction with customers spans a minimum of half an hour, the average contact with a café customer lasts less than ten seconds. Consider how specialty cafés are laid out: the customer service counter is arranged in a long line that clients move along to "use" the café. The linear coffee bar resembles an assembly line, and indeed, café labor is heavily grounded in the rationalism of Fordist manufacturing principles, which had already been tested for use in hospitality services by fast food chains. Each of the café workers is assigned a specific stage in the service process to perform exclusively, such as taking orders, using the cash registers, or handing clients cups of brewed coffee.

The specialization of tasks increases the speed of transactions and limits the duration of any one employee's interaction with the clientele. This means that in a given visit a customer might order from one worker, receive food from the next, then brewed coffee or tea from yet another, then pay a cashier before proceeding down the line of the counter, finishing the trip at the espresso machine which is always situated at its end. Ultimately, each of the café's products is processed and served by a different employee, who repeats the same preparation task for hours and attends to each customer only as they receive that one product.

Needless to say, the productive work in cafés is dreary and repetitive. Further, this style of service severely curtails interaction with the clientele, and the very brevity of each transaction precludes much chance for authentic friendliness or conversation—even asking about someone's day would slow the entire operation. The one aspect of service work that can be unpredictable— people—becomes redundant, and interaction with customers is reduced to a fatiguing eight hour long smile and the repetition of sentiments that allude to good service, such as injunctions to enjoy their purchases or to have a nice day. Rather than friendly exchanges with customers, barista workers' good

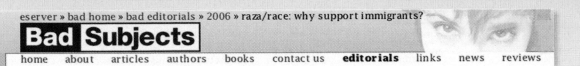

Bad Subjects

home   about   articles   authors   books   contact us   **editorials**   links   news   reviews

service is reduced to a quick rictus in the customer's direction between a great deal of friendly interaction with the espresso machine.

As the hospitality industry really took off in the sixties, good service became one of the trademarks of its advertising claims, a way for brands to distinguish themselves from the rest of the pack. One needn't think too hard to come up with a litany of service slogans that holler the good graces of their personnel—at Starbucks where the baristas make the magic, at PSA where smiles aren't just painted on, or at McDonald's where smiles are free. Employee friendliness emerged as one of the chief distinguishing brand features of personal services, which means that the workers themselves become an aspect of the product for sale.

Our notions of good service revolve around a series of platitudes about professionalism—we're at your service, with a smile, where the customer's always right—each bragging the centrality of the customer to everything "we" do. Such claims imply an easy and equal exchange between two parties: the "we" that gladly serves and the "you" that happily receives. There is, however, always a third party involved in the service exchange, and that's whoever has hired the server, the body that ultimately decides just what the dimensions of good service will be.

Like most employees, a service worker sells labor to an employer at a set rate, often minimum wage, and the employer sells the product of that labor, the service itself, at market values. In many hospitality services, where gratuities make up the majority of employment revenue, the worker directly benefits from giving good service, which of course translates to good tips. But for the vast majority of service staff, and particularly those employed in venues yielding little or no gratuities—fast food outlets, café chains, cleaning and maintenance operations—this promises many workers little more than a unilateral imperative to be perpetually bright and amenable.

The vast majority of service personnel do not spontaneously produce an unaffected display of cheer and good will continuously for the duration of a eserver » bad home » bad editorials » 2006 » raza/race: why support immigrants?

home   about   articles   authors   books   contact us   **editorials**   links   news   reviews

shift. When a company markets its products on servers' friendliness, they must then monitor and control employees' friendliness, so good service is defined and enforced from above. Particularly in chains, which are premised upon their consistent reproduction of the same experience in numerous locations, organizations are obliged to impose systems to manage employees' interaction their customers. In some chains, namely the fast food giants such as McDonald's and Burger King, employee banter is scripted into cash registers, so that as soon as a customer orders, workers are cued to offer, "would you like a dessert with that?" (an offer of dubious benefit to the customer) and to wish them a nice day. Ultimately, this has allowed corporations to be able to assimilate "good service"—or, friendly workers— into their overall brand image.

While cafés genuflect toward the notion of good service, their layouts and management styles preclude much possibility of creating the warmth that this would entail. Good service is, of course, important, but not if it interferes with throughput. What's more, these cafés have been at the forefront of a new wave of organizations that not only market themselves on service quality but also describe employees' job satisfaction as the seed from which this flowers.

Perhaps the most glaring example of this is Starbucks, where cheerful young workers are displayed behind elevated counters as they banter back and forth, calling out fancy Italian drink names and creating theatre out of their productive labor. Starbucks' corporate literature gushes not only about the good service its customers will receive, but about the great joy that its "partners" take in providing it, given the company's unique ability to "provide a great work environment and treat each other with respect and dignity," and where its partners are "emotionally and intellectually committed to Starbucks success." In the epigraph to this essay, Starbucks' chairman even describes the company's relationship with its workers as a commodity. Not only does Starbucks offer good service, but it attempts to guarantee something even better: good service provided by employees that are genuinely happy to give it.

Bad Subjects

home   about   articles   authors   books   contact us   **editorials**   links   news   reviews

Starbucks has branded a new kind of worker, the happy, wholesome, perfume-free barista. The company offers unusual benefits for service workers, including stock options, health insurance, dental plans and other perks such as product discounts and giveaways. Further, they do so very, very publicly, and the company's promotional materials are filled with moving accounts of workers who never dreamed that corporate America could care so much. With the other hand, though, the company has smashed unionization drives in New York, Vancouver and at its Seattle roaster; it schedules workers at oddly timed shifts that never quite add up to full-time hours; the company pays only nominally more than minimum wage, and their staffs are still unable to subsist schlepping lattes alone.

Starbucks is not alone in marketing itself as an enlightened employer. When General Motors introduced its Saturn line, the new brand was promoted almost entirely on the company's good relations with its staff. The company's advertising spots often featured pictures of and quotes from the union contract, describing their unique partnership between manufacturer, workers and union, which allowed blue-collar personnel to have a say in everything from automobile designs to what would be served for lunch. The company rightly guessed that this strategy would go over well with liberal consumers concerned about the ethics of their purchases. Better yet, Saturn could market its cars based on workers' happiness whether personnel were satisfied or not, because very few consumers would ever have the chance to interact with them.

At the specialty coffee chains, however, consumers have to talk to employees, yet nobody ever really asks. The café service counter runs like a smooth piece of machinery, and I found that most people preferred to pretend that they were interacting with an appliance. In such short transactions, it is exceedingly difficult for customers to remember the humanity of each of the four to seven people they might interact with to get their coffees. Even fast food counters have one server who processes each customer's order, yet in cafés the workers just become another gadget in the well-oiled café machine. This is a definite downside for the employees—clients are much ruder to café

331

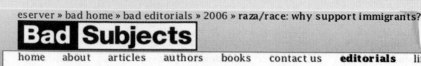

eserver » bad home » bad editorials » 2006 » raza/race: why support immigrants?

Bad **Subjects**

home   about   articles   authors   books   contact us   **editorials**   links   news   reviews

staff than in any other sector of the industry I ever worked in. I found that people were more likely to be annoyed than touched by any reference to my having a personality, and it took no small amount of thought on my part to realize why.

Barista workers are hired to represent an abstract category of worker, not to act as individuals. Because of the service system marked by short customer interaction periods and a homogenous staff, the services rendered are linked in the consumer imagination to the company and not to any one individual worker. Workers' assimilation into the company image makes employees in chain service as branded as the products they serve. The chain gang, the workers who hold these eminently collegiate after-school jobs, are proscribed sales scripts and drilled on customer service scenarios to standardize interactions with customers. The company issues protocols for hair length, color and maintenance, visible piercings and tattoos as well as personal hygiene and acceptable odorific products. Workers are made more interchangeable by the use of uniforms, which, of course, serve to make the staff just that. The organization is a constant intermediary in every transaction, interjecting its presence in every detail of the service experience, and this standardization amounts to an absorption of individuals' personalities into the corporate image.

Many of the measures that chains take to secure the homogeneity of their employees do not strike us as particularly alarming, likely because similar restrictions have been in place for several hundred years. Good service today has inherited many of the trappings of the good servant of yore, including prohibitions against eating, drinking, sitting or relaxing in front the served, entering and exiting through back doors and wearing uniforms to visually mark workers' status. These measures almost completely efface the social identities of staff during work hours, providing few clues to workers' status in their free time. Contact between service workers and their customers is thus limited to purely functional relations, so that the public only see them as workers, as makers of quality coffee, and never as possible peers.

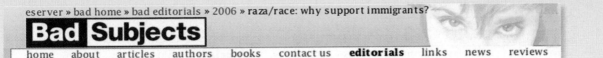

Bad Subjects

home   about   articles   authors   books   contact us   **editorials**   links   news   reviews

Maintaining such divisions is integral to good service because this display of class distinctions ultimately underlies our notions of service quality. Good service means not only serving well, but also allowing customers to feel justified in issuing orders, to feel okay about being served—which, in turn, requires demonstrations of class difference and the smiles that suggest servers' comfort with having a subordinate role in the service exchange.

Unlike the penguin-suited household servant staffs whose class status was clearly defined, service industry workers today often have much more in common from a class perspective with those that they serve. This not only creates an imperative for them to wear their class otherness on their sleeves, as it were, but also to accept their subordinate role to those they serve by being unshakably tractable and polite.

Faith Popcorn has rather famously referred to the four-dollar latte as a "small indulgence," noting that while this is a lot to pay for a glass of hot milk, it is quite inexpensive for the feeling of luxury that can accompany it. In this service climate, the class status of the server and the served—anyone who can justify spending this much on a coffee—is blurry, indeed. Coffee shops that market themselves on employee satisfaction assert the same happy servant that allows politically conscientious consumers who are in many cases the workers' own age and class peers, to feel justified in receiving good service. Good service—as both an apparent affirmation of subordinate classes' desire to serve and as an enforced one-sided politeness—reproduces the class distinctions that have historically characterized servant-served relationships so that these are perpetuated within the contemporary service market.

The specialty coffee companies are large corporations, and for the twenty-somethings who stock their counters, barista work is too temporary to bother fighting the system. Mostly, people simply quit. Dissatisfied workers are stuck with engaging in tactics that will change nothing but allow them to make the best of their lot. These include minor infractions such as taking liberties with the uniforms or grabbing little bits of company time for their own pleasure, what Michel de Certeau calls *la perruque* and the companies themselves call

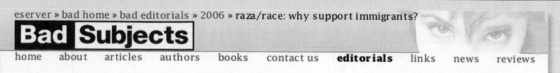

eserver » bad home » bad editorials » 2006 » raza/race: why support immigrants?

Bad Subjects

home   about   articles   authors   books   contact us   **editorials**   links   news   reviews

"time theft." As my time in the chain gang wore on, I developed my own tactic, the only one I found that jostled the customers out of their complacency and allowed me to be a barista and a person.

There is no easy way to serve without being a servant, and I have always found that the best way to do so is to show my actual emotions rather than affecting a smooth display of interminable patience and good will. For café customers, bettering baristas' lots can be as simple as asking about their day, addressing them by name—any little gesture to show that you noticed the person behind the service that they can provide. My tactic as a worker is equally simple, but it is simultaneously an assertion of individual identity at work, a refusal of the class distinctions that characterize the service environment and a rebuttal to the companies that would promote my satisfaction with their system: be rude. Not arbitrarily rude, of course— customers are people, too, and nobody gains anything by spreading bad will. But on those occasions when customer or management behavior warranted a zinging comeback, I would give it.

Rudeness, when it is demanded, undermines companies' claims on workers' personal warmth and allows them to retain their individuality by expressing genuine rather than affected feelings in at-work interpersonal exchanges. It is a refusal of the class distinctions that underlie consumers' unilateral prerogative of rudeness and servers' unilateral imperative to be nice. It runs contrary to everything that we have been taught, not only about service but about interrelating with others. But this seems to be the only method of asserting one's person-hood in the service environment, where workers' personalities are all too easily reduced to a space-time, conflated with the drinks they serve. Baristas of the world, if you want to avoid becoming a green-aproned coffee dispensary, you're just going to have to tell people off about it.

Barbie's Body May Be Perfect, but Critics Remind Us It's Plastic

(ARTICLE)

Angela Cain

Many women and girls in America suffer from poor body image, sometimes coupled with eating disorders such as anorexia and bulimia. A number of possible causes of poor body image have been identified, including the unrealistic portrayal of women through such toys as Mattel's Barbie doll. Knight-Ridder journalist Angela Cain examines the impact of Barbie and other social factors on women's body image in this article, which originally appeared in the *Albany Times-Union* on March 22, 1996.

Analyzing and Connecting

Return to these questions after you have finished reading.

1. Cain's analysis traces a plausible chain of cause and effect, but her argument is far from conclusive. How do her claims stand up to the various methods of determining causation outlined in this chapter?

2. One stakeholder is notably absent from Cain's article: Mattel, the toy company that manufactures and sells Barbie dolls. How do you think representatives of Mattel would respond to the claims in this article?

3. Drawing on your own experience as a child, what impact would you say dolls and action figures such as G.I. Joe have had on your perception of "ideal" body types? Do you think they influenced your attitude toward what men and women should look like? How do you think the impact of dolls and action figures compares with the impact of other influences, such as your parents, the television shows and movies you watched, and other factors?

4. Cain's article was published in 1996. Do you find the causal analysis still holds true or has American culture changed to the extent that her claims seem out of date?

BARBIE'S BODY MAY BE PERFECT, BUT CRITICS REMIND US IT'S PLASTIC

Barbie: With curves in all the right places and a figure that's looked flattering in fashions since 1959, the plastic doll that doesn't appear a day older than when baby boomers first pulled her out of the box.

For generations she's been the doll that little girls have aspired to be—a party girl, career woman and bathing beauty all wrapped into one. But her critics contend that the Mattel creation is one of many reasons why women are unhappy with their less-than-perfect bodies.

Barbie's unrealistic body type—busty with a tiny waist, thin thighs and long legs—is reflective of our culture's feminine ideal. Yet less than two percent of American women can ever hope to achieve such dreamy measurements.

Still, this image of thinness and beauty dominates the movie screens and fashion magazines. Unattainable or not, it's what most women think their bodies should be.

"We've let images like Barbie and slender figures on magazine covers tell us what we should look like, and since most of us don't look like supermodels, we end up feeling bad about our bodies," say Linda Brogdon, a licensed psychologist and eating-disorder specialist.

In extreme cases, this can lead to eating disorders like anorexia or bulimia. But for most women, it's simply a feeling of inadequacy because their bodies don't measure up to an unrealistic ideal.

Kristen Overman, a licensed mental-health counselor and marriage and family therapist, agrees.

"Women are groomed to compare themselves in their 5-foot-4,142-pound frames with models who are five inches taller and 20 pounds lighter than the average American woman," she says.

"The visual media plays a big role in how women see their bodies. When you look at the cover of some fashion magazine, those models are airbrushed. Nobody looks that perfect. But the magazine makes you think they do."

Whether it's breasts that sag, thighs that jiggle or a stomach that bulges, most women can point to at least one area of their bodies they dislike. In fact, studies show that more than 60 percent of women don't like what they see in the mirror.

"We always want what we don't have—straight hair if it's curly, a large chest if we have a small one," says Deby King, manager of Victoria's Secret, a lingerie shop at Governor's Square Mall in Tallahassee, Fla.

"I don't think there is any woman who is completely happy with the way she looks. If a woman said she thought she looked perfect, we would all laugh and say, 'Yeah, right.' "

What's frustrating for most women, Overman says, is that they're generally stuck with the body type they have.

"We're told that if we diet and exercise we'll get rid of the things we don't like about our bodies, that we'll actually be able to change the shape of our bodies," she says. "But that's not always true. Most women are not going to look like Suzanne Sommers if they use Thigh Master."

Overman speaks from experience. The therapist, who stands 6 feet 4 1/2 inches tall, would have given anything to have been shorter in high school.

With a frame that towered over even the tallest boy in her class, she was teased constantly.

"I was nicknamed the Jolly Green Giant," she recalls. "And I couldn't watch those commercials on television for years without feeling tremendous pain."

Body-image issues often surface during the adolescent and teen years when a sense of belonging becomes a priority for young girls. Like Overman, many girls struggle to look like and be like every other girl at school.

Studies show that children are dieting in as early as the fourth grade. And our parents play a vital role in shaping our perceptions of our bodies.

"Moms and dads almost always have an idea of what they want us to look like, and they sometimes try to project that image onto us," Brogdon says. "Then, that can turn into what you believe your body should be."

The way parents feel about their own bodies also impacts their children. Overman says her mother, who also stood over six feet tall, also felt bad about her body.

Similarly, licensed clinical social worker Katheryn Lord says her mother often made her feel badly because she didn't have an hourglass figure.

CAIN: BARBIE'S BODY MAY BE PERFECT, BUT CRITICS REMIND US IT'S PLASTIC

"My mom always said, 'I hope you don't get bigger than a size 13,'" she says. "And at ballet class, she'd say, 'Look at all those pretty girls with nice waists.'"

But when Lord turned 40, she finally learned to accept the body she was given.

"It was an enormous relief for me when I turned 40," says the therapist, now 47. "I accepted that I was never going to be tall, thin or blond, and I stopped weighing myself."

Studies have shown that black women are more comfortable with their bodies—regardless of their weight—than white women, according to a joint research project by Florida State University and Florida A&M University.

Black women, who tend to weigh ten pounds more than their white counterparts, were less likely to be influenced by images of thinness in fashion magazines. Instead, they placed more importance on acceptance from their family, friends and culture.

Studies also indicate that across the board, men are generally happier with their appearance than women.

A University of Pennsylvania study showed that most men thought their body type matched the ideal body type they believed women found attractive.

But the study revealed that most women overestimated their body size.

Lord attributes this to the way women are trained to compare their bodies.

"It would be very rare to find a woman who thinks she's smaller than she really is," she says. "We live in a very competitive world. We're constantly forced to compare ourselves to other things and other people.

"Children are encouraged to measure their looks against things like Barbie, and adults compare themselves to the supermodels."

But some say this is starting to change. To some extent, models are looking healthier, and women are beginning to recognize that they'll never fit into a size three.

"I think most people today are realistic," says Cherie Bronsky, owner of Wellness Works, a Tallahassee fitness center. "That's very different from when I started in the business 13 years ago. The fitness craze of the '80s began because of body image. It used to be that there were demands for thinness and sculpted bodies. Now people just say, 'Get me to the point where I can walk up a flight of stairs without getting winded.'

"I hear a lot of women saying, 'I don't want to look like Cindy Crawford or Barbie.' In fact, a woman just told me the other day that she knows she'll probably always be a size 13. She just wants to carry her weight well."

Television Violence and Aggression

(ARTICLE)

Thom Curtis

Thom Curtis, a Doctor of Sociology at the University of Hawaii-Hilo, and a licensed family counselor, wrote the following article on televised and domestic violence in 2001 for the journal *Family Focus*. In it, he explains how he researched detailed information on children and violence, concluding that televised violence has little or no correlation with aggressive behavior by children. Instead, Curtis found, children who behave aggressively are far more likely to have witnessed actual violence within their own family.

Analyzing and Connecting

Return to these questions after you have finished reading.

1. At the beginning of his article, Curtis states that "Contrary to popular rhetoric, there is surprisingly little empirical research that connects actual television viewing with subsequent acts of aggression or violence." Does this statement surprise you? Why or why not?

2. What arguments and evidence have you previously encountered about television violence? Who made these arguments? What do you suppose their stakes were in the debate? Which of the arguments surrounding television violence have you found to be convincing? Which did not convince you?

3. If Curtis's conclusion is correct—that domestic violence, and not television violence, is responsible for aggressive and violent behavior in children—how does the debate over television violence change? How should laws and policies be changed?

Television Violence and Aggression

by Thom Curtis, Ph.D.

Assistant Professor, Department of Sociology, University of Hawaii-Hilo

I S THERE A CONNECTION between violence on television and aggressive behavior? A longitudinal study that followed over 1,100 subjects from childhood to adulthood provided little evidence that such a connection exists. Rather than demonstrating a connection between viewing fictional televised violence and subsequent aggressive or violent behaviors, the study indicated that the leading contributor to these behaviors is the amount of family violence witnessed or experienced by the subjects as children.

Over the past 30 years, violence on television has often been cited as a key contributor to the increased violence in American society. Numerous experiments have provided evidence that children's viewing of violent behaviors on film is followed by an increase in aggression in the laboratory setting. Contrary to popular rhetoric, there is surprisingly little empirical research that connects actual television viewing with subsequent acts of aggression or violence. The few existing longitudinal surveys provide a mixed and inconclusive picture of the actual relationship between broadcast violence and aggression.

This study analyzed data regarding subjects' viewing habits as children as well as their violent behavior as teenagers and adults. It also examined the types and amounts of real violence that subjects had experienced or witnessed in their own homes.

A National Survey

The data for this study came primarily from the second and third waves of the National Surveys of Children (NSC), a longitudinal study of children selected in a probability sample of households in the United States.

The second wave of the NSC survey was conducted in 1981 as a follow-up of the first wave conducted in 1976. The second wave consisted of 1,432 children who were then 11 to 16 years old. The subsample was chosen to include all children in disrupted or high conflict families and an approximately equal number of children selected from low or moderate conflict families.

Conducted in 1987, the third wave of the survey attempted to contact the same families who had participated in the second wave. The 1,126 subjects located were then 17 to 23 years of age.

Each survey consisted of interviews with the selected child and the parent most capable of disclosing detailed information about the child and family—usually the mother. Children in the second wave were asked to identify and rank their four favorite TV programs. They were also asked how much time they spent watching television each day. As part of the third wave, subjects were asked to describe various violent or aggressive acts they had committed. The second and third wave interviews asked the parent questions about violence in their spousal relationships.

Defining TV Violence

The second wave sought information on several aspects of television viewing. The children were asked about the amount of time they spent viewing television each day. The subjects were also asked to name their four favorite programs. All together, they named 224 different programs or program types. Programs such as *Bonanza, Incredible Hulk, Kojak, Magnum P.I., Starsky and Hutch, The Six Million Dollar Man, Star Trek, Get Smart, Soap, The Three Stooges, Bugs Bunny,*

Scooby Doo, and *Tom and Jerry* were coded as violent shows. Other programs that contained no or only occasional fictional violence were deemed nonviolent.

Arguments could be made that some programs from the nonviolent category such as news or sports should have been coded as violent programming, but it was decided that only programs with fictional violence would be included in the violent category for the purposes of this study. The ratio of favored violent to nonviolent shows was multiplied by the number of hours spent viewing television to create the primary independent variable.

Answers to nine questions from the third wave interviews about violent acts perpetrated by the subjects against other persons and property were used to determine the extent to which subjects exhibited aggressive behavior.

No significant relationships were found between the television violence independent variable and interpersonal violent acts perpetrated by the subjects as teenagers or young adults. There appeared to be a small, but significant relationship between viewing habits and property damage.

Measuring Family Violence

Because this study had its theoretical basis in social learning theory, a type of modeling other than television was sought for purposes of comparison. To do this, I used answers to 18 questions from the three waves of NSC to create a "Parental Violence" scale. This scale measured the amount of violence in the form of child abuse, corporal punishment and marital violence that existed in the subject's family. The "Parent-Child Violence" subscale consisted of answers to 13 questions involving corporal punishment or child abuse. If the reported spanking, slapping, hitting or beating up resulted in the child's being physically hurt or bruised, the answers were weighted double. The "Parent's Marital Violence" subscale consisted of five questions regarding violence between spouses.

The amount of parent-child violence experienced by the child was significantly related to the child's own violence toward other persons and property. As the number and severity of violent acts directed at children increased, so did the violent acts of these children toward other people and things.

There was also a significant relationship between the violence that children witnessed in their parents' spousal relationship and violence in the children's own marriages.

Real vs. Fantasy Violence

The results of this study add to the body of research that has failed to support the theory that television violence stimulates aggressive behavior through modeling or other means. As other writers have pointed out, most children may be able to differentiate between fantasy and real life, thereby inhibiting video violence from being a model for aggressive behavior. Only those few with psychological problems or an existing proclivity to violence may lack this ability.

On the other hand, this study has demonstrated that real violence, either observed or experienced by children, is significantly correlated with later violent acts in the lives of those children. Until further research is available, it is advisable to exercise restraint in corporal discipline, spousal conflicts and other potentially violent situations, accompanied by parental wisdom in the use of the channel selector and off button on the television set.

For more information, contact thomc@hawaii.edu.

Operation Iraqi Freedom Leaflets

(LEAFLET)

In the months leading up to the second war against Iraq, which began on March 20, 2003, the United States and its allies enforced "no-fly" zones in northern and southern Iraq by increasing the number of flights. Occasionally, Iraqis shot at Coalition planes, which led to bombings of anti-aircraft sites. In October 2002, Coalition planes began dropping hundreds of thousands of propaganda leaflets on Iraqi military bases depicting what would happen if Iraqi soldiers shot at Coalition planes. (Notice that the "If" panel is on the right because Arabic is read from right to left.)

Analyzing and Connecting

Return to these questions after you have finished reading.

1. Write in words the causal argument being made in these leaflets. What is the difference between the leaflet version and your version?

2. Find other examples of extremely short causal arguments. Look for warning labels and other short texts. Identify the arguments.

3. The United States and its allies also sent email messages that urged Iraqi soldiers not to fight. What causal arguments could you make to try to convince the Iraqi soldiers not to fire upon or otherwise engage with the U.S. and allied forces?

4. Propaganda leaflets have been dropped behind enemy lines in other wars. Most seem too crude to have had much effect on morale. Do you think these leaflets or leaflets in other wars could be effective? If so, what kind of arguments would they have to make?

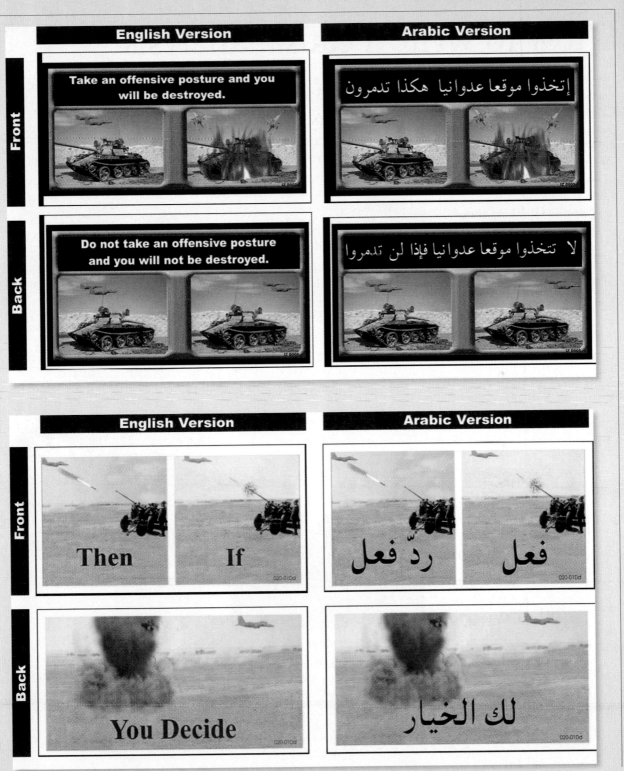

How to write a causal analysis

These steps for the process of writing a causal analysis may not progress as neatly as this chart might suggest. Writing is not an assembly-line process. As you write, you are constantly reading what you have written and rethinking.

Continue thinking about causation as you write and revise. The process of writing may lead you to additional causal relationships.

1 MAKE A CAUSAL CLAIM

- Examine a social trend, law, or policy.

- Analyze problems in your neighborhood or at your school.

- Investigate natural phenomena.

- Investigate the impact of human activity on the environment.

- Put your claim in the form "_____ causes (or does not cause) _____."

2 THINK ABOUT THE POSSIBLE CAUSES

- What are the obvious causes?

- What are the underlying causes?

- What causes might be hidden?

- What are the causes that most people have not recognized before?

Analyze your potential readers

- Who are your readers? Do they have a stake in your analysis?

- How familiar will they be with the trend, event, or phenomenon you are writing about?

- What are they likely to know and not know?

- How likely are they to accept your causal explanation?

Think about what is at stake

- What could or should change once the cause is known? What could people do differently in the future?

- If the cause is obvious to everyone, then it probably isn't worth writing about.

3 WRITE A DRAFT

- Describe the trend, event, or phenomenon.

- Give the background your readers will need.

- If the trend or event you are analyzing is unfamiliar to your readers, explain the cause or the chain of causation.

- Another way to organize the body of your analysis is to set out the causes that have already been offered and reject them one by one. Then you can present the cause or causes that you think are the right ones.

- A third method is to look at a series of causes one by one, analyzing the importance of each.

- Do more than simply summarize in your conclusion. You might consider additional effects beyond those you have previously noted, or explain to readers any action you think should be taken based on your conclusions.

- Choose a title that will interest readers in your essay.

- Include any necessary images or tables.

4 REVISE, REVISE, REVISE

- Check that your causal analysis fulfills the assignment.

- Make sure that your claim is clear and that you have sufficient evidence to convince readers.

- Look at additional potential causes, if necessary.

- Reconsider how multiple causes might interact.

- Go further back in the causal chain, if necessary, showing how the causes you examine have their roots in other events.

- Examine the organization of your analysis and think of possible better ways to organize.

- Review the visual presentation of your analysis for readability and maximum impact.

- Proofread carefully.

5 SUBMITTED VERSION

- Make sure your finished writing meets all formatting requirements.

1: Make a causal claim

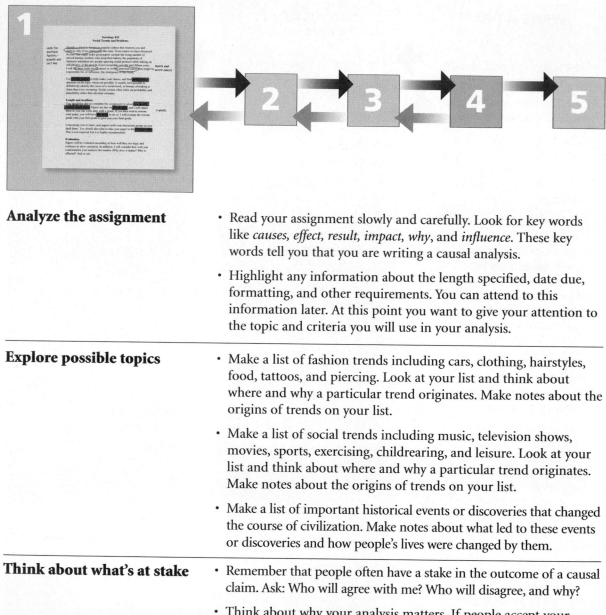

Analyze the assignment

- Read your assignment slowly and carefully. Look for key words like *causes, effect, result, impact, why,* and *influence.* These key words tell you that you are writing a causal analysis.

- Highlight any information about the length specified, date due, formatting, and other requirements. You can attend to this information later. At this point you want to give your attention to the topic and criteria you will use in your analysis.

Explore possible topics

- Make a list of fashion trends including cars, clothing, hairstyles, food, tattoos, and piercing. Look at your list and think about where and why a particular trend originates. Make notes about the origins of trends on your list.

- Make a list of social trends including music, television shows, movies, sports, exercising, childrearing, and leisure. Look at your list and think about where and why a particular trend originates. Make notes about the origins of trends on your list.

- Make a list of important historical events or discoveries that changed the course of civilization. Make notes about what led to these events or discoveries and how people's lives were changed by them.

Think about what's at stake

- Remember that people often have a stake in the outcome of a causal claim. Ask: Who will agree with me? Who will disagree, and why?

- Think about why your analysis matters. If people accept your causal claim, will anything change?

STAYING ON TRACK

Make a claim that matters

Make an arguable claim

Easy answers generally make bad arguments. If all the sources you consult agree about the cause of the effect you are interested in, there is probably no need for you to make another argument saying the same thing. Look for a phenomenon that hasn't been explained to everyone's satisfaction.

OFF TRACK

Cigarette smoke is a leading cause of lung cancer.

ON TRACK

New research indicates that childhood asthma may be linked to exposure to cockroaches.

Explain why it matters

Readers need to know why this cause-and-effect relationship is important. If we determine the cause of this phenomenon, what will change? What can we do? What might happen?

OFF TRACK

This paper will investigate the most common causes of foundation failure in U.S. residential housing.

ON TRACK

Foundation failure, especially cracked slabs, can cost anywhere from a few thousand to tens of thousands of dollars to repair. Determining the primary causes of foundation failure can help homeowners and insurers protect themselves against economic loss and inconvenience.

WRITE NOW

Think about causal factors

1. Consider trends or problems you are familiar with—in your daily life, or in the larger world.
2. List these trends and problems on the right side of a piece of paper. On the left side, write down what you think some of the causes of the problems might be. Underline the causes that you are confident about.
3. Look over your two lists. Which topics seem most interesting to you? If an entry has many underlined causes or effects, it may be too obvious to write about.

Writer at work

Sean Booker was asked to write a paper analyzing the causes of a current trend in popular culture for a course in Social Trends and Problems. He made the following notes on his assignment sheet while his class was discussing the assignment.

Sociology 032
Social Trends and Problems

Look for multiple factors – usually not just one

Identify a trend in American popular culture that interests you and analyze why it has emerged at this time. Some topics we have discussed in class that might make good papers include the rising number of unwed teenage mothers who keep their babies; the popularity of Japanese animation art; people ignoring social protocol while talking on cell phones; or the growth of pet ownership over the past fifteen years. Look for large scale social causes as well as personal causes that might be responsible for, or influence, the emergence of this trend.

Macro and micro causes

Use outside sources to help make your claims, and find authoritative opinions on the topic whenever possible. It usually isn't possible to definitively identify the cause of a social trend, so beware of making a claim that is too sweeping. Social science often relies on probability and plausibility rather than absolute certainty.

Length and deadlines
You should be able to complete this assignment in about four double-spaced, typed pages. Papers are due on March 22nd, and I will return them to you one week later with a grade. If you then wish to rewrite your paper, you will have one week to do so. I will average the rewrite grade with your first grade to give you your final grade.

2 weeks

I encourage you to share your papers with your discussion groups as you draft them. You should also plan to take your paper to the writing center. This is not required, but it is highly recommended.

Evaluation
Papers will be evaluated according to how well they use logic and evidence to show causation. In addition, I will consider how well you contextualize your analysis for readers (Why does it matter? Who is affected? And so on).

Read the assignment closely
Sean Booker began by circling the words and phrases that indicated his analytical task. Then he highlighted information about dates and processes for the project.

Choose a topic
Sean Booker made a list of trends he might write about. After each item on his list, he made notes about why the topic would matter, and to whom. He also made preliminary observations about where he might find "authoritative opinions" on each topic, wrote down any possible causes that occurred to him at the time, and noted any other observations or questions he had about that topic. Finally, he chose one trend for further research.

POPULARITY OF ANIME
- Is it more popular with certain age groups or other demographic groups?
- Is there any scholarly/authoritative research on it? Maybe in Art History?
- I've seen tons of magazines devoted to it at the bookstore.
- Could interview Sarah about the collection she has.

POPULARITY OF RAP MUSIC   ** Best research
(especially among white teenagers) possibilities**
- What percentage of sales of rap music are to white kids?
- Is it any different from white teenagers liking rock n' roll in the 50s?
- Because it annoys parents?
- Does it indicate racial tolerance?
- I know there has been research on this from an economic viewpoint.

SUV SALES
- Why do people want to drive "off-roading" cars to work every day?
- Are sales declining with rising gas prices?
- Is this even a trend any more? People are buying VWs and Mini Coopers now.

"ILLEGAL" FILE SHARING
- Why do so many people do it if it is "illegal"? (Because you get something for free.)
- What are the arguments saying that it is or isn't illegal?
- Easy answer: people are willing to "steal" in this case because there is still significant disagreement over whether it is really stealing.

2: Think about possible causes

Find the obvious causes, and then dig deeper

- **What causal factors might be hidden from the general observer, and why?** Use your imagination; hidden causes require new thinking if they are to be uncovered.

- **How do various causal factors interact?** Several causes together might contribute to an effect, rather than any single cause being the determining factor.

- **What "causes the cause" that you have identified?** What prior conditions does each cause arise from? If poor attendance is a factor in drop-out rates, what causes some students to have poor attendance in the first place?

Analyze your audience

- **Think about who is affected by the phenomenon you are investigating.** Who is in a position to react to your claims, and make changes?

- **If you don't know who your audience is, do some research to find out who is interested in your topic.** Who has offered opinions or responded to previous causal claims on this topic?

Research your analysis

- **Look for some disagreement among your sources.** If they all agree on the cause, your analysis won't matter much.

- **When your sources disagree, ask why.** Does one give more weight to some pieces of evidence than to others? Do they draw different conclusions from the same evidence? Do they use Mill's methods of determining causation in different ways?

- **Be on the lookout for new potential causes, or new findings that could help you rule out potential causes.**

Writer at work

Sean Booker began his analysis by brainstorming for all the possible causes he could think of. Then, he researched the topic to find information on the causes he had listed and also to learn about other potential causes that had been put forward.

Sean Booker thought about his own experience with the trend to help define his audience. He also noted the types of audiences his sources appeared to be writing for. Finally, Sean Booker identified what he thought were the most likely causes of rap's popularity with white teenagers. He did this analysis by applying Mill's methods of determining causation and by weighing the opinions of the authoritative sources he had read.

<u>POSSIBLE REASONS WHITE TEENAGERS LIKE RAP MUSIC:</u>

- Fashion: to look different, be noticed. Mills talks about this and uses direct evidence from interviews.

- To annoy their parents or frighten them by acting "bad." Mills also backs this up: "rebellion."

- Mills also talks about developing masculinity, which makes sense, because it's mostly males who are attracted to this music (single difference).

- To show solidarity with African Americans.

- Probably a lot would say "Because it's good," but what do they mean by that? They like the beat, lyrics, message?

- Davey D points out the marketing is skewed to a white demographic.

**Explain why kids choose hip-hop when they could choose any really different culture to look different or annoy their parents (single difference).

Most important causes to talk about: "being different," rebelling, developing masculinity. These mix personal and social factors; be sure to talk about both. Also, economic. That shows a single difference to explain why hip-hop, and not some other cultural trend, has caught on in such a big way.

3: Write a draft

Within the step 3 box:

STEP-BY-STEP

rap music develops
↓
becomes popular with African American audiences
↓
white teenagers start to notice and like rap
↓
marketers begin marketing rap to white audiences
↓
sales of rap to white teenagers rise

—What about rebelling, developing masculinity, etc.?

This really doesn't work for my analysis because there is not one straight "path" to the trend—there is a bunch of effects that feed into it simultaneously.

Introduce what you will be analyzing	• Describe the trend, event, or phenomenon you will be analyzing.
	• Give your readers any background information they will need.
	• Explain why it is important to determine the cause of this phenomenon (you can save this for the conclusion if you wish).
Describe the causal relationship	• Explain how the chain of causation works to produce the effect in question. Break down each step so readers can follow the process.
	• Alternatively, set out the causes offered by other people and show how they can be ruled out. Then, introduce your own claim and demonstrate why it is superior to others'.
	• A third method is to look at a series of possible causes one at a time, analyzing each and making a claim about its relative impact on a phenomenon.
Anticipate and address opposing viewpoints	• Acknowledge other stakeholders in the analysis, and consider their claims.
	• Demonstrate why your claim is preferable.
Conclude by doing more than summarizing	• Spell out the importance of the analysis, if you haven't already done so.
	• Consider additional effects you haven't previously discussed.
	• Explain any action you think needs to be taken based on your conclusion.

Make a claim that matters

Don't confuse correlation with causation

Mill's method of concomitant variation might lead you to conclude that any mutual relationship between two events is causal. Remember that concomitant variation only determines cause when all other variables are accounted for.

OFF TRACK

The drop in the number of Americans living in poverty during the Clinton administration was due to a number of factors.

ON TRACK

The lower number of Americans living in poverty during the Clinton administration was due to a number of factors. How much did the Welfare Reform Act contribute to this trend? The general economic prosperity experienced by the entire country during that time probably had a greater impact. Statistics show that the primary effect of the Welfare Reform Act was to simply remove people from welfare rolls, not actually lift them out of poverty.

Identify the stakeholders in your analysis

Be especially alert for opinions about your topic from people who would be adversely affected by a different causal outcome.

OFF TRACK

Can mega-doses of vitamin C prevent colds, flu, and other illnesses? Good health is important to everyone, so we should all be interested in the news that vitamin C has many important health benefits.

ON TRACK

Can mega-doses of vitamin C prevent colds, flu, and other illnesses? The supplements industry has spent millions of dollars to convince consumers that this is the case. The industry stands to make hundreds of millions more if people believe them. But evidence from independent researchers casts some doubt on the effectiveness of mega-doses of vitamin C in preventing illness.

Writer at work

Sean Booker tested three organizational patterns for his analysis. First he looked at how describing a chain of causation could illuminate his analysis. Next, he considered examining causes one by one and eliminating them before describing the cause he thought was correct. Finally, he structured his analysis as an examination of possible causes, one by one, with accompanying discussion of each cause's relative contribution to the overall effect. This seemed to Sean Booker like the best method for making his analysis, so he used it to write his draft.

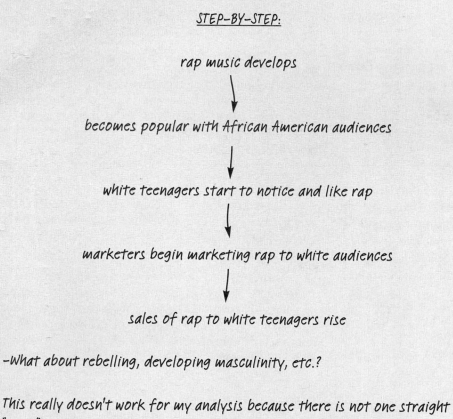

STEP-BY-STEP:

rap music develops

↓

becomes popular with African American audiences

↓

white teenagers start to notice and like rap

↓

marketers begin marketing rap to white audiences

↓

sales of rap to white teenagers rise

—What about rebelling, developing masculinity, etc.?

This really doesn't work for my analysis because there is not one straight "path" to the trend—there is a bunch of effects that feed into it simultaneously.

<u>DISPROVING ALTERNATE CAUSES:</u>

White kids like rap just because "it is good" and they are colorblind about music.
- Actually, they are acutely aware of the racial difference between themselves and the performers; that's part of why they like it.

White kids like rap because they feel sympathy with African American culture.

- I'm the only person who even thought of this reason. A lot of people I know who listen to rap know next to nothing about African American culture, so this is pretty clearly wrong. But what good does it do to bring it up and refute it if no one else would have even considered it as a possibility?

I guess the problem here is that there isn't a big controversy over which causes are "right." That kind of controversy would work better with this structure. It's more a question of how many different causes there might be, and how they might work together.

<u>ONE CAUSE AT A TIME:</u>

- Appeal of the fashion and style is one possible cause. Explain how it fills a need for white teenagers.
- Rebellion against social expectations. Explain why white kids need to do this.
- Developing masculinity. Explain how social pressures lead white male teenagers to think rap's message makes them more masculine.
- Marketing. Look at how rap is marketed to white kids, amplifying all the causes above.

This strategy is the best approach because it lets me look at all the possible causes in detail and finish with the one that sort of gathers up and amplifies the first three.

4: Revise, revise, revise

Skilled writers know that the secret to writing well is rewriting. Even the best writers often have to revise several times to get the result they want. You also must have effective strategies for revising if you're going to be successful. The biggest trap you can fall into is starting off with the little stuff first. Leave the small stuff for last.

Does your paper or project meet the assignment?	• Look again at your assignment. Does your paper or project do what the assignment asks? • Look again at the assignment for specific guidelines, including length, format, and amount of research. Does your work meet these guidelines?
Is your causal claim arguable?	• Do enough people disagree with you to make the evaluation worthwhile? • Who cares about this topic? Do you explain to readers why it is important?
Do you use logical means of determining causation?	• Do you examine common factors, single differences, and concomitant variations? • Do you use more than one method whenever possible? • Do you avoid confusing correlation with causation?
Is your evidence authoritative and convincing?	• Have you found the most accurate information about your topic available? • Have you identified stakeholders in your analysis?

	• Have you carefully examined the analysis and conclusions of people who have already expressed an opinion on this topic?
Do you address opposing views?	• Have you acknowledged the opinions of people who disagree with your claim? • Have you shown how your causal claim is preferable?
Is the writing project visually effective?	• Is the font attractive and readable? • Are the headings and visuals effective? • If you use images or tables as part of your analysis, are they legible and appropriately placed?
Save the editing for last	When you have finished revising, edit and proofread carefully.

A peer review guide is on page 31.

Writer at work

Sean Booker talked with his peer group about his analysis, and took his draft to the writing center for a consultation. He wrote notes on the draft to help him revise, and then he made some changes to the draft. His peers particularly urged him to focus his introduction. Here is the draft of Sean Booker's introduction as he originally wrote it, with notes he made, and as he revised it for his final draft.

The Appeal of Rap to Young, White Males

Need a better title

"So what?" Need a sense of why this needs explanation or why it matters

Rap music is a genre that first developed in the United States in the 1970s and has its roots in the music of West African storytellers, musicians and poets known as Griots. Rap is one of the elements of the "hip-hop" cultural movement, which includes DJing, graffiti, and breakdancing ("Hip-Hop"). While rap grew out of African traditions and the majority of rap performers are African Americans, rap music has gained the following of a large number of young, white males in the United States. Across the U.S. suburbs, white adolescent males are adopting the hip-hop style of dress, using hip-hop language, and buying millions of rap records each year. But why does rap music appeal to young, white males?

Also, need statistics/ authoritative opinion for the numbers and claims of a trend.

Borrowing Bling: The Appeal of Hip-hop to Young White Men

Rap music, a genre that developed in the United States in the 1970s, has its roots in the music of West African storytellers, musicians and poets known as Griots ("Hip-Hop"). Rap, which includes both DJing and MCing, is one of the elements of the "hip-hop" cultural movement. The other major elements of hip-hop culture are graffiti and breakdancing ("Hip-Hop"). Hip-hop has had a major impact on society through fashion as well. According to the Wikipedia entry on hip-hop fashion, "Contemporary hip-hop fashion includes the wearing of baggy jeans slung low around the waist, gold or platinum chains and boots or a fresh pair of kicks, and bandanas or doo rags tied around the head often worn with a baseball cap on top." These days, a trip to any high school or shopping mall in America will reveal numerous examples of this kind of fashion.

Hip-hop grew out of African traditions, arose in African American urban areas, and is performed almost exclusively by African Americans. Yet hip-hop has gained an audience of a large number of young, white males in the United States. Across the U.S. suburbs, white adolescent males are adopting the hip-hop style of dress, using hip-hop language, and buying millions of rap records each year. Over 70% of hip-hop music sales are made to white consumers (MacLean). What explains hip-hop's enormous appeal to young white men? A number of factors—personal, social, and economic—appear to be behind this phenomenon.

STAYING ON TRACK

Reviewing your draft

Give yourself plenty of time for reviewing your draft. For detailed information on how to participate in a peer review, how to review it yourself, and how to respond to comments from your classmates, your instructor, or a campus writing consultant, see pages 28–32.

Some good questions to ask yourself when reviewing causal analysis

- Is my causal claim clear? Have I avoided oversimplifying?
- Will my audience understand why this issue is important?
- Have I accounted for the various stakeholders in this analysis?
- Have I considered all possible causes? Have I used sound logic to evaluate them?
- Have I provided evidence to support my claim?

5: Submitted version

Booker 1

Sean Booker
Professor Martinez
SOC 032
22 March 2006

Borrowing Bling: The Appeal of Hip-hop to Young White Men

Rap music, a genre that developed in the United States in the 1970s, has its roots in the music of West African storytellers, musicians and poets known as Griots ("Hip-Hop"). Rap, which includes both DJing and MCing, is one of the elements of the "Hip-Hop" cultural movement. The other major elements of hip-hop culture are graffiti and breakdancing ("Hip-Hop"). Hip-hop has had a major impact on society through fashion as well. According to the Wikipedia entry on hip-hop, "Contemporary hip-hop fashion includes the wearing of baggy jeans slung low around the waist, gold or platinum chains and boots or a fresh pair of kicks, and bandanas or doo rags tied around the head often worn with a baseball cap on top." These days, a trip to any high school or shopping mall in America will reveal numerous examples of this kind of fashion.

Hip-hop grew out of African traditions, arose in African American urban areas, and is performed almost exclusively by African Americans. Yet hip-hop has gained an audience of a large number of young, white males in the United States. Across the U.S. suburbs, white adolescent males are adopting the hip-hop style of dress, using hip-hop language, and buying millions of rap records each year. Over seventy percent of hip-hop music sales are made to white consumers (MacLean). What explains hip-hop's enormous appeal to young white men? A number of factors—personal, social, and economic—appear to be behind this phenomenon.

On a personal level, hip-hop appeals to young, white males because it allows them to escape from the constraints of white society and experience the world of the rapper. Rap music details the life of the African American, sometimes describing a violent and gritty life on the street, or alternatively, a life filled with the glamour of flashy jewelry, nice cars, women, and money. Both of these world views differ vastly from the often insulated, predictable world of the young white adolescent. Professor Fiona Mills interviewed young white rap listeners for her essay "Rap and Young, White Males: Masculinity, Masking and Denial." She found that "young, white men are drawn to the escapist and exotic aspects of rap."

But hip-hop is more than an outlet for personal fantasy. It can also provide a highly defined alternative culture which appeals to the young, white man who may have trouble finding himself within white culture, or who may consciously reject white culture. The fact that hip-hop especially appeals to young men at a time in their lives when they are seeking to define themselves as adults supports this theory. For a white teenager trying desperately to establish himself as a unique person, hip-hop style may appeal because it is something he can easily recognize and emulate, and something which then sets him apart from his white peers. It is a means for situating himself in society.

Additionally, Mills explains that rap music, with its focus on sex, money, drugs and violence, builds a "hyper-masculine aura" that white adolescent males are drawn to because it gives them a model for establishing their masculinity. As Mills revealed in her study, white males often begin listening to music around age twelve or thirteen, just as they are entering adolescence and beginning to establish their masculine identities. In contrast, Mills found that African American males reported listening to rap music from a very young age. Mills suggests that the white adolescents she interviewed saw rap music "as a way of asserting their manhood by associating themselves with an overtly masculine culture—one in which femininity had no place."

Rap music also appeals to young white men because it is a way to rebel against their parents and white society in general. By associating themselves with a musical culture that involves heavy use of profane language and often centers on violence and drugs, white males establish their rebellion against societal standards. Many teens may like rap for the simple fact that their parents do not approve of its foul language, portrayal of violence, and treatment of women.

These factors all help explain why young white men might be drawn to hip-hop and rap music and what they might gain from adopting its cultural markers. But do these factors alone explain hip-hop's enormous popularity with white consumers? There are many other types of music and culture that might appeal to white adolescents on the same grounds as hip-hop. Why has hip-hop become such a huge cultural phenomenon?

Marketing may well be the answer. Hip-hop historian and journalist Davey D has chronicled the economic pressures that led to hip-hop being marketed directly to white audiences. Historically, advertisers and record companies have cared little about young African American consumers, who typically have less disposable income than white consumers. Young white males, on the other hand, are a key demographic that all marketers pursue. As Davey D puts it, "As major corporations saw lots of white kids getting down with hip-hop, they decided to do whatever it took to appeal to what is considered a lucrative demographic. . . . What this all boiled down to was there was a premium placed on white/more affluent listeners. Many corporations simply did want to attract a young African American clientele." To attract a white clientele, Davey D argues, record companies and promoters began putting out hip-hop acts that fed white stereotypes about African Americans. As a result, "in 2003 you have a genre of music that was born in the harshest ghettos outselling any other music and now attracting the desired Holy Grail for corporate advertisers—white folks 18-34 [translation: Generation X]."

If Davey D's argument is correct, then the popularity of hip-hop among young white men is cause for concern. While cultural crossover is in many ways a good thing and can help promote understanding among people, some feel that hip-hop is being used to manipulate consumers and even promote racial stereotypes. If true, this would be a sad statement about today's white hip-hop fans. Like white audiences at a 1920s vaudeville show, they could be exposed to a parody of African American culture and think it was the real thing.

Works Cited

D, Davey. "Hip-Hop's Ultimate Battle: Race and the Politics of Divide and Conquer."
    Davey D's Hip Hop Daily News 10 Jan. 2003. 13 Mar. 2006.
    <http://www.daveyd.com/FullArticles%5CarticleN1370.asp>.

"Hip-Hop Music." Wikipedia, the Free Encyclopedia. 2005. 10 Mar. 2006
    <http://en.wikipedia.org/wiki/Hip_hop_music>.

MacLean, Natalie. "Bring on the Bling—Rappers Give Cristal and Hennessy Street
    Cred." San Francisco Chronicle 16 Dec. 2004. 10 Mar. 2006
    <http://sfgate.com/cgi-bin/article.cgi?file=/c/a/2004/12/16/WIGNCAC0AG1.DTL>.

Mills, Fiona. "Rap and Young, White Males: Masculinity, Masking and Denial."
    Americana: The Journal of American Popular Culture Dec. 2001. 13 Mar. 2006
    <http://www.americanpopularculture.com/archive/music/rap_white_men.htm>.

Projects

A causal analysis answers the question: How did something get that way? They first have to identify what that something is: an event, an object, a phenomenon, or a trend. Once they have identified the **what,** then they move to the **how** and **why**.

Causal analyses have several different purposes. Sometimes we are just curious about why something happened. In some cases, we may want to repeat something, such as the successful sales of a product. In other cases, we may want to prevent potentially bad effects from occurring. And in still other cases, we might want to forecast the future.

The following projects give you a range of opportunities for causal analysis.

CAUSAL ANALYSIS OF A TREND

For an example of analyzing a trend, see pages 335–338.

Identify a significant change in human behavior over a period of months or years. Why have mega-churches grown rapidly? Why has reality television become popular? Why have the wealthiest one percent of Americans grown significantly richer over the past twenty years? Why have homicide rates dropped to levels not seen since the 1960s? Why are children increasingly obese?

Determine the time span of the trend. When did it start? When did it stop? Is it still going on? You likely will need to do research.

Analyze the possible causes of the trend, arguing for the ones you think are most likely the true causes. Look for underlying and hidden causes.

Remember that providing facts is not the same thing as establishing causes, even though facts can help support your causal analysis.

ANALYZING CLAIMS AND STAKEHOLDERS

For an example of analyzing claims and stakeholders, see pages 320–325.

Identify a causal relationship that is now generally accepted but was once in doubt, such as Galileo's explanation of the phases of the moon, the link between DDT and the decline of bald eagle populations, or the effects of vitamin B12 on developing fetuses.

Research the arguments that were made for and against these causal relationships. Who initially proposed the cause? What was the reaction? Who argued against them, and why? How did the causal relationship come to be accepted as real? Write a short essay outlining the stakeholders in the issue you have chosen.

Explain the arguments made for and against the now-accepted cause, and the evidence presented. Which of Mill's methods of determining causation did each party use (see pages 306–307)? Why were the arguments of the now-accepted cause more effective?

CAUSAL ANALYSIS OF A HUMAN-INFLUENCED NATURAL PHENOMENON

For an example of analyzing a human-influenced natural phenomenon, see pages 315–319.

Find a natural phenomenon or trend that is (or may be) the result of human activity. Is the growing hole in the earth's ozone layer the result of human-produced chemicals in the atmosphere? Why have populations of American alligators rebounded in the southern United States? Are sinkholes in a Kentucky town the result of new mining activity in the area? Why are more and more bacteria developing resistance to antibiotics? Choose a topic that interests you and which you feel is important. If you think the topic is important, it will be easier to convince your audience that your analysis is important.

Research the possible causes of the phenomenon, focusing on the ones you think are most likely the true causes. Remember to look at underlying and hidden causes.

Think about possible alternative causes. Do you need to incorporate them? If you don't think they are valid causes, then you need to refute them.

Recognize that causal relationships between humans and the natural world are complex, and play out on such a large scale, and that it is often difficult to prove them definitively. Don't oversimplify or make sweeping claims that can't be proven.

12

Evaluating

Convincing evaluations rely on selecting criteria
and supporting a claim with reasons and evidence.

Chapter contents

Writing to evaluate

You make evaluations every day. You choose a favorite CD, a favorite restaurant, a favorite ring tone on your cell phone. Newspapers and Web sites feature "best of" polls that let people vote for the restaurant, movie, television show, or band they think is the "best." To some extent, these judgments are a matter of personal taste. Yet, if you look into the reasons people give for their preferences, you often find that different people use similar criteria to make evaluations.

For example, think about a restaurant you like. What are your reasons for feeling this way? Is it clean? The food fresh? The prices low? Is it convenient to your home or campus? Do you like the atmosphere? These are criteria that most people will use to judge a restaurant. That's why some restaurants are always crowded, while many others quickly go out of business.

Goals of evaluation

When you write an evaluation, your goal is usually to convince readers to agree with your judgment. Convincing other people that your judgment is sound depends on the validity of the criteria you will use to make your evaluation. Will the criteria you're using as the basis of your evaluation be convincing to other people? You may think a movie is good because it has exceptional cinematography, but an action-movie fan is less likely to go see a movie just because it is visually beautiful. Sometimes you must argue for the validity of your criteria before readers will accept them. If they don't accept your criteria, they won't agree with your conclusions.

An evaluative claim

An evaluation can be stated in the form "SOMETHING is good (or bad, the best or the worst) if measured by these criteria." Usually, the most important task when writing an evaluation is to determine the kind of criteria to use.

Suppose you want to convince your student Speakers' Committee to host a talk by a well-known filmmaker whom you believe would be a better choice than other potential speakers. You could argue that, because she is famous, the filmmaker will draw many students to her talk, thus raising the profile of the Speakers' Program, and generating more money in ticket sales. You could also argue that the filmmaker's talk would be a culturally enriching experience for students because she has made many critically acclaimed movies. You might argue that a large number of students on campus have expressed their desire to hear the filmmaker, and that the Speakers' Committee has an obligation to provide speakers the students want to hear.

Criteria for evaluation

Each of these arguments uses a different kind of criteria. An argument that the filmmaker will draw students and make money is based on **practical criteria.** An argument that her artistic achievement makes her a worthwhile speaker is based on **aesthetic criteria.** An argument that the committee is bound to consider the wishes of students is based on **ethical criteria.** These are the three basic categories of criteria for all evaluative arguments.

Things are usually judged to be good (or bad) either because they work well (practicality), because they are beautiful (aesthetics), or because they are morally fair or just (ethics). An evaluative argument may use any or all of these types of criteria, and can emphasize them in different ways. For example, if you want to convince your roommate to go to an expensive sushi restaurant, you would probably emphasize the aesthetic experience of enjoying fresh sushi in a fashionable atmosphere. You would want to downplay practical criteria like cost, especially if your roommate's budget requires that he usually dine on Ramen noodles instead of sushi.

Components of evaluations

What will make a good subject to evaluate?	**Find something to evaluate** Listing is one way to identify possible subjects for evaluation. You might list restaurants, buildings, cars, computers, and other objects. You might evaluate a film, a book, a TV show, a presidential speech, or certain policies or courses at your school.
What is my working thesis?	**Write a working thesis** Your thesis should argue that something is good/better/best or bad/worst, successful or unsuccessful on the basis of criteria that you name.
What values are most important for my readers?	**Consider your readers** How interesting will this topic be to your readers? What criteria will be most convincing to them?
What are the appropriate criteria for my subject?	**Choose the appropriate criteria** **Practical criteria** will demand that the thing being evaluated work efficiently or lead to good outcomes (profits, satisfied customers, improved conditions, lower costs, and so on). **Aesthetic criteria** hinge on the importance and value of beauty, image, or tradition. **Ethical criteria** are used to evaluate whether something is morally right, consistent with the law and with rules of fair play.
Who would disagree with me?	**Consider other views** Has anyone evaluated your subject before? What criteria did they use? For example, you might hate horror movies because they give you bad dreams, but many other people love them. You should consider why they have such a strong following.
What is the most engaging way to begin?	**Start fast** You may have to give some background but get quickly to your subject.
What is the most effective way to end?	**Finish strong** If you have not announced your stance, then you can make your summary evaluation. If your readers know where you stand, you might end with a compelling example.

Keys to evaluations

The Transamerica Building in San Francisco remains controversial on aesthetic criteria. Some citizens find it a worthy symbol of their city; others object to it because they find it out of scale with the surrounding neighborhood.

Describe briefly your subject
Your readers may be unfamiliar with what you are evaluating. Give your readers a brief description.

Explain your criteria
The importance of many criteria may not be evident to your readers. You may need to state explicitly each criterion you use and explain why it is relevant.

Be fair
Be honest about the strengths and weaknesses of what you are evaluating. Rarely is anything perfectly good or absolutely bad. Your credibility will increase if you give a balanced view.

Support your judgments with evidence
Back up your claims with specific evidence. If you write that a restaurant serves inedible food, describe examples in detail.

Define criteria for visual evaluations
Criteria for visual evaluations may require additional work to define and explain.

WORKING TOGETHER
What makes an effective review?

In a group of three or four students

- Look at a selection of short, amateur online reviews, such as customer book reviews at Amazon.com, consumer reviews on a site like Epinions.com, or user comments on a film at www.imdb.com.

- Select several examples of reviews that you think are persuasive and several that are not (see if you can find some persuasive reviews that you don't necessarily agree with).

- As a group, discuss the following: What criteria do reviewers of similar products share? What types of criteria do the persuasive reviews use? What types do the less persuasive reviews use? Do you see any patterns that make reviews persuasive?

An effective evaluation

A successful evaluation makes a claim about the value of something. It supports its main claim with criteria that the audience will agree are important.

The Providence Journal

The Aesthetics of Wind Power
Lefteris Pavlides

People argue that wind turbines are good or bad depending on the criteria they select. Proponents of wind power argue that they produce energy without creating pollution and reduce dependence on foreign oil (practical criteria). Opponents argue that they drive down real estate values (a practical criterion), are ugly (an aesthetic criterion), and kill birds (an ethical criterion). The proposed Cape Wind project on Nantucket Sound in Massachusetts has provoked an especially contentious debate. Lefteris Pavlides, who is a professor of architecture at Roger Williams University, published this evaluation in the *Providence Journal* in March 2005.

The Aesthetics of
Wind Power

by Lefteris Pavlides

"Wind turbines are not pretty," said Massachusetts Governor Romney late last year, to the applause of about half of the emotional crowd at an Army Corps of Engineers public hearing on Cape Wind Park.

Yet the Corps's 3,800-page report was an overwhelmingly positive evaluation of the 130 modern windmills proposed for Horseshoe Shoal, in Nantucket Sound. And despite the governor's attempt to speak for the public's aesthetic, the truth is that most people love the elegance of the slow-moving giants that quietly turn wind into electricity.

The author assumes his readers are familiar with the controversy, so the evaluation begins with an opposing view—that wind turbines are bad because they are ugly.

371

Whose visual judgment matters on this issue? And how do we know that most people see modern windmills as visual assets?

Blind impartial market indicators provide indirect evidence that modern windmills are seen as beautiful. Surveys on real-estate prices and on tourism cited in the Army Corps's draft Environmental Impact Study (section 5) clearly show the strong visual appeal of modern windmills in many places around the world.

A boon to real estate values and tourism

And a study of 29,000 real-estate transactions in America found that the property values of homes with views of wind turbines rose faster than those of nearby homes with no such views.

The Corps's report also examined surveys of visitors to sites around the globe where wind energy is well established—modern windmills in such places as Scotland, Australia and California, and off Denmark and Sweden. Installation of wind turbines increases tourism, it was found, providing evidence that most people see them as attractive additions to land- and seascapes. From Scotland to New Zealand, and from California to the Greek Isles, people pay to visit wind turbines and be photographed with them.

As a professor of architecture, I understand the visual logic of this phenomenon. I teach that forms made to move in wind—such as sailboats and Porsches—are inherently beautiful. Experts discuss the artistic qualities of aerodynamic lines and the kinetic grace of modern windmills, using such terms as proportion, contrast, rhythm and movement to express what we all experience.

The aesthetics of wind power

From an abstract view, the graceful modern windmills are even more beautiful than their ancient

Pavlides questions the opposing view, claiming that most people find wind turbines elegant.

Pavlides challenges the assertions that wind turbines lower the value of surrounding homes and harm tourism.

The author builds his credibility as an authority.

He returns to aesthetic criteria and offers more evidence of the beauty of modern windmills.

counterparts. A Cape Cod sculptor recently wrote to me, "[T]he beauty of modern windmills is a joyous scene to behold. As sail boats provide visual delight while transforming air into propulsion, so will windmills that catch ambient breezes for essential power."

Non-experts in aesthetics also discuss the delight of watching windmills. An engineer with no artistic training sent me his unsolicited opinion that the Danish Horns Rev offshore wind park was "one of the most inspiring and thrilling sights seen from the Blavaand lighthouse observatory deck."

To adapt an adage, beauty is in the eye and also the mind of the beholder. Our judgment of what is beautiful is based not just on abstract qualities of form. Modern windmills, for instance, have acquired a broad range of connotations.

For some, they are worse than ugly, evoking deep fear in their enormous scale. For others, they are beyond magnificent, evoking deep religious feelings. More common associations with modern windmills include economic benefits or threats to market share (for fossil-fuel interests); reduction of disease in the reduction of polluting emissions; and real or bogus environmental threats.

Visual delight accompanies connotations of:

- Economic benefits, such as fixed energy prices for years to come. The Army Corps reported that Cape Wind would have a significant positive impact on the local economy.
- Health benefits from reduced pollution, including fewer people with asthma and bronchitis, and fewer premature deaths. The Corps reported a probable $53 million in health savings.

Visual blight is an impression that accompanies connotations of:

- Loss of market share. Modern windmills are a constant reminder of eroding market share for executives of coal and oil companies, such as Douglas Yearly, a former chairman of Phelps Dodge who is on the board of Marathon Oil. Mr. Yearly, who has a summer place in Cape Cod's Osterville, has spearheaded opposition to Cape Wind.

The Army Corps's report indicates that Cape Wind would produce three-quarters of the electricity needed by Cape Cod and the Islands.

Regarding wildlife, when people are told that modern windmills offer protections to animals, they see them as beautiful, while those who believe widespread misinformation about dangers to birds have reservations.

The Corps's exhaustive avian studies conclude that there is no basis for concern. Further scientific studies

The strongest arguments for wind turbines are based on practical criteria. They provide a dependable, pollution-free source of energy.

Pavlides questions the motives of some critics of wind power.

He counters the ethical argument of harm to birds by pointing to benefits to wildlife from reduced pollution.

show that wind energy is hugely beneficial to birds and other wildlife, in that it reduces:

- acid rain, which causes regional bird extinctions by killing the snails that are critical to bird diets;
- mercury contamination, which has caused extinction of loons on the Great Lakes;
- oil spills, which kill all manner of wildlife;
- and global warming, the biggest threat of all.

There is every indication that the opposition to Cape Wind will evolve much the way public attitudes toward the Statue of Liberty evolved over a century ago. The statue's installation was resisted and delayed because, as newspapers declared, it "was neither an object of art [n]or beauty." Now an adored icon, the statue significantly raises the value of properties with views of it. It is seen as beautiful because of its sculptural qualities and also because of the freedom and human rights that it represents.

He ends with the analogy to the Statue of Liberty, which many people initially found ugly when it was installed in New York Harbor but soon grew to love.

As an architect who has been studying public perception of wind turbines, I predict that most people would similarly come to see Cape Wind's turbines as breath-givingly beautiful.

The vast majority of people around Nantucket Sound would see Cape Wind as a magnificent addition to the sound—making visible the reduction of invisible toxic gases that despoil the region's environment.

And the windmills would visually communicate, now and to future generations, our commitment to energy freedom and a disease-free environment.

New Englanders have a responsibility to express their support for this project.

How to read evaluations

Make notes as you read, either in the margins, if it is your own copy, or on paper or a computer file. Circle any words or references that you don't know and look them up.

What is it?	• What kind of a text is it? A review? an essay? a blog? an editorial? What are your expectations for this kind of text? • What media are used? (Web sites, for example, often combine images, words, and sounds.)
Where did it come from?	• Who wrote the evaluation? • What do you know about the writer's background that might have influenced the evaluation?
What is the writer's thesis or main idea?	• What clues do you find about whom the writer had in mind as the readers? • What does the writer assume that the readers already know about the subject? • What new knowledge is the writer providing?
Who is the intended audience?	• What clues do you find about whom the writer had in mind as the readers? • What does the writer assume that the readers already know about the subject? • What new knowledge is the writer providing?
Does the writer make a clear evaluative claim?	• What exactly is the writer's evaluative claim?
What are the criteria used in the evaluation?	• Does the writer use practical criteria? aesthetic criteria? ethical criteria? (See page 368.) • Does the writer argue for how these criteria apply to the subject? • Does the writer acknowledge opposing views?
How is it composed?	• How does the writer represent herself or himself? • How would you characterize the style? • If there are any photographs or other graphics, what information do they contribute?

Learning to Love PowerPoint
(OPINION)
David Byrne

Musician, author, artist, and producer David Byrne has worked in multiple media, often challenging his audience to inspect or question convention. In this article, published in *Wired* magazine in 2003, he shares his discoveries about the potential artistic uses of PowerPoint software.

Analyzing and Connecting

Return to these questions after you have finished reading.

1. Byrne's evaluation of PowerPoint is based largely on aesthetic criteria. Notice, however, that he does not claim PowerPoint necessarily makes beautiful images (though he says it is possible to do so). What exactly does Byrne feel makes PowerPoint aesthetically valuable?

2. What is Byrne's assessment of PowerPoint's practical value? Why do you think he discusses this aspect of the software early in the essay?

3. Byrne provides several still examples of his work in PowerPoint to demonstrate the potential he sees in the program. How do these images help him make his case? Do you find them helpful in understanding the value Byrne sees in PowerPoint?

Learning to Love PowerPoint

A while ago, I decided to base the book-tour readings from my pseudoreligious tract *The New Sins* on sales presentations. I was going for a fair dose of irony and satire, and what could be better than using PowerPoint and a projector, the same tools that every sales and marketing person relies on?

Having never used the program before, I found it limiting, inflexible, and biased, like most software. On top of that, PowerPoint makes hilariously bad-looking visuals. But that's a small price to pay for ease and utility. We live in a world where convenience beats quality every time. It was, for my purposes, perfect.

I began to see PowerPoint as a metaprogram, one that organizes and presents stuff created in other applications. Initially, I made presentations about presentations; they were almost completely without content. The content, I learned, was in the medium itself. I discovered that I could attach my photographs, short videos, scanned images, and music. What's more, the application can be made to run by

* David Byrne. "Learning to Love PowerPoint."
Written by David Byrne, artist and musician.
Originally written for and Publish by *Wired.*
Reprinted by permission.

itself—no one even needs to be at the podium. How fantastic!

Although I began by making fun of the medium, I soon realized I could actually create things that were beautiful. I could bend the program to my own whim and use it as an artistic agent. The pieces became like short films: Some were sweet, some were scary, and some were *mysterioso.* I discovered that even without text, I could make works that were "about" something, something beyond themselves, and that they could even have emotional resonance. What had I stumbled upon? Surely some techie or computer artist was already using this dumb program as an artistic medium. I couldn't really have this territory all to myself—or could I?

In thinking about graphic design,

industrial design, and what might really be the cutting-edge of design, I realized it would have to be genetic engineering. Dolly* (God rest her soul) represents the latest in design, but it is, in her case, design we cannot see. Dolly looks like any other sheep, which is precisely the point. The dogma of some graphic designers is that their work be invisible. This perfection has been achieved with Dolly.

I began this project making fun of the iconography of PowerPoint, which wasn't hard to do, but soon realized that the pieces were taking on lives of their own. This whirlwind of arrows, pointing everywhere and nowhere—each one color-coded to represent God knows what aspects of growth, market share, or regional trends—ends up capturing the excitement and pleasant confusion of the marketplace, the everyday street, personal relationships, and the simultaneity of multitasking. Does it really do all that? If you imagine you are inside there it does.

This is Dan Rather's profile. Expanded to the nth degree. Taken to infinity. Overlayed on the back of Patrick Stewart's head. It's recombinant phrenology. The elements of phrenology recombined in ways that follow the rules

of irrational logic, a rigorous methodology that follows nonrational rules. It is a structure for following your intuition and your obsessions. It is the hyperfocused scribblings of the mad and the gifted. The order and structure give it the appearance of rationality and scientific rigor. This appearance is easy to emulate.

Phrenology sought to reveal criminal propensities—and those of potential leaders and geniuses—in the shapes and bumps of the head and face. Nowadays we see it as a scientific justification for racist and cultural biases. A dangerous pseudoscience. But if phrenology was the genetic profiling of a previous era, what will supplant genetic profiling when that too appears as ridiculous as phrenology does to us now? Nonrational logic will not go away.

---

* Dolly, a sheep born in 1996, became famous as the first mammal to be cloned from an adult cell.

PowerPoint Is Evil
(OPINION)
Edward Tufte

Edward Tufte, professor emeritus of political science, computer science and statistics, and graphic design at Yale University, is well-known as a proponent of simpler, clearer graphical information. His publishing company, Graphics Press, has produced many books on the importance of good graphic design and ways to achieve it. The following essay appeared in response to David Byrne's article on PowerPoint, in the same 2003 issue of *Wired* magazine

Analyzing and Connecting

Return to these questions after you have finished reading.

1. Tufte and Byrne come to different conclusions on the value of PowerPoint. What criteria does each writer use to evaluate the software? Are these criteria the cause of their disagreement? Or do they have different opinions about how well PowerPoint meets their criteria?

2. Tufte's essay is a good example of how aesthetic, practical, and ethical criteria can overlap. Ugly charts, he argues, do not communicate information well, and therefore fail practically as well as aesthetically. Respect for one's audience, an ethical consideration, also has practical implications: If your audience feels insulted, they will not listen to you. If you were writing this essay, would you weigh the ethical, practical, and aesthetic criteria the same way Tufte does? Why or why not?

3. Tufte's argument centers on the responsibilities of the presenter to his or her audience, while Byrne's piece focuses on the creative possibilities PowerPoint offers to the presenter. What kind of audience is more likely to be persuaded by Tufte's piece? What kind of audience is more likely to appreciate Byrne's?

4. After reading both essays, consider your own experiences with PowerPoint. Are you more inclined to agree with Byrne or with Tufte? Can you see ways in which their essays share some common ground? Have the two writers left out any points that you think are important?

IMAGINE a widely used and expensive prescription drug that promised to make us beautiful but didn't. Instead the drug had frequent, serious side effects: It induced stupidity, turned everyone into bores, wasted time, and degraded the quality and credibility of communication. These side effects would rightly lead to a worldwide product recall.

Yet slideware—computer programs for presentations—is everywhere: in corporate America, in government bureaucracies, even in our schools. Several hundred million copies of Microsoft PowerPoint are churning out trillions of slides each year. Slideware may help speakers outline their talks, but convenience for the speaker can be punishing to both content and audience. The standard PowerPoint presentation elevates format over content, betraying an attitude of commercialism that turns everything into a sales pitch.

Of course, data-driven meetings are nothing new. Years before today's slideware, presentations at companies such as IBM and in the military used bullet lists shown by overhead projectors. But the format has become ubiquitous under PowerPoint, which was created in 1984 and later acquired by Microsoft. PowerPoint's pushy style seeks to set up a speaker's dominance over the audience. The speaker, after all, is making power points with bullets to followers. Could any metaphor be worse? Voicemail menu systems? Billboards? Television? Stalin?

Particularly disturbing is the adoption of the PowerPoint cognitive style in our schools. Rather than learning to write a report using sentences, children are being taught how to formulate client pitches and infomercials. Elementary school PowerPoint exercises (as seen in teacher guides and in student work posted on the Internet) typically consist of 10 to 20 words and a piece of clip art on each

TUFTE: POWERPOINT IS EVIL

slide in a presentation of three to six slides—a total of perhaps 80 words (15 seconds of silent reading) for a week of work. Students would be better off if the schools simply closed down on those days and everyone went to the Exploratorium or wrote an illustrated essay explaining something.

In a business setting, a PowerPoint slide typically shows 40 words, which is about eight seconds' worth of silent reading material. With so little information per slide, many, many slides are needed. Audiences consequently endure a relentless sequentiality, one damn slide after another. When information is stacked in time, it is difficult to understand context and evaluate relationships. Visual reasoning usually works more effectively when relevant information is shown side by side. Often, the more intense the detail, the greater the clarity and understanding. This is especially so for statistical data, where the fundamental analytical act is to make comparisons.

Consider an important and intriguing table of survival rates for those with cancer relative to those without cancer for the same time

Estimates of relative survival rates, by cancer site[12]

	5 year		10 year		15 year		20 year	
Prostate	98.8	0.4	95.2	0.9	87.1	1.7	81.1	3.0
Thyroid	96.0	0.8	95.8	1.2	94.0	1.6	95.4	2.1
Testis	94.7	1.1	94.0	1.3	91.1	1.8	88.2	2.3
Melanomas	89.0	0.8	86.7	1.1	83.5	1.5	82.8	1.9
Breast	86.4	0.4	78.3	0.6	71.3	0.7	65.0	1.0
Hodgkin's disease	85.1	1.7	79.8	2.0	73.8	2.4	67.1	2.8
Corpus uteri, uterus	84.3	1.0	83.2	1.3	80.8	1.7	79.2	2.0
Urinary, bladder	82.1	1.0	76.2	1.4	70.3	1.9	67.9	2.4
Cervix, uteri	70.5	1.6	64.1	1.8	62.8	2.1	60.0	2.4

(% survival rates and their standard errors)

GOOD
A traditional table: rich, informative, clear.

BAD
PowerPoint chartjunk: smarmy, chaotic, incoherent.

period. Some 196 numbers and 57 words describe survival rates and their standard errors for 24 cancers.

Applying the PowerPoint templates to this nice, straightforward table yields an analytical disaster. The data explodes into six separate chaotic slides, consuming 2.9 times the area of the table. Everything is wrong with these smarmy, incoherent graphs: the encoded legends, the meaningless color, the logo-type branding. They are uncomparative, indifferent to content and evidence, and so data-starved as to be almost pointless. Chartjunk is a clear sign of statistical stupidity. Poking a finger into the eye of thought, these data graphics would turn into a nasty travesty if used for a serious purpose, such as helping cancer patients assess their survival chances. To sell a product that messes up data with such systematic intensity, Microsoft abandons any pretense of statistical integrity and reasoning.

Presentations largely stand or fall on the quality, relevance, and integrity of the content. If your numbers are boring, then you've got the wrong numbers. If your words or images are not on point, making them dance in color won't make them relevant. Audience boredom is usually a content failure, not a decoration failure.

At a minimum, a presentation format should do no harm. Yet the PowerPoint style routinely disrupts, dominates, and trivializes content. Thus PowerPoint presentations too often resemble a school play—very loud, very slow, and very simple.

The practical conclusions are clear. PowerPoint is a competent slide manager and projector. But rather than supplementing a presentation, it has become a substitute for it. Such misuse ignores the most important rule of speaking: Respect your audience.

McNasty: The New "Healthy" Fast Food Items Taste Bad (and Aren't So Healthy Either)

(REVIEW)

Dan Crane

In response to criticism from health advocates, many fast food restaurants have recently begun offering "healthy" menu choices. Dan Crane, a writer and musician, decided to evaluate some of these products in a 2003 review he wrote for the online magazine *Slate*.

Analyzing and Connecting

Return to these questions after you have finished reading.

1. The "taste test" is a staple of advertising and consumer culture. What criteria are privileged in a taste test? Which criteria are usually not considered? And if everyone's tastes differ, why do people find taste tests so convincing?

2. When choosing "healthy" foods, consumers often feel they must sacrifice aesthetic satisfaction (taste) for practical considerations (their health). Crane begins his taste test with a similar assumption. What does he discover in the course of his investigation that upsets this taste-versus-healthiness assumption?

3. Of the criteria and evidence Crane provides, which do you feel would be most likely to influence your decisions about food choice? How do you think different audiences would react to Crane's assessment?

Print | E-mail | Discuss | Newsletters | Podcast | RSS | Help

food What to eat. What not to eat.

McNasty:
The New "Healthy" Fast Food Items Taste Bad
(and Aren't So Healthy Either)
Dan Crane

Be it hangover cure, road-trip fuel, or lunchtime guilty pleasure, I have always been a sucker for salty, greasy, finger-lickin'-good, run-for-the-border-to-have-it-my-way fast food. Recently, however, I've started to feel guilty about eating at fast food restaurants. Sure, the obesity lawsuits brought against McDonald's were laughed out of court in less time than it takes to digest a No. 2 Value Meal, but with nearly two-thirds of Americans over-weight, 30.5 percent considered obese, and 2,500 Americans dying from heart disease every day, I can no longer blissfully ignore the facts: Fast food kills.

Apparently I am not the only one getting the message. Diet and health industries are thriving, half the people you know are on Atkins or the South Beach diet, and in order to stay profitable (and presumably to avoid further lawsuits), McDonald's, Burger King, Taco Bell, Pizza Hut, and Wendy's have all recently tacked on putatively healthy items to their menus. (Rather than trouble themselves with a new healthy menu line, KFC launched a featherbrained ad campaign comforting consumers with the news that "they can enjoy fried chicken as part of a healthy, balanced diet.")

But are these new lighter options tasty enough to change our eating habits? And are they actually healthy? Is the Big Mac doomed to extinction?

Though I've always believed in the dictum once quoted to me by a chef that "fat is where the flavor's at," I decided to set my skepticism aside and taste-test some of

McNASTY: "HEALTHY" FAST FOODS TASTE BAD

Slate

Home
News & Politics
Arts & Life
Business & Tech
Health & Science
Style & Shopping
Travel & Food
Sports
Slate on NPR
Output Options
About Us

Search Slate
[   ] Go
Advanced Search

food What to eat. What not to eat.

these new lower-fat foods. Rather than branching out into unknown territory (though they all now offer lower-fat and lower-calorie items, I've never been a big fan of Wendy's, Pizza Hut, or Blimpie), I decided to stick to my usual fast food triumvirate of Mickey D's, the BK Lounge, and Taco Hell. Curious to see how the new fare would fare against stalwarts like the Big Mac, Whopper, and Gordito, I set my sights on the McDonald's premium salads, Burger King's grilled chicken baguettes, and Taco Bell's "Fresco Style" menu items (which are the same as its regular menu items, except that fat-filled cheese and sauces are replaced with *pico de gallo* salsa).

A recent *New York Times* article by Marion Burros heralded the arrival of the new "healthful" menu items from all the major fast food chains mentioned above: "Some of this food was quite edible. Most gave healthy food a bad name." Based on my own "research," I'd say that aside from the obviously *not* healthy Cobb salad at McDonald's, the new menu items were almost inedible and for the most part revolting. I found it nearly impossible to get beyond the third bite. At least when I chug down an O'Doul's, it still tastes like a beer.

Burros proclaims Burger King's Smoky Barbeque and Santa Fe chicken sandwiches the "winners" of the new healthy crop. But feast your eyes on this Smoky Barbeque sandwich for a moment. And remember, eye appeal is half the meal.

Burger King's chicken baguette ad campaign promises "flavor from grilling, not from fat." At least they seemed to be moving away from painting the meat with faux grill stripes, à la Mighty Dog brand dog food. Still, the chicken, albeit eerily tender, tasted as if it had been *food*   What to eat. What not to eat.

boiled and treated with some kind of fabric softener. There was flavor, but it didn't seem to come from grilling. More likely it resulted from the whopping 1,450 milligrams of sodium—more than three orders of Supersize McDonald's french fries. Plus, the sandwich's topping, a mixture of sautéed peppers and onions, was sweet, sticky, and nausea-inducing, and the baguette it was served on was mushy, bland, and undercooked.

With the chicken sandwich baguette line, Burger King offers two different value-meal options: One comes with a bottle of water and a side salad, the other with a soft drink and medium fries. Who has the will power to resist ordering the fatty option? "Hey, I'm eating a healthy low-fat sandwich! A few fries won't kill me!" Indeed, a study by the National Alliance for Nutrition and Activity in 2002 showed that "fast-food bundling generally steers customers toward calorically-dense, low-nutrition foods like french fries and soda, rather than toward healthier options such as salads and yogurt parfaits." Creating value meals by combining seemingly healthy items with unhealthy items like fries and soft drinks, as Burger King does, lets people continue to make bad eating decisions while feeling as if they are doing something healthy.

Taco Bell's "Fresco Style" option can be applied to any of Taco Bell's menu items. Though this did reduce the fat in my grilled steak soft taco from 17 to 5 grams, and the calories from 280 to 170, the taco was extraordinarily soggy and tasted a little bland. It wasn't horrible compared to the original, but it made me wonder if one can really call something a "taco" if no cheese is involved. My biggest mistake was getting suckered into ordering the Zesty Chicken Border Bowl (thinking it was Taco Bell's answer to Atkins), an artery-clogging culinary atrocity featuring 42 grams of fat and 730 calories.

McNASTY: "HEALTHY" FAST FOODS TASTE BAD

Slate

Home
News & Politics
Arts & Life
Business & Tech
Health & Science
Style & Shopping
Travel & Food
Sports
Slate on NPR
Output Options
About Us

Search Slate
[_____] Go
Advanced Search

food What to eat. What not to eat.

The new McDonald's salads ran the gamut in taste from nearly inedible to almost delicious. The salad line leaps dramatically in taste when one moves from the salty, arid, and bland Grilled Chicken Caesar Salad (the option lowest in fat and calories of all the chicken salads, with 210 calories and 7 grams of fat)—which is sprinkled with plastic-tasting Parmesan cheese flourished with frisée and topped with Newman's Own low-fat balsamic vinaigrette (with 40 calories and 3 grams of fat of its own)—to the surprisingly tasty Crispy California Cobb, which comes with blue cheese, bacon bits, and hard-boiled egg (as well as 380 calories and 23 grams of fat). Adding the packet of butter-and-garlic croutons that accompanies the Cobb salad (50 calories, 1.5 grams of fat) and the Newman's Own ranch dressing (290 calories, 30 grams of fat) made the numbers skyrocket to 720 calories and 54.5 grams of fat. Predictably, the Crispy Chicken California Cobb was the only salad for which I'd consider a trip back through the Golden Arches, but then I might as well have eaten what I wanted in the first place: a Quarter Pounder with cheese and a medium fries—160 more calories, but 3.5 fewer grams of fat.

But McDonald's is going a step beyond salad. They have recently hired Oprah's personal trainer, exercise physiologist Bob Greene, to promote their new "Go Active" meals (currently being tested in Indiana)—Happy Meals for adults—which will include a salad, an exercise booklet, and a pedometer meant to encourage walking. A pedometer? I predict these will get about as much long-term use as the plastic toys that come in the kids' Happy Meals. (This also makes you wonder: Why isn't there a single healthy option being marketed to children, a susceptible—and overweight—audience? Why

Slate

Print | E-mail | Discuss | Newsletters | Podcast | RSS | Help

food   What to eat. What not to eat.

Home
News & Politics
Arts & Life
Business & Tech
Health & Science
Style & Shopping
Travel & Food
Sports
Slate on NPR
Output Options
About Us

Search Slate
[   ] Go
Advanced Search

not revamp the old McDonaldland characters as healthier, up-to-date versions: Grimace becomes a svelte purple hottie, Grimace D'Lite; Mayor McCheese gets promoted to Governor McLean.)

Yet the smartest healthy move McDonald's has made is actually replacing the Chicken McNugget with a new version that contains lower-calorie, lower-fat all-white meat. With 260 calories down from 310 calories, and 16 total grams of fat down from 20 grams, the new six-piece McNuggets tasted as good as, in fact better than, the processed mixture of light- and dark-meat McNuggets I once knew.

According to McDonald's sales figures, the new healthy approach is working. Third-quarter earnings were up 12 percent, attributed largely (so claimed McDonald's press releases) to these new menu options. Wouldn't it make sense, then, to simply reduce the calorie and fat count of their entire menu? Since I began ordering the Quarter Pounder with cheese in the mid-1970s, America's total daily calorie intake has increased by 10 percent, and McDonald's has begun supersizing everything. Isn't the better way to stave off the obesity epidemic to eliminate the gigantic portions and reduce fat in side items like french fries?

If America's major fast food chains are going to succeed in trimming the corpulent beast they helped create, they'll need to do more than simply add a few unpalatable palliatives to their menus. They should continue lowering the fat of the items we already love (as McDonald's has done with Chicken McNuggets) and find a way to make these new so-called low-fat and low-calorie alternatives not only healthier, but tastier as well.

Gangsta Rap and American Culture
(ESSAY)

Michael Eric Dyson

The New York Times Professor and Baptist minister Michael Eric Dyson was one of the first academics to defend rap music as a complex cultural art form. The following essay, from the 2004 collection *The Michael Eric Dyson Reader*, is based on a 1994 editorial Dyson wrote for the *New York Times*. Dyson responds to criticism from Congress and social activists aimed at censoring gangsta rap's sometimes violent and obscene images.

Analyzing and Connecting

Return to these questions after you have finished reading.

1. Dyson spends much of the essay discussing aspects of rap music and culture which trouble him: its violent imagery, misogyny, and fixation on material wealth. He describes rap's positive values much more briefly: "At their best, rappers shape the tortuous twists of urban fate into lyrical elegies. They represent lives swallowed by too little love or opportunity." How well does Dyson make his case that this quality of rap makes it worth defending? What else does he do in the essay to convince readers that rap's good qualities outweigh its bad ones?

2. Look through the essay and identify places where Dyson makes an effort to show rap's critics that he shares their concerns. How does Dyson use this shared concern to argue against rap's opponents?

3. What is Dyson's real purpose in writing this essay? The kinds of criteria he uses should give you some sense of this. Is it an evaluation of rap music on artistic principles, or something more?

Gangsta Rap and American Culture

The recent attacks on the entertainment industry, especially gangsta rap, by Senator Bob Dole, former Education Secretary William Bennett, and political activist C. Delores Tucker, reveal the fury that popular culture can evoke in a wide range of commentators. As a thirty-five-year-old father of a sixteen-year-old son and as a professor and ordained Baptist minister who grew up in Detroit's treacherous inner city, I too am disturbed by many elements of gangsta rap. But I'm equally anguished by the way many critics have used its artists as scapegoats. How can we avoid the pitfall of unfairly attacking black youth for problems that bewitched our culture long before they gained prominence? First, we should understand what forces drove the emergence of rap. Second, we should place the debate about gangsta rap in the context of a much older debate about "negative" and "positive" black images. Finally, we should acknowledge that gangsta rap crudely exposes harmful beliefs and practices that are often maintained with deceptive civility in much of mainstream society, including many black communities.

If the fifteen-year evolution of hip-hop teaches us anything, it's that history is made in unexpected ways by unexpected people with unexpected results. Rap is now safe from the perils of quick extinction predicted at its humble start. But its birth in the bitter belly of the '70s proved to be a Rosetta stone of black popular culture. Afros, "blunts," funk music, and carnal eruptions define a "back-in-the-day" hip-hop aesthetic. In reality, the severe '70s busted the economic boom of the '60s. The fallout was felt in restructured automobile industries and collapsed steel mills. It was extended in exported employment to foreign markets. Closer to home, there was the depletion of social services to reverse the material ruin of black life. Later, public spaces for black recreation were gutted by Reaganomics or violently transformed by lethal drug economies.

Hip-hop was born in these bleak conditions. Hip-hoppers joined pleasure and rage while turning the details of their difficult lives into craft and capital. This is the world hip-hop would come to "represent": privileged persons speaking for less visible or vocal peers. At their best, rappers shape the tortuous twists of urban fate into lyrical elegies. They represent lives swallowed by too little love or opportunity. They represent themselves and their peers with aggrandizing anthems that boast of their ingenuity and luck in surviving. The art of "representin" that is much ballyhooed in hip-hop is the witness of those left to tell the afflicted's story.

As rap expands its vision and influence, its unfavorable origins and its relentless quest to represent black youth are both a consolation and challenge to hip-hoppers. They remind rappers that history is not merely the stuff of imperial dreams from above. It isn't just the sanitizing myths of those with political power. Representing history is within reach of those who seize the opportunity to speak for themselves, to represent their own interests at all costs. Even rap's largest controversies are about representation. Hip-hop's attitudes toward women and gays continually jolt in the unvarnished malevolence they reveal. The sharp responses to rap's misogyny and homophobia signify its central role in battles over the cultural representation of other beleaguered groups. This is particularly true of gangsta rap.

While gangsta rap takes the heat for a range of social maladies from urban violence to sexual misconduct, the roots of our racial misery remain buried beneath moralizing discourse that is confused and sometimes dishonest. There's no doubt that gangsta rap is often sexist and that it reflects a vicious misogyny that has seized our nation with frightening intensity. It is doubly wounding for black women who are already beset by attacks from outside their communities to feel the thrust of musical daggers to their dignity from within. How painful it is for black women, many of whom have fought valiantly for black pride, to hear the dissonant chord of disdain carried in the angry epithet "bitch."

The link between the vulgar rhetorical traditions expressed in gangsta rap and the economic exploitation that dominates the marketplace is real. The circulation of brutal images of black men as sexual outlaws and black females as "ho's" in many gangsta rap narratives mirrors ancient stereotypes of black sexual identity. Male and female bodies are turned into commodities. Black sexual desire is stripped of redemptive uses in relationships of great affection or love.

Gangsta rappers, however, don't merely respond to the values and visions of the marketplace; they help shape them as well. The ethic of consumption that pervades our culture certainly supports the rapacious materialism shot through the narratives of gangsta rap. Such an ethic, however, does not exhaust the literal or metaphoric purposes of material wealth in gangsta culture. The imagined and real uses of money to help one's friends, family, and neighborhood occupy a prominent spot in gangsta rap lyrics and lifestyles.

Equally troubling is the glamorization of violence and the romanticization of the culture of guns that pervades gangsta rap. The recent legal troubles of Tupac Shakur, Dr. Dre, Snoop Doggy Dogg, and other gangsta rappers chastens any defense of the genre based on simplistic claims that these artists are merely performing roles that are divorced from real life. Too often for gangsta rappers, life does indeed imitate and inform art.

But gangsta rappers aren't *simply* caving in to the pressure of racial stereotyping and its economic rewards in a music industry hungry to exploit their artistic imaginations. According to this view, gangsta rappers are easily manipulated pawns in a chess game of material dominance where their consciences are sold to the highest bidder. Or else gangsta rappers are viewed as the black face of white desire to distort the beauty of black life.

Some critics even suggest that white record executives discourage the production of "positive rap" and reinforce the desire for lewd expressions packaged as cultural and racial authenticity.

But such views are flawed. The street between black artists and record companies runs both ways. Even though black artists are often ripe for the picking—and thus susceptible to exploitation by white and black record labels—many of them are quite sophisticated about the politics of cultural representation. Many gangsta rappers helped to create the genre's artistic rules. Further, they have figured out how to financially exploit sincere and sensational interest in "ghetto life." Gangsta rap is no less legitimate because many "gangstas" turn out to be middle-class blacks faking homeboy roots. This fact simply focuses attention on the genre's essential constructedness, its literal artifice. Much of gangsta rap makes voyeuristic whites and naive blacks think they're getting a slice of authentic ghetto life when in reality they're being served colorful exaggerations. That doesn't mean, however, that the best of gangsta rappers don't provide compelling portraits of real social and economic suffering.

Critics of gangsta rap often ignore how hip-hop has been developed without the assistance of a majority of black communities. Even "positive" or "nation-conscious" rap was initially spurned by those now calling for its revival in the face of gangsta rap's ascendancy. Long before white record executives sought to exploit transgressive sexual behavior among

blacks, many of us failed to lend support to politically motivated rap. For instance, when political rap group Public Enemy was at its artistic and popular height, most of the critics of gangsta rap didn't insist on the group's prominence in black cultural politics. Instead, Public Enemy, and other conscientious rappers, were often viewed as controversial figures whose inflammatory racial rhetoric was cause for caution or alarm. In this light, the hue and cry directed against gangsta rap by the new defenders of "legitimate" hip-hop rings false.

Also, many critics of gangsta rap seek to curtail its artistic freedom to transgress boundaries defined by racial or sexual taboo. That's because the burden of representation falls heavily on what may be termed the race artist in a far different manner than the one I've described above. The race artist stands in for black communities. She represents millions of blacks by substituting or sacrificing her desires and visions for the perceived desires and visions of the masses. Even when the race artist manages to maintain relative independence of vision, his or her work is overlaid with, and interpreted within, the social and political aspirations of blacks as a whole. Why? Because of the appalling lack of redeeming or nonstereotypical representations of black life that are permitted expression in our culture.

This situation makes it difficult for blacks to affirm the value of nontraditional or transgressive artistic expressions. Instead of viewing such cultural products through critical eyes—seeing the good and the bad, the productive and destructive aspects of such art—many blacks tend to simply dismiss such work with hypercritical disdain. A suffocating standard of "legitimate" art is thus produced by the limited public availability of complex black art. Either art is seen as redemptive because it uplifts black culture and shatters stereotypical thinking about blacks, or it is seen as bad because it reinforces negative perceptions of black culture.

That is too narrow a measure for the brilliance and variety of black art and cultural imagination. Black folk should surely pay attention to how black art is perceived in our culture. We must be mindful of the social conditions that shape perceptions of our cultural expressions and that stimulate the flourishing of one kind of art versus another. (After all, die-hard hip-hop fans have long criticized how gangsta rap is eagerly embraced by white record companies while "roots" hip-hop is grossly underfinanced.)

But black culture is too broad and intricate—its artistic manifestations too unpredictable and challenging—for us to be *obsessed* with how white folk view our culture through the lens of our art. And black life is too differentiated by class, sexual identity, gender, region, and nationality to fixate on "negative" or "positive" representations of black culture. Black culture is good and bad, uplifting and depressing, edifying and stifling. All of these features should be represented in our art, should find resonant voicing in the diverse tongues of black cultural expressions.

Gangsta rappers are not the first to face the grueling double standards imposed on black artists. Throughout African-American history, creative personalities have sought to escape or enliven the role of race artist with varying degrees of success. The sharp machismo with which many gangsta rappers reject this office grates on the nerves of many traditionalists. Many critics argue that since gangsta rap is often the only means by which many white Americans come into contact with black life, its pornographic representations and brutal stereotypes of black culture are especially harmful. The understandable but lamentable response of many critics is to condemn gangsta rap out of hand. They aim to suppress gangsta rap's troubling expressions rather than critically engage its artists and the provocative issues they address. Thus the critics of gangsta rap use it for narrow political ends that fail to enlighten or better our common moral lives.

Tossing a moralizing *j'accuse* at the entertainment industry may have boosted Bob Dole's standing in the polls over the short term. It did little, however, to clarify or correct the problems to which he has drawn dramatic attention. I'm in favor of changing the moral climate of our nation. I just don't believe that attacking movies, music, and their makers is very helpful. Besides, right-wing talk radio hosts wreak more havoc than a slew of violent films. They're the ones terrorist Timothy McVeigh was inspired by as he planned to bomb the federal building in Oklahoma City.

A far more crucial task lies in getting at what's wrong with our culture and what it

HOW TO READ EVALUATIONS

needs to get right. Nailing the obvious is easy. That's why Dole, along with William Bennett and C. Delores Tucker, goes after popular culture, especially gangsta rap. And the recent attempts of figures like Tucker and Dionne Warwick, as well as national and local lawmakers, to censor gangsta rap or to outlaw its sale to minors are surely misguided. When I testified before the U.S. Senate's Subcommittee on Juvenile Justice, as well as the Pennsylvania House of Representatives, I tried to make this point while acknowledging the need to responsibly confront gangsta rap's problems. Censorship of gangsta rap cannot begin to solve the problems of poor black youth. Nor will it effectively curtail their consumption of music that is already circulated through dubbed tapes and without the benefit of significant airplay.

A crucial distinction needs to be made between censorship of gangsta rap and edifying expressions of civic responsibility and community conscientiousness. The former seeks to prevent the sale of vulgar music that offends mainstream moral sensibilities by suppressing the First Amendment. The latter, however, is a more difficult but rewarding task. It seeks to oppose the expression of misogynistic and sexist sentiments in hip-hop culture through protest and pamphleteering, through community activism, and through boycotts and consciousness raising.

What Dole, Bennett, and Tucker shrink from helping us understand—and what all effective public moralists must address—is why this issue now? Dole's answer is that the loss of family values is caused by the moral corruption of popular culture, and therefore we should hold rap artists, Hollywood moguls, and record executives responsible for our moral chaos. It's hard to argue with Dole on the surface, but a gentle scratch reveals that both his analysis and answer are flawed.

Too often, "family values" is a code for a narrow view of how families work, who gets to count as a legitimate domestic unit, and consequently, what values are crucial to their livelihood. Research has shown that nostalgia for the family of the past, when father knew best, ignores the widespread problems of those times, including child abuse and misogyny. Romantic portrayals of the family on television and the big screen, anchored by the myth of the Benevolent Patriarch, hindered our culture from coming to grips with its ugly domestic problems.

To be sure, there have been severe assaults on American families and their values, but they have not come mainly from Hollywood, but from Washington with the dismantling of the Great Society. Cruel cuts in social programs for the neediest, an upward redistribution of wealth to the rich, and an unprincipled conservative political campaign to demonize poor black mothers and their children have left latter-day D. W. Griffiths in the dust. Many of gangsta rap's most vocal black critics (such as Tucker) fail to see how the alliances they forge with conservative white politicians such as Bennett and Dole are plagued with problems. Bennett and Dole have put up roadblocks to many legislative and political measures that would enhance the fortunes of the black poor they now claim in part to speak for. Their outcry resounds as crocodile tears from the corridors of power paved by bad faith.

Moreover, many of the same conservative politicians who support the attack on gangsta rap also attack black women (from Lani Guinier to welfare mothers), affirmative action, and the redrawing of voting districts to achieve parity for black voters. The war on gangsta rap diverts attention away from the more substantive threat posed to women and blacks by many conservative politicians. Gangsta rap's critics are keenly aware of the harmful effects that genre's misogyny can have on black teens. Ironically, such critics appear oblivious to how their rhetoric of absolute opposition to gangsta rap has been used to justify political attacks on poor black teens.

That doesn't mean that gratuitous violence and virulent misogyny should not be opposed. They must be identified and destroyed. I am wholly sympathetic, for instance, to sharp criticism of gangsta rap's ruinous sexism and homophobia though neither Dole, Bennett, nor Tucker has made much of the latter plague. "Fags" and "dykes" are prominent in the genre's vocabulary of rage. Critics' failure to make this an issue only reinforces the inferior, invisible status of gay men and lesbians in mainstream and black cultural institutions: Homophobia is a vicious emotion and practice that links mainstream middle-class and black institutions to the vulgar

expressions of gangsta rap. There seems to be an implicit agreement between gangsta rappers and political elites that gays, lesbians, and bisexuals basically deserve what they get.

But before we discard the genre, we should understand that gangsta rap often reaches higher than its ugliest, lowest common denominator. Misogyny, violence, materialism, and sexual transgression are not its exclusive domain. At its best, this music draws attention to complex dimensions of ghetto life ignored by many Americans. Of all the genres of hip-hop—from socially conscious rap to black nationalist expressions, from pop to hardcore—gangsta rap has most aggressively narrated the pains and possibilities, the fantasies and fears, of poor black urban youth. Gangsta rap is situated in the violent climes of postindustrial Los Angeles and its bordering cities. It draws its metaphoric capital in part from the mix of myth and murder that gave the Western frontier a dangerous appeal a century ago.

Gangsta rap is largely an indictment of mainstream and bourgeois black institutions by young people who do not find conventional methods of addressing personal and social calamity useful. The leaders of those institutions often castigate the excessive and romanticized violence of this music without trying to understand what precipitated its rise in the first place. In so doing, they drive a greater wedge between themselves and the youth they so desperately want to help.

If Americans really want to strike at the heart of sexism and misogyny in our communities, shouldn't we take a closer look at one crucial source of these blights—religious institutions, including the synagogue, the temple, and the church? For instance, the central institution of black culture, the black church, which has given hope and inspiration to millions of blacks, has also given us an embarrassing legacy of sexism and misogyny. Despite the great good it has achieved through a heroic tradition of emancipatory leadership, the black church continues to practice and justify *ecclesiastical apartheid*. More than 70 percent of black church members are female, yet they are generally excluded from the church's central station of power, the pulpit. And rarely are the few ordained female ministers elected pastors.

Yet black leaders, many of them ministers, excoriate rappers for their verbal sexual misconduct. It is difficult to listen to civil rights veterans deplore the hostile depiction of women in gangsta rap without mentioning the vicious sexism of the movements for racial liberation of the 1960s. And of course the problem persists in many civil rights organizations today.

Attacking figures like Snoop Doggy Dogg or Tupac Shakur—or the companies that record or distribute them—is an easy out. It allows scapegoating without sophisticated moral analysis and action. While these young black males become whipping boys for sexism and misogyny, the places in our culture where these ancient traditions are nurtured and rationalized—including religious and educational institutions and the nuclear family—remain immune to forceful and just criticism.

Corporate capitalism, mindless materialism, and pop culture have surely helped unravel the moral fabric of our society. But the moral condition of our nation is equally affected by political policies that harm the vulnerable and poor. It would behoove Senator Dole to examine the glass house of politics he abides in before he decides to throw stones again. If he really wants to do something about violence, he should change his mind about the ban on assault weapons he seeks to repeal. That may not be as sexy or self-serving as attacking pop culture, but it might help save lives.

Gangsta rap's greatest "sin" may be that it tells the truth about practices and beliefs that rappers hold in common with the mainstream and with black elites. This music has embarrassed mainstream society and black bourgeois culture. It has forced us to confront the demands of racial representation that plague and provoke black artists. It has also exposed our polite sexism and our disregard for gay men and lesbians. We should not continue to blame gangsta rap for ills that existed long before hip-hop uttered its first syllable. Indeed, gangsta rap's in-your-face style may do more to force our nation to confront crucial social problems than countless sermons or political speeches.

The Nitpicking Nation
(ARTICLE)
Stephanie Rosenbloom

The New York Times In addition to being a journalist for the *New York Times*, 1997 Colgate graduate Stephanie Rosenbloom began acting at a young age and has directed plays since she was a senior in high school. She writes articles about real estate and about how people adapt new technologies for their own purposes. "The Nitpicking Nation" appeared in the *New York Times* in May 2006.

Analyzing and Connecting
Return to these questions after you have finished reading.

1. In one way "The Nitpicking Nation" is not a classic evaluation but rather a look at how people make evaluations on Craigslist. But it also indirectly evaluates Craigslist. What positive and negative aspects of Craigslist are given?

2. Visit Craigslist.org, and compare housing and roommate ads for a city in the United States with those in a city in another country. Make a list of what is desirable and undesirable in roommates or house-sharing partners for both cities. Which criteria are the same on both lists? Which are different?

3. What criteria do you use to evaluate roommates? What makes an ideal roommate in your view?

4. Think of a product that you already own or would like to own. Enter the name of the product on Google followed by the word *review*. If you don't find many reviews, try consumersearch.com. Read several reviews and make a list of the criteria most frequently used to evaluate the product.

THE NITPICKING NATION

THEY are single, gay, straight, biracial, conservative, liberal and tattooed—and they have as many preferences for a potential roommate as an online dater has for a potential lover. They are bankers, fetishists, self-declared nerds and drug users. They have old wounds and new hopes, and are willing to barter their cooking and sexual expertise for free or discounted rent.

They are all seeking and selling housing on Craigslist.org, the electronic listing service with sites in all 50 states and more than 200 worldwide. And because users pay nothing (for now) and are able to go on at length about who they arc and what they want, their postings provide a sociological window into housing trends and desires across the country, from the neon cityscape of the Las Vegas Strip to the wheat fields of Wichita, Kan.

Myriad other sites provide roommate-matching services, but in the last decade Craigslist has emerged as the gold standard. It is easy to navigate, has an extensive number of listings and does not require people to complete an online sign-up sheet to view postings in their entirety. And the intimate and sometimes politically incorrect nature of Craigslist postings can make them fun to read—amusing, frank and even kinky.

Perhaps the most eyebrow-raising thing about the housing listings is the abundance of users—even young, savvy residents of anything-goes metropolises like Los Angeles and Miami—who want mellow, nonpartying roommates. Las Vegas sounds more like Snore City if you judge it by its housing listings. And New Yorkers can come off sounding square. "No parties" and "no drama" are common refrains.

There are exceptions, but even club-hopping Paris Hilton hopefuls seem to have their limits. As four women (ages 19 to 22) seeking a fifth roommate in Boston wrote, "We want a partier, not a puker."

People in their 20's often list their alma maters and request a roommate in their own age group. Cleanliness is a must, or at least "clean-ish," "decently clean" or "clean in public spaces." And spending life with a "professional" appears to be just as important to users of Craigslist's housing listings as it is to users of Match.com.

Some listings have stirred up trouble, however, and the Chicago Lawyers' Committee for Civil Rights Under Law, a nonprofit group, has filed a lawsuit in federal court against Craigslist for "publishing housing advertisements which exclude prospective tenants on the basis of race, gender, family status, marital status, national origin and religion."

A news release issued by the organization said that the Craigslist postings contained such language as "no minorities," "African-Americans and Arabians tend to clash with me so that won't work out," "ladies, please rent from me," "requirements: clean godly Christian male," "will allow only single occupancy," and "no children."

The suit is addressed on Craigslist: "Although in all likelihood this suit will be dismissed on the grounds that Internet sites cannot legally be held liable for content posted by users, Craigslist has no need to hide behind this well-established immunity."

The statement also says that Craigslist respects constitutionally protected free speech rights and that "discriminatory postings are exceedingly uncommon, and those few that do reach the site are typically removed quickly by our users through the flagging system that accompanies each ad."

Craig Newmark, the founder of Craigslist, said that its "culture of trust" inspires users to be straightforward. In fact, some users do not even feel compelled to embellish the descriptions of their spaces, as housing advertisements commonly do. Rather, they take a certain pride in the gritty crudeness of their offerings. A small room for rent in the East Village is described as "definitely a young person's apartment" with "two small junky TV's that we have cheap antennas on, but we get the normal channels, and that is enough for us."

"There is no window," the listing says, "but you have a full-sized door."

And where else do you find housing listings that include candid photographs of the owner or leaseholder instead of the property they are advertising? (A man in Fort Lauderdale, Fla., compromised and included images of his bare room and his bare chest.)

Indeed, Craigslist is where sex and real estate can truly merge. Near Dallas, a married couple are looking for a female roommate "with benefits." A listing for Astoria, Queens, reads: "I am offering a free room for up to three months for any females who are ticklish." A single man in Los Angeles is offering foot massages and free rent to women with comely feet.

Those are some of the tamer overtures, though the majority of roommate listings are not suggestive.

But just who are the most desirable roommates?

Many people prefer women to men. There are women who feel more comfortable sharing a home with someone of the same sex, men who say they get along better with female housemates, and a few cyberspace Casanovas who want to take a shot at turning a roommate into a bedmate. Interns are also desirable, apparently because they are thought to be hard-working, responsible and willing to pay good money for cramped rooms.

But couples are sometimes lumped into a list of the unacceptable, like cigarette smoking. Overall, Democrats are more vocal than Republicans in expressing a desire not to live with the opposing party, though two "hip professional guys" found elusive harmony on Capitol Hill: "One guy is straight, and one is gay. One is a Republican, and the other is a Democrat," they wrote in a listing for a third roommate. "We appreciate and welcome diversity."

Users in the San Francisco Bay Area appear to be among the least interested in rooming with a pet. This area had the highest percentage of "no pets" listings during a key-word search last Thursday (slightly more than 16 percent of 32,295 housing listings). In Boston, about 14 percent of 45,880 listings said "no pets."

Dallas, Wyoming and Birmingham, Ala., seemed quite pet-friendly by comparison: only about 1 percent of the housing listings in each location said "no pets." But Wichita, Kan., emerged as one of the most accepting places, with less than 1 percent of the listings snubbing pets.

In some parts of the country Craigslist housing postings are an essential part of the real estate biosphere. New York is by far the leader in this regard (it had some 180,245 housing listings last Thursday).

Mr. Newmark said there were two reasons for that. "New York real estate is kind of a blood sport," he said, "and also, because our site is free, brokers tend to post a lot of redundant ads."

He said he hoped to address that problem in a matter of weeks by beginning to charge a fee.

Although Mr. Newmark has not studied how the number of housing listings fluctuates day to day, he believes they remain fairly steady on weekdays and drop off on weekends.

Boston had 45,880 housing listings last Thursday, and the San Francisco Bay Area had 32,295. In other places like Montana and Louisville, Ky., there were just a few hundred postings, and North Dakota had fewer than 100.

The New York listings include some of the most expensive, precarious sleeping arrangements in the country. A sofa bed in the living room/kitchen of a one-bedroom apartment on 55th Street between Eighth and Ninth Avenues is $683 a month. You could get a 780-square-foot one-bedroom cottage in Savannah, Ga., for $665 a month. A couch on the West Coast, in a Los Angeles apartment belonging to three actors, is merely $400 a month and includes utilities, cable, Netflix membership, Starbucks wireless membership and wireless Internet, as well as household staples like toothpaste and shampoo.

New Yorkers are also adept at constructing what the military calls a zone of separation. A woman with an apartment at Union Square posted a photograph, not of the bedroom she wanted to rent out for $1,150 a month, but of a large divider she planned to use to create the bedroom from part of her living room.

Near Columbus Circle, a "very small, but cozy space enclosed by tall bookshelves and bamboo screens" is listed for $1,700 a month.

Potential occupants are advised that they must be older than 30 and cannot wear shoes inside the apartment, smoke, consume alcohol, invite guests over or have "sleepovers."

A plethora of "no smokers" statements in the New York housing listings make it appear that the public smoking ban has infiltrated private spaces, too.

But while cigarettes are a deal breaker for some, a number of Craigslist users across the country (Denver and Boulder, Colo.; San Francisco; Boston; and Portland, Ore., to name but a few) say that they are "420 friendly," slang for marijuana use. References to 420 were nonexistent in other cities, including Little Rock, Ark.; Santa Fe, N.M.; and Boise, Idaho.

There are also myriad references to amenities, everything from the use of old record collections and video games to a trapeze suspended in a Brooklyn loft. A posting for a room for rent in Detroit lacks images of the property, though there is a photograph of the L.C.D. television.

And if nothing else, Craigslist housing postings in the United States confirm the zaniness of the hunt and provide a taste of the free-spirited, random connections that have always been part of the experience.

A posting in Asheville, N.C., says that two 21-year-old women are planning to drive almost 20 hours to Austin, Tex., this summer, where they will rent a two-bedroom apartment for $550 a month. "We are looking for one or two (yeah, you can bring a buddy) cool people to ride out there and split an apartment with us," the listing reads. "Are you up for being spontaneous?"

Would-be Jack Kerouacs, take note: they hit the road at the end of the month.

How to write an evaluation

These steps for the process of writing an evaluation may not progress as neatly as this chart might suggest. Writing is not an assembly-line process.

As you write and revise, think about how you might sharpen your criteria and better explain how they apply to what you are evaluating. Your instructor and fellow students may give you comments that help you to rethink your argument from the beginning.

1 CHOOSE A SUBJECT

- Analyze the assignment.
- Explore possible subjects by making lists.
- Analyze a subject.

2 THINK ABOUT YOUR CRITERIA

- Find the obvious criteria, then dig deeper.
- Research your argument by finding evidence and reliable sources.

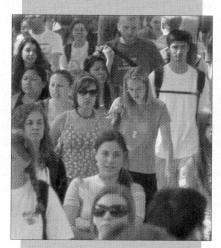

Think about what is at stake

- Who will agree with you?
- Who will disagree? Why?
- Why does your evaluation matter?

Analyze your readers

- How familiar will your readers be with your topic? How much background information will they need?
- Which of your criteria are most likely to appeal to your audience? Which criteria might they find unconvincing or unimportant?

3 WRITE A DRAFT

- Introduce the issue and give the necessary background.
- Describe your criteria and offer evidence.
- Anticipate and address opposing viewpoints.
- Conclude with either your position, a compelling example, or who is affected.
- Choose a title that will interest readers in your essay.

4 REVISE, REVISE, REVISE

- Check that your paper or project fulfills the assignment.
- Is your evaluative claim arguable?
- Are your criteria reasonable, and will your audience accept them?
- Is your evidence convincing and sufficient?
- Do you address opposing views?
- Review the visual presentation of your paper or project.
- Proofread carefully.

5 SUBMITTED VERSION

- Make sure your finished writing meets all formatting requirements.

1: Choose a subject

Analyze the assignment

- Read your assignment slowly and carefully. Look for key words like *evaluate, rank, review,* and *assess.* These key words tell you that you are writing an evaluative essay.
- Mark off any information about the length specified, date due, formatting, and other requirements. You can attend to this information later.

Explore possible subjects by making lists

- Make a list of goods and services you consume, sports, entertainment, or hobbies you enjoy, books you have read recently, films you have seen, speeches you have heard, or policies and laws that affect you or concern you.
- Consider which items on your list you might evaluate. Which are interesting to you? Which would likely interest your readers? Put checkmarks by these items.
- Choose something to evaluate that people can disagree on. You will learn the most, and interest readers most, if you build a strong evaluation that persuades your opponents to re-think their position.

Analyze a subject

- What does your subject attempt to achieve? What do other similar subjects attempt to achieve? (For example, a mountain bike is designed to climb and descend trails, but a good mountain bike will be lightweight, durable, and have good suspension.)
- Who is the audience for your subject? (Mountain bikes appeal to people who prefer to ride on trails rather than pavement.)

Think about what's at stake

- Who will agree with you? Who will disagree, and why?
- Think about why your evaluation matters.

STAYING ON TRACK

Make an arguable claim

A claim that is too obvious or too general will not produce an interesting evaluation. Don't waste your time—or your readers'.

OFF TRACK
Michael Jordan was a great basketball player.
ON TRACK
Bill Russell was the best clutch player in the history of professional basketball.

OFF TRACK
Running is great exercise and a great way to lose weight.
ON TRACK
If you start running to lose weight, be aware of the risks: your body running exerts eight times its weight on your feet, ankles, legs, hips, and lower back, often causing injury to your joints. Swimming, biking, or exercise machines might be the better choice.

WRITE NOW

Finding a subject to evaluate

1. Make a list of possible subjects to evaluate, and select the one that appears most promising.
2. Write nonstop for five minutes about what you like and dislike about this particular subject.
3. Write nonstop for five minutes about what you like and dislike about things in the same category (Mexican restaurants, world leaders, horror movies, mountain bikes, and so on).
4. Write nonstop for five minutes about what people in general like and dislike about things in this category.
5. Underline the likes and dislikes in all three freewrites. You should gain a sense of how your evaluation stacks up against those of others. You may discover a way you can write against the grain, showing others a good or bad aspect of this subject that they may not have observed.

Writer at work

Rashaun Giddens began by circling the words and phrases that indicated his evaluative task and highlighting information about dates and processes for the project. He then made notes and a list of possible subjects. He selected the military's stop loss policy, which he knew about firsthand.

English 1302
Evaluating Policy and Law

Write an essay that evaluates a government or corporate policy, or a law. Explain the policy in some detail, and assess it in terms of its impact. Write with the goal of persuading an informed but uncommitted audience to share your opinion. Your paper should be about 4–6 pages long.

Some factors you may want to consider in your assessment are: the people directly affected by the policy; the people indirectly affected; the cost of the policy; the impact of the policy on national security, the environment, international relations, or other sectors of society; and the policy's original purpose. Do not base your assessment solely on practical criteria. Remember that law and policy are intended to effect some good, whether for the public at large, for the benefit of shareholders–for someone.
                    Remember to look for all types of criteria.
Think about who will be interested in your topic. Who are you talking to? Who has a stake in this issue? How do you need to tailor your argument to reach your audience?
                                        AUDIENCE

Peer review
You will discuss drafts of your essay in your peer groups during class two weeks from today. Final drafts will be due the following week.

Grading Criteria
I will grade your essay according to how well it does the following:
   • Accurately describes the policy or law under consideration.
   • Presents persuasive criteria and evidence.
   • Appeals to its intended audience.

<u>CLAIMS COULD BE:</u>

1. The "don't ask, don't tell" policy in the military is ineffective and discriminatory.

2. The Washington, DC, Metro is one of the best subway systems in the world.

3. <u>The "stop loss" policy that forbids thousands of soldiers from leaving the military when their volunteer commitment ends is not an effective policy.</u>

4. The movie <u>War of the Worlds</u> does not hold up to the original radio broadcast.

5. The current policy regarding steroid use in professional sports does not effectively deter steroid use.

<u>FREEWRITE:</u>

I remember the Army recruiter who came to my high school during my last year. He made a really good pitch about joining the reserves. He said it was a chance to serve our country and get a start on paying for college. That was a big one at my school because most of us had jobs in high school to pay for food and clothes. That's one thing people don't think about--even when you get a scholarship that pays tuition, you still have to eat and have a place to stay. Anyway, my cousin jumped at the chance to join. The recruiter told us 15 months of active duty, but my cousin now knows the Army can keep him much longer.

2: Think about your criteria and your audience

Find the obvious criteria, and then dig deeper

- Write down the criteria you already know you will use in your evaluation. For example, a good study location is quiet, well-lit, safe, and easy to get to.

- Consider other criteria you might not be aware you're using to judge by. Perhaps you gravitate toward the student union rather than the library because you are allowed to drink coffee there. Maybe you began avoiding the library when its blue and orange carpet started to hurt your eyes.

- Think about whether these criteria are practical, aesthetic, or ethical. It isn't that important for you to classify each criterion exactly because there is often overlap between these categories. But you may run into trouble with your audience if you rely too much on one type of criteria, such as aesthetics, and neglect others, like practicality, such as a beautiful chair that hurts your back.

Research your argument

- Find evidence to show how the thing you are evaluating meets or doesn't meet your criteria. If you claim that a symphony has a compelling melodic theme in the first movement, describe the passage in detail.

- Go to reliable sources to find out how others have evaluated the same thing. Do other reviewers tend to agree or disagree with you? Do they use criteria that you don't? Are they addressing the same audience you are?

Analyze your audience

- Consider which of your criteria are most likely to appeal to your audience. Which criteria might they find unconvincing or unimportant?

- How familiar will readers be with your topic? How much background information will they need?

STAYING ON TRACK

Specify and argue for your criteria

Specify your criteria
Show exactly how your criteria apply to what you are evaluating.

OFF TRACK
Border collies make the best pets because they are smart, friendly, and easy to train. *[Vague; many pets are smart, friendly, and easy to train.]*

ON TRACK
Border collies are ideal family pets because their intelligence and trainability enable them to fit into almost any household, no matter how crowded.

Support your criteria
Give evidence to demonstrate why your criteria are valid.

OFF TRACK
Swimming is better exercise than running because you get a better workout. *[How so?]*

ON TRACK
Health professionals maintain that for those who have access to pools or lakes, swimming is the best workout because it exercises all major muscle groups and it's not prone to causing injuries.

Don't assume your audience shares your criteria
It's easy to forget that other people have different concerns and priorities. Your challenge as a writer is finding common ground with people who think differently.

OFF TRACK
Coach X is a bad coach who should be fired because he has lost to our rival school three years in a row. *[For some fans beating the big rival is the only criterion, but not all fans.]*

ON TRACK
While coach X hasn't beaten our big rival in three years, he has succeeded in increasing attendance by 50%, adding a new sports complex built by donations, and raising the players' graduation rate to 80%.

Writer at work

Rashaun Giddens made the following notes about his evaluative claim.

WHAT IS "STOP LOSS"?

The armed services can force volunteer soldiers to remain in service beyond their contractually agreed-upon term.

WHO IS AFFECTED?

- Servicemen and women who make sacrifices for their country.
- The armed forces as a whole.
- National security, because a demoralized army can't fight as well, and if troops are treated unfairly they won't re-enlist. (Also, new recruits will not sign up.)

MY EXPERIENCE

- Recruiters came to my high school.
- My cousin enlisted in the Army Reserves.

CRITERIA

Practical

- Good policy would consider the wellbeing of military families (and economic livelihood)--Practical and ethical.
- Good policy would consider the state of small businesses--Practical (ethical in that the government always says they want to help small businesses).
- Practical and ethical end up overlapping because if people see unethical behavior then they react to it and that has practical results.

Ethical

- The word of the government (a good policy does not require the government to lie or hide information).
- A good policy would prioritize the safety of servicemen and women in Iraq and elsewhere.

Aesthetic

- There really are not any aesthetic criteria. Life and death issues are too important, I guess.

<u>AUDIENCE</u>

Who has a stake in this issue? What do they know about it? How should I appeal to them?

Military families

- Families feel direct effect.
- Military families will probably have a strong sense of duty. They are likely to feel upset if the government does not treat them fairly.

All citizens

- Citizens are responsible for the way our government treats our soldiers. Appeal to people's sense of fair play.
- Citizens have concerns on moral or ideological grounds.
- All citizens need to feel a sense of empathy with the military families; that "This could be me or my child."

<u>BACKGROUND</u>

People may or may not have basic knowledge of policy. Perhaps don't know the specifics or the origin (bring in the history to ground it). May not be aware of how bad it can be in the details.

<u>TO RESEARCH</u>

- Need to get info on how stop loss originated, when it has been used, and what impact it had. Were situations in the past comparable to now?
- Find evidence of hardships for troops. Personal anecdotes from news articles and figures about effects on enlistment.
- Find evidence and testimony about effects on families and small businesses.

3: Write a draft

Introduce the issue	• Give your readers any background information they will need. • State your stance up front, if you wish. Some evaluations work better if the writer's judgment is issued at the beginning; sometimes, it is more effective to build up a mass of evidence and then issue your verdict at the end.
Describe your criteria and offer evidence	• Organize the criteria you present to be as effective as possible. Do you want to start with the most important one, or build up to it? Try both ways, and see which seems more convincing. • Explain each criterion and give reasons to support its use, if readers are unlikely to automatically accept it. • Analyze how well the thing you are evaluating meets each criterion. Provide specific examples.
Anticipate and address opposing viewpoints	• Acknowledge why others may have a different opinion than you do. • Demonstrate why your evaluation is better by pointing out either why your criteria are better or why you have better evidence and reasons.
Conclude with strength	• State your position at the end of your argument if you haven't done so previously. • Offer a compelling example or analogy to end your essay. • State explicitly what is at stake in your evaluation, especially if you are evaluating a policy or issue that affects many people.
Choose a title that will interest readers in your essay	• A bland, generic title like "An Evaluation of X" gives little incentive to want to read the paper.

Writer at work

Based on his lists of criteria, his conclusions about his audience, and his research, Rashaun Giddens sketched out a rough outline for his essay.

1. Personal anecdote (and high school). End with claim.

2. Specific example about the real issues regarding stop loss.

3. Look at stop loss
   a. What is it?
   b. Why is it in effect?
   c. Where did it come from (Civil War, Vietnam, Gulf War, 9/11)?

4. First criteria: good policy should give people faith in the military (those serving and those watching from the sidelines).
   a. Truth, justice and the American way
   b. Pressure on the reserves
   c. How they are manipulating troops

5. Second criteria: good policy protects troops and helps them do their job.
   a. Physical and mental exhaustion
   b. Pushing part-timers beyond what they have been trained for (while going lighter on the fulltime Army).
   c. Emotionally taxing the troops by repeatedly disappointing the already strained through changes in policy and changes in out time.

6. Third criteria: good policy avoids negative impacts on families and businesses
   a. Families left alone
   b. Families left alone and with less money
   c. Destroying small businesses

7. Conclusion and perspective

4: Revise, revise, revise

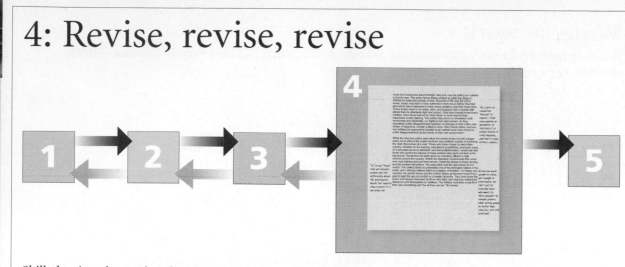

Skilled writers know that the secret to writing well is rewriting. Leave correcting errors for last.

Does your paper or project meet the assignment?	• Look again at your assignment. Does your paper or project do what the assignment asks? • Look again at the assignment for specific guidelines, including length, format, and amount of research. Does your work meet these guidelines?
Is your evaluative claim arguable?	• Do enough people disagree with you to make the evaluation worthwhile? • Does anyone but you care about this topic?
Are your criteria reasonable, and will your audience accept them?	• Do you provide compelling reasons for readers to accept your criteria for evaluation, if they weren't predisposed to do so? • Do you weight criteria appropriately, balancing aesthetic, ethical, and practical considerations in a way likely to appeal to your audience?
Is your evidence convincing and sufficient?	• Will readers believe what you say about the thing you are evaluating? What proof do you offer that it does or doesn't meet your criteria? • Are your descriptions clear and accurate?
Do you address opposing views?	• Have you acknowledged the opinions of people who disagree with you? • Where do you show why your evaluation is better?
Is the writing project visually effective?	• Is the font attractive and readable? • Are the headings and visuals effective? • If you use images or tables as part of your evaluation, are they legible and appropriately placed?
Save the editing for last	When you have finished revising, edit and proofread carefully.

A peer review guide is on page 31.

Writer at work

Working with a group of his fellow students, Rashaun Giddens made comments on his rough draft, and used them to help produce a final draft.

Aside from being less than forthright, stop loss may be putting our soldiers in harm's way. The policy forces these soldiers to suffer the strain of combat for extended periods of time. Because of the way the policy works, troops may learn of tour extensions mere hours before they had planned to return stateside to lower stress positions and their loved ones. These troops need to be ready, alert, and equipped with a morale which allows them to effectively fight and protect. Stop loss instead forces these soldiers--often those trained for short stints--to work beyond their experience and/or training. This policy may prove to overextend, both emotionally and physically, our fighting men and women. As they repeatedly suffer disappointment because of changes in their orders and delays of departure, morale is likely to drop. War breeds stress, but how can soldiers be expected to function at an optimal level when forced to suffer disappointments at the hands of their own government?

This starts to sound like "hearsay" or rumors--find some quotes or anecdotes to illustrate it so people believe it really happens, and that it really bothers soldiers.

While the stop loss policy does allow the armed forces to build a larger active force without the public backlash (and political suicide) of instituting the draft, this comes at a cost. Those who have chosen to serve their country--whether for the training, educational possibilities, economic need, or a personal sense of patriotism--are being bamboozled. I would ask that those who control the futures of these soldiers step back and look at the big picture. Remember the pitch given by recruiting officers in high schools around the country. Watch the television commercials that--even now--tout training and part-time service. Read the stories of those serving and the families left behind. The sales pitch and the real picture do not match. The United States is undeniably one of the strongest nations in the world, and I strongly believe that it is a bastion of freedom. For these very reasons, the armed forces and the United States government must find a way to lead this war (or conflict or crusade) honestly. They must show the honor and respect deserved by those who fight, and stop loss undeniably dishonors and disrespects our soldiers. The military must take a cue from their own advertising and "be all they can be." Be honest.

"Us" versus "them" tone will alienate people who feel differently about the government. Maybe "we" need to show respect--it is our army too

Giving too much weight to ethics, not enough to practicality. We can't just let everyone leave who wants to; there wouldn't be enough soldiers. What option would be better than stop loss, but still practical?

5: Submitted version

Giddens 1

Rashaun Giddens

Professor Chen

English 1302

21 April 2006

Stop Loss or "Loss of Trust"

Looking back on my high school career, my social and extracurricular lives were filled with countless highs: hanging out with my friends, prom, and varsity track to name a few. My academic career, however, was a bit shakier. So busy with what I saw then as the important things in life, I often procrastinated or altogether avoided my schoolwork. My senior year, the recruiter from the U.S. Army Reserves spoke at a school assembly. He asked that we as seniors consider the prospect of becoming "weekend warriors." In the wake of September 11, we could help protect our country and simultaneously work toward paying for a college education, which seemed like a great idea to many students. For those who could not otherwise afford college, the prospect of receiving a higher education in return for patriotism and some good hard work sounded fair enough. My life, however, took a different turn. When I received my track scholarship, I decided to head off to college right away. Many of my friends, however, heeded the call to service. So far, their realities have been far from the lives that were pitched to them; rather, this was the beginning of a path to broken dreams and broken promises.

My cousin, moved to action by a charismatic recruiter, an Army announcement of fifteen-month active tours, and the prospect of a paid college education, chose to join the United States Army Reserves. The Army, suffering from a recruitment shortfall, had recently announced a policy that would allow recruits to serve in active duty for a mere fifteen months. For serving for just over a year, my cousin could do his national duty and put himself on a path to self-improvement. The recruiter did not, however, highlight the fine print to this new program. No one told my cousin that he could be called back to active duty for up to eight years under the government's stop loss policy. Further, no one told him that just one day after the Army announced the incentive program, an appeals court ruled that the Army could, under "stop loss," compel soldiers to remain beyond the initial eight-year obligation (Wickham).

The "stop loss" policy forces thousands of soldiers to serve beyond their volunteer enlistment contracts. The all-volunteer army—on which the government prides itself—is slowly developing into a disgruntled mass of men and women being held against their wills. These men and women wanted to serve their countries, their families, and they signed what they believed were binding agreements with a trustworthy employer—the United States government—only to find that their government didn't bargain in good faith.

As far back as the Civil War, the government needed incentives to retain its troops. (Although we all want freedom, few actually want to put our own lives on the line in the pursuit of that goal.) Both the Union and the Confederacy needed to make tough decisions to maintain strong armed forces when soldiers' contracts were expiring. The Union chose to offer financial incentives to keep its young men in uniform, while the Confederacy instituted a series of (not so) "voluntary" reenlistment policies (Robertson). During World War II all soldiers were forced to remain active until they reached a designated number of "points." Vietnam saw the last stage of a mandatory draft, with soldiers serving one-year tours (Hockstader). Today's military relies on "stop loss," making soldiers stay in the military after their commitment ends. Congress first gave the military the authority to retain soldiers after the Vietnam War when new volunteers were too few to replace departing soldiers. In November 2002 the Pentagon gave stop loss orders for Reserve and National Guard units activated to fight terrorism (Robertson).

This policy is neither forthcoming, safe, nor compassionate toward those most directly impacted—the soldiers and their families. As the United States became more and more entrenched in the conflict in Iraq, the military was stretched thinner and thinner. By 2004, approximately 40% of those serving in Iraq and Afghanistan came from the ranks of the part-time soldiers: the Reserves and the National Guard (Gerard). While these individuals did know that their countries could call if they enlisted, they continue to bear an inordinate burden of actual combat time, and this new policy continues to create situations further removed from the job for which they had enlisted. Recruiters often pitch the military—including the Reserves and the Guard—to young, impressionable, and often underprivileged kids. I have experienced this pitch firsthand and seen the eyes of my classmates as the recruiter promised them a better and richer tomorrow. Seeing a golden opportunity for self-respect and achievement, young men and women sign on the dotted line. Today, other young men and women are buying a bill of goods. These recruits—and those who came before them—deserve to have an honest relationship with the government they protect. As policymakers tout the all-volunteer Army, those who serve find their rights threatened. The military claims to teach soldiers respect and honor. Is misleading your employees honest?

Aside from being less than forthright, stop loss may be putting our soldiers in harm's way. The policy forces these soldiers to suffer the strain of combat for extended periods of time. Because of the way the policy works, troops may learn of tour extensions mere hours before they had planned to return stateside to lower stress positions and their loved ones. These troops need to be ready, alert, and equipped with a morale with allows them to fight effectively. Stop loss instead forces these soldiers—often those trained for short stints—to work beyond their experience and training. This policy may prove to overextend, both emotionally and physically, our fighting men and women. As they repeatedly suffer disappointment because of changes in their orders and delays of departure, morale is likely to drop. Based on reports from families, this practice has been devastating to their soldiers. Nancy Durst, wife of United States Reservist Staff Sergeant Scott Durst, told *Talk of the Nation's* Neal Conan that the military detained her husband's unit just thirty minutes before it was to board the bus scheduled to deliver it to a stateside flight. The unit was later informed that tours had been extended for another four months (Durst). War breeds stress, but how can soldiers be expected to function at an optimal level when forced to suffer disappointments at the hands of their own government?

Finally, this policy simply runs contrary to the current administration's stated interest in the preservation of family and the bolstering of small businesses. First (and most obviously), this less-than-forthright policy keeps families separated. Husbands, wives, and children find themselves separated for longer periods of time, left with uncertainty and ambiguity for comfort. How does this aid in preserving the family? Second, when the government deploys reservists, soldiers often take a severe pay cut. Forced to leave their regular jobs, soldiers—and their families—must survive on often a much smaller government wage. Stop loss extends tours of duty and consequently the economic struggles of the families in question. Third, the policy has proven detrimental to the small business owner. Men and women have used their military experience, discipline, and training to further themselves economically. America prides itself on the power of the small businessman; however, individuals such as Chief Warrant Officer Ronald Eagle have been hurt by this policy. After twenty years of service, Eagle was set to retire from the Army and focus on his aircraft-maintenance business. Instead, the Army has indefinitely moved his retirement date. As a consequence, Eagle has taken a $45,000 pay cut and wonders whether his business will survive his hiatus (Hockstader). Is this the way the government and military fight to preserve the family—emotionally and economically?

Because American men and women risk their lives in the name of bettering those of Iraqis, the military should think about how their policy affects the lives of their soldiers and those back home. While the stop loss policy does allow the armed forces to build a larger active force without the public backlash (and political suicide) of instituting the draft, this policy comes at a cost. Those who have chosen to serve their country—whether for the training, educational possibilities, economic need, or a personal sense of patriotism—are being bamboozled.

Watch the television commercials that, even now, tout training and part-time service. Read the stories of those serving and the families left behind. The sales pitch and the real picture do not match. The United States is undeniably one of the strongest nations in the world and a bastion of freedom. For these very reasons, the armed forces and the United States government, which represents all citizens, must find a way to lead this war (or conflict or crusade) honestly. If we have to pay soldiers double what they currently make in order to get them to re-enlist, we should do so. Even a draft would at least be aboveboard and honest. But we cannot continue to trick people into risking their lives for our national security. Our country must show the honor and respect deserved by those who fight, and stop loss undeniably dishonors and disrespects our soldiers. The military must take a cue from their own advertising and "be all they can be." Be honest.

Works Cited

Durst, Nancy. Interview with Neal Conan. Talk of the Nation. NPR. 19 Apr. 2004.

Gerard, Philip. "When the Cry Was 'Over the Hill in October.'" Charleston Gazette 16
        May 2004: 1E.

Hockstader, Lee. "Army Stops Many Soldiers from Quitting; Orders Extend
        Enlistments to Curtail Troop Shortages." Washington Post 29 Dec. 2003: A01.

Robertson, John. "The Folly of Stop Loss." Pittsburgh Post-Gazette 19 Dec. 2004: J1.

Wickham, DeWayne. "A 15-Month Enlistment? Check Army's Fine Print." USA
        Today 17 May 2005: 13A.

Projects

You likely have a great deal of experience making consumer evaluations, and when you have time to do your homework to compare features, quality, and price, probably you will make a good decision. For other evaluations, however, the criteria may not be obvious. Often the keys are finding the right criteria and convincing your readers that these criteria are the best ones to use.

These projects are frequently written kinds of evaluations.

The Aesthetics of Wind Power
by Lefteris Pavlides

EVALUATE A CONTROVERSIAL SUBJECT

For an example of an evaluation of a controversial subject, see pages 371–375.

Think of controversial subjects on your campus or in your community for which you can find recent articles in your campus or local newspaper. For example, is your mayor or city manager an effective leader? Is your campus recreational sports facility adequate? Is a new condominium complex built on city land that was used as a park good or bad?

Identify what is at stake in the evaluation. Who thinks it is good or effective? Who thinks it is bad or ineffective? Why does it matter?

List the criteria that make something or someone good or bad. Which criteria are the most important? Which will you have to argue for?

Analyze your potential readers. How familiar will they be with what you are evaluating? Which criteria will they likely accept and which might they disagree with?

Write a draft. Introduce your subject and give the necessary background. Make your evaluative claim either at the beginning or as your conclusion. Describe each criterion and evaluate your subject on each criterion. Be sure to address opposing viewpoints by acknowledging how their evaluations might be different.

EVALUATE A CAMPUS POLICY

For an example of an evaluation essay, see pages 390–397.

FILM REVIEW

For an example of a review, see pages 384–389.

Identify a policy on your campus that affects you. Examples include the way your school schedules classes and has students register; the way parking spaces are allotted on campus; the library's late fee and returns policy; housing or admissions policies; or rules regulating student organizations.

Select a film to review. Choose a specific magazine, newspaper, or online publication as the place where you would publish the review. Read some reviews in that publication and notice the criteria that they use. You will need to keep the audience in mind.

Consider your target audience as the readers of your campus newspaper. Who else besides you is affected by this issue? What office or division of the school is responsible for the program? Who implemented it in the first place? Keep in mind that your school's administration is part of your audience.

Watch the film more than once and take notes. Analyze the film's genre. What makes a good horror movie? a good action-adventure movie? a good documentary? a good comedy? These will be your criteria for evaluation.

Determine the criteria for your evaluation. Which criteria will be most important for other students? for the faculty and staff? for the administration?

Find information on the film. The Internet Movie Database (**www.imdb.com**) is a good place to start. Look at the director's credits to find other films that he or she has done. Look at the information about the actors and locations.

Take a clear position about the policy. If you think the policy is unfair or ineffective, acknowledge why it was put into place. Sometimes good intentions lead to bad results. If you think the policy is fair or effective, explain why according to the criteria you set out. In either case, give reasons and examples to support your judgment.

Write a thesis that makes an evaluative claim: the film is a successful or unsuccessful example of its genre. Go beyond the obvious in selecting criteria. A comedy is supposed to make you laugh, but movies that are only gags tend to wear thin. Comedies that have engaging characters keep your interest. Acting often makes the difference between a good movie and a great movie. Use evidence from the film to support your claim.

13

Arguing for a Position

Position arguments aim to change readers' attitudes and beliefs or at least get them to consider a view different from their own.

424

Chapter contents

Writing a position argument

Many people think of the term *argument* as a synonym for *debate*. College courses and professional careers, however, require a different kind of argument—one that, most of the time, is cooler in emotion and more elaborate in detail than oral debate. At first glance an argument in writing doesn't seem to have much in common with debate. But the basic elements and ways of reasoning used in written arguments are similar to those we use in everyday conversations. Let's look at an example of an informal debate.

SEAN: I think students should not pay tuition to go to state colleges and universities.

CARMEN: Cool idea, but why should students not pay?

SEAN: Because you don't have pay to go to high school.

CARMEN: Yeah, but that's different. The law says that everyone has to go to high school, at least to age 16. Everyone doesn't have to go to college.

SEAN: Well, in some other countries like the United Kingdom, students don't have to pay tuition.

CARMEN: Their system of education is different. Plus you're wrong. Students started paying tuition at British universities in fall 1998.

SEAN: OK, maybe the United Kingdom isn't a good example. But students should have a right to go to college, just like they have the right to drive on the highway.

CARMEN: Why? What evidence do you have that things would be better if everyone went to college? It would put an enormous drain on the economy. People would have to pay a lot more in taxes.

In this discussion Sean starts out by making a claim that students should not have to pay tuition. Carmen immediately asks him why students should not have to pay tuition. She wants a reason to accept his claim. Scholars who study argument maintain that *an argument must have a claim and one or more reasons to support that claim.* Something less might be persuasive, but it isn't an argument.

If Sean's assertion were a bumper sticker, it might read "MAKE COLLEGE FREE FOR ALL." The assertion is a claim but it is not an argument, because it lacks a reason. Many reasons are possible for arguing for free tuition:

- College should be free for all because everyone is entitled to a good education.

- College should be free for all because the economy will benefit.

- College should be free for all because a democracy requires educated citizens.

When a claim has a reason attached, then it becomes an argument.

A reason is typically offered in a **because-clause,** a statement that begins with the word *because* and that provides a supporting reason for the claim. Sean's first attempt is to argue that students shouldn't have to pay to go to college because they don't have to pay to go to high school.

The word *because* signals a **link** between the reason and the claim. Just having a reason for a claim, however, doesn't mean that the audience will be convinced. When Sean tells Carmen that students don't have to pay to go to public high schools, Carmen does not accept the link. Carmen asks

"So what?" every time Sean presents a new reason. Carmen will accept Sean's claim only if she accepts that his reason supports his claim. Carmen challenges Sean's links and keeps asking "So what?" For her, Sean's reasons are not good reasons.

Benjamin Franklin observed, "so convenient a thing it is to be a rational creature, since it enables us to find or make a reason for every thing one has a mind to do." It is not hard to think of reasons. What is difficult is to convince your audience that your reasons are *good reasons.* In a conversation, you get immediate feedback that tells you whether your listener agrees or disagrees. When you are writing, there usually is not someone who can give you immediate feedback. Consequently, if you are going to convince someone who doesn't agree with you or know what you know already, you have to be more specific about what you are claiming, you have to connect with the values you hold in common with your readers, and you have to anticipate what questions and objections your readers might have.

Components of position arguments

What exactly is my issue?	**Define the issue** Your subject should be clear to your readers. If readers are unfamiliar with the issue, you should give enough examples so they understand the issue in concrete terms.
What exactly is my stand on the issue?	**State your position** You may want to state your thesis in the opening paragraph to let readers know your position immediately. If your issue is unfamiliar, you may want to find out more before you state your position. In any case, you should take a definite position on the issue.
What are the reasons for my position?	**Find one or more reasons** You need to give one or more reasons for your position. Write as many because-clauses as you can think of. Use the ones that are most convincing.
Where can I find evidence?	**Provide evidence** In support of your reasons, provide evidence—in the form of examples, statistics, and testimony of experts—that the reasons are valid. When the issue is unfamiliar, more evidence than usual is required.
Who disagrees with my position?	**Acknowledge opposing views and limitations of the claim** If everybody thinks the same way, then there is no need to write a position argument. Anticipate what objections might be made to your position. You can answer possible objections in two ways: that the objections are not valid or that the objections have some validity but your argument is stronger.

Keys to position arguments

Understand your goal

A well-written and well-reasoned position argument may not change minds entirely, but it can convince readers that a reasonable person can hold this point of view. Position arguments do not necessarily have winners and losers. Your goal is to invite a response that creates a dialog.

Be sensitive to the context

Even position arguments that have become classics and in a sense "timeless" frequently were written in response to a historical event; for example, Martin Luther King Jr. wrote his powerful argument for civil disobedience, "Letter from Birmingham Jail," in response to a published statement by eight Birmingham clergymen. A careful analysis of a recent or historical event often provides your argument with a sense of immediacy.

Rely on careful definitions

What exactly does *freedom of speech* mean? What exactly does *privacy* mean? What exactly does *animal rights* mean? Getting readers to accept a definition is often the key to a position argument. For example, torturing animals is against the law. Animal rights activists argue that raising and slaughtering animals for food is torture and thus would extend the definition. If you can get readers to accept your definition, then they will agree with your position.

Use quality sources

Find the highest-quality sources for citing evidence. Recent sources are critical for current topics, such as the relationship of certain diets to disease.

Create credibility

You have probably noticed that many times in the course of reading, you get a strong sense of the writer's character, even if you know nothing about the person. Be honest about strengths and weaknesses and about what you don't know, and avoid easy labels. If readers trust you are sincere, they will take you seriously.

Cultivate a sense of humor and a distinctive voice

A reasonable voice doesn't have to be a dull one. Humor is a legitimate tool of argument, especially when the stakes are high and tempers are flaring.

Argue responsibly

When you begin an argument by stating "in my opinion," you are not arguing responsibly. Readers assume that if you make a claim in writing, you believe that claim. More important, it is rarely just your opinion. Most beliefs and assumptions are shared by many people. When other members of your community share your opinion, your readers should consider your position seriously.

Provide visuals if needed   Images can supply relevant examples for some issues. If you have statistical data to present, consider including a table or chart.

If you choose to argue that graffiti should be considered art, you will need to provide images as examples.

WORKING TOGETHER

Identify reasons that support conflicting claims

In a group of three or four students

Select a controversial issue for which there are multiple points of view. You can find a list of issues at **www.dir.yahoo.com/ Society_and_Culture/Issues_and_Causes/.** Explore the links for one of the issues to get a sense of the range of opinion. Then decide which Web sites will give your group a range of views on the issue.

Each member of your group will analyze two Web sites. Write down the following for each site.

• What is the main claim of the Web site?

• What reason or reasons are given?

• What evidence (facts, examples, statistics, and the testimony of authorities) is offered?

Bring your answers to class and compare them with other members of your group. How do the reasons differ for opposing claims? What assumptions underlie the reasons? How does the evidence differ?

429

An effective position argument

Position arguments succeed when readers consider the writer's position as one to take seriously.

The New York Times **Take My Privacy, Please!**
Ted Koppel
Ted Koppel joined ABC News in 1963 and served from 1980 until 2005 as the anchor and managing editor of *Nightline*, the first late-night network news program. He has had a major reporting role in every presidential campaign since 1964. "Take My Privacy, Please!" which appeared in June 2005 in the *New York Times*, is an example of a position argument that doesn't begin with a thesis but first gives a series of examples.

Take My Privacy, Please!

by Ted Koppel

THE PATRIOT ACT—brilliant! Its critics would have preferred a less stirring title, perhaps something along the lines of the Enhanced Snooping, Library and Hospital Database Seizure Act. But then who, even right after 9/11, would have voted for that?

Precisely. He who names it and frames it, claims it. The Patriot Act, however, may turn out to be among the lesser threats to our individual and collective privacy.

There is no end to what we will endure, support, pay for and promote if only it makes our lives easier, promises to save us money, appears to enhance our security and comes to us in a warm, cuddly and altogether nonthreatening package. To wit: OnStar, the subscription vehicle tracking and assistance system.

Koppel announces his stance and his subject in the first two paragraphs. He questions the Patriot Act and then suggests that there may be bigger threats to privacy.

Part of its mission statement, as found on the OnStar Web site, is the creation of "safety, security and peace of mind for drivers and passengers with thoughtful wireless services that are always there, always ready." You've surely seen or heard their commercials, one of which goes like this:

ANNOUNCER -- The following is an OnStar conversation. (Ring)

ONSTAR -- OnStar emergency, this is Dwight.

DRIVER -- (crying) Yes, yes??!

ONSTAR -- Are there any injuries, ma'am?

DRIVER -- My leg hurts, my arm hurts.

ONSTAR -- O.K. I do understand. I will be contacting emergency services.

ANNOUNCER -- If your airbags deploy, OnStar receives a signal and calls to check on you. (Ring)

EMERGENCY SERVICES -- Police.

ONSTAR -- This is Dwight with OnStar. I'd like to report a vehicle crash with airbag deployment on West 106th Street.

EMERGENCY SERVICES -- We'll send police and E.M.S. out there.

DRIVER -- (crying) I'm so scared!

ONSTAR -- O.K., I'm here with you, ma'am; you needn't be scared.

The OnStar commercial is described in detail as the first example.

In the ad, OnStar is portrayed as a technology that can save lives.

431

KOPPEL: TAKE MY PRIVACY, PLEASE!

Well, maybe just a little scared. Tell us again how Dwight knows just where the accident took place. Oh, right! It's those thoughtful wireless services that are always there. Always, as in any time a driver gets into an OnStar-equipped vehicle. OnStar insists that it would disclose the whereabouts of a subscriber's vehicle only after being presented with a criminal court order or after the vehicle has been reported stolen. That's certainly a relief. I wouldn't want to think that anyone but Dwight knows where I am whenever I'm traveling in my car.

Of course, E-ZPass and most other toll-collecting systems already know whenever a customer passes through one of their scanners. That's because of radio frequency identification technology. In return for the convenience of zipping through toll booths, you need to have in your car a wireless device. This tag contains information about your account, permitting E-ZPass to deduct the necessary toll—and to note when your car whisked through that particular toll booth. They wouldn't share that information with anyone, either; that is, unless they had to.

Radio frequency identification technology has been used for about 15 years now to reunite lost pets with their owners. Applied Digital Solutions, for example, manufactures the VeriChip, a tiny, implantable device that holds a small amount of data. Animal shelters can scan the chip for the name and phone number of the lost pet's owner. The product is now referred to as the HomeAgain Microchip Identification System.

Useful? Sure. Indeed, it's not much of a leap to suggest that one day, the VeriChip might be routinely implanted under the skin of, let's say, an Alzheimer's patient. The Food and Drug Administration approved the VeriChip for use in people last October. An Applied Digital Solutions spokesman estimates that about 1,000 people have already had a VeriChip implanted, usually in the right triceps. At the moment, it doesn't carry much information, just an identification number

Koppel uses critical thinking to question the main assumption of the ad: Is it necessarily good that OnStar always knows where you are while driving?

Convenient technologies also keep track of our movements. Koppel gets his readers to think about what happens to personal information that is passively collected.

that health care providers can use to tap into a patient's medical history. A Barcelona nightclub also uses it to admit customers with a qualifying code to enter a V.I.P. room where drinks are automatically put on their bill. Possible variations on the theme are staggering.

Technologies used to track pets can also track people.

And how about all the information collected by popular devices like TiVo, the digital video recorder that enables you to watch and store an entire season's worth of favorite programs at your own convenience? It also lets you electronically mark the programs you favor, allowing TiVo to suggest similar programs for your viewing pleasure. In February, TiVo announced the most frequently played and replayed commercial moment during the Super Bowl (it involves a wardrobe malfunction, but believe me, you don't want to know), drawing on aggregated data from a sample of 10,000 anonymous TiVo households. No one is suggesting that TiVo tracks what each subscriber records and replays. But could they, if they needed to? That's unclear, although TiVo does have a privacy policy. "Your privacy," it says in part, "is very important to us. Due to factors beyond our control, however, we cannot fully ensure that your user information will not be disclosed to third parties."

The popular TiVo service admits that it does not fully protect the privacy of its subscribers.

Unexpected and unfortunate things happen, of course, even to the most reputable and best-run organizations. Only last February, the Bank of America Corporation notified federal investigators that it had lost computer backup tapes containing personal information about 1.2 million federal government employees, including some senators. In April, LexisNexis unintentionally gave outsiders access to the personal files (addresses, Social Security numbers, drivers license information) of as many as 310,000 people. In May, Time Warner revealed that an outside storage company had misplaced data stored on computer backup tapes on 600,000 current and former employees. That same month, United Parcel Service picked up a box of computer tapes in New Jersey from CitiFinancial, the consumer finance subsidiary of

Numerous accidents and data thefts have given private information to unauthorized people.

KOPPEL: TAKE MY PRIVACY, PLEASE!

Citigroup, that contained the names, addresses, Social Security numbers, account numbers, payment histories and other details on small personal loans made to an estimated 3.9 million customers. The box is still missing.

Whoops!

CitiFinancial correctly informed its own customers and, inevitably, the rest of the world about the security breach. Would they have done so entirely on their own? That is less clear. In July 2003, California started requiring companies to inform customers living in the state of any breach in security that compromises personally identifiable information. Six other states have passed similar legislation.

No such legislation exists on the federal stage, however—only discretionary guidelines for financial institutions about whether and how they should inform their customers with respect to breaches in the security of their personal information.

Both the House and Senate are now considering federal legislation similar to the California law. It's a start but not nearly enough. We need mandatory clarity and transparency; not just with regard to the services that these miracles of microchip and satellite technology offer but also the degree to which companies share and exchange their harvest of private data.

We cannot even begin to control the growing army of businesses and industries that monitor what we buy, what we watch on television, where we drive, the debts we pay or fail to pay, our marriages and divorces, our litigations, our health and tax records and all else that may or may not yet exist on some computer tape, if we don't fully understand everything we're signing up for when we avail ourselves of one of these services.

Koppel hopes by this point he has raised concerns about privacy for his readers. He now gives his thesis: The public has the right to know what is being done with private information they give to companies and services.

How to read position arguments

Make notes as you read, either in the margins or on paper or a computer file. Circle any words or references that you don't know and look them up.

What is it?	• What kind of a text is it? An article? an essay? a chart? a scientific report? a Web site? an executive summary? What are your expectations for this kind of text? • What media are used? (Web sites, for example, often combine images, words, and sounds.)
Where did it come from?	• Who wrote the analysis? • Where did it first appear? In a book, newspaper, magazine, online, in a company, or in an organization?
What is the writer's thesis or main idea?	• What is the writer's topic? What effect is he or she trying to determine the cause of? • Why is this topic important? • What are the key ideas or concepts that the writer considers? • What are the key terms? How does the writer define those terms?
Who is the intended audience?	• What clues do you find about whom the writer had in mind as readers? • What does the writer assume that the readers already know about the subject? • What new knowledge is the writer providing?
What are the reasons that support the claim?	• Is there one primary reason? • Are multiple reasons given? • Do you find any fallacies in the reasons (see pages 18–19)?
What kinds of evidence are given?	• Is the evidence from books, newspapers, periodicals, the Web, or field research? • Is the evidence convincing that the causes given are the actual causes?
How is it composed?	• How does the writer represent himself or herself? • How would you characterize the style? • How effective is the design? Is it easy to read? • If there are any photographs, charts, or other graphics, what information do they contribute?

What to the Slave Is the Fourth of July?

(SPEECH)

Frederick Douglass

On the fifth of July, 1852, former slave Frederick Douglass spoke at a meeting of the Ladies' Anti-Slavery Society in Rochester, New York. In this excerpt from his lengthy oration (published shortly thereafter as a pamphlet), Douglass reminds his audience of the irony of celebrating freedom and liberty in a land where much of the population was enslaved.

Analyzing and Connecting

Return to these questions after you have finished reading.

1. Douglass spends considerable time telling his audience what points do *not* need to be argued: that a slave is human, that man is entitled to liberty, and so on. If in fact these points are agreed upon by all, why do you think Douglass spends so much time talking about them?

2. Douglass was speaking in the last few years before the American Civil War began. How did the vivid imagery in this speech likely affect listeners? Read carefully through Douglass's descriptions of the slave trade and its impact on individuals and families. What values is he appealing to?

3. What impact does Douglass's personal history have on his credibility? Would the argument in this speech have been as compelling if it had been made by someone who had never experienced slavery first-hand?

4. What words would you use to describe the overall tone of Douglass's speech? Is it angry? threatening? hopeful? pessimistic? Why do you think Douglass chose the tone he used in this argument?

Fellow-citizens, pardon me, allow me to ask, why am I called upon to speak here to-day? What have I, or those I represent, to do with your national independence? Are the great principles of political freedom and of natural justice, embodied in that Declaration of Independence, extended to us? And am I, therefore, called upon to bring our humble offering to the national altar, and to confess the benefits and express devout gratitude for the blessings resulting from your independence to us?

But, such is not the state of the case. I say it with a sad sense of the disparity between us. I am not included within the pale of this glorious anniversary! Your high independence only reveals the immeasurable distance between us. The blessings in which you, this day, rejoice, are not enjoyed in common. The rich inheritance of justice, liberty, prosperity, and independence, bequeathed by your fathers, is shared by you, not by me. The sunlight that brought life and healing to you has brought stripes and death to me. This Fourth [of] July is yours, not mine. You may rejoice, I must mourn. To drag a man in fetters into the grand illuminated temple of liberty, and call upon him to join you in joyous anthems is inhuman mockery and sacrilegious irony. Do you mean, citizens, to mock me, by asking me to speak to-day?

Fellow-citizens, above your national, tumultuous joy, I hear the mournful wail of millions whose chains, heavy and grievous yesterday, are, to-day, rendered more intolerable by the jubilee shouts that reach them. To forget them, to pass lightly over their wrongs, and to chime in with the popular theme, would be treason most scandalous and shocking, and would make me a reproach before God and the world. My subject, then fellow citizens, is AMERICAN SLAVERY. I shall see, this day, and its popular characteristics, from the slave's point of view. Standing, there, identified with the American bondman, making his wrongs mine, I do not hesitate to declare, with all my soul, that the character and conduct of this nation never looked blacker to me than on this 4th of July!

Whether we turn to the declarations of the past, or to the professions of the present, the conduct of the nation seems equally hideous and revolting. America is false to the past, false to the present, and solemnly binds herself to be false to the future. Standing with God and the crushed and bleeding slave on this occasion, I will, in the name of humanity which is outraged, in the name of liberty which is fettered, in the name of the constitution and the Bible, which are disregarded and trampled upon, dare to call in question and to denounce, with all the emphasis I can command, everything that serves to perpetuate slavery—the great sin and shame of America! "I will not equivocate; I will not excuse;" I will use the severest language I can command; and yet not one word shall escape me that any man, whose judgment is not blinded by prejudice, or who is not at heart a slaveholder, shall not confess to be right and just.

But I fancy I hear some one of my audience say, it is just in this circumstance that you and your brother abolitionists fail to make a favorable impression on the public mind. Would you argue more, and denounce less, would you persuade more, and rebuke less, your cause would be much more likely to succeed. But, I submit, where all is plain there is nothing to be argued. What point in the anti-slavery creed would you have me argue? On what branch of the subject do the people of this country need light? Must I undertake to prove that the slave is a man? That point is conceded already. Nobody doubts it. The slaveholders themselves acknowledge it in the enactment of laws for their government. They acknowledge it when they punish disobedience on the part of the slave. There are seventy-two crimes in the State of Virginia, which, if committed by a black man, (no matter how ignorant he be), subject him to the punishment of death; while only two of the same crimes will subject a white man to the like punishment. What is this but the acknowledgement that the slave is a moral, intellectual and responsible being? The manhood of the slave is conceded. It is admitted in the fact that Southern statute books are covered with enactments forbidding, under severe fines and penalties, the teaching of the slave to read or to write. When you can point to any such laws, in reference to the beasts of the field, then I may consent to argue the manhood of the slave. When the dogs in your streets, when the fowls of the air, when the cattle on your hills, when the fish of the sea, and the reptiles that crawl, shall be unable to distinguish the slave from a brute, there will I argue with you that the slave is a man!

For the present, it is enough to affirm the equal manhood of the negro race. Is it not astonishing that, while we are ploughing, planting and reaping, using all kinds of mechanical tools, erecting houses, constructing bridges, building ships, working in metals of brass, iron, copper, silver and gold; that, while we are reading, writing and ciphering, acting as clerks, merchants and secretaries, having among us lawyers, doctors, ministers, poets, authors, editors, orators and teachers; that, while we are engaged in all manner of enterprises common to other men, digging gold in California, capturing the whale in the Pacific, feeding sheep and cattle on the hillside, living, moving, acting, thinking, planning, living in families as husbands, wives and children, and, above all, confessing and worshipping the Christian's God, and looking hopefully for life and immortality beyond the grave, we are called upon to prove that we are men!

Would you have me argue that man is entitled to liberty? That he is the rightful owner of his own body? You have already declared it. Must I argue the wrongfulness of slavery? Is it to be settled by the rules of logic and argumentation, as a matter beset with great difficulty, involving a doubtful application of the principle of justice, hard to be understood? How should I look to-day, in the presence of Americans, dividing, and subdividing a discourse, to show that men have a natural right to freedom? speaking of it relatively, and positively, negatively, and affirmatively. To do so would be to make myself ridiculous and offer an insult to your understanding. There is not a man beneath the canopy of heaven that does not know that slavery is wrong for him.

What, am I to argue that it is wrong to make men brutes, to rob them of their liberty, to work them without wages, to keep them ignorant of their relations to their fellow men, to beat them with sticks, to flay their flesh with the lash, to load their limbs with irons, to hunt them with dogs, to sell them at auction, to sunder their families, to knock out their teeth, to burn their flesh, to starve them into obedience and submission to their masters? Must I argue that a system thus marked with blood, and stained with pollution, is wrong? No! I will not. I have better employments for my time and strength, than such arguments would imply.

What, then, remains to be argued? Is it that slavery is not divine; that God did not establish it; that our doctors of divinity are mistaken? There is blasphemy in the thought. That which is inhuman, cannot be divine! Who can reason on such a proposition? They that can, may; I cannot. The time for such argument is past.

What, to the American slave, is your 4th of July? I answer: a day that reveals to him, more than all other days in the year, the gross injustice and cruelty to which he is the constant victim. To him, your celebration is a sham; your boasted liberty, an unholy license; your national greatness, swelling vanity; your sounds of rejoicing are empty and heartless; your denunciations of tyrants, brass fronted impudence; your shouts of liberty and equality, hollow mockery; your prayers and hymns, your sermons and thanksgivings, with all your religious parade, and solemnity, are, to him, mere bombast, fraud, deception, impiety, and hypocrisy—a thin veil to cover up crimes which would disgrace a nation of savages. There is not a nation on the earth guilty of practices, more shocking and bloody, than are the people of these United States, at this very hour.

Go where you may, search where you will, roam through all the monarchies and despotisms of the old world, travel through South America, search out every abuse, and when you have found the last, lay your facts by the side of the everyday practices of this nation, and you will say with me, that, for revolting barbarity and shameless hypocrisy, America reigns without a rival.

Take the American slave-trade, which we are told by the papers, is especially prosperous just now. Ex-Senator Benton tells us that the price of men was never higher than now. He mentions the fact to show that slavery is in no danger. This trade is one of the peculiarities of American institutions. It is carried on in all the large towns and cities in one-half of this confederacy; and millions are pocketed every year, by dealers in this horrid traffic. In several states, this trade is a chief source of wealth. It is called (in contradistinction to the foreign slave-trade) "the internal slave trade." It is, probably, called so, too, in order to divert from it the horror with which the foreign slave-trade is contemplated. That trade has long since been denounced by this government, as piracy. It has been denounced with burning words, from the high places of the nation, as an execrable traffic. To arrest it, to put an end to it, this nation keeps a squadron, at immense cost, on the coast of Africa. Everywhere, in this country, it is safe to speak of this foreign slave-trade, as a most inhuman traffic, opposed alike to the laws of God and of man. The duty to extirpate and destroy it is admitted even by our DOCTORS OF DIVINITY. In order to put an end to it, some of these last have consented that their colored brethren (nominally free) should leave this country, and establish themselves on the western coast of Africa! It is, however, a notable fact that, while so much execration is poured out by Americans upon those engaged in the foreign slave-trade, the men engaged in the slave-trade between the states pass without condemnation, and their business is deemed honorable.

Behold the practical operation of this internal slave-trade, the American slave-trade, sustained by American politics and American religion. Here you will see men and women reared like swine for the market. You know what is a swine-drover? I will show you a man-drover. They inhabit all our Southern States. They perambulate the country and crowd the highways of the nation, with droves of human stock. You will see one of these human flesh-jobbers, armed with pistol, whip and Bowie-knife, driving a company of a hundred men, women, and children from the Potomac to the slave market at New Orleans. These wretched people are to be sold singly, or in lots, to suit purchasers. They are food for the cotton-field, and the deadly sugar-mill. Mark the sad procession, as it moves wearily along, and the inhuman wretch who drives them. Hear his savage yells and his blood-chilling oaths, as he hurries on his affrighted captives! There, see the old man, with locks thinned and gray. Cast one glance, if you please, upon that young mother, whose shoulders are bare to the scorching sun, her briny tears falling on the brow of the babe in her arms. See, too, that girl of thirteen, weeping, yes! weeping, as she thinks of the mother from whom she has been torn! The drove moves tardily. Heat and sorrow have nearly consumed their strength; suddenly you hear a quick snap, like the discharge of a rifle; the fetters clank, and the chain rattles simultaneously; your ears are saluted with a scream, that seems to have torn its way to the centre of your soul! The crack you heard, was the sound of the slave-whip; the scream you heard, was from the woman you saw with the babe. Her speed had faltered under the weight of her child and her chains! that gash on her shoulder tells her to move on. Follow this drove to New Orleans. Attend the auction; see men examined like horses; see the forms of women rudely and brutally exposed to the shocking gaze of American slave-buyers. See this drove sold and separated forever; and never forget the deep, sad sobs that arose from that scattered multitude. Tell me citizens, WHERE, under the sun, you can witness a spectacle more fiendish and shocking. Yet this is but a glance at the American slave-trade, as it exists, at this moment, in the ruling part of the United States.

I was born amid such sights and scenes. To me the American slave-trade is a terrible reality. When a child, my soul was often pierced with a sense of its horrors. I lived on Philpot Street, Fell's Point, Baltimore, and have watched from the wharves, the slave ships in the Basin, anchored from the shore, with their cargoes of human flesh, waiting for favorable winds to waft them down the Chesapeake. There was, at that time, a grand slave mart kept at the head of Pratt Street, by Austin Woldfolk. His agents were sent into every town and county in Maryland, announcing their arrival, through the papers, and on flaming "hand-bills," headed

CASH FOR NEGROES. These men were generally well dressed men, and very captivating in their manners. Ever ready to drink, to treat, and to gamble. The fate of many a slave has depended upon the turn of a single card; and many a child has been snatched from the arms of its mother by bargains arranged in a state of brutal drunkenness.

Allow me to say, in conclusion, notwithstanding the dark picture I have this day presented of the state of the nation, I do not despair of this country. There are forces in operation, which must inevitably work the downfall of slavery. "The arm of the Lord is not shortened," and the doom of slavery is certain. I, therefore, leave off where I began, with hope. While drawing encouragement from the Declaration of Independence, the great principles it contains, and the genius of American Institutions, my spirit is also cheered by the obvious tendencies of the age. Nations do not now stand in the same relation to each other that they did ages ago. No nation can now shut itself up from the surrounding world, and trot round in the same old path of its fathers without interference. The time was when such could be done. Long established customs of hurtful character could formerly fence themselves in, and do their evil work with social impunity. Knowledge was then confined and enjoyed by the privileged few, and the multitude walked on in mental darkness. But a change has now come over the affairs of mankind. Walled cities and empires have become unfashionable. The arm of commerce has borne away the gates of the strong city. Intelligence is penetrating the darkest corners of the globe. It makes its pathway over and under the sea, as well as on the earth. Wind, steam, and lightning are its chartered agents. Oceans no longer divide, but link nations together. From Boston to London is now a holiday excursion. Space is comparatively annihilated. Thoughts expressed on one side of the Atlantic are distinctly heard on the other. The far off and almost fabulous Pacific rolls in grandeur at our feet. The Celestial Empire, the mystery of ages, is being solved. The fiat of the Almighty, "Let there be Light," has not yet spent its force. No abuse, no outrage whether in taste, sport or avarice, can now hide itself from the all-pervading light.

Treaty Oration
(SPEECH)
Chief Seattle

Chief Seattle's treaty oration was not published at the time it was originally given. This version appeared in the *Seattle Sunday Star* on October 29, 1887, in a column by Dr. Henry A. Smith. Dr. Smith was present at the treaty negotiations where Chief Seattle spoke and took notes; thirty-three years later, he reconstructed the speech from those notes.

Analyzing and Connecting

Return to these questions after you have finished reading.

1. Historians who have studied the Puget Sound Indians note that this speech was probably embellished by Dr. Smith, who was himself a poet. The flowery language may not be original to Chief Seattle, but the core of the argument is presumably his. What are Chief Seattle's claim and his primary reasons? What is the effect of the poetic language in this version of the speech?

2. In stating his people's willingness to cede their lands to the United States government, Chief Seattle also makes the claim that the lands will still ultimately belong to his people. What reasons does he use to support this claim?

3. Many different versions of this speech have been attributed to Chief Seattle, including one written by a Hollywood scriptwriter. Which parts of this speech sound authentic? Which don't?

4. Chief Seattle is clearly aware of the historical importance of his speech, and he speaks as someone who knows that what he says will be remembered in years to come. But he also speaks as a politician and as a leader of his people, with very practical, immediate goals. How does Chief Seattle frame his argument so as to procure the best advantage possible for his followers? What is he seeking, and what is he promising?

YONDER SKY that has wept tears of compassion upon my people for centuries untold, and which to us appears change-less and eternal, may change. Today is fair. Tomorrow it may be overcast with clouds. My words are like the stars that never change. Whatever Seattle says, the great chief at Washington can rely upon with as much certainty as he can upon the return of the sun or the seasons. The white chief says that Big Chief at Washington sends us greetings of friendship and goodwill. This is kind of him for we know he has little need of our friendship in return. His people are many. They are like the grass that covers vast prairies. My people are few. They resemble the scattering trees of a storm-swept plain. The great and I presume good White Chief sends us word that he wishes to buy our land but is willing to allow us enough to live comfortably. This indeed appears just, even generous, for the Red Man no longer has rights that he need respect, and the offer may be wise, also, as we are no longer in need of an extensive country.

There was a time when our people covered the land as the waves of a wind-ruffled sea cover its shell-paved floor, but that time long since passed away with the greatness of tribes that are now but a mournful memory. I will not dwell on, nor mourn over, our untimely decay, nor reproach my paleface brothers with hastening it, as we too may have been somewhat to blame.

Youth is impulsive. When our young men grow angry at some real or imaginary wrong, and disfigure their faces with black paint, it denotes that their hearts are black, and that they are often cruel and relentless, and our old men and old women are unable to restrain them. Thus it has ever been. Thus it was when the white man began to push our forefathers ever westward. But let us hope that the hostilities between us may never return. We would have everything to lose and nothing to gain. Revenge by young men is considered gain, even at the cost of their own lives, but old men who stay at home in times of war, and mothers who have sons to lose, know better.

Our good father in Washington—for I presume he is now our father as well as yours, since King George has moved his boundaries further north—our great and good father, I say, sends us word that if we do as he desires he will protect us. His brave warriors will be to us a bristling wall of strength, and his wonderful ships of war will fill our harbors, so that our ancient enemies far to the northward—the Haidas and Tsimshians—will cease to frighten our women, children, and old men. Then in reality he will be our father and we his children. But can that ever be? Your God is not our God! Your God loves your people and hates mine! He folds his strong protecting arms lovingly about the paleface and leads him by the hand as a father leads an infant son. But, He has forsaken His Red children, if they really are His. Our God, the Great Spirit, seems also to have forsaken us. Your God makes your people wax stronger every day. Soon they will fill all the land. Our people are ebbing away like a rapidly receding tide that will never return. The white man's God cannot love our people or He would protect them. They seem to be orphans who can look nowhere for help. How then can we be brothers? How can your God become our God and renew our prosperity and awaken in us dreams of returning greatness? If we have a common Heavenly Father, He must be partial, for He came to His paleface children. We never saw Him. He gave you laws but had no word for His Red children whose teeming multitudes once filled this vast continent as stars fill the firmament. No, we are two distinct races with separate origins and separate destinies. There is little in common between us.

To us the ashes of our ancestors are sacred and their resting place is hallowed ground. You wander far from the graves of your ancestors and seemingly without regret. Your religion was written upon tablets of stone by the iron finger of your God so that you could not forget. The Red Man could never comprehend or remember it. Our religion is the traditions of our ancestors—the dreams of our old men, given them in solemn hours of the night by the Great Spirit; and the visions of our sachems, and is written in the hearts of our people.

Your dead cease to love you and the land of their nativity as soon as they pass the portals of the tomb and wander away beyond the stars. They are soon forgotten and never return. Our dead never forget this beautiful world that gave them being. They still love its verdant valleys, its murmuring rivers, its magnificent mountains, sequestered vales and verdant lined lakes and bays, and ever yearn in tender fond affection over the lonely hearted living, and often return from the happy hunting ground to visit, guide, console, and comfort them.

Day and night cannot dwell together. The Red Man has ever fled the approach of the White Man, as the morning mist flees before the morning sun. However, your proposition seems fair and I think that my people will accept it and will retire to the reservation you offer them. Then we will dwell apart in peace, for the words of the Great White Chief seem to be the words of nature speaking to my people out of dense darkness.

It matters little where we pass the remnant of our days. They will not be many. The Indian's night promises to be dark. Not a single star of hope hovers above his horizon. Sad-voiced winds moan in the distance. Grim fate seems to be on the Red Man's trail, and wherever he will hear the approaching footsteps of his fell destroyer and prepare stolidly to meet his doom, as does the wounded doe that hears the approaching footsteps of the hunter.

A few more moons, a few more winters, and not one of the descendants of the mighty hosts that once moved over this broad land or lived in happy homes, protected by the Great Spirit, will remain to mourn over the graves of a people once more powerful and hopeful than yours. But why should I mourn at the untimely fate of my people? Tribe follows tribe, and nation follows nation, like the waves of the sea. It is the order of nature, and regret is useless. Your time of decay may be distant, but it will surely come, for even the White Man whose God walked and talked with him as friend to friend, cannot be exempt from the common destiny. We may be brothers after all. We will see.

We will ponder your proposition and when we decide we will let you know. But should we accept it, I here and now make this condition that we will not be denied the privilege without molestation of visiting at any time the tombs of our ancestors, friends, and children. Every part of this soil is sacred in the estimation of my people. Every hillside, every valley, every plain and grove, has been hallowed by some sad or happy event in days long vanished. Even the rocks, which seem to be dumb and dead as the swelter in the sun along the silent shore, thrill with memories of stirring events connected with the lives of my people, and the very dust upon which you now stand responds more lovingly to their footsteps than yours, because it is rich with the blood of our ancestors, and our bare feet are conscious of the sympathetic touch. Our departed braves, fond mothers, glad, happy hearted maidens, and even the little children who lived here and rejoiced here for a brief season, will love these somber solitudes and at eventide they greet shadowy returning spirits. And when the last Red Man shall have perished, and the memory of my tribe shall have become a myth among the White Men, these shores will swarm with the invisible dead of my tribe, and when your children's children think themselves alone in the field, the store, the shop, upon the highway, or in the silence of the pathless woods, they will not be alone. In all the earth there is no place dedicated to solitude. At night when the streets of your cities and villages are silent and you think them deserted, they will throng with the returning hosts that once filled them and still love this beautiful land. The White Man will never be alone.

Let him be just and deal kindly with my people, for the dead are not powerless. Dead, did I say? There is no death, only a change of worlds.

The Color of Mayhem
(ARTICLE)
Michael Marriott

The New York Times Michael Marriott writes on technology and its impact for the *New York Times*. In this article, he examines evidence of racial and ethnic stereotyping in some of the most popular video games currently on the market. "The Color of Mayhem" appeared on August 12, 2004.

Analyzing and Connecting
Return to these questions after you have finished reading.

1. Marriott uses a straightforward reporting style in this article, primarily allowing other people to express their opinions but not expressing one himself. Instead, he arranges the various voices of people he has interviewed to provide the semblance of a back-and-forth argument. How would this piece change if Marriott wrote it instead as an editorial, taking a stand of his own and backing it with quotes from his interviewees?

2. Marriott also supplies evidence to clarify the issue. How compelling do you find the facts he presents? How credible do you feel his sources are? Were some more credible than others?

3. How many different claims can you find in this article? Who are the parties making each claim What reasons do they use to support their arguments? And how do the various parties in the debate respond to one another's claims?

The Color of Mayhem

by Michael Marriott

THE SCREEN CRACKLES WITH CRIMINALITY as a gang of urban predators itch for a kill. The scene erupts into automatic-weapons fire in a drive-by nightmare of screaming car engines, senseless death and destruction set to a thumping rap soundtrack.

The action is not part of a new film, but of a video game in development—the latest permutation of *Grand Theft Auto,* one of the most popular game series ever. Partly set in a city resembling gang-ridden stretches of Los Angeles of the 1990's, it features a digital cast of African-American and Hispanic men, some wearing braided hair and scarves over their faces and aiming Uzis from low-riding cars.

The sense of place, peril and pigmentation evident in previews of the game, *Grand Theft Auto: San Andreas,* underscores what some critics consider a disturbing trend: popular video games that play on racial stereotypes, including images of black youths committing and reveling in violent street crime.

"They are nothing more than pixilated minstrel shows," said Joe Morgan, a telecommunications executive in Manhattan who is black and is helping rear his girlfriend's 7-year-old son, who plays video games. Mr. Morgan argues that games like the *Grand Theft Auto* sequel, which was described glowingly and at length in a game magazine the boy recently brought home, are dangerously reinforcing stereotypes.

"A lot of young people are unable to discern between reality and satirical depictions," he said. "It makes them very vulnerable."

His complaint echoes a concern that many civil rights and other groups, including the National Association for the Advancement of Colored People, have long raised about stereotyping in movies, and the detrimental impact it may have on racial understanding and relations.

The issue, critics say, is not that the games' representation of racial and ethnic minorities is as blatantly threatening as the sort found at hate sites on the Web, where players are asked to gun down virtual black or Jewish characters. Rather, the racial and ethnic depictions and story lines are more subtle, and therefore, some say, more insidious.

"It's not just the kinds of stereotyping people generally think of," said Eileen Espejo, a senior associate at Children Now, an advocacy group in Oakland, Calif., that has studied video games. "It is the kind of limiting what characters of color can do and cannot do in the games that sends a message to kids."

Video game developers counter that no offense is intended. They say their games are simply parodies, or a reflection of a sort of "browning" of popular culture that transcends race and sells to all in a marketplace captivated by hip-hop styles, themes and attitude.

Several games scheduled for wide release this fall or early next year are notable for their portrayal of urban black culture:

Def Jam Fight for NY, from Electronic Arts, a sort of "MTV Raps" meets "W.W.E. SmackDown!" in which mostly hip-hop-style characters (one with the voice of the rapper Snoop Dogg) slap, kick and pummel one another in locations like a 125th Street train station in Harlem.

25 to Life, from Eidos Interactive, an "urban action game" set to a hip-hop soundtrack that allows gamers to play as police officers or criminals, and includes lots of images of young gun-toting black gangsters.

Notorious: Die to Drive, described by its developer, Ubisoft, as featuring "gangsta-style car combat" with players seeking to "rule the streets of four West Coast neighborhoods." Ubisoft's Web site describes the payoff succinctly: "High-priced honeys, the finest bling, and millionaire cribs are just some of the rewards for the notorious few who can survive this most dangerous game. Once you go *Notorious,* there's no going back."

The prominence of black characters in those story lines is all the more striking because of the narrow range of video games in which blacks have been present, if present at all, over the years. A 2001 study by Children Now, for example, found that of 1,500 video-game characters surveyed, 288 were African-American males—and 83 percent of those were represented as athletes.

The portrayal of blacks as athletes has taken on a new wrinkle in *NBA Ballers,* released in April by Midway Games (with an "all ages" rating). It not only pits stars of the National Basketball Association, most of them black, in fierce one-on-one matches, but also encourages players to experience a millionaire lifestyle off the court—accumulating virtual cash that can buy mansions, Cadillac Escalades, yachts and attractive "friends." The style of play emphasizes a street-edged aggression, sizzling with swagger and showboating moves on the court.

John Vignocchi, a lead designer with Midway who worked on *NBA Ballers,* contends that the world portrayed in such games is one that gamers take for granted. "Hip-hop culture has kind of crossed over," said Mr. Vignocchi, who is white. "Look at what everyone is wearing, at what everyone is listening to." Racial stereotyping, he insisted, is "not the intention of the game."

Leon E. Wynter, a cultural critic and author of *American Skin: Big Business, Pop Culture, and the End of White America* (Crown, 2002), said that the infusion of popular aspects of black youth culture into the mainstream American media was a double-edged sword. On one hand, Mr. Wynter said, the game characters bristle with aspects "solidly associated with nonwhite people."

"The bad news is that the larger aspects of the humanity of people who happen to be nonwhite are not always transferred," he noted. "This is an extension and reflection of what we're seeing in other forms of entertainment, especially filmed entertainment aimed particularly at predominantly young male audiences."

As video games extend their prominence as a mainstream form of entertainment—the *Grand Theft Auto* series alone has sold more than 30 million games since 1998—their share of consumer dollars rivals Hollywood box-office revenues.

Video game sales in the United States reached $7 billion last year, according to the Entertainment Software Association. Game hardware, including consoles, added more than $3 billion to that total, industry analysts estimate. But with Hollywood-scale success have come Hollywood-style pressures, including the need for games to "open big" and achieve enough success to sustain lucrative sequels.

"Games are attempting to drive market share beyond the traditional 8- to 14-year-old male player," said Michael Gartenberg, research director for Jupiter Research, an Internet consulting firm. Part of that drive, he suggested, involves having video games reflect what has proved to work in popular films. And as in Hollywood, that may mean subject matter that drives sales even as it draws criticism for gratuitous violence, sexual exploitation or racial insensitivity.

In any case, limiting content to realistic, multidimensional portrayals of racial minorities may be unfair to game developers, Mr. Gartenberg suggested. "Video games are fantasies," he said, "and are not attempting to mirror any reality whatsoever."

But Esther Iverem, editor and film critic for www.seeingblack.com, a Washington-based Web site offering black opinion on cultural and political matters, said she worried about the effects of games like earlier versions of *Grand Theft Auto* on black youngsters, including her 11-year-old son. "These games don't teach them anything about respect, tolerance and responsibility," Ms. Iverem said, but are instead "validating a much-too-accepted stereotype, an accepted caricature."

Others, like the cultural critic Michael Eric Dyson, point out that racial stereotypes conveyed through video games have an effect not only on the self-image of minority youths but also on perceptions among whites. Dr. Dyson, a professor of religious studies and African studies at the University of Pennsylvania, describes some video games as addictive "video crack."

"They are pervasive, and their influence profound," he said.

Def Jam's co-founder, Russell Simmons, said the images of hip-hop culture, even those played out in video games, had been good for the country. "The most important thing for race relations in America in the last I don't know how many years is hip-hop."

"Now Eminem and 50 Cent think they are the same people," Mr. Simmons said, comparing a popular white rapper with a popular black rapper. "They're faced with the same struggle, and they recognize their common thread of poverty."

Mr. Morgan, the telecommunications executive, rejects that argument. In fact, he limits the 7-year-old gamer in his household, Elijah Wilson, to the cartoonish games for Nintendo Game Boy to avoid exposure to content he finds objectionable.

"They ingest these images," Mr. Morgan said of racial stereotypes he had found in games like *NBA Ballers*. "The result is a self-fulfilling prophecy, something straight out of central casting."

"It won't," Mr. Morgan added emphatically, "happen in my house."

Hillary vs. *Grand Theft Auto*
(LETTER)
Steven Johnson

Steven Johnson writes about the zones where media, digital technologies, and culture intersect. His books include *Interface Culture: How New Technology Transforms the Way We Create and Communicate* (1997), *Emergence: The Connected Lives of Ants, Brains, Cities, and Software* (2001), *Mind Wide Open: Your Brain and the Neuroscience of Everyday Life* (2005), and *Everything Bad Is Good for You: How Today's Popular Culture Is Actually Making Us Smarter* (2005). Johnson's letter to Senator Clinton was published in the *Los Angeles Times*.

Analyzing and Connecting
Return to these questions after you have finished reading.

1. Position arguments are sometimes written as rebuttals to the position arguments of others. What exactly does Johnson find wrong with Senator Clinton's argument for controlling video games?

2. Is Johnson serious about wanting Congress to investigate high school football and its connection to violence? If not, why does he make this comparison?

3. Johnson gives a number of reasons to justify his claim that video games are beneficial to children. Identify his reasons throughout the essay. Which are most convincing? Can you think of any others?

4. How might Senator Clinton or others who disagree with Johnson's claim respond to this essay? What sort of reasons and evidence would they need to produce to counter Johnson's argument?

Friday, July 29, 2005

Dear Sen. Clinton:

I'm writing to commend you for calling for a $90-million study on the effects of video games on children, and in particular the courageous stand you have taken in recent weeks against the notorious *Grand Theft Auto* series.

I'd like to draw your attention to another game whose nonstop violence and hostility has captured the attention of millions of kids—a game that instills aggressive thoughts in the minds of its players, some of whom have gone on to commit real-world acts of violence and sexual assault after playing.

I'm talking, of course, about high school football.

I know a congressional investigation into football won't play so well with those crucial swing voters, but it makes about as much sense as an investigation into the pressing issue that is Xbox and PlayStation 2.

Your current concern is over explicit sex in *Grand Theft Auto: San Andreas*. Yet there's not much to investigate, is there? It should get rated appropriately, and that's that. But there's more to your proposed study: You want to examine how video games shape children's values and cognitive development.

Kids have always played games. A hundred years ago they were playing stickball and kick the can; now they're playing *World of Warcraft, Halo 2* and *Madden 2005*. And parents have to drag their kids away from the games to get them to do their algebra homework, but parents have been dragging kids away from whatever the kids were into since the dawn of civilization.

So any sensible investigation into video games must ask the "compared to what" question. If the alternative to playing *Halo 2* is reading *The Portrait of a Lady,* then of course *The Portrait of a Lady* is better for you. But it's not as though kids have been reading Henry James for 100 years and then suddenly dropped him for *Pokemon*.

Another key question: Of all the games that kids play, which ones require the most mental exertion? Parents can play this at home: Try a few rounds of *Monopoly* or *Go Fish* with your kids, and see who wins. I suspect most families will find that it's a relatively even match. Then sit down and try to play *Halo 2* with the kids. You'll be lucky if you survive 10 minutes.

The great secret of today's video games that has been lost in the moral panic over *Grand Theft Auto* is how difficult the games have become. That difficulty is not merely a question of hand-eye coordination; most of today's games force kids to learn complex rule systems, master challenging new interfaces, follow dozens of shifting variables in real time and prioritize between multiple objectives.

In short, precisely the sorts of skills that they're going to need in the digital workplace of tomorrow.

Consider this one fascinating trend among teenagers: They're spending less time watching professional sports and more time simulating those sports on Xbox or PlayStation. Now, which activity challenges the mind more—sitting around rooting for the Green Bay Packers, or managing an entire football franchise through a season of *Madden 2005:* calling plays, setting lineups, trading players and negotiating contracts? Which challenges the mind more—zoning out to the lives of fictional characters on a televised soap opera, or actively managing the lives of dozens of virtual characters in a game such as *The Sims?*

On to the issue of aggression, and what causes it in kids, especially teenage boys. Congress should be interested in the facts: The last 10 years have seen the release of many popular violent games, including *Quake* and *Grand Theft Auto;* that period also has seen the most dramatic drop in violent crime in recent memory. According to Duke University's Child Well-Being Index, today's kids are less violent than kids have been at any time since the study began in 1975. Perhaps, Sen. Clinton, your investigation should

explore the theory that violent games function as a safety valve, letting children explore their natural aggression without acting it out in the real world.

Many juvenile crimes—such as the carjacking that is so central to *Grand Theft Auto*—are conventionally described as "thrill-seeking" crimes. Isn't it possible that kids no longer need real-world environments to get those thrills, now that the games simulate them so vividly? The national carjacking rate has dropped substantially since *Grand Theft Auto* came out.

Crime statistics are not the only sign that today's gaming generation is doing much better than the generation raised during the last cultural panic—over rock 'n' roll. SAT scores have never been higher; verbal scores have been climbing steadily for the last five years; nearly every indicator in the Department of Education study known as the Nation's Report Card is higher now than when the study was implemented in 1971.

By almost every measure, the kids are all right.

Of course, I admit that there's one charge against video games that is a slam dunk. Kids don't get physical exercise when they play a video game, and indeed the rise in obesity among younger people is a serious issue. But, of course, you don't get exercise from doing homework either.

Life Without Health Insurance
(ARTICLE)
Meredith Clark

Figures and statistics about the number of Americans without health insurance are available in just about any newspaper. In this essay Meredith Clark, a freelance writer living in New York City, gives a firsthand account of the problem, based on her experience with serious illness shortly after she graduated from college. The essay originally appeared in *The Nation* in February 2005.

Analyzing and Connecting
Return to these questions after you have finished reading.

1. Clark places her primary claim—that young adults should have affordable health insurance options—near the end of her argument. Why does she wait so long to make her claim? Would the impact of this piece change if the claim were made at the beginning?

2. The statistics Clark cites in her essay are readily available, and she is making a claim others have already made. What does her personal experience add to this debate?

3. How does Clark's experience with health care compare to your own? Have you ever been in a situation similar to what she describes? Does your own experience make you more or less inclined to agree with Clark?

4. What aspects of Clark's argument are most likely to provoke criticism? For example, she cites a range of $65 to $130 billion that could be saved by providing health care for all uninsured Americans. Do you think this is likely to be an accurate estimate?

CLARK: LIFE WITHOUT HEALTH INSURANCE

Between the ages of 18 and 25, young adults like myself mark several major milestones—high school and college graduation, entry into the working world, perhaps even marriage and children. In recent years, another far more frightening rite of passage has crept into the lives of millions of young people—life without health insurance.

Fifty percent of all Americans between 18 and 24 spent part of 2002 and 2003 uninsured, yet this age group rarely appears in the national healthcare debate. We may be young and fairly likely to stay healthy, but one poorly timed illness or accident can cripple us financially before we've had the chance to establish ourselves. It's a harrowing but familiar scenario to many, including myself.

I knew that my health insurance would run out shortly after I finished college, but I couldn't find any affordable options that provided more than catastrophic care. If the best I can get will only help in an emergency, I thought, what's the point of having any? Faced with what was essentially a choice between insurance and food, I opted for food and hoped for the best. It was just bad luck that I got sick in January 2004, less than three weeks after my parent's insurance stopped covering me.

I waited for over a month to visit a doctor for tests, and I only went then because I was starting to feel too sick to work. It took two more months, multiple appointments, one visit to an emergency clinic, and four rounds of antibiotics to treat the infection that I had, although none of the physicians I saw ever gave me a specific diagnosis. On at least one occasion the doctor listened to my list of symptoms and wrote a prescription without doing any tests because she said they didn't want me to incur any unnecessary expenses.

In the end I spent nearly $3,500 on care and prescriptions between January and April, and another $1,500 in November and December when I got sick again. After struggling to avoid excessive student loans in college, I found myself with another school year's worth of debt. In many ways I'm lucky. I didn't need hospitalization, I don't have a

chronic condition like diabetes, and my parents helped me with some of my bills. It is a testament to how broken the American health-care system is that I feel fortunate to not be financially ruined after my experience.

For people who face bleaker outcomes, there are serious consequences. According to a study done in June 2004 by Families USA, of all the healthcare uninsured Americans receive, two-thirds comes from hospitals. Uninsured people are a great deal more likely to delay seeking care when they are ill, and they often end up in the emergency room for conditions that could have been treated easily at an earlier time.

This substandard care takes a heavy toll: uninsured adults are 25 percent more likely to die prematurely than those with private health insurance. With the numbers of uninsured Americans increasing, young people face the prospect of being sicker and less economically productive throughout their lives. Immense economic benefits can be gained by making sure all Americans have healthcare, somewhere between $65 and $130 billion dollars, even more significant when you take into account that the government spends approximately $30 billion annually to compensate healthcare providers for assisting the uninsured.

Current discussions about healthcare have focused on people over 65 and under 18 but have largely ignored the issues of younger Americans. Children and the elderly do require more care than younger adults; children especially should be the first to benefit from any healthcare reforms that take place. However, the generation currently entering the workforce should not have to wait until offspring or old age bring steady health insurance in the form of government sponsored programs.

A lack of health insurance is not a problem that only worries me when I feel a cold coming on or cross a busy intersection; it is a topic that comes up when I have drinks with friends, while I watch some network TV drama, while I chop vegetables for dinner. Uncertainty about the future has always been a part of being young, but now fear of medical debt is a part of the mix; it's a scary new addition.

(ADVERTISEMENTS)
Buff Daddy,
Food Cops Bust Cookie Monster

"Buff Daddy" was created by the Ad Council **(www.adcouncil.org)** as part of its public service campaign to fight obesity. Supported by corporations, foundations, and individuals, the Ad Council has a goal of advertising in the public interest. Its campaigns are produced without charge by advertising agencies.

The Center for Consumer Freedom **(www.ConsumerFreedom.com)**, an organization sponsored by restaurants and food companies, has produced a series of ads taking a different position on obesity, including "Food Cops Bust Cookie Monster." These ads defend what the organization describes as "the right of adults and parents to choose what they eat, drink, and how to enjoy themselves."

Analyzing and Connecting

Return to these questions after you have finished reading.

1. Both of these ads make visual arguments. Why do you think the producers of each ad chose the image they did? How effective is each visual in communicating the ad's central message?

2. The ads also seek to appeal to their audiences through humor. Who is the target of humor in each ad? What is the tone of the humor? How successful do you think it is in convincing each audience that the ad's claims are valid?

3. The ConsumerFreedom.com ad refers to "food cops" and "nutrition nags." Why did the creators of this ad choose these terms? What type of audience are they trying to appeal to with these kinds of labels? And since the Center for Consumer Freedom is itself merely an advocacy group, like the health advocates it is lampooning, how responsibly is it arguing its case by using such terms to describe its opponents?

4. The Ad Council image invites viewers to make a direct connection between actions ("Started shooting hoops with son") and physical changes in the person acting. How would this argument sound if it were stated as a simple claim plus reasons? Would the ad be as effective in non-visual form?

BUFF DADDY

STARTED SHOOTING HOOPS WITH SON

EATS HEALTHIER AND SKIPS DESSERT

CONSIDERING CHANGING NAME TO "BUFF DADDY"

Ad Council

TAKE A SMALL STEP TO GET HEALTHY. Get started at www.smallstep.gov

ConsumerFreedom.com Editorial Infographic

Food Cops Bust Cookie Monster

Farce again became reality as the children's TV show *Sesame Street* has bowed to obesity hysteria from nutrition nags. In a nod to calorie killjoys, Cookie Monster will tout health foods, and his famous song, "C is For Cookie, That's Good Enough For Me," will be replaced with "A Cookie Is a Sometimes Food." This U-Turn may not be the last. Predictions:

Big Bird becomes Svelte Bird

Miss Piggy becomes Miss Moderation

Mayor McCheese voted out of office and replaced with Mayor McSoy-Slice

Keebler elves to make only unflavored rice cakes

Cap'n Crunch forced to sail in only skim milk

Count Chocula stabbed through heart with a carrot stick

Fat Albert becomes "Weight Watchers patient #00873-Albert"

© 2005 The Center For Consumer Freedom

How to write a position argument

These steps for the process of writing a position argument may not progress as neatly as this chart might suggest. Writing is not an assembly-line process.

As you write and revise you may think of additional reasons to support your position. Your instructor and fellow students may give you comments that help you to rethink your argument. Use their comments to work through your paper or project again, strengthening your content and making your writing better organized and more readable.

1 FIND AN ISSUE

- Make a list of possible issues.
- Select a possible issue.
- Read about your issue.

2 DEVELOP REASONS AND WRITE A WORKING THESIS

- Take a definite position.
- Develop reasons by considering whether you can argue from a definition, compare or contrast, consider good and bad effects, or refute objections.
- Support your reasons by making observations and finding facts, statistics, and statements from authorities.
- Write a working thesis.

Analyze your potential readers

What do your readers likely know about the issue?

What views do your readers likely have about the issue?

Do your readers likely agree or disagree with your position? If they disagree, why exactly do they disagree?

3 WRITE A DRAFT

- Introduce the issue and give the necessary background.
- Think about how readers will view you, the writer.
- If you argue from a definition, set out the criteria.
- Avoid fallacies.
- Address opposing views.
- Make counterarguments if necessary.
- Conclude with strength.
- Choose a title that will interest readers.

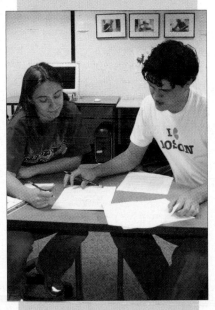

4 REVISE, REVISE, REVISE

- Check that your position argument fulfills the assignment.
- Make sure that your claim is arguable and focused.
- Check your reasons and add more if you can.
- Add additional evidence where reasons need more support.
- Examine the organization.
- Review the visual presentation.
- Proofread carefully.

5 SUBMITTED VERSION

- Make sure your finished writing meets all formatting requirements.

1: Find an issue

Analyze the assignment

- Read your assignment slowly and carefully. Look for key words like *argue for, take a stand,* and *write on a controversial issue.* These key words tell you that you are writing a position argument.
- Mark off any information about the length specified, date due, formatting, and other requirements. You can attend to this information later. At this point you want to give your attention to finding an issue if one is not specified.

Make a list of possible campus issues

Think about issues that are debated on your campus such as these.

- Should smoking be banned on campus?
- Should varsity athletes get paid for playing sports that bring in revenue?
- Should admissions decisions be based exclusively on academic achievement?
- Should knowledge of a foreign language be required for all degree plans?
- Should fraternities be banned from campuses if they are caught encouraging alcohol abuse?

Make a list of possible community issues

Think about issues that are debated in your community such as these.

- Should people who ride bicycles and motorcycles be required to wear helmets?
- Should high schools be allowed to search students for drugs at any time?
- Should bilingual education programs be eliminated?
- Should bike lanes be built throughout your community to encourage more people to ride bicycles?
- Should more tax dollars be shifted from building highways to public transportation?

Make a list of possible national and international issues

Think about national and international issues such as these.

- Should advertising be banned on television shows aimed at preschool children?
- Should the Internet be censored?
- Should the government be allowed to monitor all phone calls and all email to combat terrorism?
- Should handguns be outlawed?
- Should people who are terminally ill be allowed to end their lives?
- Should the United States punish nations with poor human rights records?

Read about your issue

- What are the major points of view on your issue?
- Who are the experts on this issue? What do they have to say?
- What major claims are being offered?
- What reasons are given to support the claims?
- What kinds of evidence are used to support the reasons?

Analyze your potential readers

- For whom does this issue matter? Whose interests are at stake?
- What attitudes and beliefs will your readers likely have about this issue?
- What key terms will you need to define or explain?
- What assumptions do you have in common with your readers?
- Where will your readers most likely disagree with you?

WRITE NOW

Choose an issue that you care about

1. Make a list of issues that fulfill your assignment.
2. Put a checkmark beside the issues that look most interesting to write about or the ones that mean the most to you.
3. Put a question mark beside the issues that you don't know very much about. If you choose one of these issues, you will probably have to do in-depth research—by talking to people, by using the Internet, or by going to the library.
4. Select a possible issue. What is your stand on this issue? Write nonstop for five minutes about why this issue is important and how it affects you.

Writer at work

Chris Nguyen received a writing assignment in her government class, and made the following notes on her assignment sheet.

GOV 322—Issues in Contemporary Society
Paper 3: Arguing for a Position

"We should or shouldn't do X" is one possible thesis.

Choose a current public controversy that has affected you or your friends in some way. Investigate the issues at stake and then write a 4–6 page essay that takes a stand: defending an action or policy, condemning it, recommending it, or making some other claim about the controversy. The bulk of your paper should be concerned with supporting your claim, using facts and reasons.

Use outside sources to back up your opinion, and find the most authoritative sources possible. Do not simply cite the opinions of people who agree with you. Respect your readers by showing them the full spectrum of opinion on your issue, not just one or two sides.

Deadlines

2 weeks

Papers are due on March 24, and I will return them to you one week later with a grade. If you then wish to rewrite your paper, you will have one week to do so. I will average the rewrite grade with your first grade to give you your final grade.

I encourage you to share your papers with your discussion groups as you draft them. You should also plan to take your paper to the writing center. This is not required, but it is highly recommended.

Evaluation

Papers will be evaluated according to how thoroughly they assess all the angles of a controversy. A strong paper will look closely at more than one or two "sides" of an issue, and will use credible sources that carry significant weight in the public debate over the issue in question.

Read the assignment closely
Chris Nguyen began by marking information about due dates and requirements. She noted her instructor's suggestion that students might phrase their thesis in a particular way. She also wrote down her teacher's advice to avoid oversimplifying the controversy.

Choose a topic
Chris made a list of potential topics for her paper. She began by thinking of controversies she and her friends had talked about in the recent past. She chose to write about a recent event on campus, in which a number of students had been ejected from a public talk because they were wearing T-shirts critical of the speaker.

Explore the issue
Chris looked for news articles about similar events, and court proceedings that followed. As she researched, she made a list of events she wanted to compare to the event at her school. She also found references to a number of court cases, which she researched as well.

Identify key terms
Chris compiled a list of key terms to help her think about her issue.

POSSIBLE TOPICS

Should military recruiting on campus be allowed if the military discriminates against gays? What is college's responsibility to students/country?

Peer-to-peer music downloading—should it be legal?

Students thrown out of speech for wearing T-shirts—violation of free speech?

NOTES
Two people wearing anti-Bush T-shirts at a rally at the West Virginia Capitol were arrested for trespassing, but charges were dropped.

High school student sent home from school for wearing a T-shirt with the word "redneck" was vindicated by court ruling.

A man is arrested for trespassing in a mall for wearing a shirt he had bought there reading "Give peace a chance."

1969 Tinker v. Des Moines ISD
Supreme Court: In order to censor, a high school must show evidence of substantial disruption as a result of speech, or invasion of others' rights.

1969 Brandenburg v. Ohio
Supreme Court: to prohibit speech, it must be "directed at inciting or producing imminent lawless action" or "likely to incite or produce such action."

1986 Bethel v. Fraser
Supreme Court: vulgar speech can be prohibited at a school assembly.

1988 Hazelwood School District v. Kuhlmeier
Supreme Court: school-sponsored speech (like school papers) can be censored.

What is free speech?
What is an invasion of someone else's rights?
What is a "substantial disruption"?
What is vulgar speech?
What is school-sponsored speech? [what about protest of it?]
What is "socially inappropriate behavior"?

2: Develop reasons and write a working thesis

Take a definite position
- Why do you take this position? Write down the first things you think of that form your thinking on this issue.

Develop reasons
- Can you argue from a definition? Is _____ a _____? Are cheerleaders athletes? Are zoos guilty of cruelty to animals?
- Can you compare and contrast? Is _____ like or unlike _____? Should health care in the United States be more like health care in Canada? Is the war in Iraq like the Vietnam War?
- Can you argue that good things will result from your position or bad things can be avoided? Is ecotourism the long-term answer to preserving endangered rain forests?
- Can you refute objections to your position?

Support your reasons
- Can you support your reasons by going to a site and making observations?
- Can you find facts to support your reasons?
- Can you find statistics to support your reasons?
- Can you find statements from authorities to support your reasons?

Write a working thesis
- Is your thesis arguable? Statements of fact are not arguable unless the facts are disputed.

  NOT ARGUABLE: The population of the United States grew faster in the 1990s than in any previous decade because Congress increased the level of legal immigration and the government stopped enforcing most laws against illegal immigration in the interior of the country.

  ARGUABLE: Allowing a high rate of immigration helps the United States deal with the problems of an increasingly aging society and helps provide funding for millions of Social Security recipients.

ARGUABLE: The increase in the number of visas to foreign workers in technology industries is the major cause of unemployment in those industries.

- Is your thesis specific? A thesis may be arguable but too broad to be treated adequately in a short paper.

ARGUABLE, BUT TOO BROAD: We should take action to resolve the serious traffic problem in our city.

ARGUABLE AND FOCUSED: The existing freight railway that runs through the center of the city should be converted to a passenger railway because it is the cheapest and most quickly implemented way to decrease traffic congestion downtown.

STAYING ON TRACK

Evaluate your thesis

Once you have a working thesis, ask these questions:

1. Is it arguable?
2. Is it specific?
3. Is it manageable in the length and time you have?
4. Is it interesting to your intended readers?

OFF TRACK

Over 60% of Americans play video games on a regular basis.

ARGUABLE? The thesis states a commonly acknowledged fact.

SPECIFIC? The thesis is a bland general statement.

MANAGEABLE? A known fact is stated in the thesis, so there is little to research. Several surveys report this finding.

INTERESTING? Video games are interesting as a cultural trend, but nearly everyone is aware of the trend.

ON TRACK

Video games are valuable because they improve children's visual attention skills, their literacy skills, and their computer literacy skills.

ARGUABLE? The thesis takes a position contrary to the usual view of video games.

SPECIFIC? The thesis gives specific reasons for the claim.

MANAGEABLE? The thesis is manageable if research can be located and observations of game playing included.

INTERESTING? The topic is interesting because it challenges conventional wisdom.

Writer at work

I believe school administrators were wrong to eject the students wearing T-shirts.

HOW TO ARGUE?????

Chris Nguyen knew how she felt, but she didn't know at first how to make a convincing case. She read more about events similar to the one that happened on her campus, and she became convinced that her school's administrators had acted improperly, and perhaps illegally, in ejecting the students. She examined the cases she had researched and drew an idea map.

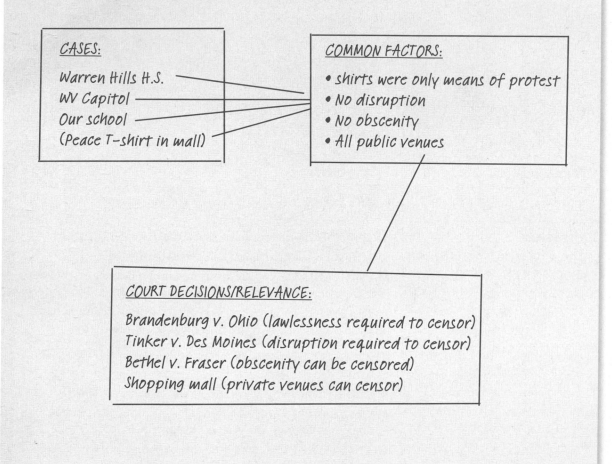

CASES:

Warren Hills H.S.
WV Capitol
Our school
(Peace T-shirt in mall)

COMMON FACTORS:

• shirts were only means of protest
• No disruption
• No obscenity
• All public venues

COURT DECISIONS/RELEVANCE:

Brandenburg v. Ohio (lawlessness required to censor)
Tinker v. Des Moines (disruption required to censor)
Bethel v. Fraser (obscenity can be censored)
Shopping mall (private venues can censor)

Chris used the idea map to define the conditions in which speech can be restricted.

CRITERIA FOR FREE SPEECH
• Cannot incite violence
• Cannot threaten violence
• Cannot be obscene (although what exactly is obscene isn't clear)
• Only on public property
• Only for adults

Ejecting students would be justified if
• The students were doing something "directed to and likely to incite imminent lawless action" NO
• They used vulgar or obscene language NO
• They were in a private venue NO
• They were minors NO

WORKING THESIS
The college was wrong to eject the six protesting students from last month's speakers' event because the students were not inciting lawless action, did not use vulgar or obscene language, were in a public venue, and were not minors.

Chris's research supported a more specific claim than the one she initially made: that the college was "wrong" to remove the students. She revised her thesis to focus on this stronger and, she thought, more interesting claim. In addition to claiming the students' right to free speech was violated, she argued that her school should apologize to the students involved. Here is the final working thesis Chris used to begin drafting her essay:

The University administration should drop trespassing charges against the six students arrested last month and offer them a formal apology, because their ejection and arrest was a violation of the students' constitutionally protected right to free speech.

469

3: Write a draft

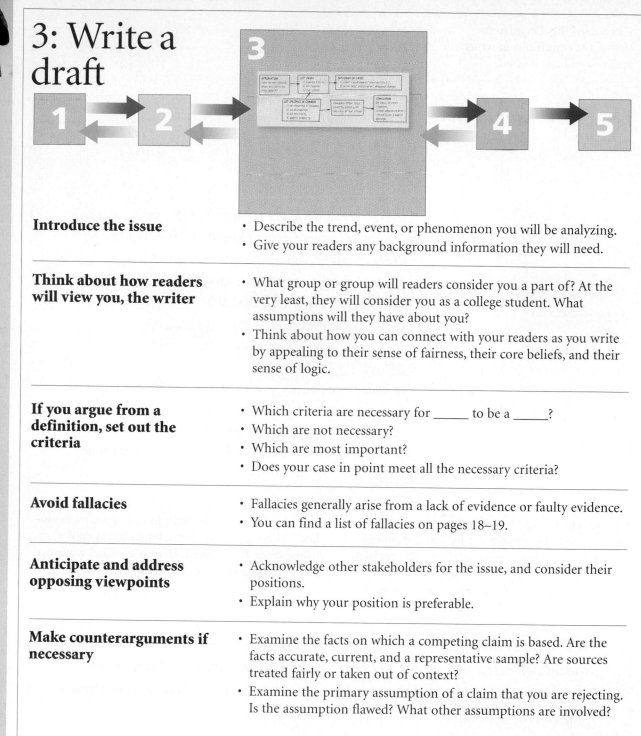

Introduce the issue	• Describe the trend, event, or phenomenon you will be analyzing. • Give your readers any background information they will need.
Think about how readers will view you, the writer	• What group or group will readers consider you a part of? At the very least, they will consider you as a college student. What assumptions will they have about you? • Think about how you can connect with your readers as you write by appealing to their sense of fairness, their core beliefs, and their sense of logic.
If you argue from a definition, set out the criteria	• Which criteria are necessary for _____ to be a _____? • Which are not necessary? • Which are most important? • Does your case in point meet all the necessary criteria?
Avoid fallacies	• Fallacies generally arise from a lack of evidence or faulty evidence. • You can find a list of fallacies on pages 18–19.
Anticipate and address opposing viewpoints	• Acknowledge other stakeholders for the issue, and consider their positions. • Explain why your position is preferable.
Make counterarguments if necessary	• Examine the facts on which a competing claim is based. Are the facts accurate, current, and a representative sample? Are sources treated fairly or taken out of context? • Examine the primary assumption of a claim that you are rejecting. Is the assumption flawed? What other assumptions are involved?

Conclude with strength

- Avoid summarizing what you have just said.
- Spell out the importance of the analysis, if you haven't already done so.
- Consider additional effects you haven't previously discussed.
- Explain any action you think needs to be taken based on your conclusion.

Choose a title that will interest readers

- Make your title specific.
- Engage your readers with the issue.

STAYING ON TRACK

Facts vs. your opinion

Distinguish facts from opinions

Find facts to support what you think. You may be surprised to find that the facts are not what you anticipated.

OFF TRACK
I believe that Americans have the best medical care in the world.

ON TRACK
On one of the most trusted indicators of health—life expectancy at birth—in 2005 the United States ranks 48th behind nearly all of Europe, Japan, Singapore, Hong Kong, and even countries like Jordan, Cuba, and Costa Rica.

OFF TRACK
It is obvious from watching television news that violent crime is on the rise.

ON TRACK
While violent crime remains the staple of local news, FBI statistics show a 24 percent drop in violent crimes in the United States between 1995 and 2004.

Writer at work

Chris mapped the ideas she would need to include in her paper.

INTRODUCTION
Case on our campus: What are limits on free speech?

LIST CASES
1) Warren Hills H.S.
2) WV Capitol
3) Our school

OUTCOMES OF CASES
1) Court ruled against Warren Hills H.S.
2) In WV case, prosecutors dropped charges.

LIST SPECIFICS IN COMMON
1) no shouting or banners
2) no disruption
3) no obscenity
4) public property

Compare other cases point by point with the case at our school.

Chris began by writing the common factors in the cases because they would be the core of her paper. She would build the rest of the paper around these four factors.

These are the factors the three cases have in common:

1) In each case, the wearers of the shirts did not express themselves in any way other than by wearing the shirts. They did not speak, shout, hold up banners or signs, or call attention to themselves in any way.

2) None of the events were disrupted by the shirts. Any disruption that occurred was due to the removal of the wearers by authority figures.

3) None of the T-shirts featured obscene language or imagery.

4) All took place in government-funded venues: a public school, a state capitol, and a state-funded university.

Chris next made a working outline, which she used to write her paper.

1) start with a brief mention of our case where students were
   ejected

2) describe limits on free speech

3) introduce the three T-shirt cases; end with claim that ejection at
   our school was unconstitutional

4) list factors that the cases have in common

5) introduce standard of lawless action for restricting free speech

6) discuss the Warren Hills High School case

7) discuss the West Virginia Capitol case

8) discuss the issue of what is offensive or considered obscene

9) compare the West Virginia Capitol incident to our campus
   because both involve political speech

10) make the distinction between public and private venues

11) point out that all cases were at public venues

12) raise the issue of minors and point out that college students
    are of legal age

13) conclude with a call for an apology

4: Revise, revise, revise

4

Speech Doesn't Have to be Pretty to be Protected

Our school administrators violated the Constitutional rights of six students last month, forcibly removing them from a public event, in a public building. The University administration should immediately drop the trespassing charges against the students and apologize to them. Generally, courts have found that, in order for the restriction of free speech to be justified, the speech must incite imminent lawless action (such as a riot), and it must take place on public property. Even in public high schools, where the government has an obligation to protect minors, "imminent lawless action" must be threatened before the speech can be repressed.

Skilled writers know that the secret to writing well is rewriting. Even the best writers often have to revise several times to get the result they want. You also must have effective strategies for revising if you're going to be successful. The biggest trap you can fall into is starting off with the little stuff first. Leave the small stuff for last.

Does your position argument fulfill the assignment?	• Look again at your assignment. Does your paper or project do what the assignment asks? • Look again at the assignment for specific guidelines, including length, format, and amount of research. Does your work meet these guidelines?
Is your claim arguable and focused?	• Is your position arguable? Statements of fact and statements of religious belief are not arguable. • Can you make your claim more specific to avoid ambiguous language and situations where your claim may not apply?
Are your reasons adequate?	• Are your reasons clear to your readers? • Can you add additional reasons to strengthen your argument? • Have you acknowledged the views of people who disagree with your position? • Have you shown how your position is preferable?
Are your reasons supported with evidence?	• Have you found the most accurate information available about your issue? • Can you find additional evidence in the form of examples, quotations from experts, statistics, comparisons, and on-site observations?

Is your organization effective?	• Are your reasons in the best possible order?
	• Do you get off to a fast start with your title and introduction? Can you do more to gain and keep the reader's interest?
	• Is your conclusion only a summary of what you have said? If so, can you think of an implication or an example that gets at the heart of the issue?
Is the writing project visually effective?	• Is the font attractive and readable?
	• Are the headings and visuals effective?
	• If you use images or tables as part of your analysis, are they legible and appropriately placed? Do you have captions for each?
Save the editing for last	When you have finished revising, edit and proofread carefully.

A peer review guide is on page 31.

A peer review guide is on page 31.

Writer at work

Chris Nguyen took her first draft of the essay to her school's writing center. In particular, she asked to discuss the paper's opening, which she felt was too abrupt. The consultant at the writing center suggested that one possible strategy was to move the thesis statement to the end of the introductory section. Chris found this change worked well for her essay, giving her claim more weight.

Chris had her thesis in the second sentence in her first draft. Moving it to the end of the introductory section allowed her to explain the issue of restricting free speech before announcing her position. Her revised paper is on the next page.

Speech Doesn't Have to Be Pretty to Be Protected

Our school administrators violated the Constitutional rights of six students last month, forcibly removing them from a public event, in a public building. The University administration should immediately drop the trespassing charges against the students and apologize to them. Generally, courts have found that, in order for the restriction of free speech to be justified, the speech must incite imminent lawless action (such as a riot), and it must take place on public property. Even in public high schools, where the government has an obligation to protect minors, "imminent lawless action" must be threatened before the speech can be repressed.

475

5: Submitted version

Nguyen 1

Chris Nguyen
Professor Conley
GOV 322
24 March 2006

Speech Doesn't Have to Be Pretty to Be Protected

Last month six students on our campus were ejected from a university auditorium for wearing T-shirts with "war criminal" on the front. Was the university justified in removing our fellow students who were not disruptive in any other way?

The First Amendment to the Constitution of the United States of America guarantees the right to freedom of expression. This important right is one of the foundations of our democracy. Yet many Americans do not understand what the right to free speech really means. Free speech is your right to say what you think—within limits. It is not the right to cause mayhem, or to threaten violence, or to incite others to violence. Authority figures also need to understand the limits on free speech. Generally, courts have found that, in order for the restriction of free speech to be justified, the speech must incite imminent lawless action (such as a riot), and it must take place on public property. Even in public high schools, where the government has an obligation to protect minors, "imminent lawless action" must be threatened before the speech can be repressed.

Clearly, it's not always easy to tell when restriction of free speech is justified. Consider these recent controversies over free speech:

- A student at Warren Hills Regional High School in New Jersey was suspended for wearing a T-shirt that featured the word "redneck" ("Federal Court").
- Jeff and Nicole Rank attended an official visit by President Bush at the West Virginia Capitol and were charged with trespassing when they refused to remove T-shirts that read "Love America, Hate Bush" (Bundy).
- Six students were removed from a university auditorium and charged with trespassing during a speech by former U.S. Secretary of State, Henry Kissinger, for wearing T-shirts that referred to the speaker as a "war criminal."

In the first two cases, it has been established that authorities did not have the right to curtail the speech of the people involved: a federal appeals court decided the first case in favor of the student, and the prosecutor in the second case dropped the charges, admitting that no law had been broken. If we examine the similarities and differences among these three cases, it becomes clear that in the third case, which happened on our own campus last month, the administration's ejection of the students was unconstitutional.

These are the factors the three cases have in common:

1. In each case, the wearers of the shirts did not express themselves in any way other than by wearing the shirts. They did not speak, shout, hold up banners or signs, or call attention to themselves in any way.
2. None of the events where the shirts were worn were disrupted by the shirts. Any disruption that occurred was due to the removal of the wearers by authority figures.
3. None of the T-shirts featured obscene language or imagery.
4. All took place in government-funded venues: a public school, a state capitol, and a state-funded university.

These similarities are important because they show how, in each case, the T-shirt wearers acted within their constitutionally protected right to free expression.

The first two factors above show how each of these cases fails to meet the standard of "imminent lawless action," set in the 1969 case of Brandenburg v. Ohio.

In that case, the Supreme Court ruled that in order to ban forms of expression, the government had to prove the expression was "directed to and likely to incite imminent lawless action." If the act of expression did not seem likely to cause a riot, for example, it could not be restricted. Simply making people angry or uncomfortable is not justification for censorship.

In the first case, at Warren Hills High School, the only person who objected to the "redneck" T-shirt was a vice principal, who claimed the term "redneck" was offensive to minority students and violated the school's racial harassment policy ("Federal Court"). The U.S. Court of Appeals for the Third Circuit, however, ruled that the school failed to prove "that the shirt might genuinely threaten disruption or, indeed, that it violated any of the particular provisions of the harassment policy." This decision followed the precedent of another landmark case, Tinker v. Des Moines, in which the Supreme Court ruled that, even in public schools, the government must provide evidence that the speech would cause "(a.) a substantial disruption of the school environment, or (b.) an invasion of the rights of others" (Haynes).

In the second case, the government never even made a claim that the T-shirts worn by Jeff and Nicole Rank were inciting lawlessness. The only people who were upset by the Ranks' T-shirts were two Secret Service officers, who ordered the couple to remove the shirts. When they refused, the officers ordered Charleston city police to arrest them, which the police did. The Ranks were charged with trespassing ("Secret Service"). The irony of arresting U.S. citizens for standing peacefully on public, state-owned property was even clear to the prosecutor, who dropped the charges (Bundy).

Moreover, none of the cases met the test for "vulgar or obscene" language. Vulgar and obscene language can be regulated, to some extent, without violating the First Amendment. In 1986, the Supreme Court ruled in the case of Bethel v. Fraser that public school officials could prohibit vulgar speech at a school assembly. The court said that "[T]he undoubted freedom to advocate unpopular and controversial views in schools and classrooms must be balanced against the society's countervailing interest in teaching students the boundaries of socially appropriate behavior." The vice principal in the Warren Hills Case was the only one who thought "redneck" was offensive, and the fact that the word is used constantly on television and other media shows that it is not considered obscene by society at large.

The Ranks' arrest is a better comparison to the situation at our school, because their shirts were clearly singled out for their political content, not for vulgarity. They carried a message that might have been offensive to some of the supporters of the president who were present, but under no circumstances could the content of the shirts be considered obscene. The same is true of the shirts that got my fellow students kicked out of a public event. Calling someone a war criminal is a serious accusation, but it is not obscene.

Finally, public versus private venue is an important factor in the protection of free speech. The Constitution guarantees that the state will not infringe the right to free expression. Private entities are free to do so, however. For example, protestors can be thrown out of a private meeting of club members. Even a shopping mall owner can deny entry to protesters or even people without shoes. Of course, anyone with private property also has to consider the economic impact of limiting speech. Recently a shopping mall owner had police arrest a man wearing a "Give Peace a Chance" T-shirt ("Man Arrested") that he had just bought in the mall. Not surprisingly, the mall owner received a great deal of bad publicity about this decision. Concerned citizens who felt this action by the mall owner went too far wrote letters to newspapers publicizing the act. They even wrote letters to the police who arrested the man ("Big Support"). The trespassing charges against the man were dropped. This incident illustrates how free speech is negotiated in the marketplace.

In the Ranks' case, the trespassing charges against them were dropped because they were on the statehouse grounds. How can a citizen trespass on public property? In the same vein, how can students be trespassing on their own campus? The six people arrested at our school were students, whose tuition and fees helped pay for the building they were in. What's more, the event was advertised in flyers and newspaper ads as "free and open to the public." How can anyone be charged with trespassing at a public event?

The Warren Hills case was decided in favor of the student, even though the expression took place in a public school. As Bethel v. Fraser shows, courts generally feel that schools can take special steps to protect minors: vulgar or obscene speech can be censored, and school-sponsored forms of expression, like newspapers, can be censored. But these actions are justified because the students are minors.

Presumably, they need more guidance as they learn about the boundaries of socially acceptable behavior. But most if not all college students are legally adults, so it does not make sense to say our school was "teaching students the boundaries of socially appropriate behavior" by throwing them out of a public event because of their shirts. It is not the job of a college administration to teach manners.

Our school administrators violated the Constitutional rights of six students last month. They forcibly removed them from a public event, in a public building. The students were not causing a commotion in any way before their arrests; there was no indication whatsoever that "imminent lawless action" might be provoked by their T-shirts. Because the students in this case were clearly exercising their Constitutional right to free speech, the university administration should immediately drop the trespassing charges against the students. Evidence from prior cases indicates the charges will not stand up in court in any case, so the legal battle will be a waste of money for the college. Furthermore, as an institution of learning that supposedly safeguards the free exchange of ideas, the college should offer a sincere apology to the arrested students. The administrators would send an important message to all students by doing this: Your right to free speech is respected at this school.

Nguyen 6

Works Cited

Bethel School Dist. v. Fraser. No. 478-674. Supreme Ct. of the US. 7 Jul. 1986.

"Big Support for 'Peace' T-shirt Arrestees." 25 Mar. 2003. The Smoking Gun.
    8 Mar. 2006 <http://www.thesmokinggun.com/archive/shirtmail1.html>.

Brandenburg v. Ohio. No. 395-444. Supreme Ct. of the US. 9 Jun. 1969.

Bundy, Jennifer. "Trespass Charges Dropped Against Bush Protesters." 15 Jul. 2004.
    CommonDreams.org. 10 Mar. 2006 <http://www.commondreams.org/
    head lines04/0715-07.htm>.

"Federal Court Says NJ School Can't Ban Redneck T-shirt." 6 Nov. 2003. Center for
    Individual Rights. 7 Mar. 2006 < http://www.cir-usa.org/releases/66.html>.

Haynes, Charles C. "T-shirt Rebellion in the Land of the Free." 14 Mar. 2004. First
    Amendment Center. 10 Mar. 2006 <http://www.firstamendmentcenter.org/
    commentary.aspx?id=12854>.

"Man Arrested for 'Peace' T-shirt." 4 Mar. 2003. CNN (Reuters) 7 Mar. 2006
    <http://www.cnn.com/2003/US/Northeast/03/04/iraq.usa.shirt.reut/>.

"Secret Service and White House Charged with Violating Free Speech Rights in
    ACLU Lawsuit." 14 Sep. 2004. American Civil Liberties Union. 9 Mar. 2006
    <http://www.aclu.org/freespeech/protest/11462prs20040914.html>.

Projects

Much of what passes for position arguments on television talk shows and on talk radio is little more than shouted assertions and name calling. Arguments in writing are different in character. They are not merely statements of someone's opinion, but are reasoned arguments backed by evidence. They aim not to get in the last word but rather to advance the discussion on an issue so that all benefit from hearing different points of view. These projects are frequently written kinds of position arguments.

The New York Times

POSITION ARGUMENT
For an example of a position argument, see pages 448–451.

Make a position claim on a controversial issue. See pages 462–463 for help on identifying an issue.

Think about what's at stake. Would everyone agree with you? Then your claim probably isn't interesting or important. If you can think of people who would disagree, then something is at stake.

Identify the key term. Often position arguments depend on the definition of the key term. What criteria are necessary for something to meet this definition? How would others benefit from a different definition?

Analyze your potential readers. How does the claim you are making affect them? How familiar are they with the issue? How likely will they be to accept your claim or the definition that underlies your claim?

Write an essay on a controversial issue that takes a stand supported by developed reasons.

For additional reading, writing, and research resources, go to **www.mycomplab.com** and choose **Lester Faigley's** *Writing*.

mycomplab

REBUTTAL ARGUMENT

Los Angeles Times

For an example of a rebuttal argument, see pages 452–454.

Identify a position argument to argue against. What is its main claim or claims? A fair summary of your opponent's position should be included in your finished rebuttal.

Examine the facts on which the claim is based. Are the facts accurate? Are the facts current? Can the statistics be interpreted differently? How reliable are the author's sources?

Analyze the assumptions on which the claim is based. What is the primary assumption of the claim you are rejecting? What are the secondary assumptions? How are these assumptions flawed? What fallacies does the author commit (see pages 18–19)?

Consider your readers. To what extent do your potential readers support the claim you are rejecting? If they strongly support that claim, then how do you get them to change their minds? What beliefs and assumptions do you share with them?

Write a rebuttal. Make your aim clear in your thesis statement. Identify the issue you are writing about and give background information if the issue is likely to be unfamiliar to your readers. Question the evidence and show the flaws in the argument you are rejecting. Conclude on a strong note with your counterargument or counterproposal.

NARRATIVE POSITION ARGUMENT

For an example of a narrative position argument, see pages 455–456.

Think about an experience you have had that makes an implicit causal argument. Have you ever experienced being stereotyped? Have you ever had to jump through many unnecessary bureaucratic hoops? Have you ever been treated differently because of your perceived level of income? Have you ever experienced unfair application of laws and law enforcement?

How common is your experience? If other people have similar experiences, probably what happened to you will ring true.

Describe the experience in detail. When did it happen? How old were you? Why were you there? Who else was there? Where did it happen? If the place is important, describe what it looked like.

Reflect on the significance of the event. How did you feel about the experience when it happened? How do you feel about the experience now? What long-term effects has it had on your life?

Write an essay. You might need to give some background, but if the story is compelling, often it is best to jump right in. Let the story do most of the work. Avoid drawing a simple moral lesson. Your readers should feel the same way you do if you tell your story well.

14

Arguing for Change

Arguments for change begin with questioning. We can make many changes in our lives if we convince ourselves that the effort is worth it. Convincing others to take action for change is always harder.

Chapter contents

Making an argument for change

Every day we hear and read arguments that some action should be taken. We even make these arguments to ourselves: We should exercise more; we should change our work habits. We can make many changes in our lives if we convince ourselves that the effort is worth it.

Convincing others to take action for change is always harder. Other people might not see the same problem that you see or they might not think that the problem is important. And even if they do see the same problem and think it is important, they may not want to commit the time and resources to do something about it. In the short term, at least, doing nothing is the easy choice. Nevertheless, most people aren't satisfied with doing nothing about a problem they think is important. We are impatient when we believe something is wrong or something could be improved. We expect things to change; indeed, we have even designed our political system to guarantee a new president of the nation at least every eight years. The problem we face in persuading others is not so much people are resistant to change but that the change we propose is the right one and worthy of their effort to make it happen.

Every major construction project, every large-scale product, every major scientific endeavor starts with an argument for change—an argument to do something that we are not currently doing and to take action. Arguments for change can even involve changing an entire government (think of the Declaration of Independence). These kinds of arguments are called proposal arguments, and they take the classic form: *We should (or should not) do SOMETHING.*

Components of proposal arguments

What exactly is the problem?	**Identify the problem** Sometimes, problems are evident to your intended readers. If your city is constantly tearing up the streets and then leaving them for months without doing anything to repair them, then you shouldn't have much trouble convincing the citizens of your city that streets should be repaired more quickly. But if you raise a problem that will be unfamiliar to most of your readers, you will first have to argue that the problem exists and it is in their interest that something should be done about it.
What is my solution?	**State your proposed solution** You need to have a clear, definite statement of exactly what you are proposing. Say exactly what you want others to do. You might want to place this statement near the beginning of your argument, or later, after you have considered and rejected other possible solutions. VAGUE: Our city should encourage all citizens to conserve water. SPECIFIC: Our city should provide incentives to conserve water, including offering rain barrels for the minimal cost of $10, replacing at no cost old toilets with water-efficient toilets, and providing rebates up to $500 dollars to those who replace grass with plants that require little water.

Will my solution work?	**Convince your readers that your solution will work**
	When your readers agree that a problem exists and a solution should be found, your next task is to convince them that your solution is the best one to resolve the problem. Many college campuses suffer from transportation and parking problems. If your campus is one of them, then your readers likely will agree that the problems exist. The question is what to do about them. One possible solution is to add a light-rail line to campus from your city's planned light-rail system. If you argue for adding a light-rail line, you must project how many people will ride it and how many car trips will be reduced as a result.
Why is my solution better than others?	**Show why your solution is better than other possible solutions**
	An obvious solution to a lack of parking is to build a parking garage. But parking garages also cost money, and they might even encourage more people to drive, further aggravating the traffic problem. Another solution is to provide more buses, which would not require building a light-rail line and likely would be cheaper. You must think why rail would be preferable. You might argue that students would be more likely to use light rail and that light rail encourages people and businesses to locate close to stations.
Will people be willing to implement my solution?	**Demonstrate that your solution is feasible**
	Your solution not only has to work; it must have a realistic chance of being implemented. Can we afford it? Will it take too long to do? Will people accept it? What else might not get done? A light-rail link might be ideal for getting students to and from campus, but it would cost a great deal of money to construct. The rail proposal is feasible only if you have a concrete proposal for how it would be funded. If the money is to come partly from students, you must argue that students would be willing to pay for the convenience.
How can I convince my readers?	**Focus on the audience**
	All effective writing attends to the audience, but in no form of writing is the audience more important than in arguments for change. Readers have to be convinced that "we really have a problem, and we need to do something about it." It's not enough just to get readers to agree that the problem exists. They have to believe that the problem is worth solving. Arguments for change must appeal to the heart as well as the mind.
Keys to proposal arguments	**Convince readers that you can be trusted**
	To gain the trust of your readers, you first must convince them that you are well informed. You also must convince them that you are fair and sincere and that your heart is in the right place. Readers think favorably of good writers. Poor writers lose readers on all counts, even with the same ideas as a good writer.

Convince your readers that you have their best interests in mind

At the outset many readers may not have much interest in the problem you identify. If you are proposing adding bike lanes to streets in your city, you likely will need the support of people who will never use them. Indeed, they may be initially opposed to converting vehicle lanes to bike lanes. You have to think about the problem from their perspective. You could argue that if more people rode bicycles, there would be more parking places for those who drive and less air pollution for everyone.

Convince your readers with evidence

You may need a great deal of evidence for a problem that is unfamiliar to your readers. A problem well known to other students may be unknown to faculty, staff, and other members of the community. Statistics are often helpful in establishing that a problem affects many people. Likewise, you will need evidence that your solution will work and that it can be accomplished. Most actions require money. Often you will need evidence about how much what you propose will cost and where the money will come from.

Emphasize what you have in common with your readers and be honest about differences

You may not share the assumptions and beliefs of your audience. Think about what may separate you from your audience and what you have in common. When you can establish common ground with your readers because you live in the same community, have similar goals, or share experiences, then you can be frank about any differences you might have. Readers appreciate honesty.

Show exactly how your proposal will have good consequences and possibly reduce bad consequences

Predicting the future is never easy. Think about how your proposal can make good things happen or reduce bad things. Has a solution similar to the one that you are proposing been tried elsewhere? Can you connect to other good consequences? For example, saving water also saves the energy required to run a water treatment plant and to pump it to a home or business.

End with strength

Remember that you want your readers to take action. If you have a powerful example, use it in the conclusion. Inspire your readers to want something better than the status quo. Leave them with a strong impression.

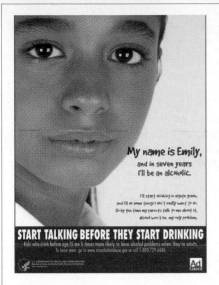

My name is Emily,
and in seven years
I'll be an alcoholic.

I'll start drinking in eighth grade,
and I'll do some things I don't really want to do.
So by the time my parents talk to me about it,
alcohol won't be my only problem.

START TALKING BEFORE THEY START DRINKING
Kids who drink before age 15 are 5 times more likely to have alcohol problems when they're adults.
To learn more, go to www.stopalcoholabuse.gov or call 1.800.729.6686

Campaigns against underage drinking frequently use images of children.

Use visuals for supporting evidence

Pictures alone don't make arguments for change. But they often provide vivid evidence for arguments for change. For example, photographs of children working in factories and mines helped to get child labor laws adopted in the early 1900s.

Charts, graphs, and maps also can be important as supporting evidence for arguments for change. They should be clearly labeled, and a caption should explain their significance and connection to the argument.

WORKING TOGETHER

Make a list of problems to solve

In a group of three or four students

First make a list of all the things you can think of that are problems: your library closes too early for late-night study, there is too little work-study aid on your campus, your roommate is a slob, the weather stays too hot or too cold for too long, store clerks are rude, and on and on. Share your list with the group. Then discuss the following.

• Which items turned up on more than one list?

• Which problems are the most important?

• Which are possible to solve?

• Which problems are the most interesting to your group?

• Which problems are the least interesting to your group?

An effective argument for change

Readers have to be motivated to take action to solve a problem.

The Declaration of Independence

Thomas Jefferson

The American Revolution had already begun with the battles of Lexington, Concord, and Bunker Hill, and George Washington had been named to head the colonial army by June 7, 1776, when the Continental Congress moved to draft a Declaration of Independence. Thomas Jefferson was given eighteen days to complete the task with the help of Benjamin Franklin and John Adams.

In CONGRESS, July 4, 1776.

The unanimous Declaration of the thirteen united States of America.

When, in the Course of human events, it becomes necessary for one people to dissolve the political bands which have connected them with another, and to assume among the powers of the earth, the separate and equal station to which the laws of nature and of nature's God entitle them, a decent respect to the opinions of mankind requires that they should declare the causes which impel them to the separation.

We hold these truths to be self-evident: That all men are created equal; that they are endowed by their Creator with certain unalienable rights; that among these are life, liberty and the pursuit of happiness. That, to secure these rights, governments are instituted among men, deriving their just powers from the consent of the governed; that, whenever any form of government becomes destructive of these ends, it is the right of the people to alter or to abolish it, and to institute new Government, laying its foundation on such principles, and organizing its powers in such form, as to them shall seem most likely to effect their safety and happiness. Prudence,

Jefferson maintains that the drastic solution of declaring independence is justified if the problem is of great magnitude.

The rationale for the proposal is a definition argument. According to Jefferson, the purpose of a government is to ensure the rights of the governed. When a government fails to achieve its defined purpose—to ensure the rights of the people—the people have the right to abolish it. The British used similar arguments to justify the revolution against King James II in 1688.

indeed, will dictate that governments long established should not be changed for light and transient causes; and accordingly all experience hath shown, that mankind are more disposed to suffer, while evils are sufferable, than to right themselves by abolishing the forms to which they are accustomed. But when a long train of abuses and usurpations, pursuing invariably the same object evinces a design to reduce them under absolute despotism, it is their right, it is their duty, to throw off such government and to provide new guards for their future security. Such has been the patient sufferance of these colonies, and such is now the necessity which constrains them to alter their former systems of government. The history of the present king of Great Britain is a history of repeated injuries and usurpations, all having in direct object the establishment of an absolute tyranny over these States. To prove this, let facts be submitted to a candid world.

He has refused his assent to laws, the most wholesome and necessary for the public good.

He has forbidden his governors to pass laws of immediate and pressing importance, unless suspended in their operation till his Assent should be obtained, and, when so suspended, he has utterly neglected to attend to them.

He has refused to pass other laws for the accommodation of large districts of people, unless those people would relinquish the right of representation in the legislature–a right inestimable to them and formidable to tyrants only.

He has called together legislative bodies at places unusual, uncomfortable, and distant from the depository of their public Records, for the sole purpose of fatiguing them into compliance with his measures.

He has dissolved representative houses repeatedly, for opposing with manly firmness his invasions on the rights of the people.

The burden for Jefferson is to convince others of the severity of the problem—that life is intolerable under the King. He goes on to detail a long list of complaints. His goal is to prove the need for change rather than to outline how the solution will work.

He has refused for a long time, after such dissolutions, to cause others to be elected; whereby the legislative powers, incapable of annihilation, have returned to the people at large for their exercise; the State remaining in the mean time exposed to all the dangers of invasion from without, and convulsions within.

He has endeavored to prevent the population of these states; for that purpose obstructing the laws for naturalization of foreigners; refusing to pass others to encourage their migrations hither, and raising the conditions of new appropriations of lands.

He has obstructed the administration of justice by refusing his assent to laws for establishing judiciary powers.

He has made judges dependent on his will alone, for the tenure of their offices, and the amount and payment of their salaries.

He has erected a multitude of new offices, and sent hither swarms of officers to harass our people, and eat out their substance.

The legalistic list of charges is made more vivid by the use of metaphors such as "swarms of officers," which likens the British to a plague of insects.

He has kept among us, in times of peace, standing armies without the consent of our legislatures.

He has affected to render the military independent of and superior to the civil power.

He has combined with others to subject us to a jurisdiction foreign to our constitution, and unacknowledged by our laws; giving his assent to their acts of pretended legislation:

For quartering large bodies of armed troops among us;

For protecting them, by a mock trial, from punishment for any murders which they should commit on the inhabitants of these States;

For cutting off our trade with all parts of the world;

For imposing taxes on us without our consent;

For depriving us in many cases, of the benefits of trial by jury;

For transporting us beyond seas to be tried for pretended offences;

For abolishing the free system of English laws in a neighboring province, establishing therein an arbitrary government, and enlarging its boundaries so as to render it at once an example and fit instrument for introducing the same absolute rule into these colonies;

For taking away our charters, abolishing our most valuable laws, and altering fundamentally the forms of our governments;

For suspending our own legislatures, and declaring themselves invested with power to legislate for us in all cases whatsoever.

He has abdicated government here, by declaring us out of his protection and waging war against us.

He has plundered our seas, ravaged our coasts, burnt our towns, and destroyed the lives of our people.

He is at this time transporting large armies of foreign mercenaries to complete the works of death, desolation and tyranny, already begun with circumstances of cruelty and perfidy scarcely paralleled in the most barbarous ages, and totally unworthy the head of a civilized nation.

He has constrained our fellow citizens taken captive on the high seas to bear arms against their country, to become the executioners of their friends and brethren, or to fall themselves by their hands.

The strongest charges against the king are placed at the end of the list.

He has excited domestic insurrections amongst us, and has endeavored to bring on the inhabitants of our frontiers, the merciless Indian savages, whose known rule of warfare is an undistinguished destruction of all ages, sexes and conditions.

In every stage of these oppressions we have petitioned for redress in the most humble terms; our repeated petitions have been answered only by repeated injury. A prince, whose character is thus marked by every act which may define a tyrant, is unfit to be the ruler of a free people.

Nor have we been wanting in attentions to our British brethren. We have warned them from time to time of attempts by their legislature to extend an unwarrantable jurisdiction over us. We have reminded them of the circumstances of our emigration and settlement here. We have appealed to their native justice and magnanimity, and we have conjured them by the ties of our common kindred to disavow these usurpations, which would inevitably interrupt our connections and correspondence. They too have been deaf to the voice of justice and of consanguinity. We must, therefore, acquiesce in the necessity, which denounces our separation, and hold them, as we hold the rest of mankind, enemies in war, in peace, friends.

To build credibility Jefferson makes a case that the colonists' frustration with the British government is justified. He argues that the colonists have tried the peaceful approach only to be rebuffed.

We, therefore, the representatives of the United States of America, in general congress, assembled, appealing to the Supreme Judge of the world for the rectitude of our intentions, do, in the name, and by authority of the good people of these colonies, solemnly publish and declare, that these united colonies are, and of right ought to be free and independent states; that they are absolved from all allegiance to the British crown, and that all political connection between them and the state of Great Britain, is and ought to be totally dissolved; and that as free and independent states, they have full power to levy war, conclude peace, contract alliances, establish commerce, and to do all other acts and things which independent states may of right do. And for the support of this declaration, with a firm reliance on the protection of Divine Providence, we mutually pledge to each other our lives, our fortunes and our sacred honor.

The proposal is that the colonies no longer have any political connection to Great Britain and possess all the rights of an independent country.

How to read arguments for change

Make notes as you read, either in the margins or on paper or a computer file. Circle any words or references that you don't know and look them up.

What is it?	• What kind of a text is it? An editorial? an essay? an advertisement? a grant proposal? a Web site? a business proposal? What are your expectations for this kind of text? • What media are used? (Web sites, for example, often combine images, words, and sounds.)
Where did it come from?	• Who wrote this material? • Where did it first appear? In a book, newspaper, magazine, online, in a company, or in an organization?
What is the problem?	• Where is the evidence for the problem? Does this evidence establish that the problem exists? • How important is the problem? • Whom does the problem affect? (These people are called the stakeholders.) • What else has been written about the problem?
What is the solution?	• What exactly is the solution that the writer proposes? • Where is the evidence for the proposed solution? Does this evidence convince you that the proposal will solve the problem? • What kinds of sources are cited? Are they from books, newspapers, periodicals, or the Web? Are they completely documented?
How feasible is the proposed solution?	• Does the writer make a case that this is practical, and will people support the solution? • If the solution costs money, where does the money come from?
How is it composed?	• How is the piece of writing organized? • How does the writer represent herself or himself? • How would you characterize the style? • How effective is the design? Is it easy to read? • If there are any photographs, charts, or other graphics, what information do they contribute?

A Trail of DNA and Data

(ESSAY)

Paul Saffo

The Washington Post Paul Saffo writes frequently about the long-term impacts of technological change on business and society. His essays have appeared in *Fortune, Harvard Business Review,* the *Los Angeles Times, Newsweek,* the *New York Times,* and the *Washington Post,* where this argument appeared in April 2005.

Analyzing and Connecting

Return to these questions after you have finished reading.

1. Saffo does not give specific proposals at the end of this essay but rather makes a general proposal. Would specific proposals make the essay stronger? Why or why not?

2. How might Saffo answer a critic who might say, "You can't outlaw technology; the technology will get out there anyway"?

3. Saffo gives a negative scenario for identification technology. Can you think of a positive scenario? For example, the miniaturization of computers can be used for cell imaging and therapeutics for treating cancer. Is Saffo's essay weaker because he doesn't offer a positive scenario?

4. Many facilities that store money, weapons, nuclear materials, biohazards, or other restricted materials now use digital face recognition systems to authenticate everyone who walks in the door, which nearly everyone agrees is a good idea. But using face recognition systems in public places has created controversy. For example, the city of Tampa deployed a face-recognition system in the nightlife district of Ybor City in an effort to catch criminals. The people who attended clubs and restaurants were unaware their images were being entered into databases. Should the practice be allowed? What are the risks of false identifications? What policy would you recommend that would catch criminals without invading the privacy of every visitor?

5. If you shop online, you must enable "cookies," which keep track of what you put into your shopping cart and allow the online store to recognize you when you return. But the cookies also can be used to monitor what other Web sites you visit, and your email address can be used to disclose your identity, even if you give no credit-card information. This information can be and often is sold to other companies without your knowledge. Many European countries ban these practices. Propose a policy for the United States that would protect privacy.

A Trail of DNA
and Data

If you're worried about privacy and identity theft, imagine this:

The scene: Somewhere in Washington.

The date: April 3, 2020.

You sit steaming while the officer hops off his electric cycle and walks up to the car window. "You realize that you ran that red light again, don't you, Mr. Witherspoon?" It's no surprise that he knows your name; the intersection camera scanned your license plate and your guilty face, and matched both in the DMV database. The cop had the full scoop before you rolled to a stop.

"I know, I know, but the sun was in my eyes," you plead as you fumble for your driver's license.

"Oh, don't bother with that," the officer replies, waving off the license while squinting at his hand-held scanner. Of course. Even though the old state licensing system had been revamped back in 2014 into a "secure" national program, the new licenses had been so compromised that the street price of a phony card in Tijuana had plummeted to five euros. In frustration, law enforcement was turning to pure biometrics.

"Could you lick this please?" the officer asks, passing you a nanofiber blotter. You comply and then slide the blotter into the palm-sized gizmo he is holding, which reads your DNA and runs a match against a national genomic database maintained by a consortium of drug companies and credit agencies. It also checks half a dozen metabolic fractions looking for everything from drugs and alcohol to lack of sleep.

The officer looks at the screen, and frowns, "Okay. I'll let you off with a warning, but you really need more sleep. I also see that your retinal implants are past warranty, and your car tells me that you are six months overdue on its navigation firmware upgrade. You really need to take care of both or next time it's a ticket."

This creepy scenario is all too plausible. The technologies described are already being developed for industrial and medical applications, and the steadily dropping cost and size of such systems will make them affordable and practical police tools well before 2020. The resulting intrusiveness would make today's system of search warrants and wiretaps quaint anachronisms.

Some people find this future alluring and believe that it holds out the promise of using sophisticated ID techniques to catch everyone from careless drivers to bomb-toting terrorists in a biometric dragnet. We have already seen places such as Truro, Mass., Baton Rouge, La. and Miami ask hundreds or thousands of citizens to submit to DNA mass-testing to catch killers. Biometric devices sensing for SARS symptoms are omnipresent in Asian airports. And the first prototypes of systems that test in real time for SARS, HIV and bird flu have been deployed abroad.

The ubiquitous collection and use of biometric information may be inevitable, but the notion that it can deliver reliable, theft-proof evidence of identity is pure science fiction. Consider that oldest of biometric identifiers—fingerprints. Long the exclusive domain of government databases and FBI agents who dust for prints at crime scenes, fingerprints are now being used by electronic print readers on everything from ATMs to laptops. Sticking your finger on a sensor beats having to remember a password or toting an easily lost smart card.

But be careful what you touch, because you are leaving your identity behind every time you take a drink. A Japanese cryptographer has demonstrated how, with a bit of gummi bear gelatin, some cyanoacrylic glue, a digital camera and a bit of digital fiddling, he can easily capture a print off a glass and confect an artificial finger that foils fingerprint readers with an 80 percent success rate. Frightening as this is, at least the stunt is far less grisly than the tale, perhaps aprocryphal, of some South African crooks who snipped the finger off an elderly retiree, rushed her still-warm digit down to a government ATM, stuck it on the print reader and collected the victim's pension payment. (Scanners there now gauge a finger's temperature, too.)

Today's biometric advances are the stuff of tomorrow's hackers and clever crooks, and anything that can be detected eventually will be counterfeited. Iris scanners are gaining in popularity in the corporate world, exploiting the fact that human iris patterns are apparently as unique as fingerprints. And unlike prints, iris images aren't left behind every time someone gets a latte at Starbucks. But hide something valuable enough behind a door protected by an iris scanner, and I guarantee that someone will

figure out how to capture an iris image and transfer it to a contact lens good enough to fool the readers. And capturing your iris may not even require sticking a digital camera in your face—after all, verification requires that the representation of your iris exist as a cloud of binary bits of data somewhere in cyberspace, open to being hacked, copied, stolen and downloaded. The more complex the system, the greater the likelihood that there are flaws that crooks can exploit.

DNA is the gold standard of biometrics, but even DNA starts to look like fool's gold under close inspection. With a bit of discipline, one can keep a card sale or a PIN secret, but if your DNA becomes your identity, you are sharing your secret with the world every time you sneeze or touch something. The novelist Scott Turow has already written about a hapless sap framed for a murder by an angry spouse who spreads his DNA at the scene of a killing.

The potential for DNA identity theft is enough to make us all wear a gauze mask and keep our hands in our pockets. DNA can of course be easily copied—after all, its architecture is designed for duplication—but that is the least of its problems. Unlike a credit card number, DNA can't be retired and swapped for a new sequence if it falls into the hands of crooks or snoops. Once your DNA identity is stolen, you live with the consequences forever.

This hasn't stopped innovators from using DNA as an indicator of authenticity. The artist Thomas Kinkade signs his most valuable paintings with an ink containing a bit of his DNA. (He calls it a "forgeryproof DNA Matrix signature.") We don't know how much of Tom is really in his paintings, but perhaps it's enough for forgers to duplicate the ink, as well as the distinctive brush strokes.

The biggest problem with DNA is that it says so much more about us than an arbitrary serial number does. Give up your Social Security number and a stranger can inspect your credit rating. But surrender your DNA and a snoop can discover your innermost genetic secrets—your ancestry, genetic defects and predispositions to certain diseases. Of course we will have strong genetic privacy laws, but those laws will allow consumers to "voluntarily" surrender their information in the course of applying for work or pleading for health care. A genetic market-place not unlike today's consumer information business will emerge, swarming with health insurers attempting to prune out risky individuals, drug companies seeking customers and employers managing potential worker injury liability.

Faced with this prospect, any sensible privacy maven would conclude that DNA is too dangerous to collect, much less use for a task as unimportant as turning on a laptop or working a cash machine. But society will not be able to resist its use. The pharmaceutical industry will need our DNA to concoct customized wonder drugs that will fix everything from high cholesterol to halitosis. And crime fighters will make giving DNA information part of our civic duty and national security. Once they start collecting, the temptation to use it for other purposes will be too great.

Moreover, snoops won't even need a bit of actual DNA to invade our privacy because it will be so much easier to access its digital representation on any number of databanks off

in cyberspace. Our Mr. Witherspoon will get junk mail about obscure medical conditions that he's never heard of because some direct marketing firm "bot" will inspect his digital DNA and discover that he has a latent disease or condition that his doctor didn't notice at his annual checkup.

It is tempting to conclude that Americans will rise up in revolt, but experience suggests otherwise. Americans profess a concern for privacy, but they happily reveal their deepest financial and personal secrets for a free magazine subscription or cheesy electronic trinket. So they probably will eagerly surrender their biometric identities as well, trading fingerprint IDs for frequent shopper privileges at the local supermarket and genetic data to find out how to have the cholesterol count of a teenager.

Biometric identity systems are inevitable, but they are no silver bullet when it comes to identity protection. The solution to identity protection lies in the hard work of implementing system-wide and nationwide technical and policy changes. Without those changes, the deployment of biometric sensors will merely increase the opportunities for snoops and thieves—and escalate the cost to ordinary citizens.

It's time to fix the problems in our current systems and try to anticipate the unique challenges that will accompany the expanded use of biometrics. It's the only way to keep tomorrow's crooks from stealing your fingers and face and, with them, your entire identity.

Coal in a Nice Shade of Green
(ARTICLE)

Thomas Homer-Dixon and S. Julio Friedmann

Thomas Homer-Dixon is director of the Center for Peace and Conflict Studies at the University of Toronto.

S. Julio Friedmann directs the carbon sequestration project at Lawrence Livermore National Laboratory in Livermore, California. The article appeared in the *New York Times* on March 25, 2005.

Analyzing and Connecting
Return to these questions after you have finished reading.

1. Thomas Homer-Dixon and S. Julio Friedmann give only two sentences at the beginning of the first paragraph to describing the problem. The rest of the first paragraph and the next six paragraphs deal with other solutions. Why do the authors bring up other solutions at the beginning?

2. In paragraph 7 the authors mention improving energy conservation and efficiency as something we need to do, but they do not discuss how much energy we might save. Is their neglect of potential energy savings a problem?

3. The authors do not discuss the relative cost of coal gasification compared to other types of energy production. Does this omission hurt their credibility?

4. The main objections the authors raise are safety and environmental concerns with coal mining. Strip mining especially damages the environment. The authors hope for more environmentally friendly methods, but it is hard to imagine what they might be. Do they make an adequate case—that the trade-off of ripping up huge tracts of land for less carbon dioxide in the atmosphere is a good one?

When it comes to energy, we are trapped between a rock and several hard places. The world's soaring demand for oil is pushing against the limits of production, lifting the price of crude nearly 90 percent in the last 18 months. Congress's vote in favor of drilling in the Arctic National Wildlife Refuge won't make much difference because the amount of oil there, at best, is tiny relative to global or even American needs. And relief isn't likely to come anytime soon from drilling elsewhere: oil companies spent $8 billion on exploration in 2003, but discovered only $4 billion of commercially useful oil.

Sadly, most alternatives to conventional oil can't give us the immense amount of energy we need without damaging our environment, jeopardizing our national security or bankrupting us. The obvious alternatives are other fossil fuels: natural gas and oil products derived from tar sands, oil shale and even coal. But natural gas supplies are tightening, at least in North America.

And, of course, all fossil fuels have a major disadvantage: burning them releases carbon dioxide, a greenhouse gas that may contribute to climate change. This drawback is especially acute for tar sands, oil shale and coal, which, joule for joule, release far more carbon dioxide than either conventional oil or natural gas.

As for energy sources not based on carbon, it would be enormously hard to meet a major percentage of America's energy needs at a reasonable cost, at least in the near term. Take nuclear power—a source that produces no greenhouse emissions. Even assuming we can find a place to dispose of nuclear waste and deal with the security risks, to meet the expected growth in total American energy demand over the next 50 years would require building 1,200 new nuclear power plants in addition to the current 104—or one plant every two weeks until 2050.

Solar power? To satisfy its current electricity demand using today's technology, the United States would need 10 billion square meters of photovoltaic panels; this would cost $5 trillion, or nearly half the country's annual gross domestic product.

How about hydrogen? To replace just America's surface transportation with cars and trucks running on fuel cells powered by hydrogen, America would have to produce 230,000 tons of the gas—or enough to fill 13,000 Hindenburg dirigibles—every day. This could be generated by electrolyzing water, but to do so America would have to nearly double its electricity output, and generating this extra power with carbon-free renewable energy would mean covering an area the size of Massachusetts with solar panels or of New York State with windmills.

Of course technology is always improving, and down the road some or all of these technologies may become more feasible. But for the near term, there is no silver bullet. The scale and complexity of American energy consumption are such that the country needs to look at many different solutions simultaneously. On the demand side, this means huge investments in conservation and energy efficiency—two areas that policy makers and consumers have sadly neglected.

On the supply side, the important thing is to come up with so-called bridge technologies that can power our cities, factories and cars with fewer emissions than traditional fossil fuels while we move to clean energy like solar, wind and safe nuclear power. A prime example of a bridge technology—one that exists right now—is gasification.

Here's how it works: in a type of power plant called an integrated gasification combined-cycle facility, we change any fossil fuel, including coal, into a superhot gas that is rich in hydrogen—and in the process strip out pollutants like sulfur and mercury. As in a traditional combustion power plant, the heat generates large amounts of electricity; but in this case, the gas byproducts can be pure streams of hydrogen and carbon dioxide.

This matters for several reasons. The hydrogen produced could be used as a transportation fuel. Equally important, the harmful carbon dioxide waste is in a form that can be pumped deep underground and stored, theoretically for millions of years, in old oil and gas fields or saline aquifers. This process is called geologic storage, or carbon sequestration, and recent field demonstrations in Canada and Norway have shown it can work and work safely.

The marriage of gasified coal plants and geologic storage could allow us to build power plants that produce vast amounts of energy with virtually no carbon dioxide emissions in the air. The Department of Energy is pursuing plans to build such a zero-emission power plant and is encouraging energy companies to come up with proposals of their own. The United States, Britain and Germany are also collaborating to build such plants in China and India as part of an effort by the Group of 8. Moreover, these plants are very flexible: although coal is the most obvious fuel source, they could burn almost any organic material, including waste cornhusks and woodchips.

This is an emerging technology, so inevitably there are hurdles. For example, we need a crash program of research to find out which geological formations best lock up the carbon dioxide for the longest time, followed by global geological surveys to locate these formations and determine their capacity. Also, coal mining is dangerous and strip-mining, of course, devastates the environment; if we are to mine a lot more coal in the future we will want more environmentally friendly methods.

On balance, though, this combination of technologies is probably among the best ways to provide the energy needed by modern societies—including populous, energy-hungry and coal-rich societies like China and India—without wrecking the global climate.

Fossil fuels, especially petroleum, powered the industrialization of today's rich countries and they still drive the world economy. But within the lifetimes of our grandchildren, the age of petroleum will wane. The combination of gasified coal plants and geologic storage can be our bridge to the clean energy—derived from renewable resources like solar and wind power and perhaps nuclear fusion—of the 22nd century and beyond.

Building the Interstate Highway System
(SPEECH)
Richard Nixon

In July 1954, President Eisenhower was scheduled to deliver a speech to the annual conference of United States Governors held at Lake George, New York, but was called away by a death in the family. Then-Vice President Richard Nixon filled in for the president and, speaking from Eisenhower's notes, unveiled a startling plan: the federal government proposed to dedicate $50 billion—an enormous sum in 1954—to create a system of interstate highways connecting the country from coast to coast, and from border to border. The proposal was electrifying news, and led directly to the creation of the Interstate Highway System we use today. Below is an excerpt from the vice president's speech. (The entire speech can be found online at **www.fhwa.dot.gov/ infrastructure/rw96m.htm**.)

Analyzing and Connecting
Return to these questions after you have finished reading.

1. What evidence does the vice president present that the state of America's highways is indeed a problem? What are the specific problems this plan is intended to solve?

2. Traffic in many locations today is more congested than it was when Nixon delivered his speech in 1954. Some politicians today argue for building more roads. How are arguments for more roads today similar to and different from Nixon's arguments?

3. Nixon's speech was covered in the media for the general public, whose approval was needed in order for the proposal to pass through Congress into law. But the immediate audience for the speech consisted of forty-eight state governors. What gestures do you see in this speech that show the vice president and president wanted to appeal to them specifically, and understood their unique concerns?

4. How many of the problems outlined by the vice president do you feel were actually solved by our Interstate Highway System?

NIXON: BUILDING THE INTERSTATE HIGHWAY SYSTEM

A Cabinet committee has just been established by the President to explore and to help formulate a comprehensive transportation policy for the Nation, taking into account the vital interests of carriers, shippers, the States and communities, the public at large. But more specifically, our highway net is inadequate locally, and obsolete as a national system.

To start to meet this problem at this session of the Congress, we have increased by approximately 500 million dollars the Federal monies available to the States for road development. This seems like a very substantial sum. But the experts say that 5 billion dollars a year for ten years, in addition to all current, normal expenditures, will pay off in economic growth; and when we have spent 50 billion dollars in the next ten years, we shall only have made a good start on the highways the country will need for a population of 200 million people.

A 50 billion dollar highway program in ten years is a goal toward which we can—and we should—look.

Now, let us look at the highway net of the United States as it is. What is wrong with it? It is obsolete because in large part it just happened. It was governed in the beginning by terrain, existing Indian trails, cattle trails, arbitrary section lines. It was designed largely for local movement at low speeds of one or two horsepower. It has been adjusted, it is true, at intervals to meet metropolitan traffic gluts, transcontinental movement, and increased horsepower. But it has never been completely overhauled or planned to satisfy the needs ten years ahead.

At this point in his notes, the President had a personal anecdote illustrating the problem. Thirty-five years ago this month, the Secretary of War initiated a transcontinental truck convoy to prove that the gas engine had displaced the mule, even on our relatively primitive roads. A Second Lieutenant named Dwight Eisenhower went along as an observer. All-weather roads in the United States at that time totaled 300,000 miles. The autos and trucks numbered 7.6 million. That truck convoy left Washington July the 7th. It arrived in San Francisco on September the 5th, sixty days and 6000 breakdowns later.

Today, all-weather mileage is approximately 1.8 million as compared with 300,000 miles. But autos and trucks number more than 56 million, as compared with 7.6 million.

It is obvious, then, that the increase in mileage has lagged behind the increase in vehicles. The road system, moreover, is fundamentally the same, either haphazard or completely arbitrary in its origin, designed for local movement, in an age of transcontinental travel.

Now, what are the penalties of this obsolete net which we have today? Our first most apparent [is] an annual death toll comparable to the casualties of a bloody war, beyond calculation in dollar terms. It approaches 40,000 killed and exceeds 1.3 million injured annually.

And second, the annual wastage of billions of hours in detours, traffic jams, and so on, measurable by any traffic engineer and amounting to billions of dollars in productive time.

Third, all the civil suits that clog up our courts. It has been estimated that more than half have their origins on highways, roads and streets.

Nullification of efficiency in the production of goods by inefficiency in the transport of goods is another result of this obsolete net that we have today.

And finally, the appalling inadequacies to meet the demands of catastrophe or defense, should an atomic war come.

These penalties warrant the expenditures of billions to correct them.

Now, let us look at the highway net as it should be. The President believes that the requirements are these: a grand plan for a properly articulated system that solves the problems of speedy, safe, transcontinental travel; intercity communication; access highways; and farm-to-market movement; metropolitan area congestion; bottlenecks; and parking.

Second, a financing proposal based on self-liquidation of each project, wherever that is possible, through tolls or the assured increase in gas tax revenue, and on Federal help where the national interest demands it.

And third, and I would emphasize this, particularly at this Conference, because I know how deeply the President believes in this principle: a cooperative alliance between the Federal government and the states so that local government and the most efficient sort of government in the administration of funds, will be the manager of its own area.

And the fourth, very probably, a program initiated by the Federal government, with State cooperation, for the planning and construction of a modern State highway system, with the Federal government functions, for example, being to advance funds or guarantee the obligations of localities or States which undertake to construct new, or modernize existing highways.

And then I would like to read to you the last sentence from the President's notes, exactly as it appears in them, because it is an exhortation to the members of this Conference: "I hope that you will study the matter, and recommend to me the cooperative action you think the Federal government and the 48 States should take to meet these requirements, so that I can submit positive proposals to the next session of the Congress."

And I know that in making this request to the Governors Conference, that the President believes it is essential that we have cooperation in this field. He believes that only with cooperation, and with the maximum of State and local initiative and control can we make a program which will deal with the problem and deal with it effectively.

Breaking the Fire Department's Language Barrier

(GRANT PROPOSAL)

Monterey County Fire Chiefs Association

Monterey County
Fire Chiefs Association

BREAKING THE
FIRE DEPARTMENT'S
LANGUAGE BARRIER

GRANT PROPOSAL

Grant proposals are one of the most common uses of proposal arguments. Their goal is to persuade someone—usually a foundation, corporation, or government agency—to give money for a charitable purpose. Grant proposals follow a specific format to achieve this goal. The proposal below, which was successful in gaining funding, was produced by the Monterey County Fire Chiefs Association of Monterey, California, in April 2001.

Analyzing and Connecting

Return to these questions after you have finished reading.

1. The four major components of a successful proposal are identifying the problem, stating the proposed solution, showing that the solution is fair, and demonstrating that it is workable. How does this proposal organize these components? Which does it spend the most time on?

2. The Problem Statement in this proposal lists seven citizens who initially approached the Fire Chiefs Association to talk about the language barrier. Why are these individuals, and their professional affiliations, listed in the proposal? What sort of impact is this information likely to have on a grant-funding institution?

3. The audience for this proposal are people assigned to give money for worthy purposes. If you were on the Board of Directors of a grant-giving organization, what further questions would you have for the authors of this proposal? How needed is the project? Look at the budget carefully. Look at the qualifications of people involved. Look at their goals and schedule.

GRANT PROPOSAL

Monterey County
Fire Chiefs Association

Executive Summary

The Monterey County Chiefs Association proposes to provide a fire safe public education program for the Spanish speaking community based on Hispanic language and cultural expectations. Our goal is to provide quality access to all members of our community. We are seeking $48,500 to fund a portion of this valuable project which will provide long lasting benefits to both the local community and our Association members.

Introduction

The Monterey County Chiefs Association is an organization of 29 fire agencies. This association encompasses over 458 square miles and services communities along the California central coast from Moss Landing to Big Sur and inland from Salinas to King City. The departments, paid and volunteer, serve a mix of urban, rural and farming communities.

The mission of the Monterey County Fire Chiefs Association is to enhance the development of local programs to insure greater protection of life and property from fire and natural disaster. This is accomplished through the development and delivery of programs such as Fire Prevention, Public Education, Emergency Response and Training.

Problem Statement

"What we have here is a failure to communicate!"
—*From the movie* Cool Hand Luke

On September 16, 1999, leaders from the Spanish speaking community of Monterey County addressed the Monterey County Fire Chiefs Association (MCFCA). The leaders, listed below, expressed their concern that the fire agencies of the county excluded the Spanish speaking population from actively participating in community efforts to develop and maintain a fire safe environment. Specifically, the leaders believe that the Spanish speaking citizens do not understand the fire safe messages transmitted from the fire agencies whose primary language and culture is English based. They also expressed their belief that the fire agencies display little understanding of the Spanish speaking culture, further complicating efforts of cross communication.

Gerardo Ramirez – ALLSTATE INSURANCE
Laura Vega – DIRECTOR HISPANIC CHAMBER OF COMMERCE, SALINAS
Cosme Padilla – LEAGUE OF UNITED LATIN AMERICAN CITIZENS (LULAC)
Dr. Henry Villanueva – CALIFORNIA STATE UNIVERSITY OF MONTEREY BAY
Dr. Jose Amaro – CALIFORNIA STATE UNIVERSITY OF MONTEREY BAY
Sergio Santos – ORGANIZER, UNITED FARM WORKERS, MONTEREY COUNTY
Carlos Ortiz – STATION MANAGER, RADIO CAMPESINA 107.9

In defense, the Fire Chiefs cited instances where nationally produced public education campaigns were translated into Spanish and distributed to the Spanish speaking community of the county. The meeting ended amicably, but without conclusion. The 2000 U.S. Federal Census reflects that of the 47% countywide Hispanic population, just under 62% of the Hispanic population is under the age of 18. "The 2000 U.S. Federal Census counted 48,389 Salinas residents under the age of 18, enough to become the second largest city in the County if the children formed their own town," reported *The Salinas Californian*.

The 1990 U.S. Federal Census reflects an annual median income in Monterey County for a family of 4 to be $50,000, leaving 11% of Monterey Counties population to fall below the Poverty level. The 2000 U.S. Federal Census numbers are not yet available, but believed to be significantly higher. According to the FEMA report Socioeconomic Factors and the Incidents of Fire, "Socioeconomic factors are among the best predictors of fire rates at the neighborhood level." "Virtually every study of Socioeconomic Characteristics has shown that lower levels of income are either directly or indirectly tied to an increased risk of fire." The relationship between low-income status and the presence of operational smoke detectors has not been firmly established. "At this point, it is known that neighborhoods with proportions of low income households also have proportionately more fires than neighborhoods with more middle and high income residents. Households without operational detectors are almost two and one half times more likely to have reported fires than those with operational detectors. Taken together these facts suggest that low income households may have fewer operational smoke detectors and thus face higher fire risk" (*1994 NFIRS, Smoke detector status in households reporting fires*). Of critical note, the community leaders reporting the communications failure represented every economic strata of Monterey County's Spanish speaking community, 47% of the county's total 450,000 population. Noting this the MCFCA has posed the following question: *"In Monterey County, is the failure to provide for a fire safe environment in the Spanish speaking community based on language and cultural barriers instead of economic status?"*

Objectives

"Lo Que Tenemos es a La Problemo Para Communicar!"
"What we have here is a failure to communicate!"

In the 1970's GM Corporation attempted to sell the Nova Chevrolet coupe in Mexico. In spite of climbing sales within the U.S., sales for the Nova were dismal there. The reason cited was that in Spanish the word Nova literally means, "Won't go." Who would purchase a vehicle that "does not go"?

The goal of this program is to develop a fire safe public education program based on the cultural expectations and the language familiar to the Hispanic community.

A. Identify the cultural and language barriers that prevent the Spanish-speaking members of the Monterey County population from active participation in providing for a fire safe community.

B. Train Monterey County firefighters in the cultural diversity of Spanish speaking residents, which potentially prevents the accurate exchange of information.

C. Partner with local Spanish language media agencies to develop a television, radio and elementary school campaign which explains the role of the fire department in the Spanish speaking community and educates Spanish speaking children in safe preventative actions for self protection.

Methods: YEAR ONE

- Recruit Hispanic Community Leaders and members of the following organizations to endorse program:

  League of United Latin American Citizens, LULAC
  Hispanic Chamber of Commerce of Monterey County
  United Farm Workers of Monterey County

- Hire consultant to identify and address the communication deficiencies in the relationship between the Fire Departments and the Spanish speaking population of Monterey County.

- Consultant to develop a Bi-lingual Public Education program for the MCFCA, which addresses the Fire & Life safety needs specific to the Spanish speaking community.

- Monterey County Fire Agencies will establish a baseline through National Fire Information Reporting System (NFIRS) for fire deaths, injuries and property loss in Monterey County prior to start of Grant Funding or implementation.

Methods: YEAR TWO

- Implement training for local fire department personnel on the delivery of the developed Bi-lingual Public Education program.

- Fire Agencies begin delivery of Bi-Lingual Public education to the Monterey County community.

Evaluation

Monthly status reviews from fire agencies participating in the proposed program will be submitted to Monterey County Fire Chiefs Association (MCFCA), enabling the Association and Program Manager to monitor program status and results of the program. During the two-year implementation of the program, 7 quarterly reviews will be conducted. A final report will be generated at the end of the two-year program period. Final results will be measured as follows:

- A comprehensive report will be completed by the consultant and distributed to MCFCA and local fire agencies

- Train 50 Monterey County firefighters in the cultural diversity of Spanish speaking residents and direct these firefighters to train an additional 250 firefighters within the County

- Produce 5 public service announcements and run them throughout the two-year implementation period

- Evaluate effectiveness of program through NFIRS and CFIRS statistics for the two-year program

- Evaluate response from target groups by conducting a survey

Future Funding

Maintain the program through existing Monterey County Fire Agencies, Training and Prevention Officers. These Staff positions should not need additional funds, as they would only change the language of delivery not the number of deliveries. Evaluation of the program will continue through an annual check of NFIRS and CFIRS for fire deaths, injuries and property loss in Monterey County. Expectations that the need for English printed materials in these existing programs would be reduced and allow a corresponding increase in printed material in Spanish.

Budget

FIRST YEAR

BUDGET ITEMS	IN KIND MATCH	DONOR	FIRE ACT
STAFF	$40,000	$24,000	$56,000
Existing staff positions within Monterey County Fire Agencies	Consultant fees	Consultant fees	
Facilities (offices)	$6,000	$5,000	$0.00
Printed Materials	$0.00	$5,000	$0.00
TOTAL	$46,000	$34,000	$56,000

SECOND YEAR

BUDGET ITEMS	IN KIND MATCH	DONOR	FIRE ACT
Staff	$40,000	$24,000	$56,000
Existing staff positions within Monterey County Fire Agencies	Consultant fees	Consultant fees	
Facilities (offices)	$6,000	$5,000	$0.00
Printed Materials	$0.00	$5,000	$0.00
TOTAL	$46,000	$34,000	$56,000

PROGRAM TOTALS

	IN KIND MATCH	DONOR	FIRE ACT
TOTAL	$64,500	$48,500	$56,000

United States Marine Corps Recruitment

(WEB SITE)

U.S. Armed Forces

The U.S. armed forces produce recruiting materials in various media, all of which aim to persuade young men and women to make a life-changing decision by enlisting. These pages from the Marine Corps Web site demonstrate the essential components of a proposal argument.

Analyzing and Connecting

Return to these questions after you have finished reading.

1. This Web site focuses on the problem of young adults who are "seeking a challenge and the opportunity to become a success." Joining the Marine Corps is presented as a potential solution to that problem. The Marine Corps, however, does not exist merely to provide opportunities for young people; it is a fighting force. Why do you think the creators of this site chose to frame the "problem" as they did?

2. What is the effect of the quotations in "Testimonials from Recruit Training"? What do they contribute to the proposal? What impact do you think they are intended to have on the audience?

3. The Web site tells readers that "Leadership and personal character are among the greatest benefits to becoming a marine. These traits not only assure your success within the Corps—they ensure success throughout life." But then it goes on to describe some more tangible benefits, such as pay, health insurance, vacation, and educational funding. Considering the authors' target audience, how important is this information, compared to the rest of the information on the site?

4. How do the images contribute to the message? How do they appeal to readers' emotions?

You can view the entire Marine Corps recruiting site at **www.marines.com.**

U.S. ARMED FORCES: UNITED STATES MARINE CORPS RECRUITMENT

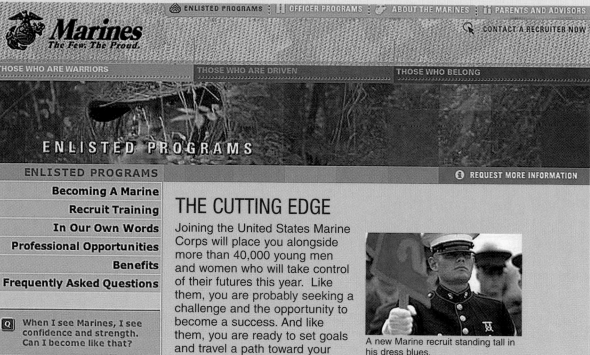

ENLISTED PROGRAMS : OFFICER PROGRAMS : ABOUT THE MARINES : PARENTS AND ADVISORS

Marines
The Few. The Proud.

CONTACT A RECRUITER NOW

THOSE WHO ARE WARRIORS   THOSE WHO ARE DRIVEN   THOSE WHO BELONG

ENLISTED PROGRAMS

ENLISTED PROGRAMS

REQUEST MORE INFORMATION

Becoming A Marine

Recruit Training

In Our Own Words

Professional Opportunities

Benefits

Frequently Asked Questions

Q When I see Marines, I see confidence and strength. Can I become like that?

Answer

THE CUTTING EDGE

Joining the United States Marine Corps will place you alongside more than 40,000 young men and women who will take control of their futures this year. Like them, you are probably seeking a challenge and the opportunity to become a success. And like them, you are ready to set goals and travel a path toward your destiny.

A new Marine recruit standing tall in his dress blues.

On the way to becoming a Marine, you will be trained in the art of self-mastery, acquiring self-discipline, the courage to undertake difficult tasks, and a steadfast commitment to overcoming the challenges before you. More than that, you will become part of a very special organization built on a foundation of honor, courage and commitment. At the core of every Marine is the warrior spirit, a person imbued with the special kind of personal character that has defined greatness and success for centuries. And in this organization, you will be regarded as family.

ENLISTED PROGRAMS | OFFICER PROGRAMS | ABOUT THE MARINES | PARENTS AND ADVISORS

CONTACT A RECRUITER NOW

THOSE WHO ARE WARRIORS   THOSE WHO ARE DRIVEN   THOSE WHO BELONG

BECOMING A MARINE

REQUEST MORE INFORMATION

ENLISTED PROGRAMS

- **Becoming A Marine**
- Delayed Entry Program
- **Recruit Training**
- **In Our Own Words**
- **Professional Opportunities**
- **Benefits**
- **Frequently Asked Questions**

Q I like the idea of being a Marine, but I'm afraid I'm not tough enough to be one. Should I forget the whole thing?

Answer

BECOMING A MARINE

The challenges associated with becoming a Marine are significant. But if you possess the will and determination to successfully overcome the obstacles that stand between you and the title of Marine, you'll have something no one can ever take away. You'll have the courage and the skills to face all of life's challenges.

Marines are devoted to both country and Corps.

A recruiter will meet you in order to understand your needs and goals and will show you the many ways the Marine Corps can help you to accomplish both. When you decide to become a Marine, you will agree to a Term of Enlistment (TOE), generally between 4 and 6 years, and then enter the Delayed Entry Program that will allow you to reserve your departure for training for up to one year. Your recruiter will help you to uncover careers, technical skills and educational opportunities that support your goals. Initial screening, a physical examination and aptitude test establish your eligibility for various programs.

Upon successful completion of Recruit Training, Marines begin Military Occupational Specialties (MOS) training.

Following MOS training, Marines are stationed to a variety of duty assignments and locations while continuing to serve Corps and country for the duration of their term of enlistment.

U.S. ARMED FORCES: UNITED STATES MARINE CORPS RECRUITMENT

TESTIMONIALS FROM RECRUIT TRAINING

Hear what Marines have to say about their experiences before, during and after Recruit Training.

"Before I came to boot camp there were things that I've done here that I never thought I'd be able to do in my life. It is tough, and it is hard. They do demand a lot out of you, but everything they do is for a reason."
- Andrew T.

A transformation: From the unknown to the invincible.

"I was really nervous when I first got here. I was scared. Before I didn't have any confidence at all. It was the greatest experience I ever had in my life. I'm a lot more confident in myself than when I first came here."
- Heather C.

There are no limits to what you'll find. In yourself.

"I knew that once I did finish and complete I'd have something that no one could ever take away from me."
- Alan B.

"It was a bit more than I expected. Easily the hardest thing I have ever done from start to finish, and I'm thrilled to death that I got through boot camp."
- Matthew F.

"Before I came here I'd always second guess my abilities. Now I'm given a task, I just go out and do it and I know I can do it well."
- Kevin O

"If you can get through this training, you can get through anything."
- Karli R.

ENLISTED PROGRAMS | OFFICER PROGRAMS | ABOUT THE MARINES | PARENTS AND ADVISORS

CONTACT A RECRUITER NOW

THOSE WHO ARE WARRIORS   THOSE WHO ARE DRIVEN   THOSE WHO BELONG

MARINE BENEFITS

REQUEST MORE INFORMATION

ENLISTED PROGRAMS

- Becoming A Marine
- Recruit Training
- In Our Own Words
- Professional Opportunities
- Benefits
- Educational Opportunities
- Frequently Asked Questions

Q Being a Marine sounds like a round-the-clock thing. Do Marines ever get down time?

Answer

MARINE BENEFITS

Leadership and personal character are among the greatest benefits to becoming a Marine. These traits not only assure your success within the Corps – they ensure success throughout life.

In addition, you and your family members are well provided for with a competitive salary and benefits, as well as medical and dental insurance. Upon enlistment, you will receive a regular Marine Corps salary, scaled according to your rank. During Recruit Training, your salary will be calculated at the Private level.

Marines enjoying some downtime

You and your family will have medical insurance for as long as you remain in the service of the U.S. government. If you remain in the Marine Corps through retirement, your medical benefits will extend throughout your lifetime and that of your spouse.

You will receive 30 days paid vacation each year. On-base shopping is tax-free at shopping outlets with substantial discounts on name-brand items. In addition, bases have fitness centers, swimming pools and recreational facilities. Life insurance is provided to all Marine personnel.

Housing on base is included as part of the compensation package. If you are married and would like to live off base, a monthly housing allowance will be provided. The Marine Corps pays all travel and expenses for required moves.

A generous retirement plan is available for those who qualify. For instance, a 20-year career in the Marine Corps will often result in retirement in your 40s. In addition to continuing commissary and post-exchange privileges, military members are often eligible for low interest loans by many banks.

Mirror, Mirror on the Wall . . . Are Muscular Men the Best of All?

(MAGAZINE ARTICLE)

Nancy Clark

Nancy Clark is a nutrition consultant for both casual exercisers and competitive athletes. She published this article in *American Fitness,* a magazine published by Aerobics and Fitness Association of America, the largest organization of the fitness professionals.

Analyzing and Connecting

Return to these questions after you have finished reading.

1. In paragraph 2, the author, Nancy Clark, cites a study that concludes young men are highly influenced by media images. In your experience do you believe that the media has that much influence? Think of examples pro and con.

2. In "Barbie's Body May Be Perfect, but Critics Remind Us It's Plastic" (see pages 335–338), Angela Cain argues that Barbie's thin waist, thin thighs, and long legs remain the ideal body image for women, reinforced by models on television and magazine covers and a multitude of media images. Less than 2 percent of women, however, have the genes to achieve this image. Cain cites studies that conclude most women don't like what they see in the mirror. Do body issues differ with gender?

3. The solution proposed is media education. If media images are the problem, then how effectively can media be the solution?

4. How does the fact that Americans are the most obese people on the planet jibe with the fitness obsession? Are these facts two sides of the same coin? Explain.

Mirror, mirror on the wall ...are muscular men the best of all?

The hidden turmoil of muscle dysmorphia – Nutrition

BY NANCY CLARK

MUSCLE DYSMORPHIA IS A NEW SYNDROME EMERGING BEHIND GYM DOORS. You might notice it in your gym's weight room. Some weightlifters pathologically believe their muscles are too small. They have poor body image (i.e., are ashamed of, embarrassed by and unhappy with their bodies) and a passionate desire to not only build muscle, but also avoid gaining fat. This preoccupation with building muscles manifests itself in excessive weightlifting (e.g., spending four or more hours per day at the gym), attention to diet (e.g., consuming protein shakes on a rigid schedule), time spent "body-checking" (e.g., looking in mirrors, CDs, window reflections, etc.), excessively weighing themselves (i.e., 10 to 20 times per day), too little time spent with family

and friends and, not uncommonly, anabolic steroid use.

Is this overconcern with body size a new obsession? Perhaps. In the past few years, we have been increasingly exposed to half-naked, muscular male bodies (e.g., Calvin Klein underwear ads). Evidently, even brief exposure to these images can affect a man's view of his body. In a study of the media's effect on male body image, a group of college men viewed advertisements featuring muscular men, while another group viewed neutral advertisements without partially naked male bodies. Then, the men (unaware of the hypothesis being tested) were given a body image assessment. Those exposed to the muscular images showed a significantly greater discrepancy between the body they ideally want to have and their current body size (Leit, Gray and Pope 2002). Another study suggests up to a third of teenage boys are trying to gain weight to be stronger, fitter, attain a better body image and perform better in sports (O'Dea and Rawstone 2001).

The irony is while college-age men believe a larger physique is more attractive to the opposite sex, women report desiring a normal-sized body. In a study of men from the United States, Austria and France, the subjects were shown a spectrum of body images and asked to choose:

- the body they felt represented their own
- the body they would ideally like to have
- the body of an average man their age and
- the male body they felt women preferred.

The men chose an ideal male body that was about 28 pounds more muscular than their current bodies. They also reported believing women prefer a male body with 30 pounds more muscle than they currently possessed. Yet, an accompanying study indicated women actually preferred an ordinary male body without added muscle (Pope 2000).

At the 2003 Massachusetts Eating Disorders Association's (MEDA) annual conference, Dr. Roberto Olivardia shared his research on adolescent boys' body image. Olivardia is a psychology instructor at Harvard Medical School and co-author of *The Adonis Complex: The Secret Crisis of Male Body Obsession* (Free Press, 2000). The title alludes to Adonis, the Greek god who exemplifies ideal masculine beauty and desire of all women. Olivardia

explained that adolescence is a time for exploring "Who am I?" Without a doubt, so much of who a teen is, is defined by his body. Because today's boys have been exposed from day one to GI Joe action figures, Hulk Hogan and Nintendo's Duke Nukem, they have relentlessly received strong messages that muscular bodies are desirable. Those at risk for muscle dysmorphia include adolescent boys who were teased as children about being too fat or short. Individuals at highest risk are those who base their self-esteem solely on their appearance."

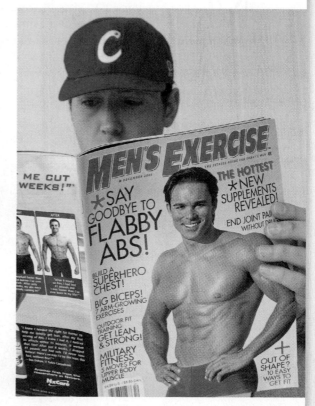

In our society, muscularity is commonly associated with masculinity. According to Olivardia, compared to ordinary men, muscular men tend to command more respect and are deemed more powerful, threatening and sexually virile. Muscular men perceive others as "backing off" and "taking them seriously." Not surprisingly, men's desire for muscles has manifested itself in a dramatic increase in muscle (and penile) implants.

Olivardia expressed concern the "bigger is better" mindset can often lead to anabolic steroid use. He cited statistics from a study with 3,400 high school male seniors: 6.6 percent reported having used steroids; more than two thirds of that group started before age 16 (Buckley et al. 1988). Olivardia regrets males commonly use steroids in secrecy and shame. "Men will tell someone they use cocaine before they admit to using 'juice.'" This commonly keeps them from seeking help.

Steroids carry with them serious medical concerns: breast enlargement, impotence, ache, mood swings, risk of heart disease, prostate cancer, liver damage and AIDS (from sharing needles)—not to mention sudden death, although it may occur 20 years from current use. "Roid rage," the fierce temper that contributes to brutal murders and violence against women, is an immediate danger.

What's the solution? According to Olivardia, young men need education about realistic body size to correct the distorted thought "if some muscle is good, then more must be better." They might also need treatment for obsessive-compulsive disorder. Sadly, most men believe they are the only ones with this problem and, thereby, take a long time to admit needing therapy. When they do, too few programs exist to help them explore the function this obsession serves in their lives—a sense of control. They mistakenly believe control over their bodies equates to control over their lives.

If you are a male struggling with dysmorphia, read *The Adonis Complex: The Secret Crisis of Male Body Obsession* and other books available at **www.gurze.com**. A Web search on "muscle dysmorphia" can also yield hundreds of articles with helpful information. Most importantly, know you are not alone—seek help and find peace.

REFERENCES

Buckley, W.E., et al. "Estimated prevalence of anabolic steroid use in high school seniors." JAMA, 260 (1988): 3441–5.

Leit, R.A., Gray, J.J. and Pope, H.G. "The media's representation of the ideal male body: A cause for muscle dysmorphia?" Int'l. J. Eating Disorders, 31 (April 2002): 334–8.

O'Dea, J.A. and Rawstone, P. "Male adolescents identify their weight gain practices, reasons for desired weight gain, and source of weight gain information." J. Am. Diel. Assoc. 101, no. 1 (January 2001): 105–7.

Pope, H.J., et al. "Body image perception among men in three countries." Am. J. Psychiatry, 157 (August 2000): 1297–301.

How to write an argument for change

These steps for the process of writing an argument for change may not progress as neatly as this chart might suggest. Writing is not an assembly-line process.

As you write and revise, imagine that you are in a conversation with an audience that contains people who both agree and disagree with you. Think about what you would say to both and speak to these diverse readers.

1 IDENTIFY THE PROBLEM

- Identify the problem, what causes it, and whom it affects.

- Describe what has been done or not done to address the problem.

- Make a claim advocating a specific change or course of action. Put the claim in this form: We should (or should not) do _____.

2 PROPOSE YOUR SOLUTION

- State your solution as specifically as you can.

- Consider other solutions and describe why your solution is better.

- Examine if the solution will have enough money and support to be implemented.

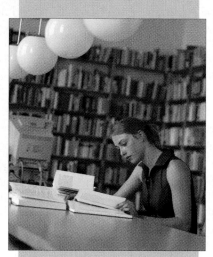

Do background research

What has been written about the problem?

What other solutions have been proposed?

Where have other solutions been effective or ineffective?

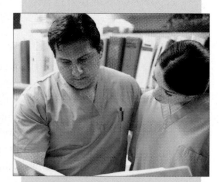

Analyze your potential readers

Whom are you writing for?

How interested will your readers be in this problem?

How would your solution benefit them directly and indirectly?

3 WRITE A DRAFT

- Define the problem. Give the background your readers will need.

- Discuss other possible solutions.

- Present your solution.

- Argue that your proposal will work.

- Conclude with a call for action.

- Write a title that will interest readers.

- Include any neccessary images, tables, or graphics.

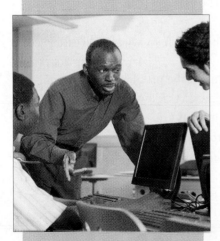

Participate in peer review, meet with your instructor, or visit your writing center.

4 REVISE, REVISE, REVISE

- Recheck that your proposal fulfills the assignment.

- Make sure that your proposal claim is clear and focused.

- Add detail or further explanation about the problem.

- Add detail or further explanation about how your solution addresses the problem.

- Make sure you have considered other solutions and explain why yours is better.

- Examine your organization and think of possible better ways to organize.

- Review the visual presentation of your report for readability and maximum impact.

- Proofread carefully.

5 SUBMITTED VERSION

- Make sure your finished writing meets all formatting requirements.

1: Identify the problem

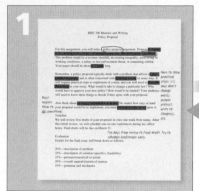

Analyze the assignment

- Read your assignment slowly and carefully. Look for the key words *propose* or *problem* and *solution*. These key words tell you that you are writing a proposal.
- Highlight any information about the length specified, date due, formatting, and other requirements. You can attend to this information later. At this point you want to zero in on the subject and your proposal claim.

Identify the problem

- What exactly is the problem?
- Who is most affected by the problem?
- What causes the problem?
- Has anyone tried to do anything about it? If so, why haven't they succeeded?
- What is likely to happen in the future if the problem isn't solved?

Do background research in online and print library sources, Web sources, government documents, experts in the field, and possibly field research such as a survey

- What has been written about the problem?
- What other solutions have been proposed?
- Where have other solutions been effective?
- Where have other solutions failed?

Make a proposal claim

- Proposal claims advocate a specific change or course of action. Put the claim in this form: We should (or should not) do _____.

WRITE NOW

Make an idea map

When you have a number of ideas and facts about a topic, write them on sticky notes. Then post the sticky notes and move them around, so you can begin to see how they might fit together. When you find an organization that suits your subject, make a working outline from your sticky notes.

PROBLEM:
Citizens of the United States born in another country cannot run for president

EXCEPTION:
Foreign-born citizens whose parents are American citizens

REQUIRED:
2/3s majority of Congress and 2/3s of state legislatures must approve

SOLUTION:
Amend the U.S. Constitution to allow foreign-born American citizens to run for and serve as the president of the United States

HOW WOULD IT WORK?
Grass-roots campaign

WHO WOULD SUPPORT?
Probably Asian Americans, Mexican Americans, and other recent immigrant groups

WHO WOULD OPPOSE?
1) politicians afraid of angering voters
2) Americans who are afraid of foreigners

HOW LONG WOULD IT TAKE?
Probably years because of the approval process

PRO ARGUMENTS
1) Fairness
2) America's image of itself as a land of opportunity

COUNTERARGUMENT
Point out that foreign born doesn't mean untrustworthy

Writer at work

Kim Lee was asked to write a proposal argument for her Rhetoric and Writing course. Upon receiving the assignment, she made the following notes and observations.

RHE 306 Rhetoric and Writing
Policy Proposal

Change an old policy or make a new one.

For this assignment, you will write a policy proposal argument. Propose a change to an existing policy or law, or propose a new law, that will correct a problem. This problem might be a revenue shortfall, an existing inequality, poor living or working conditions, a safety or law-enforcement threat, or something similar. Your paper should be about 5–7 pages long.

Remember, a policy proposal typically deals with a problem that affects a large number of people, and is often concerned with bettering society in some way. It will require practical steps to implement of course, and you will need to describe these steps in your essay. What would it take to change a particular law? Who would have to approve your new policy? How would it be funded? Your audience will need to know these things to decide if they agree with your proposal.

have to show practical steps. U.S. laws don't change unless people protest, write to Congress, etc.

Must inspire them to do something.

Also think about moving your audience to action. No matter how easy or hard your proposal would be to implement, you must persuade people to act upon it.

Timeline
We will review first drafts of your proposals in class one week from today. After this initial review, we will schedule one-on-one conferences during my office hours. Final drafts will be due on March 31.

Ten days from review to final draft. Try to schedule conference early.

Evaluation
Grades for the final essay will break down as follows:

20%—description of problem
25%—description of solution (specifics, feasibility)
25%—persuasiveness/call to action
20%—overall support/citation of sources
10%—grammar and mechanics

Read the assignment closely
Kim Lee began by highlighting key words in the assignment and noting specifics about the length and due date.

Choose a topic
Kim listed possible topics and then considered the strengths and weaknesses of each. She chose one that could be developed adequately and could motivate her audience.

Plan research strategies
Kim made a list of possible sources of information to begin her research.

POSSIBLE TOPICS
— Create a standardized form of testing for steroid use in all American sports (professional, educational, recreational).

> Might be too broad. Also, the science involved might be hard to explain in 5–7 pages

— Move the U.S. capital to Nashville, Tennessee.

> Too regional?

— Amend the Constitution to allow foreign-born American citizens (or naturalized citizens) to serve as president of the United States.

An issue of fair treatment.
Good for motivating audience.

*

— Revitalize Youngstown, Ohio, by building a tourist trade around its previous Mafioso reputation as "Little Chicago." Could give lots of specific steps (funding, building plans, tourist info).

— Reformulate the means by which the Corporation for Public Broadcasting receives federal funds. Would be very dry, though T.V. shows like Sesame Street could be used to provoke interest/make people want to act.

To Do:
— Search Internet for current discussion on this topic. What kinds of sites are discussing the "natural-born" clause? AmendforArnold.com, Orin Hatch.
— Search periodicals for discussions of this topic.
— Search academic and law journals for more sophisticated discussions.
— Any books???
— What groups (political, ideological) are discussing this right now?

2: Propose your solution

State your solution as specifically as you can

- What exactly do you want to achieve?
- How exactly will your solution work?
- Can it be accomplished quickly, or will it have to be phased in over a few years?
- Has anything like it been tried elsewhere?
- Who will be involved?
- Can you think of any reasons why your solution might not work?
- How will you address those arguments?
- Can you think of any ways of strengthening your proposed solution in light of those possible criticisms?

Consider other solutions

- What other solutions have been or might be proposed for this problem, including doing nothing?
- What are the advantages and disadvantages of those solutions?
- Why is your solution better?

Examine the feasibility of your solution

- How easy is your solution to implement?
- Will the people who will be most affected be willing to go along with it? (For example, lots of things can be accomplished if enough people volunteer, but groups often have difficulty getting enough volunteers to work without pay.)
- If it costs money, how do you propose paying for it?
- Who is most likely to reject your proposal because it is not practical enough?
- How can you convince your readers that your proposal can be achieved?

Analyze your potential readers

- Whom are you writing for?
- How interested will your readers be in this problem?
- How much does this problem affect them?
- How would your solution benefit them directly and indirectly?

STAYING ON TRACK

Acknowledging other points of view

Write for readers who may disagree with you

Proposal arguments that ignore other points of view and other possible solutions tend to convince only those who agree with you before you start writing. Your goal is to convince those who haven't thought about the problem and those who might disagree at the outset but can be persuaded. Think about why readers might disagree.

- Are they misinformed about the problem? If so, you will need to provide accurate information.
- Do they have different assumptions about the problem? If so, can you show them that your assumptions are better?
- Do they share your goals but think your solution is not the right one? If so, you will need to explain why your solution is better.

You might have to do some research to find out the views of others. If you are writing about a local problem, you may need to talk to people.

Deal fairly with other solutions and other points of view

OFF TRACK

Free tuition for all state high school graduates who attend state colleges is an idea too ridiculous to consider.
(No reason is given for rejecting an alternative solution, and those who propose it are insulted.)

ON TRACK

Free tuition for all state high school graduates is a desirable solution to get more students to attend college, but is not likely to be implemented because of the cost. A solution targeted to low-income students similar to the HOPE scholarship program in Georgia, which is funded by state lottery money, could be implemented in our state.
(The author offers a reason for rejecting an alternative solution and proposes a solution that has some common ground with the alternative.)

Writer at work

Kim Lee began laying out her proposal by first stating her solution as specifically as possible. She used the following list of questions to guide her proposal argument.

<u>PROPOSAL:</u> Amend the U.S. Constitution to allow foreign-born American citizens to run for and serve as the president of the United States.

- **How exactly will my solution work?**

Through a nonpartisan grassroots campaign, we will work to pressure members of the U.S. Congress to propose the following amendment. Ultimately, this proposal is both for the people of the United States and the governmental body.

- **Can it be accomplished quickly, or will it have to be phased in over a few years?**

This is a tricky area. An amendment such as lowering the voting age to 18 during the Vietnam War did pass within four months. It often takes at least a couple years to work a proposed amendment through Congress.

- **Who will be involved?**

This will have to be a two-front battle. (1) the American people (specifically underrepresented voting blocks such as Asian Americans, Mexican Americans, etc., who are most directly affected by the limitations put forth by the current regulation. (2) the members of the United States Congress.

- **Are any reasons why my solution might not work?**

This has been brought up a number of times and never really gotten very far. It is a hot-button topic, especially as related to national security. Congressmen/women may not want to ruffle their constituents who may see this as a national threat and direct decrease in their own personal rights.

- **How will I address those arguments?**

Through pointing out the faulty logic which states foreign born=shifty and natural-born=patriotic.

- **Can I think of any ways of strengthening my proposed solution in light of those possible criticisms?**

I believe the strength in this is pointing to the (a) contradictions that exist between the rule and the governing notion of the United States as "melting pot," "land of freedom," and "a land where everyone can grow up to be president." The heart of this argument is to drive home its illogical nature, highlight contradictions in its logic, and include stipulations which ensure that the individual who is running for president is not merely a drop-in from another country.

<u>OTHER SOLUTIONS</u>
- Solutions that have been discussed recently seem to differ in the length of required residence.

Not necessarily disadvantages, but have been ineffective in achieving the goal.
It comes from the people and not in support of one candidate, but an idea.

<u>FEASIBILITY</u>
- How easy is my solution to implement?

    It all depends on the people's ability to move Congress to action.

- Will the people who will be most affected be willing to go along with it?

    I believe the answer is yes.

- How will we pay for it?

Again, grass roots political fundraising. A major source may be ethic/immigrant groups, etc.
- Who is most likely to reject my proposal because it is not practical enough?

Most likely (a) politicians who see support of the change as a threat to their positions (due to voter dissent) and (b) citizens who live in a state of fear.

- How can I convince my readers that my proposal can be achieved?

    It must be proposed as being about the people and their ability to enact change.
    It is about empowerment.

<u>POTENTIAL READERS</u>
- Whom am I writing for?

    American people (specifically the immigrant population).

- How interested will my readers be in this problem?

It is currently a hot topic and hopefully making it more personally relevant will peak interest (not just about Governor Schwarzenegger).

- How much does this problem affect them?

    Withholds a basic right for them and their children.

- How would my solution benefit them directly and indirectly?

Directly, it allows for naturalized citizens to run for president (or vice president).
Indirectly, it fosters a sense of pride in one's ethnic identity and helps (through visibility and legislative legitimacy) to create an image of diversity and success.

3: Write a draft

Define the problem

- Set out the issue or problem. If the problem is local, you might begin by telling about your experience or the experience of someone you know. You might need to argue for the seriousness of the problem, and you might have to give some background on how it came about.

Present your solution

- Describe other solutions that have been attempted and others that are possible. Explain why other solutions either don't solve the problem or are unrealistic.

- Make clear the goals of your solution. Many solutions cannot solve problems completely.

- Describe in detail the steps in implementing your solution and how they will solve the problem you have identified. You can impress your readers by the care with which you have thought through this problem.

- Explain the positive consequences that will follow from your proposal. What good things will happen and what bad things will be avoided if your proposal is implemented?

Argue that your solution can be done

- Your proposal for solving the problem is a truly good idea only if it can be put into practice. If people have to change the ways they are doing things now, explain why they would want to change. If your proposal costs money, you need to identify exactly where the money would come from.

Conclude with a call for action

- Make a call for action. You should put your readers in a position such that if they agree with you, they will take action. You might restate and emphasize what exactly they need to do.

Writer at work

Here is the outline upon which Kim Lee built the first draft of her proposal essay.

I. SET UP PROBLEM
  A. Story about son not being able to run
  B. Statistics
  C. Why it goes beyond just the hype

II. BACKGROUND
  A. Historical
      1. How this came about
      2. What is the historical logic behind it
  B. Current - Arnold

III. PROPOSAL
  A. Why
      1. Nation built on the melting pot
      2. Why now > improved image
      3. What have foreign-born Americans achieved
      4. Who has it barred
      5. Haven't we learned anything from past biases
          a. Gitmo and Japanese American internment
          b. Natural-born traitors
      6. Tie to raising of voting age during Vietnam War
      7. Not a threat
  B. What
      1. Remove the "natural-born" clause
      2. Replace that clause with a different stipulation for president
          a. Must have been living in residence of the United States for at least 25 years
          b. Preserves the spirit of the clause
  C. How to do so in the most efficient and secure fashion
      1. Grassroots campaign to effect change with men and women of Congress
          a. We elect them
          b. Make this a major issue
          c. Use the minority voices who are often marginalized
      2. Ultimately it must be driven to Congress while keeping voices heard
  D. The actual governmental process

IV. CONCLUSION
  A. This will provide hope for the disenfranchised
  B. This will right an illogical wrong
  C. This will not place the country at risk
  D. This will create role models
  E. This will be one more step toward making this country what it professes to be

4: Revise, revise, revise

Take a break from your writing and come back to it with "fresh eyes." When you return, imagine you are someone who has never seen your proposal before. Read the proposal out loud. When you are done, ask yourself: Do I understand the problem? Does it really seem like a problem that must be dealt with? Is the solution clear? Does it seem like it is worth the trouble? Do I think it will really work? How much will it cost me, in money, effort, or inconvenience? The biggest trap you can fall into is starting off with the little stuff first. Leave the small stuff for last.

Does your paper or project meet the assignment?

- Look again at your assignment. Does your paper or project do what the assignment asks?
- Look again at the assignment for specific guidelines, including length, format, and amount of research. Does your work meet these guidelines?

Is the proposal claim clear and focused?

- Does the proposal claim address the problem?
- Does the proposal claim issue a clear call to action?

Do you identify the problem adequately?

- Do you need more evidence that the problem exists and is a serious concern?
- Will your readers find credible any sources you include? Can you think of other sources that might be more persuasive?

Is it clear how your solution will address the problem?

- Can you find more evidence that your solution will resolve the problem?
- Do you address potential objections to your solution?
- Do you provide evidence that your solution is feasible? For example, if your solution requires money, where will the money come from?

Do you consider alternative solutions?	• Do you explain why your solution is better than the alternatives?
Is your organization effective?	• Is the order of your main points clear to your reader? • Are there any places where you find abrupt shifts or gaps? • Are there sections or paragraphs that could be rearranged to make your draft more effective?
Is your introduction effective?	• Can you get off to a faster start, perhaps with a striking example? • Can you think of a better way to engage your readers to be interested in the problem you identify? • Does your introduction give your readers a sense of why the problem is important?
Is your conclusion effective?	• Does your conclusion have a call for action? • Do you make it clear exactly what you want your readers to do?
Do you represent yourself effectively?	• To the extent you can, forget for a moment that you wrote what you are reading. What impression do you have of you, the writer? • Does "the writer" create an appropriate tone? • Has "the writer" done his or her homework?
Is the writing project visually effective?	• Is the font attractive and readable? • Is the overall layout attractive and readable? • If headings are used, do they make clear what comes under each of them? • Is each photograph, chart, graph, map, or table clearly labeled? Does each visual have a caption?
Save the editing for last	When you have finished revising, edit and proofread carefully.

A peer review guide is on page 31.

Writer at work

During peer review of her paper with fellow classmates, and in her meeting with her instructor, Kim Lee made notes on her rough draft. She used these comments to guide her revision of the essay.

The history of the United States of America is punctuated with rhetoric which positions the nation as one which embraces diversity and creates a land of equal opportunity for all of those who choose to live here. As the Statue of Liberty cries out "bring us your tired, your poor, your huddled masses yearning to breathe free," American politicians gleefully use such images to frame the United States a bastion for all things good, fair, and equal. As a proud American, however, I must nonetheless point out one of the cracks in this façade of equality (and that is without even mentioning the repeated failed ratification of the women's Equal Rights Amendment). What flaw could this be? Any foreign-born person with foreign parents is not eligible to be elected our president, even if that person became an American as a baby through adoption.

> *Opening sentence is too clunky. Need something more engaging.*

> *Stay focused. Don't ask unnecessary questions. Give an example.*

The 2003 election of action film star Arnold Schwarzenegger to the gubernatorial seat in California stirred up a drive for a change to this Constitutional statute. Politicians such as Senator Orrin Hatch (R-Utah) and grassroots campaigns such as the group Amend for Arnold appear to dream of reading the political slogans of the Terminator-cum-president's campaign ("I'll be back (for four more years") or "Hasta la vista, baby (and hasta la vista to high taxes)". Consequently, they have been vocally pushing for an amendment that would alter this element of the qualifications for president.

We as a nation must take this time to take a stand against this discriminatory and antiquated aspect of the Constitution.

> *Transition—the info on Schwrz. does not lead naturally into the renewed call for change. Need a link to show the relationship between this info and my proposal.*

Look for ways to focus

Kim Lee responded to suggestions from her teacher and her peers to make her opening paragraph less wordy and better focused on her main point. She removed material that did not obviously inform readers about the problem she was interested in.

Check transitions

She also worked on strengthening transitions between paragraphs.

Read your paper aloud

Finally, Kim Lee read her essay aloud to check for misspelled words, awkward phrasing, and other mechanical problems.

STAYING ON TRACK

Reviewing your draft

Give yourself plenty of time for reviewing your draft. For detailed information on how to participate in a peer review, how to review it yourself, and how to respond to comments from your classmates, your instructor, or a campus writing consultant, see pages 29–32.

Some good questions to ask yourself when reviewing an argument for change

- Do you connect the problem to your readers? Even if the problem doesn't affect them directly, at the very least you should appeal to their sense of fairness.
- Can you explain more specifically how your solution will work?
- If resources including people and money are required for your solution, can you elaborate where these resources will come from?
- Do you include other possible solutions and discuss the advantages and disadvantages of each? Can you add to this discussion?
- Does your conclusion connect with the attitudes and values of your readers in addition to making clear what you want them to do? Can you add an additional point? Can you sharpen your call to action?

5: Submitted version

Kim Lee

Professor Patel

RHE 306

31 March 2006

Let's Make It a Real Melting Pot with Presidential Hopes for All

The image the United States likes to advertise is a country that embraces diversity and creates a land of equal opportunity for all. As the Statue of Liberty cries out "give me your tired, your poor, your huddled masses yearning to breathe free," American politicians gleefully evoke such images to frame the United States a bastion for all things good, fair, and equal. As a proud American, however, I must nonetheless highlight one of the cracks in this façade of equality. Imagine an infertile couple decides to adopt an orphaned child from China. They follow all of the legal processes deemed necessary by both countries. They fly abroad and bring home their (once parentless) six-month-old baby boy. They raise and nurture him, and while teaching him to embrace his ethnicity, they also teach him to love Captain Crunch, baseball, and The Three Stooges. He grows and eventually attends an ethnically diverse American public school. One day in the fifth grade his teacher tells the class that anyone can grow up to be president. To clarify her point, she turns to the boy, knowing his background, and states, "No, you could not be president, Stu, but you could still be a senator. That's something to aspire to!" How do these parents explain this rule to this American-raised child? This scenario will become increasingly common. Senator Larry Craig of Idaho states that Americans adopt over 25,000 foreign-born children annually (Epstein A5). As the Constitution currently reads, only "natural-born" citizens may run for the offices of president and vice president. Neither these children nor the thousands of hardworking Americans who chose to make America their official homeland may aspire to the highest political position in the land. While the huddled masses may enter, it appears they must retain a second-class citizen ranking.

The "natural-born" stipulation regarding the presidency stems from the self-same meeting of minds which brought the American people the Electoral College. During the Constitutional Convention of 1787, the Congress formulated the regulatory measures associated with the office of the president. A letter sent from John Jay to George Washington during this period read as follows:

> "Permit me to hint," Jay wrote, "whether it would not be wise and seasonable to provide a strong check to the admission of foreigners into the administration of our national government; and to declare expressly that the Command in Chief of the American army shall not be given to, nor devolve on, any but a natural-born citizen." (Mathews A1)

Shortly thereafter, Article II, Section I, Clause V of the Constitution declared that "No Person except a natural born Citizen, or a Citizen of the United States at the time of the Adoption of this Constitution, shall be eligible to the Office of President." Jill A. Pryor states in The Yale Law Journal that "some writers have suggested that Jay was responding to rumors that foreign princes might be asked to assume the presidency" (881). Many cite disastrous examples of foreign rule in the eighteenth century are the impetus for the "natural born" clause. For example, in 1772—only fifteen years prior to the adoption of the statute—Poland had been divided up by Prussia, Russia, and Austria, (Kasindorf). Perhaps an element of self-preservation and not ethnocentrism led to the questionable stipulation. Nonetheless, in the twenty-first century this clause reeks of xenophobia.

The 2003 election of action film star Arnold Schwarzenegger as governor of California stirred up movement to change this Constitutional statute. Politicians such as Senators Orrin Hatch (R-Utah) and Ted Kennedy (D-Massachusetts and Arnold's uncle by marriage) have created a buzz for ratifying a would-be twenty-eighth amendment. In addition, grassroots campaigns like "Amend for Arnold" are trying to rally popular support as they dream of the Terminator-cum-president's political slogans ("I'll be back . . . for four more years" or "Hasta la vista, baby, and hasta la vista to high taxes"). Schwarzenegger has become the face—and the bulked-up body—of the viable naturalized president.

We as a nation should follow the lead set by those enamored of the action star, but distance the fight from this one extremely wealthy actor. We must instead take a stand against the discriminatory practice applied to all foreign-born American citizens by this obsolete provision of the Constitution. Congress has made minor attempts to update this biased clause. The Fourteenth Amendment clarified the difference between "natural-born" and "native born" citizens by spelling out the citizenship status of children born to American parents outside of the United States (Ginsberg 929). (Such a clause qualifies individuals such as Senator John McCain—born in Panama—for presidency.) This change is not enough. I propose that the United States abolish the "natural born" clause and replace it with a stipulation that allows naturalized citizens to run for president. This amendment would state that a candidate must have been naturalized and lived in residence in the United States for a period of at least twenty-five years. The present time is ideal for this change. This amendment could simultaneously honor the spirit of the Constitution, protect and ensure the interests of the United States, promote an international image of inclusiveness, and grant heretofore withheld rights to thousands of legal and loyal United States citizens.

In our push for change, we must make clear the importance of this amendment. It would not provide special rights for would-be terrorists. To the contrary, it would fulfill the longtime promises of the nation. The United States claims to allow all people to blend into the great stew of citizenship. It has already suffered embarrassment and international cries of ethnic bias as a result of political moves such as Japanese American internment and the Guantanamo Bay detention center. This amendment can help mend the national image as every American takes one more step toward equality. Naturalized citizens have been contributing to the United States for centuries. Many nameless Mexican, Irish, and Asian Americans sweated and toiled to build the American railroads. The public has welcomed naturalized Americans such as Bob

Hope, Albert Pujols, and Peter Jennings into their hearts and living rooms. Individuals such as German-born Henry Kissinger and Czechoslovakian-born Madeleine Albright have held high posts in the American government and served as respected aides to its presidents. The amendment must make clear that it is not about one man's celebrity. Approximately 700 foreign-born Americans have won the Medal of Honor and over 60,000 proudly serve in the United States military today (Siskind 5). The "natural-born" clause must be removed to provide each of these people—over half a million naturalized in 2003 alone—with equal footing to those who were born into citizenship rather than working for it (U.S. Census Bureau).

Since the passing of the Bill of Rights, only seventeen amendments have been ratified. This process takes time and overwhelming congressional and statewide support. To alter the Constitution, a proposed amendment must pass with a two-thirds "super-majority" in both the House of Representatives and the Senate. In addition, the proposal must find favor in two-thirds (thirty-eight) of state legislatures. In short, this task will not be easy. In order for this change to occur, a grassroots campaign must work to dispel misinformation regarding naturalized citizens and force the hands of senators and representatives wishing to retain their congressional seats. We must take this proposal to ethnicity-specific political groups from both sides of the aisle, business organizations, and community activist groups. We must convince representatives that this issue matters. Only through raising voices and casting votes can the people enact change. Only then can every American child see the possibility for limitless achievement and equality. Only then can everyone find the same sense of pride in the possibility for true American diversity in the highest office in the land.

Works Cited

Epstein, Edward. "Doubt About a Foreign-Born President." San Francisco Chronicle 6 Oct. 2004: A5.

Ginsberg, Gordon. "Citizenship: Expatriation: Distinction Between Naturalized and Natural Born Citizens." Michigan Law Review 50 (1952): (926-29). JSTOR. U of Texas Lib. 8 Mar. 2006 <http://www.jstor.org/>.

Mathews, Joe. "Maybe Anyone Can Be President." Los Angeles Times 2 Feb. 2005: A1.

Kasindorf, Martin. "Should the Constitution Be Amended for Arnold?" USA Today 2 Dec. 2004. 9 Mar. 2006 < http://www.usatoday.com/news/politicselections/2004-12-02-schwarzenegger-amendment_x.htm>.

Pryor, Jill A. "The Natural Born Citizen Clause and Presidential Eligibility: An Approach for Resolving Two Hundred Years of Uncertainty." The Yale Law Journal 97 (1988): 881-99.

Siskind, Lawrence J. "Why Shouldn't Arnold Run?" The Recorder 10 Dec. 2004: 5.

United States. Department of Commerce. Census Bureau. "Facts for Features: The Fourth of July." 27 June 2005. 9 Mar. 2006 < http://www.census.gov/Press-Release/www/releases/archives/facts_for_features_special_editions/004772.html>.

Projects

If you want to persuade your readers to do something, you must convince them that a problem exists and that something needs to be done about it. You'll likely make the best argument for change if the problem matters to you. Most groups and organizations are faced with problems. You'll be able to argue with conviction, and you might even bring about change.

The following projects will give you experience in the kinds of proposals frequent in the workplace and in public life.

PROPOSAL ESSAY

For an example of a proposal essay, see pages 496–499.

Write a proposal of 1000–1250 words (about five to seven double-spaced pages) that would solve a problem that you identify.

Choose a problem with which you have personal experience, but you should also think about how many other people this problem affects. Your proposal should take them into account as part of your audience.

Find out who would be in a position to enact your proposal. How can you make your solution seem like a good idea to these people?

Propose your solution as specifically as you can. What exactly do you want to achieve? How exactly will your solution work? Has anything like it been tried elsewhere? Who will be involved?

Consider other solutions that have been or might be proposed for this problem, including doing nothing. What are the advantages and disadvantages of those solutions? Why is your solution better?

Examine how easy your solution is to implement. Will the people most affected be willing to go along with it? Lots of things can be accomplished if enough people volunteer, but groups often have difficulty getting enough volunteers to work without pay. If it costs money, how do you propose paying for it?

RECONSTRUCTING A PROPOSAL

For an example proposal, see pages 507–512.

You may not have a lot of experience writing proposals. Nevertheless, proposals have had a profound impact on your life. Almost every program, law, policy, or business that affects you had to be proposed before it became a reality.

Think of some things in your life that were proposed by people: the building where you attended high school, for example. At some point, that building was proposed as a way of solving a certain problem—perhaps your town had one old, overflowing high school, and your building was proposed to solve the overcrowding. Its location was probably chosen carefully, to avoid causing more problems with traffic, and to ensure that it was easy for students to reach.

Choose something you are familiar with that went through a proposal process. Try to reconstruct the four components of the original proposal. What problem do you think people were trying to solve? How did concerns about fairness and feasibility shape the program, building, or policy?

Outline your re-created proposal in a page or two.

Ask yourself if this policy, program, or business truly solved the problem it was intended to solve? Clearly, the proposal itself was successful, for the school was built, the law was passed, or the business was started. But how successful was the proposed solution in reality?

TEAMWORK: COUNTERPROPOSALS

For an example of an alternative proposal, see pages 500–502.

Find a proposal argument that you and three or four classmates are interested in. This might be a proposal to widen a road in your town, to pass a law making English the official language of your state government, or something similar.

As a group discuss the four components of the proposal as outlined in this chapter: What is the problem being addressed? What is the solution? Is it workable and fair? Is it feasible?

Then have each person in the group construct a one- or two-page counterproposal. Your counterproposals should address the same problem as the original proposal, but should offer different solutions. Your analysis of the workability, fairness, and feasibility of the original proposal will help you shape your counterproposals. Is there a way to solve the problem that is cheaper? less disruptive? more fair? less risky?

Present your counterproposals to the rest of your group, and discuss which is the most appealing. You may find that a combination of elements of the different proposals ends up being the best.

Part 3

The Writer as Researcher

15

Planning Research

When you begin a research project in a college course, you need to understand the different kinds of possible research and to plan your strategy in advance.

Analyze the research task

If you have an assignment that requires research, look closely at what you are being asked to do. The assignment may ask you to review, compare, survey, analyze, evaluate, or prove that something is true or untrue. You may be writing for experts, for students like yourself, or for the general public. The purpose of your research and your potential audience will help guide your strategies for research.

The key is understanding what is expected of you. You are being asked to

1. Determine your goals.
2. Find a subject.
3. Ask a question about the subject.
4. Find out what has been said about this subject.
5. Make a contribution to the discussion about this subject.

Determine your goals

Often your assignment will tell you how to get started. Look for key words:

- An *analysis* or *examination* requires you to look at an issue in detail, explaining how it has evolved, who or what it affects, and what is at stake.
- A *survey* requires you to gather opinions about a particular issue, either by a questionnaire or by interviews.
- An *evaluation* requires you to make critical judgments.
- An *argument* requires you to assemble evidence in support of a claim you make.

Ask your instructor for guidance if you remain unsure what is expected.

Find a subject that interests you

When you ask meaningful questions, your research will be enjoyable. Your courses may give you some ideas about questions to ask. Personal experience is often a good source of questions related to your research topic: What was the cause of something that happened to you? Was your experience typical or atypical? How can you solve a problem you have? What do experts think about the issues that concern you? Working with a topic that has already aroused your curiosity makes it more likely that your findings will interest others.

A good way to begin is by browsing a subject directory, either in your library or on the Web. Subject directories can show you many different aspects of a single topic.

549

Ask a question

Often you'll be surprised by the amount of information your initial browsing uncovers. Your next task will be to identify in that mass of information a question for your research project. This researchable question will be the focus of the remainder of your research and ultimately of your research project or paper. Browsing on the topic of solid waste recycling might lead you to a researchable question such as

- Do cities save or lose money on recycling programs?
- Why can't all plastics be recycled?
- Are Americans being persuaded to recycle more paper, aluminum, and plastic?

Focus your research question

Think about how to make your research question specific enough so that you can treat it thoroughly in a paper. Reading about your subject will help you to focus your research question.

- Why did the number of tons of recycled plastic and glass in our city peak in 2002 and decline slightly ever since?
- Should our state mandate the use of degradable plastics that decay along with kitchen and yard waste in compost heaps?
- Besides paper bags that deplete forests, what are the alternatives to plastic bags that contaminate soil in landfills and sabotage the recycling system by jamming the machinery that sorts bottles and cans?

Determine what kinds of research you need to do

Once you have formulated a research question, begin thinking about what kind of research you will need to do to address the question.

Secondary research

Most researchers rely partly or exclusively on the work of others as sources of information. Research based on the work of others is called **secondary research**. In the past this information was contained almost exclusively in collections of print materials housed in libraries (see Chapter 16), but today enormous amounts of information are available through library databases (see Chapter 17) and the World Wide Web (see Chapter 18).

Primary research

Much of the research done in college creates new information through **primary research**: experiments, data-gathering surveys and interviews, detailed observations, and the examination of historical documents. Although some undergraduates do not do primary research, sometimes you may be researching a question that requires you to gather first-hand information. For example, if you are researching a campus issue such as the impact of a new library fee on students' budgets, you may need to conduct interviews, make observations, or take a survey (see Chapter 19).

Determine what you need

Is the scope of your issue...	Then research might include...
Local? (Inadequate bike lanes, local noise ordinances, school policies)	• interviews and observations • local newspapers • other local media: television, radio
Regional? (County taxes, toll road construction, watershed protection)	• some of the sources above • state government offices • regional organizations, clubs, or associations, e.g., the Newark Better Business Bureau, Brazos Valley Mothers Against Drunk Driving
National? (Federal agricultural subsidies, immigration, major league sports)	• some of the sources above • federal government offices • national organizations, clubs, or associations, e.g., the American Automobile Association • national network news on television and radio • national newspapers or magazines, e.g., such as the *New York Times* or *Rolling Stone*
International? (Trade imbalances, military conflicts, global climate change)	• some of the sources above • federal government offices • international agencies such as UNICEF • international news outlets such as Reuters • foreign newspapers or magazines like *Le Monde* and *der Spiegel*

You can also find sources you need by thinking about people affected by your issue. Where is your issue being discussed?

Who is interested in this issue?	Where would they read, write, talk, or hear about it?	In what different media might the information appear?
scientists teachers voters minors senior citizens policy makers stock brokers	scientific journals political journals scholarly journals newspapers books Web forums government documents	online television radio print film/DVD

Set a Schedule

Use your assignment, your personal schedule, and your knowledge of the sources you'll need to schedule your research. Allow yourself some large blocks of uninterrupted time, especially during the browsing stage.

Project: Research paper for a government course, analyzing a recent financial fraud

Days until first draft is due: 17

Days 1-3:
PRELIMINARY research, one hour each evening

Days 4-6:
IN-DEPTH library research—Schedule appointment with reference librarian for periodicals search tutorial

Days 7-9:
Go over collected material, think about research question/hypothesis

Days 10-12:
Begin drafting

Days 13-14:
Revise rough draft for clarity, organization, and ideas

Days 15-16:
Follow-up research or verify questionable sources as needed

Day 17:
Fine-tune draft

Project: Paper utilizing field research for an introduction to social research course

Weeks until project due: 7

Week 1:
Research and brainstorm topics; discuss short list of possible topics/methods with professor; make final decision

Week 2:
Research survey/interview methods; design appropriate method

Week 3:
Conduct field research

Week 4:
Analyze data and do follow-up if necessary

Week 5:
Draft paper—go back to library if necessary

Week 6:
Take draft to writing center; revise

Week 7:
Proofread, fine tune, and make sure all charts and images print correctly

Draft a working thesis

Once you have done some preliminary research into your question, you need to craft a working thesis. Perhaps you have found a lot of interesting material on the home economics movement of the 1950s and 60s. You have discovered that food companies—particularly makers of packaged foods—were deeply involved in shaping and funding the movement. As you research the question of why food companies fostered the home economics movement, a working thesis begins to emerge.

Write your topic, research question, and working thesis on a note card or sheet of paper. Keep your working thesis handy. You may need to revise it several times until the wording is precise. As you research, ask yourself, does this information tend to support my thesis? Information that does not support your thesis is still important! It may lead you to adjust your thesis, or even abandon it altogether. You may need to find another source or reason that shows your thesis is still valid.

TOPIC:

The Home Economics Movement of the 1950s and 60s.

RESEARCH QUESTION:

Why did the major American food corporations fund the Home Economics movement of the 50s and 60s?

WORKING THESIS:

Major American food corporations invested in the development and spread of Home Economics in order to create a ready market for their products by teaching women to rely on prepared foods instead of cooking "from scratch." They used Home Economics programs to change the way Americans thought about food and cooking.

WORKING TOGETHER

Determine what information you need

Select one of the possible topics below or identify a topic that will work for your assignment. Write a brief list or paragraph describing the types of research that might be used to investigate the question. What kinds of information would you need? Where would you look for it?

1 How much does an average American couple spend to adopt a child from overseas?

2 How have recent cuts in library funding affected students at your school?

3 How effective was drafting soldiers in the North and South during the Civil War?

4 Why does the U.S. Postal Service spend part of its budget to encourage stamp collecting?

553

How to plan research

When you receive a research assignment, your first instinct might be to start gathering information right away. If you take a little time to set goals, explore your subject, narrow your subject, and determine what you need, you will be more efficient in searching and you will obtain better results.

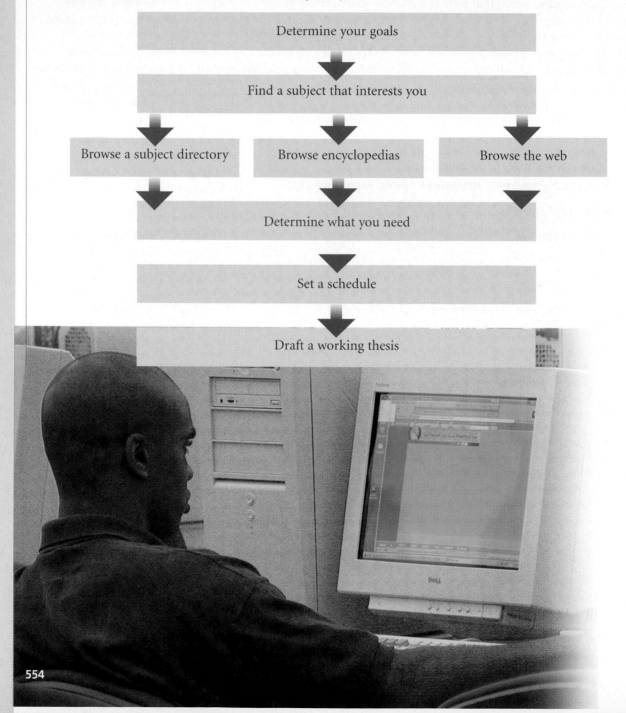

Determine your goals

Find a subject that interests you

Browse a subject directory | Browse encyclopedias | Browse the web

Determine what you need

Set a schedule

Draft a working thesis

Researcher at work

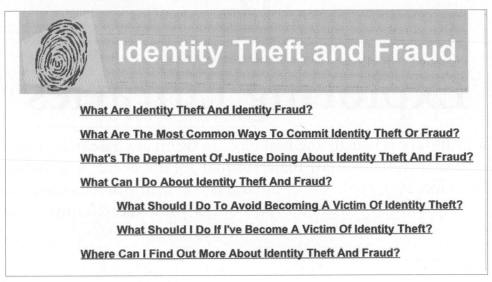

George Abukar chose the topic of identify theft because a friend's identify was stolen. He began his research for a proposal essay by finding informative Web sites on identity theft. On this Web site for the Department of Justice, he found information on current attempts to prevent and punish identity theft. George was interested in why identity theft was such a difficult crime to stop, and he came up with a short list of reasons.

- *technical weak spots in Internet transactions and storage of personal data*
- *vast scope of problem--so many people have information in electronic form and Internet makes it all accessible*
- *government's own advice for protecting against ID theft is unrealistic and ineffective*

This last reason intrigued George. He had a friend who had been an identity theft victim, and was interested in how her experience related to the national discussion of identity theft. After talking to his friend, he decided to look more closely at the way identity theft is handled by banks, credit card companies, and credit-reporting agencies. The researchable question he used to guide his search was

- *Could the companies that collect, use, and sell consumer information do more to prevent identity theft?*

After further research, George came to the conclusion that these companies could indeed do more to solve the identity theft problem. His research led him to frame the following working thesis for his paper:

- *Companies that traffic in consumers' personal data should be legally responsible if their negligence results in harm to the consumer.*

16

Exploring Libraries

Your library is usually the best place to begin any research project because it contains some materials that are not available anywhere else. Moreover, professional librarians will help you locate sources quickly so you get the most out of your research time.

Determine the print sources you need

You will have a hard time finding the information you need if you don't know what you're looking for. To guide you in your library research, think about these questions:

Who are the parties involved in the issue?
- Who are the experts?
- Who else is talking about it?
- Who is affected by the issue?

What is at stake?
- How or why does this issue matter?
- What stands to be gained or lost?
- Who is likely to benefit or suffer?

What kinds of arguments are being made about the issue?
- Are people making proposals?
- Are they trying to define terms?
- What kinds of reasons do they offer?
- What kinds of evidence is provided?
- What arguments are people not making that they could be making?

Who are the audiences for this debate?
- Do people already have strong opinions?
- Are they still trying to make up their minds?
- How well-informed are people about the issue?

Where is the issue being discussed?
- Is the issue being discussed in newspapers and on television?
- Are experts writing about the issue in scholarly journals?
- Has the issue been around long enough for books to be published about it?

What is your role?
- What is your position?
- What else do you need to know?
- What do you think should be done?

Your answers to these questions will provide you with keywords and phrases to use as you begin your search for information. Searches for print sources, online library sources, and Web sources begin with keyword searches.

Search using keywords

In most cases, you will begin your research with a keyword search or a subject search. A keyword search looks for words anywhere in the record. Subject searches use only the subject terms in the record.

Single keyword searches

The simplest keyword searches will return the most results, but often they are not the results you need.

> **EXAMPLE:**
> Type the word **capitalism** into the subject search window on your library's online catalog, and you likely will find more than a thousand items.

Multiple keyword searches

If you start with only one keyword, chances are the search will give you too many items to be useful. To narrow your search, you can combine search terms with the word AND.

> **EXAMPLE:**
> You may have read or heard that post-traumatic stress disorder is linked to visual memory.
>
> Type **post-traumatic stress disorder** AND **visual memory** to narrow the topic. (Some search engines now automatically use the AND function for any combination of words.)

Find keywords

Entries for subjects in your library's online catalog and in databases will help you find keywords. If you find a book or article that is exactly on your topic, use the subject terms to locate additional items.

> **EXAMPLE:**
> AUTHOR:
> Solove, Daniel J., 1972-
> TITLE:
> The digital person : technology and privacy in the information age / Daniel J. Solove.
> PUBLISHED:
> New York : New York University Press, c2004.
> SUBJECTS:
> Data protection–Law and legislation–United States.
> Electronic records–Access control–United States.
> Public records–Law and legislation–United States.
> Government information–United States.
> Privacy, Right of–United States.

Subject searches

When you know the exact subject terms for what you are looking for, a subject search will limit the number of items a search retrieves.

> **EXAMPLE:**
> See the subject terms at the bottom of the left column. This search—SUBJECT: Data protection AND Electronic records—would retrieve Daniel Solove's *The Digital Person.*

Limit searches

Another strategy to limit your search is to specify what you don't want, by using NOT.

> **EXAMPLE:**
> If you are interested in air pollution control policies, but not those used in the state of California.
>
> Type **air pollution control policies** NOT **California**

Find books

Nearly all college libraries now shelve books according to the Library of Congress Classification System, which uses a combination of letters and numbers to give you the book's unique location in the library. The Library of Congress call number begins with a letter or letters that represent the broad subject area into which the book is classified.

The Library of Congress system groups books by subject, and you can often find other items relevant to your search shelved close to the particular one you are looking for. You can search the extensive Library of Congress online catalog (catalog.loc.gov) to find out how your subject might be indexed, or you can go straight to your own library's catalog and conduct a subject search. The call number will enable you to find the item in the stacks. You will need to consult the locations guide for your library to find the book on the shelves.

When you find a book in your library catalog, take time to notice the subject headings under which it is indexed. For example, if you locate Jeff Hawkins's *On Intelligence*, you will probably find it cross-listed under several subject categories, including

```
Brain

Intellect

Artificial intelligence

Neural networks (Computer science)
```

Browsing within these categories, or using some of their keywords in a new search, may lead you to more useful sources.

LIBRARY OF CONGRESS

TS 171

through

Z

50 B

Find journal articles

Searching for articles in scholarly journals and magazines works much the same way as searching for books. Indexes for scholarly journals and magazines are located in the reference area of your library, and many may also be available on your library's Web site. Online indexes are databases, fully searchable by author, title, subject, or keywords. Some online indexes even contain the full text of articles, allowing you to copy the contents onto your computer. Others give you a citation, which you then have to find in your library. Follow these steps to find articles:

1 Select an index appropriate to your subject.

2 Search the index using relevant subject heading(s).

3 Print or copy the complete citation to the article(s).

4 Print or copy the full text if it is available.

5 If the full text is not available, check the periodicals holdings to see if your library has the journal.

Many specialized indexes list citations to journal articles in various fields. For example, *Medline* indexes articles in medical journals. Your library will probably have handouts that tell you which specialized index to use for a particular subject. Ask a librarian who works at the reference or information desk to help you.

Knowing what kinds of articles you want to look for—scholarly, trade, or popular—will help you select the right index. Many indexes include more than one type of journal. Although the difference among journals is not always obvious, you should be able to judge whether a journal is scholarly, trade, or popular by its characteristics. Some instructors frown on using popular journals as sources in a research paper, but these journals can be valuable for researching current opinion on a particular topic. They cannot, however, be substituted for serious research articles written by accredited scholars.

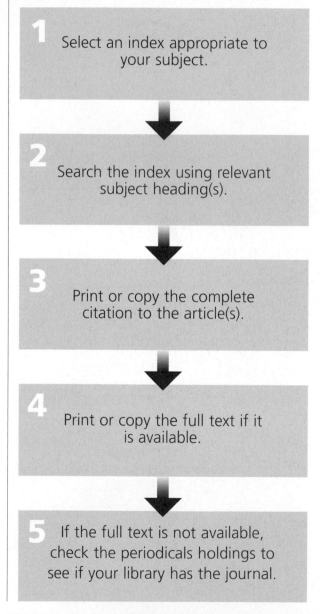

Scholarly journals

Scholarly journals are shelved in the periodicals section of your library. They

- Contain long articles typically written by scholars in the field, usually affiliated with a university or research center

- Usually include articles that report original research and have footnotes or a list of works cited at the end

- Are reviewed by other scholars in the field

- Assume that readers are also experts in the field

- Display few advertisements or illustrations

- Usually are published quarterly or biannually

Examples of scholarly journals include *American Journal of Mathematics; College English; JAMA: Journal of the American Medical Association; PMLA: Publication of the Modern Language Association;* and *Psychological Reports.*

Trade journals

- Publish articles related to particular fields, occupations, and interests

- Often give practical information

- Usually include articles that do not report original research and have few or no footnotes, and do not have a list of works cited at the end

- Contain advertisements aimed at people in specific fields

- Are published weekly, monthly, or quarterly

Examples of trade journals include *Advertising Age, Byte, PC Computing,* and *Teacher Magazine.*

Popular journals

Popular journals are found primarily on newsstands. They

- Publish short articles aimed at the general public

- Contain many advertisements and photos

- Seldom include footnotes or the source of information in detail

- Are published weekly or monthly

Examples of popular journals include *Cosmopolitan, GQ, Rolling Stone, Sports Illustrated,* and *Time.*

Evaluate print sources

Whether you use print or online sources, a successful search will turn up many more items than you can expect to use in your final product. You have to make a series of decisions about what is important and relevant. Return to your research question and working thesis (see Chapter 15) to determine which items are relevant.

How reliable are your sources? Books are expensive to print and distribute, so book publishers generally protect their investment by providing some level of editorial oversight. Print sources in libraries have an additional layer of oversight because someone has decided that a book or journal is worth purchasing and cataloging. Web sites, in contrast, can be put up and changed quickly, so information can be—and often is—posted thoughtlessly.

But print sources contain their share of biased, inaccurate, and misleading information. Over the years librarians have developed a set of criteria for evaluating print sources.

Source	Who published the book or article? Scholarly books and articles in scholarly journals are reviewed by experts in the field before they are published. They are generally more reliable than popular magazines and books, which tend to emphasize what is entertaining at the expense of comprehensiveness.
Author	Who wrote the book or article? What are the author's qualifications?
Timeliness	How current is the source? If you are researching a fast-developing subject such as vaccines for Asian bird flu, then currency is very important. Currency might not be as important for a historical subject, but even historical figures and events are often reinterpreted.
Evidence	Where does the evidence come from: facts, interviews, observations, surveys, or experiments? Is the evidence adequate to support the author's claims?
Biases	Can you detect particular biases of the author? How do the author's biases affect the interpretation offered?
Advertising	Is advertising a prominent part of the journal or newspaper? How might the ads affect what gets printed?

WRITE NOW

Evaluate information

Think of three or four different types of writing you have read recently: a novel, textbook, blog, letter, flyer, comic book, or online review. Evaluate each source according to the criteria above. Which item is the most reliable? For what purpose? Which is the least reliable?

Start a working bibliography

As you begin to collect your sources, make sure you get full bibliographic information for everything you might want to use in your project: articles, books, Web sites, and other materials. This will save you a great deal of time and trouble later. Determine which documentation style you will use. If your instructor does not tell you which style is appropriate, ask. (Two major documentation styles—MLA and APA—are explained in detail in Chapters 21 and 22.). You can compile this information in a computer file, a notebook, or on note cards.

For books

You will need, at minimum, the following information. This information can typically be found on the front and back of the title page:

- Author's name
- Title of the book
- Place of publication
- Name of publisher
- Date of publication

You will also need:

- page numbers if you are quoting directly or referring to a specific passage
- title and author of the individual chapter if your source is an edited book with contributions by several people.
- call numbers for the book or journal so you can find it easily in the future.

> HQ
> 799.7
> K36
> 2006
>
> Kamenetz, Anya. *Generation Debt: Why Now Is a Terrible Time to Be Young.* New York: Penguin, 2006.

For journals

You will need

- Author's name
- Title of the article
- Title of the journal
- Volume and issue of the journal
- Date of the issue
- Page numbers of the article

> Brazina, Paul R. "On the Trail: How Financial Audits Mark the Path for Forensic Teams." *Pennsylvania CPA Journal.* 77 (2006): 13–16.

How to explore libraries

You may have heard people say that you can find any information you want on the Web. In fact, most books, films, recordings, scholarly journals, and older copies of newspapers that you can find in a large library are not on the Web.

Talk with a librarian

Determine the print sources you need

Identify keywords

Find books

Find journal articles

Evaluate print sources

Start a working bibliography

Researcher at work

George Abukar used a title keyword search to look for books on the subject. The keyword combination "privacy AND technology" yielded the results shown here.

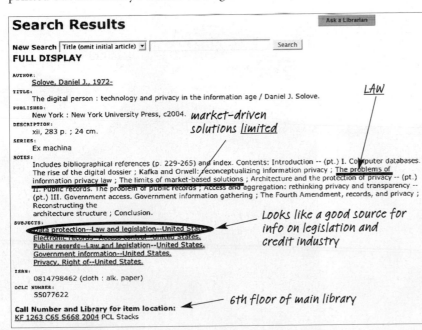

Search Results

Ask a Librarian

New Search Title (omit initial article) ▾ [   ] [Search]

KEYWORD Search Results Brief Display

YOUR SEARCH: TK PRIVACY TECHNOLOGY found 56 item(s).
(Records 1 - 10) For Full Display, click on number.

1 H.R. 1281, War Crimes Disclosure Act, Health Information Privacy Protection Act, and S. 1090, Electronic Freedom of Information Improve / United States. Congress. House. Committee on Government Reform and Oversight. Subcommittee on Government Managem / Washington / 1997
DOCS Y4.G74/7:W19 U.S. Congressional Documents PCL Stacks 5H-5J

2 Protecting health information : legislative options for medical privacy : hearing before the Subcommittee on Government Management, Inf / United States. Congress. House. Committee on Government Reform and Oversight. Subcommittee on Government Managem / Washington / 1999
DOCS Y4.G74/7:L52/4 U.S. Congressional Documents PCL Stacks 5H-5J

3 Safeguarding privacy in the fight against terrorism report of the Technology and Privacy Advisory Committee. / United States. Dept. of Defense. Technology and Privacy Advisory Committee / (Washington, D.C. / 2004
DOCS-CDROM D1.95:P93/CD Electronic Information Center PCL 2.200

4 The digital person : technology and privacy in the information age. / Solove, Daniel J., 1972- / New York / 2004
KF 1263 C65 S668 2004 PCL Stacks

5 Invited papers on privacy : law, ethics, and technology, presented at the National Symposium on Personal Privacy and Information Techno / National Symposium on Personal Privacy and Information Technology (1981 : Amelia Island Plantation) / Washington, D.C. / 1982
LAW JC 596.2 U5 N37 1981 Law Library

George knew he needed recent sources to get current information on identity theft. Because he already had several government sources covering his topic, George was particularly interested in the fourth item on the list: a fairly recent, full-length book on technology and privacy. He printed out the library's online catalog for the book.

Search Results

Ask a Librarian

New Search Title (omit initial article) ▾ [   ] [Search]
FULL DISPLAY

AUTHOR:
Solove, Daniel J., 1972-
TITLE:
The digital person : technology and privacy in the information age / Daniel J. Solove.
PUBLISHED:
New York : New York University Press, c2004.
DESCRIPTION:
xii, 283 p. ; 24 cm.
SERIES:
Ex machina
NOTES:
Includes bibliographical references (p. 229-265) and index. Contents: Introduction -- (pt.) I. Computer databases. The rise of the digital dossier ; Kafka and Orwell : reconceptualizing information privacy ; The problems of information privacy law ; The limits of market-based solutions ; Architecture and the protection of privacy -- (pt.) II. Public records. The problem of public records ; Access and aggregation : rethinking privacy and transparency -- (pt.) III. Government access. Government information gathering ; The Fourth Amendment, records, and privacy ; Reconstructing the architecture structure ; Conclusion.

SUBJECTS:
Data protection--Law and legislation--United States.
Electronic records--Access control--United States.
Public records--Law and legislation--United States.
Government information--United States.
Privacy, Right of--United States.

ISBN:
0814798462 (cloth : alk. paper)
OCLC NUMBER:
55077622

Call Number and Library for item location:
KF 1263 C65 S668 2004 PCL Stacks

LAW

market-driven solutions limited

Looks like a good source for info on legislation and credit industry

6th floor of main library

From this information, George could see that the book address two key issues for his thesis: legislation surrounding identity theft, and the problem of why market forces alone were not solving the problem. He used the printout to find the book on the library shelves.

17

Exploring Online Libraries

Electronic databases make it faster and easier than ever before to find library materials and to discover valuable sources you didn't even know existed. Databases put you in touch with the very latest information on a subject. Library databases also have the advantages of high quality and no commercial intrusion along with the convenience of Web delivery.

Find information in databases

You can learn how to use databases in your library with the help of a reference librarian. Your library may also have online and printed tutorials on using databases. Once you know how to access the databases you need, you can work from computers in other locations.

Most databases are by subscription only and must be accessed through your library's Web site, but a few like Google Scholar are free to everyone.

Academic Search Premier	Provides full text articles for thousands of scholarly publications, including social sciences, humanities, education, computer sciences, engineering, language and linguistics, literature, medical sciences, and ethnic studies journals.
ArticleFirst	Indexes journals in business, the humanities, medicine, science, and social sciences.
EBSCOhost Research Databases	Gateway to a large collection of EBSCO databases, including Academic Search Premier and MasterFILE Premier.
Expanded Academic ASAP	Indexes periodicals from the arts, humanities, sciences, social sciences, and general news, with full-text articles and images.
Factiva	Provides news and business information from over 10,000 sources including the *Wall Street Journal.*
FirstSearch	Offers millions of full-text articles from many databases.
Google Scholar	Searches scholarly literature according to criteria of relevance.
InfoTrac OneFile	Contains millions of full-text articles on a wide range of academic and general interest topics.
JSTOR	Provides scanned copies of scholarly journals.
LexisNexis Academic	Provides full text of a wide range of newspapers, magazines, government and legal documents, and company profiles from around the world.
MasterFILE Premier	Provides indexes and abstracts for business, consumer health, general science, and multicultural periodicals with many full-text articles.

567

Construct effective searches

To use databases effectively, make a list of keywords in advance (see page 558). For example, if you are researching the effects of hunting on deer populations, you could begin with the words *deer*, *hunting*, and *population*. If you are researching obesity in children, you might begin with *obesity*, *children*, and one more word such as *trend* or *Europe* or *fast food*, depending on your focus.

Select a database

Your next decision is to choose a database to begin your research. Newspapers might include stories on local deer populations and changes in hunting policy. Popular journals such as *Field and Stream* might have articles on national trends in deer hunting, and might also summarize scholarly research on the subject. Scholarly journals, perhaps in the field of wildlife biology, would contain articles about formal research into the effects of deer hunting on population density, average size and weight of animals, range, and other specific factors.

To find newspaper stories, begin with LexisNexis Academic. To find popular and scholarly journal articles, go Academic Search Premier, EBSCOhost, Expanded Academic ASAP, FirstSearch, or InfoTrac OneFile.

Evaluate database sources

Databases collect print sources and put them in digital formats. Evaluate database sources the same way you evaluate print source.

1. **Source:** Is the source a scholarly or popular journal?
2. **Author:** What are the author's qualifications?
3. **Timeliness:** How current is the source?
4. **Evidence:** Where does the evidence come from?
5. **Biases:** Can you detect particular biases?
6. **Advertising:** Is advertising prominent?

Evaluate for relevance

Even reliable sources may not pertain to your topic. Consider the relevance of each source for your subject.

LexisNexis

Home | Sources | How Do I? | Site Map | What's New | Help

Search Terms: myspace, teenagers

FOCUS™ [   ] [Search Within Results]   Edit Search

Jump to Documents [1-25]   [Print] [Email]

Document List | Expanded List | KWIC | Full   Documents 1 - 25 of 58. next ▶

Tag for delivery / Clear   ▶▶ Sorted by **Date** | Sort by: ▶ Relevance

- ☐ 1. Giving teens their space, The Daily Telegraph (Australia), June 23, 2006 Friday, State Edition, WORLD; Pg. 24, 89 words
- ☐ 2. Safety net on MySpace.com tightened, but parents hold key, The Atlanta Journal-Constitution, June 22, 2006 Thursday, Main Edition, NEWS; Pg. 1A, 1338 words, ANDREA JONES
- ☐ 3. Child protection fears hit online social networks Reports of sexual predators exploiting sites to make contact with teenagers have led to calls for tighter security, says Aline van Duyn, Financial Times (London, England), June 22, 2006 Thursday, London Edition 1, THE AMERICAS; Pg. 9, 719 words, By ALINE VAN DUYN, NEW YORK
- ☐ 4. MySpace to Add Restrictions To Protect Younger Teenagers, The New York Times, June 21, 2006 Wednesday, Late Edition - Final, Section C; Column 1; Business/Financial Desk; Pg. 2, 399 words, By SAUL HANSELL
- ☐ 5. Young love, young foolishness, Buffalo News (New York), June 20, 2006 Tuesday, FINAL EDITION, VIEWPOINTS; Pg. A11, 614 words, By Mitche Albom - Detroit Free Press
- ☐ 6. Bebo battles for the hearts and minds of nation's teenagers, Financial Times (London, England), June 19, 2006 Monday, London Edition 1, NATIONAL NEWS; Pg. 3, 485 words, By TOM BRAITHWAITE
- ☐ 7. Basic rules help ensure kids' safety, The Seattle Times, June 12, 2006 Monday, Fourth Edition, ROP ZONE; Business; Pg. C1, 805 words, Brier Dudley, Seattle Times technology columnist
- ☐ 8. MUSIC; Classical music goes new-school on Web, The Boston Herald, June 10, 2006 Saturday, ALL EDITIONS, THE EDGE; Pg. 025, 502

Results of a search on LexisNexis for MySpace AND teenagers. If your topic is the danger of predators taking advantage of younger teenagers on MySpace, probably articles 2, 3, 4, and 7 would be the first ones to examine.

Locate elements of a citation

To cite a source from a database, you will need the

- Author if listed
- Title of article
- Name of periodical
- Date of publication (and edition for newspapers)
- Section and page number

- Name of database
- Date of access (the day you found the article in the database)
- URL of the vendor (for MLA-style citations)

A sample article from the Academic Search Premier search for "steroids" and "high school." The confusing part of citing this example is distinguishing between the database and the vendor. The vendor's name often appears at the top of the screen, making the vendor's name look like the name of the database. In this case, EBSCO is the vendor—the company that sells your library access to Academic Search Premier and many other databases. Often you have to look carefully to find the name of the database.

Name of vendor / Title of article / Author

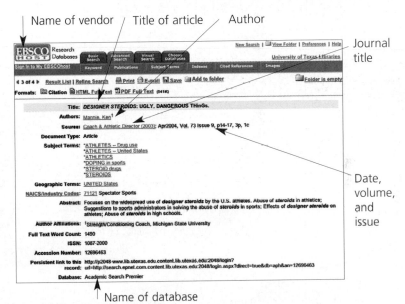

Journal title

Date, volume, and issue

Name of database

A citation for an article that you find on a database looks like this in MLA style:

Mannie, Ken. "Designer Steroids: Ugly, Dangerous Things." <u>Scholastic Coach and Athletic Director</u> 73.9 (Apr. 2004). <u>Academic Search Premier</u>. EBSCO. Perry-Casteñeda Lib., U of Texas at Austin. 26 July 2006 <http://www.epnet.com/>.

WORKING TOGETHER

Compare databases

In a group of three or four students

Identify keywords for your research topic, and use the same keywords for searches on three or more databases. If the search yields too many items, use AND to connect the terms or add another keyword plus AND. Copy the results from each search and paste it into a file. Which database turned up more items? Which turned up more scholarly articles? Which turned up more articles in popular journals? Which will be most helpful for your research topic?

How to explore online libraries

Libraries are increasingly becoming digital archives. Books remain mostly in print, but articles in scholarly journals and in newspapers are read more and more on-screen. You can access a mountain of information through your library databases, but to get to the top of the mountain, you must know how to search efficiently.

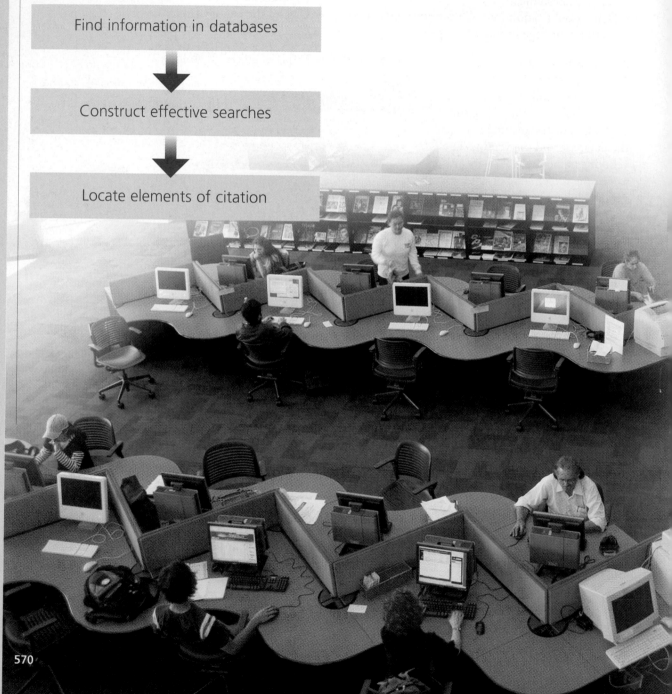

Find information in databases

Construct effective searches

Locate elements of citation

Researcher at work

George Abukar's earlier research for his proposal argument led him to a narrower focus on the credit-reporting industry. To search for articles on identity theft, he chose the comprehensive general index Business Source Premiere.

Results of a search for identity theft on Business Source Premiere.

After clicking on several entries and reading the abstracts of the articles, he found one, a recent piece in *American Banker*, which was especially appropriate for his paper. Its abstract indicated that it touched on an important component of his thesis: legislation intended to prevent identity theft. George skimmed the entire article online and then emailed it to himself so he could print it out from his home computer.

Abstract of article on Business Source Premiere.

18

Exploring the Web

Chances are that you use the Web regularly to find information about products, restaurants, stores, services, jobs, people, maps, hobbies, music, films, and other entertainment. But researching an academic paper on the Web is different from such everyday tasks. The Web can be a powerful tool for research, but it also has many traps for the unwary.

NATIONAL AERONAUTICS AND SPACE ADMINISTRATION

Solar System Exploration

SSE Home > Multimedia > Gallery > Saturn's Spectrum

Saturn
March 7, 2003

Ultraviolet

Visible

Infrared

Sitemap
Search
Home
News & Events
Planets
Missions
Science & Technology
Multimedia
Our Top 10
Planets
Spacecraft
Technology
Historical Images
Kids' Gallery
Videos
Interactive
Downloads
More NASA Galleries
People
Kids
Education
History

Hubble Space Telescope
Wide Field Planetary Camera 2
NASA and E. Karkoschka (University of Arizona)
STScI-PRC03-23

Hi-Res (1.38

Rate this Image ★ ★ ★ ★ ★ (about ratings)

Saturn's Spectrum
This is a series of images of Saturn, as seen at many different wavelengths, when the planet's rings wer
maximum tilt of 27 degrees toward Earth. Saturn experiences seasonal tilts away from and toward the S
much the same way Earth does. This happens over the course of its 29.5-year orbit. This means that
approximately every 30 years, Earth observers can catch their best glimpse of Saturn's South Pole and
southern side of the planet's rings. Between March and April 2003, researchers took full advantage to s
gas giant at maximum tilt. They used NASA's Hubble Space Telescope to capture detailed images of Sa
Southern Hemisphere and the southern face of its rings.

2 used 30 filters to snap these images on March 7, 200
best spectral coverage

Find information on the Web

Because anyone can publish on the Web, there is no overall quality control and there is no system of organization as there are in a library. Nevertheless, the Web offers you some resources for current topics that would be difficult to find in a library. The keys to success are knowing where you are most likely to find current and accurate information about the particular question you are researching, and knowing how to access that information.

Search engines

Search engines designed for the Web work in ways similar to library databases and your library's online catalog, but with one major difference. Databases typically do some screening of the items they list, but search engines potentially take you to every Web site that isn't password protected—millions of pages in all. Consequently, you have to work harder to limit searches on the Web or you can be deluged with tens of thousands of items.

Kinds of search engines

A search engine is a set of programs that sort through millions of items at incredible speed. There are four basic kinds of search engines.

1. Keyword search engines (e.g., Ask.com, Answers.com, Google)	Keyword search engines give different results because they assign different weights to the information they find. Google, for example, ranks Web sites according to how many other sites link to them and the quality of the linking sites.
2. Web directories (e.g., Best of the Web, Yahoo!, Yemoo.net)	Web directories classify Web sites into categories and are the closest equivalent to the cataloging system used by libraries. On most directories professional editors decide how to index a particular Web site. Web directories also allow keyword searches.
3. Metasearch agents (e.g., Dogpile, Metacrawler, WebCrawler)	Metasearch agents allow you to use several search engines simultaneously. While the concept is sound, metasearch agents are limited by the number of hits they can return and their inability to handle advanced searches.
4. Specialized search engines (e.g., Froogle [shopping], Google Scholar [academic], Monster.com [jobs], Pubmed [medicine], Thomasnet [business], WebMD [medicine])	Specialized search engines have been developed in recent years for specific subjects.

Advanced searches

Search engines often produce too many hits and are therefore not always useful. If you look only at the first few items, you may miss what is most valuable. The alternative is to refine your search. Most search engines offer you the option of an advanced search, which gives you the opportunity to limit numbers.

The advanced searches on Google and Yahoo! give you the options of using a string of words to search for sites that contain (1) all the words, (2) the exact phrase, (3) any of the words, or (4) that exclude certain words. They also allow you to specify the language of the site, the date range, the file format, and the domain. For example, government statistics on crime are considered the most reliable, so if you want to find statistics on murder rates, you can specify the domain as .gov in an advanced search.

An advanced search on Google for government sites only (.gov).

Discussion forums, groups, and blogs

The Internet allows you to access other people's opinions on thousands of topics. The Groups section of Google (groups.google.com) has an archive of several hundred million messages that can be searched. Much of the conversation on these sites is undocumented and highly opinionated, but you can still gather important information about people's attitudes and get tips about other sources, which you can verify later.

Web logs, better known as blogs, also are sources of public opinion. Several tools have been developed recently to search blogs: Blogdigger, Bloglines, Feedster, Google Blog Search, PubSub, Technorati, and IceRocket. Blogs are not screened and are not considered authoritative sources, but blogs can sometimes lead you to quality sources.

Evaluate Web sources

All electronic search tools share a common problem: They often give you too many sources. Web search engines not only pull up thousands of hits, but these hits may vary dramatically in quality. No one regulates or checks information put on the Web, and it's no surprise that much information on the Web is highly opinionated or false.

Misleading Web sites

Some Web sites are put up as jokes. Other Web sites are deliberately misleading. Many prominent Web sites draw imitators who want to cash in on the commercial visibility. The Web site for the Campaign for Tobacco-Free Kids (www.tobaccofreekids.org), for example, has an imitator (www.smokefreekids.com) that sells software for antismoking education. The .com URL is often a tip-off that a site has a profit motive.

Biased Web sites

Always approach Web sites with an eye toward evaluating content. For example, Web sites with .com URLs that offer medical information often contain strong biases in addition to the motive to make money. The Web site Thinktwice.com, sponsored by the Global Vaccine Institute, opposes the vaccination of children. On the site you can find claims that the polio vaccine administered to millions in the United States causes cancer because it was contaminated with Simian Virus 40. Always look for other sources for verification. The U.S. Centers for Disease Control publishes fact sheets on the latest information about diseases and their prevention, including one on polio vaccine and Simian Virus 40.

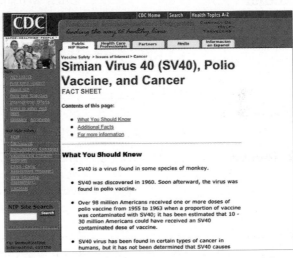

Fact sheet on Simian Virus 40, Polio Vaccine, and Cancer from the Centers for Disease Control (http://www.cdc.gov/nip/vacsafe/concerns/cancer/sv40-polio-cancer-facts.htm).

Locate elements of a citation

To cite a Web site you will need
- Author if listed
- Title of the Web page
- Date the site was posted
- Sponsoring organization if listed
- Date you visited
- Complete URL

Waskom, R. <u>Graywater Reuse and Rainwater Harvesting</u>. 8 Feb. 2006. Colorado State University Cooperative Extension—Natural Resources. 1 Apr. 2006 <http://www.ext.colostate.edu/pubs/natres/06702.html>.

A citation for a Web page looks like this in MLA style.

Criteria for evaluating Web sources

The criteria for evaluating print sources can be applied to Web sources if the special circumstances of the Web are acknowledged. For example, when you find a Web page by using a search engine, often you go deep into a complex site without having any sense of the context for that page. To evaluate the credibility of the site, you would need to examine the home page, not just the specific page you saw first.

Source	Look for the site's ownership in the Web address. If a Web site doesn't indicate ownership, then you have to make judgments about who put it up and why. The suffix can offer clues: .gov is used by government bodies, and .edu by educational institutions, generally colleges and universities. These sites are generally more reliable than .com sites.
Author	Often Web sites give no information about their authors other than an email address, if that. In such cases it is difficult or impossible to determine the author's qualifications. Look up the author on Google. If qualifications are listed, is the author an expert in the field? Some sites, such as Wikipedia, a popular online encyclopedia, allow anyone to add or delete information.
Timeliness	Many Web pages do not list when they were last updated; thus you cannot determine their currency.
Evidence	The accuracy of any evidence found on the Web is often hard to verify. The most reliable information on the Web stands up to the tests of print evaluation, with clear indication of the sponsoring organization and the sources of any factual information.
Biases	Many Web sites announce their viewpoint on controversial issues, but others conceal their attitude with a reasonable tone and seemingly factual evidence such as statistics. Citations and bibliographies do not ensure that a site is reliable. Look carefully at the links and sources cited.
Advertising	Many Web sites are infomercials aimed at getting you to buy a product or service. While they might contain useful information, they are no more trustworthy than other forms of advertising.

Other Internet sources

Other Internet sources, such as online newsgroups, can give you useful ideas but are generally not considered authoritative. Email communication from an expert in the field might be considered an authoritative source, but personal emails are generally not considered worthy of inclusion in a research paper. Remember that a key reason to cite sources is so other researchers can read and evaluate the sources you used.

Find visual sources online

You can find images published on the Web using Google and other search engines that allow you to specify searches for images. For example, if you are writing a research paper on invasive plant species, you might want to include an image of kudzu, an invasive vine common in the American South. In Google, choose Images and type *kudzu* in the search box. You'll find a selection of images of plant, including several from the National Park Service.

Some search engines such as Ditto (www.ditto.com) are designed specifically to find images. Yahoo! Picture Gallery has over 400,000 images that can be searched by subject (gallery.yahoo.com). In addition to images, you can find statistical data represented in charts and graphs on government Web sites. Especially useful is the *Statistical Abstract of the United States* for finding charts and graphs of population statistics (www.census.gov/compendia/statab/). You can also find thousands of maps on the Web (See www.lib.utexas.edu/maps/map_sites/map_sites.html for a directory of map sites.)

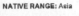

Kudzu

Pueraria montana var. lobata (Willd.) Maesen & S. Almeida
Pea family (Fabaceae)

NATIVE RANGE: Asia

DESCRIPTION: Kudzu ia a climbing, semi-woody, perennial vine in the pea family. Deciduous leaves are alternate and compound, with three broad leaflets up to 4 inches across. Leaflets may be entire or deeply 2-3 lobed with hairy margins. Individual flowers, about 1/2 inch long, are purple, highly fragrant and borne in long hanging clusters. Flowering occurs in late summer and is soon followed by production of brown, hairy, flattened, seed pods, each of which contains three to ten hard seeds.

Kudzu was planted widely in the South to reduce soil erosion but has itself become a major pest, smothering native trees and plants.

Follow copyright requirements

Just because images are easy to download from the Web does not mean that you are free to use every image you find. Look for the image creator's copyright notice and suggested credit line. This notice will tell you if you can reproduce the image. You should acknowledge the source of any image you use.

In many cases you will find a copyright notice that reads something like this, "Any use or re-transmission of text or images in this Web site without written consent of the copyright owner constitutes copyright infringement and is prohibited." You must write to the creator to ask permission to use an image from a site that is not in the public domain, even if you cannot find a copyright notice.

WRITE NOW

Evaluate Web sites

Hoaxbusters (http://hoaxbusters.ciac.org/) provides an index of Internet hoaxes sorted into categories. Read several of the hoaxes, and select one to explore further. Use the criteria for evaluating Web sources on page 576 to evaluate your site. On which criteria does it fail to be reliable?

Next do a Google search for Ritalin, a commonly prescribed drug for attention deficit disorder (ADD) and attention deficit hyperactivity disorder (ADHD). You will find that the drug is quite controversial. Look at five different Web sites. Which sites do you find most reliable and the least reliable according to the criteria on page 576?

How to explore the Web

The Web offers a staggering amount of information about nearly any topic you can think of, but the Web also has two major drawbacks. Much of the information on the Web is unreliable because no one independently verifies information for accuracy, and much of the information is unstable because Web sites appear and disappear overnight. Doing research on the Web will test your skills in evaluating and recording information.

Find information on the Web

↓

Evaluate Web sources

↓

Find visual sources online

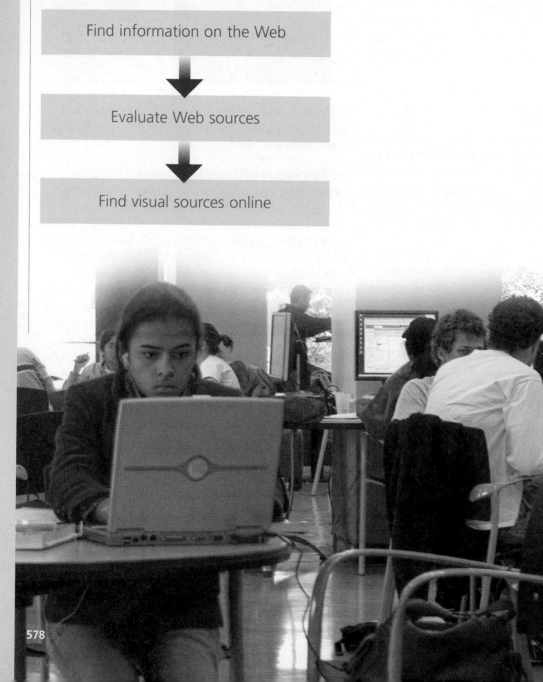

Researcher at work

Researching his proposal paper on identity theft, George Abukar realized that the topic was especially important to people who do business online, and that a great deal of information about identity theft existed solely on the Internet. He thought his paper would benefit from the inclusion of some of these sources.

George performed an initial search on Google.com using the keywords "identity theft." That search returned many results from government offices and commercial sites that sought to warn consumers about identity theft and fraud. George already had plenty of material like this, so he added two more keywords, "credit industry," to his search in order to narrow his results.

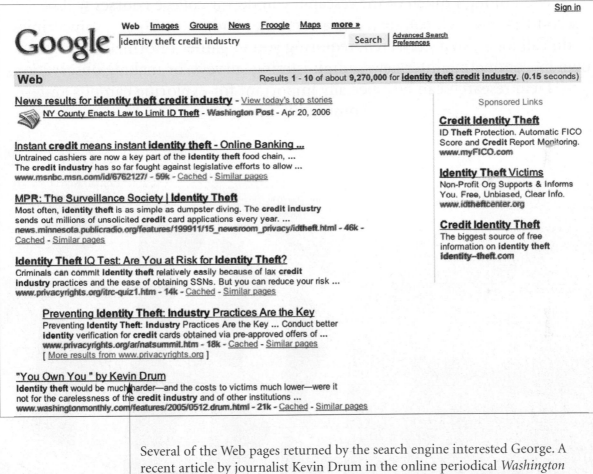

Several of the Web pages returned by the search engine interested George. A recent article by journalist Kevin Drum in the online periodical *Washington Monthly* makes a strong case for a solution similar to the one George proposes in his paper. He printed a copy of the article to work from as he drafted his paper.

You can read the final draft of George's paper on pages 624–631.

19

Exploring in the Field

Even though much of the research you do for college courses will be secondary research conducted at a computer and in the library, some topics do call for primary research, requiring you to gather information on your own by conducting interviews, administering surveys, or making observations. Field research can be especially important for exploring campus and community issues.

Conduct interviews

College campuses are a rich source of experts in many areas, including people on the faculty and in the surrounding community. Interviewing experts on your research topic can help build your knowledge base. You can use interviews to discover what the people most affected by a particular issue are thinking, such as why students object to some fees and not others.

Arrange interviews

Before you contact anyone, think carefully about your goals; knowing what you want to find out through your interviews will help you determine whom you need to interview and what questions you need to ask. To prepare for an interview

- Decide what you want or need to know and who best can provide that for you.

- Ask the person to grant an interview in advance, and let the person know why you are conducting the interview. Estimate how long your interview will take, and tell your subject how much time you will need.

- Choose a location that is convenient for your subject, but not too chaotic or loud. An office or study room is better than a noisy cafeteria.

- If you want to record the interview, ask for permission in advance.

Plan questions

- Start writing questions in advance.

- Ask some specific questions such as "What exactly are your responsibilities in your position?"

- Ask some open-ended questions such as "How have the administration's new policies changed your relationship with the people you serve?"

Conduct interviews

- Come prepared with your questions, a notebook, and a pen or pencil.

- If you plan to record the interview (with your subject's permission), make sure whatever recording device you use has an adequate power supply and will not run out of tape, disk space, or memory.

- Listen carefully so you can follow up on key points. Make notes when important questions are raised or answered, but don't attempt to transcribe every word the person is saying.

- When you are finished, thank your subject, and ask his or her permission to get in touch again if you have additional questions.

Analyze interviews

- Schedule at least 30 minutes after the interview to flesh out the notes you took while the interview is still fresh in your mind.

- Think about you own reactions including what you found unusual or suprising.

- When you are ready to incorporate the interview into a paper or project, think about what you want to highlight about the interview and which direct quotations to include.

Administer surveys

Extensive surveys that can be projected to large populations, like the ones used in political polls, require the effort of many people. Small surveys, however, often can provide insight on local issues, such as what percentage of students might be affected if library hours were reduced.

Plan surveys

Decide what exactly you want to know: What information do you need for your research question? Then design a survey that will provide that information. Likely you will want both close-ended questions (multiple choice, yes or no, rating scale) and open-ended questions that allow detailed responses. To create a survey

- Write a few specific, unambiguous questions. People will fill out your survey quickly, and if the questions are confusing, the results will be meaningless.

- Include one or two open-ended questions, such as "What do you like about X?" "What don't you like about X?" Open-ended questions can be difficult to interpret, but sometimes they turn up information you had not anticipated.

Test surveys in advance

- Make sure your questions are clear by testing them on a few people before you conduct the survey.

- Think about how you will interpret your survey. Multiple-choice formats make data easy to tabulate, but often they miss key information. Open-ended questions will require you to figure out a way to sort responses into categories.

Administer surveys

- Decide on the people you will need to survey and how many your survey will require.

- Decide how you will contact participants in your survey. If you are conducting your survey on private property, you will need permission from the property owner.

- If you mail or email your survey, include a statement about what the survey is for.

Analyze surveys

- Tally the results of the specific questions.
- Analyze the open-ended questions by determining categories for the responses to each question and assigning each answer to a category.
- When writing about the results, be sure to include information about who participated in the survey, how the participants were selected, and when and how the survey was administered.

Make surveys appealing

So many people want information from us—marketers, politicians, pollsters, corporations—that we often feel bombarded by surveys and polls. To keep people from tuning out your survey, you need to appeal to them without annoying them.

Technique	Less Effective	More Effective
Get attention with a title or subject heading that interests people and makes clear that they have something to contribute. However, don't resort to exclamations and capitalized words; these will remind people of spam email and advertising pitches.	• Survey for part-time students • Please take our survey • Important: student survey • Take this survey and WIN A FREE CAR!!!!!	• Share your opinion on cafeteria food. • Help the Biology Department improve lab classes. • Sound off about bus service.
Ask people for their help, and tell them why you need it.	• We appreciate your taking the time to answer this survey.	• Your answers to this survey will provide insight into the strengths and weaknesses of our school's current admissions policy.
Briefly describe the project and its audience.	• I'm taking this survey for a class I'm in.	• This survey is part of a group research project for Business Administration 118. We hope to present our final report to the University Student Services Committee.
Most people prefer to take surveys anonymously. Ensure confidentiality if necessary.	• Please note your name and phone number below for follow-up.	• Your answers will be kept confidential and your identity will not be associated with your answers in any way.
State up front how long the survey will take the respondent to complete.		• We estimate this survey will take you 5 to 10 minutes to complete.
Provide your contact information so respondents can learn more about your project or results.		• Please feel free to contact us at 123-4567 or bizkids@mail.edu if you have any questions about this survey.
Thank your respondents by reminding them what they are helping you accomplish.		• Thank you once again for taking the time to share your opinions. Your contribution will help to improve student services at our school.

Make observations

Observing can be a valuable source of data. For example, if you are researching why a particular office on your campus does not operate efficiently, observe what happens when students enter and how the staff responds to their presence.

Choose a place

- Choose a place where you can observe with the least intrusion. The less people wonder about what you are doing, the better.

Collect obsevations

- Carry a notebook and write extensive field notes. Record as much information as you can, and worry about analyzing it later.

- Record the date, exactly where you were, exactly when you arrived and left, and important details like the number of people present.

- Write on one side of your notebook so you can use the facing page to note key observations and analyze your data later.

Analyze observations

You must interpret your observations so they make sense to your audience. Ask yourself the following questions:

- What patterns of behavior did you observe?

- How was the situation you observed unique? How might it be similar to other locations? What constituted "normal" activity during the time when you were observing? Did anything out of the ordinary happen?

- Why were the people there? What can you determine about the purposes of the activities you observed?

THE PYRAMID TENT. COLDEST NIGHT OF THE TRIP FORCED ME TO WAKE UP AND PUT ON MORE CLOTHES.

July 26 (12) WEDNESDAY
13 MILES

WOKE UP ON A SUNNY MORNING OUR FIRST SINCE COMING TO ALASKA. OUR STREAK OF RAIN DAYS SINCE ARRIVAL ENDED AT 13. I TOOK ADVANTAGE OF THE SUNSHINE TO WASH OUR SHORTS AND POLYPRO TOPS. WE LEFT AT 1 TO PADDLE TO THE TIGER GLACIER. WE HAD TO DODGE THE ICE ALMOST ALL THE WAY. THE COLD WIND OFF THE GLACIER CHILLED US AS WE APROACHED, AND WE HEARD THE SQAKING OF HUNDREDS OF KITYWAKES ON THE ICE NEAR THEIR ROOKERY. WE HAD LUNCH ON A GRAVEL BAR ABOUT A MILE FROM THE GLACIER, THEN WE WENT

Compose interview questions

Think of a specific person who fits one of the categories below and a specific purpose. For example, write a series of interview questions for your U.S. Senator on immigration policy. Write 5–10 interview questions.

- A celebrity you admire
- A potential employee
- A potential employer
- The author of a book you have read recently
- A Fortune 500 CEO
- A professional athlete
- A well-known scientist in a field you don't know much about
- An "invisible person"—a custodian, gardener, security guard, or other person who has an impact on your life but with whom you never or rarely interact

How to conduct field research

Successful field research, like research in libraries and on the Web, requires planning. Thinking about the research question you want to answer will help you select the best method and determine your strategy.

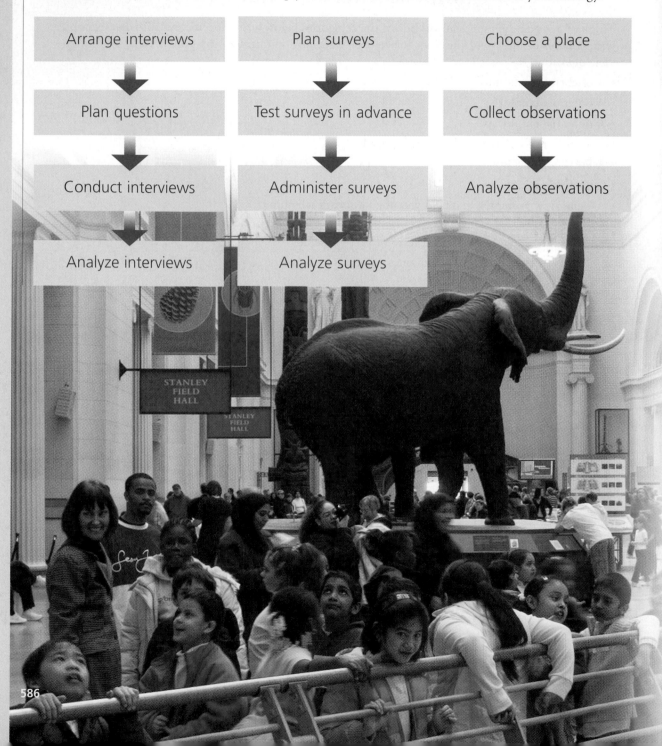

Arrange interviews	Plan surveys	Choose a place
↓	↓	↓
Plan questions	Test surveys in advance	Collect observations
↓	↓	↓
Conduct interviews	Administer surveys	Analyze observations
↓	↓	
Analyze interviews	Analyze surveys	

Researcher at work

To show that his proposal of reducing identity theft could and should be enacted, George Abukar needed evidence that other people thought it was an appropriate solution. In addition, because his proposal called for the creation of new laws, he needed to show that his proposal was supported by registered voters. George created a brief survey to measure support for his proposal.

George originally planned to administer the survey in his dormitory. However, after talking to a number of his fellow residents, he realized that a high percentage of them had not yet registered to vote. In order to have a percentage of voters similar to that of the overall population, George decided to conduct his survey in the student union food court from 11 to 2 over two days. There, he would have access to more faculty, staff, and older students, who would be more likely to have registered to vote.

Here are the results of George's survey in table form.

What do you think about identity theft?

Your answers to these four short questions will help me determine if the university community wants new laws to prevent identity theft.

	YES	NO
1) Have you, or has someone you know, ever been the victim of identity theft?		
2) Do you feel identity theft is an important problem?		
3) If a credit-reporting company reports false information about you, and you suffer as a result, should the company be held responsible?		
4) Are you registered to vote?		

Thank you for your opinions! If you would like more information about this survey, please contact George Abukar at g.abukar@mail.com

What do you think about identity theft?

Your answers to these four short questions will help me determine if the university community wants new laws to prevent identity theft.

	YES	NO
1) Have you, or has someone you know, ever been the victim of identity theft?	4	46
2) Do you feel identity theft is an important problem?	31	19
3) If a credit-reporting company reports false information about you, and you suffer as a result, should the company be held responsible?	45	5
4) Are you registered to vote?	32	18

Thank you for your opinions! If you would like more information about this survey, please contact George Abukar at g.abukar@mail.com

20

Writing the Research Paper

If you have chosen a subject you're interested in, asked questions about it, and researched it thoroughly, you will have a wealth of ideas and information to communicate to your audience.

Plan your organization

Review your goals and thesis

Before you begin writing your paper, review the assignment and your goals (see Chapter 15). Your review of the assignment will remind you of your purpose, your potential readers, your stance on your subject, and the length and scope you should aim for.

By now you should have formulated a working thesis, which will be the focus of your paper. You should also have located, read, evaluated, and taken notes on enough source material to write your paper. At this stage in the writing process, your working thesis may be rough and may change as you write your draft, but having a working thesis will help keep your paper focused.

Determine your contribution

A convincing and compelling research paper does not make claims based solely on the word of the writer. It draws on the expertise and reputations of others as well. Thus it is critical to show your readers which elements of your paper represent your original thinking.

Determine exactly what you are adding to the larger conversation about your subject.

- Who do you agree with?
- Who do you disagree with?
- What can you add to points you agree with?
- What original analysis or theorizing do you have to offer?
- What original findings from field research do you have to offer?

Determine your main points and group your findings

Look back over your notes and determine how to group the ideas you researched. Decide what your major points will be, and how those points support your thesis. Group your research findings so that they match up with your major points.

Now it is time to create a working outline. Always include your thesis at the top of your outline as a guiding light. Some writers create formal outlines with roman numerals and the like; others compose the headings for the paragraphs of their paper and use them to guide their draft; still others may start writing and then determine how they will organize their draft when they have a few paragraphs written. Experiment and decide which method works best for you.

Avoid plagiarism

You know that copying someone else's paper word for word or taking an article off the Internet and turning it in as yours is plagiarism. That's plain stealing, and people who take that risk should know that the punishment can be severe. But plagiarism also means using the ideas, melodies, or images of someone else without acknowledging them, and it is important to understand exactly what defines plagiarism.

What you don't have to document

Fortunately, common sense governs issues of academic plagiarism. The standards of documentation are not so strict that the source of every fact you cite must be acknowledged. Suppose you are writing about the causes of maritime disasters and you want to know how many people drowned when the *Titanic* sank on the early morning of April 15, 1912. You check the *Britannica Online* Web site and find that the death toll was around 1,500. Since this fact is available in many other reference works, you would not need to cite *Britannica Online* as the source.

But let's say you want to challenge the version of the sinking offered in the 1998 movie *Titanic*, which repeats the usual explanation that the *Titanic* sideswiped an iceberg, ripping a long gash along the hull that caused the ship to go down. Suppose that, in your reading, you discover that a September 1985 exploration of the wreck by an unmanned submersible did not find the long gash previously thought to have sunk the ship. The evidence instead suggested that the force of the collision with the iceberg broke the seams in the hull, allowing water to flood the ship's watertight compartments. You would need to cite the source of your information for this alternative version of the *Titanic's* demise.

What you do have to document

For facts that are not easily found in general reference works, statements of opinion, and arguable claims, you should cite the source. You should also cite the sources of statistics, research findings, examples, graphs, charts, and illustrations. For example, if you state that the percentage of obese children aged 6 to 11 in the United States rose from 4% in 1974 to 15% in 2000, you need to cite the source.

As a reader you should be skeptical about statistics and research findings when the source is not mentioned. When a writer does not cite the sources of statistics and research findings, there is no way of knowing how reliable the sources are or whether the writer is making them up.

From the writer's perspective careful citing of sources lends credibility. If you take your statistics from a generally trusted source, your readers are more likely to trust whatever conclusions or arguments you are presenting. When in doubt, always document the source.

Be careful when taking notes and copying material online

The best way to avoid unintentional plagiarism is to take care to distinguish source words from your own words.

- Don't mix words from the source with your own words. If you copy anything from a source when taking notes, place those words in quotation marks and note the page number(s) where those words appear.

- Write down all the information you need for each source for a list of works cited or a list of references (see Chapters 21 and 22).

- If you copy words from an online source, take special care to note the source. You could easily copy online material and later not be able to find where it came from.

- Photocopy printed sources and print out online sources. Having printed copies of sources allows you to double-check later that you haven't used words from the source by mistake and that any words you quote are accurate.

Quote sources without plagiarizing

Effective research writing builds on the work of others. You can summarize or paraphrase the work of others, but often it is best to let the authors speak in your text by quoting their exact words. Indicate the words of others by placing them inside quotation marks.

Most people who get into plagiarism trouble lift words from a source and use them without quotation marks. Where the line is drawn is easiest to illustrate with an example. In the following passage, Steven Johnson takes sharp issue with the metaphor of surfing applied to the Web:

> The concept of "surfing" does a terrible injustice to what it means to navigate around the Web. . . . What makes the idea of cybersurf so infuriating is the implicit connection drawn to television. Web surfing, after all, is a derivation of channel surfing—the term thrust upon the world by the rise of remote controls and cable panoply in the mid-eighties. . . . Applied to the boob tube, of course, the term was not altogether inappropriate. Surfing at least implied that channel-hopping was more dynamic, more involved, than the old routine of passive consumption. Just as a real-world surfer's enjoyment depended on the waves delivered up by the ocean, the channel surfer was at the mercy of the programmers and network executives. The analogy took off because it worked well in the one-to-many system of cable TV, where your navigational options were limited to the available channels.
>
> But when the term crossed over to the bustling new world of the Web, it lost a great deal of precision. . . . Web surfing and channel surfing are genuinely different pursuits; to imagine them as equivalents is to ignore the defining characteristics of each medium. Or at least that's what happens in theory. In practice, the Web takes on the greater burden. The television imagery casts the online surfer in the random, anesthetic shadow of TV programming, roaming from site to site like a CD player set on shuffle play. But what makes the online world so revolutionary is the fact that there are connections between each stop on a Web itinerant's journey. The links that join those various destinations are links of association, not randomness. A channel surfer hops back and forth between different channels because she's bored. A Web surfer clicks on a link because she's interested.
>
> Steven Johnson. *Interface Culture: How New Technology Transforms the Way We Create and Communicate.* New York: Harper, 1997. 107–09.

If you were writing a paper or putting up a Web site that concerned Web surfing, you might want to mention the distinction that Johnson makes between channel surfing and surfing on the Web. You could then expand on the distinction.

Use quotation marks for direct quotations

If you quote directly, you must place quotation marks around all words you take from the original:

> One observer marks this contrast: "A channel surfer hops back and forth between different channels because she's bored. A Web surfer clicks on a link because she's interested" (Johnson 109).

Notice that the quotation is introduced and not just dropped in. This example follows Modern Language Association (MLA) style, where the citation–(Johnson 109)–goes outside the quotation marks but before the final period. In MLA style, source references are made according to the author's last name, which refers you to the full citation in the list of works cited at the end. Following the author's name is the page number where the quotation can be located. (Notice also that there is no comma after the name.)

Attribute every quotation

If the author's name appears in the sentence, cite only the page number, in parentheses:

> According to Steven Johnson, "A channel surfer hops back and forth between different channels because she's bored. A Web surfer clicks on a link because she's interested" (109).

Quoting words that are quoted in your source

If you want to quote material that is already quoted in your source, use single quotes for that material:

> Steven Johnson uses the metaphor of a Gothic cathedral to describe a computer interface: "'The principle of the Gothic architecture,' Coleridge once said, 'is infinity made imaginable.' The same could be said for the modern interface" (42).

Summarize and paraphrase sources without plagiarizing

Summarizing

When you summarize, you state the major ideas of an entire source or part of a source in a paragraph or perhaps even a sentence. The key is to put the summary in your own words. If you use words from the source, you have to put those words within quotation marks.

PLAGIARIZED

Steven Johnson argues in *Interface Culture* that the concept of "surfing" is misapplied to the Internet because channel surfers hop back and forth between different channels because they're bored, but Web surfers click on links because they're interested.

[Most of the words are lifted directly from the original; see page 591.]

ACCEPTABLE SUMMARY

Steven Johnson argues in *Interface Culture* that the concept of "surfing" is misapplied to the Internet because users of the Web consciously choose to link to other sites while television viewers mindlessly flip through the channels until something catches their attention.

Paraphrasing

When you paraphrase, you represent the idea of the source in your own words at about the same length as the original. You still need to include the reference to the source of the idea. The following example illustrates what is not an acceptable paraphrase.

PLAGIARIZED

Steven Johnson argues that the concept of "surfing" does a terrible injustice to what it means to navigate around the Web. What makes the idea of Web surfing infuriating is the association with television. Web surfing and channel surfing are truly different activities; to imagine them as the same is to ignore their defining characteristics. A channel surfer skips around because she's bored while a Web surfer clicks on a link because she's interested (107–09).

Even though the source is listed, this paraphrase is unacceptable. Too many of the words in the original are used directly here, including much or all of entire sentences.

When a string of words is lifted from a source and inserted without quotation marks, the passage is plagiarized. Changing a few words in a sentence is not a paraphrase. Compare these two sentences:

SOURCE

Web surfing and channel surfing are genuinely different pursuits; to imagine them as equivalents is to ignore the defining characteristics of each medium.

UNACCEPTABLE PARAPHRASE

Web surfing and channel surfing are truly different activities; to imagine them as the same is to ignore their defining characteristics.

The paraphrase takes the structure of the original sentence and substitutes a few words. It is much too similar to the original.

A true paraphrase represents an entire rewriting of the idea from the source

ACCEPTABLE PARAPHRASE

Steven Johnson argues that "surfing" is a misleading term for describing how people navigate on the Web. He allows that "surfing" is appropriate for clicking across television channels because the viewer has to interact with what the networks and cable companies provide, just as the surfer has to interact with what the ocean provides. Web surfing, according to Johnson, operates at much greater depth and with much more consciousness of purpose. Web surfers actively follow links to make connections (107–09).

Even though there are a few words from the original in this paraphrase, such as *navigate* and *connections*, these sentences are original in structure and wording while accurately conveying the meaning of the source.

Frame each paraphrase

Each paraphrase should begin by introducing the author and conclude with a page reference to the material that is paraphrased.

Incorporate quotations

Quotations are a frequent problem area in research papers. Review every quotation to ensure that each is used effectively and correctly.

- Limit the use of long quotations. If you have more than one blocked quotation on a page, look closely to see if one or more can be paraphrased or summarized.

- Check that each quotation supports your major points rather than making major points for you. If the ideas rather than the original wording are what's important, paraphrase the quotation and cite the source.

- Check that each quotation is introduced and attributed. Each quotation should be introduced and the author or title named. Check for verbs that signal a quotation: Smith *claims*, Jones *argues*, Brown *states*.

- Check that you cite the source for each quotation. You are required to cite the sources of all direct quotations, paraphrases, and summaries.

- Check the accuracy of each quotation. It's easy to leave out words or mistype a quotation. Compare what is in your paper to the original source. If you need to add words to make the quotation grammatical, make sure the added words are in brackets.

- Read your paper aloud to a classmate or a friend. Each quotation should flow smoothly when you read your paper aloud. Put a check beside rough spots as you read aloud so you can revise later.

When to quote directly and when to paraphrase

Use direct quotations when the original wording is important.

DIRECT QUOTATION

Smith notes that

> Although the public grew to accept film as a teaching tool, it was not always aware of all it was being taught. That was because a second type of film was also being produced during these years, the "attitude-building" film, whose primary purpose was to motivate, not instruct. Carefully chosen visuals were combined with dramatic story lines, music, editing, and sharply drawn characters to create powerful instruments of mass manipulation. (21)

Prose quotations longer than four lines (MLA) or forty words (APA) should be indented ten spaces in MLA style or five spaces in APA style. Shorter quotations should be enclosed within quotation marks.

PARAPHRASE

Smith points out that a second kind of mental hygiene film, the attitude-building film, was introduced during the 1940s. It attempted to motivate viewers, whereas earlier films explicitly tried to teach something. The attitude-building films were intended to manipulate their audiences to feel a certain way (21).

PARAPHRASE COMBINED WITH QUOTATION

In his analysis of the rise of fascism in twentieth-century Europe, George Mosse notes that the fascist movement was built on pre-existing ideas like individualism and sacrifice. It "scavenged" other ideologies and made use of them. "Fascism was a new political movement but not a movement which invented anything new," Mosse explains (xvii).

In the second example, the original wording provides stronger description of the attitude-building films. The direct quotation is a better choice.

Often, you can paraphrase the main idea of a lengthy passage and quote only the most striking phrase or sentence.

Verbs that introduce quotations and paraphrases

acknowledge	claim	emphasize	offer
add	comment	explain	point out
admit	compare	express	refute
advise	complain	find	reject
agree	concede	grant	remark
allow	conclude	illustrate	reply
analyze	contend	imply	report
answer	criticize	insist	respond
argue	declare	interpret	show
ask	describe	maintain	state
assert	disagree	note	suggest
believe	discuss	object	think
charge	dispute	observe	write

STAYING ON TRACK

Quotations don't speak for themselves

Off track

Don't rely on long quotations to do the work of writing for you.

These quotations are picked up out of context and dropped into the paper. Readers have no clue about why they are relevant to the writer's text.

Richard Lanham writes:
> Economics . . . studies the allocation of scarce resources. Normally we would think that the phrase "information economy," which we hear everywhere nowadays, makes some sense. It is no longer physical stuff that is in short supply, we are told, but information about it. So, we live in an "information economy." but information is not in short supply in the new information economy. We're drowning it. What we lack is the human attention needed to make sense of it all. (xi)

Lanham goes on to say:
> "Rhetoric" has not always been a synonym for humbug. For most of Western history, it has meant the body of doctrine that teaches people how to speak and write and, thus, act effectively in public life. Usually defined as "the art of persuasion," it might has well have been called "the economics of attention." It tells us how to allocate our central scarce resource, to invite people to attend to what we would like them to attend to. (xii–xiii)

On track

When sources are used effectively, they are woven into the fabric of a research project but still maintain their identity.

Most of the source is paraphrased, allowing the discussion to be integrated into the writer's text. The writer centers on how two key concepts, the "information economy" and "rhetoric," are reinterpreted by Richard Lanham. Only those words critical to representing Lanham's position are quoted directly.

In The Economics of Attention, Richard Lanham begins by pointing out that the "information economy" stands traditional economics on its head because there is no shortage of information today. Instead Lanham argues that attention is what is in short supply and that the discipline of rhetoric can help us to understand how attention is allocated. Rhetoric historically has meant the art and study of speaking and writing well, especially for participating in public life. Lanham maintains that what rhetoric has really been about is what he calls "the economics of attention" (xii). The central goal of rhetoric, according to Lanham, is "to invite people to attend to what we would like them to attend to" (xii–xiii).

Incorporate visuals

Here are a few guidelines to keep in mind for incorporating visual sources into your research paper.

- Use visuals for examples and supporting evidence, not for decoration. For example, if the subject of your research is Internet crime in San Francisco, including a picture of the Golden Gate Bridge is irrelevant and will detract from your paper.

- Refer to images and other graphics in the body of your research paper. Explain the significance of any images or graphics in the body of your paper.

- Respect the copyright of visual sources. You may need to request permission to use a visual from the Web.

- Get complete citation information. You are required to cite visual sources in your list of works cited just as you are for other sources.

- Describe the content of the image or graphic in the caption.

Façade of the Last Judgment, Orvieto, Italy, c. 1310–1330. Medieval churches frequently depicted Christ as a judge, damning sinners to hell.

WRITE NOW

Summarize, paraphrase, and quote directly

Read this quotation and then
- Write a summary of it;
- Write a paraphrase of it;
- Incorporate a direct quotation from it into a sentence.

There is no strife, no prejudice, no national conflict in outer space as yet. Its hazards are hostile to us all. Its conquest deserves the best of all mankind, and its opportunity for peaceful cooperation many never come again. But why, some say, the moon? Why choose this as our goal? And they may well ask why climb the highest mountain? Why, 35 years ago, fly the Atlantic? Why does Rice play Texas?

We choose to go to the moon. We choose to go to the moon in this decade and do the other things, not because they are easy, but because they are hard, because that goal will serve to organize and measure the best of our energies and skills, because that challenge is one that we are willing to accept, one we are unwilling to postpone, and one which we intend to win, and the others, too. (President John F. Kennedy, September 12, 1962).

Review your research project

Read your project aloud and put checks in the margin in places where you think it sounds rough or might need more development. When you finish, try to imagine yourself as a reader who doesn't know much about your subject or has a different viewpoint. What could you add to benefit that reader?

Reviewing another student's research project

Read through a paper twice. The first time you read through a paper, concentrate on comprehension and overall impressions. On your second reading show the writer where you got confused or highlight parts that were especially good by adding comments in the margins.

Questions for reviewing a research project

- Does the title describe the subject of the paper? Does it create interest in the subject?

- Are the introductory paragraphs effective and relevant to the paper that follows?

- Is the thesis clearly stated in the beginning paragraphs of the paper?

- Does the writer offer support for the thesis from a variety of valid and reliable sources?

- Does the paper go into enough detail to support the thesis, and are the details relevant to the thesis?

- Do the arguments presented in the paper flow logically? Is the paper well organized?

- Is the tone of the paper consistent throughout? Is the word choice varied and appropriate throughout?

- Did you have to read some parts more than once to fully understand them?

- Are quotations properly introduced and integrated into the text?

- Are all facts and quotations that are not common knowledge documented?

- Is the documentation in the correct form?

- Is the paper free of errors of grammar and punctuation?

Revise your research project

From your review and possibly reviews of other students, make a list of changes you might make. Start with the large concerns—reorganizing paragraphs, cutting unnecessary parts, and adding new sections. When you have finished revising, edit and proofread carefully.

How to write a research paper

Many people have described writing a research paper as entering a conversation. To create a conversation with those who have written about your subject, you must distinguish your words from the words of others. Paraphrasing, summarizing, and quoting directly are the key moves for bringing other voices into your paper.

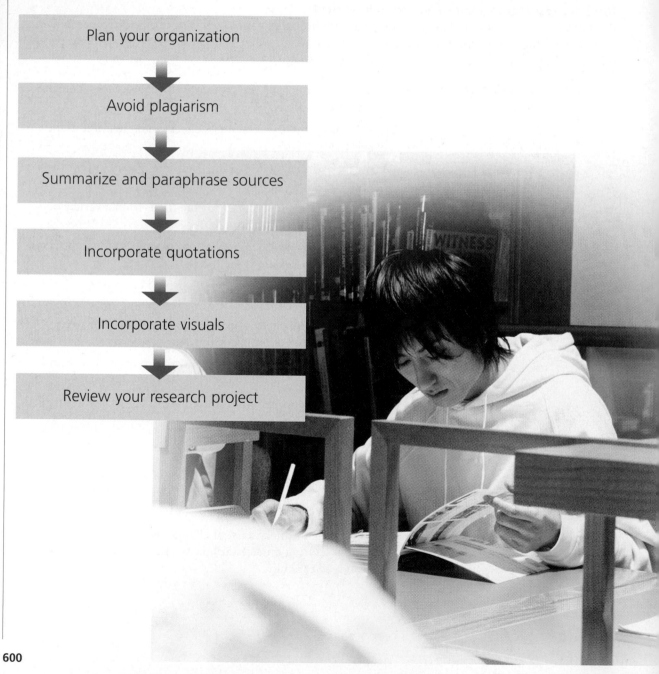

Plan your organization

Avoid plagiarism

Summarize and paraphrase sources

Incorporate quotations

Incorporate visuals

Review your research project

Researcher at work

George Akubar wanted to show that the Federal Trade Commission offers exhaustive, but not always useful, advice to consumers. He selected a number of direct quotations from the FTC's Web site, which he wove together with his own commentary:

> The FTC has an entire Web site devoted to telling consumers how to minimize their risk of identity theft. Some of their advice is obvious, like "keep your purse or wallet in a safe place at work." Some tips are more obscure: "Treat your mail and trash carefully." Some assume that people have a lot more time, patience, and knowledge than they really do:
>
> > Ask about information security procedures in your workplace or at businesses, doctor's offices or other institutions that collect your personally identifying information. Find out who has access to your personal information and verify that it is handled securely. Ask about the disposal procedures for those records as well. Find out if your information will be shared with anyone else. If so, ask how your information can be kept confidential. (<u>Identity</u>)
>
> Not many people are prepared to spend twenty minutes grilling the checkout person at Old Navy when she asks for their phone number.

George included a lengthy quotation from author Daniel Solove about the problem of identity theft. However, because Solove's proposal for dealing with identity theft was complex, and differed somewhat from the solution George was proposing, he summarized this part of Solove's argument rather than quoting directly:

> Solove's proposal for reducing identity theft is to change the structure, or "architecture," of the systems we use to collect and store personal information. He recommends giving individuals more control over their personal information, and requiring the companies that use that information to inform people whenever something unusual happens to their files.

You can read the final draft of George's paper on pages 624–631.

21

MLA Documentation

The two styles of documentation used most frequently are the American Psychological Association (APA) style and the Modern Language Association (MLA) style. The APA style is followed in the social sciences and education (see Chapter 22), while the MLA style is the norm for the humanities and fine arts disciplines. If you have questions that this chapter does not address, consult the *MLA Handbook for Writers of Research Papers*, sixth edition (2003), and the *MLA Style Manual and Guide to Scholarly Publishing*, second edition (1998).

Works Cited

s Mouth." Trans. Margaret Say

goes: Stories from Latin Americ

, 1992. 83-88.

"The Importance of Beethoven."

uly 1996. Transcript. Broadcast Ne

Chapter contents

Elements of MLA documentation

In MLA style, quotations, summaries, and paraphrases from outside sources are indicated by in-text citations in parentheses. When readers find a parenthetical reference in the body of a paper, they can turn to the list of works cited at the end of the paper to find complete publication information for the cited source.

Walker 3

... But how important is face-to-face interaction to maintaining good, "social" behavior in a group?

Describing humans as "innate mind readers," one observer argues that "our skill at imagining other people's mental states ranks up there with our knack for language and our opposable thumbs" (Johnson 196). The frequency of "flame wars" on Internet message boards and list serves, however, indicates that our innate skill at reading minds isn't always

The writer quotes a passage from page 196 of Johnson's book.

crucial information must be
these forums that causes people
ers' mental states. for language
able thumbs"

Walker 5

Works Cited

Agre, Phil. "The Internet and Public Discourse." *First Monday* 3.3 (1998) 14 July 2001 <http://www.firstmonday.dk/issues/issue3_3/agre/>.

Johnson, Steven. Emergence: The Connected Lives of Ants, Brains, Cities, and Software. New York: Scribner, 2001.

Kleiner, Kurt. "Calling All Geeks." New Scientist 15 May 1999: 10.

Mallia, Joseph. "Authorities React to Abuse of Tax-funded Internet." Boston Herald 13 May 1999: 6.

Murphy, Dervla. Full Tilt: Ireland to India with a Bicycle. London: Murray, 1965.

---. Through the Embers of Chaos: Balkan Journeys. London: Murray, 2002.

The reader can find the source by looking up Johnson's name in the list of works cited. The information there can be used to locate the book, to check whether the writer accurately represents Johnson, and to see how the point quoted fits into Johnson's larger argument.

Entries in the works-cited list

The list of works cited is organized alphabetically by authors or, if no author is listed, the first word in the title other than *a*, *an*, or *the* (see page 612). MLA style uses four basic forms for entries in the list of works cited: books, periodicals (scholarly journals, newspapers, magazines), online sources, and database sources.

1. WORKS-CITED ENTRIES FOR BOOKS

Entries for books have three main elements:

1. Author's name.

2. Title of book.

3. Publication information.

Sterling, Bruce. Shaping Things. Cambridge: MIT P, 2005

1. Author's name.
- List the author's name with the last name first, followed by a period.

2. Title of book.
- Find the exact title on the title page, not the cover.
- Separate the title and subtitle with a colon.
- Underline the title and put a period at the end.

3. Publication information.
Publication information for books includes
- The place (usually the city) of publication,
- The name of the publisher,
- The date of publication.

Use a colon between the place of publication and the publisher's name (using accepted abbreviations), followed by a comma and then the publication date.

2. WORKS-CITED ENTRIES FOR PERIODICALS

Entries for periodicals have three main elements:

1. Author's name.

2. "Title of article."

3. Publication information.

Swearingen, C. Jan. "Feminisms and Composition." College Composition and Communication 57 (2006): 543-51.

1. Author's name.
- List the author's name with the last name first, followed by a period.

2. "Title of article."
- Place the title of the article inside quotation marks.
- Insert a period before the closing quotation mark.

3. Publication information
- Underline the title of the journal.
- Follow immediately with the volume number.
- List the date of publication, in parentheses, followed by a colon.
- List the page numbers, followed by a period.

3. WORKS-CITED ENTRIES FOR ONLINE SOURCES

Basic entries for online sources have five main elements:

1. **Author's name.**

2. **"Title of document"** and/or title of Web site.

3. **Date of publication.**

4. **Date of access**

5. **<URL>.**

There are many formats for the different kinds of electronic publications. Here is the format of an entry for an online article.

Smith, Sonia. "Biting the Hand That Doesn't Feed

Me: Internships for College Credit Are a Scam."

Slate. 8 June 2006. 24 July 2006

<http://www.slate.com/id/2143298/>.

4. WORKS-CITED ENTRIES FOR DATABASE SOURCES

Basic entries for database sources have six main elements:

1. **Author's name.**

2. **Print publication information.**

3. **Name of the database (underlined) and name of the vendor.**

4. **Name of library or library system.**

5. **Date of access.**

6. **<URL of vendor>.**

Bayly, Christopher A. "Moral Judgment: Empire,

Nation, and History." European Review 14 (2006):

385-91. Academic Search Premier. EBSCO. U of

Texas Lib. 3 Aug. 2006 <http://www.epnet.com/>.

1. Author's name.
- List the author's name with the last name first, followed by a period.

2. Title of document and/or title of Web site.
- Place the title of the Web page inside quotation marks.
- Insert a period before the closing quotation mark.
- Underline the title of the entire site or the online journal, followed by a period.

3. Publication information.
- Give the date of electronic publication.
- List the date of access just before the URL.
- Place the URL inside angle brackets, followed by a period.

1. Author's name
- List the author's name with the last name first, followed by a period.

2. Print publication information.
- Give the print publication information in standard format, in this case for a periodical (see page 615).

3. Name of database and name of vendor.
- Underline the name of the database, which you will have to look for.
- Give the name of the vendor, which is usually at the top.

4. Name of library or library system.
- Give the name of the library or library system you used.

5. Date of access.
- List the date you looked at the source just before the URL. No period follows.

6. <URL>.
- Put the URL of the vendor inside angle brackets followed by a period.

In-text citations in MLA style

1. Author named in your text	Put the author's name in a signal phrase in your sentence.

> Sociologist Daniel Bell called this emerging U.S. economy the "postindustrial society" (3).

2. Author not named in your text	

> In 1997, the Gallup poll reported that 55% of adults in the United States think secondhand smoke is "very harmful," compared to only 36% in 1994 (Saad 4).

3. Work by one author	The author's last name comes first, followed by the page number. There is no comma.

> (Bell 3)

4. Work by two or three authors	The authors' last names follow the order of the title page. If there are two authors, join the names with *and*. If there are three, use commas between the first two names and a comma with *and* before the last name.

> (Francisco, Vaughn, and Lynn 7)

5. Work by four or more authors	You may use the phrase *et al.* (meaning "and others") for all names but the first, or you may write out all the names. Make sure you use the same method for both the in-text citations and the works-cited list.

> (Abrams et al. 1653)

6. Work by no named author	Use a shortened version of the title that includes at least the first important word. Your reader will use the shortened title to find the full title in the works-cited list.

> A review in The New Yorker of Ryan Adams's new album focuses on the artist's age ("Pure" 25).

Notice that "Pure" is in quotation marks because it refers to the title of an article. If it were a book, the short title would be underlined.

7. Work by a group or organization	Treat the group or organization as the author. Try to identify the group author in the text and place only the page number in the parentheses.

> According to the Irish Free State Handbook, published by the Ministry for Industry and Finance, the population of Ireland in 1929 was approximately 4,192,000 (23).

8. Quotations longer than four lines	NOTE: When using indented ("block") quotations of longer than four lines, the period appears *before* the parentheses enclosing the page number.

> In her article "Art for Everybody," Susan Orlean attempts to explain the popularity of painter Thomas Kinkade:
>> People like to own things they think are valuable. . . .The high price of limited editions is part of their appeal: it implies that they are choice and exclusive, and that only a certain class of people will be able to afford them. (128)
>
> This same statement could possibly also explain the popularity of phenomena like PBS's Antiques Road Show.

If the source is longer than one page, provide the page number for each quotation, paraphrase, and summary.

9. Online sources	If an online source includes paragraph numbers rather than page numbers, use *par.* with the number.

> (Cello, par. 4)

If the source does not include page numbers, consider citing the work and the author in the text rather than in parentheses.

> In a hypertext version of James Joyce's Ulysses, . . .

10. Work in an anthology	Cite the name of the author of the work within an anthology, not the name of the editor of the collection. Alphabetize the entry in the list of works cited by the author, not the editor. For example, Melissa Jane Hardie published the chapter "Beard" in *Rhetorical Bodies*, a book edited by Jack Selzer and Sharon Crowley.

> In "Beard," Melissa Jane Hardie explores the role assumed by Elizabeth Taylor as the celebrity companion of gay actors including Rock Hudson and Montgomery Cliff (278-79).

Note that Hardie, not Selzer and Crowley, is named in parenthetical citations.

> (Hardie 278-79)

11. Two or more works by the same author

Use the author's last name and then a shortened version of the title of each source.

> The majority of books written about coauthorship focus on partners of the same sex (Laird, Women 351).

Note that *Women* is underlined because it is the name of a book.

---

12. Different authors with the same last name

If your list of works cited contains items by two or more different authors with the same last name, include the initial of the first name in the parenthetical reference. Note that a period follows the initial.

> Web surfing requires more mental involvement than channel surfing (S. Johnson 107).

---

13. Two or more sources within the same sentence

Place each citation directly after the statement it supports.

> Many sweeping pronouncements were made in the 1990s that the Internet is the best opportunity to improve education since the printing press (Ellsworth xxii) or even in the history of the world (Dyrli and Kinnaman 79).

---

14. Two or more sources within the same citation

If two sources support a single point, separate them with a semicolon.

> (McKibbin 39; Gore 92)

---

15. Work quoted in another source

When you do not have access to the original source of the material you wish to use, put the abbreviation *qtd. in* (quoted in) before the information about the indirect source.

> National governments have become increasingly what Ulrich Beck, in a 1999 interview, calls "zombie institutions"—institutions which are "dead and still alive" (qtd. in Bauman 6).

---

16. Literary works

To supply a reference to literary works, you sometimes need more than a page number from a specific edition. Readers should be able to locate a quotation in any edition of the book. Give the page number from the edition that you are using, then a semicolon and other identifying information.

> "Marriage is a house" is one of the most memorable lines in Don Quixote (546; pt. 2, bk. 3, ch. 19).

Books in MLA-style works cited

COLLAPSE

HOW SOCIETIES CHOOSE
TO FAIL OR SUCCEED

JARED DIAMOND

VIKING

TITLE PAGE

Title of book

Subtitle of book

Author's name

Publisher's imprint

VIKING
Published by the Penguin Group
Penguin Group (USA) Inc. 375 Hudson Street
New York, New York 10014, U.S.A.
Penguin Group (Canada), 10 Alcorn Avenue, Toronto, Ontario, Canada M4V 3B2
(a division of Pearson Penguin Canada Inc.)
Penguin Books Ltd, 80 Strand, London WC2R 0RL, England
Penguin Ireland, 25 St. Stephen's Green, Dublin 2, Ireland
(a division of Penguin Books Ltd)
Penguin Books Australia Ltd, 250 Camberwell Road, Camberwell, Victoria 3124, Australia
(a division of Pearson Australia Group Pty Ltd)
Penguin Books India Pvt Ltd, 11 Community Centre, Pancheel Park,
New Delhi–110 017, India
Penguin Group (NZ), Cnr Airborne and Rosendale Roads, Albany,
Aukland 1310, New Zealand
(a division of Pearson New Zealand Ltd)
Penguin Books (South Africa) (Pty) Ltd, 24 Sturdee Avenue,
Rosebank, Johannesburg 2196, South Africa

Penguin Books Ltd, Registered Offices: 80 Strand, London WC2R 0RL, England

First published in 2005 by Viking Penguin, a member of Penguin Group (USA) Inc.

20 19 18

Copyright © Jared Diamond, 2005
All rights reserved

Maps by Jeffrey L. Ward

COPYRIGHT PAGE

Place of publication
(When more than one city is listed
for the publisher, use the first city.)

Copyright date
(usually indicates date of original
publication)

Diamond, Jared. Collapse: How Societies Choose to Fail or Succeed.
New York: Viking, 2005.

1. Author's or editor's name
- The author's last name comes first, followed by a comma and the first name.
- For edited books, put the abbreviation *ed.* after the name, preceded by a comma:

Kavanaugh, Peter, ed.

2. Book title
- Use the exact title, as it appears on the title page (not the cover).
- Underline the title.
- All nouns, verbs, pronouns, adjectives, and subordinating conjunctions, and the first word of the title are capitalized. Do not capitalize articles, prepositions, coordinating conjunctions, or *to* in an infinitive, unless they are the first word of the title.

3. Publication information

Place of publication
- If more than one city is given, use the first.
- For cities outside the U.S. add an abbreviation of the country or province if the city is not well known.

Publisher
- Omit words such as Press, Publisher, and Inc.
- For university presses, use UP:

New York UP

- Shorten the name. For example, shorten W.W. Norton & Co. to Norton.

Date of publication
- Give the year as it appears on the copyright page.
- If no year is given, but can be approximated, put a *c.* ("circa") and the approximate date in brackets: [c. 1999].
- Otherwise, put *n.d.* ("no date"):

Boston: Harvard UP, n.d.

Sample works-cited entries for books

ONE AUTHOR

17. Book by one author

The author's last name comes first, followed by a comma, the first name, and a period.

> Doctorow, E. L. The March. New York: Random, 2005.

18. Two or more books by the same author

In the entry for the first book, include the author's name. In the second entry, substitute three hyphens and a period for the author's name. List the titles of books by the same author in alphabetical order.

> Grimsley, Jim. Boulevard. Chapel Hill: Algonquin, 2002.
> ---. Dream Boy. New York: Simon, 1995.

MULTIPLE AUTHORS

19. Book by two or three authors

The second and subsequent authors' names appear first name first. A comma separates the authors' names. If all are editors, use eds. after the names.

> Cruz, Arnaldo, and Martin Manalansan, eds. Queer Globalizations: Citizenship and the Afterlife of Colonialism. New York: New York UP, 2002.

20. Book by four or more authors

You may use the phrase *et al.* (meaning "and others") for all authors but the first, or you may write out all the names. You need to use the same method in the in-text citation as you do in the works-cited list.

> Britton, Jane et al. The Broadview Anthology of Expository Prose. New York: Broadview, 2001.

ANONYMOUS AND GROUP AUTHORS

21. Book by an unknown author

Begin the entry with the title.

> The Baseball Encyclopedia. 10th ed. New York: MacMillan; 1996.

22. Book by a group or organization

Treat the group as the author of the work.

> United Nations. The Charter of the United Nations: A Commentary. New York: Oxford UP, 2000.

23. Religious texts

> Holy Bible. King James Text: Modern Phrased Version. New York: Oxford UP, 1980.

EDITIONS, REPRINTS, AND UNDATED BOOKS

24. Book with an editor

List an edited book under the editor's name if your focus is on the editor. Otherwise, cite an edited book under the author's name.

> Lewis, Gifford, ed. The Big House of Inver. By Edith Somerville and Martin Ross. Dublin: Farmar, 2000.

25. Book with no publication date

If no year of publication is given, but can be approximated, put a c. ("circa") and the approximate date in brackets: [c. 1999]. Otherwise, put n.d. ("no date").

> O'Sullivan, Colin. Traditions and Novelties of the Irish Country Folk. Dublin [c. 1793].
> James, Franklin. In the Valley of the King. Cambridge: Harvard UP, n.d.

26. Reprinted works

For works of fiction that have been printed in many different editions or reprints, give the original publication date after the title.

> Wilde, Oscar. The Picture of Dorian Gray. 1890. New York: Norton, 2001.

PARTS OF BOOKS

27. Introduction, Foreword, Preface, or Afterword

Give the author and then the name of the specific part being cited. Next, name the book. Then, if the author for the whole work is different, put that author's name after the word By. Place inclusive page numbers at the end.

> Benstock, Sheri. Introduction. The House of Mirth. By Edith Wharton. Boston: Bedford-St. Martin's, 2002. 3-24.

28. Single chapter written by same author as the book

> Ardis, Ann. "Mapping the Middlebrow in Edwardian England." Modernism and Cultural Conflict: 1880-1922. Cambridge: Cambridge UP, 2002. 114-42.

29. Selection from an anthology or edited collection

> Sedaris, David. "Full House." The Best American Nonrequired Reading 2004. Ed. Dave Eggers. Boston: Houghton, 2004. 350–58.

Periodicals in MLA-style works cited

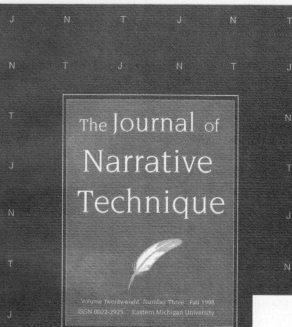

The Journal of Narrative Technique

Volume Twenty-eight Number Three Fall 1998
ISSN 0072-2925 Eastern Michigan University

Author's name

Title of article

Punish Her Body to Save Her Soul:
Echoes of the Irish Famine in *Jane Eyre*

Susan Schorn

> *Ravenous, and now very faint, I devoured a spoonful or two of my portion without thinking of its taste, but the first edge of hunger blunted, I perceived I had got in hand a nauseous mess—burnt porridge is almost as bad as rotten potatoes; famine itself soon sickens over it.*—Brontë's *Jane Eyre*

In 1846, the second year of the Irish Potato Famine, Charles Trevelyan, Assistant Secretary in charge of the relief of Ireland, stated "The great evil with which we are to contend is not the physical evil of famine, but the moral evil of the selfish, perverse and turbulent character of the people" (Clarity). That same year, Charlotte Brontë penned the following speech for the character of Mr. Brocklehurst in her novel *Jane Eyre*: "Oh, madam, when you put bread and cheese, instead of burnt porridge, into these children's mouths, you may indeed feed their vile bodies, but you little think how you starve their immortal souls!" The similarity between the sentiment and policy of these two men, one fictional, one very real indeed, is no coincidence. Both express ideas that were then common currency with regard to "the Irish Problem." The connections between starvation, moral improvement, discipline, and nationality were familiar ones in Victorian England, and Brontë's use of this public, political sentiment in her novel—and of numerous other images borrowed from accounts of the

Name of journal, volume number, issue number, date of publication, page number

The Journal of Narrative Technique 28.3 (Fall 1998): 350–365. Copyright © 1998 by *The Journal of Narrative Technique*.

Schorn, Susan. "'Punish Her Body to Save Her Soul': Echoes of the Irish
Famine in Jane Eyre." The Journal of Narrative Technique 28 (1998):
350–65.

1. Author's or editor's name
- The author's last name comes first, followed by a comma and the first name.

2. Title of Article
- Use the exact title, which appears at the top of the article.
- Put the title in quotation marks. If a book title is part of the article's title, underline the book title. If a title requiring quotation marks is part of the article's title, use single quotation marks around it.
- All nouns, verbs, pronouns, adjectives, and subordinating conjunctions, and the first word of the title are capitalized. Do not capitalize articles, prepositions, coordinating conjunctions, or *to* in an infinitive, unless they are the first word of the title.

3. Publication information

Name of journal
- Underline the title of the journal.
- Abbreviate the title of the journal if it commonly appears that way.

Volume, issue, and page numbers
- For journals paginated separately by issue, list the volume number, a period, and then the issue number before the year and page numbers.
- For continuously paginated journals, include the volume number before the year, but do not include the issue number (as in the example above).

Date of publication
- For magazines and journals identified by the month or season of publication, use the month (or season) and year in place of the volume.
- For weekly or biweekly magazines, give both the day and month of publication, as listed on the issue. Note that the day precedes the month and no comma is used.

Sample works-cited entries for periodicals

JOURNAL ARTICLES

30. Article by one author

Mallory, Anne. "Burke, Boredom, and the Theater of Counterrevolution." PMLA 119 (2003): 329-43.

31. Article by two or three authors

Higgins, Lorraine D., and Lisa D. Brush. "Personal Experience Narrative and Public Debate: Writing the Wrongs of Welfare." College Composition and Communication 57 (2006): 694-729.

32. Article by four or more authors

You may use the phrase *et al.* (meaning "and others") for all authors but the first, or you may write out all the names.

Breece, Katherine E. et al. "Patterns of mtDNA Diversity in Northwestern North America." Human Biology 76 (2004): 33-54.

PAGINATION IN JOURNALS

33. Article in a journal paginated by volume

Include the volume number before, but do not include the issue number.

Lerer, Seth. "Medieval English Literature and the Idea of the Anthology. PMLA 118 (2003): 1251-67.

34. Article in a journal paginated by issue

List the volume number, a period, and then the issue number (here, 2/3) before the year and page numbers.

Davis, Jim. "Rethinking Globalization." Race and Class 40.2/3 (1999): 37-48.

MAGAZINES

35. Monthly or seasonal magazines

Use the month (or season) and year in place of the volume. Abbreviate the names of all months except May, June, and July.

Barlow, John Perry. "Africa Rising: Everything You Know about Africa Is Wrong." Wired Jan. 1998: 142-58.

36. Weekly or biweekly magazines

Give both the day and month of publication, as listed on the issue.

Toobin, Jeffrey. "Crackdown." New Yorker 5 Nov. 2001: 56-61.

NEWSPAPERS

37. Newspaper article by one author

The author's last name comes first, followed by a comma and the first name.

> Marriott, Michel. "Arts and Crafts for the Digital Age." New York Times 8 June 2006, late ed.: C13.

38. Article by two or three authors

The second and subsequent authors' names are printed in regular order, first name first:

> Davis, Howard, June Allstead, and Jane Mavis. "Rice's Testimony to 9/11 Commission Leaves Unanswered Questions." Dallas Morning News 9 Apr. 2004, final ed.: C5.

39. Newspaper article by an unknown author

Begin the entry with the title.

> "The Dotted Line." Washington Post 8 June 2006: final ed.: E2.

REVIEWS, EDITORIALS, LETTERS TO THE EDITOR

40. Review

If there is no title, just name the work reviewed.

> Mendelsohn, Daniel. "The Two Oscar Wildes." Rev. of The Importance of Being Earnest, dir. Oliver Parker. The New York Review of Books 10 Oct. 2002: 23–24.

41. Editorial

> "Stop Stonewalling on Reform." Editorial. Business Week 17 June 2002: 108.

42. Letter to the editor

> Patai, Daphne. Letter. Harper's Magazine Dec. 2001: 4.

Online sources in MLA-style works cited

Name of journal

Author's name

Title of article

Print | E-mail | Discuss | Newsletters | Podcast | RSS | Help

hey, wait a minute The conventional wisdom debunked.

Home
News & Politics
Arts & Life
Business & Tech
Health & Science
Style & Shopping
Travel & Food
Sports
Slate **on NPR**
Output Options
About Us

Search Slate

Go

Advanced Search

**LET'S BE THE
BEARER OF
GOOD NEWS.**

Visit the Good News
Gallery on *Slate*,
sponsored by MINI.

My Mommy War
The reader said she didn't want children. I urged her to reconsider. Here's what happened next.
By Emily Yoffe
Posted Wednesday, June 14, 2006, at 12:32 PM ET

Hundreds of people have written demanding an apology and a retraction for the "disgusting," "offensive," "hurtful," "appalling," and "shocking" reply I gave in a recent <u>Dear Prudence column</u>. The letter I got was from a woman in her 30s who was about to marry a wonderful man, and they did not want children. What should she tell friends and family members who were asking when they were going to have kids? I gave some advice on how to fend them off—then added five sentences to this effect: Now that her life circumstances were changing, I wrote, she might want to re-examine this decision not to have kids.

I expected my answer would annoy people, but I was surprised by the fury of the response. You would think my reply was the equivalent of running around the streets with a turkey baster full of sperm, impregnating happy childless women.

What I didn't say in the column was that I understood exactly how the young woman felt. In my 30s, I, too, was comfortably committed to being childless. I, too, had never felt the maternal imperative everyone promised me I would. I, too, looked at my friends with children and concluded, "No, thanks!" Then *my* circumstances changed when I fell in love with a man who wanted kids. I had to decide whether to let him go, or marry him and agree to have a child.

Continue Article ▾

Also in Slate

News & Politics

**A Banner Day at the
White House**
Boy, that Josh Bolten is
good. Since taking over as
White House chief of staff,
he has ... **More**

Health & Science

A Few Good Doctors
About this time every year,
doctors across New York City
begin to cast a wary eye at
local ... **More**

News & Politics

Endangered Elitist

Yoffe, Emily. "My Mommy War." Slate. 14 June 2006. 11 Aug. 2006 <http://www.slate.com/id/2143659/>.

1. Author's name

- Authorship is sometimes hard to discern for online sources. If you know the author or creator, follow the rules for books and journals.
- If the only authority you find is a group or organization, list its name after the date of publication or last revision.

2. Name of the site and title of page or article

- The name of a Web site will usually be found on its index or home page. If you cannot find a link back to the home page on the page you are on, look at the URL for clues. You can work your way back through the URL, deleting sections (separated by slashes) until you come to a home or index page.
- If there is no title for the Web site, list it by author or creator. If it is a personal home page, place the words *Home page* after the name of the owner of the page.

3. Publication information
Volume and issue

- For online scholarly journals, the volume and issue number follow the name of the journal.

Dates
List two dates for each Web site:
1. List the date the site was produced or last revised (often at the bottom of the page; this may also appear as a copyright date) after the name of the site.
   The date might be simply a year, which is placed inside parentheses for scholarly journals.
2. List the date you accessed the site. Place this second date just before the URL. Notice that there is no period after the date of access.

URLs

- Copy the address exactly as it appears in your browser window. You can even copy and paste the address into your text for greater accuracy. Put it in angle brackets followed by a period.

Common questions about citing online sources

Where do I find the title?

Web sites are often made up of many separate pages or articles. Each page or article on a Web site may or may not have a title. If you are citing a page that has a title, treat the title like that of an article in a periodical. Otherwise, treat the name of the Web site itself as you would a book.

How do I handle very long URLs?

If the URL is excessively long and complicated, give the URL of the site's search page. If the document is from a subscription service, give the URL of the service's home page or the keyword assigned, preceded by the word *Keyword*. You can also give the sequence of links you followed, preceded by the word *Path*. Place a colon after *Keyword* or *Path*.

Note: Be sure to test your URLs as part of your proofreading process.

Sample works-cited entries for online sources

ONLINE PUBLICATIONS

43. Publication by a known author

If you know the author or creator, follow the rules for periodicals and books.

> Boerner, Steve. "Leopold Mozart." The Mozart Project: Biography. Ed. Steve Boerner. 21 Mar. 1998. The Mozart Project. 30 Dec. 2005 <http://www.mozartproject.org/biography/mozart_l.html>.

44. Publication by a group or organization

If the only authority you find is a group or organization, list its name after the date of publication or date of revision.

> "State of the Birds, USA 2004." Audubon. 2004. National Audubon Society. 19 Aug. 2006 <http://www.audubon.org/bird/stateofthebirds/>.

45. Publication with an author and a group affiliation

If both an author and an organization or institution are affiliated with the site, list the name of the organization or institution after the publication date or revision date.

> Edwards, Rebecca. "Socialism." 1896. 2000. Vassar College. 20 Nov. 2001 <http://iberia.vassar.edu/ 1896/socialism.html#debs>.

46. Publication where the author's name is a pseudonym

If the author's or creator's name is a pseudonym or is unconventional, list it exactly as it appears on the Web site.

> Akma. "Still Recouping." Akma's Random Thoughts. Weblog posting. 16 Feb. 2005. 21 Sept. 2006 <http://akma.disseminary.org>.

ONLINE PERIODICALS

47. Article in a scholarly journal

The volume and issue number follow the name of the journal. The date in parentheses is the date of publication.

> Caramanica, Laura. "Shared Governance: Hartford Hospital's Experience." Online Journal of Issues in Nursing 9.1 (2004). 12 Apr. 2006 <http://www.nursingworld.org/ojin/topic23/tpc23_2.htm/>.

48. Article in a newspaper

The first date is the date of publication, the second is the date of access.

> Erard, Michael. "A Colossal Wreck." Austin Chronicle 16 Nov. 2001. 21 Mar. 2006 <http://www.austinchronicle.com/issues/dispatch/2001-11-16/pols_feature.html>.

49. Article in a popular magazine

The first date is the date of publication, the second is the date of access.

> Cohen, Jesse. "When Harry Met Maggie." Slate 16 Nov. 2001. 21 Feb. 2006 <http://slate.msn.com/?id=2058733&>.

ONLINE BOOKS AND SCHOLARLY PROJECTS

50. Online book

> Prebish, Charles S. and Kenneth K. Tanaka. The Faces of Buddhism in America. Berkeley: U of California P, 2003. 22 May 2006 <http://ark.cdlib.org/ark:/13030/ft1v19n7k4/>.

51. Document within a scholarly project

Give the author and title of the work first, as well as its date and place of publication if it is a book. Then give the name of the project or database, its editor, version or revision date, affiliation, and date of access. The URL is the Web address of the document itself.

> Calhoun, John C. "The Southern Address." Nineteenth Century Documents Project. Ed. Lloyd Bensen. 2000. Furman U. 21 Apr. 2006 <http://www.furman.edu/~benson/docs/calhoun.htm>.

LIBRARY DATABASE

52. Work from a library database

Begin with the print publication information, then the name of the database (underlined), the name of the vendor, the name of the library or library system, date of access, and the URL of the vendor's home page.

> Snider, Michael. "Wired to Another World." Maclean's 3 Mar. 2003: 23-24. Academic Search Premier. EBSCO. Harold B. Lee Lib., Brigham Young U. 14 Jan. 2006 <http://www.epnet.com/>.

Other sources in MLA-style works cited

53. Email communication

Give the name of the writer, the subject line, a description of the message, and the date.

> Wilson, Samuel. Email to the author. 18 Sept. 2002.

54. Course home page

Begin with the instructor's name, the name of the course, the words *Course home page*, the dates of the course, the name of the department, school, date of access, and URL.

> Kirkpatrick, Judith. American Literature Online. Course home page. Jan.-May 2003. Dept. of English. Kapi'olani CC. 21 Feb. 2006. <http://www2.hawaii.edu/~kirkpatr/s03/s03250syllabus.html>.

55. Personal home page

If there is no title for the Web site, list it by author or creator. If it is a personal home page, place the words *Home page* after the name of the owner of the page.

> Stallman, Richard. Home page. 21 Mar. 2004. 8 Apr. 2004 <http://www.stallman.org/>.

56. Sound recording

> Ochs, Phil. There But for Fortune. Elektra Records, 1989.

57. Film

> Lost in Translation. Dir. Sofia Coppola. Perf. Bill Murray and Scarlett Johansson. Focus Features, 2003

58. Video or DVD

List the medium (DVD, VHS, etc) before the name of the distributor.

> House of Flying Daggers. Dir. Yimou Zhang. Perf. Takeshi Kaneshiro and Ziyi Zhang. DVD. Columbia Tristar, 2005.

59. Television or radio program

Provide the title of the episode or segment, followed by the title of the program and series (if any). After the titles, list any performers, narrators, directors, or others who might be pertinent. Then give the name of the network, call numbers and city for any local station, and the broadcast date.

> "Kaisha." The Sopranos. Perf. James Gandolfini, Lorraine Bracco, and Edie Falco. HBO. 4 June 2006.

Visual sources in MLA-style works cited

60. Cartoon

> Chast, Roz. "Are you in Your Goddess Years?" Cartoon. <u>New Yorker</u> 10 Mar. 2004: 113.

61. Advertisement

> Discover Card. Advertisement. <u>Newsweek</u> 29 Oct. 2001: 40-41.

62. Map, graph, or chart

Treat a map, graph, or chart as an anonymous book, but add the appropriate descriptive label.

> <u>Baltimore Street Map and Visitor's Guide</u>. Map. Baltimore: MAP, 1999.

63. Painting, sculpture, or photograph

Provide the artist's name, the title of the work, the name of the institution or individual who owns the work, and the city.

> Cloar, Carroll. <u>Odie Maude</u>. 1990. David Lusk Gallery, Memphis.

If you are citing a photograph of a work, give the information for the work, followed by the publication information for the source that you got the photograph from. Include the slide, plate, figure, or page number, as relevant. In the text, mentioning the work and the artist in the text itself is preferable to a parenthetical citation.

VISUAL SOURCES ONLINE

64. Online map

> Xpeditions Atlas. Map. Map. <u>National Geographic.com</u>. 2003. National Geographic Society. 24 July 2006 <http://www.nationalgeographic.com/xpeditions/atlas/>.

65. Online work of art

> Bontecou, Lee. <u>Untitled</u>. 1997. Museum of Modern Art, New York. 11 Sept. 2006 <http://www.moma.org/exhibitions//2004/LeeBontecou.html>.

66. Online cartoon

> Kelley, Steve. "The Swan." Cartoon. Daryl Cagle's Professional Cartoonist's Index. 9 Apr. 2004. 12 Aug. 2006 <http://cagle.slate.msn.com/politicalcartoons/PCcartoons/kelley.asp>.

Sample MLA paper

Abukar 1

George Abukar
Professor Hernandez
English 1102
5 May 2006

It's Time to Shut Down the Identity Theft Racket

For many college students, a credit rating is something
you'll start to worry about after you graduate and get a job.
A friend of mine, whom I'll call "Donna," has never had a
credit card in her life, and protecting her credit rating was the
last thing on her mind her junior year. That is, until she started getting disturbing calls from debt collectors accusing her of
not paying her credit card bill.

The first few times she got these calls, Donna explained to
the callers that she didn't have a credit card and didn't know
what account they were talking about. Then one debt collector
threatened to tell Donna's boss about her bad debts and take
her to court. Donna got scared.

It took several days of phone calls to her parents, her bank,
the police, and a credit-reporting agency before Donna found
out what was going on. During spring break of her sophomore
year, Donna had lost her wallet at a beach in South Carolina.
She got a new driver's license from the Department of Motor
Vehicles when she returned home, but she didn't report the
lost wallet to the police because it didn't have any money or
credit cards in it.

But whoever found Donna's wallet used her driver's license
information to apply for a credit card, and got one, with
Donna's name on it. He or she used the card to rack up several
thousand dollars in bills, mostly for clothes and stereo equipment. When this criminal didn't pay the bill, the creditors
came looking for Donna instead.

It's bad enough that someone stole Donna's identity. What
was worse, to her, was that none of the people who should have
helped stop the crime did. The credit card company that issued

Include your last name
and page number as
page header, beginning
with the first page,
1/2" from the top.

Center the title. Do not
underline the title, put
it inside quotation
marks, or type it in all
capital letters.

Indent each paragraph
five spaces (1/2" on the
ruler in your word
processing program).

Specify 1" margins all
around. Double-space
everything.

MLA style does not
require a title page.
Check with your
instructor to find out
whether you need one.

Abukar 2

the card did not bother to check the applicant's identity. The credit reporting agencies did nothing to help her get the bad information off her files. In fact, even after she has filled out forms for all three national credit reporting agencies, asking to have the information about the unpaid credit card bills removed from her file, the bad debts are still showing up. Donna worries that she will never have a clean credit record, and that she'll have trouble buying a house or car after she graduates. "All this information about me has been falsified," Donna said in an interview, "and I don't even get to set the record straight." Only the credit reporting agencies have the ability to do that, and since they do not stand to make any money from helping Donna, they are in no hurry to do it.

As long as credit-reporting agencies are protected from the effects of identity theft, they will not take steps to protect consumers. Therefore, I propose that the United States Congress pass federal legislation making credit-reporting agencies liable for damages when their actions or negligence lead to loss from identity theft.

This legislation is necessary. Identity theft is out of control. In a report to Congress, the General Accounting Office of the United States estimated that check-related fraud losses in 1999 were $2.2 billion (Identity Theft: Prevalence 40). That was double the figure for 1997, so it is reasonable to assume costs are even higher today. Fraud losses from credit card fraud for Mastercard and Visa were over $1 billion in 2000 (43). Clearly, identity theft is a huge and expensive problem. What is being done to prevent it?

Mostly, consumers are being told to protect themselves. The FTC has an entire Web site devoted to telling consumers how to minimize their risk of identity theft. Some of their advice is obvious, like "Keep your purse or wallet in a safe place at work." Some tips are more obscure: "Treat your mail and trash carefully." Some assume that people have a lot more time, patience, and knowledge than they really do:

> Ask about information security procedures in your workplace or at businesses, doctor's offices or other institutions that collect your personally identifying information. Find out who has access to your personal information and verify that it is handled securely.

Akubar states his thesis in this paragraph after he has described the problem using the example of Donna.

If more than one publication is by the same author, include a short title in the reference.

Quotations of more than four lines should be indented 1" or ten spaces.

Abukar 3

Ask about the disposal procedures for those records as well. Find out if your information will be shared with anyone else. If so, ask how your information can be kept confidential. (Identifying Theft: Minimizing)

Do not include a page number for items without pagination, such as Web sites.

Not many people are prepared to spend twenty minutes grilling the checkout person at Old Navy when she asks for their phone number. But even if someone takes all these steps and avoids even a simple mistake like Donna made by losing her wallet, is that enough?

Daniel J. Solove, in his book The Digital Person: Technology and Privacy in the Information Age, argues that it is not. "The underlying cause of identity theft," he says, "is an architecture that makes us vulnerable to such crimes and unable to adequately repair the damage" (115). He notes that

Introduce blocked quotations rather than just dropping them into the text.

> We are increasingly living with digital dossiers about our lives, and these dossiers are not controlled by us but by various entities, such as private-sector companies and the government. These dossiers play a profound role in our existence in modern society. The identity thief taps into these dossiers and uses them, manipulates them, and pollutes them. The identity thief's ability to so easily access and use our personal data stems from an architecture that does not provide adequate security to our personal information and that does not afford us with a sufficient degree of participation in its collection, dissemination, and use. (115)

Do not place blocked quotations within quotation marks.

Solove's proposal for reducing identity theft is to change the structure, or "architecture," of the systems we use to collect and store personal information. He recommends giving individuals more control over their personal information and requiring the companies that use that information to inform people whenever something unusual happens to their files. This sounds like a good plan, but I think the second half of it is far more important. Solove says that any new system should be "premised on the notion that the collection and use of personal information is an activity that carries duties and responsibilities" (121). This statement is an indirect way of saying,

Abukar 4

"Companies that handle personal information ought to be held liable for damages caused by identity theft." I would argue that if you make companies responsible to consumers by making them liable (the second half of Solove's plan), then they will automatically give consumers more control over their own information (the first half).

As Solove himself points out, "Credit reporting agencies don't work for the individuals they report on; rather they are paid by creditors" (117). Individuals already have the motivation to take care of their credit rating. But companies that make huge profits by collecting and selling our personal information have absolutely zero motivation to take even minimal steps to protect us.

How big are the profits? There are only three major American credit reporting agencies: Equifax, Experian, and TransUnion. Equifax reported an annual profit of $246.5 million in 2005 ("Equifax"). TransUnion, the smallest of the three, is privately held and does not report its annual revenue, but it employs 3,600 people. Experian, the largest of the three companies, had an annual revenue of $2.5 billion dollars last year (Moyer). These companies are raking in money while they do next to nothing about identity theft. Why would they want to change things? It is much easier, and more profitable, for them to place the burden on consumers and blame them whenever identity theft occurs. If these companies actually lost money every time identity theft occurred, would they change their attitude?

To answer that question, let's look at the banking industry. American Banker reports that bankers in Colorado are working to create an identity theft task force that would include bankers. The task force would let them work with law-enforcement officials in the state. Why are they doing this?

> "Fraud from identity theft is a huge issue," said Don A. Childears, the president and chief executive officer of the Colorado Bankers Association. "We estimate that our banks lose up to $150 million each year to fraud, so we're very motivated to find a solution." (Kuehner-Herbert 3)

The article also points out that "Along with consumers, financial institutions are hit hardest by fraud from identity theft because they have to assume most of the losses." Credit reporting agencies, by contrast, see little or no loss from identity theft. At most, they may spend some extra time processing paperwork when fraud has occurred. But Donna's experience shows they don't even take this responsibility very seriously.

It gets worse. The credit reporting agencies are not content with letting consumers and banks foot the bill for their sloppy handling of our digital identities. They want to make more money off the insecurity they have created. Kevin Drum reports in Washington Monthly,

> For their part, the major credit-reporting bureaus—Experian, Equifax, and TransUnion—don't seem to care much about the accuracy of their credit reports. In fact, they actually have a positive incentive to let ID theft flourish. Like mobsters offering "protection" to frightened store owners, credit-reporting agencies have recently begun taking advantage of the identity-theft boom to offer information age protection to frightened consumers. For $9.95 a month, Equifax offers "Credit Watch Gold," a service that alerts you whenever changes are made to your credit report. Experian and TransUnion offer similar services. In effect, customers are being asked to pay credit agencies to protect them from the negligence of those same agencies.

Unlike consumers, who usually at least try to act responsibly to protect their credit rating, credit-reporting agencies avoid responsibility for, and profit from, identity theft. Therefore, the most important step to take in reducing identity theft is to implement legislation that holds credit reporting agencies responsible for the damage their actions or inactions cause consumers.

Legislation, of course, must be passed by the government. And because of the Fair and Accurate Credit Transactions Act (FACTA) passed by the U.S. Congress in 2003, states cannot pass any laws that are stricter than the federal laws on identity theft (Solove 113). Therefore, a new federal law is needed. To determine whether U.S. Representatives and Senators could be convinced to pass such a law, I conducted a sample survey asking

Cite publications by the name of the author (or authors).

Abukar 6

people about this issue. I asked fifty people who were sitting or walking on the University Commons the following questions:

1. Have you, or has someone you know, ever been the victim of identity theft?
2. Do you feel identity theft is an important problem?
3. If a credit-reporting company reports false information about you, and you suffer as a result, should the company be held responsible?
4. Are you registered to vote?

The results of this survey indicate that most people, and the vast majority of registered voters, believe credit-reporting agencies should be held responsible for the damage they cause (see fig. 1). Furthermore, registered voters felt even more strongly about the issue than non-voters (see figs. 2-5).

Fig. 1. Identity theft survey results

Fig. 2. Is ID theft an important problem? (Overall response)

Fig. 3. Is ID Theft an important problem? (Registered voters only)

Fig. 4. Should credit-reporting companies be held responsible for harm? (Overall results)

Fig. 5. Should credit-reporting companies be held responsible for harm? (Registered voters only)

Abukar 7

Although this survey was very limited, I believe its results could be replicated on a much larger scale. Almost 13% of Americans surveyed by the FTC had gone through the same ordeal as Donna (Identity Theft Survey 4), and the frequency of identity theft is increasing. Each of those victims has friends and family. As this problem touches more and more people, there will be more and more awareness that the victim is not to blame.

Drum points out that the type of law I am proposing is very similar to the Truth in Lending Act passed in 1968, which regulated banks and lending institutions. He explains,

> One notably simple provision was that consumers could be held liable for no more than $50 if their credit cards were stolen and used without their authorization. For anything above that, it was the credit-card issuer who had to pay. The result was predictable: Credit-card companies have since taken it upon themselves to develop a wide range of effective anti-fraud programs. Congress didn't tell them to do it, or even how. It just made them responsible for the losses, and the card issuers did the rest themselves.

So it would be hard for anyone to claim (as the credit-reporting agencies probably will) that a law like this would bankrupt the credit-reporting companies. The credit-card business has flourished since 1968, and is now a multi-billion dollar industry. The lesson here is that responsible behavior is even better for business than irresponsible behavior.

The person who took Donna's driver's license still hasn't been caught. The credit-reporting agencies still haven't repaired her credit rating. The thief made money by stealing Donna's identity. The credit-reporting agencies are still making money by selling Donna's name and the false information associated with it. Donna's financial history is a wreck, and she worries about it constantly. Why is one person who profited from her misery labeled a criminal, while the others are considered good corporate citizens? It's time to shut down the identity theft racket, and make corporate responsibility the law of the land.

Abukar 8

Works Cited

"Donna." Personal interview. 30 Mar. 2006.

Drum, Kevin. "You Own You." Washington Monthly (Dec. 2005).
9 Apr. 2006 <http://www.washingtonmonthly.com/
features/2005/0512.drum.html>.

"Equifax Annual Profit at $246.5 Million." Atlanta Business
Chronicle. 2 Feb. 2006. 9 Apr. 2006 <http://www.bizjournals.
com/atlanta/stories/2006/01/30/daily33.html>.

Identity Theft: Minimizing Your Risk. 2005. United States,
Department of Commerce, Federal Trade Commission.
9 Apr. 2006 <http://www.consumer.gov/idtheft/
con_minimize.htm>.

Kuehner-Herbert, Katie. "Colorado Banks Would Fund ID
Theft Task Force." American Banker 21 Mar. 2006: 1-4.
Business Source Premier. EBSCO. U of Texas Lib. 7 April
2006 <http://web3.epnet.com>.

Moyer, Liz. "Credit Agencies in the Clover." Forbes.com June
2005. 10 Apr. 2006 <http://www.forbes.com/business/2005/
06/07/cx_lm_0608equifax.html>.

Solove, Daniel J. The Digital Person: Technology and Privacy
in the Information Age. New York: NYU P, 2004.

United States. General Accounting Office. Identity Theft:
Prevalence and Cost Appear to be Growing. Report to
Congressional Requesters. Washington, D.C.: GAO, 2002.

---. Federal Trade Commission. Identity Theft Survey Report.
McLean, VA: Synovate, 2004.

Center "Works Cited" on a new page.

Double-space all entries. Indent all but the first line in each entry five spaces.

Alphabetize entries by the last names of the authors or by the first important word in the title if no author is listed.

Underline the titles of books and periodicals.

If an author has more than one entry, list the entries in alphabetical order by title. Use three hyphens in place of the author's name for the second and subsequent entries.

Go through your text and make sure all the sources you have used are in the list of works cited.

22

APA Documentation

Social sciences disciplines—including government, linguistics, psychology, sociology, and education—frequently use the American Psychological Association (APA) documentation style. For a detailed treatment of APA style, consult the *Publication Manual of the American Psychological Association*, fifth edition (2001).

IN HYPOTHESIS GENERATION

., & Fisher, S. D. (1979). Hypothesis plausibility and hypothesis ration. *Organizational Behavior and Human Performance, 24,* 93–110.

J., & Klayman, J. (1992). Recognition of uncertainty in emotional in- ences: Reasoning about emotionally equivocal situations. *Developmental sychology, 28,* 145–158.

nan, M. E. (1989). Error, falsification and scientific inference: An experimen- tal investigation. *Quarterly Journal of Experimental Psychology, 41,* 385–412.

empel, C. G. (1966). *Philosophy of natural science.* Englewood Cliffs, NJ: Pren- tice Hall.

Kerr, N. L. (1997). HARKing: Hypothesizing after the results are known. *Per- sonality and Social Psychology Review, 2,* 196–217.

Kerr, N. L., & Harris, S. E. (2000). HARKing (hypothesizing after the results are known): Views from three disciplines. Unpublished manuscript, Michigan State University, Lansing.

Klahr, D., & Dunbar, K. (1988). The psychology of scientific discovery: Search in two problem spaces. *Cognitive Science, 12,* 1–48.

Klayman, J. (1995). Varieties of confirmation bias. In D. L. Medin, J. R. Buse- meyer, & R. Hastie (Eds.), *The psychology of learning and motivation: Decision making from a cognitive perspective.* New York: Academic Press.

Koehler, J. J. (1993). The influence of prior beliefs on scientific judgments of evidence quality. *Organizational Behavior and Human Decision Processes, 56,* 28–55.

Lakatos, I. (1978). *The methodology of scientific research programmes.* Cambridge, UK: Cambridge University Press.

Laughlin, P. R., & McGlynn, R. P. (1986). Collective ind... and individual influence by exchange of k...

Laughlin, P. R., Vander... of Experimental Social Psycholo... vs. indiv...

Chapter contents

APA citations

APA style emphasizes the date of publication. When you cite an author's name in the body of your paper, always include the date of publication. Notice too that APA style includes the abbreviation for page (p.) in front of the page number. When multiple pages are cited, give the full page range (Zukin, 2004, pp. 151–153). A comma separates each element of the citation.

Zukin (2004) observes that teens today begin to shop for themselves at age 13 or 14, "the same age when lower-class children, in the past, became apprentices or went to work in factories" (p. 50).

One sociologist notes that teens today begin to shop for themselves at age 13 or 14, "the same age when lower-class children, in the past, became apprentices or went to work in factories" (Zukin, 2004, p. 50).

When you cite an author's name in the body of your paper, always include the date of publication.

APA style includes the abbreviation for page (p.) in front of the page number.

If the author's name is not mentioned in the sentence, the reference looks like this.

References

Zukin, S. (2004). *Point of purchase: How shopping changed American culture*. New York: Routledge.

The corresponding entry in the references list would be

Where do you put the date?

You have two choices. You can put the date in your text in parentheses

Zhang, Liu, and Cao (2006) specify . . .

or between the author's name and the page number in the citation note.

. . . visual languages (Zhang, Liu, & Cao, 2006, p. 192).

When do you need to give a page number?

- Give the page number for all direct quotations.

- For electronic sources that do not provide page numbers, give the paragraph number when available. Use the abbreviation para. or the symbol ¶.

- If the source does not include page numbers, it is preferable to reference the work and the author in the text.

In Wes Anderson's 1998 film *Rushmore*, . . .

In-text citations in APA style

1. Author named in your text

Influential sociologist Daniel Bell (1973) noted a shift in the United States to the "postindustrial society" (p. 3).

2. Author not named in your text

In 1997, the Gallup poll reported that 55% of adults in the United States think secondhand smoke is "very harmful," compared to only 36% in 1994 (Saad, 1997, p. 4).

3. Work by a single author

(Bell, 1973, p. 3)

4. Work by two authors

Notice that APA uses an ampersand (&) with multiple authors' names rather than *and*.

(Suzuki & Irabu, 2002, p. 404).

5. Work by three to five authors

The authors' last names follow the order of the title page.

(Francisco, Vaughn, & Romano, 2001, p. 7).

Subsequent references can use the first name and *et al*.

(Francisco et al., 2001, p. 17)

6. Work by six or more authors

Use the first author's last name and *et al*. for all in-text references.

(Swallit et al., 2004, p. 49)

7. Work by a group or organization

Identify the group author in the text and place only the page number in the parentheses.

The National Organization for Women (2001) observed that this "generational shift in attitudes towards marriage and childrearing" will have profound consequences (p. 325).

8. Work by an unknown author

Use a shortened version of the title (or the full title if it is short) in place of the author's name. Capitalize all key words in the title. If it is an article title, place it in quotation marks.

("Derailing the Peace Process," 2003, p. 44)

9. Quotations 40 words or longer	Indent long quotations five spaces and omit quotation marks. Note that the period appears before the parentheses in an indented "block" quote.

> Orlean (2001) has attempted to explain the popularity of the painter Thomas Kinkade:
>> People like to own things they think are valuable. . . . The high price of limited editions is part of their appeal; it implies that they are choice and exclusive, and that only a certain class of people will be able to afford them. (p. 128)

10. Two works by one author with the same copyright date	Assign the dates letters (a, b, etc.) according to their alphabetical arrangement in the references list.

> The majority of books written about coauthorship focus on partners of the same sex (Laird, 2001a, p. 351).

11. Two or more sources within the same sentence	Place each citation directly after the statement it supports.

> Some surveys report an increase in homelessness rates (Alford, 2004) while others chart a slight decrease (Rice, 2003a) . . .

If you need to cite two or more works within the same parentheses, list them in the order they appear in the references list and separate them with a semicolon.

> (Alford, 2004; Rice, 2003a)

12. Work quoted in another source	Name the work and give a citation for the secondary source.

> Saunders and Kellman's study (as cited in McAtee, Luhan, Stiles, & Buell, 1994)

Books in APA-style references list

TITLE PAGE

The World of Cities ◄

Title of book

Places in Comparative and ◄
Historical Perspective

Subtitle of book

ANTHONY M. ORUM AND XIANGMING CHEN ◄

Author's name

Publisher's imprint

b Blackwell
Publishing

© 2003 by Anthony M. Orum and Xiangming Chen

350 Main Street, Malden, MA 02148-5018, USA
108 Cowley Road, Oxford OX4 1JF, UK
550 Swanston Street, Carlton South, Melbourne, Victoria 3053, Australia
Kurfustendamm 57, 10707 Berlin, Germany

The right of Anthony M. Orum and Xiangming Chen to be identified as the Authors
of this Work has been assewrted in accordance with the UK Copyright, Designs and
Patents Act 1988.

First published 2003 by Blackwell Publishers Ltd, a Blackwell Publishing company

COPYRIGHT PAGE

Date

Place of publication

Orum, A. M., & Chen, X. (2003). *The world of cities: Places in comparative and historical perspective*. Malden, MA: Blackwell.

1. Author's or editor's name
- The author's last name comes first, followed by a comma and the author's initials.
- Join two authors' names with an ampersand.
- If an editor, put the abbreviation *Ed.* in parentheses after the name:

Kavanaugh, P. (Ed.).

2. Year of publication
- Give the year the work was copyrighted in parentheses. If no year of publication is given, write *n.d.* ("no date") in parentheses:

Smith, S. (n.d.).

- If it is a multivolume edited work published over a period of more than one year, put the span in parentheses:

Smith, S. (1999–2001).

3. Book title
- Italicize the title.
- Capitalize only the first word, proper nouns, and the first word after a colon.
- If the book is part of a series, list the series name immediately after the title. Do not italicize or underline it.
- Use the same rules for capitalization as for the title.
- Close with a period.
- If the title is in a foreign language, copy it exactly as it appears on the title page.

4. Publication information
Place of publication
- List the city without a state abbreviation or country for major cities known for publishing (New York, Boston).
- Add the state abbreviation or country for other cities (as in this example). If the publisher is a university named for a state, omit the state abbreviation.
- If more than one city is given on the title page (as in this example), list only the first.

Publisher's name
- Do not shorten or abbreviate words like *University* or *Press*.
- Omit words such as *Co., Inc.,* and *Publishers*.

Sample references for books

13. Book by one author

The author's last name comes first, followed by a comma and the author's initials.

> Ball, E. (2000). *Slaves in the family*. New York: Ballantine Books.

If an editor, put the abbreviation *Ed.* in parentheses after the name.

> Kavanagh, P. (Ed.). (1969). *Lapped furrows*. New York: Hand Press.

14. Book by two authors

Join two authors' names with a comma and ampersand.

> Hardt, M., & Negri, A. (2000). *Empire*. Cambridge, MA: Harvard University Press.

If editors, use (*Eds.*) after the names.

> McClelland, D., & Eismann, K. (Eds.).

15. Book by three or more authors

Write out all of the authors' names up to six. The seventh and subsequent authors can be abbreviated to *et al.*

> Anders, K., Child, H., Davis, K., Logan, O., Petersen, J., Tymes, J., et al.

16. Chapter in an edited collection

Add the word *In* after the selection title and before the names of the editor(s).

> Howard, A. (1997). Labor, history, and sweatshops in the new global economy. In A. Ross (Ed.), *No sweat: Fashion, free trade, and the rights of garment workers* (pp. 151–172). New York: Verso.

17. Published dissertation or thesis

If the dissertation you are citing is published by University Microfilms International (UMI), provide the order number as the last item in the entry.

> Price, J. J. (1998). Flight maps: Encounters with nature in modern American culture. *Dissertation Abstracts International, 59*(5), 1635. (UMI No. 9835237)

18. Government document

When the author and publisher are identical, use the word *Author* as the name of the publisher.

> U.S. Environmental Protection Agency. (2002). *Respiratory health effects of passive smoking: Lung cancer and other disorders*. (EPA Publication No. 600/6-90/006 F). Washington, DC: Author.

Periodicals in APA-style references

JOURNAL COVER

Name of journal

Social Science Quarterly

December 1993
Volume 74, Number 4

Date

Issue number

Volume

OF GENERAL INTEREST

Foreign Debt and Economic Growth in the World System	GLASBERG/WARD
Household Out-of-Pocket Health Expenditures	RUBIN/KOELLN
Imprisonment in the American States	TAGGART/WINN
Political Opportunity and Peace and Justice Advocacy	IMIG/MEYER
Offshore Assembly in Developing and Developed Countries	CLARK/SAWYER/SPRINKLE
Alcohol Prohibition and Motor Vehicle Accidents	WINN/GIACOPASSI
Saturn Comes to Tennessee: Citizen Perceptions of Impacts	FOLZ/GADDIS/LYONS/SCHEB
Reciprocity and South Africa's Foreign Policy Behavior	VAN WYK/RADLOFF

CURRENT RESEAR...
ETHNICITY

American Women Who W...
Policy Effects of Suffrage E...
Health and Pension Benefi...
Labor Supply of Puerto Ric...
Black-White Differences i...
Accent Penalties and the E...

FIRST PAGE OF ARTICLE

Title of article

Author's names

Abstract

Publication information

Effects of County-Level Alcohol Prohibition on Motor Vehicle Accidents*

Russell G. WINN, *New Mexico State University*
David GIACOPASSI, *Memphis State University*

All motor vehicle accidents in Kentucky were analyzed over a four-year period to determine if counties that prohibit the sale of alcohol have lower crash rates. The data reveal that dry counties have a lower rate of alcohol-related fatalities and significantly lower rates of alcohol-related nonfatal and property accidents. The authors caution that the results should not be taken as a general prescription for alcohol regulation since the counties studied are dry by choice.

Over the past 90 years more than 2.5 million Americans have died in automobile crashes, many of them alcohol-related (Jacobs, 1989). Based on the commonly assumed relationship between alcohol availability and a wide range of social problems, both state and local governments have sought to reduce the number of alcohol-related accidents by enacting regulations to limit alcohol use. These policy changes have included increasing legal drinking age and taxes; restrictions on hours of sale, type, and density of outlets; and changing criminal justice enforcement practices. Researchers have evaluated the effects of the restrictive policies in terms of alcohol-related behavior, principally driving under the influence (DUI), public drunkenness, and various health conditions such as cirrhosis. These studies have yielded inconsistent results (Moskowitz, 1989; Smith, 1988).

While numerous studies have analyzed the effects that tightened alcohol regulations have on deleterious conditions, few studies have looked at the impact of modern alcohol prohibition on alcohol-related behaviors and conditions. Currently, 15 states have local jurisdictions that prohibit the public sale of beverage alcohol. The proportion of dry population in these 15 states ranges from less than 1 percent of the population of Nebraska to over 40 percent of the population in Arkansas and Kentucky (Distilled Spirits Industry, 1983).

* Direct all correspondence to Russell Winn, Department of Government, Box 3BN, New Mexico State University, Las Cruces, NM 88003.

SOCIAL SCIENCE QUARTERLY, Volume 74, Number 4, December 1993
© 1993 by the University of Texas Press

Winn, R. G., & Giacopassi, D. (1993). Effects of county-level alcohol prohibition on motor vehicle accidents. *Social Science Quarterly, 74,* 783–792.

1. Author's name
- The author's last name comes first, followed by the author's initials.
- Join two authors' names with a comma and an ampersand.

2. Date of publication
- Give the year the work was published in parentheses.
- Most popular magazines are paginated per issue. These periodicals might have a volume number, but are more often referenced by the season or date of publication.

3. Title of article
- Do not use quotation marks.
- If there is a book title in the article title, italicize it.
- The first word of the title, the first word of the subtitle, and any proper nouns in the title are capitalized.

4. Publication information
Name of journal
- Italicize the journal name.
- All nouns, verbs, and pronouns, and the first word of the title are capitalized.
- Do not capitalize any article, preposition, or coordinating conjunction unless it is the first word of the title or subtitle.
- Put a comma after the journal name.
- Italicize the volume number and follow it with a comma.

Volume, issue, and page numbers
- See sample references 22 and 23 for more on different types of pagination.

Sample references for periodical sources

19. Article by one author

Kellogg, R. T. (2001). Competition for working memory among writing processes. *American Journal of Psychology, 114*, 175–192.

20. Article by multiple authors

Write out all of the authors' names, up to six authors. The seventh and subsequent authors can be abbreviated to *et al.*

Blades, J., & Rowe-Finkbeiner, K. (2006). The motherhood manifesto. *The Nation, 282*(20), 11–16.

21. Article by a group or organization

National Organization for Women (2002). Where to find feminists in Austin. *The NOW guide for Austin women*. Austin, TX: Chapter Press.

22. Article in a journal with continuous pagination

Include only the volume number and the year, not the issue number.

Engen, R., & Steen, S. (2000). The power to punish: Discretion and sentencing reform in the war on drugs. *American Journal of Sociology, 105*, 1357–1395.

23. Article in a journal paginated by issue

List the issue number in parentheses (not italicized) after the volume number. For a popular magazine that does not commonly use volume numbers, use the season or date of publication.

McGinn, D. (2006, June 5). Marriage by the numbers. *Newsweek*, 40–48.

24. Monthly publications

Barlow, J. P. (1998, January). Africa rising: Everything you know about Africa is wrong. *Wired*, 142–158.

25. Newspaper article

Hagenbaugh, B. (2005, April 25). Grads welcome an uptick in hiring. *USA Today*, p. A1.

Online sources in APA-style references list

Author's name

Title of Web page

Department of Justice
Federal Bureau of Investigation

Contact Us | Methodology | UCR Homepage | FBI Homepage

HATE CRIME **Statistics 2004**

Report Summary

Published annually since 1992, *Hate Crime Statistics* is the byproduct of the joint effort between the FBI and the law enforcement agencies that identify and report hate crimes. This partnership and, ultimately, this publication serve as the cornerstone in raising the Nation's awareness about the occurrence of bias-motivated offenses. The publication has also become a statistical tool for those involved in the advocacy or the study of persons persecuted because of their inherent traits, such as the color of their skin, or the personal decisions they make, like what church they attend.

Hate Crime Statistics, 2004, chronicles 7,649 criminal incidents that law enforcement agencies reported—as motivated by a bias against a race, religion, disability, ethnicity, or sexual orientation—and includes information on 9,035 offenses, 9,528 victims, and 7,145 known offenders. Eleven of the 14 tables in this publication present various information about hate crime incidents, the types of offenses committed, and some aspects of the victims and the offenders. The remaining tables contain hate crime data aggregated by state or agency type and show the parameters of participation for law enforcement agencies that contributed data to the program.

Section I
The UCR Program collects data for crimes motivated by biases against a race, religion, sexual orientation, ethnicity/national origin, or disability. This section presents Tables 1 through 11, which present data about the number and types of these offenses broken down by bias motivation, by offense type, by location, and by participating state.

Section II
The data in this section provide aggregate state totals and individual agency breakdowns of bias-motivated incidents. Table 12 furnishes for each state the total number of participating agencies, the population represented, the number of agencies that submitted hate crime incidents, and the number of incidents reported. Table 13 provides data from those agencies that submitted one or more hate crime incidents in any of their reports, and Table 14 shows those agencies that submitted reports indicating that no instances of hate crimes occurred.

Appendices
The Hate Crime Statistics Act is presented in Appendix A. Appendix B is the directory of State Uniform Crime Reporting Programs, which contains the addresses and telephone numbers of the state UCR Programs and U.S. Territories that contribute data to the FBI.

Appendix A
Appendix B
Download Files (PDFs, Excels)

Web sites are often made up of many separate pages or articles. Each page or article on a Web site may or may not have a title. If you are citing a page or article that has a title, treat the title like an article in a periodical.

> Heiney, A. (2004). A gathering of space heroes. Retrieved April 29, 2006, from the National Aeronautics and Space Administration Website: http://www.nasa.gov/missions/shuttle/f_ahofpreview.html

Otherwise, treat the name of the Web site itself as you would a book.

> American Psychological Association (2004). *APA Online*. Retrieved September 23, 2005, from http://www.apa.org/

If there is no title for the Web site, list it by author or creator. If it is a personal home page, place the words *Home page* after the name of the owner of the page.

> Zhao, Hongyu. Home Page. Retrieved April 1, 2006, from http://www.geocities.com/ky_jane/

Department of Justice. Federal Bureau of Investigation. (2004). Hate crime statistics 2004: Report summary. Retrieved June 1, 2006, from http://www.fbi.gov/ucr/hc2004/openpage.htm

1. Author's name, associated institution, or organization

- Authorship is sometimes hard to determine for online sources. If you do have an author or creator to cite, follow the rules for periodicals and books.
- If the only authority you find is a group or organization (as in this example), list its name as the author.
- If the author or organization is not identified, begin the reference with the title of the document.

2. Dates

You need to list two dates for a Web site.

- First, list the date the site was produced or last revised (sometimes this is the copyright date) after the author. This date might be simply a year.
- Second, list the date you accessed the site. Place this second date just before the URL, preceded by the word *Retrieved* and followed by a comma and the word *from*. Note that the month comes before the day and year. The day and year are separated by a comma.

3. Name of site and title of page or article

- Web sites are often made up of many separate pages or articles. Each page or article on a Web site may or may not have a title. If you are citing a page or article that has a title, treat the title like an article in a periodical (as in this example). Otherwise, treat the name of the Web site itself as you would a book.
- The name of a Web site will usually be found on its index or home page. If you cannot find a link back to the home page, look at the address for clues. You can work your way backward through the URL, deleting sections (separated by slashes) until you come to a home or index page.
- If there is no title for the Web site, list it by author or creator. If it is a personal home page, place the words *Home page* after the name of the owner of the page.

4. URL

- Copy the address exactly as it appears in your browser window. You can even copy and paste the address into your text for greater accuracy.
- Note that there are no angle brackets around the URL and no period after it.

Sample references for online sources

26. Online publication by a known author

Authorship is sometimes hard to discern for online sources. If you do have an author or creator to cite, follow the rules for periodicals and books.

> Carr, A. (2003, May 22). AAUW applauds senate support of title IX resolution. Retrieved April 1, 2006, from http://www.aauw.org/about/newsroom/press_releases/030522.cfm

27. Online publication by a group or organization

If the only authority you find is a group or organization, list its name as the author.

> Girls Incorporated. (2003). Girls' bill of rights. Retrieved April 28, 2006, from http://www.girlsinc.org/gc/page.php?id=9

28. Article in an online scholarly journal

> Brown, B. (2004). The order of service: the practical management of customer interaction. *Sociological Research Online*, *8*(4). Retrieved December 16, 2005, from http://www.socresonline.org.uk/9/4/brown.html.

29. Article in an online newspaper

> Slevin, C. (2005, April 25). Lawmakers want to put limits on private toll roads. *Boulder Daily Camera*. Retrieved April 25, 2006, from http://www.dailycamera.com/bdc/legislature/article/0,1713,BDC_16336_3720378,00.html

30. Article in an online magazine

> Pein, C. (2005, April 20). Is Al-Jazeera ready for prime time? *Salon*. Retrieved April 25, 2006, from http://www.salon.com/news/ feature/2005/04/22/aljazeera/index.html

31. Document from an index or database

Increasingly, articles are read online through indexes and databases. APA recommends giving the original publication information and the date of retrieval from the database.

> Woznicki, K. (2004). Disciplines team to study race relations. *Monitor on Psychology* 35. Retrieved March 15, 2006, from Expanded Academic ASAP database.

Other sources in APA-style references list

32. Television program

> Burgess, M., & Green, M. (Writers). (2004). Irregular around the margins. [Television series episode]. In D. Chase (Producer), *The sopranos*. New York: HBO.

33. Film, Video, or DVD

> Kaurismäki, A. (Director). (1999). *Leningrad cowboys go America* [DVD]. United States: MGM.

34. Musical recording

List both the title of the song and the title of the album or CD. In the in-text citation, include side or track numbers.

> Lowe, N. (2001). Lately I've let things slide. On *The convincer* [CD]. Chapel Hill, NC: Yep Roc Records.

APA reports of research

Reports of experimental research follow a specific organization in APA style, with a title page and an abstract that gives a brief summary of the contents and four distinct sections—introduction, method, results, and discussion—followed by the list of references. This organization allows other researchers to identify information quickly.

- **The introduction** identifies the problem, reviews previous research, and states the hypothesis that was tested.

- The **methods** section describes how the experiment was conducted and how the participants were selected.

- The **results** section reports the findings of the study. This section often includes tables and figures that provide statistical results and tests of statistical significance. Tests of statistical significance are critical for experimental research because they give the probability that the results could have occurred by chance.

- The **discussion** section interprets the findings and often refers to previous research.

Sample APA paper

A common type of APA paper is the review of research. Research reports in APA style have abstracts; reviews of research often do not have abstracts. This review of research, commissioned by the Women's Sports Foundation (www.WomensSportsFoundation.org), is an executive summary of a long report that examines physical activity and sport as solutions for many of the serious health and social problems faced by American girls.

Her Life   1

APA style uses a title page.

Include page header and page number, beginning with the title page.

Running Head: HER LIFE

Type the running head (the shortened title) for publication in all caps, flush left.

Her Life Depends on It: Executive Summary
Don Sabo, Kathleen E. Miller, Merrill J. Melnick, and
Leslie Heywood

Center the title and names of authors.

Her Life Depends On It: Executive Summary

An appreciable mass of evidence-based knowledge about girls' involvement with sport and physical activity has been generated during the last decade. The amount and quality of this research are uneven and varied. For example, a good deal of research examines the associations between physical activity and risk for coronary heart disease, but studies that focus on risk for Alzheimer's disease are just beginning to appear. Researchers have verified links between high school athletic participation and teen pregnancy prevention, although more longitudinal research is needed to thoroughly confirm the connections. Overall, however, this report shows that the current state of knowledge on the relationship of physical activity to the health and social needs of American girls warrants the serious attention of public health officials, educators and sport leaders. American girls are confronted by a daunting array of health risks in their youth and in later life:

- Obesity: In 1970, only 1 out of every 21 girls was obese or overweight; today that figure is 1 in 6 (National Center for Health Statistics, 2002).
- Heart Disease: Cardiovascular disease is the number-one cause of death among American women (44.6% of all deaths), and the death rate is 69% higher for black women than for white women (American Heart Association, 2003).
- Cancer: Breast cancer is the most common cancer among women, accounting for nearly one of every three cancers diagnosed in American women (Jemal et al., 2004).
- Osteoporosis: Of the 10 million Americans estimated to have osteoporosis, eight million are women (National Osteoporosis Foundation, 2003).
- Tobacco Use: In grades 9-12, 29.5% of female students report current tobacco use (Centers for Disease Control and Prevention, 2002).
- Drug Use: Thirty-eight percent of twelfth-grade girls and 18% of eighth-grade girls have used an illicit drug at least once during the past year (Johnston, O'Malley, & Bachman, 2002).

Continue to use the running head with the page number in the top right.

Give the full title at the beginning of the body of the report.

Specify 1-inch margins on all sides.

Her Life 3

- Sexual Risk: About one-quarter of sexually active adolescents are infected with a sexually transmitted disease each year (Kirby, 2001).
- Teen Pregnancy: The United States has the highest teen pregnancy and birth rates in the industrialized world. About 80% of teen pregnancies are unintended (National Campaign to Prevent Teen Pregnancy, 2002).
- Depression: By age 15, girls are twice as likely as boys to have experienced a major depressive episode. This gender gap continues for the next 35 to 40 years, until menopause (Cyranowski et al., 2000). ◄

  Include authors and date in parentheses when you do not mention authors in the text.

- Suicide: In 2001, about 1 in 4 U.S. high school girls seriously considered suicide, and 1 in 10 actually attempted to kill herself (National Center for Health Statistics, 2003).
- Pathogenic Weight Loss Behavior: Over 90% of victims of eating disorders are female, and 86% report onset by age 20 (National Association of Anorexia Nervosa and Associated Disorders, 2004).

◄ The U.S. Institute of Medicine has defined the mission of public health as "fulfilling society's interest in assuring conditions in which people can be healthy" (Committee for the Study of the Future of Public Health, 1988). This research compiled in this report strongly suggests that sport and physical activity provide conditions that help to assure girls' health and well-being. Some findings identified in this report include:

Indent each paragraph five to seven spaces (1/2" on the ruler in the word processing program).

- Breast Cancer Risk: One to three hours of exercise a week over a woman's reproductive lifetime (the teens to about age 40) may bring a 20–30% reduction in the risk of breast cancer, and four or more hours of exercise a week can reduce the risk almost 60% (Bernstein et al., 1994).
- Smoking: Female athletes on one or two school or community sports teams were significantly less likely to smoke regularly than female non-athletes. Girls on three or more teams were even less likely to smoke regularly (Melnick et al., 2001).
- Illicit Drug Use: Two nationwide studies found that female school or community athletes were significantly less likely to use marijuana, cocaine or most other illicit drugs, although

they were no less likely to use crack or inhalants. This protective effect of sports was especially true for white girls (Miller et al, 2000; Pate et al., 2000).

- Sexual Risk: Female athletes are less likely to be sexually active, in part because they tend to be more concerned about getting pregnant than female non-athletes (Dodge & Jaccard, 2002).
- Depression: Women and girls who participate in regular exercise suffer lower rates of depression (Nicoloff & Schwenk, 1995; Page & Tucker, 1994).
- Suicide: Female high school athletes, especially those participating on three or more teams, have lower odds of considering or planning a suicide attempt (Sabo et al., 2004).
- Educational Gains: The positive educational impacts of school sports were just as strong for girls as for boys including self-concept, educational aspirations in the senior year, school attendance, math and science enrollment, time spent on homework, and taking honors courses (Marsh, 1993).

Despite the growing research evidence, girls do not have enough encouragement or opportunity to participate in sports and fitness activities. Nearly one out of every two high school boys plays sports, while only one in three high school girls participates (National Federation of State High School Associations, 2003). Special interventions aimed at increasing the physical activity level of girls are essential (National Women's Law Center & Harvard School of Public Health, 2004). Every girl deserves the opportunity to be healthy, happy, and herself. But the solutions to meeting girls' health needs stretch far beyond education and individual choice. There has been a serious erosion of infrastructural supports for physical fitness and athletics.

- Sedentary School Life: Recess and physical education are disappearing from urban schools, and only about one-third of students nationwide attend physical education class daily.
- Safety Concerns: Parents worry about the safety of their young daughters who attend after-school exercise or sport programs.
- Lack of Women in Leadership: The majority of youth programs and drop-in centers for older children and adolescents have male-oriented, if not male-dominated, cultures.

- Persistent Inequalities: Gender inequalities remain a feature of the sport and physical activity landscape. In many towns and cities, the parks and recreation departments are serving more boys than girls. Very few high schools and universities are providing participation opportunities for female athletes in proportion to the number of women in the general student body.
- Lack of Space and Facilities: In urban areas the amount of available space for exercise and athletics is often limited. Advocates for girls' programs, moreover, often have to compete with politically entrenched male administrators of boys' programs for a share of the available courts, swimming pools and fields.

This report shows that this backsliding is not just about failing to provide more girls with athletic and fitness opportunities—it's about endangering the public health. Health processes and outcomes are influenced by a multitude of factors. While researchers have made admirable progress identifying links between physical activity and girls' health, the scientific journey has just begun. And researchers are also learning more about the negative health outcomes associated with sport and exercise: e.g., overtraining can lead to permanent injury; female athletes in certain sports are especially prone to develop eating disorders; female college athletes binge drink more often than female non-athletes. Research findings that pertain to both favorable and unfavorable health impacts from sport and exercise are included in this report.

Economic inequalities exert powerful influences on health and illness. Not all girls have the same sports and fitness opportunities due to the economic circumstances of their families, schools, and communities. As some of the findings in this report suggest, the fitness and athletic experiences of poor girls and many girls of color are often mediated by poverty and racial discrimination.

The knowledge that physical activity and sport can help to prevent illness and problem behaviors is only the first step in enhancing the health and well-being of American girls. Knowledge must be transformed into policies and practice. Meeting the challenge of inactivity among girls will require a consistent, diverse and multifaceted commitment.

Her Life 6

References

American Heart Association & American Stroke Association. (2003). *Heart disease and stroke statistics, 2003 update.* Dallas, TX: Author.

Bernstein, L., Henderson, B., Hanisch, R., Sullivan-Halley, J., & Ross, R. (1994). Physical exercise and reduced risk of breast cancer in young women. *Journal of the National Cancer Institute, 86,* 1403–1408.

Centers for Disease Control and Prevention. (2002). Annual smoking-attributable mortality, years of potential life lost, and economic costs—United States, 1995–1999. *Morbidity and Mortality Weekly Report, 51,* 300–303.

Committee for the Study of the Future of Public Health. (1988). *The future of public health.* Washington, D.C.: National Academy Press.

Cyranowski, J. M., Frank, E., Young, E., & Shear, M. K. (2000). Adolescent onset of the gender difference in lifetime rates of major depression: A theoretical model. Archives of *General Psychiatry, 57*(1), 21–27.

Dodge, T., & Jaccard, J. (2002). Participation in athletics and female sexual risk behavior: The evaluation of four causal structures. *Journal of Adolescent Research, 17,* 42–67.

Jemal, A., Tiwari, R. C., Murray, T., Ghafoor, A., Samuels, A., Ward, E., et al. (2004). Cancer statistics 2004. *CA: Cancer Journal for Clinicians, 54,* 8–29.

Johnston, L. D., O'Malley, P. M., and Bachman, J. G. (2002). Demographic subgroup trends for various licit and illicit drugs, 1975–2001. Monitoring the Future Occasional Paper No. 57. Ann Arbor, MI: Institute for Social Research.

Kirby, D. (2001). Do abstinence-only programs delay the initiation of sex among young people and reduce teen pregnancy? Washington, DC: National Campaign to Prevent Teen Pregnancy.

Marsh, H. W. (1993). The effects of participation in sport during the last two years of high school. *Sociology of Sport Journal, 10,* 18–43.

Center "References" heading.

Alphabetize entries by last name of the author.

Double-space all entries.

Indent all but the first line of each entry five spaces.

Melnick, M .J., Miller, K. E., Sabo, D., Farrell, M. P., and Barnes, G. M. (2001). Tobacco use among high school athletes and nonathletes: Results of the 1997 Youth Risk Behavior Survey. *Adolescence, 36,* 727–747.

Miller, K. E., Sabo, D., Melnick, J. J., Farrell, M. P., & Barnes, G. M. (2000). The Women's Sports Foundation report: Health risks and the teen athlete. East Meadow, NY: Women's Sports Foundation.

National Association of Anorexia Nervosa and Associated Disorders (2004). *General information: Facts about eating disorders.* Online. Retrieved April 12, 2004, from http://www.anad.org

National Campaign to Prevent Teen Pregnancy. (2002). Not just another single issue: Teen pregnancy prevention's link to other critical social issues. Washington, DC: Author.

National Center for Health Statistics. (2002). *Health, United States, 2002.* Hyattsville, MD: Author.

National Center for Health Statistics. (2003). *Health, United States, 2003.* Hyattsville, MD: Public Health Service. Available online at http://www.cdc.gov/nchs/data/hus/tables/2003/03hus058.pdf

National Federation of State High School Associations. (2003). *The 2003 high school athletics participation survey.* Indianapolis, IN: National Federation of State High School Associations.

National Osteoporosis Foundation (2003). *Osteoporosis statistics.* Online. Retrieved February 2004 from http://www.nof.org/osteoporosis/stats.htm

Nicoloff, G., & Schwenk, T. S. (1995). Using exercise to ward off depression. *Physician Sports Medicine, 23*(9), 44–58.

Page, R. M., & Tucker, L. A. (1994). Psychosocial discomfort and exercise frequency: An epidemiological study of adolescents. *Adolescence, 29*(113), 183–191.

Pate, R. R., Trost, S. G., Levin, S., & Dowda, M. (2000). Sports participation and health-related behaviors among U.S. youth. Archives of *Pediatric and Adolescent Medicine, 154,* 904–911.

Sabo, D., Miller, K. E., Melnick, M. J., Farrell, M. P., & Barnes, G. M. (in press). High school athletic participation and adolescent suicide: A nationwide study. *International Review for the Sociology of Sport.*

Go through your text and make sure that everything you have cited, except for personal communication, is in the list of references.

Part 4

The Writer as Designer

23

Thinking Visually

The principles of good design, like those of good writing, begin with your audience and what you are trying to accomplish.

Communicate with visuals and words

The word *writing* makes us think of words, yet in our daily experience reading newspapers, magazines, advertisements, posters, and signs, we find words combined with images and graphics. Similarly, the dominant visual medium of our time, television, uses words extensively; think of the words you see on commercials when you have the sound off and the running text across the bottom of the screen on news, sports, and financial programs. Understanding the relationships of words and visuals will make you a better writer.

What do visuals do best?

We've become accustomed to deciding whether we'll need to wear a sweater outside tomorrow by looking at the colors on a weather map. But even then, we depend on words to tell us whether the forecast is for today or tomorrow, and what each color signifies. Visuals work well when they

- Deliver spatial information, especially through maps, floor plans, and other graphic representations of space
- Represent statistical relationships
- Produce a strong immediate impact, even shock value
- Emphasize a point made in words

What do words do best?

Words can do many things that images cannot. Written words work best when they

- Communicate abstract ideas
- Report information
- Persuade using elaborated reasoning
- Communicate online using minimal bandwidth

What can words and visuals do together?

Combining words and visuals allow writers to present very complex ideas: how the quick thinking of Union generals to rush soldiers to high ground at the battle of Gettysburg led to a decisive victory; how atomic structure influences ionic bonding; how the warming of oceans in the Arctic and Antarctic affects weather worldwide.

Understand visual and verbal concepts

We use many of the same terms to talk about texts with words and texts with visuals.

Emphasis

In words

Writers have many tools for creating emphasis, including headings, type size, boldfacing, italics, and other enhancements. Whatever comes at the beginning or the end receives more emphasis, whether it be a sentence, a paragraph, an essay, or a book.

In images

Emphasis is created by composition, by arranging elements so the attention goes where the designer wants it to go.

Balance

In words

People unconsciously expect balance, as when they move the knife to one side of the plate and the fork to the other. Balance in words can refer to parallelism, such as John F. Kennedy's famous words: "Ask not what your country can do for you; ask what you can do for your country." Balance can also mean that a writer presents more than one position on an issue.

In images

Balance in images is most often achieved by the placement of objects.

Contrast

In words

We often explain something unfamiliar by comparing and contrasting it to something more familiar. For example, a human's short-term memory is like a computer's random access memory in serving as an intermediate stop to long-term storage, but humans are far more limited than computers in capacity.

In images

Contrast is achieved with color, size, shape, number, and position.

Repetition

In words

We expect certain elements to be repeated after they are announced in writing; for example, if there is a heading beginning with I, we expect to find a heading beginning with II later in the document.

In images

Architects use repetition to create visual patterns in buildings.

Point of view

In words

Point of view refers to the perspective of the writer: the first person singular *I*, the second person *you*, the third person *he, she, my cat*, or the first person plural *we*. It can also mean the writer is directly interacting with the subject or taking a distant view.

In images

Point of view refers to the vantage point of the photographer or artist.

Motion

In words

Motion is expressed with verbs. The train *sped, roared, whooshed, thundered, slowed, glided* through the station.

In images

Blurring suggests the motion of the train and the people on the platform.

Details

In words

Although images can show accurately what something looks like, images cannot tell us what it smells, sounds, tastes, or feels like. Furthermore, words can describe what we cannot see.

In images

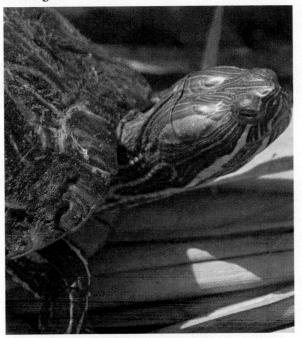

The glistening moss on the shell of a red-eared slider indicates that it just emerged from the water.

WRITE NOW

Identifying visual and verbal concepts

Find a magazine article, a book chapter, or another text that contains several pictures. Go through the text to find examples of as many of the seven concepts listed here as you can locate in both words and pictures. Note the page and paragraph number where you find the concept and how exactly the concept is used. Which concepts are used most effectively?

Concept	In words	In images
Emphasis		
Balance		
Contrast		
Repetition		
Point of view		
Motion		
Details		

24
Creating Visuals

Pictures and other visuals can have a powerful impact on readers. They can support or emphasize a writer's point and make concrete the ideas expressed in words.

Know when to use images and graphics

Personal computers, digital cameras, scanners, printers, and the Web have made it easy to include images and graphics in what we write. But these technologies don't tell us when or how to use images and graphics.

Think about what an image or graphic communicates

- Think about your readers' expectations for the medium you are using. Most essays don't use images. Most Web sites and brochures do use images.
- Think about the purpose for an image or graphic. Does it illustrate a concept? highlight an important point? show something that is hard to explain in words alone? If you don't know the purpose, you may not need the image.
- Think about the placement of an image or graphic in your text. It should be as close as possible to a relevant point in your text.
- Think about the focus of an image. Will readers see the part that matters? If not, you may need to crop the image.
- Provide informative captions for the images and graphics you use and refer to them in your text.

Format images for the medium you are using

Images that you want to print need to be of higher quality than those intended for the Web or the screen. Pay attention to the settings on your camera or scanner.

Digital cameras frequently make images with 72 dpi (dots per inch), which is the maximum you can display on the screen. Most printers use a resolution from 300 to 600 dpi. Use the high-quality setting on your camera for images you intend to print.

Scanners typically offer a range of resolution from 72 to 1600 dpi. The higher the number, the finer the image, but the file size becomes larger. Images on the Web or a screen display at 72 dpi, so higher resolutions do not improve the quality but do make the image slow to load.

Take pictures that aren't boring

No matter how easy it is now to take photographs, the great majority of pictures look the same. Why? It's because most people think pictures should look the same, taken at eye level with the subject in the center.

The result is boring, boring, boring.

This kind of picture has been taken many, many times. How else might you see this subject?

Change the angle

Find a new eye level

Kneel

Squat

Lie down

Climb a tree

Most people never stop to experience the visual richness of the world. Look for detail. Be open to what you see.

Compose images

A common misperception is that photographs are a direct representation of reality. Nothing could be further from the truth. A photograph shows not so much *what* the photographer sees but rather *how* the photographer sees. The key to becoming a good photographer is not to take pictures that show things exactly as they appear but to take pictures that convey meaning, organization, and an emotional response to the subject.

Eliminate nonessential elements

Most people include too much in their photographs. Decide what is essential and concentrate on getting those elements in the frame.

The mud on a tired horse after a race shows his exhaustion.

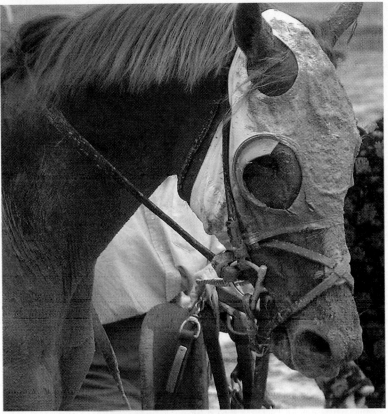

Framing

If you are taking a portrait, usually the closer you can get to your subject, the better. If your camera has a zoom, use it.

Decide what you want in a frame. If your goal is to show the habitat of pelicans, you'll need a wide shot.

But if you want a portrait of a pelican, get in tight.

665

Edit images

If you own a digital camera, you likely have an image-editing program that came with your camera. Image editors are now standard software on most new computers.

Cropping

Most images can be trimmed to improve visual focus and file size. To crop an image, select the rectangle tool, draw the rectangle over the area you want to keep, and select the Crop or Trim command. The part of the image outside the rectangle will be discarded.

Rotating

Often you'll find that you held your camera at a slight angle when taking pictures, especially if your subjects were moving. You can make small adjustments by using the Rotate Image command. You can also rotate images 90° to give them a vertical orientation.

Rotate Canvas ▶	180°
Crop	90° CW
Trim...	90° CCW
Reveal All	Arbitrary...
Variables ▶	Flip Canvas Horizontal
Apply Data Set...	Flip Canvas Vertical

Resizing

All photo editors will tell you the height and width of an image. You can resize images to fit in a particular area of a Web page or printed page. You can also change the resolution in the dpi window.

Adjusting color

You can adjust color using controls for brightness, contrast, and saturation that are similar to those on your color TV. Be aware that colors look different on different monitors and what you print may not look like the colors on your screen.

Image Size

Pixel Dimensions: 23.4M

Width: 3504 pixels
Height: 2336 pixels

OK
Cancel
Auto...

Document Size:

Width: 14.6 inches
Height: 9.733 inches
Resolution: 240 pixels/inch

Hue/Saturation

Edit: Master

Hue: 0
Saturation: 0
Lightness: 0

OK
Cancel
Load...
Save...

☐ Colorize
☑ Preview

Create tables, charts, and graphs

Software makes it easy to create tables, charts, and graphs, which are often effective in conveying statistical information at a glance. Select the type of visual that best suits your purpose.

Table 25.1 Population Change for the Ten Largest U.S. Cities, 1990 to 2000				
	Population		Change, 1990 to 2000	
City and State	April 1, 2000	April 1, 1990	Number	Percentage
New York, NY	8,008,278	7,322,564	685,714	9.4
Los Angeles, CA	3,694,820	3,485,398	209,422	6.0
Chicago, IL	2,896,016	2,783,726	112,290	4.0
Houston, TX	1,953,631	1,630,553	323,078	19.8
Philadelphia, PA	1,517,550	1,585,577	-68,027	-4.3
Phoenix, AZ	1,321,045	983,403	337,642	34.3
San Diego, CA	1,223,400	1,110,549	112,851	10.2
Dallas, TX	1,188,580	1,006,877	181,703	18.0
San Antonio, TX	1,144,646	935,933	208,713	22.3
Detroit, MI	951,270	1,027,974	-76,704	-7.5

Source: U.S. Census Bureau, Census 2000; 1990 Census, Population and Housing Unit Counts, United States (1990 CPH-2-1).

Tables

A table is used to display numerical data and similar types of information. It usually includes several items as well as variables for each item.

Bar Graphs

A bar graph compares the values of two or more items.

Line Graphs

A line graph shows change over time.

Pie Charts

A pie chart shows the parts making up a whole.

WORKING TOGETHER

Communicate with images and graphics

In a group of three or four students

Look at your textbooks for your other courses. Find one example where an image or graphic helps you to understand the material. Write briefly what exactly the image or graphic does that words alone could not. Find a second example where you think an image or graphic could be added. Write why an image or graphic would help.

Bring your examples to class and compare them with other group members. When do words work best? When is it more appropriate to communicate information through graphics and other visual media?

25

Designing for Print

We know at a glance who is telling the truth.

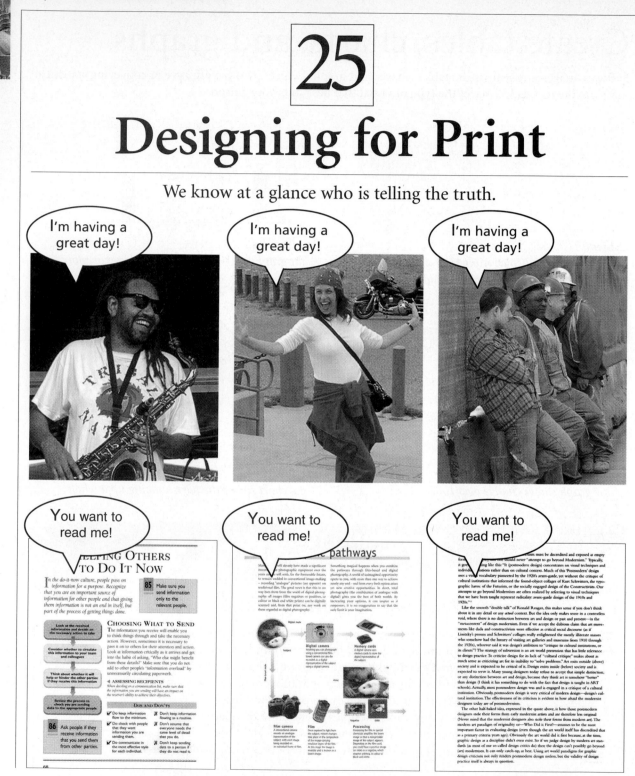

Start with your readers

Imagine yourself in the shoes of your reader. Pretend for a moment that someone else has written about your subject. What do you, the reader, want from the writer?

Tell your reader what you are writing about

An accurate and informative title is critical for readers to decide if they want to read what you have written. Furthermore, the title is critical to allow the reader to return to something read earlier.

Some genres require **abstracts**, which are short summaries of a document. Abstracts are required for scholarly articles in the sciences and social sciences as well as dissertations. Business reports and other reports often have executive summaries, which are similar to abstracts but often briefer.

Make your organization visible to readers

Most longer texts and many shorter ones include headings, which give readers an at-a-glance overview and make the text easier to follow and remember. Headings visually indicate the major and subordinate sections of a text.

Some genres have specific formats for organization, such as the APA-style report of research that is divided into four parts: introduction, method, results, and discussion. If you are writing in a genre that requires a specific format, follow it. Readers will be irritated if you don't.

Help your reader to navigate your text

Do the little things that help readers. Remember to include page numbers, which word processing software can insert for you. Make cross references to other parts of your document when a subject is covered elsewhere. If you are citing sources, make sure they are all in your list of works cited.

Help your reader to understand the purposes for different parts of your text

A traditional way to add information that you don't want to interrupt your running text is with footnotes. Today writers often use boxes or side-bars to supply extra information. If you use boxes or sidebars, indicate them with a different design or a different color. The key is to make what is different look different.

You do research every day. If you compare prices online before you buy an airline ticket, or if you look up a detailed course description before registering for a class, you are doing research. If you want to settle an argument about the first African American to win an Olympic gold medal, you need to do research. In college, research means both investigating existing knowledge that is stored on computers and in libraries, and creating new knowledge through original analysis, surveys, experiments, and theorizing. When you start a research task in a college course, you need to understand the different kinds of possible research and to plan your strategy in advance.

If you have an assignment that requires research, look closely at what you are being asked to do.

The assignment may ask you to review, compare, survey, analyze, evaluate, or prove that something is true or untrue. You may be writing for experts, for students like yourself, or for the general public. The purpose of your research and your potential audience will help guide your strategies for research.

Pull quotes are often set off from the body text with a larger font and a different color.

Use headings and subheadings effectively

Readers increasingly expect you to divide what you write into sections and label those sections with headings. A system of consistent headings should map the overall organization.

Determine levels of headings

Determine the level of importance of each heading by making an outline to see what fits under what. Then make the headings conform to the different levels by choosing a font size and an effect such as boldfacing for each level. The type, the size, and the effect should signal the level of importance.

Phrase headings consistently

Headings should be similar in how they are worded. For example, if you are writing heading for an informative brochure about a service, you might use the most frequently asked questions as your headings.

TITLE

Saepe et multum hoc mecum cogitavi, bonine an mali plus attulerit hominibus et civitatibus copia dicendi ac summum eloquentiae studium.

Major Heading

Ac me quidem diu cogitantem ratio ipsa in hanc potissimum sententiam ducit, ut existimem sapientiam sine eloquentia parum prodesse civitatibus, eloquentiam vero sine sapientia nimium obesse plerumque, prodesse numquam.

Level 2 heading Ac si volumus huius rei, quae vocatur eloquentia, sive artis sive studii sive exercitationis cuiusdam sive facultatis ab natura profectae considerare principium, reperiemus id ex honestissimis causis natum atque optimis rationibus profectum.

Be a Quitter! Join Quitters

Why quit smoking?
- You'll lower your risk for heart attack, stroke, and cancer.
- You'll look, feel, and smell a whole lot better.
- You'll have extra money to spend on things other than cigarettes.

How will the Quitters class help me?
- You'll find out your individual level of nicotine-dependence.
- You'll utilize a brand-switching technique.
- You'll explore the use of nicotine replacement therapies.

Headings function like gateways from one section to another.

Design pages

Word processing programs design pages for you with their default settings for margins, paragraph indentations, and justification. Even if you use the default settings, you still have a range of options. Thinking about design will lead to better decisions.

Choose the orientation, size of your page, and columns

You can usually use the defaults on your word processing program for academic essays (remember to select double-spacing for line spacing if the default is single-spaced). For other kinds of texts you may want a horizontal rather than a vertical orientation, a size other than a standard sheet of paper, and two columns or more rather than one.

Divide your text into units.

The paragraph is the basic unit of extended writing, but think also about when to use lists. This list is a bulleted list. You can also use a numbered list.

Use left aligned text with a ragged right margin.

Fully and justified text aligns the right margin, which gives a more formal look but can also leave unsightly rivers of extra white space running through the middle of your text.

Be conscious of white space.

White space can make your text more readable and set off more important elements. Headings stand our more with white space surrounding them. Leave room around graphics. You don't want words to crowd too close to graphics because both the words and the visuals will become hard to read.

Be aware of MLA and APA design specifications.

MLA and APA styles have specifications for margins, indentations, reference lists, and other things. See the sample papers in Chapters 21 and 22 if you are using MLA or APA style.

Giddens 3

stay in the military after their commitment ends. Congress first gave the military the authority to retain soldiers after the Vietnam War when new volunteers were too few to replace departing soldiers. In November 2002 the Pentagon gave stop-loss orders for Reserve and National Guard units activated to fight terrorism (Robertson).

- This policy is neither forthcoming, safe, nor compassionate toward those most directly impacted–the soldiers and their fami lies.
- As the United States became more and more entrenched in the conflict in Iraq, the military was stretched thinner and thinner.
- By 2004, approximately 40% of those serving in Iraq and Afghanistan came from the ranks of the part-time soldiers: the Reserves and the National Guard (Gerard).

While these individuals did know that their countries could call if they enlisted, they continue to bear an inordinate burden of actual combat time, and this new policy continues to create situations further removed from the job for which they had enlisted. Recruiters often pitch the military–including the Reserves and the Guard–to young, impressionable, and often underprivileged kids.

The Pitch

I have experienced this pitch firsthand and seen the eyes of my classmates as the recruiter promised them a better and richer tomorrow. Seeing a golden opportunity for self-respect and achievement, young men and women sign on the dotted line. Today, other young men and women are

Understand typography

Just as people communicate with body languages, texts have a look and feel created by the layout, type-faces, type size, color, density, and other elements.

Typography is the designer's term for letters and symbols that make up the print on the page. You are already using important aspects of typography when you use capital letters, italics, boldface, or different sizes of type to signal a new sentence, identify the title of a book, or distinguish a heading from the body text.

Word processing programs and personal computers now enable you to use dozens of different type-faces (fonts), bold and italic versions of these fonts, and a range of font sizes. Fortunately, you can rely on some simple design principles to make good typographic choices for your documents.

Choosing a font

A font family consists of the font in different sizes as well as in its boldface and italic forms. Although computers now make hundreds of font styles and sizes available to writers, you should avoid confusing readers with too many typographical features. Limit the fonts in a document to one or two font families. A common practice is to choose one font family for all titles and headings and another for the body text.

A Font Family

Arial Narrow
Arial Narrow Italic
Arial Regular
Arial Italic
Arial Bold
Arial Bold Italic
Arial Black

The font family Arial, shown above in 14 point, is composed of style variations on the Arial design that include a variety of weights.

Serif and sans serif typefaces

Typefaces are normally divided into two groups—serif and sans serif. Serif typefaces include horizontal lines—or serifs—added to the major strokes of a letter or character such as a number. Sans serif typefaces, by contrast, do not have serifs. Notice the difference opposite.

The typical use and stylistic impact of the typefaces vary considerably. Serif typefaces are more traditional, conservative, and formal in appearance. By contrast, sans serif typefaces offer a more contemporary, progressive, and informal look. Serif is often used for longer pieces of writing, such as novels and textbooks. It is also the best bet for college papers.

The difference between serif and sans serif fonts

The horizontal lines make serif easier to read because they guide the eye from left to right across the page.

This **SERIF** font is called Garamond

This **SANS SERIF** font is called Helvetica

Think about font style

Not all fonts are suitable for extended pieces of writing. Sentences and paragraphs printed in fonts that imitate calligraphy or handwriting are not only difficult to read but also informal in appearance. For most academic and business writing, you will probably want to choose a traditional font, such as **Times Roman**, that is easy to read and does not call attention to itself. This book is set in 10.5 point **Minion**.

Choosing the best font for the job

This piece of text is in a calligraphic font, and may be right for some special situations, but there is no doubt that every single reader will be aware of the struggle to decipher it.

This font is is **28 point Palace Script**

This piece of text is in a handwriting font, and although easier to read than the above is still very difficult in large amounts.

This font is **17 point Feltpen**

This is about as normal a font as you can find. It is called Times Roman, for the simple reason that it was designed for use in the *London Times* newspaper, and so had to be as readable as possible.

This font is is **14 point Times Roman**

```
This font is also very
readable and is very
common as it is the
default font on most
computer software. It
does however, require
much more space than
other faces.
```

This font is **14 point Courier**

Think about font size

It's easy to change the size of a font when you write on a computer. For most types of writing in college, a 12-point font is the standard size for the main (body) text, with headings in a larger font.

Type sizes

8 point

12 point

18 point

36 point

48 point

Height can make a difference

To ensure that what you write can be read easily, you need to choose an appropriate size. Fonts differ by height, called the x-height, as well as point size. Fonts of the same point size can look different because of height. Effective size depends on the appearance of a font, not merely its point size.

To ensure that what you write can be read easily, you need to choose an appropriate size. Fonts differ by height, called the x-height, as well as point size. Fonts of the same point size can look different because of height. Effective size depends on the appearance of a font, not merely its point size.

Both texts are set the same "size" (12 point) but they appear different because of the x-heights. Bembo, left, looks much smaller and takes much less space than Glypha, right.

Type sizes for computer monitors

For Web pages, you should consider using a larger font to compensate for the added difficulty of reading from a computer monitor. For overhead transparencies and computer-projected displays, you should use an even larger size (such as 32 point) to ensure that the text can be read from a distance.

Pixilation on the computer screen breaks up the font; thus the 12-point type in this example is too small.

You should consider enlarging to 18-point type as in this example.

Or even 32 point if using an overhead projector or a computer-projected display.

Checklist for evaluating document design

1. Audience — Who is the intended audience? Will the design be appealing to them? How does the design serve their needs?

2. Genre — What is the genre? Does the design meet the requirements of the genre? For example, a brochure should fit in your pocket.

3. Organization — Is the organization clear to readers? If headings are used, are they in the right places? If headings are used for more than one level, are these levels indicated consistently?

4. Readability — Is the typeface attractive and readable? Are the margins sufficient? Is any contrasting text, such as boldface, italics, or all caps, brief enough to be legible? If color is used, does it direct emphasis to the right places?

5. Layout — Can the basic layout be made more effective? Is there adequate white space around headings, images, and graphics?

WRITE NOW

Design a menu

Collect menus from a few restaurants, either in print or on the Web. Study the design of each menu.

Design a menu of your own. First, you have to decide what kind of food you will serve: burgers, Italian, Thai, seafood, and so on. Second, think about the clientele you want to attract: college students, families, office lunch crowd, or another demographic. Third, list a few food items for your menu. Fourth, name your restaurant and give it a theme.

Make a sketch of your menu. Decide what graphics, clip art, and backgrounds you want to use. Then create your menu using word processing software.

WRITE NOW

Create a brochure

Create a brochure for a subject that you know about—a building, a park, a hobby, or a campus service—using the front and back of a sheet of paper. Follow these steps to create a handsome brochure.

5	6	1
2	3	4

1 Develop a layout

A typical brochure has six panels—three on the front and three on the back.

- Take two pieces of standard 8½ x 11 paper, place them together, and fold them into three sections.
- Separate them, lay one page above the other, and label the sections by number, so you will know which panel fits where.

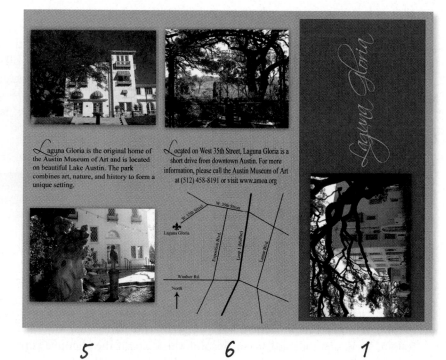

Laguna Gloria is the original home of the Austin Museum of Art and is located on beautiful Lake Austin. The park combines art, nature, and history to form a unique setting.

Located on West 35th Street, Laguna Gloria is a short drive from downtown Austin. For more information, please call the Austin Museum of Art at (512) 458-8191 or visit www.amoa.org

5   6   1

2 Make a sketch

Plan out what you want to put on each panel.

- Draw boxes where you want to insert art.
- Plan where the text will go.

3 Prepare the template

• In Word, under View, select Page Layout, which will allow you to see the graphics.

• Under File, select Page Setup, then select Landscape which will change the orientation of your page to horizontal.

4 Create text boxes

• In the Insert menu, select Text Box.

• Make three text boxes for the panels on each side. Do this by selecting Text Box under the Insert menu. Your pointer will change to a cross tool, which if you click and drag, creates a box.

• Resize each box to fit the layout.

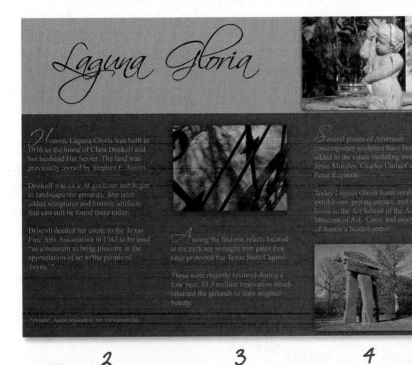

5 Insert the images

• Choose appropriate images and scan them.

• Put the images and other graphics into the layout by selecting options under Picture in the Insert menu.

• Think carefully about their size at this stage.

6 Check the formatting

When you finish you will have two pages with three panels each.

• Print them out and place them together.

• Fold, and check the panels are in the correct order.

• Check the alignment of the panels and the readability of the text. If you have extra space, consider enlarging the type or setting apart the key points.

7 Edit and proofread

Carefully check your work; errors destroy the effect of an otherwise handsome brochure.

8 The finished brochure

Once printed, the brochure is a very effective informational document. This informational brochure offers a visual and verbal introduction to Laguna Gloria, an art museum. It was created by David Crumley for a course assignment in Multimedia Writing. Crumley chose background colors that work in harmony with his original photographs.

26
Designing a Web Site

With over 100 million Web sites in the world, the biggest challenge for a Web designer is to make your visitors interested and keep them interested.

AUSTIN CITIZENS FOR SIGNS

Home — ST 1000

Missing Signs — AV 2000

Unreadable — RD 3000

Consequences — BLVD 4000

History — HWY 5000

TheCost — CIR 6000

What To Do — PKWY 7000

Contact — LN 8000

Austin Citizens for Signs

The Capitol of Texas is large enough to be visible from many points in Austin, which is fortunate because if you were looking for it by relying on street signs, you might never find it.

A leisurely stroll around the Capitol will reveal no less than eight intersections with either no street signs or barely visible ones. Even at Eleventh and Congress, the intersection direcly in front of the Capitol, there is no street sign to tell you where you are (see photo at the top of this page).

Visitors and citizens alike find Austin frustrating to navigate because so many street signs are missing. For a city that has become quite image conscious in recent years, the absence of street signs is an annoying blemish.

Fortunately, the citizens of Austin are not powerless. We can act by informing our others about the problem, by calling traffic administrators to let them know about missing signs, and by urging the City Council to take action.

Plan a Web site

Web authoring software makes it easy to compose Web pages, but the software doesn't tell you how to design an effective Web site. Visitors to Web sites often don't read pages one after the other as they often do in books. Visitors expect to be able to move through your site according to their own interests.

Determine your structure

Think in advance about the structure of your site. Decide on the major topics that should be on separate pages. Draw a map of your site that shows the pages and the links to other pages.

Kat Schwegel created the multipage *Austin Citizens for Signs* for a course project. Her subject was something that bothered her: the absence of street signs at many intersections in her city. Her goal was persuasive. She wanted fellow students and fellow citizens to contact city council members about the problem. She composed separate pages describing the missing signs, the consequences of their absence, the history of the problem, the cost of installing signs, and what readers can do to address the problem.

"What to Do" page on Austin Citizens for Signs.

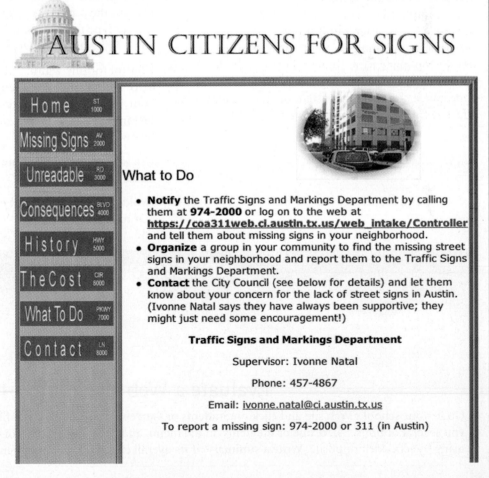

AUSTIN CITIZENS FOR SIGNS

Home ST 1000
Missing Signs AV 2000
Unreadable RD 3000
Consequences BLVD 4000
History HWY 5000
The Cost CIR 6000
What To Do PKWY 7000
Contact LN 8000

What to Do

- **Notify** the Traffic Signs and Markings Department by calling them at **974-2000** or log on to the web at **https://coa311web.ci.austin.tx.us/web_intake/Controller** and tell them about missing signs in your neighborhood.
- **Organize** a group in your community to find the missing street signs in your neighborhood and report them to the Traffic Signs and Markings Department.
- **Contact** the City Council (see below for details) and let them know about your concern for the lack of street signs in Austin. (Ivonne Natal says they have always been supportive; they might just need some encouragement!)

Traffic Signs and Markings Department

Supervisor: Ivonne Natal

Phone: 457-4867

Email: ivonne.natal@ci.austin.tx.us

To report a missing sign: 974-2000 or 311 (in Austin)

Make your site visually effective

A handsome site will result from keeping a few principles in mind.

Give your site a visual theme

A consistent look and feel makes a Web site appear unified and supports the content. A Web site does not need a loud background or flashy animations to achieve a visual theme. Instead, the little things such as selecting a simple set of colors for the text, headings, links, and background do more to create a consistent visual theme than an attention-grabbing image. Similar graphics and images should be the same size, and often their placement can be repeated from page to page.

Keep the visuals simple

A less complicated site is not only more friendly because it loads faster, but if it is well designed, it can be elegant. Simple elements are also easier to repeat. Too many icons, bullets, horizontal rules, and other embellishments give a page a cluttered appearance. A simple, consistent design is always effective for pages that contain text.

Make the text readable

Long stretches of text on the Web tend not to get read. You can make your text more readable on the Web if you do the following:

- Divide your information into chunks. If your information runs longer than a page, consider placing it on two Web pages.

- Use shorter paragraphs when possible. Long paragraphs are harder to read on the screen than in print.

- Use a sans serif typeface because it is easier to read on the screen (see page 672). You can specify type faces using the font command on your Web editing software.

- Control for line width. Lines of type that run across the entire page often are difficult to read. Your Web editing software will allow you to put text into tables, columns, or text boxes that limit line width.

- Use white space to separate elements and to give visual relief.

- Avoid dark backgrounds because it makes your text hard to read.

WRITE NOW

Evaluate a Web site

Go to your school's Web site and click on Students or Current Students. You will find a menu giving you several options. Select one of the items on the menu, and evaluate that part of the overall site using the checklist opposite. Write a summary of its overall effectiveness for students at your school.

Make navigation easy

People typically scan a Web site quickly and move around a lot. They are likely to click on links, following their interests. If you put content on more than one page, provide a navigation bar so readers can navigate easily. A navigation bar can be a simple text bar or icons that are easy to create with image editing software.

Kat Schwegel's navigation bar is prominent on all of her pages. Her use of signs as navigation icons supports the visual theme of her site.

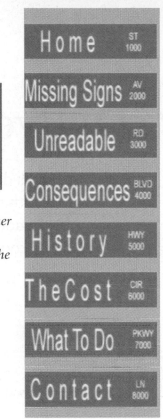

Checklist for evaluating a Web site

1. Audience and purpose	How does the site identify its intended audience? What is the purpose of this part of the overall site?
2. Content	How informative is the content? Has the site been updated recently? What do you want to know more about?
3. Readability	How readable is the text? Are there any paragraphs that go on too long and need to be divided? Are headings inserted in the right places, and if headings are used for more than one level, are these levels indicated consistently?
4. Visual design	Does the site have a consistent visual theme? Does the key information stand out on each page?
5. Navigation	How easy or difficult is it to move from one page to another on the site? Is a consistent navigation scheme used throughout the site?

27

Delivering Presentations

The best speakers draw their inspiration from their audience, and they maintain contact with their audience, communicating with body language and presentation style in addition to the content. Audience members leave feeling like they've had a conversation with the speaker even if they have been silent through the presentation.

Plan a presentation

A successful presentation, like successful writing, requires careful planning. Look closely at what you are being asked to present and how long you will have. Decide early on what kind of presentation you will give and what visuals you will incorporate.

Select your topic

Choosing and researching a topic for a presentation is similar to choosing and researching a topic for a written assignment. Ask these questions:

- Will you enjoy speaking on this topic?
- Does the topic fit the assignment?
- Do you know enough to speak on this topic?
- If you do not know enough, are you willing to do research to learn more about the topic?

Remember that if your presentation requires you to do any research, then you will need to develop a written bibliography as you would for a research assignment. You will need to document the sources of your information and provide those sources in your presentation.

Think about your audience

Unlike writing, when you give a speech, you have your audience directly before you. They will give you concrete feedback during your presentation by smiling or frowning, by paying attention or losing interest, by asking questions or sitting passively. Ask these questions:

- Will your audience likely be interested in your topic?
- Are there ways you can get them more interested?
- What is your audience likely to know or believe about your topic?
- What does your audience probably not know about your topic?
- What key terms will you have to define or explain?
- Where is your audience most likely to disagree with you?
- What questions are they likely to ask?

Organize your presentation

Make a list of your key points	Think of the best way to order your key points.
Plan your introduction	You have to get the audience's attention, introduce your topic, convince the audience that it is important to them, present your thesis, and give your audience either an overview of your presentation or a sense of your direction.
Plan your conclusion	End on a strong note. Simply summarizing is a dull way to close. Think of an example or an idea that your audience can take away with them.

Design effective visuals

Visual elements can both support and reinforce your major points. They give you another means of reaching your audience and keeping them stimulated. Visuals should communicate content and not just be eye candy. Some of the easier visuals to create are outlines, statistical charts, flow charts, photographs, and maps.

At a minimum, consider putting an outline of your talk on a transparency or on a PowerPoint slide. An outline allows an audience to keep track of where you are in your talk and when you are moving to your next point.

Create visuals

Follow these guidelines to create better visuals.

Keep the text short	You don't want your audience straining to read long passages on the screen and neglecting what you have to say. Except for quotations, use short words and phrases on transparencies and slides.
Always proofread	Typos and misspelled words make you look careless and can distract the audience from your point.
Use dark text on a white or light-colored background	Light text on a dark background is hard to read.
Use graphics that reproduce well	Some graphics do not show up well on the screen, often because there isn't enough contrast.
Plan your timing when using visuals	Usually you can leave a slide on the screen for one to two minutes, which allows your audience time to read the slide and connect its points to what you are saying.

Know the advantages and disadvantages of presentation software

Presentation software allows you to combine text, images, sounds, animations, and even video clips on *computer-generated* slides, which can be projected onto a large screen. Presentation software, such as Microsoft PowerPoint, allows you to import charts and other graphics that you have created in other programs, and it gives you several options for presentation, including printed handouts and Web pages.

The major drawback of presentation software is perhaps that it is too easy to use. An attractive presentation can be empty of content. You can quickly get carried away with all the special effects possible—such as fade-ins, fade-outs, and sound effects. Presentations with many special effects often come off as heavy on style and light on substance. They also can be time-consuming to produce.

Give a memorable presentation

What makes an effective presentation?

Usually more effective	Usually less effective
Talk	Read
Stand	Sit
Make eye contact	Look down
Move around	Stand still
Speak loudly	Mumble
Use visual elements	Lack visual elements
Focus on main points	Get lost in details
Give an overview of what you are going to say in the introduction	Start your talk without indicating where you are headed
Give a conclusion that summarizes your main points and ends with a key idea or example	Stop abruptly
Finish on time	Run overtime

WRITE NOW

Moving across media

Convert either a paper you have written or one of the readings in Part Two into a presentation using visuals. Presentation software can help you create the visuals.

Think about your main points and how to support each point with facts, statistics, or other evidence. Think too about how to engage your audience at the beginning. Perhaps you will need to find a vivid example or anecdote to get your audience interested.

Avoid making the common mistake of putting too much text on your slides. Cutting and pasting from your written text often produces a dull, wordy presentation.

28
Working as a Team

Much writing in the workplace and in organizations—especially important writing tasks like reports, analyses, and proposals—is done by teams of people. The better you understand how to write effectively with others, the more enjoyable and more productive the process will be for you.

Organize a team

Unlike sports teams where a coach is in charge, writing team members often have to organize themselves.

Analyze the assignment

- Identify what exactly you are being asked to do.
- Write down the goals as specifically as you can and discuss them as a team.
- Determine which tasks are required to meet those goals. Be as detailed as you can. Write down the tasks and arrange them in the order they need to be completed.

Make a work plan

- Make a time line. List the dates when specific tasks need to be completed and distribute it to all team members. Charts are useful tools for keeping track of progress.
- Assign tasks to all team members. Find out if anyone possesses additional skills that could be helpful to the team.

Keep goals in mind

- Revisit the team's goals often. To succeed, each team member must keep in mind what the team aims to accomplish.
- Communicate often. Most writing teams will not have an assigned leader. Each team member shares responsibility.

What makes a good team?

In sports, in the workplace, and in everyday life, successful teams have well-defined goals and work together to achieve these goals. Successful teams communicate well, make good decisions together, act quickly on their decisions, and continuously evaluate their progress. Successful teams achieve the right balance so that each team member can contribute.

Successful teams work well together. All the members share responsibility and commitment to the team's goals.

Understand the team process

Analyze
Take time to analyze the writing assignment with your team members. Discuss the goals of the assignment as a group.

Question
Ask as many questions as you can think of about the assignment and about how the team will work together.

Listen
Listen carefully to each team member's ideas and how they can contribute to achieving the goals.

Decide
Write down the team's goals. Make a work plan that lists dates when each task needs to be completed. Assign tasks to team members.

Create
Work closely together in creating content. It's more fun to work with other people, and you'll have help when you get stuck.

Evaluate
Evaluate often if you are meeting the goals on your time line. If something isn't getting done, find out why. When you complete a draft, each member of the team should evaluate it.

Revise
Compare your evaluations and decide as a group what revisions and additions need to be made. Decide who will revise each section.

Review
Arrange for one or more people outside your group to review your work. Meet to decide what additional changes need to be made in light of the external review.

Work as a team

Work closely together in creating and revising content. You'll enjoy writing more and you'll have the benefit of more ideas.

Carry out the plan

- Decide on a process for monitoring progress. Set up specific dates for review and assign team members to be responsible for reviewing work that has been done.
- When you have a complete draft, each team member should evaluate it by providing written comments.
- Meet to compare evaluations and decide on a plan for revising and adding content.
- After revising, arrange for one or more people to review the project. Meet again to determine if additional changes are needed.

Be aware of team dynamics

Teamwork requires some flexibility. Different people have different styles and contribute in different ways. Keep talking to each other along the way.

- Deal with problems when they come up.
- If a team member is not participating, find out why.
- If team members have different ideas about what needs to be done, find time to meet so that the team can reach an agreement.
- Get the team together if you are not meeting the deadlines you established in the work plan and, if necessary, devise a new plan.

WORKING TOGETHER

What to do when problems arise in teams

Working together in a team is most often a rewarding experience, but you need to know how to deal with problems when they arise. Generally it is better to make an effort to resolve problems within the team before asking your instructor to intervene. In a group of four or five students, discuss how you might respond as a group to a team member who

1. is "missing in action,"
2. doesn't come prepared,
3. doesn't answer email,
4. is disrespectful to others,
5. refuses to allow any to critique or revise his or her work.

Appendix A: Writing Essay Examinations

Like any writing task, writing essay exams is a learned skill. Practice and careful preparation are your keys to success.

Preparing for the examination

Use common sense before an essay exam. Get a good night's sleep. Don't wait until the last minute to study. Be prepared.

1. Learn what to expect. Ask the instructor about the exam format. How much time will you have? How many points will each question be worth?

2. Study early and often. Review your notes and assigned readings to determine the major concepts and terms being tested. Practice explaining, applying, and analyzing them. Think about how the texts or concepts relate to one another.

3. Anticipate possible questions. Generate essay questions you think might appear on the exam, and outline possible responses.

4. Make a plan. Have a plan for budgeting your time and approaching the questions. You may want to tackle questions worth the most points first. Allow time to plan, revise, and proofread in addition to actually writing the essay.

Writing a successful exam

After "Be Prepared," the best piece of advice for writing essay examinations is "Don't Panic." It's easy to feel pressure as you hear the clock ticking away during an exam. Although time is limited, don't forsake the writing process during an essay exam.

Understand the question

Take the time to read the question carefully. Underline important words or phrases. If the question asks you to address more than one issue, number them. Be on the lookout for prompting words, which tell you what kind of essay the instructor wants.

analyze:

Analyze the good and bad effects of requiring students to mandatory standardized tests to graduate from high school.

Make an original argument that seeks to illuminate some aspect of the issue at hand for the reader. Will students be better educated if they must pass a test at the end of high school? Or will they be less well educated because teachers will be forced to teach what's on the test and neglect other essential knowledge?

assess or evaluate:

The president's long-standing rationale for recommending most-favored nation (MFN) status for trade relations with China is that our openness encourages human rights reforms in China. Assess whether China's MFN status for the past four years has been a success on those grounds.

Make judgment based on well-supported reasons. For example, has China's human rights record improved with increased trade with the United States?

compare/contrast:
Compare Jamaica Kincaid's relationship with her mother in Annie John *with Amy Tan's relationship with her mother in* Joy Luck Club.

Make an argument about similarities or differences between texts or issues. A compare and contrast essay should not simply describe similarities or differences; it should argue for what can be learned by comparing the two books.

describe:
Describe how aphasia can affect sufferers' language skills.

"Describe" questions usually ask you to present relevant material from the course readings and lectures.

discuss:
Discuss Giotto's reputation as a transitional figure between medieval and renaissance painting.

Make a specific and manageable argument with plenty of detail. Since *discuss* can be a vague prompting word, ask your instructor if you need clarification.

explain:
Explain why we would die of thirst if we only drank salt water.

Take on the role of teacher. Your goal is to make the reader understand a concept. Begin by breaking the subject down into categories or steps. Carefully detail and illustrate those categories or steps. Use the terms covered in the course where appropriate.

explore:
Explore how antitrust laws affected the telecommunications industry in the 1980s.

Like "discuss" questions, "explore" questions tend to be vague. Develop a focused argument. Avoid the temptation to respond with an equally vague thesis. ("Antitrust laws had a considerable effect on the telecommunications industry during the 1980s.")

Plan your essay

After you read the essay question, take a few minutes to sketch an outline of your answer. Decide what argument you want to make. Break the argument into manageable chunks, logical steps, or categories. Note the examples you want to analyze in order to illustrate each chunk of the argument.

Write the essay

An essay exam is not the place to be subtle. Your instructor probably won't have time to hunt for your argument. Highlight your argument clearly toward the beginning of the essay and map out the upcoming paragraphs. Use strong transitions between paragraphs. Relate the point of each paragraph clearly to the larger argument. Offer examples to prove your point. And remember, examples aren't self-explanatory. Analyze your examples to support your argument. Then write a conclusion that once again emphasizes the argument and the steps you took to prove it.

Revise and proofread

While your instructor won't expect essay exam answers to be as polished as other types of writing, your prose still affects your credibility. Reserve time at the end of the exam period to revise your essay, expanding on explanations, adding any examples that strengthen your argument, and clarifying muddled sentences. Then read the essay for errors in spelling, punctuation, and grammar.

Appendix B: Creating Portfolios

Your instructor may ask you to submit a portfolio of written work as part of your grade. Some schools also require a writing portfolio in the junior or senior year. A portfolio includes a range of documents, giving readers a broader, more detailed picture of your writing than a single document could.

Portfolios have different purposes and different requirements. For some portfolios, you might assemble a notebook of printed writing, while for others you might submit documents online into an electronic portfolio system. For any kind of portfolio, your goal is to provide tangible evidence of your learning. You may be asked to submit earlier drafts of your submitted papers and projects to show the revisions you made to them. Your instructor should give you instructions about the purpose of your portfolio, what it should contain, and how you should arrange and submit it.

Types of portfolios

What you choose to include will depend on your portfolio guidelines. Here are some common portfolio types, their purposes, and documents they might contain.

Developmental

A developmental writing portfolio demonstrates a writer's developing skills over a given period of time—perhaps a semester, a year, or several years. Developmental portfolios may focus on skills like critical thinking, research, argument, style, collaboration, and mechanical competence. A developmental portfolio will usually include examples of revised work, providing evidence to readers that you have learned to evaluate and improve your own work. Often, writing in a developmental portfolio ranges from simple, short pieces to longer, more complex work. Your selections may demonstrate how you built upon or combined earlier ideas to produce a more substantial project.

Disciplinary

A disciplinary or professional writing portfolio demonstrates the writer's mastery of important writing forms in a field or discipline. An engineering writing portfolio might include examples of a survey, an accident report, an email to clients, a competitive bid, and similar documents. A business writing portfolio might include examples of a complaint resolution letter, an interoffice memo, a prospectus, an executive summary, and a PowerPoint presentation. A portfolio for a creative writing class might include examples of different genres, such as personal essays, short fiction, poetry, drama, and criticism.

Like a developmental portfolio, a disciplinary portfolio may also reflect how your knowledge about a subject progressed over a period of time. To show how you learned, you might provide examples of informal writing where you wrestle with new concepts; short papers where you research, expand, or connect your growing knowledge; and drafts or sections of longer analytical papers that demonstrate how you have learned to manipulate complex ideas.

Stylistic

Some portfolios are used to give readers a sense of the various styles and genres a writer can employ. Such a portfolio might include humorous writing, formal oratory, descriptive writing, and other types of writing that aim to produce different effects for the reader.

The reflective letter or summary

Usually, a portfolio includes a reflective letter, a summary statement, or some other written document in which you provide an overview of the material and your experience in the course. You may be asked to explain why you chose the pieces you did, or to discuss what you feel you have accomplished. The reflective letter is your opportunity to frame the different documents in the portfolio and explain how they add up to a single, comprehensive picture of your performance as a writer.

The letter does not simply make a claim that you performed well; it tracks your experience in the course, using the writing samples as a step-by-step guide to your learning. You will get the most out of your reflective letter if you perform an honest, impartial examination of your challenges, setbacks, and successes in the course.

Sample portfolio

Here is a sample portfolio assignment for a rhetoric class, including the Table of Contents and reflective letter submitted by Grace Bernhardt.

End of Semester Portfolio Requirements
Rhetoric 309: 19th Century rhetoric—Professor Morrison

Your grade for the semester will be based upon a portfolio of your writing, chosen by you, and submitted the final week of class. I will meet individually with each of you at least twice during the semester to talk about your portfolios and answer any questions you have about them. I will also make periodic suggestions about work that you should include in your portfolio.

I will evaluate your portfolio for evidence of the following:
- Awareness of rhetorical terms and techniques.
- Comprehension of the ways rhetoric was used in the 19th century, and ability to discuss individual examples.
- A growing ability to use and to discuss the use of rhetorical techniques in your own writing and in that of your peers.
- Steady improvement in the power and readability of your own prose, including mechanical facility and vocabulary.

Of course, I do not expect you to know all the course material the minute you walk through the door. Nor do I expect you to be a perfect writer on the first day of class. That is what this class is for: to teach you about rhetoric and to help you improve your writing. Therefore, your portfolio should demonstrate to me how you have approached each element of the class—the readings, the class discussions, the writing process, and the research—and what you have learned from it. You should begin your portfolio with a reflective letter that sums up your experience in the class. In particular, I am interested in how the class experience might be useful to you in the future.

Please follow the letter with a list of your portfolio contents. Arrange your materials in whatever order you like, and place them in a three-ring binder with your name on the outside. The portfolio is due at the beginning of class on Monday, May 1.

Grace Bernhardt's reflective letter:

Dear Professor Morrison,

I learned a great deal about writing, speaking, and thinking this semester. When I first started this class I had only done freewriting in a creative writing workshop. The exercises we did almost every day showed me how writing can get me started thinking and can help get me out of feeling stuck when I am not sure where to go next. I have included two examples of my freewriting from the beginning and the end of semester so you can see how much more useful they became to me.

I also learned how to take criticism. I was proud of my first draft of the paper on Frederick Douglass, and was shocked to get it back with many comments and suggestions from you. But when I sat down and read your comments, I realized how much better the paper could be. Your help, along with our peer review and a session with a consultant in the writing center, helped me improve the paper. The experience taught me that I can improve any paper and that I should always try to do so. My final research paper is probably the best writing I've done so far in my life, but I hope to get even better.

I discovered how helpful my peers could be to my learning. Writing peer reviews taught me how to look closely at someone else's words and consider how they could be stronger. The discussions were the best part of class, and it was on the online class discussion forum that I worked out the focus for my final research project. I have included a transcript of this forum discussion.

The research we did for our final project was difficult and time consuming, but I learned much about the resources in our library. You can see from my annotated bibliography that I finally figured out the difference between primary and secondary sources!

Finally, this class taught me so much about history and the power of words. I feel like I know more about why America is the way it is. I am considering majoring in Radio, Television, and Film, and this class helped me understand the impact of words on audiences.

Thanks for a great class!
Sincerely,
Grace Bernhardt

Portfolio Contents

1. First informal writing assignment: What do I know about rhetoric?

2. Last informal writing assignment: What would you do with your final research project if you had another semester to work on it?

3. First draft (with instructor comments): Investigating "Independence": An Analysis of Frederick Douglass's Speech, "What to the Slave Is the Fourth of July?"

4. Peer review of Investigating "Independence": An Analysis of Frederick Douglass's Speech, "What to the Slave Is the Fourth of July?"

5. Final draft: Investigating "Independence": An Analysis of Frederick Douglass's Speech, "What to the Slave Is the Fourth of July?"

6. Peer review for Kevin Gi

7. Discussion forum transcript: "Special Elements of Oratory"

8. Proposal and annotated bibliography for final research paper.

9. Final draft of research paper: "Discrepancies in Newspaper Transcriptions of Abolitionist Orations."

Image Credits

p. 5 (bottom): © Dorling Kindersley; **p. 78:** U.S. Army; **p. 85:** Frank Capri/Hulton Archive/Getty Images; **p. 91 (right):** © Dorling Kindersley; **p. 118:** Library of Congress; **p. 123:** David Hume Kennerly/Getty Images; **p. 124–127:** Library of Congress; **p. 144:** NASA; **p. 178, 180, 181, 183:** Taylor Crothers; **p. 211:** © Dorling Kindersley; **p. 245:** AP Images; **p. 257:** Corbis; **p. 258:** Library of Congress; **p. 261:** Ted Soqui/Corbis; **p. 267 (top):** Hoffmann/Getty Images; **p. 267 (bottom left):** Gaslight Ad Archives; **p. 267 (bottom right):** Volkswagen AG; **p. 268 (top left):** PhotoFest; **p. 268 (bottom):** © 2006 Volkswagen of America, Inc.; **p. 269:** Keith Beford/Reuters/Corbis; **p. 281:** © Miriam Berkley; **p. 316:** Mario Tama/Getty Images; **p. 317:** Mike Theiss/Jim Reed Photographer/Corbis; **p. 319:** Jim Reed/Corbis; **p. 327:** Scott Olson/Getty Images; **p. 335–338:** © Judith Miller/Dorling Kindersley/Wallis and Wallis; **p. 378:** David Bryne; **p. 381:** Inge Druckrey; **p. 436–437:** Getty Images; **p. 444–445:** PoodlesRock/Corbis; **p. 503–504:** Wally McNamee/Corbis; **p. 519 (top):** Janni Chavakis/Zefa/Corbis; **p. 519 (bottom):** Tim Pannell/Corbis; **p. 522 (left):** Ausloeser/Zefa/Corbis; **p. 522 (right):** © Royalty Free/Corbis; **p. 523 (left):** © Royalty Free/ Corbis; **p. 560–561:** © Dorling Kindersley; **p. 564:** Getty Images; **p. 600:** Getty Images; **p. 603:** JLP/Deimos/Zefa/Corbis; **p. 633:** Getty Images; **p. 668 (bottom):** © Dorling Kindersley; **p. 682:** Getty Images; **p. 687:** Dynamic Graphics Group/IT Stock Free/Alamy.

Unless otherwise credited, all photos © Lester Faigley Photos.

Text Credits

Rick Bass. "Why I Hunt: A Predator's Meditation." As it appeared in *Esquire,* October, 1990. Copyright © 1990 Rick Bass. Reprinted by permission of the author.

Gail Bederman. "Race, Gender, and Civilization at the Columbian Exhibition." From "Race, Gender and Civilization at the Columbian Exposition" in *Manliness and Civilization.* Copyright © 1995 by The University of Chicago. Reprinted by permission.

Angela Cain. "Barbie's Body May Be Perfect, but Critics Remind Us It's Plastic." From the *Albany-Times Union*, March 26, 1996. Copyright © Knight-Ridder/Tribune Media Information Services. All Rights Reserved. Reprinted with permission.

Meredith Clark. "Life Without Health Insurance." Reprinted by permission from the February 3, 2005 issue of *The Nation.* For subscription information, call 1-800-333-8536. Portions of each week's Nation magazine can be accessed at http://www.thenation.com.

Nancy Clark. "Mirror, Mirror on the Wall, Are Muscular Men the Best of All?" From *American Fitness*, Jan/Feb 2004. Copyright © 2004 American Fitness. Reprinted by permission.

Tim Collins. "Straight from the Heart." From *The Guardian*, July 13, 2005. Copyright Guardian Newspapers Limited 2005. Reprinted by permission.

Dan Crane. "McNasty: The New 'Healthy' Fast Food Items Taste Bad (and Aren't so Healthy Either)." From *Slate magazine*, November 25, 2003. Copyright © 2006 Washington Newsweek Interactive CO LLC. Reprinted by permission.

Thom Curtis. "Television Violence and Aggression." From *Family Focus.* Copyright © 2001. Reprinted by permission of the author.

Stentor Danielson. "Pesticides, Parasite May Cause Frog Deformities." From *National Geographic News*, July 9, 2002. Copyright © 2002. Reprinted by permission of The National Geographic Society.

Jared Diamond. Title page from *Collapse: How Societies Choose to Fail or Succeed.* Copyright © 2005 by Jared Diamond. Used by permission of Viking Penguin, a division of Penguin Group (USA) Inc.

Anne Dillard. "Living Like Weasels." From *Teaching a Stone to Talk: Expeditions and Encounters.* Copyright © 1982 by Annie Dillard. Reprinted by permission of HarperCollins.

Michael Eric Dyson. "Gangsta Rap and American Culture." From *Michael Eric Dyson Reader.* Copyright © 2004 Michael Eric Dyson. Reprinted by permission of BASIC BOOKS, a member of Perseus Books, L.L.C

EBSCO. Screen images from EBSCO Database are used by permission of EBSCO Publishing.

EBSCO. Screen images from Business Source Premier are used by permission of EBSCO Publishing.

Sue Kunitomi Embrey. "Some Lines for a Younger Brother." Originally published in *Gidra,* vol. II, no. 5, May 1970. Copyright © 1970 by Sue Kunitomi Embrey. Reprinted by permission.

Harold Evans. "Russell Simmons." From *They Made America.* Copyright © 2004 by Harold Evans Associates LLC. By permission of Little, Brown and Co., Inc.

Dagoberto Gilb. "Love in LA." From *The Magic of Blood.* Copyright © 1993 by University of New Mexico Press. Reprinted by permission.

Google. Screen images are used by permission from Google.

Lori Gottlieb. "How Do I Love Thee?." From *The Atlantic Monthly*, March 2006. Copyright © 2006. Reprinted by permission of the author.

Salman Hameed. "Travelogue of an Astronomer." As it appeared in *Chowk*, May 2004. Reprinted by permission of the author.

Jason Christopher Hartley. "Just Another Soldier." From *Just Another Soldier: A Year on the Ground in Iraq.* Reprinted by permission of HarperCollins Publishers.

Thomas Homer-Dixon and S. Julio Friedman. "Coal is a Nice Shade of Green." From *The New York Times*, March 25, 2005, Science Section. Copyright © 2005 by The New York Times Co. Reprinted by permission.

Pam Houston. "A Blizzard Under Blue Sky." From *Cowboys Are My Weakness.* Copyright © 1992 by Pam Houston. Used by permission of W.W. Norton & Company, Inc.

Steven Johnson. "Hillary vs. 'Grand Theft Auto'." Special to the *Los Angeles Times*, Friday, July 29, 2005. Copyright © 2005 Steven Johnson. Reprinted by permission of the author.

The Journal of Narrative Technique. "cover and excerpt." From *The Journal of Narrative Technique*, Fall 1998. Copyright © 1998 by The Journal of Narrative Technique. Reprinted with permission.

Ari Kelman. "City of Nature: New Orleans' Blessing, New Orleans' Curse." From *Slate* magazine, August 31, 2005. Copyright © 2006 Washington Newsweek Interactive CO LLC. Reprinted by permission.

Jamaica Kincaid. "A Small Place." From *A Small Place.* Copyright © 1988 by Jamaica Kincaid. Reprinted by permission of Farrar, Straus and Giroux, LLC.

Index